Turn to learn . . .

WHAT'S INSIDE
This College Prowler Book?

IVY LEAGUE CONTRIBUTORS . . .

EXPERT OPINIONS

Jeffrey Orleans
Executive Director, Council of Ivy Group Presidents (The Ivy League) since 1984

Yale Alumnus

Answers questions and clears up misperceptions on the Ivy League.

Shannon Duff
Former Yale admissions essay reader & founder of Collegiate Compass Counseling Services

Yale Alumna

Gives key insight and tips on applying to the Ivy League.

Ivy League Admissions Officers
Identities protected

Promised to speak off the record about what really goes on in the admissions office only if we keep their names a secret.

ALUMNI INTERVIEWS

Ruth Bader Ginsburg
Supreme Court Justice

Columbia & Cornell Alumna

Reflects on diversity and her days in the Ivy League.

Jeffrey Lehman
Former Cornell University President

Explains his role as a key defendant in the Supreme Court's case on affirmative action and looks at the verdict's impact.

STUDENT INSIDERS

Marc Zawel

& Research Team

Cornell Alumnus

Former managing editor of the *Cornell Daily Sun*. Primary author and guiding voice of this book.

Priya Radjev

Illustrations

Harvard Student

Harvard Crimson political cartoonist. Puts her spin on the issues.

College Insiders

A student writer from each Ivy gives you the inside scoop on life at their school. Each student contributed over 100 pages of information and used peer surveys, thorough research, and personal experience to tell it like it is.

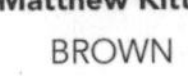
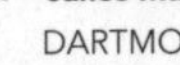

Matthew Kittay	**Julia Green**	**Oliver Striker**	**Janos Marton**	**Dominic Hood**	**Jennifer Klein**	**Alison Fraser**	**Melissa Doscher**
BROWN	COLUMBIA	CORNELL	DARTMOUTH	HARVARD	PENN	PRINCETON	YALE

1000s of Current Ivy League Students Share Their Thoughts.

Special thanks to: Roland Allen, Chris Babyak, Babs Carryer, Jared Cohon, The Donald H. Jones Center for Entrepreneurship, Bill Ecenberger, Thomas Emerson, Mark Exler, Daniel Fayock, Julie Fenstermaker, Andy Hannah, Paul Kelly, David Koegler, LaunchCyte, Dave Lehman, Bert Mann, Nick Mason, Orlando Mason, Veronica Mason, Jerry McGinnis, McGinty, Glen Meakem, Abu Noaman, Gabriela Oates, Tim O'Brien, Jon Reider, Kyle Russell, Bob Sehlinger, Andrew Skurman, Barbara Skurman, Terry Slease, Daniel Steinmeyer, Team Evankovich, Tri Ad Litho, Lauren Varacalli, Larry Winderbaum, Jacque Zaremba, and the College Prowler student authors.

College Prowler®
5001 Baum Blvd.
Suite 750
Pittsburgh, PA 15213

Phone: 1(800) 290-2682
Fax: 1(800) 772-4972
E-mail: info@collegeprowler.com
Web: www.collegeprowler.com

Untangling the Ivy League 2006

Primary Author
Marc Zawel

Concept & Development
Christopher Mason

Illustrations
Priya Radjev

Editing
Adam Burns, Omid Gohari, Christina Koshzow, Christopher Mason, Kimberly Moore, Joey Rahimi, Luke Skurman, and Robert Williams

ISBN # 1-59658-500-5
ISSN # 1557-1203

Printed in the U.S.A.
www.collegeprowler.com

Table of Contents

Introduction

Nobody has ever done a book on the Ivy League like this before.

We were tired of reading college guides based on one expert's perspective, or from the view-point of a major publishing house. So we set out to create a book on the Ivy League written by its students and alumni. We figured they would know more from experience. That is why every section in this guide, every expert opinion, and every major insight is from the people who know best. The section on Harvard is by a Harvard student; admissions advice comes from a Yale admissions officer; and important issues such as affirmative action and legacy admission policy receive attention from no less than an Ivy League university president and a Supreme Court justice.

– Christopher Mason, Co-Founder, College Prowler

SECTION 1

Defining the Ivy League

What is the Ivy League?

The Ivy League—made up of Brown, Columbia, Cornell, Dartmouth, Harvard, Penn, Princeton, and Yale—was not always the way it is today. What began merely as an athletic conference has since evolved into what many believe to be a collection of the world's most elite institutions of higher education.

How elite?

- Some high school students are now paying $30,000 for Ivy admissions counseling.
- Graduation from an Ivy League school has become synonymous with success.
- Most of the Ivies were established before the signing of the Declaration of Independence in 1776.

So where did the name come from?

Good question; although you might get a different answer depending on whom you ask. There are three popular explanations for how the Ivy League got its name.

First up, **Story Number One**. According to the *Morris Dictionary of Word and Phrase Origins*, the answer can be traced to the Roman numeral IV:

> Over a century ago, an interscholastic athletic league was formed by Harvard, Yale, Columbia, and Princeton. It was officially known as the "Four League." The Roman number "IV" was often used instead of the word four, and the term "IV League" came into use.

THE Ivies Through the Ages

THE "IVY" APPEARS

1933

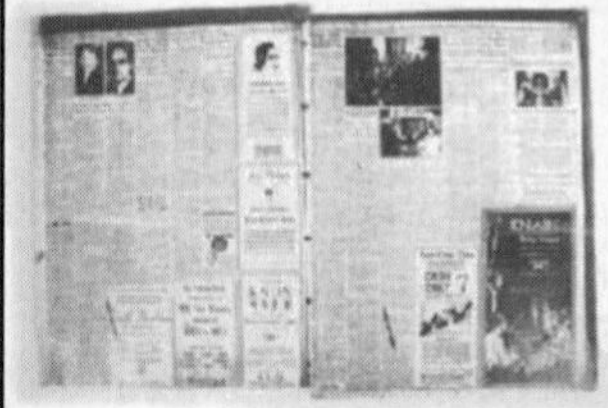

Stanley Woodward of the *New York Herald Tribune* first uses the phrase "Ivy colleges" in print to describe the eight current Ivy schools (plus Army).

THE NAME "IVY LEAGUE" IS COINED

1935

AP sports editor Alan Gould first uses the exact term "Ivy League."

When spoken, the IV was spelled out and sounded like "Ivy League." Brown, Dartmouth, Cornell, and Pennsylvania were the major opponents of the IV league, and in the early 1900s were members of the league.

There is very little evidence, however, that backs up this claim. According to the third edition of the *New Dictionary of Cultural Literacy*, the explanation is an urban legend.

Story Number Two sounds like this:
We're in the newsroom of the *New York Herald-Tribune* on a lazy Thursday afternoon, mid-October 1937. The *Tribune*'s sports editors gather writers in their department to assign coverage for that coming week's college football games. Stanley Woodward, a respected veteran reporter, is assigned the coveted, most widely-anticipated game of the week—Pittsburgh versus Fordham at the Polo Grounds in New York. Caswell Adams, the *Tribune's* boxing correspondent, is assigned to the weekend's Columbia-Pennsylvania bout at Columbia's Baker Field. As the story goes, Adams, not thrilled with his assignment, turns to his editors to voice his dissatisfaction and asks, "Why in hell do I have to watch the ivy grow every Saturday afternoon? How about letting me see some football away from the ivy-covered halls of learning for a change?" Woodward, who was working nearby, overheard the comment and realized that a group of schools that had long shunned a conference could now be named. The next week, he began to work the term into his columns.

Story Number Three, however, seems to indicate that this account is also flawed. According to Mark F. Bernstein, the author of *Football: The Ivy League Origins of an American Obsession*, the correct story is a little different. After Harvard and Princeton announced that they would resume athletic competitions against one another in 1933 (following a seven-year hiatus), reporters began to speculate about the creation of another athletic conference. Woodward, our reporter from the *Herald-Tribune*, wrote on October 14, 1933 that, "A proportion of our eastern ivy colleges are meeting little fellows another Saturday before plunging into the strife and the turmoil." This was, according to Bernstein, the first public use of the "Ivy" tag.

Bernstein notes, however, that the full "Ivy League" term didn't appear until February 8, 1935, when Alan Gould, sports editor of the Associated Press, first used it in a story. It was adopted slowly by other writers, and in 1936, Ivy newspaper editors at seven of the schools published a joint editorial calling for an "Ivy League." This account places the term's creation almost an entire year before Woodward apparently overheard Adams' comment in the *Herald-Tribune*'s newsroom. Speculation aside, the Ivy League, itself, seems to agree with Bernstein; his dates appear on their Web site, *www.ivyleaguesports.com*.

So those are the stories. The first appears to be a myth, and the second is more widely accepted and circulated, despite the evidence presented in Bernstein's third account. Regardless, the first formal agreement between the schools did not occur until 1945, when all eight officially joined together to participate in the "Ivy Group Agreement." For more information about this pact and the development of the Ivy League, check out the timeline below:

THE FIRST "IVY GROUP AGREEMENT" IS SIGNED

1945

Applying only to football, it affirms the observance of common academic standards and eligibility requirements and outlines the administration of need-based financial aid with no athletic scholarships. The agreement creates the Presidents Policy Committee, including the eight Presidents; the Coordination and Eligibility Committee, made up of one senior non-athletic administrator from each school; and the committee on Administration, comprised of the eight directors of athletics.

THE AGREEMENT IS EXTENDED

1954

The Ivy Presidents extend the Ivy Group Agreement to all intercollegiate sports. Their statement also focuses on presidential governance of the League, the importance of intra-League competition, and a desire that recruited athletes be academically "representative" of each institution's overall student body. Although this is the League's official founding date, the first year of competition is 1956-57.

→

Snapshots in Time

BONUS POINTS!

Now that you understand where the Ivies come from, it's time to see how they've impacted history. Take a look at these snapshots in time . . .

African American Firsts.

Like women, African Americans were admitted to Ivy League schools at varying rates. At Dartmouth, it took student protests to persuade college administrators to admit Edward Mitchell, who had been a servant for University President Francis Brown, in **1824**. In **1870**, Richard T. Greener became the first African American to graduate from Harvard; and in **1876**, Edward Bouchet became the first African American to graduate from Yale and receive a Ph.D. from an American school.

Inman Page and George Washington Milford both became Brown's first African American

graduates in **1877**. William Adger was the first African American to graduate from Penn in **1883**; and the first African American Cornellian, Charles Cook, received his degree in **1890**.

Manhattan Project.

As fascism rose in Germany and Italy during the 1930s, a large group of European scientists and mathematicians, many of them Jews, left their countries for America's institutions. The most famous was Albert Einstein, who came to the town of Princeton in 1933. Although Einstein was a faculty member of the Institute for Advanced Study, an institution independent of Princeton University, his presence attracted many other scientists and mathematicians, which in turn, helped transform the small college town into one of the world's leading intellectual centers.

Enrico Fermi and Leo Szilard wound up at Columbia, Hans Bethe went to Cornell, Stanislaw Ulam attended Harvard, and Eugene Wigner and John von Neumann enrolled at Princeton. These names may be unfamiliar to you, but **all were indispensable members of the Manhattan Project**, which built the atomic bomb at Los Alamos, NM from 1942-46 (under the direction of J. Robert Oppenheimer, also a Harvard man).

THE Ivies Through the Ages

1971 — WOMEN NOW ENROLLED AT ALL EIGHT IVIES

With women now enrolled as undergraduates at all eight Ivy institutions, the Presidents unanimously approve the proposal of the Coordination and Administration committees that, "The Ivy Group rules of eligibility shall not be construed to discriminate on grounds of sex."

1979 — THE "STATEMENT OF PRINCIPLES" IS ISSUED

On the 25th anniversary of the 1954 Agreement, the Council of Presidents issues a 10-point "Statement of Principles," reaffirming basic goals with regard to admissions, financial aid, and the role of athletics in the undergraduate educational experience.

Brain Trust.

The Brain Trust was comprised of Columbia University professors—friends from FDR's earlier life as a law student at the University. This informal group of advisors gave key insight and direction to presidential policies such as The New Deal, which helped pull the U.S. out of the Great Depression during the 1930s.

Potty Mouth.

In 1885, publishing mogul William Randolph Hearst was expelled from Harvard for allegedly giving his professors chamber pots (small, portable toilets) with their names written on the bottom.

Arrogant Excellence.

During the early years of World War II, another notable figure, **Norman Mailer, entered Harvard at the age of 16**. After graduating in 1943, cum laude, he enlisted and shipped out to the Pacific, where he saw combat in the Philippines. Mailer's fictionalized account of his wartime experience, *The Naked and the Dead*, was published in 1948 when he was only 25. Mailer remains one of America's great novelists and for decades was **known for his fiery pen** and arrogance. (Woody Allen once quipped that Mailer "bequeathed his ego to Harvard Medical School.")

Test-ees.

From 1959-62, psychologist Henry A. Murray conducted experiments on 22 Harvard undergraduates to test how they reacted under intense stress. **One young math student, code-named "Lawful," was Theodore Kaczynski, later known as the "Unabomber."**

Around the same time, Harvard professors Richard Alpert and Timothy Leary headed a study exploring the uses and "mind-expanding" benefits of hallucinogens, especially LSD. After **two undergrads ended up in psychiatric hospitals**, Harvard asked the professors to cease using undergrads as participants.

Computers, Yo.

The world's first electronic digital computer, ENIAC, was created by Penn whiz kids John Mauchy and Pres Eckert, who, at the time, were still in their mid-20s.

Monstrously massive, ENIAC occupied 15,000 square feet and contained 18,000 radio tubes. Princeton's John von Neumann, who fled Europe and helped to build the atomic bomb, encountered ENIAC (and other early computers) after the war and applied his incredible mathematical talent to improving its technology. Von Neumann continued computer work at Los Alamos and Princeton and was instrumental in the computer calculations necessary to create the hydrogen bomb by 1952.

ORLEANS BECOMES EXECUTIVE DIRECTOR

1984

Jeffrey Orleans (he appears in this book!), a Yale graduate, is appointed the third Executive Director of the Council of Ivy Group Presidents. He is authorized to hire other professional staff and create an "Ivy Office" to more effectively coordinate and serve institutional activities, represent the League nationally, and engage in League-wide sports information and championship administration.

FIRST AFRICAN AMERICAN IVY PRESIDENT

2001

Ruth J. Simmons becomes the first African American leader of an Ivy League institution when she is appointed as the president of Brown.

Ivy in the Whitehouse.

After John F. Kennedy, a Harvard man, was elected president of the United States **in 1960, he surrounded himself** with the most brilliant men of his day, culled largely from the Ivy League. As secretary of defense, he chose Robert McNamara, a Harvard MBA and Harvard Business School professor, and McGeorge Bundy as a national security advisor.

"Mac" Bundy was an outstanding mind who seemed to embody the ideal Ivy League man. He excelled at the elite prep school, Groton, where at the age of sixteen, he refused to complete the College Board exam essay questions, "How did you spend your summer vacation?" and "What is your favorite pet?" **Instead, Bundy penned an essay lambasting the inanity of the topics** and reproached the College Board for their choice of questions. He got a 100. Bundy was the first Yale student ever to enter with three perfect scores on his college entrance exams. After Yale, Bundy attended graduate school at Harvard, later taught there, and at the age of 34, became Harvard's Dean of Arts and Sciences.

Wrong Answer.

In 1957, Charles Van Doren, an assistant professor at Columbia University, achieved a record performance on the quiz show *Twenty-One.*

As it turns out, the **producers fed Van Doren the answers ahead of time**, a fact uncovered by Congressional Staff Investigator Dick Goodwin (first in his class at Harvard Law School). Van Doren resigned from Columbia, and the events were later dramatized in the 1994 film, "Quiz Show," which portrayed Goodwin's sympathy for Van Doren, a fellow Ivy man.

Lolita!

Cornell was a literary hotspot back when people used to read books. Russian-born novelist Vladimir Nabokov spent most of the decade teaching at Cornell and producing some of his best novels, including the infamous *Lolita,* which was published in **1958** and portrayed a 45-year-old college professor's sexual obsession with a 12 year-old girl.

Tyrone's Tuition.

In 1974, Cornell's Thomas Pynchon published his masterpiece, *Gravity's Rainbow,* which portrayed Lieutenant Tyrone Slothrop, a Harvard man whose college admission story seemed like something out of a prospective student's nightmare.

Slothrop's parents allowed a Harvard scientist to perform secret experiments on Tyrone when he was only a baby in exchange for Tyrone's Harvard tuition. As a grown man, Slothrop tells another character, "Harvard's there for other reasons. The 'educating' part of it is just sort of a front."

On a side note, Pynchon's stabs at Harvard may be what endear him to prominent men of literature at Yale. Yale critic Edward Mendelson called Pynchon, "the greatest living writer in the English-speaking world," while fellow Yale professor Harold Bloom, in an article called "Dumbing Down American Readers," included Pynchon is his list of four American novelists who still "deserve our praise."

Seeing Red!

Dartmouth Night, the evening of speeches, parades, and bonfires that kick off Homecoming Weekend at the school, originated in 1888 as a celebration after a baseball game win. The **events were protested** by militant feminists who threw bloody tampons in 1986 and red-dyed eggs (representing the ova) in 1987.

Women Get In.

Although some of the universities had separate women's colleges—including Radcliffe at Harvard, Barnard at Columbia, and Pembroke at Brown—one by one, Ivy League schools took steps toward fully integrating male and female student bodies.

In 1969, Yale and Princeton began to accept women, while two years later, Harvard and Brown joined with their companion schools of Radcliffe and Pembroke. Dartmouth joined the crowd later in the 1970s, while Columbia began to integrate women after a failed merger with Barnard in 1983.

Wall Street Windfalls.

During the '80s, many Ivy Leaguers put love on hold, cast philosophical discussion to the wind, and headed for Wall Street. This portrayal, which contrasts the Ivies' proud tradition with the greed and vulgarity that, in some respects, characterized the '80s, is from **Tom Wolfe's 1987 novel, *Bonfire of the Vanities***, the best single document on the Wall Street generation (Wolfe himself earned a Ph.D in American Studies at Yale before launching a distinguished career of literary journalism).

Proof in Princeton.

In 1993, Princeton professor Andrew Wiles solved the world's oldest and most difficult unsolved math problem, Fermat's Last Theorem.

His amazing proof, which weighed in at 150 pages, took Wiles a decade of solitary labor and cemented his reputation as the world's greatest living mathematician. Around the same time, Edward Witten (Princeton M.A. and Ph.D), of the Institute for Advanced Study, caused a revolution in so-called string theory, the branch of physics and math that hopes to reconcile Einstein's physics with quantum mechanics in an impressive-sounding Theory of Everything.

1975–Bill Gates Dropped Out of Harvard.

He goes on to start a little company called Microsoft and does surprisingly well for himself.

WHICH IVY IS THE OLDEST?

School:	Founded:
1. Harvard	1636
2. Yale	1701
3. Penn	1740
4. Princeton	1746
5. Columbia	1754
6. Brown	1764
7. Dartmouth	1769
8. Cornell	1865

Current Perceptions and Stereotypes

POP QUIZ!

Time for a test!
Can you name all eight Ivy schools? (No cheating!)

How'd you do? Get them all? Intrigue over this same question led us to conduct a completely informal, unscientific survey at 11 colleges and universities around the country. With a little help, we asked students a simple question—"Can you name the schools in the Ivy League?"—and purposely left out how many schools were part of the group.

Of the 100 students we polled, here are the results:

- Four—yes, only four—could name all eight Ivy League schools, although a larger number was able to provide a partial list.
- The most commonly named: Harvard, Princeton, and Yale.
- The most often forgotten: Brown and Dartmouth.
- Schools most often mistaken for an Ivy (listed alphabetically): Duke, Johns Hopkins, MIT, NYU, and Stanford.

"Ivy Plus"

The term Ivy Plus is often used to refer to the eight "original Ivies" along with several other prestigious colleges and universities for purposes of university affiliations and alumni associations. The inclusion of non-Ivy League schools under this term is commonplace for some schools and extremely rare for others. Among these other schools, Massachusetts Institute of Technology and Stanford University are almost always included. The University of Chicago and Duke University are often included as well.

Just because people might not know which schools are in the Ivy League, it doesn't mean that they don't hold stereotypes about the league in general, though.

Let's start with the students. University of Pennsylvania student, Elisabeth Kwak-Hefferan, explored these questions in a 2003 *Daily Pennsylvanian* piece titled, "Ivy League Snobs? Maybe." She wrote:

"Last week, someone who didn't even know me called me an egotistical snob. . . . At first I was indignant; hey you don't know me! How dare you judge me according to whatever prejudices you have against Penn? But after my initial anger faded, I realized something rather disturbing. I may not think I'm a snob, but I must admit some of the noses around here are turned up pretty high."

The mere fact that this columnist was approached and called a snob because of her affiliation with Penn does tell us something, although Kwak-Hefferan also acknowledges that:

> . . . Too many Ivy Leaguers mistake their luck in having the opportunity to study at some of the best schools in the world as justification for putting on airs of superiority . . . . No wonder the Ivy League has such a bad reputation when it comes to conceit. Maybe I can forgive the stranger who called me a snob. After all, he was just playing the odds.

Sheela V. Pai also examined Ivy elitism in a 1999 *Yale Herald* article, "Yale Elitism: Alive and Kickin,'" in which she discussed the Yale Club's change in policy that allowed its members to partake in casual Fridays. Members were no longer required to wear the traditional jacket and tie on Fridays, Pai reported, in an effort to draw younger members to the club. To prove the club's elitism, however, the author conducted several experiments, including placing a *Vogue* magazine in its gym and tuning a television to a soap opera. The magazine was gone in several days, and a new policy was quickly created that limited the broadcasted television channels. The ultimate test for Pai was entering the Club in jeans and a T-shirt. She wrote, "the palpable alienation was enough to drive even the most hardened rowdy back to the traditional skirt and blouse."

WHAT'S IMPORTANT?

According to a 2000 survey of incoming Cornell students:

68% considered "being very well off financially" to be "essential" or "very important."

But are these assumptions correct? Are Ivy students conceited? And what exactly do these students expect to receive in return for their investment? Of the eight Ivy League schools, only Cornell publishes data and survey responses that help address this question. A survey of its class of 2004 asked students to consider which goals were "essential" or "very important" to them. Approximately 68 percent thought "being very well off financially" fell into this category as did "becoming successful in [their] own business"—a statement supported by 40 percent of their peers. Also according to the survey, "to be able to make money" (61 percent) and "to get training for a specific career" (56 percent) were important reasons for going to college—more so for Cornell freshmen than for freshmen polled at other universities.

For Ivy students, the importance of good job placement and economic security is a concern and incentive—at least in part—for attending these schools. Alumni surveys conducted by Cornell show quite clearly the expectations of those who have attended Ivy League schools. In 2001, the class of 1989 identified their five most important goals (scaling 1 = "not at all" to 5 = "essential"). At the top of the list was "Raising a family" (4.12), although not far below was "Being very well-off financially" (3.67) and "Recognition from colleagues' contributions to a special field" (3.50).

Evolution in Pop Culture

The influence of the Ivy League reaches far beyond the schools themselves. Read on to see how everything from books to movies has been affected by the Ancient Eight.

Old School Ivy

In 1961, Frederick A. Birmingham wrote and published a book, *The Ivy League Today.* In this once modern-day guidebook, he instills a sense of great tradition and superiority to his readers. According to Birmingham,

"These schools are often called the sole hope in the fight against mediocre mass education, and the true preservers of a well-rounded curriculum in a college world rapidly becoming overspecialized. . . . [The Ivy League] became a symbol of caste. The feeling had been there all the time; now it had a name . . . In their long histories Ivy alumni included great names in the American tradition, presidents and poets and statesmen and industrialists who made unforgettable contributions to the nation . . ."

Films created in the same era mimick this sentiment of Ivy supremacy. *The Paper Chase* (1973), set at Harvard Law School, tells the life story of James Hart, a first-year law student and how he balances the pressures of law school with the pull of a relationship. In one particular scene, Hart and other members of his study group check into a hotel in order to study for exams. Once locked inside, they don't leave for three days and study day and night in their underwear, forgoing showers and contact with the outside world. Hart's classmates are what many would believe to be typical Ivy kids—Bell is a nerdy, arrogant, self-centered student, while Kevin struggles to keep on top of his work.

→

→

Love Story, a film released in the 1970s, also emphasized a very similar Ivy lifestyle. The plot goes like this: Oliver Barrett IV, wealthy Harvard hockey jock, whose last name appears on half of the buildings at the university, falls in love with Jenny Cavalerri, a poor Radcliffe music student. Oliver's parents disapprove, and his father gives him an ultimatum: "If you marry her now, I'll not give you the time of day." He chooses Jenny, who tragically dies of cancer, and he's left utterly alone, alienated from his parents and forever separated from his one true love. The film ends with an unrepentant Oliver telling his father, "Love means never having to say you're sorry." The film highlighted two increasing trends at the Ivies, going coed and accepting more low-income students.

New School Print: Ivy Scream. You Scream.

MYSTERY AND MURDER

When she's not busy running CNBC, Chairman Pamela Thomas-Graham pens mystery novels with an Ivy League twist. Published in 2000, *Blue Blood: An Ivy League Mystery* is the story of a Harvard professor, Veronica "Nikki" Chase, who awakens early one morning to learn that the wife of her friend Gary Fox, a dean at Yale, has been murdered. A year earlier, Thomas-Graham introduced readers to her Harvard protagonist in *A Darker Shade of Crimson: An Ivy League Mystery* (1999). Most recently, Thomas-Graham has published *Orange Crushed* (2004), which was promoted as a "smart and sassy" and "thoroughly engaging page-turner that will appeal to all fans of mystery." The book is the third in the author's Ivy League mystery novel series. How does she juggle it all? This Harvard grad confesses to getting only four hours of sleep a night. Sounds Ivy League to us.

MORE MYSTERY AND MORE MURDER

Additional books such as *Confessions of an Ivy League Bookie: A True Tale of Love and the Vig* by Peter Alson (1996) explore America's obsession with the secrets of the Ivy League and (perhaps) its desire to undermine its tradition and prestige. Heidi Mattson wrote *Ivy League Stripper* in 1995, while Carol Saline's true-crime story, *Dr. Snow: How the FBI Nailed an Ivy League Coke King* (2000), sought to expose what she saw as the darker side of the Ivy League—a far cry from Frederick Birmingham's book back in 1961. Clearly, sex, drugs, mystery, and scandal sell today, and for many authors, no source proves better material than the Ivy League.

At the Cinema: Sorority Girls and Pot Smokers

AMERICAN PSYCHO (2000)

Bret Easton Ellis' *American Psycho* was turned into film and presented Patrick Bateman, a Wall Street broker, preening in front of a mirror, stating, "I have all the characteristics of a human being, but not one discernible emotion except greed and disgust." In the film, Bateman is portrayed as a Harvard grad who is fiercely competitive with his co-workers and materialistic to the core. American Psycho satirized the decade's moral decay by turning Bateman into a serial killer.

LEGALLY BLOND (2001)

What sells in print also appears to sell on the big screen. *Legally Blond* was the story of Elle Woods, the quintessential beautiful, blonde, rich sorority girl. Woods is madly in love with Warner Huntington III, another stereotypical Ivy Leaguer, who breaks up with her after claiming she is neither intellectual nor serious enough for his aspiring political career. In breaking up with Woods, Huntington tells her that, "My family has five generations of senators, my brother's in the top three at Yale Law, and he just got engaged to a Vanderbilt for Christsakes." Woods is done . . . until she decides to prove Warner wrong and vows to gain admission to Harvard Law School.

But this is no James Hart or Oliver Barrett IV. This is Elle Woods, whose application to the school includes a video essay of her sitting poolside in a bikini, reciting lines from a soap opera and presiding over sorority chapter meetings. Her entrance is clinched with stellar LSAT scores. What should you take away from this? Not to ruin it for those who haven't seen it, but Woods ultimately becomes one heck of a lawyer. She proves to us that, with hard work and dedication, most everyone can do well at Harvard, and simply put, that Warner is nothing more that just another conceited Ivy Leaguer.

HOW HIGH (2001)

The sorority girl succeeds at Harvard, but what about two pot-smokers? The poorly-reviewed 2001 film, *How High*, attempts to answer that very question. Silas P. Silas and Jamal King discover a new strain of marijuana that magically aids them in acing their college entrance exam. Their choice destination: Cambridge, MA.

How do these slackers fare? Surprisingly, they do pretty darn well, at least until their special stash runs dry. Like *Legally Blond*, though, what should we make of a film that appears to attack the academic rigor of schools like Harvard? If Silas and King can get in, who can't? Admissions parody aside, how does this film portray Ivy League students? If Gerald, one of the film's stereotypical Ivy League students, is any indication, the answer is not too highly (no pun intended). Described by filmmakers as "a hall monitor since the first grade," and "a very annoying little tattletale who has no friends and many enemies," Gerald might be a good example of how many view Ivy Leaguers today.

THE SKULLS (2000)

This film follows the life of Luke McNamara, a student from a working-class background, who joins a secret elite fraternity, the Skulls, at a school strikingly similar to Yale. The society has its perks upon joining—namely, a $20,000 cash gift and a new sports car; but then, it has its drawbacks—namely, murder and conspiracies. By the film's end, McNamara has found himself

→

embroiled in an attempt to uncover the murder of his journalist friend, Will Beckford, and expose the Skulls for who they are. Surprise, surprise! The Ivy League and murder—you haven't read or seen anything like this recently, have you?

While we're at it, here's some interesting food for thought: Bateman, America's "psycho," loses himself in a string of murders after he finds little value or meaning in his life. McNamara is given a shot at greatness, aspiring to become everything that Bateman is, and becomes entangled in the same type of death games that characterize Bateman's life. Both are products of the Ivy League, which according to these films, might not always churn out America's finest and brightest.

Fraternities and Clubs

The concept of a fraternity or social club tends to bring various images to mind. Most common, perhaps, are the stereotypes. We think of John Belushi as "Bluto" Blutarsky in "Animal House" or Will Ferrell as Frank Ricard in "Old School" and the associated partying, drugs, secrets, and sex. We might also think of what is reported to us by the media—the hazing of pledges that leads to deaths or the underage binge drinking that leads to rape. So far in this guidebook, we have learned that the Ivy League—and its students, governing bodies, and portrayals—is far more complicated and complex than it initially appears. This is perhaps no truer than when approaching the Ivies' organizations—and their secrets.

Ivy Greeks

The Greek system, with its history and traditions dating back over 250 years, has grown and evolved over time. With this growth has come another change—a refocusing of goals and a redefinition of what fraternity or sorority membership entails. So, what is the Greek system about? What is its role in the Ivy League—where, for the most part, fraternities and sororities appear to have been truest to their founding traditions and principles?

Greek houses on Ivy campuses today face increased media scrutiny and university regulation, in large part due to issues of drinking on college campuses. While some students are drawn to fraternities and sororities because of their social component, this is not to say that Greeks are all about partying. For example, at Cornell, which has the largest Ivy Greek system and one of the largest systems in the country, Greeks contributed 46,000 hours of community service and $125,000 to charity in 2000-20001. Even if some argue that the literary aspects of the Greek system have faded with time, philanthropy has certainly survived.

"If it's secret and elite, it can't be good."

— Will Beckford, played by actor Hill Harper, in *The Skulls* (2000).

"Part of what makes a fraternity different from a bunch of friends that live and socialize together is a commitment to giving back to the community and the development of its brothers."

— Mike Hamilton, brother of Sigma Alpha Epsilon fraternity at Dartmouth College

BROWN "UNDERCOVER"

Literary societies have existed at Brown since the 18th century. One of these was the Philermenian Society (founded as the Misokosmian Society in 1794). In reaction to the Federalist Philermenians, a Democratic-Republican society called the United Brothers Society was formed in 1806, and in 1824 a third, the Franklin Society, was formally recognized by the university president.

All of these societies had libraries and meeting rooms on the top floor of Hope College, where they guarded their documents against inter-society espionage.

By the late 19th century, these societies diminished and eventually dissolved on account of the growth in the number of originally-secret Greek letter fraternities. Only the Franklin Society survived, evolving into the Society of the Pacifica House (Societas Domi Pacificae) after the Civil War. Pacifica House, today a secret society, is the only such society at Brown.

Recruitment for fraternities and sororities in the Ivy League has also evolved—in many ways becoming more inclusive than it once was. Informal recruitment begins the very first day of the year at many schools, when Greeks host gatherings and impromptu social events for prospective members. "Rush," or formal recruitment, begins at varying times throughout the year—some Ivies offer it in the fall, others in the spring, or both. Exactly when a student can make the decision to join a fraternity or sorority also varies by school. For some, it is an option freshman year, while others must wait until they are sophomores. During rush, interested students visit Greek houses to meet members, get tours of the house, and learn more about the priorities, activities, and principles of the organization. This is also the time when Greek members are putting on their best faces to "rushees"—and vice versa. If you become a "rushee," or a perspective member, prepare to be wined and dined by fraternities and sororities that want to prove why you should join their house. At the same time, as a "rushee," you, too, will have to be on your best behavior at the houses you are most interested in joining. At the end of rush, prospective members rank their top choices and then wait to see which houses offer a "bid," or an invitation of membership. Bids are not always offered from the houses "rushees" wish to join the most, so prospective Greeks should be prepared for disappointment, but also understand that they might not have been the best match for the house—and there is always next year . . .

After students have selected a house, bids are "signed," or affirmed, and prospective members now become "pledges." "Pledging," the time between when a student decides to join a house and when they are initiated and become a full-fledged member, varies greatly from school to school and from house to house. Within the Ivy League, there are some similarities though; most pledges are assigned a "big brother" or "big sister." This tends to be an older student in the house who guides, helps, and offers support to the pledge. New members should expect pledging to be exciting, fun, and also a lot of work—they will spend a lot of time simply learning of the history, traditions, values, and members that make each house so unique. Pledges bond with other pledges during this time but also come to know all of the brothers or sisters quite well throughout the process. As they grow older, many brothers and sisters will reflect fondly on their time spent as a pledge and remember it as a definitive period in their collegiate lives.

There is no definitive answer as to whether one should or should not join a fraternity or sorority. It depends almost entirely on your own situation. Are you at a big or a small Ivy? Does Greek life dominate the social scene or not? What are you looking to get out of your four years in college?

I've already mentioned some of the advantages that students have cited about joining—there is the camaraderie, the ability to achieve goals with the help of a team, the support network, and lest we forget, the fun. Emerged in a fraternity or sorority, you will quickly develop a strong group of friends with whom you'll eat dinner, take classes, and spend your free time. There will be opportunities to join intramural sports leagues, do community service, and host parties. If you're lucky, you'll be in a beautiful, spacious home (many Greek houses in the Ivies date back over a century), and you'll quickly learn how to live independently with others. Many houses also have their own cooks, so you can expect home-style cooking and the company of friends in your house's dining room. There will be leadership opportunities, a strong support network when you need it, and come graduation, a tight group of alumni willing to offer guidance and help in pursuing what you want to do with your life.

To be fair, we should also point out some of the most often-cited shortcomings—hazing, drinking, and conformity. You've likely heard or read of fraternity and sorority hazing at some point. According to Hank Nuwer, author of *Wrongs of Passage: Fraternities, Sororities, Hazing and Binge Drinking,* the first reported hazing fraternity death occurred at Cornell in 1873 when a Kappa Alpha Society pledge fell into an Ithaca gorge after being left alone in the woods. While incidents like these have been relatively rare in the Ivy League in the last several years, the *Dartmouth* reported in 2004 that members of one of the school's fraternities hazed sorority pledges "as part of a pledge activity gone awry." A year prior, in January 2003, the *Dartmouth* reported another incident involving the alleged hazing of sorority members in two fraternity houses at the school. "Male students used red markers to sign their names on the bodies of three pledges at the urging of both the pledges themselves and two other . . . members," the newspaper reported.

In 2002, it was reported by CNN that drinking by American college students resulted in 1,400 deaths a year and nearly 70,000 cases of sexual assault. The issue of drinking, underage drinking, and binge drinking are all areas that have recently come under increased scrutiny by university administrators. While this problem centers around *all* college students (Greeks and non-Greeks) at many schools, Greek houses tend to provide an environment conducive to drinking with their ready and easy access to alcoholic beverages. Also, according to a *2001 College Alcohol Study* by the Harvard School of Public Health, fraternity members are twice as likely to drink as other students. The response has been significant: just as there has been increased vigilance in monitoring and punishing houses that haze, many schools have now instituted monitoring systems at parties and enforced mandatory alcohol education for Greek members. Fraternities and sororities that fail to comply are placed on probation, and in some instances, shut down.

Alexandra Robbins, author of *Pledged: The Secret Life of Sororities,* spent a year undercover as she sought to expose what goes on in Greek houses, including rampant conformity. She concludes that "[sororities] promote the organizations as groups that enrich life experiences and further the development of women, yet at the same time they enforce regressive standards and strip sisters of their sense of self-empowerment." In the book's conclusion, Robbins cites a 1994 study in the *Journal of College Student Development* that found Greeks to have had "significantly less independence, liberalism, social conscientiousness, and cultural sophistication than the independent students, and tended to possess more sociability, hedonism, self-confidence and social conformity." This criticism, that joining Greek houses forces conformity is another potential drawback—although not one cited nearly as often as binge-drinking and hazing.

When you balance these criticisms with the positives that come from joining Greek organizations, you'll find that for every Greek who is an irresponsible drinker, there is another who savors the teamwork, experience, and motivation that goes along with joining a house. And for every Greek who falls victim to social conformity, there is yet another who wants nothing more than to bask in his/her individuality.

The choice is certainly yours. Consider your options, but choose wisely; once you make this decision, there will be no opportunity to change it.

The Inside Scoop On Eating Clubs

Eating Clubs

Eating Clubs are Princeton's version of fraternities or sororities. There are 11 active eating clubs on Prospect Avenue, or "The Street."

"Bicker"

As a noun, "bicker" refers to the several days at Princeton in which prospective, primarily sophomore, students visit selective eating clubs for interviews with members. The word can also be used as a verb (i.e., Johnny "bickered" Campus Club but didn't get in.) "Bicker" at Princeton is interchangeable with "rush" at those schools with Greek systems.

Most Selective Club

In 2003, Tower Club, with 161 candidates—the largest bicker class among the Princeton eating clubs—invited 86 members to join, for an admit rate of just over 50 percent. Runner-up: Ivy Club, accepting 64 of 106 bickerees, or around 60 percent.

Sample Menu at the Princeton Tower Club

Lunch: Spinach Salad with Ranch Dressing, Maryland Crab Soup, Burgers, Turkey Burgers, Breaded Chicken Sandwich, "Boca Burger," Grilled Portabella Sandwich, "Signature Sandwich"

Dinner: Oven-Roasted Chicken, Pot Roast, Vegetarian Stuffed Peppers, Smashed Potatoes, Corn, Pasta Bar

Princeton Tower Club

You Can't Sit Here!

SELECTIVE EATING CLUBS:

- Cap and Gown
- Cottage
- Ivy
- Tiger
- Tower

Eating Clubs

The opportunity to join the Greek system is not available to all Ivy students. At Princeton, fraternities and sororities were banned in 1855. It was this ban, coupled with the lack of decent dining options at the school, that led to the creation of small, independent eating clubs before the turn of the century. These clubs (with names like, Knights of the Round Table, Old Bourbon, and At Mrs. Van Dyne's) initially shut down almost as quickly as they were created—a lack of arrangements prevented permanency. In 1878, however, this changed when a group of upperclassmen banded together, made arrangements to have a full-time steward, and rented Ivy Hall (located on Mercer Street in Princeton) for the purpose of solidifying an independent dining facility. About four years later, this group of men—which at that point had self-perpetuated to include more people than just the founders—secured the College's permission to erect a private house on Prospect Avenue, not only establishing the first formal eating club, called Ivy Club, but also setting the trend for the rest of the clubs that followed. Prospect Avenue, in some senses, became eating club central.

These clubs quickly eroded interest in, and support of, Princeton's secret societies—the American Whig Society and the Cliosophic Society that had formed in the 18th century—to the extent that the two groups merged in 1928. The newly-formed American Whig-Cliosophic Society, still in existence today, is now the world's oldest college political, literary, and debate society. Meanwhile, the increasingly popular eating

The Ivy Club of Princeton

Membership $6,500

Membership Size 140

Connections When You Graduate.............................. Priceless clubs provided more than just a place to eat. They also offered a means of getting around the administrative ban on fraternities at the school and essentially allowed for the creation of social houses.

In his book, *This Side of Paradise*, F. Scott Fitzgerald, a member of Cottage Club, offered insight on some of the clubs that existed while he was a student at Princeton:

> Ivy, detached and breathlessly aristocratic; Cottage, an impressive mélange of brilliant adventurers and well-dressed philanderers; Tiger Inn, broad-shouldered and athletic, vitalized by an honest elaboration of prep-school standards; Cap and Gown, anti-alcoholic, faintly religious and politically powerful; flamboyant Colonial; literary Quadrangle; and the dozen others varying in age and position.

Some of these clubs are still in existence today. As of 2005, there were a total of eleven clubs on campus—all of which have been coeducational since a 1991 lawsuit brought against several of them by student Sally Frank, class of 1980. Students now visit these clubs during their freshman year; by March of their sophomore year, they link up with friends and enter their chosen club. Five of the offerings, Cap and Gown, Cottage, Ivy, Tiger and Tower, are selective. Prospective members "punch" these clubs during a period of time called "bicker"—and then wait for an answer.

The six remaining clubs, Campus, Charter, Cloister, Colonial, Quadrangle and Terrace are non-selective. At these "sign in" clubs, students place their name on a list for entrance; if too many show interest, a lottery is held. Prospective members can place their names on the lists of several clubs and are guaranteed entrance into at least one—with up to 12 of their friends.

Each club now occupies a large house on Prospect Avenue (or simply, "The Street"), with the exception of Terrace, located around the corner on Washington Road. Some clubs, like Cannon, Elm, and Dial Lodge, have fallen on hard times over the years and have been forced to shut their doors or merge with others. But for the clubs that remain, it's clear that they will continue to serve as an important component to the Princeton experience.

Saved You a Seat.

NON-SELECTIVE EATING CLUBS:

- Campus
- Charter
- Cloister
- Colonial
- Quadrangle
- Terrace

More Scoop On Eating Clubs

Daily Princetonian Review of Food at Colonial Club

"The quality of the lunches we sampled significantly outshined the dinner offerings, but variety was consistent and impressive. Our sample lunch included poboy sandwiches made from shrimp, scallops, chicken, or tofu, egg-drop soup, and a side salad of spring greens with fresh strawberries, blue cheese and walnuts. A deli sandwich bar, salad bar and fresh fruit was also available. The dinner of baked lemon codfish and lasagna was notably less gourmet than the lunch, but still of reasonable quality. A pasta bar and salad bar always accompanied dinners for pickier eaters. All-American desserts like chewy chocolate chip cookies were a staple. Overall, meals could be characterized as consistently edible American cuisine."

Sample Fees at University Cottage

- $400 initiation
- $400 advance deposit
- $500 social
- $6,025 board

Eating Club Observations

"If, at The Ivy League's southernmost school, it's Southern gentleman and ladies you seek, visit Cottage Club. Cloister Club, home to the aquatic athletes, is the place to go if you're hoping to walk through the looking glass and into the fields and football games of an Abercrombie & Fitch catalogue. If John Belushi's portrayal of John 'Bluto' Blutarsky in *Animal House* is the most moving piece of cinematic expression you've ever seen, then it's Tiger Inn ('TI' in the P'ton lexicon) for you. Just drink a lot of water." — Melissa Rose Langsam, *Harvard Crimson*

"How miserable it all was. How sad and stupid. To get into Princeton, the first school in my life where I didn't feel like a nerd for loving books, and find out that silly cliques still topped the social pyramid." — Walter Kirn, *Houston Chronicle* and Princeton alumnus

Final Clubs Revealed

Definition of "Punch"

Can be used as a verb (i.e., Julie couldn't "punch" any of the final clubs because they didn't admit women) or an adjective (i.e., Mike really enjoyed the "punch event" last night). It is similar to "rushing" or "bickering." Students punch final clubs, or try out, during their sophomore year.

According to *Harvard Magazine*

"Interestingly, club leaders privately estimate that about half the graduate membership of the final clubs would support the election of women should the undergraduate members wish it. At one club, more than 80 percent of the graduate membership said they would agree to the admission of women."

Harvard Final Clubs

- AD
- Delphic
- The Fly
- The Fox
- Owl
- Phoenix
- Porcellain
- Spee

The Ad, The Fly, and Final Clubs

Although the story behind Harvard's final clubs differs from that of Princeton's eating clubs, when examining the two closely, certain similarities become apparent. Like eating clubs, Harvard's final clubs have a very rich history. Take, for example, the AD, founded in the mid-19th century after the Alpha Delta Phi fraternity at Harvard broke into two fractions (supposedly after a disagreement over the course of the Civil War). The rift created two new social organizations, the Fly (stemming from the word Phi) and the AD (from Alpha Delta). In 1896, members and alumni of the AD raised enough money to buy property on which the club still stands, making it one of the first final clubs at the school. Its rival, the Fly, became an official club in 1910, nearly 50 years after the fraternity broke up.

As many of Harvard's fraternities folded, dismantled, or evolved into final clubs at the turn of the century, three tiers of clubs emerged. There were final clubs for upperclassmen, waiting clubs for sophomores and juniors, and freshman clubs. The AD was one of the final clubs (named because they would be the "final" clubs Harvard students would join). The other was Porcellian, an extremely selective, prestigious club founded in 1791 by a group of male undergraduate students who would talk and roast pork together. In order to be accepted into Porcellian, students were put through a rigorous screening that required them to first be members of several waiting and freshman clubs. One famous Harvard student who did not make the cut was Franklin D. Roosevelt, the 32nd President of the United States. Roosevelt failed to be accepted despite the fact that his father James, and cousin, Teddy (the 26th president of the United States), had both been members. Lathrop Brown, Roosevelt's roommate, would later write that "his not 'making' the Porcellian meant only that he was free of any restraining influences of a lot of delightful people who thought that the world belonged to them and who did not want to change anything in it." Instead, Roosevelt joined the Fly.

REJECTED!

Franklin D. Roosevelt, the 32nd president of the United States, was rejected from Porcellian, even though his father and cousin were both members.

. . . the University gave the clubs an ultimatum: go coed or go private. They decided to privatize.

Like Princeton's eating clubs, many of Harvard's final clubs have collapsed or merged over the years, either voluntarily or not. Its eight clubs today—AD, Delphic, the Fly, the Fox, Owl, Phoenix, Porcellian, and Spee—have been completely independent from the school since 1984. It was in that year that the University gave the clubs an ultimatum: go coed or go private. They decided to privatize; all of them are now owned and run by alumni organizations, and women are still refused membership, except for the all-female Bee Club. Recruitment at these clubs, similar to their counterparts at Princeton, varies greatly. At the beginning of their sophomore year, interested students "punch" (or, try out) for final clubs; most "punching" is by invitation only. Although they are often notified of their acceptance into the clubs by Thanksgiving, most new members must endure several weeks (and sometimes, months) of an integration process. This might involve, among other things, streaking across campus, washing cars in freezing cold temperatures—while wearing Speedos—pampering senior members, and drinking.

Once they have passed the integration process and are initiated, new members are treated to what current members already enjoy: fancy clubhouses, a social outlet, and an opportunity to network with those who have similar interests. At the same time, however, "there are many problems with Harvard's final clubs," according to an editorial in the school newspaper, the *Harvard Crimson.* "With their all-male membership and secretive, closed selection process, they are relics of Harvard's sexist, elitist past. That they are campus social centers is a sad reflection on Harvard's nightlife."

Secret Societies and Mysteries of Skull and Bones

We've touched on eating clubs at Princeton, final clubs at Harvard, and the largest Greek organizations at schools like Cornell, Penn, and Dartmouth—but what about senior secret societies? Senior secret societies—so named because they are clandestinely comprised of approximately 15 members of a school's senior class—are, in fact, present on each of the eight Ivy League campuses.

It's clear that, among its peers, Yale is truly the leader, with at least 10 prominent societies on campus, including Skull and Bones—a secret society that's considered by many to be the most elite and notorious in the world. This society and the others—Berzelius, Book and Snake, Elihu, Mace and Chain, Manuscript, Scroll and Key, the Society of St. Anthony Hall, St. Elmo's, and Wolf's Head—differ from fraternities and sororities (and certain eating and final clubs) in that membership is not open through rush. Instead, each year, prospective student are "tapped," or offered individual invitations to join. Also unlike Greek systems, these new members tend not to pay dues or fees; funding instead comes primarily from society alumni.

The Scroll and Key society was established in 1842 by John Addision Porter at Yale after members of Alpha Delta Phi fraternity, including Theodore Runyon, the late governor of New Jersey, Congressman Isaac Hiester, and Leonard Case, founder of Case Western Reserve University, did not gain entrance into Skull and Bones. This society is thus modeled after Skull and Bones; 15 juniors are annually tapped for membership. Unlike the other secret societies, though, whose central activity is the "audit," in which members share their life story with the group, Scroll and Key members debate. The purpose of this debate, as well as the audit, is to encourage openness and acceptance of all members, who learn about others and themselves in the process. As of fiscal year 2001, Scroll and Key, whose corporate name is Kingsley Trust, had assets of over $6.6 million dollars, making it the wealthiest of Yale's senior societies. Its tomb, or window-less home is at 444 College Street.

Shhhhh, It's a Secret (Society)...

Berzelius (Colony Club)
Book and Snake (Cloisters)
Dragon Society
Elihu
Franklin Society (dissolved)
Griffin Society
Hexagon
Lantern
Mace and Chain
Manuscript
Mortar Board
Oracle
Pacifica House
Philermenian Society
Quill and Dagger
Sage and Chalice
Scroll and Key
Skull and Bones
Skull and Dagger
Society of St. Anthony Hall
Sphinx Society
St. Elmo's
Wolf's Head

Tap = Go to Your Room!

How did this practice start?

According to Judith Ann Schiff, chief research archivist at the Yale University Library, "In the late 1870s, the juniors revolted. Instead of waiting alone in their rooms on election night, they gathered outside on the steps of the Old Campus dormitories to see which societies their friends would accept. But the seniors didn't want to announce the elections publicly, so they simply tapped each selected junior and said only, 'Go to your room.' Thus Tap Day was born."

In the 19th century, Yale College was split into two departments: the "Ac," or Academical Department for liberal arts majors, and "Sheff," the Sheffield Scientific School for engineers and scientists. Both Berzelius and Book and Snake were initially founded as Sheff final clubs before evolving into senior secret societies in 1933. Berzelius, conceived in 1848 and originally called the Colony Club, has a tomb at 78 Trumbull Street and assets through the Colony Foundation, its corporate name, of over one million dollars—although it is rumored to be in poor financial standing. Book and Snake, the other former Sheff final club, is also known as the Cloisters. Founded in 1863, its tomb now rests on Grove Street. It taps 16 new members each year, many of who are involved in athletics or the Greek system, and was the first society at Yale to accept women and minorities.

Berzelius
the party society

Book and Snake
athletes and Greeks

Elihu
the least-prestigious

St. Anthony Hall
not even secret

The Wolf's Head was created in 1883, making it the third oldest senior society at the school. Like other groups, its founders were unhappy with the offerings of Yale's societies and most likely had, themselves, been passed up by Skull and Bones and Scroll and Key. Elihu differs from other secret societies at Yale in that it invites every junior class member to interview with the group—as opposed to selectively tapping certain students. Founded in 1903, the Elihu Club, Inc. tends to be politically left-leaning. It is also the only senior society on campus whose tomb has windows. Because of this, and its open-selection procedure, Elihu is said by students to be considered less prestigious.

Manuscript is one of the newest societies at Yale, founded in 1952, and housed in a more modest-sized tomb designed by Yale architect King-lui Wu on Elm Street. As in Elihu, selection differs here as well—faculty and alumni are actively involved in the process. The society was also the location of a party in Tom Perrlotta's 2001 novel *Joe College*. Mace and Chain was recently reintroduced on campus by an alumnus of the society who longed for its return. Not much is known or reported on the group except that it conducts its activities out of an apartment on Audubon Street. Similarly, St. Elmo's, which occupies a cellar of a house on Lynwood Street, and the Society of St. Anthony Hall (St. A's), whose members conduct activities in Yale's Silliman College, are newcomers to this increasingly crowded field of societies.

Most of these senior societies are now coed and, unlike some final clubs at Harvard, appear to value the diversity of its members. Although most of the groups follow "lines" when selecting new members—for example, consistently tapping the student who holds a certain position on campus—many do not. The societies tend to follow the lead of Skull and Bones in having their 15 members meet twice a week, on Thursday and Sunday nights, for their audits. At these meetings, which take place in the spring semester, members provide oral histories of their lives, often including their histories with the opposite sex. After these meetings come to an end, students tend to hit off-campus eateries, like Naples Pizza, to relax, although not to say a word of what has transpired that evening.

Yale is not the only Ivy with secret societies. There is the Dragon Society, the Griffin Society, Skull and Dagger, and the Sphinx Society on Dartmouth's campus. At Brown, Franklin Society and Philermenian Society—in existence since the 18th century—diminished and dissolved by the late 19th century and was replaced by Greek letter societies. The Pacifica House remains the school's only secret society today. Cornell boasts of Quill and Dagger, Mortar Board, and Skull and Dagger societies. The Hexagon, Lantern, and Oracle societies are among many others on Penn's campus. But none of these senior secret societies come anywhere close to competing with the amount of intrigue and attention that has been paid to Skull and Bones at Yale.

We've already mentioned the film, *The Skulls,* a fictitious account of a secret and dangerous society at an unnamed Ivy League school in New Haven, Connecticut. But what about the documented research of *New York Observer* reporter and Yale graduate Ron Rosenbaum? He claims to have set up video cameras in the window of the tomb to record an initiation ceremony.

Alexandra Robbins, the recent Yale graduate who wrote *Pledged,* also authored one of the most comprehensive histories of the Skull and Bones, *Secrets of the Tomb: Skull and Bones, the Ivy League, and the Hidden Paths of Power,* in 2002. Clearly, we are continually drawn to and fascinated by Skull and Bones.

You Decide

Where did "322" come from?

Story 1: The concept for Skull and Bones was brought back from Germany, and a second chapter was founded in 1832.

Story 2: The society was named for Eulogia, the goddess of eloquence. She entered the Pantheon after Demosthenes died in 322 BC.

The Beginning of the Bones

Yale student William H. Russell founded Skull and Bones after he returned from a trip to Germany in 1831-1832. While overseas, he had come across a secret society known as the Brotherhood of Death (or, the Order of the Skull and Bones). This German society supposedly had connections to the Order of the Illuminati, a group of young revolutionaries who played a central role in the French Revolution and generally spread mayhem across Europe in the 1800s. Russell brought it to the States and founded the second chapter of Skull and Bones in 1832. The number 32-2 (or 322) is thus seen everywhere on Bones paraphernalia, including its silverware.

But wait. There is also an entirely different story—that Skull and Bones was founded as a "scholarly" society that had to be kept secret in order to quell faculty concerns. According to this legend, the group consisted of students who were dissatisfied with the quality of teaching and the election process for the Phi Beta Kappa society at Yale. This new club first called itself the Eulogia Club—in honor of the goddess of eloquence—which was another offshoot of a German student organization. The belief that the goddess Eulogia entered the Pantheon after Demosthenes died in 322 BC was another explanation of the presence of "322."

Two stories of its founding. One society. Which to believe? Most Bonesmen (as they're known), themselves, claim not to know how the society really started. They just know that it still holds the same mystery it had back in its early days.

In 1856, Daniel Coit Gilman, who later founded Johns Hopkins University, incorporated the society as the Russell Trust Association. In 1943, by special act of the Connecticut state legislature, its trustees were granted an exemption from filing corporate reports with the Secretary of State, which is normally a requirement. Most donations to the society are still made through this association today, and although Skull and Bones is not the richest of all secret societies, it is certainly the most famous.

There are rumors that the skulls of Apache chief Geronimo, Pancho Villa, and Martin Van Buren are housed **in the tomb.**

Inside the Tomb

Skull and Bones moved into its current residence, a small Greco-Egyptian style building on High Street in New Haven, the same year that the society was incorporated. Made of brown sandstone, the tomb looks ominous as it sits below street level, a staircase with a big black gate blocking the entrance. Only Bonesmen are allowed inside the tomb, but enough have been loose-lipped for the public to get a sense of what is really going on beyond the gate. According to accounts, the tomb relics include Nazi memorabilia, (in particular, a set of Hitler's silverware). There are also numerous Civil War and World War I artifacts, along with a pair of boots that one member wore throughout France during World War II. He shipped them to the tomb right after completing his tour of duty.

Each member is required to give a CB (short for "Connubial Bliss") and share their sexual history with fellow Bonesman.

The most prevalent decorations are rather morbid—coffins, skeletons, moose heads, skulls, and a large collection of gothic artwork. Candles and Medieval armor can also be seen everywhere. One room reportedly has old manuscripts and copies of every book ever written by a Bonesman. There are small statuettes of the god Demosthenes, which give some weight to the more realistic (and less amusing) story about the society's origins.

Probably the biggest catch in the tomb is the gravestone of Elihu Yale, founder of the University. The marker was stolen from a graveyard in Wrexham, Wales, where the man was buried and is now displayed regally in a glass case. There are also rumors that the skulls of Apache chief Geronimo, Pancho Villa, and Martin Van Buren are housed in the tomb. This speculation prompted Ned Anderson, an Apache member, to ask the FBI in 1986 to investigate the claim about Geronimo and repatriate the skull if necessary. It was discovered soon thereafter that the skull was not genuine. It still sits in the tomb.

Initiation Rites

According to accounts, the initiation process has changed dramatically over the last century and a half, although certain components have remained the same. Letting students know that they have been chosen to join Skull and Bones is now much more secretive than it used to be; names of members are no longer printed in the *Yale Daily News* as they were in the late 1800s and early 1900s.

Every spring, senior Bonesmen choose 15 third-years who they would like to tap, as well as a few extras in case some first-choice picks turn them down. Distinguished student leaders, legacies, and children of East Coast old money families are all targeted, and Protestants are often picked over Catholics. At least this is how it used to be. Over the past decade, however, Skull and Bones has made an effort to tap a more multicultural cross-section of the cream of the crop. When women were first inducted, in 1991, many alumni expressed unhappiness with the idea of accepting women into the "Old Boys' Club."

The names of new members were published in the *Yale Daily News* and the *New York Times* until 1970.

Secret Traditions REVEALED

Skull and Bones is steeped in tradition. There are so many secret rituals, words, and stories that it's hard to tell the real from the myth. Here's what we've found:

- New Bonesmen are all **assigned secret names**. These are often passed down from older students; some are traditionally given to one person each year. The most common are: Long Devil (tallest member); Boaz (varsity football captain); Magog (member with the most sexual experience); Gog (member with the least sexual experience). Some Bonesmen choose literary or mythical names like Hamlet, Thor, or Uncle Remus. Presidents Taft and George H.W. Bush were Magogs. President George W. Bush was allowed to choose his name, but rumor has it he couldn't think of one. He was given "Temporary," and it stuck.

- Skull and Bones time is **five minutes fast**. The clocks in the tomb say 8:00 while "barbarian" (non-Bones) time is really 7:55.

- There is **no alcohol** allowed in the tomb.

- All Bonesmen must **leave the room** if the words "Skull and Bones" or "322" are mentioned—no matter where they are or who they are with.

- Bonesmen used to be given **grandfather clocks** as wedding gifts. This stopped in the early 1960s, supposedly because too many members were having second and third marriages. The other notorious gift—$15,000 upon graduation—is a myth.

- Unlike other secret societies at Yale, Skull and Bones **does not give gifts**, grants, or any other money to the community.

- Current student Bonesmen take an **annual one-week trip** to Deer Island, an exclusive waterfront property on the St. Lawrence River. After a chartered boat ride, members can play tennis or softball, eat elegant meals in a private mansion, or play water sports. There is also an amphitheater on the island. Many older Bonesmen visit the island for long weekends in the summer to reconnect with old friends and relax.

- Bonesmen **do not pay dues** to the society. An annual letter is sent out, however, requesting "a voluntary contribution to the Russell Trust Association."

The initiation process changes slightly from year to year, but past Bonesmen say it always includes elaborate costumes and masks until the newly-initiated student swears an oath of secrecy. The third-year is disoriented, yelled at, and often thrown around and scared. In the Inner Temple, the most secret room of the tomb, the initiation rite takes place. Once they are initiated, new Bonesmen take turns telling their sexual histories (possibly while lying naked in a coffin) and disclosing their autobiographies. They go through group criticism sessions—the audits—that some describe to have caused nervous breakdowns.

The Bonesmen, now seniors, meet every Thursday and Sunday night during their final year of college, and the process begins once again.

This is a network unlike many—Bonesmen are also encouraged to ***intermarry****, so ties of friendship become even stronger ties of family.*

The Ties, the Network

Current and former Bonesmen include presidents, secretaries of state, ambassadors, C.I.A. operatives, journalists, media and business moguls, and members of just about every other profession out there. Conspiracy theorists and cynics consider the proliferation of Bonesmen some sort of New World Order; the Bonesmen are blamed for virtually all that occurs in the realm of politics and economics, even matters of war and peace. These theorists argue that Bonesmen and Skull and Bones is behind all that goes wrong, and occasionally right, in the world. This might be stretching their influence a bit much.

There are approximately 800 living Bonesmen in the United States, many of whom, like fraternity brothers, help guide younger Bonesmen into prominent positions elsewhere. This is a network unlike many—Bonesmen are also encouraged to intermarry, so ties of friendship become even stronger ties of family.

Skull and Bones is everywhere. Business and media leaders include Henry Luce (Class of 1920), founder of Time, Inc.; Harold Stanley (Class of 1908), founder of Morgan Stanley; Artemus Gates (Class of 1918), President of New York Trust Company, Union Pacific, Time, and Boeing; Dean Witter, Jr. (Class of 1944), investment banker; Russell W. Davenport (Class of 1923), editor of *Fortune* Magazine and creator of the Fortune 500 list; Frederick W. Smith (Class of 1966), founder of FedEx. And don't forget Pierre Jay (Class of 1892), first chairman of the Federal Reserve Bank of New York; John Thomas Daniels (Class of 1914), founder Archer Daniels Midland; Thomas Cochran (Class of 1904), another partner at Morgan Stanley; and Harry Payne Whitney (Class of 1894), investment banker.

Then, of course, there are the multi-taskers and power moguls. Andrew D. White (Class of 1853) was a successful businessman and the founding president of Cornell University. William Graham Sumner (Class of 1863) was an influential sociologist, social Darwinist, and economist. George Herbert Walker, Jr. (Class of 1927) was the financier and co-founder of the New York Mets. William Draper III (Class of 1950), a member of the Department of Defense, was also involved in the United Nations and Import-Export Bank. Supreme Court Justice Potter Stewart was in the Bones class of 1936. Evan G. Galbraith (Class of 1950) was an ambassador to France and the managing director of Morgan Stanley. Winston Lord (Class of 1959) was an ambassador to China and President Bill Clinton's assistant secretary of state. Armory Howe Bradford (Class of 1934) was the general manager for the *New York Times*. Not only do they own the newspapers, magazines, and publishing houses, Bonesmen also write for them. Conservative journalist William F. Buckley, Jr. was a 1950 Bonesman. Doonesbury writer Garry B. Trudeau (Class of 1970) and award-winning novelist Mark Salzman (Class of 1982) were both in the society. **And then, there is the Bush family . . .**

The Bush Legacy

President George W. Bush's father, former President George H.W. Bush, was in the Bones class of 1948. Up to 10 of his Presidential advisors were fellow Bonesmen. Former Connecticut Senator Prescott Sheldon Bush, who is George H.W.'s father and George W.'s grandfather, was a Bonesman in the Class of 1917. George H.W.'s brother was also a Bonesman. Bush cousins and in-laws have also been traced to the society. The Bush family has Bones financial connections in banking companies, oil, and politics dating back to the late 1920s.

The Bush family actually has the second-most names on the Skull and Bones roster, according to what we've uncovered. First is the Taft family, boasting nine members. Alphonso Taft, a U.S. Attorney General, was in the first class of Bonesmen. His son, former President William Howard Taft, was in the Bones class of 1878. His son, Robert Alphonso Taft was also a Bonesman (Class of 1910) and senator just after World War II. Henry Stimson (Class of 1888) was President Taft's secretary of war. He was also President Hoover's secretary of state. And as President Truman's chief advisor on atomic weaponry, Stimson also encouraged his boss to drop the atomic bomb—its construction and deployment was essentially overseen by a committee of Bonesmen, including Stimson, George Harrison, Robert Lovett, Harvey Bundy, and Averell Harriman.

See? You really can get lost tracing through the network of alliances. *But back to the Bushes.*

Prescott Bush, the father of George H.W. Bush and grandfather of George W., was tapped to be a Bonesman in 1916. He became managing partner of Brown Brothers, Harriman after a tour in World War I. Brown Brothers, Harriman was founded by fellow Bonesman Averil Harriman (1913). Prescott Bush was in the same Bones class as Averil's brother Ronald (1917) and was one of four Bonesmen from that class to act as managing director of the company. In 1928, W.A. Harriman and Company bought stock in Dresser Industries, an oil drilling equipment company. Prescott Bush and other Bonesmen, E. Roland Harriman and Henry Neil Mallon (a Yale graduate but not a Bonesman), were all involved at the top levels of the company. Mallon eventually hired George W. Bush to work at Dresser.

Presidential Skulls

Probably the timeliest Bones connection has to do with the recent 2004 presidential race. Massachusetts senator and presidential hopeful John F. Kerry was a Bonesman (Class of 1966). He, of course, ran against President George W. Bush, who was in the Skull and Bones class of 1968. At least five of Bush's advisors were also Bonesmen, and many other members of the administration claim membership, including Bill Donaldson (Class of 1953), chairman of the Securities and Exchange Commission; Robert McCallum (Class of 1968), the assistant attorney general; General Counsel to the Office of Homeland Security Edward McNally (Class of 1979); and Roy Austin (Class of 1968), ambassador to Trinidad and Tobago.

In a February 7, 2004 interview that was aired on NBC's *Meet the Press*, Tim Russert spoke with President Bush about his connection to Skull and Bones. Russert mentioned that Bush and Kerry were "both in Skull and Bones, the secret society." An excerpt from that interview reveals how even though membership in the society might be less than private, Bonesmen keep their lips sealed when pressed to speak:

> **Bush:** It's so secret we can't talk about it.
>
> **Russert:** What does that mean for America? The conspiracy theorists are going to go wild.
>
> **Bush:** I'm sure they are. I don't know. I haven't seen Web pages yet. (Laughs)
>
> **Russert:** Number 322.
>
> **Bush:** First of all, he's not the nominee, and—but look, I look forward . . .

Stumbling to change the topic, Bush noticeably broke a Bonesman rule by not leaving the room when "322" was mentioned. His flustered, hurried, and off-hand comment shows though that he wasn't quite prepared for Russert's test on live, national television.

Similarly, Kerry was confronted twice on national television about his involvement in Skull and Bones. In an August 31, 2003 interview also with Tim Russert on NBC, Kerry tried to make light of his connections:

> **Russert:** You were both members of Skull and Bones, a secret society at Yale. What does that tell us?
>
> **Kerry:** Uh, not much, 'cause it's a secret. (Laughs)
>
> **Russert:** Is there a secret handshake? Is there a secret code?
>
> **Kerry:** I wish there were something secret I could manifest . . .
>
> **Russert:** 322—a secret number?
>
> **Kerry:** There are all kinds of secrets, Tim. But one thing that's not a secret: I disagree with this President's direction that he's taking the country . . .

Kerry desperately tries to change the subject, smoothly transitioning back into politics. In an April 18, 2004 edition of the same show, Tim Russert interviewed Kerry again. Towards the very end of the interview, he brought up Skull and Bones:

> **Russert:** Before we go, you and George Bush were both members of Skull and Bones, the secret society at Yale. The rule is, if someone mentions Skull and Bones, you walk out of the room. If you're both in a . . .
>
> **Kerry:** You trying to get rid of me here?
>
> **Russert:** You're both in a presidential debate and the moderator says "Skull and Bones," you both leave the podiums?
>
> **Kerry:** I doubt it.
>
> **Russert:** You'll hang in there.
>
> **Kerry:** I think you'll see both of us have our two—you know I'd love to have a debate with the President right now. There's so much to talk about for our country . . .

And, just like that Kerry did it again! Veering around the questions seems to be a Bones tradition—much to the dismay of host Tim Russert—although Kerry did acknowledge the Bones law of leaving the room when "Skull and Bones" was mentioned.

It was a hot topic for those interested in Bonesmen to discuss who would side with whom in the 2004 election. Many claimed that it didn't matter one way or the other—ultimately, it would be just another connection in national and international politics, economics, and policy for the Bonesmen. After all, it doesn't seem to take much more than just a quick call and a mention of the "H.W. Russell Trust" or "322" to get you a job basically anywhere from a fellow Bonesmen.

Most Likely To Be President:

Which Ivy was attended by the most U.S. presidents?

President may have attended Ivy universities for either undergrad or grad school program. In some cases, President did not complete his education.

Rankings:

1.	Harvard	7
2.	Yale	5
3.	Princeton	3
4.	Columbia	2
5.	Penn	1
6.	Brown	0
6.	Cornell	0
6.	Dartmouth	0

Did you know?

In the '50s, Dwight Eisenhower served as Columbia's president before becoming the president of the United States.

John F. Kennedy's Educational Record

- London School of Economics – Undergraduate (transferred to Princeton*)
- Princeton University – Undergraduate (transferred to Harvard)
- Harvard University – Undergraduate
- Stanford Graduate School of Business (flunked out)

* Currently, Princeton does not accept transfers.

What college did Abraham Lincoln, Andrew Johnson, and Harry S. Truman attend?
None!

Woodrow Wilson was the only United States president to ever earn a PhD. Although his PhD was earned at John Hopkins, he attended Princeton for his undergraduate education. In 1902, he became the president of Princeton.

U.S. Presidents in the Ivy League

Columbia

Dwight D. Eisenhower
University President *(1948 to 1953)*

Franklin D. Roosevelt
Law

Theodore Roosevelt
Law (dropped out)

Harvard

John Adams
Law

John Q. Adams
Law

George W. Bush
Business

Rutherford B. Hayes
Law

John F. Kennedy
Government

Franklin D. Roosevelt
Economics

Theodore Roosevelt
History

Penn

William H. Harrison
Medicine (dropped out)

Princeton

John F. Kennedy
Law (dropped out)

James Madison
Government

Woodrow Wilson
Political Science
University President (1902-1910)

Yale

George H.W. Bush
Economics

George W. Bush
History

William J. Clinton
Law

William H. Taft
Law

Scandals and Pranks

You've heard them before. You know, the rumors involving some dirty old professor and an unassuming coed. Something sexual happens; her grade is boosted; end of story. For years after, the lesson learned is simple—the shorter your skirt, the higher your grade. But there are other stories.

One of the highest-profile cases of sexual misconduct at an Ivy League school made big headlines in early 2004. It involved an exchange between renowned Shakespeare scholar and Yale professor Harold Bloom and then-student (and now writer) Naomi Wolf in 1983. In a *New York* magazine article, Wolf claimed that her professor came to her apartment and groped her, and when she notified her alma mater years later to discuss the incident, received no response. "The man did something, at least once, that was self-centered and harmful," she wrote in the article. "But his harmless impulse would not have entered his or my real life—then or now—if Yale made the consequences of such behavior both clear and real." Bloom never responded to Wolf's claims and continues to teach at Yale.

In 1920, a secret group of top administrators at the school interviewed and then expelled anyone they suspected to be homosexual.

In spring 2004, a group of Harvard entrepreneurs and free-speech advocates created the *H Bomb*, an erotic magazine featuring fellow students in all their glory. ***(www.h-bomb.org)***

At Harvard, the student newspaper, the *Harvard Crimson*, uncovered a pretty juicy Cambridge scandal in 2002. As reported by the paper, in 1920, a secret group of top administrators at the school interviewed and then expelled anyone they suspected to be homosexual. All this was learned only after months of pressure on the University to release old records; the administration finally acquiesced and handed over hundreds of papers in 2002. Many of those questioned by the secret group never finished college; two even committed suicide. At the final tally, six students and a professor were expelled for homosexuality, two for associating with gays, and one alumnus was blacklisted.

There are plenty of other Ivy sex stories that are less disturbing, more titillating, and still very scandalous.

DID YOU KNOW?

All of the photo shoots for *Playboy*'s "Women of the Ivy League" take place off-campus.

In spring 2004, a group of Harvard entrepreneurs and free-speech advocates created the *H Bomb*, an erotic magazine featuring fellow students in all their glory. Katharina Cieplak-von Baldegg and Camilla Hardy started the magazine, which is similar to Vassar College's *Squirm* journal. The media was all over it—many journalists and reporters called the magazine pornographic and disgusting, leading the school's administration to disallow its organizational funding.

In the magazine's defense, its two founders claimed that the nudity was tasteful and called the revealing pictures "no big deal." The two simply wanted to make it known that Harvard kids cared about sex, too. They succeeded. By the time the publication's first issue hit stands, it was considered just another intellectual and artsy magazine.

Then, of course, there's another magazine featuring nude Ivy League students. In September 1995, *Playboy* magazine published its well-known "Women of the Ivy League" issue. It wasn't the magazine's first special issue, although it certainly got a lot more attention than the ones from 1979 and 1986.

Sound Minds and Rosy Cheeks

Ever since the winter of 1973-74, when the craze caught the nation with its pants down, streaking has been a mainstay on college campuses across the country. The esteemed Ivy League institutions have proven no exception in this long and venerable tradition.

In 2002, the *Dartmouth* reported that streaking was alive and well, despite an administration cited by one student as "iron-fisted" when it came to naked rights. "If Dartmouth aims at truth and honesty and, for that matter, individual integrity, shouldn't nudity be respected?" said a student quoted in the newspaper. "I put on clothes because I am cold, not because I am hiding, but if I choose to get down to the basics—I'll do it. **Why restrict freedom?**" That freedom has included the right to walk around a coffee shop, storm the football field and ride a unicycle—all au naturel.

Yale, too, upholds several great traditions, including the (naked) distribution of candy in the libraries and a swim team strip show that reportedly dates back over 130 years—25 more years than the swim team has existed. Social priggery, however, has crept into these Ivory towers and called for the abandonment of the part-prank, part-sacred, pantheistic ritual. At Princeton, after the **Board of Trustees banned the Nude Olympics**, a three-decade old tradition, school spokesman Justice Harmon told the *Daily Princetonian*, "It was only a matter of time before something really tragic happened."

→

A violation of the Board's edict now puts students at risk for a year's suspension. Harmon said that the Nude Olympics, and events like them, were "silly and spontaneous and can't be planned." In that statement alone, he perhaps captured collegians' long-standing enjoyment of streaking.

Politics and Other Frivolity

Aside from protecting the God-given right to bear skin, Ivy Leaguers have taken up other political causes from time to time.

In 1930, for example, the *Cornell Daily Sun* asked Republican leaders, from congressmen to the vice-president, to join in celebrating the **150th birthday of Hugo N. Frye**, the reported founder of the Republican Party in New York. Although none of the invited politicians could make the event, most sent kind words regarding Mr. Frye's legacy, including the vice-president and the secretary of labor. Frye, however, was a figment of the *Daily Sun* editors' imaginations, short for "You Go and Fry." The duped Republicans weren't too amused, although the editors got off with a smug apology and a smirk.

Another politically-minded prankster at Princeton founded the **Veterans of Future Wars** in 1935, in response to Great War veterans demanding their bonuses 10 years early. Lewis Gorin justified his cause by explaining: "It is but common right that this bonus be paid now, for many will be killed or wounded in the next war, and hence they, the most deserving, will not otherwise get the full benefit of their country's gratitude." The Veterans of Foreign Wars were not amused, calling the 50,000 active Future War veterans (and their spin-offs, including the Gold-Star Mothers of Future Veterans) "cowards." Time, however, would justify some of Gorin's cause, as all the Princeton VFW members, except for one injured and ineligible soul, would fight for the United States in World War II.

Grand Theft Ivy

Long known for their generally leftist leanings, Ivy scholars have also been known to "redistribute wealth" when they see fit.

In 1933, some staff members of the *Harvard Lampoon* decided that the Commonwealth of Massachusetts' Sacred Cod (hanging in the State's House of Representatives as an eternal reminder of the area's early dependence on fish) would look better in the *Lampoon* offices. In **an unprecedented cod-napping,** involving the kidnapping of a rival publication's staff member, unmarked vehicles, and anonymous phone calls, the *Lampoon* successfully stole the sanctified fish. Two days later, as public suspicion rained down on the humor magazine and regional papers decried the heinous crime against humanity, the *Lampoon* anonymously arranged the drop-off of the fish with a Harvard administrator. Happy that the fish was safe and sound, the state dropped its investigation—although it did begin to keep a tighter leash on its Sacred Cod.

Another famous theft involves Harvard, although this time the school was on the receiving end. Their Ivy competitor, Brown, has historically had a penchant for acquiring its football opponents' mascots. In 1973, several Brown students gained access to the Harvard band, claiming to be *Crimson* reporters. They lured the band into loading **the famous Big H Drum** into their truck, for "publicity photos" for possible use on ABC. As the Harvard students droned on about the band's ability and prestige, the Brown students drove off, leaving a panicked and confused bandleader in their wake. Police soon apprehended the gentlemen, although the charges were dropped after a brief stint in the Foxboro jail.

Warm Welcomes and Cold Receptions

From being sold fake elevator and pool passes, to being given slightly "modified" maps, freshmen often receive their fair share of "welcome weekend" pranks.

At Brown one year, incoming freshmen received letters informing them that there was an **11 p.m. curfew** for the first weekend and that it would be re-evaluated as the semester went on. The letter, ostensibly signed by the school's interim president Sheila Blumstein, also told freshmen that, "if you are intoxicated . . . CALL US [the administration]." Blumstein denied having anything to do with the letter. Administrators said that similar pranks, including one faked letter from the president that banned fraternities and sororities, had occurred frequently the past several years.

A similar letter-under-the-door prank was pulled at the University of Pennsylvania. There, two students left copies of a memo stating that a **dorm's water supply** would be shut down for a few days, and residents should report to the gyms for showers.

The Mysterious Pumpkin

Midnight streaking sessions and duped freshmen make good late-night laugh-fodder, but the truly great pranks, the ones that become legends in and of themselves, take things to a whole new height.

Cornell's mysterious pumpkin is one such prank. One night in 1997, shortly before Halloween, **a giant pumpkin** appeared impaled on top of McGraw Tower, the school's famous 173-foot-tall clock. For months, media outlets covered the story, and police combed the scene for clues, all to no avail. It was only three years later, when a former roommate of one of the men involved came forward with the tale, that theories involving catapults, helicopters, and aliens were finally put to rest. The true identity of the pranksters, however, was never revealed. And perhaps for the mysterious pumpkin, and other pranks of its caliber, that is part of the magic.

And if that wasn't strange enough . . .

On the morning of April 30, 2005, **a shiny disco-ball** was spotted dangling from the top of (you guessed it) McGraw Tower. The removal, which took almost four hours, cost the University around $25,000, according to the Cornell press service.

Local authorites, with the help of a 170-foot-high crane, brought down the disco ball, which was about two-feet in diameter, and a pair of climbing shoes from the roof of the clock tower. Police have yet to identify any suspects.

Want to know how they did it?

Go to **www.collegeprowler.com/Ivy** to find out!

Deconstructing Ivy Urban Legends

Although they might be locked away in a Gothic tower, legends of the Ivy League sometimes surface and reach the consciousness of the outside world, morphing into rumors that enter the realm of fact. You're probably familiar with some of these myths, the ones you've heard from a friend of a friend whose sister's boyfriend goes to an Ivy League school.

Interestingly, all of them incorporate some quirky aspect of the schools' traditions or histories that, in turn, provide additional insight into the true nature of the Ivy League.

We've stumbled across just some of the Ancient Eight's "storied" urban legends and decided to affirm the true ones and debunk the lies. Read on and see what we've uncovered . . .

LEGEND: Grade Inflation Runs Rampant at Harvard

Founded 140 years before the signing of the Declaration of Independence, Harvard has contributed significantly to our nation's history by educating some of the most famous statesmen, philosophers, artists, and scholars in American history. Harvard students are said to be among the best and brightest in the nation and around the world. In recent years, however, the school has been plagued by rumors of excessive grade inflation—prompting students at competing schools to complain that it's easier to get an "A" at Harvard than elsewhere.

So, is there any truth to this rumor? Unfortunately, or fortunately (depending on whom you speak to), yes. According to reports on CNN and in the *Boston Globe*, a record 91 percent of graduating seniors in 2002 had some kind of honors on their diploma. This number seems even greater in contrast with competing schools like Princeton and Yale, which cap total honors at about one-third of the graduating class. Why the inflation? One of the most commonly agreed-upon reasons originates from an unlikely event—the Vietnam War. It was during this era that professors gave students higher grades because those with low grades could lose their college deferments and be sent to war. Grade inflation has continued since then.

VERDICT: PERHAPS

LEGEND: Walking Through Princeton's Gate Means Failure

Any student at Princeton knows that it's best not to pass through the FitzRandolph Gate, for fear of terrible consequences. Legend stipulates that any student who passes through it prior to graduation won't graduate. In fact, a Princeton student's first time walking through the gate is supposed to be at graduation, where the gate symbolizes their transition to the outside world. The FitzRandolph Gate was constructed in 1905 in an effort to keep townspeople off Princeton's campus, although it was opened for special occasions. According to the *Daily Princetonian*, the gate was once opened for President Grover Cleveland during his visit to the University. In 1970, however, the gate was cemented open at the request of the senior class.

The legend of a gate that students should not pass through is not unique to Princeton. Both Yale and Brown have similar stories, and countless other schools have myths that prevent students from graduating. But while there is no real correlation between passing through the FitzRandolph gate and not graduating, superstitious Princeton students who follow tradition might think twice before taking the chance.

VERDICT: MYTH

LEGEND:
Side-stepping the Compass at Penn

Another failure-related Ivy League myth exists at the University of Pennsylvania, where legend states not to "walk over the compass at Locust Walk and 37th Street or you'll flunk midterms." The granite compass embedded in Locust Walk at 37th Street, in the heart of Philadelphia, is the subject of one of Penn's most popular urban legends. Although its origin is unknown, the compass legend has become widely accepted by the student body over the past 20 years. But does the myth hold true? As Penn's landscape architect Robert Lundgren, who designed the compass in 1984, told the *Penn Current* with a laugh, "It was a surprise to me. It is kind of funny. It's nice that they attached something personal to that."

VERDICT: MYTH

LEGEND:
Professor Josiah Carberry Teaches Pyschoceramics at Brown

You may not have heard of psychoceramics, the study of cracked pots, but at Brown University, legendary professor Josiah Carberry taught this discipline. Or did he? The myth behind Carberry first began in 1929, with an announcement on a bulletin board that advertised a lecture the professor would give. The story of Professor Carberry soon grew to include a family of mythical characters, such as his wife Laura, his poetical daughter Patricia, his puffin-hunting daughter Lois, and his accident-prone assistant Truman Grayson, who was always being bitten by things that began with the letter "A."

According to archives in the Brown library, the legend of Josiah Carberry continued when an anonymous gift of $101.01 was given to the University on Friday, May 13, 1955. The gift established the Josiah S. Carberry Fund in memory of his "future late wife"—all on the condition that every Friday the 13th would become "Carberry Day." Those affiliated with Brown would donate their loose change on that day in brown jugs. This money would then be added to the Carberry Fund, which would be used to purchase "such books as Professor Carberry might or might not approve of."

Over the years, Carberry has been the recipient of many awards, including *Yankee* magazine's "Absent-bodied professor" award in 1975, and an Ig Noble Prize at the First Annual Ig Noble Prize Ceremony sponsored by Massachusetts Institute of Technology and the *Journal of Irreproducible Results* in 1991. All this for a professor who never even existed.

VERDICT: MYTH

LEGEND: *Animal House* Took Place at Dartmouth

Animal House, the cult-classic movie that premiered in 1978 about an unruly college fraternity, continues to be enjoyed by filmgoers today. While the antics of the Delta house at the fictitious Faber University might be exaggerated, the story is loosely based on the Alpha Delta Phi chapter of Dartmouth College. The film's script, written by Chris Miller, a member of that house, drew from his own experiences to create some of the characters and scenes that appear in the movie. Though famous scenes, such as the parade at the end of the film, were not inspired by actual events, the name of the movie came from an Alpha Delta Phi tradition of naming pledges after animals—a tradition in place when Miller was a member.

VERDICT: KINDA

LEGEND: Secret Underground Tunnels Unite Columbia

Columbia University's urban campus is an unusual sight in New York City. It is spacious, lined with trees, and covered in grass. Underneath the University is an unusual sight as well—a comprehensive tunnel system. Many students know of the tunnel system, although not what it is used for. The oldest part of the tunnels, a passage between the school's Buell Hall and St. Paul's Chapel, predates the University's Morningside Heights campus to a time when the Bloomingdale Insane Asylum occupied the land. Perhaps the most interesting section of the subterranean system is the decommissioned first floor of Pupin Hall, a place that can be reached only through the tunnels and was once home to the Manhattan Project and other wartime research during the 1940s. According to the *Columbia Spectator*, Pupin Hall still holds parts of a cyclotron, the first machine to split the atom. And although parts of Columbia's cyclotron were given to the Smithsonian Institute, most of this device remains within the tunnel system today.

A bit more recently, the tunnels played a role during the student strike of 1968, in which activists used the underground passageways to communicate between occupied buildings on campus. Columbia administrators ultimately used the tunnels to enter the barricaded buildings. Indeed, the history of these underground tunnels might be as interesting as the history of the University itself.

VERDICT: TRUTH

LEGEND:
Cornell Has the Nation's Highest Suicide Rate

Cornell students often face taunts of "Don't jump!" or questions of "How many students committed suicide this year?" upon telling others of their alma mater. While Cornellians might find such statements irksome, they tend not to be surprised by them and often acknowledge the prevalence of a rumor that attributes Cornell with the highest suicide rate in the country. The origin of the rumor is unknown, although some credit the many gorges and suspension bridges dotting the Ithaca campus. Others believe it is the exceptionally cold winter months and dreary upstate New York weather.

Does Cornell really have the highest suicide rate in the Ivy League? The answer is no. According to a study put out by the *Boston Globe*, Cornell ranked number four out of 11 peer institutions reviewed by the newspaper. The study surveyed the decade from 1990 to 2000 and found that, on average, there were 5.7 deaths per 100,000 per year. With Cornell's 14,000 undergrads, it ranked below the Massachusetts Institute of Technology, Harvard, and Duke. The study also found the national suicide average among colleges to be 10 students per 100,000 per year.

VERDICT: MYTH

Governing the Ivies

With all these scandals, secrets, and pranks, where does the Ivy League turn for order? What great mediator can they call upon for reason and regulation? **Meet the Ivy Council and the Council of Ivy Group Presidents.**

The Ivy Council

Student governments tend to get a bad reputation. Detractors argue that these governing bodies consist of résumé-padding overachievers who have their decisions carefully guided by administrators and are more interested in hearing themselves argue than anything else. Supporters of student governments, however, claim that they allow participants to make a difference and receive valuable leadership experience. The Ivy Council, the Ivy League's student governing body, is not exempt from these two polarized stances. Originally created in 1993, the Ivy Council consists of student government leaders from each Ivy school—including Harvard, which took a brief hiatus in 2001—and continues to be a heated topic of dispute among its members and critics.

Alex Cosmas, now a Columbia grad, was the Council's president until 2004. According to him, the group convenes twice a year to meet and discuss relevant issues facing the Ivy student governments, including social and political issues. At these summit meetings, members typically draw up and vote on resolutions such as the 2002 "Resolution to Adopt Student Government's Stance on the Higher Education Act (HEA),"which denounced the Drug Free Provision of the 1998 HEA Bill and mandated that students convicted of drug-related offenses be disallowed from receiving federal financial aid packages for a period no

The Ivy Council =

An assembly of the Ivy League's student government leaders.

shorter than a year. In the spring of 2003, the Council passed a "Resolution Asserting the Importance of Affirmative Action in the College Admissions Process."

Whether student government leaders should be voting on resolutions on behalf of their constituents is, in itself, a contentious topic of debate. For example, following the affirmative action vote, the *Daily Princetonian* ran a news article headlined, "Ivy Council backs race as a factor in admissions." The story cited the fact that "Princeton was the only school that held a referendum to gauge student support for affirmative action" prior to the summit. "The Ivy Council's decision to pass a resolution sparked a debate on campus as to whether the USG (Undergraduate Student Government) should make political decisions on behalf of the student body," reporter Julie Kestenman wrote. The article went on to explain how the University had also been the only member to abstain from voting on the 2002 HEA "drug-aid" provision.

So why the controversy over Harvard?

The Ivy Council is funded primarily through donations and mandatory member school dues. This had, at least in some respects, left the group with only seven members until the spring of 2004. Following the financial handling of an Ivy summit hosted by Harvard three years prior, the Crimson decided to withdraw from the governing body. The details of the entire ordeal are murky, although those familiar with the episode explain that when Harvard went over budget with the conference, students personally footed the additional expenses and were promised quick reimbursement from other participating schools. This did not happen.

"These were costs incurred by individual members that they thought they had sponsorship for," Michael Hanson, a Cornell grad and member of the Ivy Council's board of governors told me in 2003. "Things like food and room rentals. And then the donor backed out." Complications with receipts delayed reimbursement checks for months. Hanson attributes Harvard's self-removal from the group to two factors: the financial problems associated with the summit, and also "internal policies" regarding the involvement of certain student University Council (UC) members. You see? Even Ivy student government isn't without its mindless bickering and alleged corruption.

In an "Enough is Enough" editorial published by the *Harvard Crimson* in April 2001, editors encouraged the Harvard council to "pursue the deadbeat Ivy Council for payment." The editorial continued:

> At the same time, [the Harvard council] must withdraw its support or the Ivy Council immediately. For years the council has dedicated its financial support and personal efforts to the Ivy Council while reaping returns that are dismal at best. Time and again, Ivy Council meeting have proven to be an unproductive waste of resources—at a three-day meeting in New York in 1999, Ivy Council members engaged in only three hours of meeting on tangible issues of student life . . . . With the latest mishap, the Ivy Council has proven to be not only incapable of living up to its goal of fostering productive dialogue between Ivy League schools but also has shown itself to be a major financial drain as well.

It concluded, "In January, the council committed to withdrawing from the Ivy Council unless it adopted ten demands, one of which was the creation of a budget a month in advance. Given that the Ivy Council finds itself unable to maintain basic fiscal responsibility, it is time that Harvard withdraw its support."

The Council of Ivy Group Presidents = An assembly of the eight Ivy League university presidents.

Edward Pritchett, the vice president of the Ivy Council at the time, responded in a November 2002 *Cornell Daily Sun* article. "We feel that the Ivy Council would benefit from Harvard's participation and that they, too, would receive many positive things from rejoining our ranks," he said. "We want to represent the entire Ivy League and when we are missing one of our fellow schools it is felt by all the other members."

Pritchett's wishes have been answered. According to Jennifer Choi, the former Ivy Council president, Harvard rejoined the group in the spring of 2004. "Many of the old Harvard UC members from 2000-2001 were no longer on the UC and it is my understanding that much of the old reasoning behind not being a part of the Ivy Council were no longer relevant to the UC," she said. "Also a major part of why Harvard rejoined, I imagine, has a lot to deal with the success of the Ivy Council so far."

The Opponents and Proponents

One of the harshest criticisms of the Ivy Council comes from Scott L. Glabe, a reporter for the *Dartmouth Review* and, coincidentally, also a College Prowler author. He described his experience with the organization in a May 2003 article:

> "Do you want to be a leader?" asked the e-mail. Of course I did, and, a perpetual sucker for these sorts of things, I responded immediately. Thus began my association with [the] Ivy Council, an inter-Ivy student government organization that does . . . well, I'm still trying to figure that out. My journey of discovery encompassed two states, two campuses, and two road trips.

Participating in the affirmative action summit, Glabe felt that:

> From the beginning, the focus was more on producing a statement we could disseminate to various media outlets rather than engaging in any substantive dialogue. It was explained to me by an overzealous Cornell delegate, that since the student government of each school had already lent its support to affirmative action, my personal opinion was of no import, though it was the "Ivy Council" name on the resolution.

Of course, this is only one delegate's opinion. Many other Ivy Council executive board members we spoke with would almost certainly disagree. "For those not involved, it's not an easy thing to talk about how a collaborative body can have an impact on solving campus issues," Michael Hanson, the delegate on the Council's board of governors, told me after hearing of Glabe's experience.

Choi, the group's president at the time, echoed these sentiments. In the spring of 2004, around the same time that Harvard rejoined its Ivy peers, a leadership summit held in New York was a "tremendous success," she said. With over 180 students in attendance, the theme of "Being a Leader in the Age of Technology and Globalization" brought some big-name guests to speak with participants, including Steve Forbes, the Chairman and CEO of *Forbes* magazine; Nasreen Berwari, Iraq's new minister of municipalities and general works; Jeffrey Sachs, special adviser to the UN's Millennium Development; and Dov Zakheim, U.S. undersecretary of defense.

"We are providing an avenue for interaction and communication that isn't available from any other organization," Choi asserted in response to critics. "We are unique in that we are not only engaging the student governments at each of the universities but going beyond that by also engaging the individual students at each of the universities through our collective programming that brings students from across all different campuses together to engage in an invaluable leadership experience and knowledge exchange."

Orleans's job is to *"implement all aspects of the [group's] decisions and of the administration of league-wide athletics—including internal academic rules, relations with the NCAA, administration of championships, and sports information and television."*

You've heard the arguments. Now, the decision is up to you. Is the Ivy Council just a bunch of ambitious students talking amongst themselves? Or, does the group accomplish what it intends, collaborating dialogue, discussion, and action among Ivy government leaders and students alike? Perhaps it's even a bit of both.

The Council of Ivy Group Presidents

Officially, the Ivy League is governed by the Council of Ivy Group Presidents. Never heard of it? Don't sweat it. I hadn't either. Basically, this is an organization composed of the eight Ivy League university presidents; this is the Ivy League. They meet every once in a while to shake hands, boast about their school's low admit rate, and challenge one another to intense games of Trivial Pursuit. Well, not really. But seriously, what is their role? And what kinds of decisions do they make?

Jeffrey H. Orleans is the Ivy League's Executive Director (and Yale alumnus), responsible for everything from the athletic association's rules compliance to scheduling and officiating. After several e-mail exchanges, Jeff agreed to speak with us about the Council. Here's what he had to say:

The organization dates, at least in some form, as far back as 1945, when it was first called the Presidents Policy Committee. In February of 1954, after the initial athletic agreement was expanded beyond football to include all intercollegiate sports, a statement reaffirmed and focused presidential governance of the League. Five years later, in December of 1969, Clayton Chapman, an assistant athletic director at Cornell, became executive secretary of the Council, providing its first staff assistance. In July 1973, Ricardo A. Mestres, a vice president at Princeton, became the Ivy Group's first permanent executive director. He would be succeeded by James M. Litvack, a Princeton faculty member, in 1976.

The year 1980 proved to be an important one for the Council of Ivy Group Presidents, as the "Parry-Ryan" report was unanimously adopted in order to provide a comprehensive approach to assuring that the scope of scheduling, competition, and practice opportunities remained consistent with athletes' academic priorities. This structure remains in place today. Jeff Orleans was appointed the third Ivy League executive director in 1984, a position that he continues to hold.

With his staff of six, Orleans's job is to "implement all aspects of the [group's] decisions and of the administration of league-wide athletics—including internal academic rules, relations with the NCAA, administration of championships, and sports information and television." Today, Orleans explained, the Council is still "composed of the eight presidents of the Ivy institutions, meeting as a group without a smaller executive board." The presidents meet twice annually, as does a faculty-student affairs group known as the Policy Committee. Athletic directors from the eight schools also meet frequently over the course of the year. Ivy policy changes, Orleans said, can originate within either of these groups, although final decisions can only be made by the presidents.

Some of the decisions these presidents have made in the past include approving a tenth game of football, previously limited to nine in 1977; adopting a structure in 1985, which remains in effect currently, for monitoring the academic qualifications of recruited athletes; and the agreement in 1991 to freshman eligibility in football and to 12 sessions of spring practice for football rather than one spring "media day" (this coincided with reducing the permitted number of recruited football players league-wide).

In comparing the Ivy League with other athletic conferences, Orleans cited the fact that the Ivy League regulated competitive seasons and off-season practice activities, "in order to assure that our athletes have adequate time for their academic priorities as well as for non-athletic extracurricular activities." Also, the Ivy League has always been "unique" in Division I athletics by "maintaining high admissions standards for its athletes," he said. As a result, student athletes have some of the highest graduation rates, essentially the same as non-athletes. When it comes to scholarships, again, the Ivy League differs in that it does not offer "grants-in-aid," Orleans said. Like all other Ivy students, athletes receive "need-based" financial aid that covers their full cost of attendance, but not other special financial considerations.

Not all decisions made by the presidents pertain to athletic policy, though. Asked whether a school has ever expressed interest in joining the Ivy League, Orleans replied, "Rarely and informally." And this decision, like the others, would ultimately be made by the Ivy presidents, he said.

Athletic History, Traditions, and Rivalries

A Word About the Competition

The Ivy League certainly has its roots in sports and sporting-related events. And although its name has taken on additional connotations since its creation, at its heart, the Ivy League remains an athletic organization. Over the years, it has expanded and produced national championships in 33 men's and women's sports teams among all eight schools.

On average, there are more than 35 varsity teams at each school, and many of the squads, including fencing, hockey, lacrosse, rowing, soccer, and squash have competed on the national level in the last several years. In fact, apart from 1966, 1978, and 1995, **an Ivy League athlete or team has captured at least one NCAA national title a year since 1956**.

Does the Ivy League Offer Athletic Scholarships?

Nope.

Who Has the Most Varsity Teams?

1. Harvard	**43**
2. Brown	38
3. Princeton	38
4. Cornell	36
5. Yale	35
6. Dartmouth	34
7. Penn	33
8. Columbia	29

Row, Row, Row Your Boat

In examining Ivy athletic history and traditions, it seems only appropriate to start where the league began—rowing. **The sport is quickly regaining popularity, and Ivy League teams are consistently at the top of the national rankings** in men's and women's heavyweight and lightweight competition.

It all began on August 3, 1852, at New Hampshire's Lake Winnipesauke, where Harvard and Yale competed in a two-mile boat race that marked the first time American colleges competed athletically against one another. The event was sponsored by a railroad company hoping to sell fans tickets to the White Mountains. The now-famous, annual Harvard-Yale race was generated from that competition—the year 2005 marked the 140th running of the end-of-season battle between Ivy League forces. Harvard took the crown, and falling in line with tradition, all eight rowers and coxswain in the losing boat were forced to give their racing shirts to the Harvard squad. Talk about bragging rights!

Other races, like **The Head of the Charles**, a longer race in Boston that dates back 40 years, draw national attention with crowds often numbering in the hundreds of thousands.

The 2005 Yale women's rowing team—along with Brown, Princeton, and Radcliffe—finished among the leaders in the 2005 NCAA Rowing Championship. *(ivyleaguesports.com)*

How Does Your Favorite Rowing Team Stack Up?

We looked at the results of every annual Ivy League rowing competition. Each time a school won a competition, we noted it. The rankings are below.

Which School Has the Best Men's Rowing Team in History?

Rowing champions are determined in the varsity heavyweight race at the EARC rowing regatta; if the overall winner is a non-Ivy school, the next-highest Ivy finisher is considered the Ivy champion.

Best Men's Heavy Row Team of the Past Decade *(As of '03-'04)*	Number of Championships
1. Princeton	**4**
2. Harvard	3
3. Penn	2
4. Brown	1
4. Cornell	1
6. Columbia	0
6. Dartmouth	0
6. Yale	0

Best Men's Heavy Row Team Historically *(As of '03-'04)*	Number of Championships
1. Harvard	**23**
2. Brown	6
2. Yale	6
4. Penn	5
5. Cornell	4
5. Princeton	4
7. Dartmouth	1
8. Columbia	0

Which School Has the Best Women's Rowing?

As stated on its Web site, "The crew at Harvard has continued to row under the name 'Radcliffe.'" The rowing champion is determined in varsity race at EAWRC regatta; if the winner is a non-Ivy school, the next-highest Ivy finisher is considered the Ivy champion.

Best Women's Rowing Team of the Past Decade *(As of '03-'04)*	Number of Championships
1. Brown	**6**
2. Princeton	3
3. Columbia	0
3. Cornell	0
3. Dartmouth	0
3. Harvard	0
3. Penn	0
3. Yale	0

Best Women's Rowing Team Historically *(As of '03-'04)*	Number of Championships
1. Princeton	**10**
2. Harvard	7
3. Brown	6
4. Yale	4
5. Dartmouth	2
6. Penn	1
7. Columbia	0
7. Cornell	0

Data Source: ivyleaguesports.com.

How the Ivy League Invented Football

On September 29, 1956, the first official Ivy League football game was played at Baker Field between Brown and Columbia. The visiting Brown squad blanked its opponent, 20-0. But it had been almost 100 years earlier, while still in its infancy, that the first football contest was held.

Mark F. Bernstein, in his book, **Football: The Ivy League Origins of an American Obsession**, explores in-depth the development of this American pastime. On November 6, 1869, after the Civil War and as the country was being rebuilt, Princeton met Rutgers in the first intercollegiate football game, the opener of a three-game series between the two schools. According to Bernstein, the rules for the contest were set as follows: a 360-foot long and 225-foot wide field; 25 players would be on each side; and the object was to either kick or bat the ball between two goal posts. Although players could catch the ball, four judges and two referees would ensure that there would be no throwing or running, as well as no holding or tripping. The game would be played until one team scored six goals.

Greatest Football Team of All Time

School:	Championships:
1. Dartmouth	**17**
2. Yale	14
3. Princeton	13
4. Harvard	10
5. Penn	8
6. Cornell	3
7. Brown	2
8. Columbia	1

Note: As of '03-'04. In the event of a tie, a win was recorded on both sides.

After two-initial coin tosses, one to determine possession, the other to determine sides, the game began (the Princeton team kicked off from a tee made of a dirt pile). **It was about as preliminary a game of football as was possible, although certain strategies and rules were established.** At one point, a loose scramble for the ball led players to fall through a surrounding fence, crushing some on-lookers. Almost three hours after kick-off, Rutgers defeated Princeton, 6-4, while Princeton got revenge in the second game, shutting out the Scarlet Knights 8-0. The third match was never played because school administrators canceled it—the Tigers went on to capture the first four national titles.

While the time of Ivy national champions in college football is long since over, **the impact of these schools on the development of the sport is truly undeniable**. As Bernstein writes in his book's preface, "They invented the All-America team and filled all the early ones, produced the first coaches, arranged the basic rules, conceived many of the strategies, devised much of the equipment, and even named the positions." Through many years of play, these Ivy schools have formed long-standing rivalries, none more important than that between Harvard and Yale. The annual tilt between these two schools, simply known as "The Game," is what many consider as the most heated rivalry in all of collegiate sports.

Several players died during an intense football game between Harvard and Yale in 1894. This game was later dubbed the "Springfield Massacre."

Greatest Football Team of the Last 10 Years

1. Penn	**6**
2. Harvard	2
2. Yale	2
4. Brown	1
4. Dartmouth	1
4. Princeton	1
7. Columbia	0
7. Cornell	0

Note: In the event of a tie, the win was recorded on both sides.

Spotlight on "The Game"

Yale News

Soldiers Field Jammed for Game Today
As Unbeaten Yale Team Faces Harvard

For over 120 years, the Yale Bulldogs and the Harvard Crimson have battled on the football field. The series is the third-most played in college football—after Lehigh-Lafayette and Princeton-Yale—and over two million fans have viewed it, including several presidents like John F. Kennedy, who himself was a Harvard man.

The teams first met in 1875, but the competition nearly died in its infancy after the infamous and incredibly violent "Springfield Massacre" in 1894, which resulted in the deaths of several players. **Yes, you read that right.** However, after a three-year hiatus, the two schools' intense rivalry led to the reinstatement of "The Game," in 1897. One of the most famous showdowns in all of college football occurred in 1968, when both teams came into "The Game" with unbeaten records. The sellout crowd in Cambridge saw Yale jump out to a 22-0 lead and hold a 29-13 lead with only three and a half minutes left in the game. But Harvard recovered a fumble and an onside kick and scored as time expired to close within two points. After the Crimson converted a two-point conversion, the home crowd erupted in cheers as Harvard "beat" Yale in the 29-29 tie.

The Harvard Crimson and Yale Elis renew their antagonistic yearly face-off the week before Thanksgiving, as fans pack either Harvard Stadium (the oldest stadium in the country) or the Yale Bowl in droves. After 121 some-odd meetings between the two teams, **Yale leads the all-time series** 64-49-8. The game has decided a stake in the Ivy League title on 20 different occasions.

"The Game" is, at its heart, an intense athletic rivalry, but a strange, arguably coincidental, link takes the competition into the political realm. By looking at presidential election years since 1940, it becomes apparent that a Yale victory in "The Game" means a Republican in the White House, while a Harvard win equates to a Democrat. The trend has been steady for over 60 years, with 1960, 1976, and most recently, 2004, as the only exceptions. In 1940, the Bulldogs were shut out, 28-0 by the Crimson. That same year, Democrat Franklin D. Roosevelt took 253 electoral votes, blanking his Republican opponent, Alfred Landon. With Harvard on top, the Democrats were in the Oval Office.

Who Invented the Fine Art of Tailgating?

There are two different claims to the creation of parking lot debauchery . . .

Story Number 1:

Tailgating dates back to the very first college football game between Rutgers and Princeton in 1869, when fans traveled to the game by carriage, grilling sausages and burgers at the "tail end" of the horse. Today, tailgating is a part of most athletic events, especially college football.

Story Number 2:

It all began at Yale in 1904. Well, other schools claim the honor, but the Yale story has been verified by, you guessed it . . . Yale. It seems there was a train made up of private railcars that brought fans to a Yale game. The train stopped at the station, and the fans had to walk the distance to the stadium. When they arrived at the stadium, they were hungry and thirsty, so the idea was born to bring along a picnic basket of food for the next game. Perhaps necessity *is* the mother of invention.

"The Game" Since 1940*

YEAR	WINNER	ELECTION	PARTY
1940	HARVARD, 28-0	FRANKLIN D. ROOSEVELT	Democrat
1944	NO GAME PLAYED	FRANKLIN D. ROOSEVELT	Democrat
1948	HARVARD, 20-7	HARRY S. TRUMAN	Democrat
1952	YALE, 41-14	DWIGHT D. EISENHOWER	Republican
1956	YALE, 42-14	DWIGHT D. EISENHOWER	Republican
1960	YALE, 39-6	JOHN F. KENNEDY	Democrat
1964	HARVARD, 18-14	LYNDON B. JOHNSON	Democrat
1968	TIE, 29-29	RICHARD M. NIXON	Republican
1972	YALE, 28-17	RICHARD M. NIXON	Republican
1976	YALE, 21-7	JIMMY CARTER	Democrat
1980	YALE, 14-0	RONALD REAGAN	Republican
1984	YALE, 30-27	RONALD REAGAN	Republican
1988	YALE, 26-17	GEORGE BUSH	Republican
1992	HARVARD, 14-0	WILLIAM J. CLINTON	Democrat
1996	HARVARD, 21-16	WILLIAM J. CLINTON	Democrat
2000	YALE, 34-24	GEORGE W. BUSH	Republican
2004	HARVARD, 35-3	GEORGE W. BUSH	Republican

The 117th playing of "The Game" received widespread media attention. **The election between then Texas Governor George W. Bush and Vice President Al Gore had not yet been decided.** To add to the twist, Bush graduated from Yale in 1968, while Gore had graduated from Harvard in 1969. "Why not let the 117th playing of 'The Game' determine the next leader of the free world?" read a Yale promotional press release. When the battle had ended, Yale was victorious 34-24.

And keeping with tradition, once Election 2000 had been decided, Bush, the Republican, was our 43rd President. When it came to the hotly-contested 2004 race between Bush and Senator John F. Kerry, **fans again turned to "The Game" for a prediction. Only this time, "The Game" would break from tradition**: Harvard romped Yale, 35-3 in Cambridge, the team's fourth consecutive win against the Bulldogs. But when all of the provisional ballots in Ohio had been counted, it was the Republican, Bush, who had defeated the Democrat, Kerry.

. . . it becomes apparent that a Yale victory in "The Game" means a Republican in the White House, while a Harvard win equates to a Democrat.

** The above chart summarizes the historical outcomes of "The Game" and its corresponding presidential elections.*

Rah, Rah, Rah!

Ivy League schools also **initiated the tradition of collegiate fight songs and cheers**. At the first game, according to Mark F. Bernstein, "Princeton partisans did bring with them their famous 'rocket' cheer, which hissed like an exploding rocket: 'Hooray! Hooray! Hooray! Tiger sis-boom-ah, Princeton!'" This cheer would evolve by the 1890s into the school's famous "locomotive," which according to Bernstein, "imitates the sound a train engine gathering speed and is still heard at football games today."

We Suck!

In 2004, Harvard might have outplayed Yale, winning 35-3, but they certainly didn't outsmart their opponent's fans. It was at this game, at Harvard Stadium in Cambridge, that 20 Yale students—masquerading as part of the Crimson's "Pep Squad" and carrying phony ID cards—duped Harvard fans into holding up nearly 1,800 pieces of colored construction paper. Fans were told that the paper would read "Go Harvard" when everyone raised it at the same time. With 4 minutes, 47 seconds remaining in the half, the "Pep Squad" ran up and down the stadium aisles, getting fans to hold up their pieces of paper, which amazingly spelled out: "We Suck." "It was almost sad," Dylan Davey, one of the Yale organizers told the *Yale Daily News*. "There were all these grandfather and grandmother types—and they all had big smiles, saying 'Oh, you're so cute, I'm so glad you're doing this.' **I felt bad for about two minutes. Then I got over it.**" And although the stunt will go down in prank history, it wasn't the first time that the Crimson fans had been duped: MIT has similarly tricked Harvard, and Yale pulled the same stunt in 1982.

Source: http://www.yaledailynews.com/article.asp?AID=27506

Fight! Fight! Fight!

Many football cheers reflect the time and social climate in which they were created. *Football: The Ivy League Origins of an American Football Obsession* cites several examples:

One was used in 1968, after members of Students for a Democratic Society took over the president's office at Columbia:

Who owns New York?
Why, we own New York!
Why, we own New York!
Who?
C-O-L-U-M-B-I-A!

At Harvard, a new self-mocking cheer, "Fight Fiercely, Harvard," also became popular during this time:

Fight fiercely, Harvard, fight, fight, fight,
Demonstrate to them our skill,
Albeit they possess the might, nonetheless we have the will!
Oh, we shall celebrate our victory,
We shall invite the whole team up for tea.

And 20 years ago, a song was commissioned by the Yale alumni magazine to commemorate the 100th playing of "The Game":

Oh, Harvard men have higher SATs,
And the Princeton campus has a lot of trees;
Dartmouth men know about the birds and bees.

But Yale's got a better football team,
Yale's got a better football team,
Yale's got a better football team,
And we know that's all that matters.

And if you still feel like singing along, we have more . . .

IVY LEAGUE FIGHT SONGS!

BROWN

Ever True to Brown

We are ever true to Brown,
For we love our college dear,
And wherever we may go,
We are ready with a cheer.
And the people always say,
That you can't outshine Brown men,
With their Rah! Rah! Rah! and their Ki! Yi! Yi!
And their B-R-O-W-N.

CORNELL

Give My Regards to Davy

Give my regards to Davy,
Remember me to Tee Fee Crane.
Tell all the pikers on the hill
That I'll be back again.
Tell them just how I busted
Lapping up the high highball.
We'll all have drinks at Theodore Zinck's
When I get back next fall!

DARTMOUTH

Dartmouth's in Town Again

Dartmouth's in town again, Team! Team! Team!
Echo the old refrain, Team! Team! Team!
Dartmouth, for you we sing,
Dartmouth, the echoes ring,
Dartmouth, we cheer for you!
Down where the men in Green, play on play,
Are fighting like Dartmouth men,
We have Dartmouth team, and say,
Dartmouth's in town again!

COLUMBIA

Roar, Lion

When the bold teams of old wore the blue and white,
Deeds of fame made their name here at old Columbia,
Nowadays, we can praise fighting teams again,
Hear the Lion roar his pride,
While the men of Morningside,
Follow the blue and white to victory!
Roar, Lion, Roar
And wake the echoes of the Hudson Valley
Fight on to victory evermore
While the sons of Knickerbocker
Rally 'round Columbia, Columbia!
Shouting her name forever
Roar, Lion, Roar
For Alma Mater on the Hudson shore.

Stand Up and Cheer

Stand up and cheer,
Stand up and cheer for old Columbia!
For today we raise
The Blue and White above the rest!
Our boys are fighting
And they are bound to win the fray
We've got the team! We've got the steam!

PRINCETON

The Princeton Cannon

In Princeton town we've got a team
That knows the way to play.
With Princeton spirit back of them,
They're sure to win the day.
With cheers and song we'll rally 'round
The cannon as of yore,
And Nassau's walls will echo with
The Princeton Tiger's roar:
(And then we'll) crash through that line of blue,
And send the back on 'round the end!
Fight, fight for ev'ry yard,
Princeton's honor to defend.
Rah! Rah! Rah!
Rah! Tiger sis boom bah!
And locomotives by the score!
For we'll fight with a vim
That is dead sure to win,
For Old Nassau.

PENN

Fight on, Pennsylvania

Fight on, Pennsylvania, put the ball across that line.
Fight, you Pennsylvanians, there it goes across this time.
Red and blue we're with you
And we're cheering for your men.
So it's fight, fight, fight, Pennsylvan-I-a,
Fight on for Penn!

HARVARD

Ten Thousand Men of Harvard

Ten Thousand Men of Harvard want victory today
For they know that o'er old Eli
Fair Harvard holds sway.
So then we'll conquer all old Eli's men,
And when the game ends we'll sing again:
Ten thousand men of Harvard gained vict'ry today.

YALE

Down the Field

March, march on down the field,
Fighting for Eli.
Break through that crimson line,
Their strength to defy.
We'll give a long cheer for Eli's men.
We're here to win again.
Harvard's team may fight to the end,
But Yale will win!

Dead Chicken and Fish

Moving to the rink, the Ivy League features some of the top ice hockey teams in the country today. The six schools with hockey teams—Brown, Cornell, Dartmouth, Harvard, Princeton, and Yale—make up half of the **Eastern Collegiate Athletic Conference** (ECAC), and during the 2002-2003 season, the four teams that advanced to the semifinals of the ECAC Tournament were all from the Ivy League. The two bitter rivals of the conference, Cornell and Harvard, met in the conference title game—as they have for the past two years—with both games going into overtime. Harvard won in 2002, and Cornell won in 2003. **Both schools have also reached the NCAA Frozen tournament in recent seasons.**

You can't talk about Ivy League hockey, or even college hockey in general, without mentioning Cornell's "**Lynah Faithful**" fans. After a Harvard student pelted the Cornell goalie with a dead chicken during a game in Cambridge in the 1970s, Cornell fans retaliated by throwing fish at the visiting squad when they arrived in Ithaca. This tradition continues today. Other traditions—from reading newspapers when the away team is announced over the public address, to chanting the most belligerent of insults in perfect synchronicity—have made Lynah Rink notorious as one of the most raucous hockey barns in the country.

After a Harvard student pelted the Cornell goalie with a dead chicken, Cornell fans retaliated by throwing fish.

Getting season tickets is no easy task. **Students camp outside of the distribution office for days and nights in hope of purchasing highly-coveted seats.** And, no matter how bad the notorious upstate New York weather is, come the winter months, it's guaranteed that rabid fans will pack Lynah for every home game. But while the Cornell hockey community has been largely responsible for the passion in their rivalry, the Harvard fan base is starting to grow. In response, "Lynah Faithful" fans have begun traveling to Cambridge for away games in an attempt to turn Harvard's Bright Hockey Center into "Lynah East." Cornell continues to hold the edge in the all-time series with 60 wins to Harvard's 50, and the teams have tied seven times.

How Does Your Favorite Hockey Team Stack Up?

We looked at the results of every annual Ivy League hockey competition. Each time a school won a competition, we noted it. Below are the ranked results.

Best Men's Hockey Team of the Past Decade *(As of '03-'04)*	**Number of Championships**
1. Cornell	**5**
2. Yale	3
3. Brown	2
3. Harvard	2
5. Princeton	1
6. Columbia	0
6. Dartmouth	0
6. Penn	0

→

Best Men's Hockey Team Historically *(As of '03-'04)*	Number of Championships
1. Harvard	**20**
2. Cornell	17
3. Yale	6
4. Brown	5
4. Dartmouth	5
5. Princeton	1
6. Columbia	0
6. Penn	0

Best Women's Hockey Team of the Past Decade *(As of '03-'04)*	Number of Championships
1. Dartmouth	**5**
2. Brown	3
3. Harvard	2
4. Cornell	1
5. Columbia	0
5. Princeton	0
5. Penn	0
5. Yale	0

Best Women's Hockey Team Historically *(As of '03-'04)*	Number of Championships
1. Cornell	**8**
2. Dartmouth	7
3. Brown	6
4. Harvard	5
5. Princeton	4
6. Columbia	0
6. Penn	0
6. Yale	0

Data Source: ivyleaguesports.com

Hobey Baker,

the famous hockey player for whom college hockey's top individual award is named, attended Princeton.

Hoops Dominance

Over on the hardwood, Penn and Princeton basically *are* Ivy League basketball and prove their dominance year after year. Other than the Pac-10, the Ivy League is the only conference that does not have a postseason tournament. This means that the League's automatic bid to the NCAA tournament depends solely on the regular season conference record. It is usually only the Quakers' and Tigers' records, however, that really matter. **Since 1969, only twice has the Ivy League not been represented by Penn or Princeton in the NCAA tournament.** In 2002, though, Yale shook things up a bit, finishing tied for first with Penn and Princeton, and forcing a three-game playoff. The Quakers came out victorious, extending the P-dominance of Ivy League basketball another year. The two teams have won outright or shared 42 of the 48 Ivy League titles, but Penn leads the all-time series 113-95.

When it comes to winning traditions, **it's also difficult to overlook the year 1996**, when the Princeton men's basketball team defined "March Madness" after dethroning defending NCAA champion UCLA in a low-scoring classic that advanced them to the round of 32. Looking back a few more decades, Princeton made it to the Final Four in 1965 led by now NBA Hall of Famer Bill Bradley. The school also currently holds the record for most continuous winning seasons with 50, likely the result of help from legendary coaches such as Pete Carrill and Butch Van Breda Kolff.

Guess What?

The Ivy League is the only basketball conference in the country that plays its games back-to-back on Friday and Saturday to minimize missed class time.

With each school having not only an array of great programs, but also a few select squads that gain the national spotlight, it isn't hard to see that the Ivy League is a group of eight teams proud of their sports and even prouder of the colleges they represent.

Simply put, the gap between the talent seen in national championships and an Ivy League match is pretty small. Whether it's the sports themselves or the rich traditions or rivalries that follow at each of these schools, the Ivy League truly has a cherished history—and a future—that is second to none.

SPOTLIGHT ON:
Bill Bradley

By Kevin Nash

Bill Bradley possessed a characteristic that many would expect from an Ivy League student: intelligence.

Bradley, described as a "thinking-man's player," and the type of player basketball's inventor James Naismith envisioned, had the scholarly ability to watch a play develop two or three passes ahead of time. He had the intangibles that you wouldn't and couldn't find on a stat sheet. His 12.4 points per game career average pale in comparison to Knicks Hall of Famers Willis Reed, Walt Frazier, Dave DeBusschere, Earl Monroe, and Jerry Lucas. But it was Bradley's scientific approach to basketball that allowed him to succeed at the collegiate and professional level.

During Bradley's three-year career at Princeton University, he was the focal point of the offense. After scoring 3,068 points at Crystal High School in Missouri, Bradley had many suitors, but he rejected 70 nationwide scholarship offers, including one from Kentucky's Adolph Rupp, and paid his way to Princeton. As a Tiger, he was a three-time All-American and the 1965

→

→

Player of the Year. During all three of Bradley's seasons, the school claimed the title of Ivy League champion.

One of his best games, statistically, was at the 1964 Holiday Festival, when the Tigers took on heavily-favored Michigan. Bradley scored 41 points, but fouled out with his team leading 75-63. Princeton went on to lose 80-78. Also in 1964, Bradley led the U.S. Men's Basketball Team to a gold medal at the Tokyo Games. A year later during the NCAA Tournament against Wichita State, Bradley scored 58 points—a single-game record. Top performances paved the way for him to be the first basketball player to be awarded the winner of the prestigious AAU Sullivan Award, presented to the top amateur athlete in the country. He finished his career at Princeton with 2,503 points, averaging 30.2 points per game, and as a recipient of a Rhodes Scholarship, he went to Oxford.

Bradley was drafted by the New York Knicks, and after completing his studies abroad, he returned to basketball in 1967. The Knicks forward developed into one of their most solid players and played a key role in their 1970 and 1973 NBA championships. He retired from the NBA in 1977 after a 10-year career and was elected a U.S. Senator from New Jersey in 1979. Three years later, he was elected into the Hall of Fame and in 1995, published the critically acclaimed book *Life on the Run*. In 2000, Bradley took a run at the presidency, but lost in primary elections to Al Gore, an Ivy League man himself.

How Does Your Favorite Basketball Team Stack Up?

We looked at the results of every annual Ivy League basketball competition. Each time a school won a competition, we noted it. Below are the ranked results.

Best Men's Basketball Team of the Past Decade *(As of '03-'04)*	**Number of Championships**
1. Penn	**7**
2. Princeton	6
3. Yale	1
4. Brown	0
4. Columbia	0
4. Cornell	0
4. Dartmouth	0
4. Harvard	0

Best Men's Basketball Team Historically *(As of '03-'04)*	**Number of Championships**
1. Princeton	**24**
2. Penn	22
3. Yale	4
4. Dartmouth	2
5. Brown	1
5. Columbia	1
5. Cornell	1
5. Harvard	0

Best Women's Basketball Team of the Past Decade *(As of '03-'04)*	**Number of Championships**
1. Harvard	**5**
2. Dartmouth	4
3. Princeton	2
3. Penn	2
5. Brown	1
6. Columbia	0
6. Cornell	0
6. Yale	0

Best Women's Basketball Team Historically *(As of '03-'04)*	**Number of Championships**
1. Dartmouth	**13**
2. Harvard	8
3. Brown	5
3. Princeton	5
5. Penn	2
6. Yale	1
7. Columbia	0
7. Cornell	0

Data Source: ivyleaguesports.com

Which Ivy Mascot Reigns Supreme?

(A completely subjective response)
by Christopher Mason

Answering this question was not easy.

Especially since Dartmouth doesn't even have a mascot. Back in 1968, they canned their politically-incorrect mascot, the Indian, and decided to channel their spirit through Big Green.

What exactly is Big Green? It's the celebrated color of Dartmouth, like the Harvard Crimson or Cornell Big Red (both of which also have mascots). So until the Student Assembly officially approves a new mascot, or students agree by-and-large that the Big Green Moose is the school's mascot, Dartmouth is going to have to remain at the bottom of the list for this one. Sorry guys.

As if that wasn't enough, we have copycats. Two schools—Brown and Cornell—have bears as their mascots. While Brown has Bruno the Bear, Cornell has Big Red the Bear.

Cornell's "Big Red" got its start as a live North American black bear named Touchdown. The original Touchdown was followed by Touchdown-Two, -Three, and in 1939, Touchdown-Four, before the school gave up the live bear idea and switched to costumes. According to Brian O. Earle, class of '68 and advising coordinator of the College of Agriculture and Life Sciences, "They kept him awhile, then he got mean." The University switched to bear costumes after Touchdown-Four "mauled another mascot."

Touchdown sounds tough, but let's get down to business. Even though the two schools both have bears as mascots, the next question is, obviously, "Who would win in a fight?" To settle this matter, we turned to some serious research and expert opinion. According to the Pittsburgh Zoo's mammal curator, Amos Morris, the brown bear (*Ursus arctos*) would win. It dramatically out-sizes the black bear (*Ursus americanus*) on average, and besides, Brown had theirs first.

With these matters settled, we are now proud to present our list of mascots. Yale's Bulldog, Handsome Dan, wins because his name is Handsome Dan. (Very cool.) More importantly, he is the first college mascot in existence—being a trail blazer goes a long way. While most mascots have rather bland names, "Handsome Dan" has universal appeal and works well in the streets, as well as in Ivy sporting competitions.

Handsome Dan I

1889-1898

He was purchased from a New Haven blacksmith for $5.00.

If such a mascot showdown occurred, he'd probably just let the others engage in a Battle Royal. Too cool to even bother, he'd end up as the last one around, unscratched and still handsome. The rest of the mascots were ranked based in the order of who we think would win in a fight (no weapons allowed). Here's the explanation:

The Penn Quaker is locked in at seven. There is no way that the Penn Quaker would ever want to fight John Harvard, or vise versa. But the fact remains; if anything ever went down between these two mascots, you know that John Harvard would win. He looks like he's in much better shape than the Penn Quaker. The Quaker has a double chin.

The Princeton Tiger comes in at third. The Brown and Cornell Bears would defintely take a beating from the Princeton Tiger; we don't need an animal expert to clarify this one. As would the Princeton Tiger from the Columbia Royal Lion, ranking in at second. The pecking order of these animals is stated quite clearly in *The Wizard of Oz*: Lions, Tigers, and Bears, oh my!

Who Would Win in a Fight?

School	Mascot
1. Yale University	"Handsome Dan" the Bulldog
2. Columbia University	Royal Lion
3. Princeton University	Tiger
4. Brown University	Bruno the Bear
5. Cornell University	Big Red the Bear
6. Harvard University	John Harvard
7. University of Pennsylvania	Penn Quaker
8. Dartmouth College	Big Green

Note: Since the 1988 homecoming, Cornell's unofficial mascot, the Big Red Bear has been joined on occasion by a female bear of equal stature. For the sake of keeping things interesting, we left her out of it. It just wouldn't be fair. I mean come on, two on one? Also, if Keggy-the-Keg was more popular and could have been included in this competition, he would have won. Keggy-the-Keg is the world's coolest unofficial mascot but could not be included with a straight face.

DID YOU KNOW?

Dartmouth isn't the only school to have changed its "Indian"-related nickname to something more politically-correct within the last few decades.

Stanford, Syracuse, Miami-Ohio, Marquette, and Nebraska-Omaha have all changed their "Indian" mascots to the Cardinal, Orangemen, Redhawks, Golden Eagles, and Mavericks, respectively.

Campbell's Colors

According to Greg Pratt, staff development specialist for Campus Information and Visitor Relations at Cornell University, Cornell's school colors are actually carnelian and white. The reddish color was chosen for its similarity to "Cornellian."

"The colors for the cans are the same as our colors because Mr. Campbell was at a Cornell football game one time and decided that he liked the colors so much he'd use them [himself]," Pratt explained.

Women in Ivy League Sports

The date: September 24, 2002.

The place: The East Room of the White House.

The event: The Princeton women's lacrosse team is honored by President George W. Bush for winning its second NCAA national championship, 30 years after the passage of Title IX, the landmark legislation that helped make the team's very existence possible.

Trials and Tribulations

All accomplishments aside, the Ivy League has had its share of tribulations relating to women's sports. Brown University was the subject of a federal Title IX lawsuit in 1992, *Cohen* v. *Brown*, in which due to budget constraints, the school had attempted to cut four varsity programs: women's volleyball, women's gymnastics, men's wrestling and men's golf. The lawsuit, brought by several of the gymnasts, was later settled. Brown agreed to keep all four teams, and the case became a landmark precedent for women's athletic opportunities.

Off the field, women's athletics have made a tremendous impact in the culture of the Ancient Eight. When they first became eligible to receive the prestigious Rhodes scholarship in 1976, of the 13 women who received the scholarship that first year, three were varsity athletes. All three were Ivy Leaguers. Harvard basketball and tennis stars, Alison Muscatine and Denise Thal, and Princeton field hockey player, Suzanne Perles, received the honor. In 1982, Dartmouth's Gail Koziara, a three-time Ivy League basketball player of the year, became the first Ivy League woman to win the NCAA Postgraduate Scholarship. Twenty years later, former Big Green women's lacrosse coach and senior associate athletic director JoAnn Harper was promoted to Director of Athletics and Recreation and became the first woman athletic director in the Ivy League.

Like the Princeton lacrosse team, women's athletics in the Ivy League have come a long way in a very short period of time. From humble beginnings in the late 1960s and early 1970s—while some of the Ivies were still in the process of going coeducational—to national power status after the millennium, **women's sports have had a unique place in the history of the Ancient Eight**.

With its tradition providing a culture of inclusion and fair play, the league became the first conference in the country to mandate equal participation for women in 1971. It was in that year that the Coordination and Administration Committees of the Ivy League proposed a unanimously accepted rule that, "The Ivy Group rules on eligibility shall not be construed to discriminate on grounds of sex."

But even before the league began to officially administer championships in 1974, women were an important part of the Ancient Eight's competitive and non-competitive athletic landscape. **Eight Ivy League women won Olympic gold medals prior to the 1971 rule change, and throughout the conference, accounts of women's sports early in the 20th century are abundant.** At Cornell, for example, the first women's physical training instructor, Ellen B. Canfield, was hired in that capacity and as the coach of women's rowing shortly after World War I. Elsewhere, the majority of athletics for women was unfortunately confined to intramurals, although there was great variety in offerings. The Brown Women's College Department of Physical Culture, for example, established an intricate intramural program, in which sports such as swimming, basketball, tennis, and field hockey were highly popular.

By 1971, all eight of the Ivies had either gone coeducational or merged with their affiliated women's colleges, setting the stage for the beginning of one of the most powerful women's conferences in the nation. Only a year later, future Ivy League executive director Jeffrey Orleans, as an attorney in the U.S. Equal Employment Opportunity Commission, helped to develop the groundbreaking Title IX legislation and make a policy that had already been implemented in the Ivy League federal law. While universities throughout the country scrambled to comply, the Ancient Eight was already in position to compete.

First Ivy Female Championship

The Ivy League awarded its first women's championship in May 1974, when the Radcliffe (Harvard) crew team won the Eastern Association of Women's Rowing Colleges regatta in Middletown, CT. From here, there was no place to go but up for the fledgling women's conference. In 1964, Brown had established the first women's ice hockey team in the nation. By 1976, Cornell, Dartmouth, Harvard, Princeton and Yale had followed suit, and the first Ivy League championship was awarded to Cornell. A year prior, **Princeton had won its first of four straight Ivy League basketball titles**. Before the end of the decade, the Ivy League would begin to award championships in track and field, cross country, volleyball, gymnastics, swimming and diving, soccer, field hockey, tennis, softball and lacrosse.

Through the 1980s and 1990s, **the Ivy League's rise in national prominence continued**. During these decades, the league awarded championships in fencing, indoor track and field and squash, bringing the total of sponsored women's sports to 16, by far the most in the NCAA. In 1984, the Yale women's fencing team won the first NCAA championship for any Ivy League women's team.

In 1993, Cornell became the first Ivy school to play in the NCAA volleyball tournament. Later that academic year, **Brown beat Dartmouth in the first-ever Ivy League playoff basketball game** to earn the Ancient Eight's first-ever automatic bid to the NCAA tournament. With this addition, the Ivy League gained an automatic bid to NCAA tournaments in more sports than any other conference in the country. Also in 1994, the Princeton women's lacrosse team won its first of three national championships over the next nine years.

"We Have Theodora. We Don't Really Need Anyone Else."

By Kevin Nash

As an athlete, Dr. Theodora Roosevelt Boyd played into a popular stereotype.

No, not that most blacks are in college because of their talents on the field, but that she was able to overcome adversity to put on a huge display—both on the court and in the classroom.

Dr. Boyd, an African American female, was born in 1906 in Charleston, SC, but was educated in the public school system in Newton, MA. As she came of age in the 1920s, women had just obtained the right to vote, and race relations were still contentious. It was during this time that Dr. Boyd was given a unique opportunity: to attend Radcliffe in 1923 as a black female.

She was described as outstandingly-skilled at both field hockey and basketball. At the time, Radcliffe was a member of the competing "**Seven Sisters**," consisting of Barnard, Bryn Mawr, Mount Holyoke, Smith, Vassar, Wellesley and Radcliffe itself. Dr. Boyd graduated in 1927; beneath her yearbook photo read: "I'd like to know just what our athletic record as a class would have been if Theodora had chosen some other college beside Radcliffe. What matters if two or three of the team don't show up? We have Theodora. We don't really need anyone else. At both hockey and basketball she is a very present help in trouble—present everywhere. She seems to draw the ball to her like a magnet. The worse the team is, the better she plays. Three cheers for Theodora!"

After graduation, Dr. Boyd began teaching at Clark College in Atlanta, GA where she spent two years before returning to Radcliffe to pursue a Master's degree. In 1930, she returned to teaching, this time at Texas Teacher's College in Tyler, TX. By this time, though, the Great Depression had begun to seize the country, and Dr. Boyd left Texas after only one year. Her next stop would be as a physical education and French teacher at St. Augustine's in Raleigh, NC, although it wasn't long until she was again spending her summers attending Harvard. In 1943, she received her PhD, Phi Betta Kappa, from that school and then went on to earn a Certificate de La Language Française, de Civilization Française from the Sorbonne from the University of Paris.

Looking for the Ranking List on Your Favorite Sport?

Go to **www.collegeprowler.com/Ivy** to find rankings for:

Women's Sports

Basketball	Soccer
Cross Country	Softball
Fencing	Squash
Field Hockey	Swimming
Golf	Tennis
Gym	Indoor Track
Lacrosse	Outdoor Track
Row	Volley Ball

Men's Sports

Baseball	Light Row
Basketball	Soccer
Cross Country	Squash
Fencing	Swimming
Golf	Tennis
Gymnastics	Indoor Track
Lacrosse	Outdoor Track
Heavy Row	Wrestling

Despite earning three degrees from white institutions, **Dr. Boyd was still only allowed to teach at black colleges**. She taught at a number of places after St. Augustine's, including Alabama State Teacher's College, Delaware State College, and St. Paul's University before moving to Howard University. At that school, she became the first female to serve as Chair of the Department of Romance Languages. She was also the Chairman of the Joint Graduate Reading Exam committee, a member of the faculty committee for the Study of Evaluation of Teachers, and on the Freshman Advisory Board. Before her death in 1977, Dr. Boyd's other prestigious memberships included the American Council of Teachers of English, American Association of University Women, Phi Beta Kappa, and Alpha Kappa Mu National Honor Society.

Spotlight on Current Pro Ivy Athletes

It takes an exceptional athlete to suceed in the nation's most storied athletic conference. Over the years, there have been scores of Ivy League athletes who have gone on to impact within the wide world of professional sports.

Who Invented the Golf Tee?

A Harvard man, of course. George F. Grant attended Harvard dental school in the early 1870s. In 1899, he patented the golf tee, while also running a prominent dental practice.

Some say he might have also been the first black college athlete, playing baseball for Harvard, but this cannot be confirmed due to a lack of complete records.

DID YOU KNOW?

Four Ivy Leaguers have played professional football in three different decades, and all became All-Pros. That quartet is Chuck Bednarik, Calvin Hill, Nick Lowery, and Sid Luckman.

Who Else Made It to the Pros?

Find out at:
www.collegeprowler.com/Ivy

Most Likely to Be a Pro . . .

Which Ivy Has the Most All-Time Major League Baseball Players?

(As of 2003-2004)

School	# of Pro Players
1. Penn	**60**
2. Brown	39
3. Dartmouth	29
4. Harvard	28
5. Yale	26
6. Princeton	22
7. Columbia	21
8. Cornell	12

Which Ivy Has the Most All-Time Major League Football Players?

(As of 2003-2004)

School	# of Pro Players
1. Penn	**52**
2. Brown	45
3. Dartmouth	34
4. Cornell	32
5. Columbia	30
6. Princeton	26
7. Yale	26
8. Harvard	25

➜

Which Ivy Has the Most All-Time National Basketball Association Players?

(As of 2003-2004)

School	# of Pro Players
1. Penn	**12**
2. Princeton	10
3. Dartmouth	7
4. Columbia	6
5. Brown	3
5. Cornell	3
5. Yale	3
8. Harvard	2

Which Ivy Has the Most All-Time National Hockey League Players?

(As of 2003-2004)

School	# of Pro Players
1. Harvard	**19**
2. Cornell	17
3. Yale	9
4. Brown	7
5. Princeton	6
6. Dartmouth	4
7. Columbia	0
7. Penn	0

Data Source: ivyleaguesports.com

Ivy Olympic Athletes

The Ivy League has played a vital role in the Olympics since its revitalization in 1896. In fact, Princeton professor William Milligan Sloane was a key advocate for the games and sat on the original Olympic committee. More recently, over 50 Ivy League students competed in the *Athens 2004* games. To give you an idea of how large a number that is, consider this: Ireland contributed 51 total athletes to the *Athens* games.

Members of the 1896 Olympic Committee—Sloane is believed to be seated on the right (with opened book).

DID YOU KNOW?

The only Ivy League athlete to win a Bronze medal at the *Athens 2004* games was **Jim Pedro** of Brown University in men's judo.

DID YOU KNOW?

Two Ivy League athletes won gold medals in Athens. Both had the last name Nelson (no relation):

Men's Athletics

Adam Nelson - Dartmouth College

Women's Rowing

Lianne Nelson - Princeton University

Who Else Made It to the Olympics?

Find out at:
www.collegeprowler.com/Ivy

Ivy Olympians

Which School Has the Most Olympic Athletes?

(As of 2003-2004)

School	# of Athletes
1. Harvard	**244**
2. Yale	172
3. Penn	170
4. Dartmouth	158
5. Princeton	115
6. Cornell	96
7. Brown	58
8. Columbia	48

Which School Has the Most Olympic Silver Medals?

(As of 2003-2004)

School	# of Silver Medals
1. Harvard	**31**
2. Penn	26
3. Yale	21
3. Dartmouth	21
3. Princeton	21
6. Cornell	17
7. Brown	8
8. Columbia	1

Which School Has the Most Olympic Bronze Medals?

(As of 2003-2004)

School	# of Bronze Medals
1. Yale	**27**
2. Penn	17
3. Harvard	15
3. Princeton	15
5. Brown	10
6. Dartmouth	8
7. Cornell	4
8. Columbia	3

Data Source: ivyleaguesports.com

". . . the League has produced almost **800 Olympians** with a remarkable **one-in-six capturing Gold!**"

When it began, the Penn Relay Carnival was the first and largest track and field relay meet. It is annually the best-attended track meet in the world with the exception of the Olympic Games and World Championships.

Give Me Some More

Can't get enough?

Here's one last set of sports rankings to check out:

Oh yeah? Well, Who is the Most Ivy of the Ivies?

What does All-Ivy mean?

The Ivy League honors student-athletes with Academic All-Ivy status three times a year. To be eligible for the award, the students must be either starters or key reserves on an officially-recognized varsity team and maintain a cumulative grade point average of 3.0 or better. Each institution nominates five men and five women from its eligible student-athletes at the end of the fall, winter, and spring seasons.

Which School Has the Most All-Ivy Athletes?

(As of 2003-2004)

School	# of Athletes
1. Harvard	**360**
2. Princeton	292
3. Columbia	284
4. Brown	283
5. Penn	277
6. Dartmouth	275
7. Cornell	261
8. Yale	38

What does All-American mean?

Each year the College Sports Information Directors of America choose Academic All-American teams in the sports of football, women's volleyball, men's and women's basketball, baseball, and softball. Also, men's and women's at-large teams—comprised of athletes from all sports not listed above—are chosen. To be eligible as an Academic All-American, an athlete has to maintain at least a 3.20 grade point average and be a starter or key reserve on his or her team.

Which School Has the Most All-American Athletes?

(As of 2003-2004)

School	# of Athletes
1. Cornell	**50**
2. Harvard	48
3. Dartmouth	42
3. Princeton	42
5. Yale	38
6. Brown	37
7. Penn	19
8. Columbia	14

Data Source: ivyleaguesports.com

YES!
LIL' SIB
VE RI
LUX ET
VERITAS

Getting In: Admissions Tips from Insiders and Experts

What It Takes to Get In

In late February 2003, an inadvertent e-mail sent from the undergraduate admissions office at Cornell mistakenly welcomed rejected early decision candidates to the university. The letter, sent to the 1,700 high school students who submitted early decision applications, included nearly 550 who had already been rejected in December and early January. "Greetings from Cornell, your future alma mater!" the letter began. "Congratulations on your acceptance into the class of 2007!"

"I was really excited," Danielle Foti, a high school senior from Red Hook, NY, who applied for a place in the incoming class, told the *Cornell Daily Sun*. The e-mail, from Angela Griffin-Jones, dean of undergraduate admissions, continued, "I am delighted that you will be joining us as a new freshman in the fall, and I hope you are enjoying the end of your senior year, knowing that all your college decisions are behind you." Just hours later, an apology e-mail was sent from the Undergraduate Admissions Office. The entire episode was later blamed on a "systems coding error."

So, what (besides a "systems coding error") does it take to get in? If you're applying to college, thoughts like this have already crossed your mind. In addition to evoking images of rich histories, traditions, and excellence, the Ivy League also raises numerous questions: Who gets in? Where do I stand? What are my chances?

Sound familiar?

While athletics, history, and secret societies might be interesting, several (or most) of you have probably flipped directly to this section. We might as well get down to business.

Even though everyone might have the same exact questions, there is, unfortunately, no one exact answer. There is no single formula that will get you admitted to the Ivy League, no "ideal student" who will always get in, and no one barometer to measure yourself against and predict your odds. The bottom line is that there is nothing typical or average about the Ivy League because, when it comes down to it, there is no average Ivy student. Each one is exceptional and unique; that's why they get in. That's also why it's impossible to come up with a specific, guaranteed response.

But this is not the place for the "there-is-no-answer" answer. While there might not be a guaranteed formula, there are things that you can do to better-understand the whole elusive admissions process and improve your odds. You'll need information and preparation, along with tips and lessons from people who've been there—and guess what? It's all in the following pages, so read on. The more you know, the better-equipped you'll be to give things your best shot.

Why It's So Hard

First off, it's a matter of supply and demand; it's a matter of space; and it's a matter of competition. Every year, huge numbers of applicants fight for an extremely limited number of openings.

According to the National Association for College Admission Counseling, approximately 15 million students were enrolled in college in 2004. In addition, both the number of students graduating from high school and the percentage of those students applying to college is both on the rise and expected to grow through 2010. Despite these increases, the size of freshman classes at Ivy League schools has hardly changed in the last decade, with Princeton being the sole exception. In April 2000, they approved a 10 percent, or 500-student, increase in their undergraduate student body that will be phased in, beginning with the class entering in Fall 2007.

The bottom line is that, while the number of students graduating high school and applying to college has grown over the years, the number of spots that they are competing for remains relatively the same. These more serious, prepared, and accomplished students (with rising standardized test scores) are well-aware of the increasingly high value our society places on attending a prestigious college or university. It's hard; and it's getting harder. The constant number of openings in a freshman class, combined with the increasing number of qualified high school graduates looking to attend college doesn't just mean more competitiveness in the Ivy League. It also means that, as these eight schools become more selective, a "trickle down" effect also occurs at colleges ranked just below them.

Blame History

What are some of the historical factors that have lead to these drastic changes?
Prior to World War II—when the GI Bill made the possibility of higher education more of a reality for many Americans—admission to the nation's top schools was largely lax. Students who could finance their education and had taken a predetermined number of courses at a certain level were relatively assured a spot. Since the early 1950s, though, competition for entrance into the Ivy League has increased considerably. There is today, more than ever, an emphasis placed on the importance of higher education as a key factor in the success of individuals. For many, a college degree is a precursor to a well-paying job and increased opportunities.

At the same time, college has become more affordable for many students through financial aid and government grants.
Once largely reserved for the wealthy, higher education has opened its doors to all, and as a result, demographics have shifted. These two factors have created a frenetic, highly-competitive admissions process—one that places additional pressures on high school students to assume numerous extracurricular activities, achieve high College Board scores, and consistently make the Dean's List.

Competition is growing, and rates of admission are dropping at such a pace that if many current seniors at Ivy League schools (who applied just four years ago) were to reapply, **they would not be accepted.**

47% **of valedictorians** who applied to the University of Pennsylvania were accepted into the **Class of 2008**.

How to Get a Leg Up on the Competition

Now what? You know that the Ivy admissions process is competitive, but what can you do about it, and how can you improve your odds? In order to gain more insight, we turned to former and current admissions officers throughout the Ivy League and gathered advice from some of the top college counselors in the country. After many phone calls, e-mails, and visits, we have collected a wealth of advice and suggestions on approaching admissions. Additionally, Shannon Duff, a former reader in Yale's Admissions Office and the founder of Collegiate Compass LLC, a college admissions consulting firm, agreed to speak with us. Here's what everyone had to say.

Who Is Shannon Duff?

Shannon Duff is the founder of Collegiate Compass LLC (*www.collegiatecompass.com*), an educational consulting firm specializing in college admissions consulting.

Collegiate Compass offers a variety of services ranging from advice on specific aspects of the admissions process, to comprehensive advising throughout the entire college search and selection process. Students from across the United States and around the world have turned to Collegiate Compass for guidance as they apply to college.

Not only is Shannon a top college admissions consultant, she is also an Ivy League grad and a former reader for Yale's Undergraduate Admissions Office. She received both a BA and an MBA from Yale, where she was a nine-time varsity letter winner (cross-country, indoor and outdoor track) and captain of the 1998 women's cross country team. **During business school, Shannon read, reviewed, and rated applications for Yale's Admissions Committee.**

Shannon also earned a Certificate in College Counseling from UCLA Extension (2004) and worked as a private GMAT tutor and admissions consulting specialist (2003-2004) for Veritas, a test prep company. Shannon is the author of two academic papers relating to college admissions and college athletics: "The Value of Legacy Preferences in Admissions at Selective Private Colleges" (2004), and "Collegiate Athletics: Comparing Stanford, Duke, and the Ivy League" (2005). An excerpt from her first paper appears at the end of this section.

When we asked Shannon for some general tips for students applying to the Ivy League, she offered the following advice:

1. Get involved.

If there's one characteristic that Ivy students share, it is **passion and a relentless commitment to whatever inspires that passion**—whether it is squash, the cello, photography, or sports reporting. By heightening your commitment to the issues, subjects, and activities that interest you most, you will increase your chances of standing out amidst a pool of high achievers. It is up to you to take the initiative to increase your involvement in the activities that interest you most, whether it means taking a summer history class at a university, working as an intern for a member of the state legislature, hosting a soccer clinic for younger players in your area, or organizing a benefit for a local charity.

GET AHEAD EARLY ON:

1. Get involved.
2. Challenge yourself academically.
3. Stay abreast of current events.
4. Make the most of your summer.

2. Challenge yourself academically.

There is no need to harp on this topic, as it is not any sort of revelation—great grades in challenging courses and high scores are the baseline for competition in Ivy League admissions. When admissions officers at the nation's top universities see strong transcripts and standardized test scores, they say, **great, but so what? What else does this applicant offer? What would he bring or contribute to the life of the campus community?** Nonetheless, to qualify for and succeed at this higher level of competition where acceptance letters are awarded, you must make the most of the opportunities at your school by taking and receiving high grades in the most challenging courses your school (and in some cases, neighboring schools) offers.

3. Stay abreast of current events.

Start to read a local or national newspaper at least several times a week, or follow a weekly current events and news magazine. It doesn't matter which newspaper or magazine it is, but stay abreast of what is going on in the world beyond your high school. If you don't already do this, you may be surprised by how it will expand your awareness and also your horizons.

It might also be a good idea to occasionally browse through the online editions of Ivy student newspapers. They are fun to read and can be a great source of information about current issues and events on campus. Once you are in the midst of the college application process, they can also provide helpful ideas for essays or questions for your admissions interviews. The above list contains the Web sites of each Ivy League school's daily newspaper:

Brown University
The Brown Daily Herald
www.browndailyherald.com

Columbia University
The Columbia Spectator
www.columbiaspectator.com

Cornell University
The Cornell Daily Sun
www.cornelldailysun.com

Dartmouth College
The Dartmouth
www.thedartmouth.com

Harvard University
The Harvard Crimson
www.thecrimson.com

Princeton University
The Daily Princetonian
www.dailyprincetonian.com

University of Pennsylvania
The Daily Pennsylvanian
www.dailypennsylvanian.com

Yale University
Yale Daily News
www.yaledailynews.com

4. Make the most of your summer.

Free from the daily routine of school and homework assignments, you should use the summertime to pursue the subjects or activities that interest you the most. How students choose to spend their free time is a telling indicator of what they value most, and consequently, colleges—through essay questions and interviews—will want to gain a sense of how you spend your time beyond school, both in the summer and during the school year. Jobs, internships, camps, summer classes, and travel are all great chances to expand your horizons. Colleges want students who take full advantage of the resources and opportunities available to them. While financial constraints can sometimes limit some of your options, there are many scholarships for summer programs and paid internships that you can find if you start looking early enough.

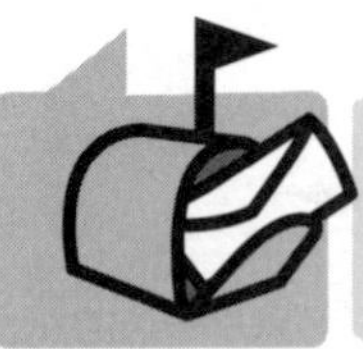

Figuring Out What's Important

Keeping in mind Shannon's tips for getting ahead, it is now time to turn to the three evaluative areas—academics, extracurricular, and personal—that admissions officers use to admit, reject, or waitlist an applicant. First on the list: academics.

The Top 3 Evaluative Areas:

1. **Your academic record**
2. **Your extracurricular record**
3. **Your personal characteristics**

Your Academic Record: Course Loads

Your academic record—which includes the classes you have taken, the grades you have received, your standardized test scores, and any awards or honors—is obviously one of the most important components to your application. Many of the other prospective students you will be competing with will have top-notch records. But how do you achieve one in the first place?

Challenge yourself, and start early.

Our experts recommend that high school students take the most challenging curriculum offered at their high school to get into and succeed at Ivy schools. For many students, this means Advanced Placement, Honors, or International Baccalaureate courses, although you won't be penalized if your school or area doesn't offer these kinds of classes.

The college guidance counselors we spoke with recommended that students meet with them early in their high school careers, during freshman year, or even before, to discuss preliminary course plans and make a tentative outline of what they will need to do during their freshman and sophomore years in order to become eligible for more advanced courses as juniors and seniors. Why start so soon? Simply put, to get to an advanced level by senior year, you need to start early in your high school career. Remember that college admissions officers will focus on your first three to three-and-a-half years of high school when they make their admission decisions. While substantial declines in a student's grades during his or her senior year can be grounds for revoking an acceptance decision, the initial admissions decisions will be made without the benefit of your final semester grades. So to think as a freshman that you can always make up for lackluster performance later on is naïve—excelling throughout those first three years, and then maintaining that rigorous course schedule during your senior year, is extremely important.

> "We pay close attention to the **types and levels of courses** taken and the grades achieved, particularly as they relate to your educational interests and the availability of courses at your high school."
>
> **—Cornell University**
>
> *http://www.admissionsug.upenn.edu*

In addition to talking to your high school counselor, another good idea is to check the Web sites of the specific Ivies, since many of their admissions sections suggest general guidelines and recommended course loads. For example, according to *http://www.studentaffairs.columbia.edu/admissions*, the Web site for Columbia College, an undergraduate school at Columbia University:

> The College has no explicit number of unit requirements for admission, but applicants must present evidence that they are prepared for college work in the humanities, mathematics, social sciences, foreign languages, and natural sciences. Accordingly, the College strongly recommends the following preparation:
>
> - English literature and composition—four years
> - Mathematics—three to four years

> "Although schools provide different opportunities, students should pursue **the most demanding** college-preparatory program available."
>
> **—Harvard University**
>
> *http://www.admissions.college.harvard.edu*

- History and social studies—three to four years
- One foreign language (ancient or modern)—three to four years
- Laboratory science—three to four years

Students who plan to become scientists, engineers, physicians, or dentists should be as solidly grounded in mathematics and the sciences as their high school schedules and curricula have permitted. The study of mathematics at least through precalculus is strongly advised wherever possible.

Modifying the preparatory program just outlined—by taking more work in some subjects and less in others—is not only acceptable but may be desirable in individual cases. The vast majority of successful applicants to the College have taken five academic courses per term for all four years of secondary/high school.

And according to Princeton's undergraduate admission site, *http://www.princeton.edu/main/admission-aid/undergraduate*:

The admission staff seeks to understand how candidates have excelled within the context of their respective schools and communities, asking how well they have made use of the resources at their disposal.

Therefore, there are no fixed unit or course prerequisites that must be completed before admission. We recognize that not all high schools offer the same opportunities and we will give full consideration to any applicant who has been unable to pursue studies to the extent recommended below if the record otherwise shows clear promise.

The following is recommended as basic preparation for study at Princeton:

- Four years of English (including continued practice in writing)
- Four years of mathematics
- Four years of one foreign language
- At least two years of laboratory science
- At least two years of history (including that of a country or an area outside the United States)
- Some study of the visual arts, music, or theater

We also encourage students to take the most rigorous courses possible in their secondary schools, including honors and advanced placement courses where available. . . . In no case is a particular course an absolute requirement for admission to Princeton.

Applicants who intend to pursue a B.S.E. degree in the School of Engineering and Applied Science or to major in a physical science should complete not only four years of mathematics, preferably including calculus, but also one year of physics or chemistry (preferably both).

For more information about courseload recommendations, check out each school's admissions Web site:

Brown University
http://www.brown.edu/Administration/Admission/

Columbia University
http://www.columbia.edu/prospective_students/index.html

Cornell University
http://www.cornell.edu/admissions/

Dartmouth College
http://www.dartmouth.edu/apply/admissions/

Harvard University
http://www.harvard.edu/admissions/

Princeton University
http://www.princeton.edu/main/admission-aid/

University of Pennsylvania
http://www.upenn.edu/admissions/

Yale University
http://www.yale.edu/admissions/

Average GPAs & Class Standings

(Class of 2007)

School	Avg. GPA	Top 10% of High School Class
Brown	N/A	90%
Columbia	3.8	86%
Cornell	N/A	85%
Dartmouth	3.7	88%
Harvard	N/A	96%
Penn	3.9	93%
Princeton	3.8	94%
Yale	N/A	95%

Your Academic Record: Standardized Tests

Another critical component of your academic record is your standardized test score, which usually consists of the SAT or ACT. Not only are these tests the cause of headaches for high school students across the country, they are also the source of much controversy. While College Board studies, including one released in 1999, show a relatively high correlation between SAT scores and freshman year academic performance, critics challenge the ability of standardized tests to effectively measure and predict academic success. These people feel that there are many flaws to the test and say that it favors wealthy students who can better prepare for it, as well as non-minorities who might be able to relate better to the actual questions. Regardless, the debate is not really important right now. Love it or hate it, Ivy League schools use the SAT as another component to assess your academic record.

Our admissions experts told us that standardized tests provide them with perhaps their only opportunity to compare one student against another. With grade inflation and the varying degrees of difficulty at high schools around the world, the SAT (or sometimes the ACT) is the single test that all applicants take, thus it aids admissions officers in gauging the academic credentials of prospective students. However, like all other components of an application, your scores must

A Brief History of the SAT

In 1900, the College Entrance Examination Board (College Board) was set up by 12 university presidents, many of them Ivy League, to administer college admissions tests.

These first tests—administered at 69 locations around the world over a week in June of 1901—were subject-specific and in essay form. The first 973 test-takers could choose from English, French, German, Latin, Greek, history, mathematics, chemistry, and physics exams. Perhaps more interesting, however, were the demographics of these students: over one third hailed from New York, New Jersey, or Pennsylvania; 38 percent was from private schools, 27 percent from public school, 22 percent from academies and endowed schools, and the remainder from other institutions. Students were graded by experts in each subject who rated them "Excellent," "Good," "Doubtful," "Poor," and "Very Poor." Sixty percent of this group applied to Columbia, although 22 other colleges and universities were also chosen.

Then, in 1926, Carl C. Brigham, who had previously worked on creating IQ tests for the United States Army, was put in charge of a recently-established College Board committee tasked with developing an objective test to be administered to high school students. The result was the Scholastic Aptitude Test (SAT), first given on June 23, 1926 to 8,040 candidates, 60 percent of who were male. There were nine sub-tests that comprised this SAT I: Definitions, Arithmetical Problems, Classification, Artificial Language, Antonyms, Numbers Series, Analogies, Logical Inference, and Paragraph Reading. Of the male students who took that first test at 353 locations, 26 percent applied to Yale, while 27 percent of women applied to Smith College. Ivy League schools were receptive to the testing—so much so, that by the late 1930s, it was being used by all eight schools as a scholarship test.

On January 1, 1948, Educational Testing Services (ETS) became the administrator of the SAT I. In four years' time, the SAT structure progressed—the Verbal section had been

→

SAT & ACT Scores

School	SAT Scores (25-75 Percentile)	ACT Scores (25-75 Percentile)
Brown	Verbal: 690-760 Math: 690-760 Combined: 1380-1520	English: N/A Math: N/A Composite: 26-31
Columbia	Verbal: 660 - 760 Math: 670 -780 Combined: 1330-1540	English: 26-33 Math: 26-32 Composite: 26-32
Cornell	Verbal: 650-730 Math: 690-740 Combined: 1340-1470	English: 27 - 33 Math: 27 - 33 Composite: 28 - 32
Dartmouth	Verbal: 660-760 Math: 670-770 Combined: 1330-1530	English: N/A Math: N/A Composite: 27-33
Harvard	Verbal: 700-800 Math: 700-790 Combined: 1400-1590	English: 30-35 Math: 30-35 Composite: 31-34
Penn	Verbal: 660-750 Math: 680-780 Combined: 1340-1530	English: 28 - 33 Math: 28 - 34 Composite: 28 - 33
Princeton	Verbal: 700-790 Math: 700-800 Combined: 1400-1590	English: N/A Math: N/A Composite: N/A
Yale	Verbal: 690-790 Math: 690-790 Combined: 1380-1580	English: N/A Math: N/A Composite: 30-34

All SAT scores are for the Class of 2008, with the exception of Columbia and Dartmouth, whose data is for 2009. All ACT scores are for the Class of 2007, with the exception of Penn and Yale, whose data is for 2008.

expanded to include sentence completion, analogies, antonyms, and reading comprehension questions. By 1957, the number of students taking the SAT I each year had passed 500,000. In 1959, another standardized testing player, American College Testing (ACT), would enter the market.

Since this time, the SAT I and the subject-specific SAT II tests have continued to evolve and change. In June 2002, the College Board announced an overhaul to the SAT I, and beginning in March 2005, the revamped test was administered. The Verbal section is now called "Critical Reading," with both short and long reading passages and no more analogies. The

new Math section has eliminated quantitative comparisons and expanded to include topics from Algebra II. Finally, a new Writing section has been added with dual parts. The College Board made these changes to better reflect what students study in high school.

be taken with a grain of salt. In 2003, for example, 673 students scored a perfect 1600 on the SAT I in one sitting. Impressive. Two-thirds of these students applied to Harvard, yet fewer than 200 received admission. So a perfect score does not guarantee entry. Do the best you can on your tests, but understand that they won't be the sole factor that accepts or rejects you from an Ivy League school. Check out the SAT and ACT ranges (above) of students who have recently become a part of the Ancient Eight.

What About the New SAT?

One of the biggest challenges students have faced in taking the current SAT is the sheer length of the new test. The actual time students are given to take the test has increased from three hours to three hours and 45 minutes. Including breaks between sections, this means that students are in the testing rooms for about 4.5 hours, versus about 3.5 with the old SAT—a substantial difference. The ability to maintain focus and concentration definitely plays an important role in this test. Also, the test will be scored out of a total of 2400 points (vs. the old 1600 points). Now when your older siblings brag about their "stellar" 1450 scores, they just won't sound as impressive.

The College Board won't release percentile rankings associated with scores until 2006 because they want to base these calculations on a full year of data. Thus, in the 2005-2006 admissions season, colleges will really only be able to compare students' scores within their applicant pools (though there will be some data sharing among colleges).

In the **Critical Reading Section** (formerly known as Verbal), a selection of reading comprehension questions will be added along with a few short passages. Analogies will be cut from this section.

In the **Math Section**, more questions from Algebra II and other third-year college preparatory math classes will be added, while Quantitive Comparisons will be altogether eliminated.

The **Writing Section** (an entirely new segment) will include multiple-choice questions on grammar and usage along with a student-written essay:*

The multiple choice questions will call upon students to improve given sentences and paragraphs. Students will also be asked to identify mistakes in diction, grammar, sentence construction, subject-verb agreement, proper word usage, and run-on sentences.

Students will be given 25 minutes to respond to a open-ended question and construct a well-organized essay that effectively addresses the task. The essay question may require students to react to a quote or an excerpt, or to agree or disagree with a point of view. In any case, a good essay will support the chosen position with specific reasons and examples from literature, history, science, current affairs, or even a student's own experiences.

* The highest possible score on the new Writing section will be 800. Scores on the essay and multiple-choice section will be combined to produce a single score.

SAT vs. ACT

While students' SAT and ACT scores generally serve the same purpose in the college admissions process—that is, providing a standard means of comparing applications from many different high schools—they are quite different tests. The ACT is a content-based test, while the SAT is an aptitude test—this means that the majority of the ACT tests students on material that they have learned in high school, while the SAT tests critical thinking and problem solving abilities. Many admissions officers encourage students to take both tests—some score better on one than the other.

SAMPLE QUESTIONS

FROM THE FIRST PHYSICS COLLEGE ENTRACE TEST:

A balloon contains 300 cubic meters of hydrogen, each cubic meter of which weighs 90 grams. The material of the balloon weighs 250 kilograms. Each cubic meter of the surrounding air weighs 7290 grams. How many kilograms in addition to its own weight will the balloon lift?

Describe a method of finding the specific gravity of a solid heavier than water; of a liquid.

"The ultimate goal is the creation of a **well-rounded** freshman class, one that includes not only well-rounded students but also those of narrower focus whose achievements are judged exceptional."

—Yale University

http://www.yale.edu/admit/

Ask Shannon
SAT x3?

Q: Does it matter how many times I take the SAT?

A: If a student takes the SAT more than three times without some sort of extenuating circumstance, admissions officers will begin to wonder why he is spending so much time taking tests when he could (and should) be dedicating that time to his academic and extracurricular pursuits.

Ask Shannon
And what about . . .

Q: Does it really matter if you take the SAT instead of the ACT (or vice-versa)?

A: Generally, if a college states no preference for one test over the other and leaves the decision to students, it is fine to take either. The main exception to this would be that students from metropolitan areas on the east and west coasts are generally expected to have taken the SAT—they may take the ACT in addition to the SAT, but not taking the SAT may lead admissions officers to wonder why these students did not take this test with the rest of their classmates.

Your Extracurricular Activities

Because admissions officers are not just admitting individuals, but also seeking to assemble a diverse class of students when they make their decisions, your involvement outside of the classroom will also be important in determining whether you are accepted or rejected.

An Ivy League admissions officer told us that his school does not need or want applicants who have engaged in a dozen—or, in some cases, dozens—of activities. Instead, his team looks for students who have participated in a variety of activities and wants applicants who have shown dedicated participation or leadership over three or four years. Ivy League admissions officers tend to see a lot of "typical" activities listed: newspaper or yearbook editor, varsity athlete, and president of the spirit club. While these activities are all great, they're not exactly unique. One way to stand out and get a leg up on the competition is by participating or founding interesting, unusual, or unique clubs.

Don't join clubs just for the sake of building a huge activity list.

It's more important to be seriously-committed to a few select causes than to have tons of activities that don't really *excite* you.

If you have a specific interest or passion, make an effort to explore it as much as possible.
For example, students who love art can teach classes to kids, volunteer at museums or galleries, participate in shows, or develop exhibits and projects in their neighborhoods and schools. Students who connect their activities to an underlying theme and concentrate their efforts in a particular area demonstrate a strong commitment and focus that is desirable to many admissions officers.

"We don't want to see a four page activities résumé, as I've seen several times," said one admissions officer. "We care first and foremost about academic performance and challenge. The extracurricular activities are secondary to us." Work experience is also looked upon favorably, although it won't be held against you if you haven't had any. According to the same officer, "If a student can work, say, 15-20 hours a week for a year or more and still has excellent grades, then we certainly take note of that."

Recruited athletes enjoy a large advantage in admissions,

according to the *New York Times*. A study of intercollegiate athletes found that for men, the odds of admission to the Ivies were more than four times greater than non-athletes. **The advantage for female recruits was even higher.**

Your Personal Demographics and Characteristics

Beyond academics and extracurricular activities, student demographics and personal characteristics can also play a role in the admissions decision. The good news is that, because the Ivy League focuses on creating a diverse student body, applicants from many different backgrounds have a shot at admission. The trick is to show what makes you different.

You see, schools today are looking for all types of applicants from every ethnicity, geographic corner of the world, and socioeconomic background. Students who are the first person in their family to attend college can be just as important to the makeup of the freshman class as those who are fourth- or even fifth-generation legacies. The Ivies want students who are active and who will contribute positively to the community, maybe play an instrument in the wind ensemble, row for the crew team, or found a club or two. They want politically-active students, musicians, and scientists. Perhaps most importantly, the Ancient

Eight wants and needs ambitious students—students who have proven that they can do the work and succeed. They want students who will become important, contributing members of society.

While you can control some personal factors, such as your levels of dedication, motivation, or contribution, there are other characteristics and demographics that are more fixed. One such example involves location.

Because students from New York City can have a much different high school experience than students from, say, Nebraska, many schools give consideration to where each prospective student is from in order to provide a degree of parity among regions. Also, the Ivies, all located in the Northeast, will often try to compensate for factors such as distance by offering a few more slots to students living further away (since these long-distance applicants are less likely to enroll if accepted).

Once the application deadline has arrived, applicants are often divided according to their region so that students from the same high school can be evaluated alongside their classmates who have also applied.

This, like the SAT, gives admissions readers some sense of the rigor at the high school and a better understanding of how each student compares within the group. For example, if one applicant from a given high school has taken six Advanced Placement courses, and other applicants from that high school have taken only one or two, then admissions officers will view much more favorably the student who challenged himself—provided, of course, that the student who took six did well in those classes. In the case where a prospective student is the only applicant from their high school, other factors are used such as guidance counselor assessments, past judgment from the particular high school (if applicable), and the school profile. All students from a given region are then compared, overall, with one another.

> "**Diversity** within the student body is important as well, and the Committee works very hard to select a class of able and contributing individuals from as broad a range of backgrounds as possible."
>
> **—Yale University**
>
> *http://www.yale.edu/admit*

Diversity is important, so figure out what makes you *unique*.

With all this in mind, remember that you still apply to college as an individual. You have a 2130 on your SATs. Or an 1890. You have taken two AP courses. Or eight. You were president of the student body. Or an accomplished chemist. You live in Massachusetts. Or Alaska. You went to public school. Or boarding school. Your mom is a housewife. Or a lawyer. Your Dad is a contractor. Or unemployed. Your older brother went to Harvard. Or you're an only child. You are, well, you. And although there might be applicants similar to you, every prospective student is different. Use this to your advantage.

When it comes time to evaluate your application, you will obviously be reviewed as an individual, but admissions officers are also tasked with "building a class."

According to one admissions dean, "It's a very exciting process when we admit a student and think that they can be that student. Sometimes we take a risk—sometimes we see the diamond in the rough and hope that the applicant will take every opportunity that we as a university can offer them. Usually, hopefully, we are right!" In other words, apply. It's worth a shot. Just a little over one in 10 gets in, but if you don't apply, your odds drop to zero.

How to Use Campus Visits to Your Advantage

If you're thinking about applying, you should also be thinking about visiting. Before we get into a more detailed discussion about applying to the Ivies, we should point out that one of the best ways to gather information about schools is to visit their campuses.

Throughout high school, if your family is on a vacation or another type of trip that takes you close to a college, it's worthwhile to try to stop and visit the campus, even if it's only briefly. Seeing a variety of colleges of different sizes, each within different environments (urban, suburban, or rural) and in different parts of the country will help you to develop perspective in comparing schools. This will be helpful as you begin to refine the list of colleges in which you are interested.

Even though visiting campuses can seem overwhelming, if you're going to take the time to check out a school, you should do more than just wander around. So, grab the College Prowler guide to your school, see what the students are saying, learn about the places to check out, and get moving. In order to help you plan your time, Shannon listed five important things that you should try to do on each campus visit.

Five Important Parts of a Campus Visit:

1. Tours
2. Information sessions
3. Classes
4. Interviews
5. Overnight stays

1. Tours

Use the tour as both an opportunity to see the campus and a chance to ask the guide (usually a student) questions. The tours sponsored by the admissions office will be a great way for you to see the academic, residential, and dining facilities; if there is something not included on the tour that you would like to see, just ask the guide for directions once the tour has ended. Your stops along the way will also often include a freshman room, enabling you to see what the living accommodations of first year students are like. If you have a choice between student guides as the tour commences, you should try to choose the guide whose academic or extracurricular interests are most similar to your own.

2. Information sessions

Make an effort to attend information sessions, as they are usually hosted by admissions officers who will go into substantial detail about academics, extracurricular life, and the admissions process.

Bring a list of questions—this is your chance to have them answered in person by an admissions officer at the college. Take good notes; as you visit several colleges, you will find that it can become hard to remember which college said what.

3. Classes

Try to attend a class or two by making arrangements in advance through the admissions office. Or contact an older friend, maybe a graduate of your high school, to see if there is a class you could attend with him or her. Most professors welcome visitors—just be on time!

4. Interviews

If the Ivy school you're applying to offers on-campus interviews, and you are a rising senior, call the admissions office in advance to schedule an interview.

5. Overnight stays

Try to plan your college trip at a time when school is in session, and you can stay overnight with a current student. If you have a friend or a family friend who attends the college, don't hesitate to ask if you could stay with them for a night. Most students are excited to share their school with prospective students—don't be shy! Plus, it'll surely beat sharing a room with your parents.

Now that you know what to do on campus, here are some of Shannon's tips for a successful visit:

1. Visit the campus while school is in session.

It is difficult to gain a sense of a college when students are not around, as you will not have the benefit of being able to talk to people, attend class, or observe campus life. Do not pass up your one chance to see a college just because it is over the summer break, but do your best to plan college visits during the academic year.

2. Always call ahead to sign up for tours and information sessions.

If, for some reason, it's a last-minute visit and you haven't signed up in advance, be sure to sign in at the admissions office. While it is less common in the Ivy League, many colleges today use demonstrated interest in the school as a minor distinguishing factor among applicants, and visiting the campus is one of the best ways to show your interest. Signing in is easy to do and can only help you, so remember to do this.

3. Do your homework on the college before your visit.

Have some general knowledge of the information from the college's Web site, its view-book, or the individual College Prowler guide to that school. This way, during your visit, you can focus on asking questions that will help you to gain perspective on the school beyond just printed facts and figures.

4. Be on time!

Do not be late for tours, information sessions, classes, and any other meetings you have set up.

5. Talk to students.

Tours and information sessions can only tell you so much. Talk to the students to find out what they really think about their school.

6. Thank your admissions hosts for their time.

Ask for the business card (or contact information) of the admissions representative who hosts your information session. Write a short note or e-mail to thank him and note your level of interest, especially if the school is one of your top choices.

COLLEGE VISIT "DO"S:

1. **Visit the campus while school is in session.**
2. **Always call ahead to sign up for tours and information sessions.**
3. **Do your homework on the college before your visit.**
4. **Be on time.**
5. **Talk to students.**
6. **Thank your admissions hosts for their time.**

Early Decision: Is it for You?

As you refine your list of colleges, you'll also have to think about whether or not you're going to apply under any type of early admissions program. There are two types of early admissions programs used in the Ivy League: Early Decision and Single Choice Early Action. When applying under an Early Decision policy at a given college, students agree that, if they are accepted to that college, they will enroll. Single Choice Early Action policies differ in that they are non-binding; the timeline for these application policies is similar except for the fact that students applying Single Choice Early Action have until May 1 to commit to the school.

Much controversy and debate has surrounded early admissions programs—mainly Early Decision programs—over the last 10 years largely because colleges can and do use them to increase their yield (the percentage of accepted students who eventually enroll). While colleges do have an interest in ensuring that their student bodies are comprised of students who are excited to be there, and Early Decision policies allow students to reveal to a college that it is their first choice, several effects of Early Decision policies are undesirable.

First, college rankings such as *U.S. News and World Report* initially used yield as a criterion in ranking schools, which in turn, escalated colleges' desire to produce the highest yield possible (easily achieved through Early Decision). This yield competition eventually reached a level beyond what was generally considered to be healthy, and in 2004, *U.S. News* subsequently discontinued its use as a metric in college rankings. Next, students whose college choice depends on which school offers them the best financial aid package do not have the opportunity to compare awards under binding early decision policies, and therefore are often unable to apply early. As a result, it is argued that Early Decision applicant pools have been historically comprised of affluent students who are not dependent on financial aid and have the benefit of advice from college counselors who are aware of the advantages of applying early.
According to this argument, the benefits of applying early are realized disproportionately by students from wealthier socioeconomic groups and better schools. Further, when a significant portion of an incoming class is accepted under Early Decision policies, the result can be less than advantageous for students whose financial constraints necessitate that they apply in the Regular Decision round, as they must compete for the limited number of remaining spots in the class.

In an effort to reduce the alleged discriminatory effects of Early Decision policies and the pressure being placed on students to make college decisions very early in their senior year, Harvard and Yale (and a number of other schools outside the Ivy League) have switched to non-binding Single Choice Early Action policies. These programs permit students to apply early to that school only and receive notification in

Ivy Early Admissions Programs

Early Decision

Students submit their application to one college by November 15 and agree to enroll at that college if accepted. Applicants receive notification of the admissions decision by mid-December. Students can apply Early Decision to only one school.

Single Choice Early Action (Early Action):

Students submit their application to one college by November 15 and receive notification in mid-December. Students may apply to as many other schools as they wish under Regular Decision policies and do not have to decide until May 1 if they will attend the college to which they applied early. "Single Choice" means that, under this policy, students can apply Early Action to only one school.

Regular Decision:

Students apply by January 1 (different schools' deadlines vary slightly), are notified of the admissions decision by early April, and then have until May 1 to decide whether or not they will attend.

"On average, applying early increases the chances of admission at selective colleges the same amount as **a jump of 100 points or more in SAT score.**"

—Christopher Avery, Andrew Fairbanks, and Richard Zeckhauser

The Early Admissions Game. (Cambridge: Harvard University Press, 2003), p. 16.

December, but they give applicants until May 1 to decide if they will accept the offer. This allows students to apply to as many colleges as they wish during the Regular Decision round.

As the controversy suggests, there are advantages to applying early, both inside and outside of the Ivy League, especially under Early Decision (binding) policies. If you do have a clear first choice college and are willing to accept whatever financial aid package a college offers, you will most likely benefit from applying Early Decision to that school. Clearly, the admissions rates for Early (both ED and EA) applicants are higher than those for Regular Decision applicants for a variety of reasons.

After analyzing the admissions records of fourteen highly selective colleges from 1991-1992 to 1996-1997 in their 2003 book, *The Early Admissions Game*, Christopher Avery, Andrew Fairbanks, and Richard Zeckhauser assert that "on average, applying early [decision] increases the chances of admission at selective colleges the same amount as a jump of 100 points or more in SAT score." As noted before, colleges clearly enjoy benefits from being able to make admissions decisions knowing that admitted students will enroll; by accepting students early, they improve their yield rate and also reduce the risk profile of their enrollment management task in the regular decision round (meaning that colleges are never sure how many students will accept their offers of admission and must be careful not to have too many or too few students enroll). At Harvard and Yale, however, the non-binding nature of their Single Choice Early Action policies does significantly reduce the advantage conferred upon those who apply under these policies; in many cases, Harvard and Yale will defer the vast majority of students who apply Early Action to the regular round so that they can compare them to the regular applicant pool. The final consideration which must be taken into account alongside the higher admissions rates of early applicants is that certain groups of students who are admitted at higher rates in the Regular Decision round also tend to apply early—namely, recruited athletes and in many cases, legacies. The substantial presence of these groups of applicants in the early admissions pool has the effect of contributing to these higher admissions rates.

Ask Shannon
Common Apps

Q: Does it make a difference if you use the Common Application instead of the school-specific one?

A: The Ivy League is split on the Common Application. **Five of the Ivy League colleges accept it**: Cornell, Dartmouth, Harvard, Princeton, and Yale. Three do not: Brown, Columbia, and Penn.

By agreeing to accept the Common Application, a college pledges that it will give equal consideration to common application and other institutionally-endorsed application forms. Nonetheless, some suggest that it might be better to use the college's own application even if the college accepts the common application so as to emphasize your interest in the school.

If you have time, it is never a bad idea to complete your top choice colleges' own applications even though using the Common Application is perfectly acceptable (note that a number of colleges across the U.S. solely use the Common Application). Keep in mind that there are many more powerful ways to express your interest in a college than through the type of application you use. You should demonstrate your interest to colleges by visiting, speaking to admissions officers at college fairs and presentations, and writing a compelling response to the question "Why are you interested in attending College X?"

The following chart summarizes the type of early admission program offered at each Ivy League school and compares the admit rates for these programs with overall admission statistics:

Class of 2009 Admissions Statistics

(As of April 2005)

School	EA/ED Acceptance Rate	Regular Decision Acceptance Rate *(Commonly published)*	Regular Decision Acceptance Rate *(Including deferred early applicants)*	Overall Acceptance Rate
Brown	28% (ED)	12.7%	~11.8%	14.6%
Columbia*	23.2% (ED)	8.6%	~8.3%	10.4%
Cornell	41.7% (ED)	24.3%	~24.1%	26.2%
Dartmouth	33.9% (ED)	15.1%	~14.6%	16.8%
Harvard	21.4% (SCEA)	6.4%	~5.5%	9.1%
Penn	34.2% (ED)	17.9%	~16.8%	18.9%
Princeton	29.1% (ED)	8.4%	~7.7%	10.9%
Yale	18.1% (SCEA)	7.5%	~6.7%	9.7%

These statistics are the colleges' current preliminary estimates as reported in a university newspaper, a university press release, or by the admissions office in early April 2005.

** Columbia statistics are for Columbia College only.*

Regular Decision acceptance rates can be confusing, as they are sometimes listed as strictly the number of Regular Decision acceptances/number of Regular Decision applicants. For most colleges, ***this Regular Decision applicant pool includes a number (often a large number) of students who were deferred in the early round*** *and are now being re-evaluated in the regular round, increasing the size of the applicant pool in this regular round and effectively reducing what is commonly reported as the "Regular Decision acceptance rate." In the above chart, the Regular Decision columns are clearly labeled as the "Commonly Published" figures and the figures which include deferred students as part of the Regular Decision applicant pool.*

2004-2005 was an incredibly competitive year in Ivy admissions—many schools saw record numbers of applicants and record low acceptance rates.

Additionally, many more students were wait listed at colleges than have previously been, adding somewhat of a new dynamic to admissions decisions. The decision to wait list these students seems to stem from: 1) traditional uncertainty about what percentage of students offered admission will decide to attend, and 2) the desire to signal to students that their applications were too strong to reject outright. While opinion related to the second reason for wait listing students is divided—many fear that it may create false hopes among wait listed students—it seems to be a new trend in admissions decisions that will certainly be followed carefully. As it turns out, few, if any, of these students will be offered admission from the waiting list this year given colleges' high yield rates (percent of accepted students who decided to attend).

Your Application

You've performed well inside and outside of school. You stressed over (and got great scores on) your SATs. You've talked to counselors, friends, parents, and college students. And you've attended info sessions, researched, and visited (or at least checked out the College Prowler guides on) your schools. You know your strengths, and you understand what makes you unique. You've obtained a wealth of information, and you're ready to build a killer application.

Earlier in this chapter, we discussed the three evaluative areas that admissions officers consider when reviewing applications—your academic record, extracurricular activities, and personal characteristics. But just as receiving a perfect score on your SATs or being class president will not guarantee you admission, neither will your family background or state of residence. Each admissions decision is the result of a unique combination of factors, and so are you. The trick is to make sure that your application reflects this.

COLUMBIA SAYS:

1. **Read all application instructions carefully.**
2. **Be sure to meet all deadlines.**
3. **Print . . . [your] name and Social Security Number on all documents which you submit.**
4. **Keep copies of all documents which you submit.**

http://www.studentaffairs.columbia.edu

It's time to talk about the specific parts of the application and add some transparency to the whole process. If you're going to apply, you need to understand what you're getting into, so at this point, it's important to learn as much as possible. The more you know, the less confused and in the dark you'll be—also, the better prepared you'll be to give admissions officers what they're looking for. **This is the part where you learn how to make your Ivy application shine.**

The Essay

The essay, for some, is the most dreaded part of the application process. While many schools ask specific questions like, "What would be on page 367 of your autobiography?" others leave the questions more open-ended. Although the essays are just another component to your overall application, admissions officers stress that students must put time into them since, outside of an interview, they are likely the applicants' only opportunity to become an individual, someone beyond just numbers on a piece of paper. "Of anything that a student submits that is subjective, the writing really does separate the applicants," an admissions officer told us. "Writing can show personality. Writing can elicit emotion. Writing can differentiate otherwise identical candidates."

Your essay is often your only chance to stand out as an **individual.**

When evaluating the essay, these admissions officers look for "sophistication" and "likeability;" they seek students whom "we would want to interact with on campus for four years." Content can obviously help your writing stand out, although a combination of content and style can really make for a top essay. College guidance counselors suggest picking a topic that interests you—maybe even helps define you and your ambitions—and then simply writing an essay from the heart. You should not write an essay that you think admissions officers want to read. **Write about you.** Time and again, both admissions officers and guidance counselors stressed that this is perhaps your only opportunity to become someone, an individual. Take advantage of this.

Perhaps more importantly, make sure that you read, re-read, and then read again each of your essays. Get input or an opinion from someone you trust, a parent, a teacher, or a friend. And if you're planning on using the same essay for more than one college—which many students do—don't forget that the quickest and easiest way to rejection is to accidentally send an

HOW TO WRITE AN "IVY LEAGUE" ESSAY:

1. Choose a topic about which you are passionate.
2. Don't make your topic overly-broad.
3. Develop your essay around one main point.
4. Be yourself.

essay to Princeton about how much you want to go to Penn. It sounds ridiculous, but it happens every year. So check. And then double check.

Because essays are such a critical component of your application, take note of the following tips Shannon gives to Collegiate Compass clients:

1. Choose a topic about which you are passionate.

As we've mentioned, it doesn't matter what you write about—it is how you address the topic, along with your ability to express why you chose this particular topic and why it is important to you. Note that this expression of why you chose a topic should rarely be explicitly stated—rather, it is a question that you want the reader to be able to answer after having read the essay. Again, your essay can be about anything that holds special significance for you—a commonplace issue, routine, or object can be brought to life through your description of its significance to you.

> "The Committee . . . gives serious consideration to such qualities as **motivation, curiosity, energy, leadership ability**, and **distinctive talents**. An applicant's own written part of the application . . . provide[s] a great deal of insight into these personal qualities."
>
> **—Yale University**
>
> *http://www.yale.edu/admit*

2. Don't make your topic overly-broad.

Most college application essays are only about a page in length, so you have limited space in which to make your points. Remember that there are other parts of the application where you will list your accomplishments—the essay is not the place to do this. If you do, you're wasting valuable space and missing an opportunity to give admissions officers perspective on your personality, convictions, and motivations.

3. Develop your essay around one main point.

Aim to structure your essay so that the reader will come away remembering one main point or idea and associate you with this theme. This advice is helpful as you remember the context in which admissions officers read essays—that is, amidst reading hundreds or thousands of other applications. Clarity and focus are virtues in essays.

4. Be yourself.

Do not be afraid to be creative or bold, and don't worry about what you think admissions officers want to hear. Write about what you believe is important to tell them about yourself, or write about an experience that you believe illustrates something important about you. Different is good when it comes to college essays—if you have a unique idea for an essay, go for it; although if you're a bit uncertain, it can help to get the advice of a trusted teacher or advisor to make sure it's appropriate. Just don't get stuck racking your brain in an attempt to think of an essay topic that has never before been used. Simple topics often make for great essays, as they inspire the reader to look at a common object or idea in a new way.

The Interview

Interviews at Ivy League schools generally carry slightly more weight than those at many other colleges. Admissions officers use interview reports to gain insight to an applicant's ability to reflect on their interests and experiences and expand on answers to previous questions. While a fantastic interview will not resurrect the fate of a student with otherwise unimpressive credentials, a great interview can make one applicant stand out among a group of similarly-qualified candidates. Students who stand out in their interviews are genuine and expressive in describing their interests, motivations, and goals. Generally, the reasons students impress interviewers are not related

The how and why of students' responses are what define the success of the interview; it is critical, then, that students are prepared to expand upon their answers.

to their vocabulary, speaking ability, or achievements. Instead, they stem from their capacity to expand on why they enjoy or care about the issues, subjects, or activities to which they are most dedicated. The how and why of students' responses are what define the success of the interview; it is critical, then, that students are prepared to expand upon their answers.

Keep in mind that, just as it's important to have good, detailed answers, it is also important to have thoughtful questions. Not only do schools use interviews as a way to learn more about you, they also use them as a way to gauge your interest in them.

The advantage of on-campus interviews: your evaluative report will almost always be filed earlier.

There are two types of interviews used by the eight Ivy League schools: alumni interviews and on-campus interviews.

Alumni Interviews

Each Ivy League institution offers most applicants an alumni interview near their high school. In instances where a student's location makes such an interview impossible, the colleges pledge that the absence of an interview will not affect an applicant's chances for admission. On rare occasions, students will be interviewed by telephone. For Early Decision or Early Action applicants, alumni interviews are conducted from October through November, and for Regular Decision applicants, the time window is from December through February.

On-Campus Interviews

On-campus interviews in admissions offices are generally held from July to November and are available to rising seniors on a first-come, first-serve basis. Not all Ivy League colleges offer on-campus interviews (check the table on page 107 for each school's policy). Most frequently, prospective students interview with current seniors at the college who have been trained by the admissions office. In some cases, students will have the chance to interview with an admissions officer. Be sure to plan your visit early, and call ahead to try to schedule an on-campus interview, as these spots can fill up quickly during popular visiting times. There is also an advantage of interviewing on-campus: your evaluative interview report will almost always be filed in your applicant folder earlier than one submitted by an alumnus or alumna. This will allow an admissions officer the benefit of a positive (hopefully) report in your folder for each reading of the application; often alumni interview reports do not arrive in time for the first reading of the application.

Sample Interview Questions

Most interviewers start with some basic questions about you and your interests and then go into more detailed questions. Their objective is not to catch you off guard or make you nervous, but rather to learn about you. Some common interview questions are listed below. By spending some time thinking about how you would answer these questions, you can prepare yourself for a successful interview. In addition, you should also always be prepared to ask questions about the college.

1. I see that you have listed ___ as a possible major in college. What is it that interests you about ___?
2. What are your main extracurricular activities? What is it that you like most about these activities?
3. Tell me about an occasion when you have demonstrated leadership, either in school or in your extracurricular activities.

→

→

4. How would you describe your high school? If you could change one thing about your high school, what would it be?

5. What is a current issue at your school or in your community?

6. Would you tell me about your favorite book or a book you have read recently? How has the book impacted you?

7. **How would your friends or family members describe you? What three adjectives would they use?**

8. How have you changed or grown throughout high school?

9. What experiences thus far in your life have had the greatest impact on you?

10. What people in your life have had the greatest impact on you?

11. What is the best class you've taken in high school? What made it such a good class?

12. What are your strengths and weaknesses?

13. As you think about and compare colleges, what is most important to you? What things are you looking for in a college?

14. What is it that you like most about ___ (the college to which you are applying)? Do you have any questions for me about ___ (the college)?

Although interviews are often optional at many of the Ivy schools, Shannon and most college counselors encourage students to take advantage of the opportunity to interview. All schools offer some type of alumni interviews, and many offer a limited number of on-campus interviews. As we've mentioned, all of the Ivies pledge that if you live in an area of the country or the world where an alumni interview cannot be offered, it will not be used against you as your application is considered. **But, in short, if you have the chance to interview, with few exceptions, you should.**

Ask Shannon

Help Me!

Q: What am I supposed to wear to an interview?

A: Students should dress neatly for interviews, which means avoiding jeans. Younger alumni interviewers generally do not mind if students wear jeans, but it is always a good idea to be safe and wear nicer pants. Girls do not need to wear skirts—they certainly can, but pants are fine. Students should not hesitate to show their sense of style (within reason), but again should adhere to the standard of neatness, meaning clean and not cluttered.

The following table summarizes the interview policies of each Ivy League school:

Ivy League Interview Policies

SCHOOL	ON-CAMPUS INTERVIEW?	ALUMNI INTERVIEW?
Brown	Not offered.	Offered to most students who apply. About 70 percent of applicants interview with alumni close to their home or high school.
Columbia	Not offered.	Offered to most students who apply. Columbia notes that the earlier you submit your application, the better your chance of getting an interview.
Cornell	Not offered to applicants outside of the School of Hotel Administration or the College of Architecture, Art, and Planning (both of which require an interview).	Offered to most students who apply. Interview required of students applying to the School of Hotel Administration or the College of Architecture, Art, and Planning.
Dartmouth	Available to rising seniors from mid-June to mid-November with limited availability. Conducted by Dartmouth seniors.	Offered to most students who apply.
Harvard	Available to rising seniors from July to November with limited availability.	Offered to most students who apply.
Penn	Not offered unless applicant is the child or grandchild of an alumnus (which are offered through Penn's Alumni Council on Admissions).	Offered to most students who apply.
Princeton	Not offered.	Offered to most students who apply.
Yale	Available to rising seniors from July to November with limited availability.	Offered to most students who apply.

Recommendations

Recommendations are an incredibly important part of your application and help to bring it to life. These letters provide a way for colleges to gain insight to who you are, beyond your class rank, GPA, and SAT score. Many schools require both teacher recommendations as well as a letter from your guidance counselor. Sometimes, you also have the option of submitting additional letters of support—a boss, coach, or someone from your neighborhood are all good options if they know you well and are able speak to your character and personality.

Because teacher recommendations are usually written by your 11th- or 12th-grade teachers (although this is not a requirement), it is a good idea to start thinking about whom you want to ask during the end of your junior year. Because many teachers get overloaded with requests for recommendations in the fall, this is often a great time to let them know that you'd like their help. **The bottom line here is to give everyone plenty of time.** The last thing you want to do is to ask someone to write you a letter in the same week your application is due. Remember all the other students in your class? They're going to ask for letters, too.

Once you've figured out whom you want to write your recommendations and they've given their "ok," make sure that you provide all the necessary information, including the recommendation form, deadline, and a stamped/addressed envelope (if they will be returning the letter directly to the school). At this time, it is also a good idea to sit down and discuss the college and your reasons for applying with whoever will be writing your recommendation. Sometimes, it can also help to bring a list of any activities or accomplishments that you want them to keep in mind. The more information and time they receive, the better. The last thing you want is a rushed, generic-sounding letter.

"Recommendations from guidance counselors, headmasters, and teachers, considered in concert with your classroom performance, give us a more subjective evaluation of your work. **They provide a perspective** that may not be evident from mere grades and scores. These commentaries are quite important, so it is best to find persons who are **well acquainted with your work and potential**. It is also helpful to us, and beneficial to you, to obtain a recommendation from a teacher in the area in which you think you might like to continue your studies."

—University of Pennsylvania

http://www.admissionsug.upenn.edu

"These . . . letters help to personalize the application; **they go beyond** the numerical information of grade point averages and test scores and evaluate the applicant's contributions in particular classrooms and the greater school community."

—Dartmouth College

http://www.dartmouth.edu/apply

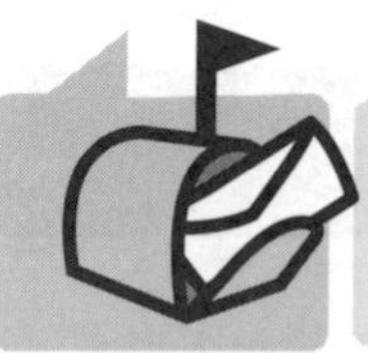

The Decision Process

You've worked days and nights on end to complete your application. Now what? At most of the Ivies, the application reading process is "internally rolling," meaning that after your folder has been reviewed for *the first time*, admissions officers have several options: acceptance, rejection, wait list, or postponement. Most often, postponement is chosen because even if an applicant is "exceptional," the admissions team will still want a chance to read through most, if not all, of the applications before making decisions—this allows them to get a feel for the overall quality of this particular pool of prospective students. Some folders, though, are below par in every respect: the grades are poor, the writing is adequate, mediocre, or poor, and the test scores and letters of recommendation are moderate. In these instances, if an admissions committee is fairly certain, given their past experiences and general idea of the "average" successful applicant, that a particular folder will be reviewed unfavorably at a future date, they refuse the application. (Remember that this happens internally—all students receive their decisions at the same time in April regardless of when their application was reviewed.) Sometimes, the opposite is true: the writing is brilliant, the grades are flawless, the standardized test scores are superb, and the letters of recommendation are stellar, among other factors. In these instances, committees might just accept the application before reading through the remainder of folders.

According to one admissions insider, his committee probably accepts about 10 percent after just one reading, refuses about 20-30 percent after one reading, and postpones the remaining 60-70 percent for a second, third, or sometimes even fourth reading.

An advantage of accepting later on—at least from the standpoint of the admissions office—is that they now know what the competition looks like, both regionally and for the class as a whole. "Acceptances are rarer in the earlier stages of reading, as committees tend to be more reserved or conservative in acceptances, not wanting to fill slots so readily, waiting to see what other applicants exist in the region," an insider told us.

"**In the end, everything in an application matters.** The good news is that so many little things figure in an admissions decision that it is fruitless to worry too much about any one of them."

—Yale University

http://www.yale.edu/admit

Towards the end of the process, after folders have been read two (or up to four) times and spaces are filled, there are often still many more excellent and qualified applicants than there is available space. These students are placed on a waiting list and will not know their fate until after accepted students have decided whether to enroll or not. During some years of under-enrollment, 100 students might be taken from the list, although most often, Ivies take between zero and 20 students.

The chart on the following pages helps to summarize the entire decision process:

INSIDE AN IVY ADMISSIONS OFFICE

Application materials are received by the admissions office both electronically and via regular mail. The materials are sorted, applicant data is entered into the computer system, and a folder is assembled for each applicant which includes all components of his application.

Once an applicant's folder is complete or nearly complete, it is read by the admissions officer responsible for the applicant's region. They will evaluate the application in various categories and then assign an overall rating to the application, which will determine the next step in the evaluation process.

EXCEPTIONAL APPLICATIONS

After the initial reading, the very strongest applications, near-certain admits, are generally sent directly to one of the admissions directors who will either support the admissions officer's evaluation of the application and make the decision to admit that candidate, or will raise questions about the application and send it to Admissions Committee, where it will be discussed and voted upon.

COMPETITIVE APPLICATIONS

The greatest number of applications fall into this middle category of "possible" admits. Within this category, admissions officers note subcategories of stronger and weaker applications—the stronger applications are usually sent to Admissions Committee, while the weaker applications may be sent to another reader or admissions officer whose opinion will also be considered in determining whether the application makes it to Admissions Committee.

UNCOMPETITIVE APPLICATIONS

The weakest applications are generally sent directly to one of the Admissions Directors who will either support the recommendation of the admissions officer to reject the candidate or raise questions that may "keep the applicant's chances alive" by sending it to another admissions officer or Admissions Committee to be considered further.

Notes: The flow chart above provides a general overview of the application evaluation process; keep in mind that the process varies significantly among Ivy League institutions. For instance, at some Ivy colleges, Admissions Committees discuss almost all applications and render the vast majority of decisions. At other colleges, Admissions Committees may be used for a smaller percentage of applicants (usually for the toughest decisions, which involve students who are right on the fence), and many more decisions are made based on the combination of the admissions officers' comments (with a final review of the application by an Admissions Director).

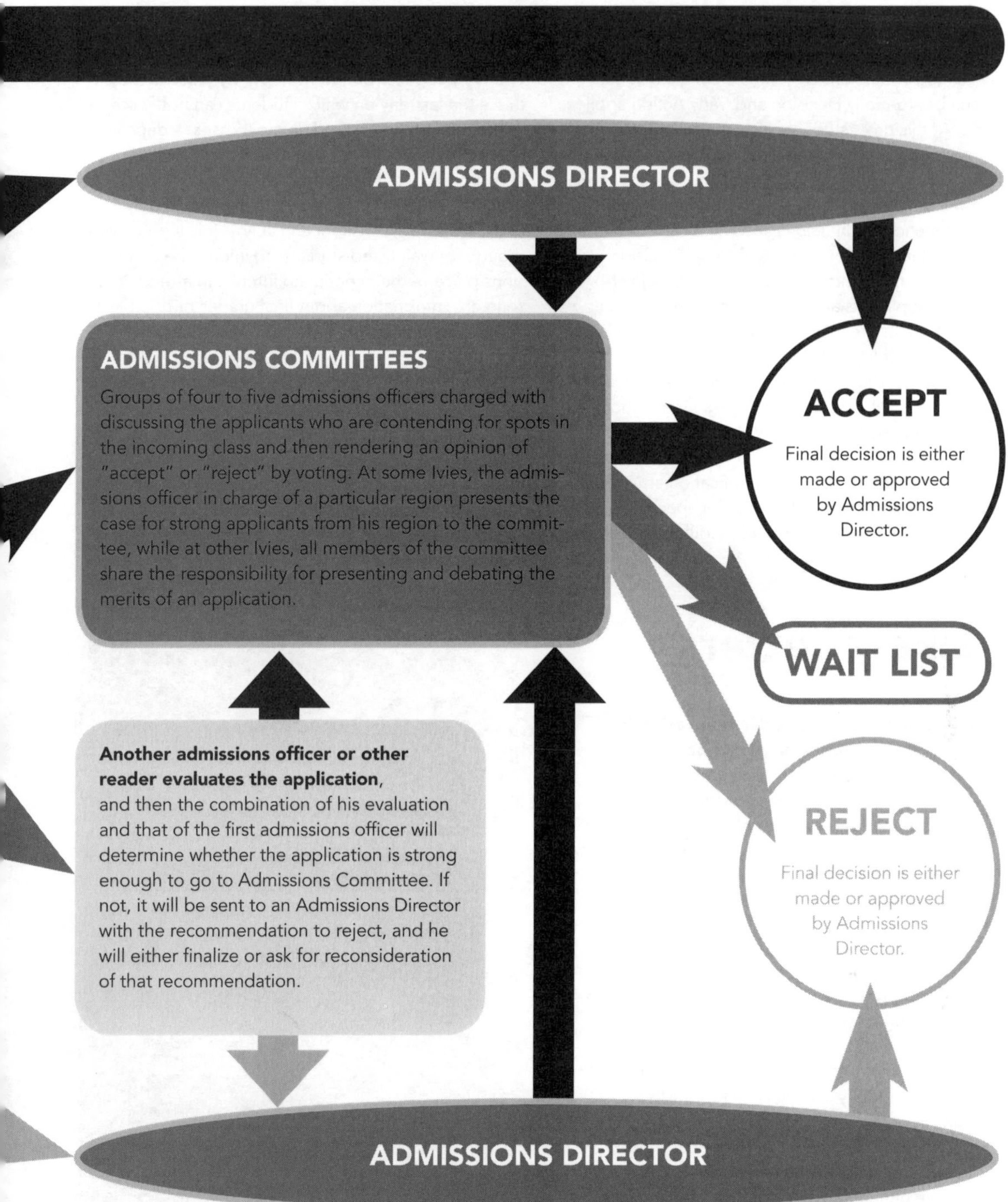

ADMISSIONS DIRECTOR

ADMISSIONS COMMITTEES

Groups of four to five admissions officers charged with discussing the applicants who are contending for spots in the incoming class and then rendering an opinion of "accept" or "reject" by voting. At some Ivies, the admissions officer in charge of a particular region presents the case for strong applicants from his region to the committee, while at other Ivies, all members of the committee share the responsibility for presenting and debating the merits of an application.

ACCEPT

Final decision is either made or approved by Admissions Director.

WAIT LIST

Another admissions officer or other reader evaluates the application, and then the combination of his evaluation and that of the first admissions officer will determine whether the application is strong enough to go to Admissions Committee. If not, it will be sent to an Admissions Director with the recommendation to reject, and he will either finalize or ask for reconsideration of that recommendation.

REJECT

Final decision is either made or approved by Admissions Director.

ADMISSIONS DIRECTOR

The Admissions Directors have final authority concerning admissions decisions, however they very rarely make or change decisions unilaterally. It is much more common for them to ask questions about the applicants in question or send an application headed for admission or rejection to Admissions Committee. Finally, the process that occurs within the Admissions Office is generally similar for both Early Action/Decision and Regular Decision candidates, though the fact that there are far fewer Early Action/Decision candidates means that the process can be completed within a shorter period of time.

Thick and Thin Envelopes

Ivy League admissions decisions are mailed in early December for Early Decision and Early Action applicants. At this time, students are notified of the college's decision to accept, defer, or deny their application. If a student is deferred, his or her application will be given further consideration during the regular round of admissions and will receive notification of a final decision with the Regular Decision candidates. Ivy admissions decisions for Regular Decision applicants are mailed in early April; at this point, students are informed of the schools' decision to accept, wait list, or deny them. Most schools pledge that students who apply Early will be given a final decision in April—in other words, a student who applied Early and is deferred will usually not be wait listed. Both Early and Regular admissions decisions are made available online before notification arrives by mail. Check admissions Web sites for specific details of notification, as the timing is slightly different each year.

The Ivy League's Common Reply-By Date is May 1; this is the last day on which students can notify schools of their decision to attend. In most cases, a deposit must accompany the reply. Students who are placed and choose to remain on an active waiting list at an Ivy League college will receive a final answer by July 1. In the time between April and July 1, it is a good idea though for wait listed students to inform the admissions office of their continued interest in attending and send any information about final grades or notable awards received.

Likely Letters

Ivy admissions offices offer some athletic recruits and a very limited number of other top candidates a "likely letter," which basically states that the applicant will be accepted so long as he or she maintains their grades and does not engage in any other sort of activity which might be the basis for acceptance to be rescinded.

These letters were originally devised as a way for the Ivy League to attract and retain recruits who were being offered scholarships and admission to colleges outside the Ivies—and must make or forego commitments to these programs by early November (early signing date for most sports), early February (for a few sports) or mid-April (regular signing date for most sports). These letters may be given anytime after October 1 but are generally sent in October and November, for students who want to make an early commitment, or in January and February, for students applying during the regular admissions round. Coaches are the ones who typically request that these letters be sent, but it is up to the admissions officers to make the final decisions and actually mail the letters.

Ask Shannon

What if . . .

Q: I'm wait listed at my dream school, but the notification date isn't until July 1, and **all my other schools want an answer before then**. What should I do?

A: If you want to be sure that you have a college to attend in the fall, you must accept the admissions offer of one of the colleges to which you were admitted. You do not know how the wait list dynamics will play out at your dream school—even if you've been told that your chances of being admitted off the wait list are good, you just never know! It is much better to be safe than sorry. Should you be admitted off the wait list of your dream school later in the summer, you can accept that offer of admission, and then should promptly call the college whose admissions offer you've accepted to tell them that you won't be enrolling after all. Colleges expect that this will happen in a number of instances, and call it "summer melt." In many cases, the college that you decided not to attend will then be able to admit someone off their waiting list.

Going Ivy League Isn't Cheap

At Yale, undergraduate tuition has increased from $19,840 in 1994-1995, to $31,460 in 2005-2006—and that's not including room and board and the school's estimate for books and other personal expenses ($2,700). At Harvard, the total undergraduate tuition (including room and board) averaged approximately $6,500 in 1977. That number was slightly over $38,000 in 2005-2006 (and excludes additional student services fees and personal expenses). **Attending college is becoming increasingly expensive, but why?**

> "Each year, Dartmouth students receive approximately $38 million in grant/scholarship aid. . . . The **range of scholarships** offered to financial aid recipients in recent years has been **as low as $1,000 to over $37,000.**"
>
> **—Dartmouth College**
>
> *http://www.dartmouth.edu/apply*

Economist Ronald Ehrenberg, author of *Tuition Rising: Why College Costs So Much*, explains that today's academic institutions are like

cookie monsters.

"They aggressively seek out all the resources that they can find and put them to use funding things that they think will make them better. They want better facilities, better faculty, improved research support, improved instructional technology and better students. All of these things take more money," he writes in a paper entitled, "Why Can't Colleges Control Their Costs?" "While they could aggressively try to increase their efficiency, reduce costs, and get better by substituting rather than growing expenditures, they don't do this. Rather they adopt the attitude that as long as large lines of high quality applicants are flocking to their doors and accepting their offers of admissions there is no reason for them to moderate their tuition increases."

According to the College Board, for the 2002-2003 academic year, the average annual cost of a four-year private college was $27,677, including tuition, room and board, books, transportation, and personal expenses. It's generally agreed upon by experts that this annual cost increases five to six percent annually, which means that if you enrolled today, your education would cost you somewhere in the neighborhood of $120,000. But analysts also predict that costs might increase seven or eight percent a year further down the line. Enrolling in 2009? Based on a seven percent tuition inflation rate, your first year of college will cost $38,818.42. Expect to pay $41,535.71, $44,443.21, and $47,554.24 for your sophomore, junior and senior years, respectively. Grand total: $172,351.59. Ten years from now, four years of college will cost $241,732.02. What about 25 years from today (2029), when many students applying now will be sending their own children to college? Costs might be somewhere over $660,000 by then. **How's that for incentive to start saving?**

> "**Our doors have long been open to talented students** regardless of financial need, but many students simply do not know or believe this. We are determined to change both the perception and the reality."
>
> **—Harvard President Lawrence H. Summers**
>
> *http://www.admissions.college.harvard.edu*

Just remember that, while costs are increasing, so is the amount of help. **All of the colleges in the Ivy League pledge to follow "need-blind admission,"** which means that your ability (or inability) to pay for school will not be a factor in determining your acceptance. And if you are accepted, there are numerous ways (including scholarships, grants, loans, and work-study) to pay for your education. In fact, many schools are taking steps to make it possible for students to receive an Ivy League education. According to Harvard's Financial Aid Initiative, which began in 2004, " . . . parents of families with incomes of less than $40,000 no longer will be asked to contribute to the cost of their child's education. . . . In addition, Harvard also is reducing substantially the expected parental contributions of families with incomes between $40,000 and $60,000" (*http://www.admissions.college.harvard.edu*).

> In September 2004, Sidney E. Frank, a member of the class of 1942, made **a gift of $100 million** . . . to establish an endowed scholarship fund that will provide financial assistance for the neediest undergraduate students at Brown University. . . ."
>
> **—Brown University**
>
> *http://financialaid.brown.edu*

> Actual difference in average yearly cost between a medium-security prison and an Ivy League education: **$0**
>
> *http://www.anotherperspective.org*

Yale, too, is implementing similar aid reforms. On March 3, 2005, Yale's President, Richard Levin, announced that "families with incomes below $45,000 will no longer be required to pay any portion of the cost of their children's education. . . . Families with incomes between $45,000 and $60,000 will see their required contribution reduced significantly . . . by about 50 percent." Be sure to visit each school's financial aid Web site and do your research. Many schools offer pages with frequently asked questions. **Paying for college does not have to be the hardest part of the admission process.**

For more information about your options, check out each school's financial aid Web site:

Brown University
http://financialaid.brown.edu/

Columbia University
http://www.studentaffairs.columbia.edu/finaid/

Cornell University
http://finaid.cornell.edu/

Dartmouth College
http://www.dartmouth.edu/home/admissions/finaid.html

Harvard University
http://www.admissions.college.harvard.edu/prospective/financial_aid/

Princeton University
http://www.princeton.edu/main/admission-aid/aid/

University of Pennsylvania
http://www.admissionsug.upenn.edu/paying/

Yale University
http://www.yale.edu/admissions/aid.html

A Historic Hook-Up

In 1995-96, the Cornell medical school admitted 249 students, but only expected 101 to 104 to enroll. When 199 students accepted, **Cornell offered one year of tuition to the first 15 students who agreed to defer admission by one year**. Not only did these lucky students receive free tuition, they also received free University housing during their year off.

Avery, Christopher, Andrew Fairbanks, and Richard Zeckhauser. *The Early Admissions Game.* (Cambridge: Harvard University Press, 2003), p. 175.

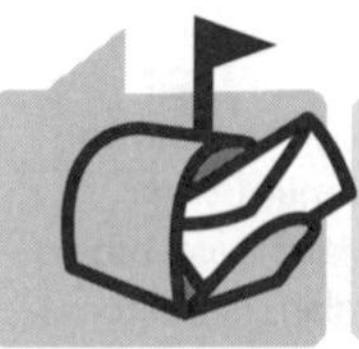

College Admissions Calendar

In short, preparing for and applying to college clearly requires much planning, but hopefully, this discussion of the many different parts of the college admissions process has shed some light on what you can expect. In order to give an overview of how to prepare for and stay on top of the process, Shannon has shared with us the following **general timeline** for high school juniors and seniors as they navigate the college search and admissions process:

BEFORE JUNIOR YEAR	**Keep in mind what colleges will be looking for on your transcript as you pick your junior year classes.** **Use your summer break to do something, or several things, about which you are passionate.** Some colleges will ask on the application what you have done for the past two summers. Explore ways to pursue your interests through internships, summer jobs, camps at colleges, classes at colleges, or prep school programs. Try to work some college visits into family trips or other travels.

JUNIOR YEAR

SEPTEMBER	**Register for the PSAT.** **Focus on your academics.** For the most part, this year's grades and class rank are the last that colleges will use in making admissions decisions. **Reflect on your extracurricular activities.** Consider ways in which you can expand your commitment to those activities you enjoy most. **Plan for the SAT Subject Tests**; they are offered in October, November, December, January, May, and June. Ideally, students plan so that they take these tests soon after completion of the courses to which they roughly correspond.
OCTOBER	**Take the PSAT.** **Attend a local college fair and/or any college admissions officers' presentations** for schools that interest you.
NOVEMBER	**Remember the importance of building relationships with your guidance counselor and teachers**; your counselor will have helpful advice for you as you sort through your college options, and they will be writing a recommendation for you for college next year—keep this in mind! **Contact the closest Social Security office** if you don't have a Social Security number yet. You will need it next fall for your college applications.

DECEMBER	You should receive your PSAT scores in December. **This is a good time to consider test-prep options in your area for the SAT Reasoning Test.** Some students will choose to take a prep class before the March test; others will take a prep class right before the May or June tests. Kaplan, Princeton Review, and Sylvan all offer test prep courses.
JANUARY	**Make a list of colleges** you want to visit and research further. **Research summer opportunities.** Many good internships, camps, and other programs fill up early, so now is the time to plan. **Plan your spring standardized testing schedule with your counselor.** The SAT Reasoning Test is offered in March, May, and June; the SAT Subject Tests are offered in May and June; and the ACT is offered in February, April, and June.
FEBRUARY	**If you will be applying for financial aid, start researching and learning about the process for federal student financial aid, as well as independent scholarships.**
MARCH	**Take the SAT Reasoning Test.** **Consider which AP tests you will take in May.**
APRIL	**Take the ACT Test.** **If possible, use at least part of spring break to visit several colleges.** (It is best to visit when school is in session and the students are there.) **Request view-books and other materials from the colleges that interest you.**
MAY	**Plan college visits for the summer. Call admissions offices** now to try to schedule interviews for when you will be on campus.
JUNE	**Take the SAT Reasoning Test and SAT Subject Tests.** **Consider which of your junior year teachers you will ask to write letters of recommendation for you.** You might want to ask them now if they would be willing to write you a letter of recommendation for college, before they are inundated with requests in the fall. Depending on the teacher, you might be able to give them recommendation forms at this point; others may prefer to wait until the fall. **For prospective collegiate student athletes— be sure to register with the NCAA Clearinghouse.** (*www.ncaa.com*)

SUMMER BEFORE SENIOR YEAR	**Visit colleges** that you were not able to see during the school year, and **refine the list of colleges you are considering.** **Talk to older friends** who are headed to college in the fall, as well as those who are already in college.

SENIOR YEAR

AUGUST	**Gather the applications as they become available online, or request them by mail.** Most colleges' applications (or supplements to the Common Application) are available by August. Think about possible topics for your personal statement, and colleges' supplemental essay questions; **begin to draft your essays.** **Research scholarships.** There are thousands of scholarships available at the national, state, and local levels. Your school's college counseling office or guidance department is a good starting place for this search.
SEPTEMBER	**Meet with teachers whom you have asked (or plan to ask) to write recommendations.** Give them the appropriate forms and discuss briefly the colleges in which you are interested. If the teacher will be sending the letter directly to the college, make sure he/she has a stamped, addressed envelope. **Check with your counselor to see if any of the colleges you are interested in will be making presentations at your school or nearby schools.** If they are, attend. Introduce yourself briefly to the admissions officer who is presenting should the opportunity present itself. **Draft an activities resumé** which includes sections dedicated to: 1. Extracurricular activities 2. Honors and awards 3. Summer activities 4. Jobs/internships
OCTOBER	**Take the SAT Reasoning Test and/or ACT again** if you are not satisfied with your scores from the spring. **Finalize the list of colleges to which you will apply**—ensure that this list includes a combination of reach, target, and safety schools. **Follow up with teachers writing recommendations for you**; ensure that teachers have all the materials and information they need. Later, check with teachers to make sure the letters have been mailed. Finally, be sure to write thank-you notes to teachers who write letters of recommendation for you.
NOVEMBER	**Take any remaining SAT Subject Tests.** **Early Decision and Early Action applications are due.** **Submit applications for any colleges you are applying to that have rolling admissions**—the earlier you submit your application to these schools, the better.

DECEMBER	**Early Decision and Early Action decisions are mailed and/or available on the Web.** **Last chance to take SAT Reasoning, SAT Subject, and ACT tests.** **If you are accepted early under a binding program, or decide to attend a college to which you are admitted early, and you have applied to other colleges, write or call these colleges to withdraw your applications.**
JANUARY	**Regular Decision applications are due.** **Complete and submit financial aid applications, including the Free Application for Federal Student Aid (FAFSA) and CSS/PROFILE.** **Follow your school's procedure for submitting Mid-Year School Reports** to colleges that require them.
FEBRUARY	**If you have not received confirmation from a college that all your application materials have been received**, send the admissions office an e-mail to confirm that they have received all your application materials.
MARCH	**Remain focused on your academics**; colleges can reverse acceptance decisions if students' grades decline substantially. **Register for May AP exams.**
APRIL	**April 1 – Most selective colleges' decisions are mailed and/or available on the Web.** **Meet with your counselor to discuss your college options.** **Re-visit any colleges** as you make your final decisions.
MAY	**May 1 – Deadline for replying to colleges' offers of admission, and/or sending a deposit.** **Complete all forms required by the college for incoming freshmen.** **Take AP exams.**

SUMMER BEFORE COLLEGE	**Ask your high school to send a final transcript** to the college you will be attending. **Make a packing list.** Talk to your roommate(s)—plan who will bring major items such as TVs and microwaves. **Enjoy your summer, and get excited for college!** Talk to older friends and any students from your school or area who know about your college to see if they have any advice for you.

What the Ivy League Wants

In their own words:

Brown University

"As you will learn, admission practices at colleges vary in terms of how test scores or interviews or courses are evaluated, which is to say that the relative weight applied to these factors does not follow some common formula. Thus, the probability of admission differs from college to college.

With so much variation in the educational opportunities among secondary schools, from state to state and country to country, we cannot possibly or fairly apply a uniform standard for achievement. **Rather, we attempt to treat each applicant individually and educate ourselves about the variety of experiences that students bring with them.**

Each year the Board of Admission is thoroughly inspired by the many dimensions of excellence that our applicants present; however, we can admit relatively few of these individuals. Thus, you should make an effort to be realistic in estimating your chances of admission. The most important actions that you may take on your own behalf are to research your colleges well and to produce a thoughtful application."

(http://www.brown.edu/Administration/Admission)

Columbia University

"In the process of selection, the Committee on Admissions asks questions about each applicant's academic potential, intellectual strength, and ability to think independently. The Committee also considers the general attitudes and character of the applicant, special abilities and interests, maturity, motivation, curiosity and whether he or she is likely to make productive use of the four years at Columbia. In its final selection, **Columbia seeks diversity of personalities, achievements and talents, and of economic, social, ethnic, racial and geographic backgrounds.**

Each applicant's academic record is examined, together with reports on personal qualities that have been supplied by the principal, headmaster or counselor and by teachers. The student's record of participation in the life of his or her school and community is also important, as is his or her performance on standardized tests."

(http://www.studentaffairs.columbia.edu/admissions)

Cornell University

"Unlike some state university systems, **Cornell does not use any single formula** for its admission decisions. In fact, the whole process can be very subjective. First and foremost, we look at your high school record, the rigor of your coursework, your grades, and your rank-in-class (don't worry if your school doesn't rank—that's quite common). The personal application you write (essays, extracurriculars, etc.) is also a very important piece of Cornell's selection process. Standardized testing plays a role, but probably not as much as you think. From there, we rely on a lot of tools that can't be quantified: recommendations, for example, and interviews (required for architecture and hotel applicants). Since all of these pieces help inform our decisions, we can't point to any master chart of GPA and test scores and automatically tell you what the decision will be. And frankly, we like it that way, because it forces us to learn as much as we can about each of our applicants."

(http://www.admissions.cornell.edu)

Dartmouth College

"There is no set formula or prescription for admission. . . . Dartmouth incorporates an individual, holistic approach to the reading of applications. In reading files from an applicant, **we thoughtfully consider the achievements of an applicant with respect to the opportunities available in his or her environment.**

Each application to Dartmouth is:

- Independently reviewed by at least two and usually three members of the Admissions staff.
- Evaluated for the tangible academic accomplishments which are represented by grades and test scores and supplemented by essays, recommendations, and interviews.
- Carefully considered for qualities such as passion for ideas, dedication to learning, leadership, compassion, integrity, motivation, and sense of humor.
- Evaluated for significant extracurricular involvements and interests beyond the classroom—ranging from community service and debate to athletics and drama."

(http://www.dartmouth.edu/apply/admissions/)

Harvard University

"**There is no formula for gaining admission to Harvard.** Academic accomplishment in high school is important, but the Admissions Committee also considers many other criteria, such as community involvement, leadership and distinction in extracurricular activities, and work experience. We rely on teachers, counselors, headmasters, and alumni/ae to share information with us about applicants' strength of character, their ability to overcome adversity, and other personal qualities—all of which play a part in the Admissions Committee's decisions."

(http://www.admissions.college.harvard.edu)

Princeton University

"Ultimately, admission is offered to those students who, in our judgment, will best take advantage of the educational opportunities at Princeton and contribute in many ways to the Princeton community. While we do not employ any formulas, the large majority of admitted students rank in the top 10 percent of their graduating classes and have given evidence of a high energy level through their pursuit of nonacademic interests and activities. In evaluating candidates, we closely review all available information, including recommendations, application responses, and the results of various standardized tests. **The most important single document in an applicant's folder, however, is the transcript showing the student's performance in his or her academic program in high school.**"

(http://www.princeton.edu/pr/admissions)

University of Pennsylvania

"As a major research and teaching institution with an emphasis on undergraduate education, Penn seeks students who will avail themselves of the rich academic, cultural and social opportunities of the academic community. As an institution, Penn prides itself on its enormous diversity—not only in the great wealth of our undergraduate and graduate programs, but in the wide variety of students and talents that such programs attract. **The student who flourishes in the Penn community possesses a history of strong academic excellence, a healthy degree of motivation, and a well-developed interest and involvement in his or her environment.**"

(http://www.admissionsug.upenn.edu)

Yale University

"We estimate that over three quarters of the students who apply for admission to Yale are qualified to do the work here. Between two and three hundred students in any year are so strong academically that their admission is scarcely ever in doubt. The great majority of students who are admitted, however, stand out from the rest because a lot of little things, when added up, tip the scale in their favor. **The difference between a successful and an unsuccessful candidate at Yale is often painfully small.**

What does matter in the admissions process? Yale is above all an academic institution, and thus academic strength is our first consideration in evaluating any candidate. The single most important document in the application is the high school transcript, which tells us a great deal about a student's academic motivation and performance over time."

(http://www.yale.edu/admit)

Who Got In

Real Profiles of Accepted Ivy Students:

Brown
Virginia, Public HS
Gender: Male
GPA: 3.9 (unweighted)
Class Rank: Top 10 in a class of over 200
SAT (old version): 1550 (750 V, 800 M)
SAT IIs: 790 Literature, 780 Writing, 750 Math IC
Extracurriculars (ECs): International recognition for filmmaking and production talent, including some documentary work

Columbia
Maryland, Public HS
Gender: Female
GPA: 3.9 (unweighted)
Class Rank: Top 5 in a class of over 400
SAT (old version): 1520 (800 V, 720 M)
SAT IIs: 800 Writing, 750 Biology, 750 Math 2C
ECs: National-level dance competitor, participated in prestigious national medical internship program that lasted through the summer and senior year

Cornell
Connecticut, Private HS
Gender: Male
GPA: 3.7 (unweighted)
Class Rank: N/A
SAT (old version): 1600
SAT IIs: 790 Math IIC, 750 Writing, 690 Biology
ECs: Varstiy basketball, varsity tennis, Young Republicans Club, substantial volunteer work abroad

Dartmouth
New York, Public HS
Gender: Male
GPA: 3.8 (unweighted)
Class Rank: N/A
SAT (old version): 1330 (660 V, 670 M)
SAT IIs: 700 History, 660 Writing, 630 Math IC
ECs: Newspaper, yearbook, wrestling, martial arts at a national level, Student Government officer, Key Club, National Honor Society

Harvard
California, Private HS
Gender: Female
GPA: 4.0 (unweighted)
Class Rank: N/A
SAT (old version): 1510 (730 V, 780 M)
SAT IIs: 800 Chemistry, 780 Math IIC, 760 Physics
ECs: Nationally-recognized musical achievements, concert performer, science research, founded musical community organization

Penn
Texas, Public HS
Gender: Male
GPA: 4.0 (unweighted)
Class Rank: 1 in a class of over 400
SAT (old version): 1500
ECs: Baseball, substantial involvement in a sports-related business, president of several HS clubs and attended their state and national competitions

Princeton
New York, Public HS
Gender: Female
GPA: 3.8 (unweighted)
Class Rank: N/A
SAT (old version): 1530
SAT IIs: 790 Math IC, 780 Chemistry, 750 Physics
ECs: Notable community service, research, school newspaper, piano

Yale
Texas, Public HS
Gender: Male
GPA: 4.2 (weighted)
Class Rank: 2 in a class of over 500
SAT (old version): 1540 (800 V, 740 M)
SAT IIs: 800 Writing, 790 US History, 740 Literature
ECs: Top-10 national ranking in speech/debate; substantial speaking-related accomplishments

An Essay By Someone Who Got In

The following student was accepted to Yale's Class of 2009:

1. Tell us about a person who has affected your life in a significant way.

My mother was driving our minivan through western Virginia. The car was navy blue and shaped like a refrigerator. We were on our way to my camp; it was to be the first time I had ever slept away from home for more than one night. I was nine. I fidgeted most of the trip, due both to undisciplined energy and apprehension.

I heard a scream, felt a tightness around my chest, and was sprayed with broken glass and the contents of our camp trunks. Our car had been rammed square on the side. A body was slumped over the steering wheel: it was my mother's. She looked asleep, except that blood was dripping from her eye. Sometimes, when I am very tired or unhappy, that image burns behind my eyelids; the effect is similar to staring at the sun too long.

She managed to rouse herself enough to get me out of the car, but then lay down on the ground and could not be reached. Two ambulances came, and I was put in one of them. I asked the emergency workers if my mother was okay. One chewed gum and drawled "Sure. Y'all will see her at the hospital. Don't worry your little head about it." One of the kidnappers tried to put her hand on my shoulder. I swatted it away. I was not to be reassured. I was enraged. I loved my mother. I felt a combination of disorientation and agony; that feeling is my most vivid memory of the event. I sat silent in the ambulance, not knowing what to do, in dejected, furious silence.

At the hospital, I asked to see my mom. My dad had been informed of the accident a quarter of an hour before, and had just begun the five hour drive to us. The doctors told me that I could not see my mother until my father arrived. I threw the only proper fit of my childhood. It was tactical, not emotional. I held my breath, again and again. I almost passed out. I was then allowed to see my mother.

I arrived at her hospital bed. At first I could not recognize her. It was as though her flesh had been carved off and put on someone else's body. I was disgusted with how she looked, and shamed that I felt so. She was distorted and her skin was colorful, like a rainbow. She turned around to face me, and stared at a 'no smoking' sign on the wall. She asked who I was. She could not recognize me because she could not see me. For the first time that day, I stopped wanting to kill something and wanted to cry.

Later, I learned that my mother had bruised her brain. I had never really thought about my mother as a character, I simply considered her a fact of my existence. She drove me places, played with me, gave me money, organized my dance lessons. Sometimes we cooked together and she told me about feminism. She was a busy person and a serious professional, but never at my expense. At nine years old and younger, I was rather more preoccupied with my mischief than my mother's twelve hour days. I didn't really care if she made partner or if she was suing somebody. I just wanted her to read me Nancy Drew on the weekends and tell me I was wonderful.

It all stopped after the accident. Mom could see enough to get around, but she couldn't read, couldn't drive, couldn't work, she wasn't fun, she wasn't healthy. Doctors gave her an appalling prognosis. Her injuries were most likely permanent. I think that the loss of her job was a greater bereavement to my mother than the diminishment of her sight itself. She was desperate to regain her professional integrity, her life, her identity before the accident. She wanted her honor back.

My mother's desperation permeated her approach to recovery. I barely noticed at the time, but she went to therapy almost every day, for hours. I didn't notice it was futile, that she made no progress, as all had predicted. I did notice that she was unhappy and frustrated. I didn't like her very much at the time because I couldn't understand her. She fought with my loving father, as if for her life. Now that sufficient years have passed to let me look back on that terrible episode with a measure of maturity and objectivity, I am overcome with the deepest respect for her vital resilience, and a regret that I could not appreciate her bravery as she lived it. If I had, one of the key sadnesses of her recovery would not have existed. She would not have been as alone as she was. She had generous disability insurance, a family who cared for her passionately, my father's income, and no prospect of recovery: her back was against the wall, the odds were against her, but she spit at the easy exit those who cared for her finally concluded she should take, and decided to fight anyway, largely alone.

There was nothing graceful about her healing. Recovery was difficult for her, and for my father. Persistent pain and therapy finally yielded fruit: my mother could read. There was no color, and no peripheral vision, but she could read. I suppose that Lincoln might have felt about Gettysburg the same way my mother felt about her victory. Both were incomplete, but enough to change the landscape of the battle.

Seven years later, my mother is still colorblind and has no peripheral vision. But her victory is total. She works towards changing the world again, every day, long hours. It was her bravery, her utter confidence in conflict which made her able to spurn the loving naysayers and achieve the unprecedented. She lives to fight another day. This was not a medical miracle; medicine was the means but not the reason for her recovery. Audacity is the fabric of her character. I saw my mother survive and conquer. Hers is the compelling example that taught me courage.

—Anonymous Student
Accepted to Yale Class of 2009

Why It Worked

Comments from Shannon Duff, independent college counselor:

This essay is incredibly powerful, poignant, and, in short, effective. Before you start to worry that your essay will be hopelessly inferior in comparison, let me promise you that this essay is probably among the top five percent of college application essays and help you break down what it is that makes it such a successful response to the prompt. Doing this will help you to think about the best ways to approach your own essays.

This essay is exemplary for four main reasons:

1. **She expresses vividly her observations** and reactions to her mother's injury and struggle to recover. She reveals how the accident transformed the way she looked at her mother, changing her perspective from a selfish one in which she viewed her mother as "a fact of [her] existence," to one in which she understood the strength of her mother's character, drive, and passion. Further, one would guess from the depth of the author's perception of her mother's commitment to her profession and ability to make a difference that this passion is something she shares.

2. She demonstrates powerfully a consciousness of other people's thoughts, feelings, and, more generally, the world around her. I emphasize the importance of this "consciousness" to students as they write their essays; **you want to demonstrate that you are aware of and learn from the people and events that surround you**. The last thing colleges are looking for is a student who sees himself as the center of the world. After all, a college provides many stimuli (experiences, interactions, classes) for its students, and it seeks to accept those that have the potential to gain the most from these stimuli.

3. She illustrates her writing talent, **but does not do so at the expense of the content of the essay**. I have seen a great many essays that showcase the tremendous writing talent of their authors, but either don't answer the question or are very abstract, and reveal little about their author. Given that you have such limited opportunity within the confines of a college application to express that which is unique about you, you cannot afford to sacrifice this space to present just a writing sample.

4. By starting with the ordinary, and progressing to a much deeper level, the author draws in the reader. The beginning of the essay is an everyday situation, which rapidly turns into a horrifying experience, which is transformative for her and her family. While many college essays attempt to accomplish too much in a short space, **she limits that which she seeks to accomplish**, contributing to the success of the essay.

ADDITIONAL NOTES

She **skips the trite**, avoiding, "My mother's accident taught me that . . ."

The closing of the essay leaves the reader with a **strong sense of its author**.

Students with Special Needs

Students with physical and learning disabilities will always find ways to excel beyond their limitations. In fact, many of the greatest minds that have shaped our modern collective history have been learning disabled. So if you have special needs, just realize that attending an Ivy League school is very possible. These pages provide the contact information for each school's learning disability department. We strongly encourage you to contact them and pursue your goal.

Brown University

Contact:
Catherine Axe
Coordinator, Disability Support Services
(401) 863-9588
dss@brown.edu

Is a smaller course load available? - **Yes**
Is more time given to finish your degree? - **Yes**
Is credit given toward the degree for remedial courses? - **No**

Services offered to students with learning disabilities: *various testing accommodations, reading machines, tape recorders, note-taking services, readers, extended time for tests, tutors*

Services offered to students with physical disabilities: *note-taking services, special transportation, tape recorders, special housing, tutors, adaptive equipment, reader services, interpreters for hearing-impaired, talking books*

Is the campus accessible to students with physical disabilities? *Mostly (some topography challenges around the west campus area, still a few inaccessible buildings on campus)*

Is housing available for disabled students? - **Yes**

Columbia University

Contact:
Colleen Lewis
Director, Office of Disability Services
(212) 854-2388
disability@columbia.edu

Is a smaller course load available? - **No**
Is more time given to finish your degree? **- No**
Is credit given toward the degree for remedial courses? - **No**

Services offered to students with learning disabilities: *various testing accommodations, reading machines, tape recorders, videotaped classes, note-taking services, readers, extended time for tests*

Services offered to students with physical disabilities: *note-taking services, special transportation, learning center*

Columbia University (continued)

Is the campus accessible to students with physical disabilities? *Yes (elevators can get crowded but are all handicap accessible, urban campus=close quarters)*

Is housing available for disabled students? - **Yes**

Cornell University

Contact:
Michele Fish
Associate Director Student Disability Services
(607) 254-4545
mdf6@cornell.edu

Is a smaller course load available? - **No**
Is more time given to finish your degree? - **Yes**
Is credit given toward the degree for remedial courses? - **No**

Services offered to students with learning disabilities: *reading machines, note-taking services, learning center, readers, extended time for tests*

Services offered to students with physical disabilities: *note-taking services, special transportation, learning center, special tutors*

Is the campus accessible to students with physical disabilities? *Yes (90 percent of disabled students on campus think so)*

Is housing available for disabled students? - **Yes**

Dartmouth College

Contact:
Kathy Trueba
Student Disabilities Coordinator
(603) 646-2014
kathy.trueba@dartmouth.edu

Is a smaller course load available? - **Yes**
Is more time given to finish your degree? **- Yes**
Is credit given toward the degree for remedial courses? - **No**

Services offered to students with learning disabilities: *various testing accommodations, learning center, speed-reading courses, extended time for tests*

Services offered to students with physical disabilities: *note-taking services, special transportation, tape recorders, special housing, tutors, adaptive equipment, reader services, braille services, interpreters for hearing-impaired, talking books*

Is the campus accessible to students with physical disabilities? *Mostly (still some inaccessible buildings on campus)*

Is housing available for disabled students? - **Yes**

Harvard University

Contact:
Louise H. Russell
Director, Student Disability Resource Center
(617) 496-8707
lrussell@fas.harvard.edu

Is a smaller course load available? - **Yes**
Is more time given to finish your degree? - **Yes**
Is credit given toward the degree for remedial courses? - **No**

Services offered to students with learning disabilities: *tape recorders, videotaped classes, untimed tests, readers, extended time for tests*

Services offered to students with physical disabilities: *note-taking services, special transportation, tape recorders, special housing, adaptive equipment, reader services, braille center and services, interpreters for the hearing-impaired*

Is the campus accessible to students with physical disabilities? *Mostly (still some inaccessible buildings on campus)*

Is housing available for disabled students? - **Yes**

Princeton University

Contact:
Maria Flores-Mills
Assistant Dean, Disabilities Coordinator
(609) 258-3054
mflores@princeton.edu

Is a smaller course load available? - **No**
Is more time given to finish your degree? - **No**
Is credit given toward the degree for remedial courses? - **No**

Services offered to students with learning disabilities: *various testing accommodations, tutors, learning center, interpreters for the hearing-impaired*

Services offered to students with physical disabilities: *note-taking services, special transportation, tape recorders, special housing, tutors, adaptive equipment, reader services, braille services, interpreters for hearing-impaired, talking books*

Is the campus accessible to students with physical disabilities? *Mostly (still a few inacessible buildings on campus)*

Is housing available for disabled students? - **Yes**

University of Pennsylvania

Contact:
Alice Nagle
Director, Student Disabilities Services
(215) 573-9235
anagle@pobox.upenn.edu

Is a smaller course load available? - **Yes**
Is more time given to finish your degree? - **Yes**
Is credit given toward the degree for remedial courses? - **No**

Services offered to students with learning disabilities: *various testing accommodations, reading machines, tape recorders, note-taking services, oral tests, learning center, readers, extended time for tests, tutors*

Services offered to students with physical disabilities: *note-taking services, special transportation, tape recorders, special housing, tutors, adaptive equipment, reader services, braille services, interpreters for hearing-impaired, talking books*

Is the campus accessible to students with physical disabilities? *Yes (all buildings on campus are deemed handicapped accessible)*

Is housing available for disabled students? - **Yes**

Yale University

Contact:
Judy York
Director, Resource Office on Disabilities
(203) 432-2324
judith.york@yale.edu

Is a smaller course load available? - **Yes**
Is more time given to finish your degree? - **Yes**
Is credit given toward the degree for remedial courses? - **No**

Services offered to students with learning disabilities: *reading machines, note-taking services, learning center, readers, extended time for tests, oral testing*

Services offered to students with physical disabilities: *note-taking services, special transportation, tape recorders, special housing, tutors, adaptive equipment, reader services, braille services, interpreters for hearing-impaired, talking books*

Is the campus accessible to students with physical disabilities? *Mostly (many science buildings are located on hills, still a few inaccessable buildings on campus)*

Is housing available for disabled students? - **Yes**

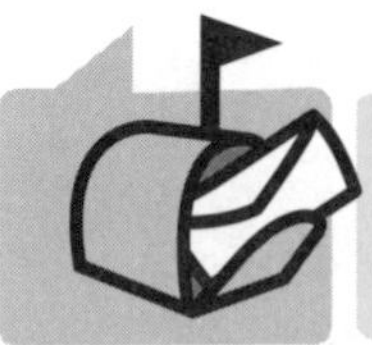

The Role of Affirmative Action

Can the color of your skin help your odds? Just as the issue of standardized testing continues to raise debate in our society, so does the practice of affirmative action.

Defined as "an active effort to improve the employment or educational opportunities of members of minority groups and women," the policy of affirmative action was introduced by President Lyndon B. Johnson in 1965. "This is the next and more profound stage of the battle for civil rights," he said. "We seek . . . not just equality as a right and a theory but equality as a fact and as a result."

Affirmative action would focus on education and jobs, requiring that steps be taken to ensure that African Americans and other minorities be given the same opportunities as whites. It was meant to temporarily "level the playing field" for all Americans. In 1974, however, Allan Bakke, a white male medical school applicant who had twice been rejected by the University of California, filed a lawsuit against the school because it had reserved 16 out of its 100 spaces for less qualified minority students. By 1978, the Supreme Court case, *Regents of the University of California* v. *Bakke*, would decide in favor of the university by a slim margin. **The court's decision stated that the use of quota systems was illegal, although affirmative action was not.** " . . . Race or ethnic background may be deemed a 'plus' in a particular applicant's file, yet it does not insulate the individual from comparison with all other candidates for the available seats," said Justice Lewis F. Powell Jr., who spoke on behalf of the Court.

The issue would be continually revisited for the next 25 years, although it would not be until 2003 that other high-profile admissions cases would be heard by the Supreme Court. In June of that year, the U.S. Supreme Court rendered its opinion on two cases involving race-based admissions preferences used to promote diversity at the University of Michigan's Law School and College of Literature, Science and the Arts. In these cases, respectively, *Grutter* v. *Bollinger*, and *Gratz* v. *Bollinger*, the **Court upheld the legitimacy of the Law School's use of race** as a part of what it found to be the school's individualized consideration of each applicant, but ruled unconstitutional the College's use of a point-based system to consider race in admissions decisions.

In a case that divided the country, even President George W. Bush weighed in, saying that although he supported "diversity of all kinds, including racial diversity in higher education . . . the method used by the University of Michigan to achieve this important goal is fundamentally flawed. . . . At their core the Michigan policies amount to a quota system that unfairly rewards or penalizes prospective students based solely on their race."

In the fall of 2003, we had the chance to sit down with Jeffrey S. Lehman, Cornell's 11th president. As the former dean of the University of Michigan Law School, he was also a named defendant in *Grutter* v. *Bollinger*. Here's what he had to say:

***Marc Zawel (MZ):* Could you start by discussing your involvement in the case?**
Jeffrey Lehman (JL): It all went back to well before the lawsuit was filed. I was a junior faculty member at the University of Michigan in 1992, and the faculty, at the request of then Dean Lee Bollinger, asked us to revisit our admissions policy. We were asked to rethink the policy from the ground up and decide what we were accomplishing and additionally, how best to promote our mission as a law school. I was a member of the committee that drafted the policy later adopted by the faculty. Two years after that, I became dean myself and was responsible for implementing that policy.

In December of 1997, a lawsuit was filed against the law school—a companion to another suit filed against Michigan's undergraduate admissions policy—arguing that the policy was unconstitutional. I was a main defendant and was engaged both in educating the public about what we did and why and also in helping to frame the legal strategy. We had outside attorneys

Affirmative Action =

An active effort to improve the employment or educational opportunities of members of minority groups and women.

who represented us throughout the litigation—but if you're an attorney, one of the things you dread is having a law professor, and even worse, a law school dean as your client because I was very, very heavily involved in the work. It was really a lot of fun. It was an extraordinary experience. I had both the opportunity to participate in the legal strategy and also in the public representation.

***MZ:* In your opinion, why was the Supreme Court case so important for higher education and society at large?**
JL: There're a couple of reasons but they all go back to what we're trying to accomplish through higher education. We're trying to inculcate and help people develop different types of skills. Some of the skills are intellectual skills, some of them are character skills and some of them are social skills. What we know is that people will be better prepared to be effective in a multi-racial, multi-ethnic, multi-cultural society if they had the opportunity to live and interact and engage in that kind of community before they enter the work force.

Most young people who are going to college have grown up in residential isolation. This is still a relatively segregated society as far as where people live and where they go to high school. So college is the time when people can suddenly say, "Oh my goodness, I am going to be interacting with all different kinds of people." But there's an intellectual dimension as well. It's important to learn to be able to see a problem or an issue and look at it from two different perspectives—at the same time knowing that they can be inconsistent without rushing to closure. Rushing to say that a certain perspective is right or wrong is not a good way of approaching things. And I'm not just talking about racial diversity; it's all kinds of diversity. Ideological diversity, religious diversity: it's all of these, but racial diversity is a part of it.

***MZ:* During the Supreme Court arguments, there were large rallies in Washington held in support of affirmative action. Were similar rallies held against the policy?**
JL: There were outspoken critics, I don't know if there were rallies, but the critics of our policy are passionate about a particular value that resonates with most people, which is the value of colorblindness: the value of not using racial categories because those have done a lot of harm in American history. I think part of what we were trying to accomplish in talking about the case is helping people to acknowledge that there are values, and it's an important value and it's a value reflected in the presumptions created in our constitutional doctrine. But it's a value that collides with a different value.

A Justice's Perspective

Supreme Court Justice Ruth Bader Ginsburg is a remarkable woman.

Born in Brooklyn, NY in 1933, she attended Cornell University and graduated with a BA in government in 1954. She was first among women in her class and was elected Phi Beta Kappa. That same year, she entered Harvard Law School and was one of only nine women alongside 500 men there. Justice Ginsburg quickly made the Harvard Law Review, and then transferred to Columbia, where she was promptly elected to the Columbia Law Review. Upon her graduation in 1959, she was tied for first in her class.

Despite her acceptance to the New York State Bar and vast accomplishments, Justice Ginsburg was not offered a job from a single New York law firm because few welcomed women at the time. Instead, she took a clerkship with a federal judge until 1961, and then was a research associate and then associate director of the Columbia Law School Project on International Procedure.

From there, Justice Ginsburg began teaching law in 1963, first at Rutgers, and then back to Columbia in 1972, where she became the first tenured law professor at the school. Simultaneously, in 1971, Ginsburg was instrumental in founding the Women's Rights Project at the American Civil Liberties Union and served as the organization's general counsel from 1973-1980. During this time, she argued six gender discrimination cases before the Supreme Court and was successful in five of them.

After serving as a Judge of the United States Court of Appeals for the District of Columbia Circuit for 13 years, she was nominated for the Supreme Court by President Bill Clinton and took her seat on August 10, 1993. The Senate confirmed her by a vote of 97 to 3. Justice Ginsburg is the first Jewish Supreme Court Justice and only the second woman justice to serve.

In October 2003, Justice Ginsburg returned to her alma mater in Ithaca, NY for the inauguration of Cornell's 11th president, Jeffrey S. Lehman '77. She would have a quick lunch with the new

→

→

president before adorning her regalia, joining the procession and offering remarks at the formal installation ceremony. Justice Ginsburg spoke with us for just a couple of minutes before the festivities began.

"This place is so incredibly beautiful, and my favorite times are the fall, when all the leaves are turning, and the spring, after a long winter, when the glorious sun warms us and turns everything green," she remarked. "Thank goodness for the winter months or people would never be able to get through their courses."

"When I graduated from law school, the major law firms were just beginning to accept Jews; they were not yet ready to accept women and they certainly weren't ready to accept mothers," Justice Ginsburg explained. "It's part of the genius of this country that our idea of 'We the People'—who we include among the doers and shakers of society—evolved and is ever-expanding. Certainly the racial strife we have had is the most stirring example of that [change]. Jews nowadays are accepted almost everywhere in the USA, and women are gaining recognition for what they can contribute in every field of human endeavor. Whatever our differences, the main point is that all people are of equal citizenship stature."

And with that, she was whisked off. But not before she had imparted some amazingly candid and insightful advice to us all.

The value of integration—the value of having these important public institutions of higher education integrated—is important to recognize. A big part of the educational goal during the litigation was to try to get both of these perspectives out on the table so that everyone could see them and hold them in their minds at the same time and understand why we were making the choices we were making. It's not that we were unaware of the value of colorblindness; it's that we recognized it but saw it as being an irreconcilable conflict with another value so we had to make a choice.

***MZ:* The Supreme Court decision was five to four in favor; a Cornell study found that only 53 percent of New York state residents supported the use of affirmative action in employment while just fewer than 50 percent supported it in admission decisions. How do you respond?**

JL: One of the things that we did learn in the course of the litigation was how many misconceptions individuals have about how these admission policies work. I don't know how many people I spoke to thought that we used quota systems in which there was a check-box system where if you said you were African American you were automatically admitted. They were stunned when I said the offer rate for African Americans at the University of Michigan Law School was actually lower than the offer rate for white applicants. And people were stunned by facts like that.

Even President George W. Bush called a press conference to criticize us and say that he thought our policy was unconstitutional, and he got the facts all wrong. So, I think what the polling data reflects is actually the fact that we have not done a great job of telling people exactly what we do and what we don't do, how the process really works and the way in which race is and is not considered. I think when people don't know what the facts are, it sounds scary and bad and they tend to respond to polls the way they did.

DID YOU KNOW?

William Howard Taft (Yale Class of 1878), president of the United States (1909-1913), was the only president also to become chief justice of the United States (1921-1930).

***MZ:* Say the ruling had gone five to four the other direction—what could colleges have done to continue to ensure diversity on campus?**

JL: Well, they couldn't have done much if the ruling had gone the other way, which is why the case was so significant. If the ruling had gone the other way and had done what the plaintiffs were asking for—which was to enforce a strict rule of absolute colorblindness no matter what—it would not be possible to have the level of integration, meaningful integration, that we have on our campus today. That's why that case was so important.

***MZ:* Did you ever doubt that Michigan was going to win this case?**

JL: I expected from the beginning that it was going to be close. I think that any time you have a case that involves a clash of deeply held values you can't predict with certainty how it's going to turn out. My expectation in the beginning was that we would win. We were following the law as it had existed since the 1978 *Bakke* decision. And I felt that it was quite unlikely that, at the end of the day, the majority of the Court would want to overturn that and disrupt a system that had emerged to reconcile these two values.

***MZ:* So the court upheld affirmative action but struck down the point system?**

JL: Right, they struck down the undergraduate system. The law school policy, which I was involved in drafting, was upheld. The undergraduate admission policy—which used a fixed number of points—was stuck down and the message there was that you really have to go person by person and case by case and consider race in a very nuanced and contextualized way.

***MZ:* If you can't use it as a plus in a point system, how do you use it then?**

JL: It really means that a point system, in general, is not workable if you want to try to value racial diversity. You can't mechanically input a point system. I think that is a good thing. Educationally, I think it's very hard to reduce an applicant to a number or to the sum of five numbers. I understand administratively that there are virtues to trying to do it that way, but look at something as simple as a high school grade point average. I think that a 3.5 grade point average can mean any of 20 different things about a student's preparation for and aptitude for a rigorous college curriculum. Everything depends on what classes they chose to take, which classes they did well in and which classes they did less well in, and it's very hard to capture those kinds of things in a point system.

***MZ:* You mentioned earlier that affirmative action is used in higher education to prepare individuals for working in diverse work environments. Should affirmative action be used in employment and job recruitment?**

JL: I think part of the message of the Supreme Court decision is that a judgment that has to be made in context, case-by-case. I think the law in this area continues to evolve; there are certainly some areas where the Court has suggested that it is appropriate for employers to be sensitive to the race of the employee, and there are some areas where I think it would be unlikely for the Court to say that it is appropriate to consider race. So I think that it will end up being context-by-context.

***MZ:* Will affirmative action always be needed?**

JL: None of us can predict the future with absolute confidence. I will say that the trends all point that way. If you look at where we are in 2003 and compare that to where we were in 1963, this has been a period of tremendous progress. And if you were to ask what would a college campus look like under a colorblind system today compared to what it would have looked like in 1963, it's entirely different. You have to remember that this country had 300 years to experience slavery and Jim Crow-legalized segregation. After that, to look at what we have done in forty years, I think there is reason for tremendous hope for the future.

Speaking of the Supreme Court . . .

Which school was attended by the most Supreme Court justices?

School	# of Justices
1. Harvard	**20**
2. Yale	18
3. Princeton	9
4. Columbia	8
5. Cornell	2
5. Dartmouth	2
5. Penn	2
8. Brown	1

Harvard

William Cushing, *Associate Justice 1790-1810*
Joseph Story, *Associate Justice 1812-1845*
Benjamin R. Curtis, *Associate Justice 1851-1857*
Horace Gray, *Associate Justice 1882-1902*
Melville Weston Fuller, *Chief Justice 1888-1910*
Henry B. Brown, *Associate Justice 1891-1906*
Oliver Wendell Holmes, Jr., *Associate Justice 1902-1932*
William H. Moody, *Associate Justice 1906-1910*
Louis D. Brandeis, *Associate Justice 1916-1939*
Edward T. Sanford, *Associate Justice 1923-1930*
Felix Frankfurter, *Associate Justice 1939-1962*
Harold H. Burton, *Associate Justice 1945-1958*
William J. Brennan, Jr., *Associate Justice 1956-1990*
Harry A. Blackmun, *Associate Justice 1970-1994*
Lewis F. Powell, Jr., *Associate Justice 1972-1987*
William H. Rehnquist, Chief Justice 1986-Present, Associate Justice 1972-1986

Harvard (continued)
Antonin Scalia, Associate Justice 1986-present
David H. Souter, Associate Justice 1990-present
Ruth Bader Ginsburg, Associate Justice 1993-present
Stephen Breyer, Associate Justice 1994-present

Yale
Oliver Ellsworth, *Chief Justice 1796-1800*
Henry Baldwin, *Associate Justice 1830-1844*
David Davis, *Associate Justice 1862-1877*
William Strong, *Associate Justice 1870-1880*
Morrison R. Waite, *Chief Justice 1874-1888*
William B. Woods, *Associate Justice 1881-1887*
David J. Brewer, *Associate Justice 1890-1910*
Henry B. Brown, *Associate Justice 1891-1906*
George Shiras, Jr., *Associate Justice 1892-1903*
William Howard Taft, *Chief Justice 1921-1930*
Benjamin Nathan Cardozo, *Associate Justice 1932-1938*
Stanley F. Reed, *Associate Justice 1938-1957*
William O. Douglas, *Associate Justice 1939-1975*
Sherman Minton, *Associate Justice 1949-1956*
Potter Stewart, *Associate Justice 1958-1981*
Byron R. White, *Associate Justice 1962-1993*
Abe Fortas, *Associate Justice 1965-1969*
Clarence Thomas, Associate Justice 1991-present

Princeton
Oliver Ellsworth, *Chief Justice 1796-1800*
William Paterson, *Associate Justice 1793-1806*
William Johnson, *Associate Justice 1804-1834*
H. Brockholst Livingston, *Associate Justice 1807-1823*
Smith Thompson, *Associate Justice 1823-1843*
James M. Wayne, *Associate Justice 1835-1867*
Peter V. Daniel, *Associate Justice 1842-1860*
Mahlon Pitney, *Associate Justice 1912-1922*
John Marshall Harlan II, *Associate Justice 1955-1971*

Columbia
John Jay, *Chief Justice 1789-1795*
Samuel Blatchford, *Associate Justice 1882-1893*
Charles Evans Hughes, *Chief Justice 1930-1941, Associate Justice 1910-1916*
Benjamin Nathan Cardozo, *Associate Justice 1932-1938*
Stanley F. Reed, *Associate Justice 1938-1957*
William O. Douglas, *Associate Justice 1939-1975*
Harlan Fiske Stone, *Chief Justice 1941-1946, Associate Justice 1925-1941*
Ruth Bader Ginsburg, Associate Justice 1993-present

Cornell
Charles Evans Hughes, *Chief Justice 1930-1941, Associate Justice 1910-1916*
Ruth Bader Ginsburg, Associate Justice 1993-present

Dartmouth
Levi Woodbury, *Associate Justice 1845-1851*
Salmon Portland Chase, *Chief Justice 1864-1873*

Penn
Owen J. Roberts, *Associate Justice 1930-1945.*
William J. Brennan, Jr., *Associate Justice 1956-1990*

Brown
Charles Evans Hughes, *Chief Justice 1930-1941, Associate Justice 1910-1916*

Data Source: Cornell Law

The Truth About Legacy Admissions

Legacy admissions are often considered affirmative action for the privileged. Just what are legacy admissions? Do your chances of getting in really depend on your family? Read on.

Connecting Debates

A connection between the University of Michigan's 2003 race-based admissions cases and legacy admissions preferences was highlighted by *Wall Street Journal* reporter Daniel Golden in an article that was part of his 2004 Pulitzer Prize-winning series on college admissions:

> As it happens, a majority of the justices are already familiar with another type of admissions preference. Five justices or their children qualified for an admissions edge known as "legacy preference," which most U.S. colleges give to the sons and daughters of their alumni . . . . Two justices, Stephen Breyer and Anthony Kennedy, have family ties to Stanford University that span three generations. A third justice, Sandra Day O'Connor, is a Stanford graduate and the mother of two Stanford alumni, and has served on the university's board of trustees. Justice John Paul Stevens attended the University of Chicago and Northwestern Law School, as did his father. Ruth Bader Ginsburg and her daughter Jane formed the first mother-daughter combination ever to attend Harvard Law School. It isn't clear whether academic lineage played a role in the admissions of these justices' children, and several of them had stellar high-school records. Yet judges—like everyone else wrestling with the affirmative-action debate—inevitably filter it through the prism of their own personal history.

Legacy Admissions =

Refers to the preferential treatment of applicants in the university admissions process on the basis of having family members as alumni.

The Debate Over Legacies

The subject of legacy admissions preferences became a hot political topic during the 2004 presidential election, no doubt owing at least in part to the 2003 U.S. Supreme Court rulings on the University of Michigan's affirmative action policies. As automatic, point-based advantages based on race were ruled unconstitutional, the nature of the consideration of college applicants' legacy status was increasingly questioned. Inevitably, discussions of legacy admissions policies in the media also mentioned President George W. Bush's own status as a legacy applicant and student at Yale. During the presidential campaign, legacy admissions preferences found few supporters as Democrats and Republicans alike spoke out against these policies. **President Bush, himself, eventually spoke out against legacy admissions preferences**. An August 6, 2004 *Associated Press* news story reported the following:

> President Bush, who followed his father and grandfather to Yale University despite an undistinguished academic record, said Friday that colleges should get rid of "legacy" admission preferences that favor the sons and daughters of alumni. "I think it ought to be based on merit," Bush told a conference of minority journalists when he was pressed about his views on affirmative action. "And I think colleges need to work hard for diversity."

Further, Senator Edward Kennedy (D-MA) has proposed legislation (*The College Quality, Affordability, and Diversity Improvement Act of 2003*, S1793) which aims to discourage universities' use of legacy admissions preferences by requiring colleges to disclose their legacy enrollments in order to receive certain federal funds. In many cases, politicians' and others' opposition to legacy admissions policies stems from a misunderstanding of how these policies have evolved from a state of having tremendous impact on admissions decisions to their current status as only a distinguishing point between otherwise similarly-qualified applicants. Turn the page to see what Shannon has to say about it all.

Excerpt

Excerpted from "The Value of Legacy Preferences in Admissions at Selective Private Colleges" by Shannon Duff (2004).

As America's premier private undergraduate institutions become ever more selective, enormous attention is focused on which students are admitted, why others are not and the reasons underlying these decisions. In a society where access to educational opportunity has far-reaching affects on individuals' futures, it is both understandable and appropriate that the college admissions process has become highly scrutinized. William Bowen and Sarah Levin are articulate in their description of the high stakes of college admissions decisions in their 2004 book entitled *Reclaiming the Game*:

> Places in the entering class are extremely valuable in the most selective colleges and universities, and the wise rationing of academic opportunity is a major challenge faced by all of them . . . . At these schools, the cost of admitting Jones is the inability to admit Smith, and this basic concept of "opportunity cost" (what an institution is giving up by following one path) is a central concept. . . .[1]

While selective private undergraduate institutions, and specifically, Ivy League colleges, usually have somewhat differing visions of exactly which students should earn spots in each year's incoming class, there is a well-advised consensus among these and most American universities that it is desirable to assemble a class of students that is diverse in many respects, including academic interests, extracurricular interests, race and level of parental education, and also to assemble a class which includes talented student-athletes and legacy students.

Though there are many subjective considerations involved in today's college admissions decisions which extend beyond the applicant's academic records and test scores, the most formalized, institutionalized and, increasingly, controversial of these subjective considerations are applicants' status as legacies, recruited athletes, or members of racial minorities. At most universities in the U.S. today, applicants falling into one or more of these categories are admitted at higher rates than students with comparable academic credentials based on the premise that these applicants possess qualities which will enable them to contribute to the university community in specific and desirable ways. But how did this come about?

History Of Legacy Admissions Preferences

Legacy policies were formalized as admission to selective private universities became more competitive in the years following World War I, and since then, have evolved at most Ivy League schools from being a heavily weighted factor in admissions decisions to their current role as a minor distinguishing characteristic among competitive applicants. To simplify this discussion of the history of legacy admissions preferences, it is helpful to focus on the policies of Harvard and Yale; it is important to note, however, that the timing and evolution of these legacy admissions policies did differ among other Ivy institutions, sometimes quite significantly.

The first two and a half centuries of Harvard's existence and the first two centuries of Yale's life were not marked with much competition among applicants, as those who could spare the time and money necessary to attend these colleges were generally accepted. Often sons of graduates did attend the same institution as their fathers, as familial wealth generally determined who could attend college, and location and family tradition influenced where one would enroll, according to Marcia Graham Synnott in *The Half-Opened Door.*[2] Policies of legacy preferences in admissions, however, were not, and did not need to be formalized at this time as there was not sufficient competition for seats in the class to necessitate a stated preference for alumni sons over other applicants.

In the 1920s, however, as a result of the flood of applications received from veterans returning home from World War I, and a growing belief in the predictive power of standardized tests as a basis for comparison, admissions at many universities, including Harvard and Yale, became somewhat more selective.[3] Yale restricted the size of its entering classes for the first time in the early 1920s, but it must be noted that this limitation did not apply equally to all applicants;

it was intended primarily to limit the number of Jewish students at the school, writes Geoffrey Kabaservice in *The Guardians*.[4] Yale's Board of Admissions affirmed the intent of the class size limitations in 1924, by a vote, resolving that "the limitation of numbers shall not operate to exclude any son of a Yale graduate who has satisfied all the requirements for admission."[5] At a time when both Yale and Harvard were very dependent on their alumni for support, legacy preferences in admissions became more formalized as a means for pleasing alumni through both the acceptance of their sons, and also for the limiting the numbers of Jewish as well as Catholic students.

At Yale in the 1920s, the wartime inflation made the school more dependent on alumni contributions. The alumni, in turn, were willing to contribute in Yale's time of need, although often based on the expected recompense in admissions. According to *The Half Opened Door*:

> In September 1929, a memorandum entitled 'The Admission Requirements as Applied to the Sons of Yale Alumni' was sent to members of the Board of Admissions. While the percentage of alumni sons admitted had indeed increased, some of those connected with the university's endowment campaign in 1927 urged that "more specific assurances" be given the alumni . . . many alumni felt that the university had committed itself during the fund drive to provide for Yale sons of good character and reasonably good record . . . regardless of the number of applicants and of the superiority of outside competitors.[6]

The information available does not point to the degree to this perception of the university "having committed itself . . . to provide for Yale sons" was created by the administration or was solely a creation of the alumni's minds. Regardless, this perception clearly existed and would shape both alumni expectations and outside perceptions of who had a realistic chance of being accepted at Yale.

Amidst this drive to increase their resources, both Yale and Harvard struggled with the questions of Jewish and Catholic students; since 1913, there had been an unstated quota capping the percentage of Jews and Catholics admitted to Yale. Similar issues regarding

"An investment in knowledge always pays the best interest."

—Ben Franklin

minority admissions also strained relations with Harvard alumni at this time. At both Yale and Harvard, increasing the proportion of alumni sons in entering classes seemed the clear way to both inspire the alumni generosity the universities needed and help limit the numbers of members of Jews and other groups considered undesirable who would be admitted. In *The Guardians*, Kabaservice asserts that "Yale's policy of favoring the admission of the sons of its graduates was, in its way, a counterpart to the immigration restrictions of the 1920s. . . ."[7]

At the same time, Harvard, under President A. Lawrence Lowell, took a somewhat more measured approach to the question of Jewish students at the University. While President Lowell himself favored restrictions on the number of Jewish students in each class, opposition from the faculty and other sources led him to commission a lengthy report on this issue led by the "Committee on Methods of Sifting Candidates for Admission."[8] When the Committee's findings showed that Jewish students performed well, if not superbly academically, the conservative forces at Harvard cited their character (combined with their increased presence on campus) as the undesirable part of Jews' presence. In 1926, Harvard decided to limit the size of its freshman class for the first time. As Synnott notes,"By the mid-1920s, Harvard had yielded to a selective system of admissions which, with no apologies, aimed at reducing the percentage of Jews in the college."[9] Nonetheless, Harvard acted with substantially less conservatism than Yale in more thoroughly considering the merits of Jewish students; this disparity would continue to characterize comparisons of the two universities' responses to challenges to tradition through the 1950s.

Thus, by the mid-to-late 1920s, both Yale and Harvard employed for the first time somewhat selective admissions policies; selective, however, did not necessarily mean merit-based—especially in the case of Yale. As these policies took hold, the percentage of alumni sons at Yale grew from 13.2 percent in 1924, to mid-twentieth percentiles in the 1930s, to a high of 31.4 percent in the Class of 1943.[10] Yale Emeritus Professor of History and Yale historian Gaddis Smith joked about the generosity of legacy admissions at this time: "To determine the suitability of a son of a Yale College graduate for admission to Yale at this time, an admissions officer might shine a flashlight in one ear, and barring the light's rays coming out the other ear, he would be offered admission to Yale."[11]

After instituting a policy of selective admissions in 1926, Harvard saw further changes in admissions policies through the 1930s under President James Bryant Conant, a staunch advocate of merit-based admissions. Conant and his assistant dean, Henry Chauncey, were intensely interested in the power of testing as a way to predict academic performance, and then sort candidates applying for admission. While it is hard today to conceive of merit-based admissions as a novelty, the newness of the idea at this time must be remembered, as "Harvard and other American colleges did not operate on the principle that an undergraduate's high school academic record equaled valor. Students who were extremely studious were considered a little peculiar," according to Nicholas Lemann's book *The Big Test.*[12] In 1934, Conant established the National Scholarship Program, which provided full four-year scholarships to Harvard based solely on academic merit and made Harvard accessible to talented students across the country without regard to their ability to pay.[13]

Nonetheless, Conant realized that the University's ability to maintain its superior resources and to offer scholarships to attract the best students depended on the generosity of its alumni, and therefore refrained from altering Harvard's policy of admitting most alumni sons. The author Lemann comments on not only this period but through the present in stating, ". . . the connection between family money and higher education was never truly severed. The level of government support for private universities never rose high enough to allow them to stop needing alumni contributions."[14] As Harvard increasingly sought to attract the best and brightest students throughout the 1930s and 1940s, it was careful to avoid upsetting its alumni and other wealthy benefactors whose sons were applying; thus, the traditional makeup of and percentage of alumni sons did not change dramatically over this period.[15] The cautious, initially limited approach to increasing the role of merit in admissions employed by Harvard would stand in marked contrast to the swift and drastic changes which would transform Yale admissions into a merit-based process in the 1960s.

Conservatism in admissions continued at Yale through the mid-1950s, when Dean of Admissions Arthur Howe (under Yale President A. Whitney Griswold) was given the mandate to "open up Yale's student body and nationalize it."[16] While admissions under Griswold and Howe saw some movement towards merit-based admissions, their major innovation in admissions, the creation of the "ABC system,"[17] represented less than a breakthrough. Through this system, prep school headmasters could give their applicants to Yale a grade of A, B or C: students who received A's were essentially automatically admitted, B's and C's were considered after. While demonstrating an increased focus on merit that represented some progress, the system effectively perpetuated the practice of admitting mostly prep school students to Yale; further, "it was understood that if a boy's father had gone to Yale and he was capable of doing the work, Yale ought to admit him,"[18]. While the changes in admissions policies at Yale under Griswold and Howe were decidedly limited in their scope and preserved sweeping preferences for alumni sons conditioned only upon their ability to do the work, they did indicate small steps towards merit-based admissions.

Dramatic changes in admissions policies at Yale did not occur until the Kingman Brewster administration. When Inky Clark took over as dean of admissions and financial aid at Yale under Brewster in 1965:

> He turned Yale admissions upside down. Twenty years earlier, when Conant and Chauncey wanted to change admissions policy at Harvard, they moved cautiously, concentrating at first on just a handful of scholarship students and leaving the rest undisturbed. Clark, operating in a more conservative institution, waged a formal assault . . . [he] and his staff visited a thousand [schools, including those] . . . in ghettos and barrios and on Indian

> reservations and in remote rural areas.
> He increased the public-school share of Yale freshman by 9 percent in a single year. . . .
> The son of Yale's biggest donor, Paul Mellon, was rejected.[19]

The resulting forty percent increase in applications to Yale was an important ingredient in providing the sheer multitude and diversity of applicants that would be critical in transforming the school's admissions into a selection process based on merit; Clark's efforts were an important part of convincing a much broader section of Americans that they had a chance of being admitted to Yale, and therefore should apply. This onslaught of applications certainly had implications for the sons of Yale alumni who were applying as the heightened competition dramatically reduced the number of legacies admitted, which not unexpectedly provoked outcries from the alumni, according to a *Yale Alumni Magazine* story "The Birth of a New Institution" by Geoffrey Kabaservice.[20]

While specific admissions policies and specific decisions have varied among institutions and over time, Yale and most of the nation's most selective private institutions have, since the late 1960s and early 1970s, used merit as the primary determinant of who gained admission, and increasingly sought to increase the diversity of the student body, primarily along racial, ethnic, and geographic lines. Thus increasingly competitive admissions, preferences for students from non-traditional (in comparison to historic applicant pools) backgrounds and increases in university endowments provide the backdrop against which legacy preferences in admissions endured during the period from the late 1960s to the present.

For many institutions, this period also saw the beginning of coeducation—a landmark victory for diversity; Yale College admitted its first freshman class which included women in 1969, while coeducation began at Harvard in 1972 (though the formal merger of Harvard and Radcliffe did not occur until 1999). Amidst this focus on increasing diversity, legacy preferences endured as a stated and practiced policy at Harvard and Yale, with the beneficiaries of such policies being held to increasingly high standards as the quality of the overall class increased and the goal of assembling a diverse class was advanced. Anecdotal evidence of legacy rejections at Yale in the late 1960s and 1970s led Professor Gaddis Smith to "wonder if it wasn't harder to be admitted as a legacy than as a non-legacy."[21] Admissions as a whole would continue to grow increasingly competitive, and legacy applicants from this time forward would have to compete with these heightened standards as they and their alumni parents continued to confront the reduced power of legacy status.

An additional dynamic affecting Harvard and Yale and many other private colleges at this time was the significant growth of their endowments, which moderated somewhat the universities' exclusive dependence on alumni support. The Yale endowment grew from just over $100 million in 1945 to over $500 million in 1967, representing exceptional growth and a dramatic increase in not only the total value of the endowment but also in the revenue from investments which would be generated on an annual basis.[22] Harvard's endowment also grew rapidly during this time: "In the mid-twentieth century, Harvard's endowment was about $215 million, roughly comparable in size to Yale's. But in subsequent decades—thanks in large part to the investment acumen of Paul Cabot, the University's Treasurer from 1949 to 1966—Harvard's capital accumulation accelerated [significantly],"[23] according to the book *Harvard A to Z*. By 1974, at the time of the formation of the Harvard Management Corporation, the endowment's value was just over $1 billion.[24] While alumni giving remains extremely important, the skillful management and resulting impressive performance of university endowments have to some extent freed universities from a state of almost complete dependence on alumni support; this degree of independence represents a healthy state which gives the university and its leaders (many of them alumni themselves) a degree of autonomy over many aspects of university policy, including admissions, as well as the ability to better plan future expenditures, with endowment income often being more predictable than alumni giving.

And While We're at It . . .

Harvard owns nearly 430 acres (1.8 km^2) of property in the Boston area.

Columbia is notably among the largest private landowners in New York City, which has some of the highest property values in the world.

Dartmouth owns 26,800 acres (108 km^2) in the northern part of New Hampshire as part of the Second College Grant, making it the largest land owner in the state.

"The Value of Legacy Preferences in Admissions at Selective Private Colleges"

(Citations)

[1] Bowen, William G., and Levin, Sarah A. Reclaiming the Game: College Sports and Educational Values. (Princeton: Princeton University Press, 2003), p. 11.

[2] Synnott, Marcia Graham. The Half-Opened Door: Discrimination and Admissions at Harvard, Yale, and Princeton, 1900-1970. (Westport: Greenwood Press, 1979), p. 4.

[3] Synnott, p. 13.

[4] Kabaservice, Geoffrey. The Guardians: Kingman Brewster, His Circle, and the Rise of the Liberal Establishment. (New York: Henry Holt and Company, 2004), p. 48.

[5] Synnott, p. 152.

[6] Synnott, p. 13.

[7] Kabaservice, p. 48.

[8] Synott, p. 65-70.

[9] Synott, p. 110.

[10] Kelley, Brooks Mather. Yale: A History. (New Haven: Yale University Press, 1974). p. 406.

[11] Smith, Gaddis. Interview with Gaddis Smith by Shannon Duff, 12 April 2004.

[12] Lemann, Nicholas. The Big Test: The Secret History of the American Meritocracy. (New York: Farrar, Strauss, and Giroux, 2000). p. 27-28.

[13] Lemann, p. 28.

[14] Lemann, p. 140.

[15] Lemann, p. 149.

[16] Kabaservice, Geoffrey. "The Birth of a New Institution." Yale Alumni Magazine, December 1999, <http://www.yalealumnimagazine.com/issues/99_12/admissions.html>

[17] Lemann, p. 144.

[18] Lemann, p. 143.

[19] Lemann, p. 149.

[20] Kabaservice, "Birth of a New Institution."

[21] Smith, Gaddis. Interview with Gaddis Smith by Shannon Duff, 12 April 2004.

[22] Pierson, George W. A Yale Book of Numbers: Historical Statistics of the College and University, 1701-1976. (New Haven: Yale University Press, 1983). p. 613.

[23] Bethell, Hunt, and Shenton. Harvard A to Z. (Cambidge: Harvard UP, 2004). p. 105

[24] Bethell et al., p. 105-106.

Who Has the Most Money?

School	Endowment
1. Harvard	**$22,587,305,000.69 ***
2. Yale	$12,740,896,000
3. Princeton	$10,251,952,000
4. Columbia	$4,493,085,000
5. Penn	$4,019,000,000
6. Darmouth	$2,863,310,718
7. Brown	$1,793,380,000
8. Cornell	$374,458,697

** Give or take a penny*

FOOD FOR THOUGHT

The combined total endowment of these institutions is over three times the total revenue brought in by McDonald's in 2004.

DID YOU KNOW?

In most Ivy League institutions, "legacies" (affirmative action for children of alumni) make up 10-15% of the freshmen class.

The Ivy League and other top colleges admit alumni's children at 2-4 times the rate of other applicants.

Ivy vs. Ivy: Reviews and Rankings

By Students. For Students.

It's time to see what the students have to say.

Throughout the creation of this section, we felt it was critical that our content be unbiased and unaffiliated with any Ivy League college or university. We think it's important that our readers get honest information and a realistic impression of the student opinions on any campus. If any aspect of a particular school is undesirable, we (unlike a campus brochure) intend to publish it. The following pages will shed light on the good and unveil the bad. Here, you'll find that the surveyed Ivy Leaguers did not show hesitation expressing their opinions on just about everything their schools have (or don't have) to offer.

This chapter—and our College Prowler guidebooks in general—is possible only through endless student contributions. Because you can't make student-written guides without the students, we had students at each campus who help write, randomly survey their peers, edit, layout, and perform accuracy checks on every book that we publish. From the very beginning, student writers gather the most up-to-date stats, facts, and inside information on their colleges. They fill each section with student quotes and summarize the findings in editorial reviews. In addition, each school receives a collection of letter grades (A through F) that reflect student opinion and help to represent contentment, prominence, or satisfaction for each of our specific categories. Just as in grade school, the higher the mark the more content, more prominent, or more satisfied the students are with the particular category.

Once a book is written, additional Ivy League students (from the school in question) serve as editors and check for accuracy even more extensively. Our bounce-back team—a group of randomly selected students who have no involvement with the project—are asked to read over the material in order to help ensure that it accurately expresses every aspect of the university and its students. This same process is applied to the other schools that College Prowler currently covers. All of this has led to the creation of a student network that continues to transcend the academic data and advice that commercials, school Web sites, traditional college guides, and even school officials and alumni are able provide.

We hope that the following section serves as a valuable tool in your college selection process.

Enjoy!

Brown University

45 Prospect Street, Providence, RI 02912
www.brown.edu (401) 863-2378

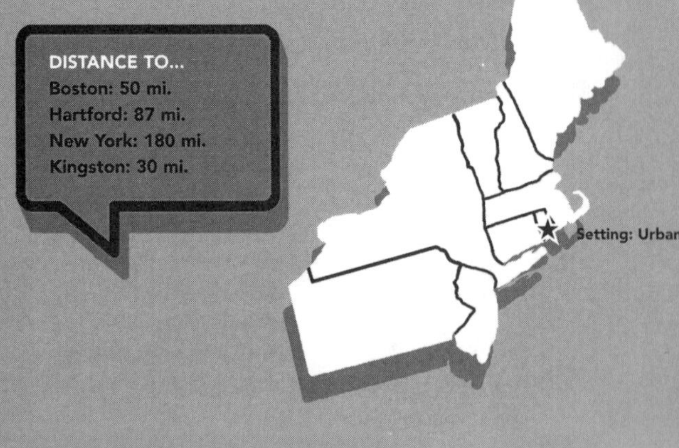

"Brown's liberal nature and open curriculum exceed that of the average liberal arts school."

Total Enrollment:
5,660 - Large
Acceptance Rate:
14.6%
Tuition:
$32,974
Top 10% of High School Class:
90%

SAT Range

Verbal	Math	Total
690 – 760	690 – 760	1380 – 1520

ACT Range

Verbal	Math	Total
N/A	N/A	26-31

Most Popular Majors:
8% History
7% International Relations and Affairs
6% Biology
6% Political Science and Government
5% Pyschology

Students Also Applied To:*
Cornell University, Harvard University
Princeton University, Stanford University
Yale University

*For more school info check out *www.collegeprowler.com*

Table of Contents

College Prowler Report Card

Academics	A
Local Atmosphere	A-
Safety & Security	C+
Computers	B+
Facilities	B
Campus Dining	C-
Off-Campus Dining	A-
Campus Housing	B+
Off-Campus Housing	A-
Diversity	B
Guys	B+
Girls	B
Athletics	C+
Nightlife	B+
Greek Life	C+
Drug Scene	B
Campus Strictness	B+
Parking	C+
Transportation	B+

The Lowdown
ON ACADEMICS

Special Degree Options

Brown's Program in Liberal Medical Education (PLME) is an eight-year program combining a liberal arts education with medical school. Freshmen are accepted to the college and medical school as freshmen and spend eight years at Brown completing their BA and MD.

Brown also offers master's degrees in some departments for undergraduates who want to add on an additional year of study.

Sample Academic Clubs

African Students Association, Asian American Student Association, Bio-medical Engineering Society, Chinese Student Association, Engineering Society, Women Students at Brown, Brown Film Society, Shakespeare on the Green, Pre-Med chapter AMSA (American Medical Student Association)

Degrees Awarded:
Bachelor, Master, Doctorate, Combined Degrees

Undergraduate Schools:
Brown College, Applied Mathematics, Engineering, Biology and Medicine

Full-Time Faculty:
762

Faculty with Terminal Degree:
96%

Student-to-Faculty Ratio:
9:1

Average Course Load:
4 courses

AP Test Score Requirements:
Possible credit for scores of 4 or 5

IB Test Score Requirements:
Possible credit for scores of 6 or 7

Did You Know?

Brown does not have any general course requirements. While you must complete a total of 30 courses and specific courses within a concentration (Brown's word for major), there are absolutely no course requirements. You'll never have to take another math class or English class if you don't want to. This system, known as the New Curriculum, started in 1969.

In line with this educational philosophy, most classes at Brown can be taken with a grade option of A/B/C/No Credit or Satisfactory/No Credit.

If one of Brown's hundreds of concentrations doesn't appeal to you, you can make up your own.

Best Places to Study:
The John D. Rockefeller Library (The Rock) or The Sciences Library (The Sci-Li), the Blue Room, Coffee shops on Thayer Street, dorm computer clusters and study rooms

Students Speak Out
ON ACADEMICS

"Brown really lets you explore whatever you want when you get here. I decided on visual arts, and I'm really happy about that. I made my own experience out of it."

"**The teachers are a mixed bag**. Most all of them are on the very high end of the intelligence scale. However, some are very interested in students and teaching, while others seem to care less as they write their grants or just appear lazy when it comes to making interesting lesson plans and assignments. Most of them, I ended up liking and learning from."

"Because **there is no core curriculum**, you aren't typically forced into any bad courses. The skills and styles of teachers at Brown vary widely—as they probably do everywhere—but Brown does tell you to judge for yourself. The first several weeks of every semester is a 'shopping period' during which you can try out as many classes as you can pack into your day. Not everyone shops around, but most students shop at least a little. Shopping can be extremely useful for weeding out the incoherent mumblers and the digressive babblers and for hunting down the best teachers."

"Almost every semester, I have taken at least one course that has had a profound impact on my life. These classes have ranged from 'Early Modern Philosophy,' to 'Intro to Object Oriented Programming,' to 'Seminar in the Teaching of Writing,' to 'Intro to Neuroscience.' **I have taken some courses that I misjudged** while scheduling classes, but I think that's part of the learning experience, too—to learn to craft your own education."

"**I didn't get a chance to develop close relationships with my professors** freshman year because I took a lot of big intro classes. I did take one class where the professor led the sections and really got to know everyone by taking pictures of all the students and putting our names on them, so when he called on someone, he knew who it was. It was a smaller class, but I felt like I got to know him that way."

"A lot of classes I have taken in my first two years have been taught by graduate students. It's not that professors don't try to get to know you, but **you have to take initiative** and go to office hours to get to know them."

"**Brown has a cross-curriculum with the Rhode Island School of Design**; you can take up to four courses there for Brown credit."

"Many of my classes were interesting. Sometimes when taking many courses in the same department, **I found that they were a bit repetitive**. I had a few that were incredible, and a few that were miserable, but overall, the course selection and courses, themselves, at Brown are great."

"I took a lecture and a seminar with my thesis advisor. At first, after the lecture, **our relationship was distant**. In the seminar, however, we had in-depth discussions and had dinner at the professor's house with a guest lecturer who was a big policy maker in his field."

"My teachers have been great. Because of the open curriculum, I think **teachers know that you are choosing to be in their class,** so they are pretty excited to have you there, and they tend to go the extra mile and help you if you need any help with things like setting work up for the summer. I've had really good experiences. I took a sociology class my first year, and the professor had just come to the U.S. a year or two before that, and we met almost every week. It was basically me helping her with her English and her teaching me the readings. It was really cool."

The College Prowler Take
ON ACADEMICS

At Brown, persistence and personal responsibility play a big role in defining the undergraduate career. Students are rewarded for learning to work within Brown's small and intimate academic departments. In other words, it is always possible to work the system. Students always have a good chance of getting into high-level classes, even if they are outside their concentration. On that note, many students come to Brown uncertain of their concentrations, and many switch their concentrations more than once in their undergraduate career. Brown's academic philosophy encourages exploration into new areas of study which can spark new interests or projects. In general, Brown believes that every student knows what's best for him- or herself.

Unlike other elite universities, Brown's primary focus is on undergraduate students. In accordance with this goal, all Brown professors are required to teach an undergraduate class which gives students access to some of the top academics in their field. Most students are able to make strong connections with at least a few professors who provide them with support as they develop their own interests. There are, of course, shortcomings to Brown's system. The lack of many professional schools, like law or business schools, can make the post-Brown transition a bit jarring. In addition, for a large university, Brown can sometimes seem to have a limited number of courses available, with some departments lacking a large enough staff to support all the students. Often, you have to try for several semesters to get into popular or limited—enrollment classes. With persistence, however, anything is possible at Brown.

The College Prowler™ Grade on

Academics: A

A high Academics grade generally indicates that professors are knowledgeable, accessible, and genuinely interested in their students' welfare. Other determining factors include class size, how well professors communicate, and whether or not classes are engaging.

Local Atmosphere

The Lowdown
ON LOCAL ATMOSPHERE

Region:
Northeast

City, State:
Providence, Rhode Island

Setting:
Urban

Distance from Boston:
45 minutes

Distance from New York:
2 hours, 30 minutes

Points of Interest:
The RISD museum, the beaches in Newport, Waterplace Park, Roger Williams Zoo, Purgatory Chasm, the outdoor ice rink downtown, Lupo's Heartbreak Hotel

Famous Rhode Islanders:
Harry Anderson, H.P. Lovecraft, Samuel Slater, Emeril Lagasse, The Farrelly Brothers

Fun Facts about Brown:

1) Brown is about a 10-minute walk from the world-famous Lupo's Heartbreak Hotel where big and small shows, from punk to jazz, happen on an almost nightly basis.

2) Once a month, Providence hosts Gallery Night. Galleries around the city, including Brown's Bell Gallery, open their doors and wine cellars to locals who want to take in a little culture. Brown and RISD student art is almost always a part of the event.

3) Recently, Providence has been the stage for numerous movies and TV shows. The obvious examples are the film *Outside Providence* and the show *Providence* on NBC. Perhaps the most accurate portrayal of Providence is in *Family Guy*, which was written by a RISD graduate.

4) A few times a semester, RISD hosts a student art sale on Benefit Street. There's no better place to buy your holiday or birthday presents.

Students Speak Out
ON LOCAL ATMOSPHERE

"Providence is an ideal city for college. It's easily navigable, not overpowering, and still has plenty to do. Students even have enough clout to influence city council elections."

"Providence is what you make of it. **The town has a lot to offer**—from parks to hang out in, to bars, clubs, and restaurants. Other universities are present, but aside from RISD, there is little interaction between Brown students and other area university students. Check out the Waterfire and the mall on rainy days!"

"The mall is right here. **You really need to get off-campus sometimes**, but you don't have to go that far; downtown is great."

"Personally, I can't imagine not going to school in a city. Brown is in the perfect location for a school. It is on a hill, so it seems secluded, but just **walking down the hill puts you in the center of downtown Providence**. Providence definitely has a city feel. There are always things to do and places to go. The Providence Place Mall, the largest mall in New England, is a 15-minute walk away."

"There is the Trinity Reperatory Center, which shows Broadway-caliber plays, the Fleet Skating Center, the Providence Convention center, Waterplace Park, and many restaurants and parks. **Providence can be considered a college town** because, other than Brown, RISD, Providence College, and Johnston and Wales. are all within short driving distance."

"It's nice that there is a social life that revolves around the school. I started college at a big university in New York, and I always felt like people were off doing their own things in their own world. **Here, you really get to know the people in your class**."

"The social options at Brown and in Providence are really very ideal. Many students become unhappy going to school in a small town where they are forced to stay on campus. Brown offers a wide array of on campus events, but **the city is so accessible if ever you are inclined to go off-campus**."

"**Providence is definitely a city that is on the up-and-up**. There are art galleries and neat movie theaters—both artsy, independent foreign places and big, multiple theaters that show Hollywood movies."

"I love Thayer Street. **There's so much to it**. I've never been anywhere quite like it."

The College Prowler Take
ON LOCAL ATMOSPHERE

Providence is a city, but it's not a big city. Sometimes the desire for the city to grow and incorporate new and exciting features is at odds with its efforts to maintain the small-town feel. If you want to go to a club one night, a museum the next day, a hip hop show after that, and then eat a few meals, you can cram it all into a weekend. Some Brown students never really explore the city, let alone the places less than an hour's drive in any direction from College Hill. There are beaches, state parks, ski areas, and vineyards close enough to make day-trips to, all surrounded by quaint New England towns. Students often complain about the lack of a drive-in theater or an all night diner, without realizing that there are several of both about 10 minutes away. There are more hip-hop, '80s, and live rock clubs and bars within walking distance of the university than Brown students can handle. And, of course, there's New York and Boston/Cambridge, both easily accessible by bus and train for weekends when you need to get out.

In short, Providence is a crowd pleaser. People from small towns may be a little intimidated at first but, with the exception of Goth night at Club Hell, the locals don't bite. Students from megalopolises such as New York, DC, or LA may scoff at the downtown area, which can be traversed in about 20 minutes, but no Brown student who puts in a little effort can honestly complain that, "there's nothing to do in Providence." The city simply has too much history, too many quirks, and too much to offer for the intrepid Brown student to find it boring.

The College Prowler™ Grade on
Local Atmosphere: A-

A high Local Atmosphere grade indicates that the area surrounding campus is safe and scenic. Other factors include nearby attractions, proximity to other schools, and the town's attitude toward students.

Safety & Security

The Lowdown
ON SAFETY & SECURITY

Number of Brown Public Safety Officers:
32

Phone:
(410) 863-3101

Health Center Office Hours:
Appointments for non-medical emergencies: Monday and Friday 8:30 a.m.-4:15 pm; Tuesday, Wednesday, and Thursday 9:30 a.m.-4:15 p.m.

Safety Services:
Blue-light phones, emergency e-mail notification, shuttle and escort service, Safewalk program

Health Services:
24-hour EMS response, routine, sports and travel physicals, gynecological exams, STD screenings, birth control counseling, Health forms for travel, employment and school applications, vaccines and medical prescriptions, allergy testing

Students Speak Out

ON SAFETY & SECURITY

"On campus, things are pretty safe. However, in the nearby periphery, it is pretty unsafe to walk alone at night. There are muggings."

"I feel safe here. Then again, I'm from New York City, so **I feel safe just about anywhere**."

"**My computer got stolen freshman year from my room**. I left my window cracked open and someone crawled in. My roommate had her jewelry stolen at the same time. Still, I feel relatively safe on campus. (I think security has improved since then.) I walk home alone sometimes. I use the shuttles but not the Safewalk program."

"**I never had a problem with security**. They respond well when you lock yourself out of your room. Also, they don't hassle you too much when drinking is involved. However, you have to watch your back at night because there have been a lot of muggings, and security isn't everywhere. There has also been much dispute over arming Brown police with firearms."

"**Safety is not one of Brown's strong points**. Campus is, after all, located in the city. If you follow basic safety procedures, however, you should be fine. Walk in groups and stay in well-lit areas. Personally, I have never had any problems with it, and I don't know anybody who has. Providence is rated one of the safest cities in the United States, but it's still a city. You just have to keep your wits about you when you're walking around."

"I think it's good that **the University uses e-mail to keep us informed about crimes** going on around campus, but I think they are a little sensationalist, and they also make it sound worse than the crime actually was. In some of the situations, I was actually part of the incident, but when I read the e-mails, I knew they made it sound worse than it actually was. It's no worse than most other urban schools."

"I think that there are certain areas off-campus that you should tend to avoid when you are walking alone, but on campus **you don't have to worry about much**."

"Last year, it really felt like **there were e-mails** from administration **coming every day about students getting jacked**."

"There are all these security guys who hang around campus in yellow jackets at night. I think they are a kind of useless. **The campus is very safe**. I like to go running, and I feel fine running all over the campus and the neighborhoods."

"I don't think there is a reason to feel unsafe, but at the same time, if you are walking alone on Benefit Street at four in the morning on a Saturday night and something happens to you, you cannot blame it on the area. It is common knowledge that the eastside is safer than any other area of Providence. I'm convinced that **the men in yellow coats aren't doing much of anything**."

The College Prowler Take
ON SAFETY & SECURITY

Brown students receive an alert by e-mail every time there is a major crime committed on campus or the University perceives a specific safety threat. In the last two years, in response to a real and perceived increase in crime on and around campus, Brown increased the hours of campus police, hired security officers to patrol at night, and hired a private consulting firm to address the problems. The University tries very hard to inform the students about the status of crimes on campus and provides services to encourage smart and safe movement on campus at night. The shuttle runs on a route all the way around campus and comes about every five minutes until 3 a.m. The escort, which picks up and drops off students from off-campus housing to any location on the University's campus, runs every night from 5 p.m. until 3 a.m. Safewalk is a student-run volunteer program that provides walking escorts for students every night. Students should feel safe, but not be naïve, about the threats that do exist in the surrounding city and on College Hill.

The campus area has all the common security features. There are many blue-light phones and well-lit public areas, and the police presence is generally strong enough to deter crime. Most students seem to feel very safe on campus, and will admit that things like theft happen when doors are carelessly left unlocked, or valuables are left in public places. Still, many students choose to leave their laptops unattended in the libraries or never lock their dorm rooms.

The College Prowler™ Grade on

Safety & Security: C+

A high grade in Safety & Security means that students generally feel safe, campus police are visible, blue-light phones and escort services are readily available, and safety precautions are not overly necessary.

Computers

The Lowdown
ON COMPUTERS

High-Speed Network?
Yes

Wireless Network?
Yes

Number of Labs:
9

Number of Media Labs:
2

Number of Computers:
200+

Operating Systems:
Mac, Windows, Unix

24-Hour Labs:
Center for Information and Technology (CIT) Building

Charge to Print?
No

Free Software

Adobe Acrobat Pro, Adobe Illustrator, Adobe, Pagermaker, Adobe Photoshop, Cs ChemDraw, ELFE, EndNote, Exceed, KaleidaGraph, Kedit, Dreamweaver, Mathematica, Matlab, PCTeX, ProDesktop, SAS, Scientific Word, SciFinder Scholar, Sigmaplot, SPSS, Symantec AntiVirus, Tecplot.

For a full listing visit *www.brown.edu/Facilities/CIS/Software_Services/software/supportlist.html*

Students Speak Out
ON COMPUTERS

"Most students have their own computer. There are enough clusters for everyone, but it just gets tight during exam periods and thesis due dates."

"The computer network is pretty good, and I believe it will get better. Occasionally, the network shuts down, but they notify you ahead of time. **It's best if you have a personal computer and printer** because labs can get crowded at times."

"Bring your own computer. If you get a laptop, **buy a wireless card**, so you can get hooked up in the libraries."

"I brought my own computer but **I end up doing all my work at computer labs** because I can't get anything done in my dorm. I don't think it's essential to have a computer because the facilities are pretty extensive. During finals, it could be hard without one."

"The **networks are good**, and you get some space on the University's file server to save your files. I never used mine, but I knew I had it."

"I think **having a computer makes it a lot easier**. I don't know anyone without a computer. I relied on the school's printers, but that's about it."

"I definitely think you need to bring your own computer to Brown. **The clusters are always full of people**. If I didn't have one, I think I would have turned a lot of papers in late. My roommate freshman year came to Brown without a computer but bought one within a month because she thought it was such a pain not to have one."

"Brown has computer clusters in the main libraries and the CIT (Center for Information Technology). **It is not absolutely necessary to have a computer on campus**. There are enough computers in the cluster to accommodate the 10 percent of students who do not have their own computers."

"I'm a Mac user, and I've found that **there are fewer resources available to me**."

"I think **it's easy to use campus computers**. I haven't needed to have my own in my three years here."

"Definitely bring your own computer. The computer clusters are accessible and generally easy to use, but, in college, **everything depends on e-mail**, and you need to be able to access it at any hour."

The College Prowler Take
ON COMPUTERS

Computers are a necessary tool at Brown. All papers, research, and communications revolve around having access to computers. The Center for Information Technology helps students adapt their own computers for use in the University network. Every Brown student has a e-mail account, server space, and full access to most of the University's computer software and hardware. All of this is in addition to all the electronic research tools available through JOSIAH, the library Web site server. The CIT also holds free group and individual training sessions to help students use specific software that the University makes available through its network. Network security is high, which has the positive effect of keeping viruses and junk mail away from people's inboxes, but also has essentially cut-off illegal file sharing on the University's network.

While many students get by without a computer, the majority of students brings a computer with them or purchases one from either the Brown Bookstore's computer center or a private company soon after they arrive. The fact that most students have their own computers decreases the traffic at the clusters at all but the busiest times of the year. If you are buying a new computer, a laptop is your best bet; it takes up less space in the cramped freshman rooms and gives you the freedom to bring your computer to any of your favorite study spots. Brown's new wireless network also gives students the chance to access the Internet with their laptop in certain places on campus. In general, Brown's computers offer more resources than most students could ever desire, and the school continues to expand its computing facilities, taking advantage of new technology as it becomes available.

The College Prowler™ Grade on
Computers: B+

A high grade in Computers designates that computer labs are available, the computer network is easily accessible, and campus computing technology is up-to-date.

The Lowdown
ON FACILITIES

Student Center:
Faunce House

Athletic Center:
The Olney-Margolies Athletic Center (the OMAC), The Smith Swim Center, The Bair's Lair Athletic Center, Meehan Auditorium ice rink, Pizzitola Sports Center, Pembroke Field

Libraries:
The John D. Rockefeller Humanities Library (The Rock), The Sciences Library (The Sci-Li), Orwig Music Library, Art Slide Library, The List Art Center, John Hay Special Collections Library, Annemarie Brown Library, John Carter Brown Library

Campus Size:
140 acres

What Is There to Do?

There are more things happening on and around campus than you could ever hope to do. It is easy for students to start any kind of club or activity if it doesn't already exist on campus, which is unlikely considering there are over 200 official University-supported organizations. All these student interests are also provided proper meeting facilities. Once buildings close for the academic day, they remain open for organizations to use as meeting places. There are also several playhouses, music practice spaces, and studios for the artistically inclined.

Movie Theatre on Campus?

The Brown Film Society has movie marathons in the evenings and on the weekend in Carmichael Auditorium.

Bowling on Campus?

No

Bar on Campus?

Brown currently enjoys two on-campus bars. The Grad Center Bar, below the Grad Center Dorm, was recently named one of the 10 hippest college bars in the country. Known to students as the GCB, the bar donates thousands of dollars in profits to charity every year. The Hourglass Cafe and concert venue is a favorite of underclassmen. The cafe is entirely student staffed and managed, offering some of the best on-campus jobs.

Coffeehouse on Campus?

The Upper Blue Room in Faunce House on the Main Green is home to the University's main coffee house, but the Rockefeller Library also has a small coffee and snack shop in the lobby.

Want to know more about places to hang out on campus? For a detailed listing on all facilities around campus, check out the College Prowler book on Brown available at *www.collegeprowler.com*.

Students Speak Out
ON FACILITIES

"The athletic facilities need some improvement. Everything else is pretty good, in my opinion."

"The facilities are very nice. They are very state-of-the-art and Ivy League-ish. **We don't have an official student center**, but Faunce Hall acts as one, since it houses the Student Activities Office, the mail room, a mini-arcade, the Campus Market, and various other things."

"I participate in gymnastics and **the facilities could use some attention**. We're donor-funded, so our facilities compared to other school's gymnastics facilities are not the best. But we can deal with it, we're fine."

"The campus is **beautiful**. Enough said."

"**Nothing is crazy nice**. They are doing better jobs on the newer classrooms, but most of the buildings from the '60s and '70s are pretty badly done, but they are doing great things when they renovate halls. The athletic center is alright; the courts are good, but the weight room and nautilus machines could use a new layout."

"**Brown needs a better central place**, something like a Student Center or Rec Center."

"The computer labs are nice, and there are many of them. I'm not an athlete, so I don't know much about the athletic facilities, but **the student center consists of a café, a market, and a bar**, which is open almost every night. It is great if you can't muster the energy to go clubbing."

"Most things are fairly centralized, and the campus is fairly compact. The only thing is that **the athletic center can be a little bit of a walk** depending on where you are living. Nothing is more than 10 minutes away, though."

The College Prowler Take
ON FACILITIES

Brown's facilities reflect Brown student's needs; the average Brown student would tell you they spend much more time in the library than at the gym. Therefore, it makes sense that the libraries and computer centers are constantly renovated and updated, while other facilities may receive less attention. That being said, Brown is not completely lacking any facilities, but it is easy to see which interests are given priority.

Compared to other Ivies, Brown's facilities are modest and reflect a certain degree of frugality. A quick glance at the campus will not necessarily showcase the somewhat obscured—but first-rate—costume shop, wood and metal working studios, or the special libraries available to all students. Overall, most Brown students have everything they need, though it may take them a little time to learn to properly navigate their surroundings.

The College Prowler™ Grade on
Facilities: B

A high Facilities grade indicates that the campus is aesthetically pleasing and well-maintained; facilities are state-of-the-art, and libraries are exceptional. Other determining factors include the quality of both athletic and student centers and an abundance of things to do on campus.

Campus Dining

The Lowdown
ON CAMPUS DINING

Freshman Meal Plan Requirement?
Yes

Meal Plan Average Cost:
$2,884

Off-Campus Places to Use Your Meal Plan:
None

Student Favorites:
The Blue Room, The Ivy Room, Josiah's

Places to Grab a Bite with Your Meal Plan

The Blue Room
Location: Faunce House, the Main Green
Food: Café
Favorite Dish: Focaccia chicken sandwich
Hours: Monday-Friday 7 a.m.-6 p.m.

The Gate
Location: Alumni Hall, Pembroke campus
Food: Pizza, subs, ice cream
Favorite Dish: Pizza and hot sandwiches
Hours: Monday-Friday 11 a.m.-2 a.m., Saturday 6 p.m.-2 a.m., Sunday 4 p.m.-2 a.m.

The Ivy Room

Location: Wriston Quad, below the Ratty

Food: Omelets, wraps, pizza and smoothie station, salads

Favorite Dish: Smoothies and falafel

Hours: Monday-Friday, Lunch: 11:30 a.m.-1:45 p.m., Snacks: 8 p.m.-Midnight

Josiah's (Jo's)

Location: New Dorm B, Main campus

Food: Grill, sushi, wraps, soup bar

Favorite Dish: Beef Carberry with cheese

Hours: Daily, 6 p.m.-2 a.m.

The Sharpe Refectory (The Ratty)

Location: Wriston Quad, Main Campus

Food: Regular, vegetarian and Kosher meals

Favorite Dish: Chicken nuggets and Magic bars

Hours: Monday-Saturday 7:30 a.m.-7:30 p.m., Sunday 10:30 a.m.-7:30 p.m.

The Verney-Woolley Cafeteria (The V-Dub)

Location: Emery-Woolley Hall, Pembroke Campus

Food: Regular and Vegetarian Meal

Favorite Dish: Cajun gumbo and tater tots

Hours: Monday-Friday 7:30 a.m.-7:30 p.m.

Other Options

If you can't leave campus to eat, you can take your chances with the notorious "silver truck," which parks in front of Wayland Arch on Wriston Quad most nights after 8:00 p.m. If you feel less adventurous, it is also easy to get Chinese and Italian food delivered to dorms.

Did You Know?

There is a Ratty Recipe Repository link off of Brown's Daily Jolt Web site which has student-invented recipes for meals using ingredients in the University's cafeteria. Recipes include "Curry Chicken Salad," "Fruity Desert Crepes," and "Macaratty and Cheese."

Students Speak Out

ON CAMPUS DINING

"The meal plan is alright. The V-Dub has recently been renovated, and the food is consistently tasty. Food quality at the Ratty, the other dining hall, is less consistent. But there is usually a decent selection."

"The main dining hall food is **below-average** to average cafeteria food. Special snack bars are pretty good and give you good variety."

"I hated the meal plan when I was on it! **The Ratty is the pits, but I hear it got better**. The VW is a better option. Josiah's and the Blue Room are better alternatives if you have points, and the Gate is a good place to get a piece of pizza."

"The **meal plan rips you off**. The Ratty was disgusting. I was on the full meal plan. I'm definitely going off of it even though I'm living in a dorm without a real kitchen, which should tell you something. I think the V-Dub is a little better. Being off the meal plan without a car might be a little difficult."

"I stayed on meal plan for all three years that I lived in the dorms. It was great to get to see people in the dining halls. **There's usually something good to eat**."

"I think the **food got progressively worse** over the time I was on the plan. I'm excited to be off the meal plan now."

"It would be **cheaper if I went off the meal plan**, but there are tradeoffs. Now that I'm off the meal plan, I eat whatever comes my way. If you don't have a car or access to a car, it would be really frustrating to be off the meal plan."

"I went to both cafeterias. I went to the Ratty more, but the V-Dub is nicer. **The atmosphere at the V-Dub is nice**; they play music, and it feels more like a restaurant. It's the same food no matter where you go."

The College Prowler Take
ON CAMPUS DINING

While most schools have contracted with Marriott or fast-food companies for their dining needs, Brown prides itself on maintaining a University-run food service. Why exactly this is a source of pride is another question entirely. The main dining halls—the "Ratty" and the "V-Dub"—serve what can only be described as average food. Chances are, you won't return home for the holidays demanding that your mom cook more like Brown Food Services (BFS). A lack of variety, and the inability to use credits in real restaurants close to campus can be frustrating. The few cafés and restaurants run by the University are equally frustrating because they are more expensive than independent cafés and diners on Thayer and Wickenden Streets. The Brown meal plan feels more like a middle school lunch program than a welcomed dining experience.

Year after year, the Ratty is the butt of new and old jokes, but as demonstrated by the Ratty Recipe Repository, many Brown students embrace the standard cafeteria-style eating. Besides, the meal plan provides much more than hot food every day. The meal plan is a state of mind. From your first week on meal plan, you will undoubtedly enjoy meals with friends, meet lots of new people, and sing karaoke with your fellow Brunonians at the V-Dub. Good or bad, surviving meal plan freshman year is a defining experience and undoubtedly a right of passage. In time, however, you'll find the right balance of splurging for off-campus meals and eating creatively at the dining halls. Students who are off the meal plan might enjoy better food, but it is costly and time consuming to fend for yourself.

The College Prowler™ Grade on
Campus Dining: C-

Our grade on Campus Dining addresses the quality of both school-owned dining halls and independent on-campus restaurants, as well as the price, availability, and variety of food.

Off-Campus Dining

The Lowdown
ON OFF-CAMPUS DINING

Student Favorites:
Spike's Junkyard Dogs, East Side Pockets, Sawadee, India, Viva

Best Pizza:
Al Forno

Best Chinese:
Apsara

Best Healthy:
The Garden Grill Cafe

Best Wings:
Ri Ra

Best Breakfast:
Julian's

Best Place to Take Your Parents:
Hemenway's, Mediterraneo

Students Speak Out

ON OFF-CAMPUS DINING

"I've always been amazed at the variety of restaurants Providence has to offer. My favorites are the Italian restaurants and the Paragon burger."

"The restaurants are very good; **that's one of the best parts about living in this city**. There are so many good places that I feel like I need a full four years to try them all. There are really too many good ones to name, but generally, I eat on Thayer Street, on Wickenden Street, or downtown. Federal Hill, Providence's Italian district, is a short trolley ride away and has fantastic Italian food. There are also some great Thai and Indian places if you like those types of food."

"The restaurants are great. Thayer and Wickenden streets are good and close. Paragon is great and cheap. Also check out Sakura for sushi and Federal Hill for more expensive Italian food. **Providence also has great Indian and Thai food**. Just steer clear of Chinese."

"On my Brown application, I literally said that one reason I wanted to come here was for the **great Italian food in the area**."

"My favorite restaurant, that I can never go to because it's so expensive, is Ten. **I go when my dad comes into town**."

"Sawadee has **amazing Masaman curry**."

"**Miss Fanny's Soul Food Kitchen is amazing**. Broad Street Tokyo is good for sushi, as is Mia Sushi on Federal Hill."

"Thayer Street is the 'college town' street of Brown. **There are lots of restaurants, small little sandwich shops, and chains**. Paragon and Andrea's are nice sit-down places that are not too expensive. D'Angelo's, Au Bon Pain, Smoothie King, Ben & Jerry's, Johnny Rockets, Eastside Pockets, Antonio's pizza, and Kabob and Curry are the chains. Meeting Street Café has really great, mega-sized sandwiches and cookies; if it's your birthday they give you a free cookie."

"There are a lot of **good breakfast places**."

"Providence can be **kind of expensive**, and the food can be a little monotonous."

"Off-campus food is spectacular. **There are ridiculous amounts of really good restaurants** in the area since Johnson & Wales [culinary school] serves up so many good local chefs. Fast-food type places are all over the place; there's falafel, pizza, and pastries everywhere. You won't have to worry about having variety."

COLLEGE PROWLER™

Want to know more about off-campus cuisine? For a detailed listing on all dining options around campus, check out the complete College Prowler book on Brown available at *www.collegeprowler.com*.

The College Prowler Take

OFF-CAMPUS DINING

Providence truly caters to the epicurean diner. One need not stray farther than the College Hill and the downtown areas to find all varieties of ethnic food, dining styles and atmospheres. Without a doubt, Providence is host to an impressive number of off-campus restaurants that offer variety in terms of price and menus. Vegetarian, Kosher, and all other diets can be easily accommodated. Great food is truly one of Providence's greatest assets.

The scariest thing about off-campus eating, however, is the lack of supermarkets that are easily within walking distance of the University. The closest supermarket is over a mile away, which will sound a lot worse in February when it snows and gets dark before dinner. There are a few specialty markets nearby, including a Saturday farmers' market at Hope High school, but you really need a car if you plan to cook on a regular basis.

The College Prowler™ Grade on

Off-Campus Dining: A-

A high Off-Campus Dining grade implies that off-campus restaurants are affordable, accessible, and worth visiting. Other factors include the variety of cuisine and the availability of alternative options (vegetarian, vegan, Kosher, etc.).

Campus Housing

The Lowdown

ON CAMPUS HOUSING

Undergrads on Campus:
80%

Number of Dormitories:
27

University-Owned Apartments:
40

Room Types

Standard residence rooms, multi-room suites, houses, and apartments.

Standard—Students share a large central bathroom facility. Most first-year students are assigned to these rooms.

Suites—Several students share a suite, which normally has single or double bedrooms, a common room, and a sink area without a toilet.

Apartments—Several students share an apartment, which has all singles, a kitchen, a common room, and a full bathroom.

Houses—A large group of students share a full, University-owned house. Each house has its own unique features, but students enjoy the advantages of living in a house without the hassles of moving off campus.

You Get

Every room has a phone jack, an Ethernet hub, and free cable with access to Brown's HBO-like movie channel. Rooms also come with a lamp or an overhead light, a desk, a dresser, a book shelf and a bed.

Also Available

Although every dorm has laundry machines, laundry service is also available through the Brown Student Agency.

Available for Rent

You can rent microwaves and small refrigerators from the Brown Student Agency. The same goes for towels and sheets.

Cleaning Service?

Most dorms have a custodial service that keeps hallways, bathrooms and other public areas reasonably clean.

Did You Know?

Brown is said to have a few secret societies in addition to the well-publicized organizations. These societies are said to be located near campus in mysterious Mansions. The most famous myth concerns the ominous Grad Center dorm. It is rumored to have been designed in 1968 by prison architects as a fortress in case of riots. Regardless of the building's design intent, it is a fact that the imposing concrete spiral staircase was actually built in the incorrect orientation because the builders read the blueprints wrong.

After talking so much about housing, Brown students have come up with their own terms for Brown's sometimes odd dorms. A "Dingle" is a room originally built as a double, but has been converted to a single. A "Trouble" is a room originally built as a double, but has been converted to a triple.

Adding to the eccentricity of the Brown housing system, Residential Life sponsors a lip-synching contest each year in February. The prize, which can go to any group, including rising sophomores, is the opportunity to select any on-campus room, suite, or apartment. As you would expect, this is a fiercely-competitive contest.

Students Speak Out
ON CAMPUS HOUSING

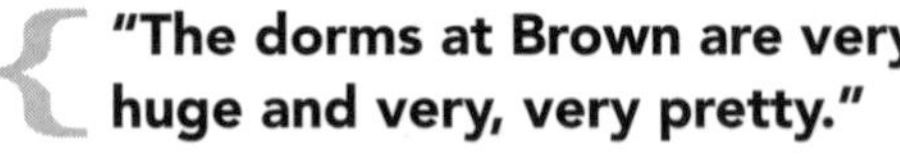

"The dorms at Brown are very huge and very, very pretty."

"All **freshman dorms are fine**. Don't worry if you get a so-called 'bad dorm' because you end up bonding with your dormmates over that anyway. There is a housing shortage, but it's really the sophomores that get screwed. As a freshman, you have no control over what dorm you get, so don't worry about it."

"Emery Woolley and Mo-Champ used to be super-gross, **bad '70s public-housing projects**. They refurnished them well. I'll cheer Keeny for its overly-social, thirsty, and frisky freshman. Since you don't pick housing as a freshman, have faith in Residential Life. Andrews has really nice rooms, but it's pretty quiet."

"I am staying on campus senior year. I live in Slater Hall, right next to University Hall, and I definitely don't want to move. I can roll out of bed and into my classes. **My room is large, with high ceilings**, and I get a view of sunset down College Hill."

"Dorms are pretty decent. Some are much nicer than others, though. **As a freshman, you'd want to be in Keeney**—that's where most freshmen are, and it's located on the convenient side of campus."

"The dorms aren't bad, and **many freshman rooms are actually very nice**. As a freshman, everyone is assigned a roommate and a dormitory, so you have no say in either matter. No matter what, housing is guaranteed all four years."

"**I've stayed on campus all four years**. I don't want to have to pay bills. I have the rest of my life to deal with real life. For a year, I feel like it's not worth it to buy a bed and furniture, and the senior dorms are nicer than a house off campus. I don't see the point when the houses are right next door to the dorms anyway."

The College Prowler Take
ON CAMPUS HOUSING

Brown guarantees housing for four years if the student wants it. They also require students to live on campus for the first six semesters of their Brown career. Although many students complain about this policy, it makes life easier for rising sophomores and juniors and relieves a lot of the stress between freshman and junior year. Starting in the spring of freshman year, students are faced with a lot of choices in terms of housing. In addition to the lottery, all the program and Greek houses give students the choice of getting around the fickle lottery system. In addition to circumventing the lottery, special housing is one more chance to meet new people and have new experiences.

Despite complaints about the frustrating lottery system, Brown's housing system is better than most. After freshman year, the system can be worked to a student's advantage—including some houses reserved specifically for sophomores. Live in the dorms first year. Live in a house or program house sophomore year. Move to a different program house junior year if you didn't love your sophomore digs. By senior year, you'll have skipped the whole lottery system, and are basically guaranteed prime on-campus housing without ever being forced to enter the lottery or move off-campus. Once again, a little finesse is all it takes to make the housing system work for you.

The College Prowler™ Grade on
Campus Housing: B+

A high Campus Housing grade indicates that dorms are clean, well-maintained, and spacious. Other determining factors include variety of dorms, proximity to classes, and social atmosphere.

Off-Campus Housing

The Lowdown
ON OFF-CAMPUS HOUSING

Undergrads in Off-Campus Housing:
20%

Average Rent for a Studio Apartment:
$600/month

Average Rent for a 1BR Apartment:
$800/month

Average Rent for a 2BR Apartment:
$1200/month

Best Time to Look for a Place:
For the best selection, look by no later than February; however, if you want the best prices, wait until late in the spring when the landlords are anxious to rent their spaces.

Popular Areas:
Fox Point, around Governor Street
Wickenden Street Area
Brook and Cushing Streets, right off Thayer

For Assistance Contact:
www.brown.edu/Administration/ResLife/index.html
(401) 863-3500
Res_Life@brown.edu

Students Speak Out
ON OFF-CAMPUS HOUSING

"It's definitely worth it. Most people live within a 10-minute walk from campus. Then there are loft, warehouse, and other house or apartment options in the city."

"Off-campus housing is definitely the way to go if you can . . . **just make sure your landlord and neighbors aren't too insane** because that does happen."

"**I lived off campus one year, and it was awesome**. I lived in Young Orchard the year before—that was a step down, but only a very small step."

"I lived off campus for two years. **Off-campus living is totally better**. The annoying thing was, I had to stay in dorms until my junior year. I would have moved off earlier if I could have."

"Many juniors and seniors live in off-campus housing. There seems to be **enough to go around**, and it's pretty nice, pretty affordable, and very convenient and close to campus. The campus is very compact, so nothing is a very far walk."

"Living off campus, I get more studio space and cheaper digs. **No one's in my business**."

"**I've never felt at home on campus**. But living off campus, I'm not as likely to go to things on campus late at night."

"You have a lot **more freedom off campus**. You are treated like an adult, not a student."

"Off-campus housing can be **extremely convenient**; it's as close to campus as a dorm. Of course, the further away from campus you go, the cheaper it is. But in general, students that live off campus find the walking commute minimal."

The College Prowler Take
ON OFF-CAMPUS HOUSING

Brown guarantees housing for all four years, even though most students opt to live on their own by senior year to gain more freedom, more space, or better facilities. Every once-in-a-while, when there is a housing crunch, the University will allow juniors to live off-campus. Officially though, only seniors are guaranteed permission to seek housing off of campus grounds. Students apply to the Office of Residential Life for off-campus permission in the early spring of their junior year, most having already signed a lease in the previous months. As a senior, getting permission is easy, but finding the perfect apartment can be a greater challenge. Within a mile radius of campus there are endless housing options, but the best available places are rarely well-advertised. Hit the pavement or ask friends if you want to find the best place. In general, students can find any kind of residence they want—historic houses, new apartments, studios, or mansions.

While most students believe they save money by moving off campus, the frustrations and complications of moving off campus often add up quickly. Summer subletting can be hard, and don't forget the astronomical heating bills during the winter. Moving off campus should be a careful choice.

The College Prowler™ Grade on
Off-Campus Housing: A-

A high grade in Off-Campus Housing indicates that apartments are of high quality, close to campus, affordable, and easy to secure.

The Lowdown
ON DIVERSITY

White: 66%

Asian American: 14%

African American: 7%

Hispanic: 7%

Native American: 1%

International: 6%

Out-of-State: 94%

Minority Clubs
The Third World Center at Brown was created in 1976 to meet the needs of all minority students and to promote racial and ethnic pluralism in the Brown community. Minority students receive a great deal of support from the pre-orientation Third World Transition Program, the presence of Minority Peer Councilors in freshman dorms, and program houses, such as Harambee House.

Political Activity
Brown is famed for its political activism and liberal atmosphere, but actual activism and demonstrations on campus have become more infrequent. While it is commonplace to find students discussing politics and volunteering for liberal causes, rallies and sit-ins are part of Brown's past.

Gay Pride

Brown students and faculty are extremely receptive and friendly to all people, and there have been very few incidences of discrimination or hate crimes related to sexual orientation. The effort to promote queer politics and acceptance is spearheaded by The Queer Aliance. Twice a year, the organization hosts huge dances which are among the most popular campus parties.

Most Popular Religions

Brown does not have a single predominant religion, and the majority of students claim to have no particular affiliation. However, some sources show that some religious minorities have particularly high numbers at Brown. The Chaplains' office provides services for students of all religions; they list Bahat, Buddhism, Christianity, Hinduism, Islam, Jainism, Judaism, and Sikhism as the most popular Brown faiths.

Economic Status

Brown recently made a major admissions policy change to accept students on a "need-blind" basis in order to promote quality of scholarship and demonstrated ability above affluence. However, the average Brown student comes from the upper-middle class.

Did You Know?

Although Brown originally was founded as a Methodist school, was the first university open to students of all religious persuasions.

Students Speak Out

ON DIVERSITY

"Diversity isn't terrible. But it's very hard to be here and forget that you are in very white, very middle-class New England."

"Compared to Berkeley, it's not diverse. **Compared to Princeton, it's very diverse**. I don't know; people have different opinions on this, too."

"Brown has a **diversity of opinions and political views**, as well as students with all types of geographical, religious, racial and educational backgrounds. If you want to meet people different from you, you have to make an effort."

"Brown is **not as diverse as it claims to be**, especially economically."

"The University is an interesting size. It's small enough that you recognize a lot of faces on campus, but your social circle doesn't change that much. You always have a home base, but **I engage with a lot of people**."

"The campus is somewhat diverse. There are a lot of people of Asian decent, but **other races and ethnicities are under-represented**."

"There are two indications that **race is still an issue around campus**. One, there is still a lot of dialogue between the students and the administration on the subject, but also, the overwhelming sense of mistrust that most white students show when it comes to minorities, I think a lot of students feel that there might be overcompensation and that 'white problems,' whatever those are, are not addressed."

"Brown is diverse. I would say **we are the most genuinely diverse student body**. We also have every possible student activity that you could want. If we don't have it, it's easy to start your own and get funding."

"Once you get here you realize that **there are so many pockets**, like hippies and hipsters. It's all here."

"There is not enough **political diversity among the professors**, and certainly not among the students."

"**I don't think it's an 'Us vs. Them' environment**, but the manifestation of relations, either racial or class, exist."

The College Prowler Take
ON DIVERSITY

The University makes an honest effort to promote socio-economic diversity among the student body—the recent change to need-blind admissions is just one example of this goal. Also, a recent endowment (the biggest single gift ever made to Brown) promises to preserve the goal of providing financial aid to deserving students. While the hard numbers indicate that there is a good deal of racial and economic diversity at Brown, the day-to-day interactions between students are the real test of diversity and tolerance at Brown. Very few outright problems or public sentiments exist that would indicate a lack of diversity at Brown. In spite of this, however, the students, left to their own devices, do not always choose to integrate themselves in different social circles.

The University gives Brown the basic ingredients to enjoy diversity in political, economic, racial, and geographical arenas. It also provides support for students who come from a variety of backgrounds. Every student, regardless of their background, will be put in situations where they are confronted with people and opinions they have not experienced before coming to Brown. The vocal nature of Brown students and the University's outstanding policies, which protect freedom of student expression, mean that Brown is as diverse as the students make it.

The College Prowler™ Grade on
Diversity: B

A high grade in Diversity indicates that ethnic minorities and international students have a notable presence on campus and that students of different economic backgrounds, religious beliefs, and sexual preferences are well-represented.

The Lowdown
ON GUYS & GIRLS

Female Undergrads: 54%

Male Undergrads: 46%

Birth Control Available? Yes

Social Scene
Brown students generally can be put into two groups: social butterflies and social caterpillars. It makes for a great dynamic. Just when you think you've exhausted your social sphere, you meet someone in a class who, it turns out, lived down the hall from you for two years, but never left their room. That being said, freshman housing units are the basis for future social interaction at Brown. In freshmen housing units personalities spill into the hallways and start friendships that may last a lifetime. At Brown, a smile really is all it takes to meet people.

Hookups or Relationships?
Brown is a school where hookups and brief flings reign supreme. Most students would say that they are simply too busy and too involved to pursue a committed relationship. Brown also seems to attract many freshmen with little or no relationship experience. It's impossible to say what combination of factors lead to the two most common sentiments about Brown students and dating: "There is no dating at Brown," and "We're just friends . . . with benefits."

Dress Code

Unshaved armpits and dreadlocks will always be a staple of the Brown hippie look, but Brown guys and girls exhibit the full range of styles and attitudes—Fake Prada and Louis Vuitton mix with real high-fashion looks. There's everything from boarding school kids who can't shake their preppy duds, to the dirty hippy garb that really makes you wonder whether all dorms are equipped with shower stalls. Unfortunately, the cold weather can get the better of fashion during the winter months, but the dress code for those who care is either designer head-to-toe or funky and artsy.

In May, shorts and short skirts distinguish between those that spring-breaked in the Bahamas and those that stayed to work on their thesis. The fashionable Brown guy looks a bit Euro, a bit bohemian, or classic Abercrombie. For girls, there's everything from perfectly-coifed designer looks to oblivious fashion victims. The fashionable Brown girl, above all, strives for her own unique style. Collectively, Brown kids definitely rock a style.

Students Speak Out

ON GUYS & GIRLS

"There isn't a ton of dating at Brown. There are plenty of attractive people here. You have to be more persistent. It's nice that there is a social life that revolves around the school."

"I'd have to say **the guys at Brown are hotter than the girls**. It's not exactly a big dating school, but people do date and hook up."

"I haven't had too much success with girls at Brown. Freshman year, I had a girlfriend. That was about it. **I meet most girls at parties**."

"Guys at Brown are flaky. I've dated enough to know. I've met a lot of people that are socially awkward, but I think that's why **we get along so well**. It's funny when we all come together."

"**There's no serious dating. Not here**. I think there's a variety of guys. Some guys like to take girls out on dates. A lot of guys don't; they're more into the hookup thing. I think that there is more going on here than at most places. It happens pretty often; it's definitely common."

"Brown is one of those places where you meet really cool people, but there's not so much casual dating going on. You are **either in a long term relationship or single**."

The College Prowler Take

ON GUYS & GIRLS

According to the rumors, the headshots Brown requires with every application are meant to ensure Brown's reputation for having most attractive Ivy League students. Whether or not you believe this rumor is entirely a matter of taste (and whether you consider "attractive Ivy League student" an oxymoron). In general, students tend to agree that the admissions office did a fabulous job choosing interesting and enjoyable classmates, but they are a little more critical when it comes to sharing anything more than intellectual curiosity with their peers. However, the truth of the matter is that the Brown student body is no more or less attractive than any other population of 20-year-old students; observers are just as likely to rave about the spectacular beauties lounging on the main green as they are to complain about the pale, four-eyed creatures that wander out of the library late at night.

The only real consensus is on the state of the dating scene: there isn't one. Students either chose between serial relationships, random hookups, or celibacy. While this is a common complaint on Friday nights, the system probably exists this way because it best suits the busy Brown lifestyle.

The College Prowler™ Grade on

Guys: B+

A high grade for Guys indicates that the male population on campus is attractive, smart, friendly, and engaging, and that the school has a decent ratio of guys to girls.

The College Prowler™ Grade on

Girls: B

A high grade for Girls not only implies that the women on campus are attractive, smart, friendly, and engaging, but also that there is a fair ratio of girls to guys.

Athletics

The Lowdown
ON ATHLETICS

Athletic Division:
Division 1

Conference:
Ivy League

School Mascot:
The Brown Bear

Men's Varsity Teams:	Women's Varsity Teams:
Baseball	Softball
Basketball	Basketball
Crew	Cross Country
Cross-Country	Ice Hockey
Equestrian	Fencing
Fencing	Field Hockey
Golf	Gymnastics
Football	Golf
Ice Hockey	Lacrosse
Lacrosse	Soccer
Soccer	Skiing
Skiing	Water Polo
Wrestling	Squash
Water Polo	Swimming & Diving
Squash	Tennis
Swimming & Diving	Track & Field
Tennis	
Track & Field	

Club Sports
Sailing, Men's Rugby, Men's and Women's Ultimate Frisbee, Men's Volleyball

Intramural Sports
Football, Volleyball, Tennis, Soccer, Basketball, Frisbee, Hockey, Softball, Squash

Students Speak Out
ON ATHLETICS

"Club sports are a lot of fun without the pressure of varsity sports. There's a huge culture that revolves around the ultimate Frisbee teams. There's no varsity team, but the club team travels a lot."

"Intramurals are pretty popular. **Varsity sports are almost like a social scene**, and like all other social scenes, it's fractious and segregated from most other things. Part of the reason is that there's less of a stigma for athletes, but it's more that, physically, the sports complex is not in the center of campus."

"If I wasn't playing a sport, I would have time to take photography. But in general, I think **I can do just about everything I want to do at the University and still be a varsity athlete**. I'm still a double concentrator."

"What's a varsity sport? No, seriously, if you're looking for colleges where you can be a celebrity on campus because you are an athlete, then look elsewhere. My friends that are varsity athletes work very, very hard, and it is **difficult for them to have social lives outside of their teams**. Some of them end up dropping the team; others stick with it and have a great experience, love their teammates, and their sport."

"The men's and women's ultimate Frisbee teams go to **the national tournament almost every year**. It can be as intense as you want it to be. There's a really great community of people who are athletically-minded but want something less intense than varsity, yet still highly-competitive. It's a great way to meet fun, active people."

"The only thing I don't like about Brown is the way the athletes are treated. I'm an athlete and people only assume I got in because I'm an athlete, and that I'm in 'dumb-jock' classes. **There's a lot of hostility toward athletes here**; not from the professors, but sometimes from other students. I feel like the athletes do just as well (if not better) in classes than non-athletes."

"As far as professors go, at the beginning of each semester, **the professors let the athletes know that if there's a conflict to let them know about it**. They're willing to work with us, and it's definitely supportive."

The College Prowler Take

ON ATHLETICS

Brown is not an overly-athletic school. Almost every student played some varsity sport in high school, but for most students, academics and other extracurricular activities come before athletics. There are, however, a full range of varsity sports and less intense club and intramural sports. Many Brown students go for runs around campus, or find themselves playing catch or Frisbee on the main green.

Sports are just one aspect of social life, but they help to relieve stress from the academic rigors of the University. Brown has facilities for non-athletes to swim, workout, and play organized sports. Brown also has gifted student athletes who may go underappreciated, despite winning records.

The College Prowler™ Grade on

Athletics: C+

A high grade in Athletics indicates that students have school spirit, that sports programs are respected, that games are well-attended, and that intramurals are a prominent part of student life.

Nightlife

The Lowdown

ON NIGHTLIFE

Student Favorites:
Fish Co., Olive's, The Steam Alley, Nick-a-Knees, The GCB, Max's, Viva

Useful Resources for Nightlife:
Brown's Daily Jolt, *www.brown.dailyjolt.com*

Bars Close At:
1 a.m. on weeknights, 2 a.m. on weekends

Primary Areas with Nightlife:
Thayer Street, Wickenden Street, Point Street Bridge area, Downtown

Students Speak Out
ON NIGHTLIFE

"Parties on campus range greatly and are widely-dispersed. The frats are definitely not the main places to go for parties, unless that's your scene."

"**Providence is a fun city**. There are lots of bars within walking distance of campus. It cuts down on driving. There are places to drink around town for freshman."

"**Bars on campus are really easy to get into**. The main ones are Max's, Kartabar, Liquid Lounge, and Viva. Kartabar and Viva have Euro and Latin music on weekends, and Max's has hip-hop night and '80s night during the week. Downtown, there are a bunch of places that you can get into if your ID is remotely okay."

"If you like dive bars, Providence is a great place to be. **There are good, cheap bars**."

"I go out Thursday nights. **I go to places that are close and don't have a cover charge**. There are lots of places that are 18-and-over. There are places to go to, but in general, I would spend most of my weekends in the dorms with my friends."

"There are certain places I like to go around campus because I have no ID problems there. **My roommate was Greek, so we spent a lot of time at Viva**."

"There's a **variety of different late-night scenes** at Brown—bars, clubs, pubs, snack bars, frat parties, campus events—whatever suits you."

"The **on-campus parties are worthwhile** checking out for underclassmen, but they're ultimately uninspiring and repetitive. House parties are great, as are a few bars and clubs. Check out Nick-a-Nee's, The Red Fez, Andreas for cocktails, the Underground, when it's open, and the GCB."

"I've never been to a club. Actually, I went to Viva once and never went back. **I'm a big fan of the GCB**."

"There are **some great bars around town**. I love Patrick's. I used to go to there by myself on Saturday mornings to watch soccer. It would be 10 o'clock on a Saturday morning, and it would be me, the bartender and an 80-year-old man. I would ask for breakfast, and the bartender would offer me a beer with it."

The College Prowler Take
ON NIGHTLIFE

Brown students are fonder of bars than clubs. If you really need to party every night, however, Providence has a few dozen clubs that will expose you to Rhode Island nightlife, which can be gritty but holds promise for hot people and decent tunes. If drinking is all you need, Providence's bars, like its restaurants, cater to all styles and tastes.

Although Brown students are not the most adventurous, the bars, clubs and other nightlife activities lurking in the city can entertain the blandest or wildest tastes any night of the week. Seven days a week, bars are swinging on College Hill, downtown, and everywhere else in the city until at least 1 a.m. Any Brown student who thinks that there's not enough to do after the sun goes down needs to open their eyes, expand their bubble, and venture out to one of Providence's eager-to-please nightspots.

The College Prowler™ Grade on
Nightlife: B+

A high grade in Nightlife indicates that there are many bars and clubs in the area that are easily accessible and affordable. Other determining factors include the number of options for the under-21 crowd and the prevalence of house parties.

Greek Life

The Lowdown
ON GREEK LIFE

Number of Fraternities:
6

Number of Sororities:
2

Number of Coed Fraternities:
2

Undergrads in Greek Houses:
Less than 10%

Fraternities on Campus:
Alpha Epsilon Pi, Delta Phi, Delta Tau, Phi Kappa Psi, Sigma Chi, Theta Delta Chi

Sororities on Campus:
Alpha Chi Omega, Kappa Alpha Theta

Coeds:
Alpha Delta Phi, Zeta Delta Xi

Other Greek Organizations:
Greek Council, Greek Peer Advisors, Interfraternity Council, Order of Omega, Panhellenic Council

Students Speak Out
ON GREEK LIFE

"Greek life exists, but It's not big. I think it's mostly a thing for freshman. It's not like other schools where it's probably cool to be in a sorority."

"The Greek life is there for parties and some other events, but it doesn't dominate. It's not a big deal if you are in a frat or sorority, and it is not a big deal if you never set foot in one. No one cares one way or another. It's nice because you can go to frat parties, which can be fun sometimes, but **it's not a status thing at all**. However, there definitely are a few real 'frat' types, but it's nice to have a little bit of every type at Brown."

"I'm in a fraternity. I never thought I would join one, but it turns out that I did. **They definitely do not dominate**, but they do provide big parties open to the whole campus that a lot of people find to be pretty fun—there's dancing, drinking, and usually some theme. There's usually always something else going on around campus, though, and bars are always open."

"Greek life is definitely there, but it in no way dominates the social scene. **They have a lot of the parties on campus**, that can be fun, but it is definitely avoidable and not seen as being a big deal at all."

"I wasn't in a sorority, but I lived in a dorm that was partially joined with a Greek house. Going into it, I was very skeptical because you hear so many stories based on stereotypes, but living in a dorm with them completely changed my perspective of Greek life. **They were very approachable.** It was intimidating at first; I thought they were going to be rowdy, but in the end, it created a great dynamic."

The College Prowler Take

ON GREEK LIFE

Greek life at Brown is about as minimized as it can be. This is due to the Greek system itself, and the University's attempts to seamlessly integrate frats and sororities into daily campus life. All Greek houses are on campus and abide by the same rules and regulations as any other organization. The parties, for the most part, are open and welcoming to all students. If a student never wants to see the Greek system, they can easily ignore it. On the flip side, if a student wants a real Greek experience, they can find it in one of the houses that do exist.

The Greek system at Brown is one of the many positive-interest groups. Banners hang around the Main Green and Wriston Quad to inform students of coming parties and events. A handful of nights during the year, you see the crazy, *Animal House*-type antics that Greek systems present at any school. However, if you want a school where who you are is defined by the three Greek letters printed on your T-shirt, Brown is simply not the place.

The College Prowler™ Grade on

Greek Life: C+

A high grade in Greek Life indicates that sororities and fraternities are not only present, but also active on campus. Other determining factors include the variety of houses available and the respect the Greek community receives from the rest of the campus.

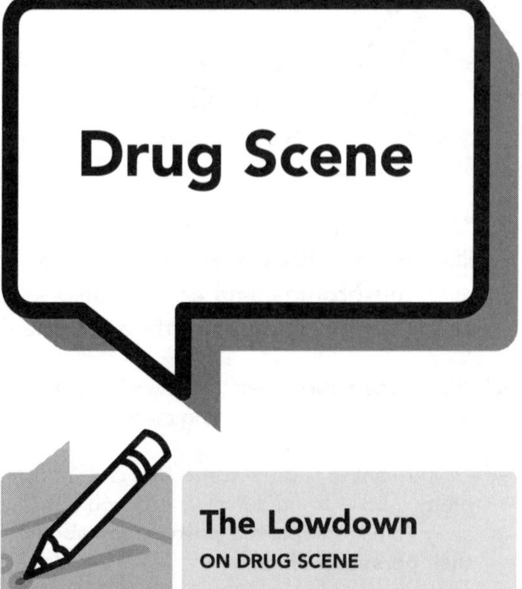

The Lowdown

ON DRUG SCENE

Most Prevalent Drugs on Campus:
Marijuana, cocaine, study drugs

Liquor-Related Referrals:
103

Liquor-Related Arrests:
1

Drug-Related Referrals:
53

Drug-Related Arrests:
6

Drug Counseling Programs

Brown's Health Service provides information about substance abuse, as well as other common health issues for college students through its Health Education office, located on the 3rd floor of Health Services. The phone number is (401) 863-2794. In addition, every freshman dorm has many undergraduate counselors who help students and provide a source of information on substance abuse issues.

Students Speak Out
ON DRUG SCENE

"Pot is the most used and accessible illicit drug at Brown. However, coke, acid, mushrooms, and ecstasy also seem to be around from time to time."

"I think **the policy is lax**, and I like it. I got in trouble one time, but nothing came of it."

"If you want to find the scene, you can find it pretty quickly. If you don't want to, you can stay away from it. **People are pretty open about their personal habits**."

"Yeah, most of my friends smoke and drink. I wouldn't date someone who doesn't smoke or drink; I think it's like that at most universities. I have friends outside of that group that I meet in class or at work to get a cup of coffee with, but **people kind of stick to their circles** here."

"I've never been busted. You hear stuff like that happening. I think Brown is really cool. They definitely give you a lot of responsibility, and they're pretty hands-off. **They expect students to make the right decision**."

"I would say **most students do drink, but not a lot**. I would say the average student would, at most, have fours drinks—I mean in a night, not in an hour."

The College Prowler Take
ON DRUG SCENE

While you can guarantee some exposure to drugs, it is by no means a social prerequisite. There is enough to do at Brown and in Providence to fight off the boredom that makes the drug scene thrive at other less-entertaining schools. Brown students, like any college student body, look to drugs for both social and academic reasons. Many students drink and smoke cigarettes and pot casually. From there, the scenes are more obscure and are neither prominent nor hard to find. Students at Brown tend to view substance use, and they abuse as a luxury that can be enjoyed with personal responsibility. The effects that abuse will have on your work, and the threat of University and police action if you get caught, means that students use drugs sensibly on campus.

In the end, students are neither excluded nor included socially based purely on their drug habits, and Brown students exhibit the full spectrum of personal habits. The most important thing to remember is that most Brown students are responsible and goal-driven kids. Drug use is more a by-product of college life than a main activity.

The College Prowler™ Grade on

Drug Scene: B

A high grade on Drug Scene indicates that drugs are not a noticeable part of campus life, drug use is not visible, and no pressure to use them seems to exist.

Campus Strictness

The Lowdown
ON CAMPUS STRICTNESS

What Are You Most Likely to Get Caught Doing on Campus?

Smoking cigarettes or pot in the dorms

Students Speak Out
ON CAMPUS STRICTNESS

"Whereas most schools have RAs or proctors in the dorms who play the disciplinary role regarding drugs and alcohol, Brown has residential counselors. They are mostly sophomores and are pretty lax."

"My best friend at school had a few parties that were broken up by the police, but that was because somebody called due to the noise. Brown is a very liberal school, and **it really trusts its students to make their own decision**."

"Sometimes **I felt like they were out to get me**. We got busted once or twice, and then it seemed like the cops made a habit of coming by my room. We had some close calls, but we still got away with a lot."

"They're **not strict about drinking**. With smoking, they've buckled down a little, but not much. You will never go to jail, but maybe just get a dean's hearing."

"Police generally don't look for people doing stuff. But it's **not like they'll pretend they didn't see it** if they happen to come upon it."

"Campus was too strict for me. I couldn't wait to get off campus where there aren't **people patrolling your lifestyle** every day."

"Many times, if you are caught drinking, the cops tell you to just pour it out and leave. It's pretty laid-back. **Brown also doesn't have RAs** in the normal sense, we have an MPC (minority peer counselor), a WPC (woman's peer counselor) and an RC (resident counselor). Each of the three exists in your freshman unit, and they don't write people up or report you. Their job is to advise you to make good decisions."

The College Prowler Take
ON CAMPUS STRICTNESS

The Brown police are not unlike those cool parents you knew in high school—they let the kids have their parties and almost never check on suspicious smells. While the police will nab students for any blatant displays of illegal behavior, they are unlikely to look for it unless staff or students notify them. These days, the main job of the Brown police is crime prevention and not student supervision. In addition, the counselor support system in the dorms provides a safe, open, and fun, environment for the students, not a tool for the University to keep an eye on the students in their rooms.

Although many people do think enforcement is lax, people do go to dean's hearings and letters of reprimand are issued every time. The first few offenses stay confidential, but if the school is aware of a real problem, they will notify your parents and require counseling for social and substance-related issues. Blatant acts of crime against other students, on the other hand, are dealt with more harshly. The University establishes safe, yet liberal, boundaries for students and uses security presence to protect, not police, the students.

The College Prowler™ Grade on

Campus Strictness: B+

A high Campus Strictness grade implies an overall lenient atmosphere; police and RAs are fairly tolerant, and the administration's rules are flexible.

Parking & Transportation

The Lowdown
ON PARKING & TRANSPORTATION

Student Parking Lot?
Yes

Freshmen Allowed to Park?
No

Approximate Parking Permit Cost:
$200-$385

Parking & Transportation Services:
Brown University Police and Security
75 Charleslfield St.
(401) 863-3157

Ways to Get Around:

Public Transportation
Rhode Island Public Transit Authority (RIPTA)
(401) 781-9400

Brown Shuttle Service
5 p.m.-3 a.m. daily
The shuttle runs a set route around campus and promises no more than a seven-minute wait for a ride.

Brown Escort Service
5 p.m.-3 a.m. daily
This service provides transportation between University buildings and off-campus residences that are within the service's boundaries.
(401) 863-1778

Students Speak Out

ON PARKING & TRANSPORTATION

"Don't bring a car. Parking is not the greatest, but you don't need a car because everything is walkable."

"Parking is **difficult but possible**. After freshman year, you can enter the 'Parking Lottery' and get a reserved spot for the following year."

"Parking is tight in Providence. It is best to **get a spot through Brown** because you will get a $10 ticket if you park at night on the street."

"Public transportation is alright. **Trolleys, busses, and cabs can get you around** the city. However, taxis can be late or stand you up, particularly when you really need them late at night or when you need to get to the airport or train station. Fortunately, on a nice day, everything is in walking distance."

"Transportation is wonderful for getting out of the city to go to New York, Boston, or Newport. **There are many trains within walking distance, and they are inexpensive, as well**. Everyone who doesn't have a car pretty much walks everywhere. Everything in downtown Providence is pretty much within walking distance."

The College Prowler Take

ON PARKING

Do you like your car? Do you have a financial or emotional incentive to keep it in peak condition? Have you become accustomed to convenient and free parking? If you answered "yes" to any of these questions you might want to seriously reconsider bringing your car to campus. The cruel winters and even crueler parking cops make street parking a dangerous proposition. Brown parking also leaves a lot to be desired. Upperclassmen are usually able to get a University parking spot in a safe, covered lot, but there are far fewer good spots than students who want them. Most underclassmen are forced to park in a lot that's so far away it is only accessible by car. Private parking lots are the most popular choice for students, but they come at a high cost; some go for up to $100 a month. Most students choose not to bring a car until senior year when they can park at an off-campus house or get a good University parking spot.

The College Prowler™ Grade on

Parking: C+

A high grade in this section indicates that parking is both available and affordable, and that parking enforcement isn't overly severe.

The College Prowler Take
ON TRANSPORTATION

For such a small city, Providence offers a lot of options to travel within the city limits, and to other big cities. If you want to get to New York or Boston, via train or bus, you can walk downhill to the station in about 10 minutes. Within the city, the trolleys that run to the other major areas of town are cheap and run regularly. Furthermore, there are a lot of people on campus brave enough to bring cars, so it's easy to bum rides. Cheap and reliable, Providence's RIPTA system will get you everywhere you need with out the hassle of having a car. Many Brown students use public transportation infrequently because most missions can be accomplished without having to leave College Hill, but when you need them, a trolley, a bus or a train are waiting to carry you off.

The College Prowler™ Grade on
Transportation: B+

A high grade for Transportation indicates that campus buses, public buses, cabs, and rental cars are readily-available and affordable. Other determining factors include proximity to an airport and the necessity of transportation.

Overall Experience

Students Speak Out
ON OVERALL EXPERIENCE

"Brown is an Ivy League school that places more emphasis on the quality of a liberal education than on the way that they are perceived by other schools."

"Given the choice to do it over again, I would definitely come to Brown. Before I came to college, I never thought that the size of the school would be something really important to me. Now I know I would never want to go to a school that was any bigger. I think the size really lets you get to know a lot of people here. All my friends who just graduated are **depressed that they're leaving**. I have friends at other schools who are thrilled to be getting out after four years."

"Students at Brown are generally not competitive with each other; **they do not feel the need to define their credibility by their GPA**. Instead, Brown students are known for choosing to study that which truly interests them, uninfluenced by economic or social pressures."

"I indulged my social life and my academic life. It was amazingly liberating. I think I'm leaving Brown knowing who I am and where I want to go. I don't have the specific plan, but I have the ability to deal with it. I think that's pretty specific to Brown. **Everyone here has a good sense of themselves**. Students go through their life at Brown and after graduation being comfortable with themselves."

"My biggest qualm about Brown is the fact that the University doesn't have a large endowment. I know **a lot of programs are in danger of being cut**."

"Before I came to Brown, I didn't think there would be a big difference between the academics, particularly advising, at the schools I was looking at. It is a big deal. The possibilities an open curriculum provides can be a big factor in your educational career. Freshman year, I took a lot of classes in a concentration I didn't end up pursuing. The switch wouldn't have been so easy if it wasn't for the open curriculum. **It makes both the students and the professors care more**. Professors know you want to be in their classes."

"I got tired of analyzing someone else's material and wanted to start producing work of my own. I was tired of reading the same readings that people had been doing for a couple hundred of years and writing the same papers that Brown students have been writing for decades. So, I switched concentrations and now I feel like I have **a real, personal impact on the department I'm in**."

The College Prowler Take
ON OVERALL EXPERIENCE

Brown has a reputation that precedes itself. As an Ivy League school, Brown carries a distinction that many students desire while knowing little about what they need or want in a liberal arts education. In that sense, Brown's liberal nature and open curriculum exceed that of the average liberal arts school. Many students redefine and rediscover themselves in college, and Brown's biggest strength is that it promotes individual development and self-discovery over the course of the undergraduate career. Internally, you have a lot of chances to make mistakes, which the University calls "discoveries," in the course of your studies. It's easy to change your concentration in the fifth, or even sixth, semester.

Few people who choose Brown regret it. While it's not the school for everyone, almost anyone can find what they are looking for at Brown. Whether you are from New England or Siberia, there are clubs, organizations, classes, and fellow students who share your academic and personal interests. Most people choose Brown for its liberal nature and its strong academic resources, and few are disappointed.

The Inside Scoop

School Spirit

School spirit at Brown is strong, but not necessarily reflected by the turnout at athletic events or other school functions. Although the bleachers may be empty and some people may not even know the school mascot is the Brown Bear, most people take advantage of other chances to show their school spirit. Brown students do attend political rallies, student rock shows, and other performances, art openings and student film screenings to support each others work. The Brown school spirit is most strongly felt in the mutual admiration among students.

The Lowdown
ON THE INSIDE SCOOP

Tips to Succeed at Brown:

- Be very persistent, whether dealing with classes or other University services.
- Always seek the council of an advisor or a dean if you need questions answered or if you are having a hard time. Deans, especially, are there to protect you when things go wrong and can help improve your overall Brown experience.
- Make connections with professors or administrators who can provide good recommendations for you.

Things I Wish I Knew Before Coming to Brown:

- Most things can be bought at school for about what it costs to ship them, so don't be a pack rat when you are moving to campus.
- Upper-level courses are not necessarily harder than lower level ones. Don't be afraid to take harder classes as a freshman if you are interested in them.
- What you take freshmen year doesn't matter, but your grades do.
- Be careful of the credit/no credit grade option. Usually, you end up getting an A anyway or you totally slack-off and get nothing out of the class.

Urban Legends

Josiah Carberry is the fabled professor of Psycho Ceramics ("Cracked Pots") at the University. Many things around campus, such as Josiah's Café and the Brown online library catalog are named after him.

There is a book bound in human leather in the special collection at the John Hay library.

If guys step on the Pembroke seal, they will never graduate. If girls step on it, they will become pregnant.

Finding a Job or Internship

The Lowdown
ON FINDING A JOB OR INTERNSHIP

Brown has the typical support to aid students looking for jobs and internships. The place to start is Career Services. Career Services tires to offer a full range of resources to students: a library with walls of books for researching internship, grant, program and job opportunities and services; a staff that will review and edit resumes, cover letters and perform mock interviews; and a few other specialized services, such as the dossier service which keeps recommendations on file for students, and a Web site with job and internship listings.

In the end, however, most students use Career Services sparingly, if at all, and have at best limited results actually finding jobs through the network. Going to career services, however, can be a great way to get motivated or receive specific advice about cover letters or resumes.

Advice

There are a few good ways to get good work around the University. An easy and surefire option is to work for the University Food and Catering Service or the library system, both of which hire students for all shifts and give good hours with decent pay. For a slightly more academic job, most professors hire students as research or administrative assistants, depending on the department. These jobs are coveted and students only get them by taking classes with the professor and demonstrating genuine interest and ability in the course, as well as developing a relationship with the professor.

Alumni

Web site:
http://www.alumni.brown.edu

Office:
Brown University Alumni Relations
Box 1859
Providence, RI 02912
Alumni_Relations@brown.edu
(401) 863-7070

Services Available:
Alumni Directory
Career Networking
Alumni College Advising
Alumni Medical and Home Insurance

Major Alumni Events:
The biggest alumni events revolve around graduation week when alums are invited to come back to the University for a weekend to participate in class and University reunions.

Alumni Publications:
BAM, Brown Alumni Magazine
BAM is published six times a year and is mailed to all alumni with active addresses.

Famous Brown Alumni:

Todd Haynes

Charles Evans Hughes

John F. Kennedy, Jr.

Laura Linney

Lisa Loeb

Prince Nikolaos and Princess Alexandra of Greece

John D. Rockefeller, Jr.

Tom Scott and Tom First, founders of Nantucket Nectars

Duncan Sheik

Ted Turner

The Best & Worst

The Ten BEST Things About Brown:

1. The new curriculum
2. The students
3. President Ruth Simmons
4. Thayer Street
5. College greens
6. The restaurants off campus
7. Cheap rent
8. Close to Boston and New York
9. Providence
10. The classes and professors

The Ten WORST Things About Brown:

1. Eight channels on-campus cable
2. The paltry endowment
3. Long winters
4. The meal plan
5. Providence parking laws
6. No liquor sales on Sunday
7. No grocery stores within walking distance
8. Bars close at 2 a.m.
9. The stress of the housing lottery
10. Lots of rain

Visiting Brown

Take a Campus Virtual Tour:

http://www.brown.edu/Students/Bruin_Club/tour/corliss.html

To Schedule a Group Information Session or Interview:

Call (401) 863-2378 on any weekday from 8:30 a.m.-5 p.m. Eastern time for information about tours.

Interviews are recommended but not required. Off-campus interviews are offered by alumni who will contact students applying for admission and arrange a time and place to meet. These interviews provide the Board of Admission with another means with which to evaluate the applicant.

Campus Tours:

Tours are offered most days at varying times in the morning and the evening and take about an hour. The office recommends contacting them for specific schedules.

Overnight Visits:

A limited number of high school students can stay with current freshman on weeknights during the semester. This is an excellent way to see firsthand the typical day of a Brown undergraduate. Registration is done online at the Admissions Web site.

Hotel Information:

The Inn at Brown University
www.brown.edu/Administration/Confernece_Services/inn.html
Vartan Gregorian Quadrangle, corner of Charleslfield St. and Thayer St.
(401) 863-7500
Price Range: Around $100

The Providence Biltmore
www.providencebiltmore.com
11 Dorrance St.
Providence, RI 02903
(401) 421-0700
Distance: 1 mile
Price Range: From $159.95

Westin Providence
www.westinprovidence.com
1 W. Exchange St.
Providence, RI 02903
(401) 598-8000
Distance: 1 mile
Price Range: From $239

Directions to Campus

Driving from the East

- Follow I-195 West, exit at South Main Street (exit 2) and proceed to the traffic light at College Street (large courthouse at the corner).
- Turn right on College Street.
- Go to the top of the hill where College Street terminates at Prospect Street, in front of Brown University's Van Wickle Gates.

Driving from the West, North, and South

- Follow I-95 to I-195 East, exit at Downtown Providence (exit 1), and follow the exit ramp along the river.
- At the second light (College Street), turn right.
- Go to the top of the hill where College Street terminates at Prospect Street, in front of Brown University's Van Wickle Gates.

Columbia University

212 Hamilton Hall, New York, NY 10027
www.columbia.edu (212) 854-2522

"Columbia has a lot of grad students and TAs, but you would never know it. They are brilliant, young, and entertaining."

Total Enrollment:
6,248 - Large
Acceptance Rate:
10.4%
Tuition:
$31,472
Top 10% of High School Class:
86%
SAT Range

Verbal	Math	Total
660 – 760	670 – 780	1330 – 1540

ACT Range

Verbal	Math	Total
26-33	26-32	26-32

Most Popular Majors:
25% Social Sciences
15% Engineering
10% English Language and Literature/Letters
9% History
7% Visual and Performing Arts
Students Also Applied To:*
Brown University, Harvard University
Princeton University, Yale University
*For more school info check out *www.collegeprowler.com*

Table of Contents

College Prowler Report Card

Academics	A-
Local Atmosphere	A-
Safety & Security	C+
Computers	B
Facilities	B-
Campus Dining	D+
Off-Campus Dining	A+
Campus Housing	C+
Off-Campus Housing	F
Diversity	B+
Guys	B-
Girls	C+
Athletics	F
Nightlife	A
Greek Life	C-
Drug Scene	B-
Campus Strictness	A+
Parking	F
Transportation	A+

Academics

The Lowdown
ON ACADEMICS

Degrees Awarded:
Bachelor, Master, Doctorate

Undergraduate Schools:
Columbia College, The Fu Foundation, School for Engineering and Applied Sciences, School of General Studies

Full-Time Faculty:
1,237

Faculty with Terminal Degree:
100%

Student-to-Faculty Ratio:
7:1

AP Test Score Requirements:
Placement with scores of 4 or 5

Special Degree Options:
Five-year combined BA/BS

Sample Academic Clubs:
Astrophysics Club, Maison Française, Society of Engineers

Average Course Load

Students can take anywhere from 12 to 22 points a term, which translates to about four to seven classes, depending on how many credits a class is worth (the system is slightly convoluted at CU). Most kids take five classes a semester, but both four and six are acceptable and certainly possible.

Did You Know?

Bring your flippers—Columbia requires all of its undergraduates to pass a swim test in order to graduate. The test consists of swimming three lengths of the pool without stopping, and it is the bane of all seniors trying to fulfill every last requirement.

Best Places to Study:
The stacks in Butler Library, a corner table at the Hungarian Pastry Shop, a comfy chair in Lerner Hall

Students Speak Out
ON ACADEMICS

"Use your own discretion. One student's heartless wench is another's ultimate educator."

"The good things about most of Columbia's TAs are that they are easily accessible to their students and they will try to work with students who are having problems in class. The bad news is that they are **notoriously hard graders** who are difficult to please, and tend to be petty."

"There is a **core curriculum that will take up about two years** of your studies. Although the classes are helpful, if you aren't so sure what you want to do with your life, the core could also hurt you because it prevents you from being able to try out a lot of different things with your credits. No matter what you think, don't take more than 19 credits in one semester. It is not worth it—trust me."

COLUMBIA UNIVERSITY

"A great Web site is *www.columbia.edu/~msd39* [CULPA Web site]. You have to have the professor's name, but **it will give you a review and can be really helpful** in picking classes. Be sure not to base all of your decisions on it because sometimes you may totally disagree. But if 10 people say that if they had a choice between lighting their hair on fire or taking some guy's class and they pick the fire, I'd say steer clear if you can."

"The teachers at Columbia are some of the world's best. However, the **overly-prestigious ones are a bunch of windbags** held afloat by their egos alone."

"I'd say the **math/science intro courses are a crapshoot** and will probably suck, regardless of whether or not your professor is competent."

"Professors here are **intelligent, provocative, and well-connected** in their respective fields."

"All of my teachers at Columbia have been **truly excellent**. However, this past semester, I had an amazing, fascinating, mesmerizing teacher who taught me the philosophy of aesthetics. I also had her for another class, and believe me when I say that this woman made me want to major in philosophy. All of my instructors have been real professors, with the exception of my teacher for a mandatory freshman writing class—that one was taught by a great teaching assistant [TA]."

The College Prowler Take

ON ACADEMICS

A college cannot be considered one of the best in the world without attracting top-notch faculty—and vice-versa. Most students are impressed with the collective knowledge and academic rigor of the professors. The major problems that Columbia students cite are the huge egos of the senior faculty and the lack of individual student-teacher interaction. If a student is sincere and persistent, however, it is possible to find stimulating mentors among the faculty. Columbia is the kind of place where you must find out—on your own, of course—who and what works for you.

Sometimes students have little choice in selecting a professor, especially if a course is offered only once a year. In these situations, students are forced to bite the bullet. Students can either ask upperclassmen for their opinions, or use CULPA to learn about a specific professor. Many view the first week of school as a tasting menu. These nomadic students go from course to course in order to find the professor who best suits their needs, and sometimes they may even find an inspiring mentor in the process. Many Columbia students find their niche in their selected curriculum, while others are equally impressed by the diversity offered within the core requirements. Overall, one can find something of interest in a classroom at Columbia, but rest-assured, it will take more effort than just flipping through the course catalogue once or twice.

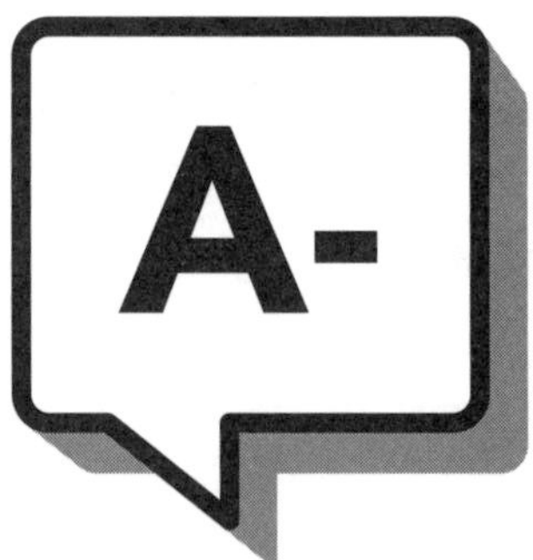

The College Prowler™ Grade on

Academics: A-

A high Academics grade generally indicates that professors are knowledgeable, accessible, and genuinely interested in their students' welfare. Other determining factors include class size, how well professors communicate, and whether or not are engaging.

Local Atmosphere

The Lowdown
ON LOCAL ATMOSPHERE

Region:
Northeast

City, State:
New York City, New York

Setting:
Big city

Distance from Philadelphia:
2 hours

Distance from Boston:
4 hours, 30 minutes

Points of Interest:
Times Square, Broadway, SoHo, Harlem, Wall Street, the list goes on . . .

Famous New Yorkers:
Kareem Abdul-Jabbar, Humphrey Bogart, Theodore Roosevelt, Barbara Streisand, Edith Wharton

Major Sports Teams:
Knicks, Rangers, Mets, Yankees, Giants

City Web sites:
www.newyork.citysearch.com

Local Slang:
The subway is referred to by New Yorkers as "the train." They also say standing "on line" instead of "in line."

Fun Facts About New York City:

1) Two of its many nicknames are "The Big Apple" and "The City That Never Sleeps."

2) It used to be called New Amsterdam.

3) It has 722 miles of subway track.

4) The *New York Post* was founded in 1803 by Alexander Hamilton and is the oldest newspaper in the United States.

5) George Washington was sworn in as president in New York City. Back then, it was the capital of the United States of America.

Students Speak Out
ON LOCAL ATMOSPHERE

"Thousands of working young people populate the surrounding areas. Columbia is located in an exciting city that has a lot to offer."

"Dude, it's New York."

"New York is one of the hottest cities in the world. Stuff to stay away from: homeless people that don't perform on the subway. We are in a recession, after all. **Give your money to the talented bums**!"

"**Manhattan itself is a vast playground** with hip jazz clubs, trendy bars, low-key coffee shops, and charming restaurants featuring every imaginable type of cuisine. And then there is the typical New York touristy stuff like the museums, Times Square, and Central Park."

"I do not like the atmosphere of Morningside Heights. It is **stuffy and overcrowded** with too many screaming children and stroller moms. Get out into the real New York away from the Upper West Side or Morningside Heights."

"New York has got to be one of the greatest cities on Earth. There are several other universities in Manhattan. **Steer clear of the trends** and try to visit the Met [Metropolitan Museum of Art] as often as possible."

"Here's a valuable New York survival tip: if you ever see **a crowd running away from something**, don't be an individual; join the crowd, get out of the street, and run away with them!"

"Columbia is located in the relatively quiet Morningside Heights neighborhood of NYC. It is **a great place to sleep and study before heading downtown** on the weekend!"

"**You really need to do research** if you don't know what is available in New York City. It is truly an amazing city! There are Broadway shows, museums, and great people."

"I love living in New York because you can taste and see all levels of status and class. You can walk off of the campus after getting a bad grade on a test and see a man begging for food and remember how lucky you are; it just **keeps things in perspective**."

The College Prowler Take

ON LOCAL ATMOSPHERE

New York City has something for everyone, and it does not take much for even the staunchest suburbanite to find their niche somewhere in Manhattan. The immediate area (Morningside Heights) is full of restaurants, shops, bars, and cafes. Those who stay close to Columbia do have access to a slice of New York's offerings, though it's clear that the rest of the city offers many more diversions for more adventurous souls.

The urban locale is part of the draw for many Columbia students, but students who prefer the quiet life may find comfort in some of the other geographic regions within the city. The trendy hipsters flock to Soho or Williamsburg in Brooklyn, while art lovers have the galleries in Chelsea, and those wishing to catch the newest play have Broadway and off-Broadway—not to mention "off-off" Broadway—at their disposal. After a little exploring, it is possible for anyone to find their "happy place" somewhere in New York. Sometimes Columbia students begin to feel like the city is going to eat them alive, but after making some friends and getting to know the environment, New York City is certainly a monster that can be tamed.

The College Prowler™ Grade on

Local Atmosphere: A-

A high Local Atmosphere grade indicates that the area surrounding campus is safe and scenic. Other factors include nearby attractions, proximity to other schools, and the town's attitude toward students.

Safety & Security

The Lowdown
ON SAFETY & SECURITY

Safety Services Phone:
(212) 854-7777

Health Center Office Hours:
Monday-Thursday 8 a.m.-6 p.m.,
Friday 8 a.m.-5 p.m.; closed on Sundays, but there is a physician on-call at all times.

Safety Services:
Blue-light phones, escort services

Health Services:
Basic medical services, women's health office, counseling and psychological services, free HIV testing

Students Speak Out
ON SAFETY & SECURITY

"Campus feels safe during the day, but if you don't keep an eye on your stuff, you will get robbed. The nearby parks aren't safe at night, and the threat of being female at college is there."

"Although the campus and the surrounding area are very safe, it is wise to **be aware of your environment**."

"It is very safe. On many early mornings I have wandered in a half-assed state-of-mind around the campus at 4 a.m. Each time, I've been able to eat at Ollie's across the street and continue on with my life as if it were during regular daytime hours. The only thing I'd like to note on this matter: **avoid taking the subway** between the hours of 2 and 7 a.m."

"Columbia is located in **the safest place in New York City**. Enough said."

"The campus itself is **like a citadel**. There are only a few ways to enter the fortress-like facilities at Columbia University, which makes it feel like its own little island village."

"I have **always felt safe on campus** despite being in NYC on September 11th."

"Security and safety are not issues at all. I feel **completely safe walking by myself** in the wee hours of the morning around campus."

"Strangely enough, although Columbia is an open campus, I have always found it to be extremely safe. **They close the main gates at 116th Street after a certain hour**, and a security guard is posted 24/7. It's a pretty small campus, and while Morningside Heights was pretty sketchy 10 years ago, it's really cleaned up since then. I mean, I've definitely walked home at like four or five in the morning by myself . . . no problem!"

"**Security on campus is pretty tight**. They always have guards doing rounds, and they always check up on visitors at the dorms."

The College Prowler Take
ON SAFETY & SECURITY

Most students feel safe at Columbia. It would be difficult not to, since Columbia security and the NYPD both have such high profiles on campus. While it is possible for almost anyone to get on campus, access to certain buildings and all residence halls is restricted to those with a Columbia ID card. With escort services and emergency phones both readily available, campus security excels at keeping students safe.

Simple common sense and street smarts are necessary to survive in any urban environment. Even though the area surrounding the school has been gentrified, there are still some sketchy areas that should be avoided at certain hours. For example, you don't want to make the mistake of getting on the wrong train and ending up in Harlem in the middle of the night. As safe as Columbia is, it is not a fortress devoid of any criminals. Keep your wits about you and keep your distance from the local panhandlers. Most are harmless, but you never know.

The College Prowler™ Grade on

Safety & Security: C+

A high grade in Safety & Security means that students generally feel safe, campus police are visible, blue-light phones and escort services are readily available, and safety precautions are not overly necessary.

Computers

The Lowdown
ON COMPUTERS

High-Speed Network?
Yes

Wireless Network?
Yes

Number of Labs:
6

Number of Computers:
500

Operating Systems
Mac, PC, Unix

24-Hour Labs:
Lerner Hall, Butler Library, Hartley, Carman, River, McBain, East Campus, Wien, Furnald, Broadway, Schapiro

Free Software:
Secure telnet and file-transfer programs, EndNote, Symantec AntiVirus

Discounted Software:
MapInfo, MATLAB, Mathematica, SAS, SPSS, Stata

Charge to Print?
Undergraduates receive 100 free printed pages each week.

Did You Know?

At Columbia, students are given a University Network ID or UNI, which is usually their initials and some combination of numbers, and it is their e-mail address and login to all computers. Students at Columbia, nerdy till the end, often jokingly refer to each other by UNIs ("Hey, jfg32! Get over here!").

Students Speak Out
ON COMPUTERS

"Having not owned a computer for my first year at Columbia, I can say with some authority, bring or buy a computer, even if it's a dinosaur!"

"The computer labs are great, though at times overcrowded. Most people respect the quiet rule—take all of your cell phone conversations outside—which they do not respect in the library. **You definitely need your own computer** in order to survive here."

"The Columbia network is **an embarrassment to higher education**."

"The **limited number of Macs** on campus is not good, but the fact that they are not always operational can really be a problem. That said, there are plenty of working PCs. However, the same cannot be said about the campus printers. There are about two printers in each computer lab, and it is rare for both—or even one—to be working properly. Expect long lines for printers."

"Finding space in a lab is usually easy, but bring your own computer. I got by without my own printer, but the network printing system isn't always that convenient. The network is fast, but **bandwidth restrictions can mess you up for no reason**—like if your roommate is on LimeWire all day, your account can suffer."

"Having your own computer is a must for convenience and academic sanity. There are **plenty of computers available** on campus, but the last thing you want to do is put all of your faith in being able to concentrate at the lab while pulling an all-nighter for a paper that's due the next morning."

"I think it is best to bring a computer, but computer labs in less-populated dorms are **well-kept secrets** and virtually always available."

The College Prowler Take
ON COMPUTERS

While it is possible to survive at Columbia without your own PC, it is certainly not recommended. There are plenty of computer rooms around campus and also terminals for a quick look at your e-mail, but they are usually packed during the day and the waits are incredibly long at crunch times. The Barnard Library is one of nicer options, and there are other rooms off the beaten path in the departments or other libraries that tend to be less crowded. The printers are not always reliable and it often becomes necessary to send a document to multiple locations, just hoping that one machine is working properly.

Procrastinators should definitely bring their own computer to school—even if it's a dinosaur with a word-processing unit. Furthermore, as more professors learn how to incorporate the Internet into their courses, it's much more pleasant to read lectures and notes or download problem sets in your room while wearing Garfield pajamas than it is to scout around for an open computer and a functioning printer.

The College Prowler™ Grade on

Computers: B

A high grade in Computers designates that computer labs are available, the computer network is easily accessible, and campus computing technology is up-to-date.

Facilities

Favorite Things to Do

Hang out on the steps of Low Library and watch the people walk by (and wait for them to trip!), or go up to the roof of a residence hall and check out the New York skyline.

Popular Places to Chill

Lerner Hall, the Hungarian Pastry Shop, Butler Library's undergraduate reading rooms

The Lowdown ON FACILITIES

Student Center:
Yes, Lerner Hall

Athletic Center:
Yes, Marcellus Hartley Dodge Fitness Center, Levien Gym

Libraries:
20

What Is There to Do?
What isn't there to do? There's campus theater, Frisbee golf, a cappella, and tons of places on and around campus to grab a bite to eat or something to drink.

Movie Theatre on Campus?
Yes, Roone-Arledge Theater, Lerner Hall

Bowling on Campus?
No

Bar on Campus?
No

Coffeehouse on Campus?
No

Students Speak Out ON FACILITIES

"The athletic center is awesome, but it can be crowded during peak hours. Lerner is pretty cool; it's the most interesting building you'll see on campus! You can study there, get some food, and meet up with people."

"The **athletic center boasts an impressive layout** and everything else is satisfactory."

"The libraries are staffed by people who actually know what they are doing, and the stacks are well-maintained. The **media centers** can be crowded, especially in the course reserve section. If you have to watch a video for a class, watch it early because there are usually only one or two copies on reserve."

"An area that receives constant complaints at Butler Library [the main library on campus] is the **digital editing equipment**. There are only two stations for the entire undergraduate population, and there is a two-hour limit per session. This makes it very difficult to finish film projects."

"Lerner Hall, the student center on campus, is the only building that does not look like it belongs here. In a community of brick and ivy stands this awkward glass structure that houses cafes, computer rooms, theaters, and general meeting space. Once you get past the offbeat design of this place, you can **enjoy the social atmosphere**."

"The gym needs a little work, but it gets the job done. **Lerner isn't much of a student center**. It's a ridiculous waste of space, and it's really inaccessible and uncomfortable compared with other student unions that I have visited."

"The facilities are beautiful. **No other campus in NYC rivals it**. And it is one of the only places in New York where grass is present. The gym is crowded but nice—truly the best place on campus to spot hotties."

"The facilities are very nice and beautiful, too. Everything is state-of-the-art and adorned in an amalgamation of Greco-Roman classicism. Forget about the Gothic embellishments of Princeton and the University of Chicago, **we've got ancient Athens**."

The College Prowler Take

ON FACILITIES

Most Columbia students agree: The facilities, albeit satisfactory, are not one of the many highlights of the University. The surrounding city does provide plenty of alternatives for those who wish to study or socialize off-campus (with the Hungarian Pastry Shop being a favorite). That said, sooner or later you will need to visit one or more of the campus libraries. The 20 or so libraries are usually full, especially Butler. But even during finals, it is quite possible to find a quiet corner to do some studying, and the staff is generally knowledgeable and helpful. Students have been critical of the media centers located within the libraries, but with a little planning, you can get what you need from these facilities.

Lerner Hall has cafes, computer labs, a bank, a copy center, club meeting spaces, music rooms, and theaters that serve the student populace. Although the modern architecture does not match the rest of the campus, the building itself is useful and the people are accommodating. Many students consider the gym one of the best facilities on campus. Even though it is often crowded, it is well-maintained and also serves as a good place to people watch. It even boasts an indoor pool and track. Lockers are rented on a first-come, first-serve basis, and the demand always exceeds the supply (so act fast).

The College Prowler™ Grade on

Facilities: B-

A high Facilities grade indicates that the campus is aesthetically pleasing and well-maintained; facilities are state-of-the-art, and libraries are exceptional. Other determining factors include the quality of both athletic and student centers and an abundance of things to do on campus.

Campus Dining

The Lowdown
ON CAMPUS DINING

Freshman Meal Plan Requirement?
Yes

Meal Plan Average Cost:
$3,456 per year

Student Favorites:
Uris Hall, Ferris Booth Commons

Other Options:
All the restaurants, from Mexican, to Japanese, to Indian, deliver to your door.

Places to Grab a Bite with Your Meal Plan

Café (212), Lerner Hall

Salads and sandwiches; it's a chaotic place to get food, as it's in the entrance to Lerner, next to the ATMs, and always full. But, they often have good soup in the winter, so it's worth looking into.

Hours: Monday-Thursday 8 a.m.-2 a.m., Friday 8 a.m.-9 p.m. Saturday, 9 a.m.-9 p.m. Sunday, 9 a.m.-2 a.m.

Ferris Booth Commons, Lerner Hall

Stir-fry, wraps, sushi; it's a little more upscale and a nice place to sit with friends or study.

Hours: Monday-Thursday 10 a.m.-9 p.m.
Friday 11 a.m.- 5 p.m.

Food Court, Wien Hall

Taco Bell, Pizza Hut, and the like make this a good choice when you need to satisfy that greasy food craving really fast.

Hours: Monday-Thursday 11 a.m.-7:30 p.m.
Friday 11 a.m.-6 p.m.

John Jay Dining Hall

Everything you could think of to serve for dinner, and a lot of things that never crossed your mind. As a freshman, this will be dinner, so be thankful that you can choose between Lucky Charms and Corn Pops every night.

Hours: Monday-Sunday 10:30 a.m.-1:30 p.m,
5 p.m.-8 p.m.

Did You Know?

Furnald Hall used to have a pub (called Furnald Pub), but the first floor is now a beautiful lounge with hardwood floors and couches where a cappella groups often perform and residents study.

Students Speak Out
ON CAMPUS DINING

"Lerner Hall has the best soup to warm you up on a cold winter day. The lines suck and the sandwiches and sushi are seriously overpriced, but they are tasty."

"The food is very good here. There is nothing to complain about in the slightest. However, the **dining plans are outrageously expensive**. For the price that you pay there, you could eat at a pretty nice restaurant every day."

"During your first year at Columbia, they make you enroll in a meal plan that includes cafeteria food at John Jay. All I can say is that you should **pick the meal plan with the least amount of meals but more points**. The food is not that bad, though. I actually had no problems with the food, and if you don't want to eat at the cafeteria in John Jay, we have about five other cafeterias that have better food."

"Food on campus is fine. The best food can be found in Uris Hall [the Business School]. It's not very junk food heavy, so it's **unlikely that you'll gain the 'Freshman 15.'**"

"**Save your money to eat downtown** on the weekends. Manhattan is rich with culinary delights for the epicurean in all of us."

"Dining hall food is the same as anywhere. **212 is a great place for sandwiches**, and Ferris Booth features healthier dining options like fresh fish with vegetable side dishes."

"Food is not at all that bad. **The dining hall is bad, I admit**. The places where you can swipe your Columbia Card to use dining points are great. There's stir-fry, sushi, sandwiches, and Pizza Hut. You can get pretty much anything you want."

"**Food on campus sucks**, but, granted, I'm generally a pretty picky eater. But I do know some graduate students who are still on a meal plan here."

The College Prowler Take
ON CAMPUS DINING

Freshmen are required to have dining plans during their first year at Columbia, and there is only one dining hall on campus where they can eat breakfast and dinner—lunch is purchased with points at the eateries mentioned previously. Conventional wisdom suggests that students should invest in the meal package with the fewest meals and the most points. While few sing the praises of cafeteria food, it is even rarer for students to totally disparage the grub at Columbia. The dining hall food is okay, and the on-campus cafés have a little something for everyone.

Sophomores and upperclassmen who go off meal plans often voice regrets about not being able to have food at their fingertips, but many rectify this problem by getting a Flex Account. This allows students to use their Columbia ID to buy food without having to worry about having cash on them. The cafes in Lerner Hall and Uris are among the student favorites for sandwiches, soups, or coffee breaks.

The College Prowler™ Grade on

Campus Dining: D+

Our grade on Campus Dining addresses the quality of both school-owned dining halls and independent on-campus restaurants, as well as the price, availability, and variety of food.

Off-Campus Dining

Fun Facts:

The exterior of Tom's Diner appears in *Seinfeld*, so watch out for tourists taking photos in front of it, but don't expect the inside to look the same as on TV—they use a different location for the interior.

Koronet's serves pizza slices as big as your head (no, actually bigger), till 4 a.m. This is a great place to stop on your way home (from the library, of course).

The Lowdown
ON OFF-CAMPUS DINING

Student Favorites:
The West End, the Heights, Caffé Taci, Symposium, Le Monde, Tom's Diner, Tomo

Best Pizza:
Koronet's

Best Chinese:
Dynasty

Best Healthy:
The Wrapp Factory

Best Wings:
The West End

Best Breakfast:
Tom's Diner

Best Place to Take Your Parents:
Le Monde

Students Speak Out
ON OFF-CAMPUS DINING

"The area around Columbia is adorable, and there is everything you can imagine from Ethiopian to French. There's Thai, Chinese, falafel, bagels, and coffee shops."

"Remember that Columbia is in New York City, where **you can get virtually any type of food you want at any time of the day**. There are some great little places around the area that have good stuff. Koronet's serves huge slices of pizza for cheap [$2-3], there's an Ollie's across Broadway for Chinese-American, Tomo for Japanese down the road, Pinnacle has pizza and sandwiches, and there's the Milano Market, as well."

"There are about 20 restaurants within a few blocks of campus. Lunch specials abound with Caffe Swish being among the best; it has tasty Asian fusion cuisine and lousy service. There are sandwich shops, pizza parlors, and diners available for quick bites. **The West End is probably the most popular place to eat**. It's only a block or two away from school, and it offers a little bit of everything, from bar food to Mexican eats, as well as French and Italian dishes."

"New York City has some of the best restaurants in the world. Grab yourself a Zagat guide and venture out! Don't have much money? Head down to **Gray's Papaya**! Best hot dogs on the planet. Want to stay close to campus? Check out the new restaurant row on Amsterdam and 123rd—Max, and Kitchenette."

"The immediate neighborhood is full of restaurants, several of which are really lackluster. For a **good deal on a sushi lunch**, go to Tomo. For Southeast Asian fare, Caffe Swish can't be beat. For an enormous slice of pizza, you've got Koronet's. And for a little bit of relaxingly aloof service, there's Toast, which serves an array of sturdy Americana dishes."

"Oh gosh! There are so many places to eat! And all are **a lot of fun to go to**. There's Le Monde, Deluxe, Tom's, Nacho Mama's, Nussbaum, Columbia Cottage, Cafe Pertutti, two supermarkets, two Starbucks, and who can forget AmCaf and West End—"the Real World New York" went there one episode."

"Although the food in this part of town is good, it's worthwhile to hop on the train and check out **Negril on 23rd and 9th**. This is the best place to eat in New York. It is a Jamaican restaurant with spicy meals that hit the spot after a rough week of classes."

"There are lots of good restaurants in the area. I am keen for salads, so I like the quick places like Strokos and Hamilton's. Both have salads made to order and sandwiches. There are also good sit-down restaurants everywhere on Broadway, including Tom's Restaurant, which is the restaurant they always show on "Seinfeld." My favorites are a French place called Le Monde, an Italian place called V&Ts, and a **noodle shop called Ollie's**."

The College Prowler Take

OFF-CAMPUS DINING

There are only a few other cities in the world that offer the same overwhelming variety of food that New York does. Within a few blocks of campus there are pizza places, sushi bars, Italian restaurants, diners, cafes and just about anything you can imagine. And of course, there's the rest of the city . . . .

Everyone has his or her own favorite local haunt, but the West End and Caffe Taci are two of the best. One special thing about New York is that almost every restaurant delivers until at least midnight, so you don't even have to leave your room to have some great food brought to your doorstep. For students on the go, there's always a local place to grab a sandwich, wrap, or a salad. Brunch is really big in New York, and although many hot spots are crowded, they are often well worth the wait. Don't be afraid to experiment with ethnic cuisines. In New York City, you can get what you want, whenever you want it. As far as food goes, it does not get any better than New York!

The College Prowler™ Grade on

Off-Campus Dining: A+

A high Off-Campus Dining grade implies that off-campus restaurants are affordable, accessible, and worth visiting. Other factors include the variety of cuisine and the availability of alternative options (vegetarian, vegan, Kosher, etc.).

Campus Housing

The Lowdown
ON CAMPUS HOUSING

Undergrads on Campus:
98%

Number of Dormitories:
16

Room Types:
Standard, suite-style

Best Dorms:
East Campus, Hogan, Ruggles

Worst Dorms:
Wien

Dormitories
Broadway, Carman, East Campus, Furnald, Hartley, Hogan, John Jay, McBain, River, Ruggles, Schapiro, Wallach, Watt, Wien, Woodbridge, 47 Claremont

Cleaning Service?
In hall-style dorms, floor bathrooms are cleaned once a day. In suite-style dorms, bathrooms are cleaned once a week.

Also Available
Single sex floors are available in hall-style dorms, smoking is by floor (except first-year dormitories, which are all smoke-free), and special-interest housing can be obtained through an application process.

You Get
A bed, a dresser, a chair, desk, a chest of drawers, Ethernet access, a campus phone, and trash can. Cable service and upgraded phones are available at additional cost.

Did You Know?
Columbia dorms are riddled with serious elevator etiquette. Because most buildings are tall, old, and have slow elevators, it is customary to walk one or two flights of stairs in lieu of taking the elevator. The same goes for walking one flight to the basement for laundry (though exceptions are made for coming up with a big bag of clothes and detergent). Those who disobey these unwritten laws will be subjected to snide comments from fellow elevator riders accompanied by frequent button pushing to "speed up" the ride.

Students Speak Out
ON CAMPUS HOUSING

"Freshman housing is better than sophomore or junior housing. It's easy for a freshman to get a decent-sized single or a sizable double."

"Dorms are fine. They're **almost like living at home**, but smaller."

"As freshmen, we don't get much choice. I mean, I am not saying these dorms are shacks, but I am also not saying they are the Four Seasons Hotel. I think **they are just fine** from what I saw."

"I lived in John Jay my freshman year. I highly recommend a single if you can get it. There's just so much to be said for privacy. I had a huge single and loved every minute of it. **Don't listen to those who tell you John Jay is anti-social.** I've made some of my closest friends on my hall there."

"The dorms are **convenient and pleasant**. Which are 'nice' is contingent on one's living style [single, suite, etc.]."

"The dorms are **hit or miss**. The apartment housing, however, is really much more hospitable and homey. If you're lucky, you'll be placed in an apartment which doesn't look like much from the outside, but that on the inside is beautifully well-kept and refurbished."

"**Furnald is the best freshmen dorm**! It's so nice! John Jay is tiny and lame, and Carman's not that bad."

"Dorms are kind of crappy. **The first-year and senior-year dorms are decent**, though."

"Dorms are nice. Columbia gives you **singles if you want them**. I have actually lived in both of the freshmen dorms. Carman is known to be more social; I liked it a lot. But having a single is really sweet, so I'd honestly go for John Jay if I had to do it over."

Need help choosing a dorm? For a detailed listing of all dorms on campus, check out the College Prowler book at *www.collegeprowler.com*.

The College Prowler Take

ON CAMPUS HOUSING

Columbia housing is not created equally. All Columbia College and SEAS freshmen are required to live on campus and the University saves decent living space for them. Once you have to undergo the housing lottery, you'd best hope that the housing gods are looking down upon you that day. Some suites are spacious with great views. Some singles resemble walk-in closets. There are as many sob stories as there are success stories in this regard. General Studies students are often housed in apartments together, though a housing shortage currently plagues all the undergraduate schools.

Most students choose to stay on campus because there is no better deal in New York. Living with friends can sometimes improve a less than ideal situation, but others say that a small room is a small room. To get satisfactory housing, a sacrifice must be made. Most Columbia students view the on-campus living situation as a character building experience—you learn your limits of socialization and how to live with someone whose feng-shui differs ever so slightly from yours. Also, when all else fails, room transfers and off-campus housing are both possible.

The College Prowler™ Grade on

Campus Housing: C+

A high Campus Housing grade indicates that dorms are clean, well-maintained, and spacious. Other determining factors include variety of dorms, proximity to classes, and social atmosphere.

Off-Campus Housing

The Lowdown
ON OFF-CAMPUS HOUSING

Undergrads in Off-Campus Housing:
2%

Average Rent for a Studio Apartment:
$1,000/month

Average Rent for a 1BR Apartment:
$1,300/month

Average Rent for a 2BR Apartment:
$2,200/month

Best Time to Look for a Place:
Right after you hit the lottery

Popular Areas:
Harlem, Washington Heights

Students Speak Out
ON OFF-CAMPUS HOUSING

"There is an office that helps you find an apartment off-campus. Columbia owns a lot of apartment buildings and the commute in New York is not bad."

"I really don't know. **I just dream of off-campus housing**."

"Not only is it very expensive to live in Manhattan, but in order to find affordable housing off-campus, you're going to have to **resign yourself to some distant corner of the city**. Off-campus housing is rarely worth it because a long commute into the city every day will kill you!"

"I've lived in Manhattan—20 blocks away from campus—and **I still chose to live on campus**. Rent in New York City is super-expensive, so if you're hoping to move off campus in an affordable place, it's going to be way uptown."

"You can definitely **sublet an apartment off campus**. However, mostly everyone lives on campus, as you're guaranteed housing for four years. A couple of my friends are renting apartments over the summer at decent prices."

"Expect to pay at least $1,400 per month for a tiny studio apartment! Sometimes you can luck out, but it usually takes a few months to find a suitable space. **Rental brokers are very expensive**—10 to 20 percent of the first year's rent must be paid to these people who help you find an apartment—and it is difficult to find an apartment without one. Some students choose to live in cheaper areas of Manhattan or Brooklyn, but the commute makes this situation less than ideal for the busy student."

"I'm sure that **housing off-campus is pretty expensive**. I only know one person who lives off campus, and his apartment costs him plenty more than my family can afford."

The College Prowler Take
ON OFF-CAMPUS HOUSING

There are two words that strike fear into the hearts of those seeking an apartment to rent in New York City: "broker's fee." A broker's fee is 10 to 20 percent of the first year's rent that gets paid to someone who has spent (for all you know) all of 15 minutes helping you find an apartment. It is difficult to find an apartment without a broker, but it is not impossible. Affordable off-campus housing is usually quite a commute from campus. Some find the extra privacy to be a benefit and use the commute to study, but the majority end up wishing for a place nearer to campus.

Most leases are for a year, but some find subletting a useful alternative. "Roommate Wanted" signs are posted all over the city, and this can be a bit dangerous (Who knows who will respond to it: the *Grand*son of Sam, maybe!) At least with Columbia housing, there is always someone to whom you can voice your complaints. When you live with strangers off campus you are on your own. Finding off-campus housing without a broker's fee requires money, patience, and a little bit of luck. On-campus housing is easily the best rental deal in New York City, but chances are you'll have to give up some autonomy in the process.

The College Prowler™ Grade on
Off-Campus Housing: F

A high grade in Off-Campus Housing indicates that apartments are of high quality, close to campus, affordable, and easy to secure.

Diversity

The Lowdown
ON DIVERSITY

White: 63%

Asian American: 16%

African American: 7%

Hispanic: 8%

Native American: 0%

International: 7%

Out-of-State: 73%

Minority Clubs
The following give an idea of the minority clubs at Columbia, but there are many, many, more: Taiwanese American Students Association (TASA), Thai Student Association, Queers of Color, Romanian Society, Russian International Association of Columbia, Korean Students Association (KSA), Latino Heritage Month, Liga Filipina, Grupo Quisqueyano (GQ), and the Haitian Students Association.

Political Activity
Columbia tends to be a liberal campus, although there are pockets of conservative strongholds that thrive, as well.

Gay Pride

Columbia is a fairly liberal school in a very diverse city, so there aren't many problems with gay tolerance.

Most Popular Religions

Judaism, Christianity

Economic Status

A lot of Columbia kids come from privileged backgrounds, but there are also a large number of students on financial aid from different countries and walks of life.

Students Speak Out
ON DIVERSITY

"I feel like I'm in Wonder Breadville. However, I heard from others that this is the most diverse Ivy League school that you will ever find. It is not diverse enough in comparison to the city in which it is located."

"It's **extremely diverse** here—it's New York City, after all."

"I'd say the campus is diverse. There are tons of minorities on campus, with **the largest groups being Jewish students and Asians**."

"With hundreds of clubs and activities, Columbia has something for everyone, from debate to fencing. Columbia attracts students from all over the globe. There are no dominant ethnic groups, be they Caucasian, Asian, or other. **The common denominator here is achievement**—not race, culture, religion, or social class."

"There are **over one hundred countries represented** in the student body. No matter what language you speak or want to speak, I would venture so far as to say that you will never have any problem finding an interlocutor."

"There are many diverse things going on **from theatrical, to political, to religious, to musical events**—anything. It's a great place."

"Columbia prides itself on diversity. However, **there isn't much racial mixing**."

"Columbia is **the most diverse of the Ivies**; that's why I chose to come here. I've met people of all types and personalities, and it's been an awesome experience from my sheltered, Catholic school background."

The College Prowler Take
ON DIVERSITY

As far as Ivy League colleges go, Columbia boasts that it is (by far) the most diverse. Many languages are spoken across campus and most cultural or religious groups have clubs or organizations to preserve and celebrate their identity. Despite representing many countries and ethnicities, Columbia still remains a college of the Caucasian persuasion.

Columbia succeeds in being diverse, but interestingly, the desire among students to succeed is a value that transcends race, nationality, and class. The school is located in New York City, which offers more diversity than probably any other location in the United States. With over eight million people and hundreds of languages spoken, any sort of people, culture, or lifestyle you can imagine is not far away.

The College Prowler™ Grade on

Diversity: B+

A high grade in Diversity indicates that ethnic minorities and international students have a notable presence on campus and that students of different economic backgrounds, religious beliefs, and sexual preferences are well-represented.

The Lowdown
ON GUYS & GIRLS

Female Undergrads: 51%

Male Undergrads: 49%

Birth Control Available?
Yes, it's at the Health Services office.

Social Scene
Drinking is what people do at Columbia, that is, if they have any social life at all. Most bars in the area draw a specific crowd, so you have a pretty good idea of who you'll see based on where you go before you even get there. But the bonus about going to school in New York is that when you tire of area bars (or if you never wanted to drink in the first place), there's a whole city out there to explore and hoards of people to meet.

Hookups or Relationships?
Like most colleges these days, Columbia isn't a place where people date. Serious relationships are not an anomaly, but few claim to have met the love of their life at CU. Hookups happen, although some might claim that some of the "nerdier" students are too bashful to be as free lovin' as kids at other schools.

Dress Code
Columbia's got room for all kinds—the indie rockers, the label whores; even the Abercrombie lovers have their support at Columbia. You can wear what you want, but for the most part, it's a laid-back jeans kind of place.

Best Place to Meet Guys/Girls
Your friends and lovers will come mostly from your participation in extracurricular activities, whether it's debate or drama.

Top Three Places to Find Hotties:
1.The library
2. The Hungarian Pastry Shop
3. The bar

Top Places to Hook Up:
1. In the stacks of Butler library
2. Your tiny single dorm room
3. At the bar

Students Speak Out
ON GUYS & GIRLS

"Hot isn't the word I'd used to describe Columbians. We are better known for our 'good personalities.' You want hot? Head down to NYU."

"The guys are bookish for the most part, and the girls are **conservative and very buttoned-up**. I often have a hard time understanding what some of them are doing in a raging city like New York, but I guess that's just one more aspect of the city's diversity. If you're looking for hotties, you've got to go and hang out down in Soho."

"Both the men and women of Columbia tend to fall into one of two categories regarding personal style: fashionistas or it-looks/smells-okay-so-I'll-just-wear-my-jeans mode. Each type is easy to spot. Men tend to wear more hair products than the women do, and it is rare to find girls who wear a lot of makeup. The **low-maintenance** appearance seems to rule the day at CU."

"The dating scene here is strange. People don't really date. They just hang out as friends and maybe a relationship develops, but that is rare. There is an abundance of **happily single people** at Columbia."

"The **good-looking ones are in short supply**, but the good news is that there are many who are very smart and very willing."

"Though it didn't stop me from trying and failing, the **women at Columbia have big egos**, and it's a huge turnoff. Everything is always about them, and it gets old after a while. Hot is a matter of opinion—it's better than high school, I'll say. I think the men aren't so great, but I'm not interested in them, so what do I know?"

"If it's stereotypical hotties you seek, then **check out the gym**. They tend to migrate there in order to admire their own beauty."

"There are definitely hot boys on campus and in New York in general. Everyone is really laid-back. It's definitely **not a school where you feel you have to have a significant other**."

"Columbia's not known for its good-looking people, but it gets better every year! I find that since there are so few really hot guys, **the ones that are hot are complete jerks**. I know this from plenty of experience with the type. Oh, and as for hot girls, guys generally seek the company of Barnard [students]."

The College Prowler Take

ON GUYS & GIRLS

Although most students believe that Columbia is not the place to find lots of hotties, they seem to agree that both the men and women who attend are rather attractive. The place on campus to spot the certifiable hotties is the gym, but people also seem to find visual fulfillment at the local bars around campus. It is not unheard of to have some lookers in class, too. And there is, of course, also all of New York City to ogle.

Many students say that they came to Columbia to study, not to focus on romance, and they are unfazed by the school's reputed lack of eye candy. That said, the students are usually ambitious and interesting, so sometimes mental attraction is more possible and even sought after. Likewise, there are plenty of hookups going on at Columbia, and serious relationships, as well. If you seek it, you can probably find it. There are all types here, from the high-maintenance princesses, to the shower-and-wear-jeans crowd. Overall, eye-candy is definitely there for the taking around campus. You just have to keep your eyes open for whoever best suits your sweet tooth.

The College Prowler™ Grade on

Guys: B-

A high grade for Guys indicates that the male population on campus is attractive, smart, friendly, and engaging, and that the school has a decent ratio of guys to girls.

The College Prowler™ Grade on

Girls: C+

A high grade for Girls not only implies that the women on campus are attractive, smart, friendly, and engaging, but also that there is a fair ratio of girls to guys.

The Lowdown
ON ATHLETICS

Athletic Division:
Division I

Conference:
Ivy League

School Mascot:
Lion

Fields:
Baker Field

Men's Varsity Teams:	Women's Varsity Teams:
Baseball	Archery
Basketball	Basketball
Cross-Country	Cross-Country
Fencing	Fencing
Field Hockey	Lacrosse
Football	Soccer
Golf	Softball
Soccer	Swimming & Diving
Swimming & Diving	Tennis
Tennis	Track & Field
Track & Field	Volleyball
Wrestling	Rowing

Most Popular Sports
The football and basketball teams are most discussed at Columbia, the latter having recently gotten a new coach.

Overlooked Teams
Most often, the women's teams are stronger than the men's (most notably the crew team) and generally don't get enough recognition for that.

Best Place to Take a Walk
Riverside Park, Central Park

Students Speak Out
ON ATHLETICS

"Nobody cares about sports here. I sometimes wish people did because then the teams might do a little better. Varsity sports are a joke. IM sports are okay; rugby and ultimate Frisbee are both popular."

"Unfortunately, sports—of any kind—**do not play a major role in undergraduate life** unless you are a participant."

"**Embarrassing**—but they try so hard."

"Many people are surprised to learn that Columbia even has football, basketball, baseball, and soccer teams. They are there for those who enjoy watching and competing in collegiate sports, but **not many people attend these events**. This is due, in part, to the fact that the fields and stadiums are nowhere near campus and the activities are not widely-publicized."

"There are many athletic opportunities at Columbia, but they are usually **not as popular as they are at other schools**."

"**We have sports** at Columbia?"

The College Prowler Take
ON ATHLETICS

Well, you heard the students; some of them are surprised to learn that Columbia has sports teams at all. Athletics are not a priority on campus, except for those who participate. Columbia is known for its academics, not its athletics, and many non-athletes (that is, most Columbians) take verbal shots about CU athletics any chance they can get. If you asked an engineering student if he went to last week's football game, he would likely look at you as if you asked him where Jimmy Hoffa was buried. Perhaps if Baker Field were not 100 blocks north of Columbia's main campus, students would be more inclined to support Columbia's athletes.

When the weather is good, it's common to see people participating in all sorts of athletics on the lawns in front of Butler Library. Crew and fencing are popular sports on campus. Those interested in athletics should check out the *Spectator* (Columbia's primary student newspaper) to learn more about our Lions. For everyone else, don't worry, if athletics don't concern you, it'll be like they were never there.

The College Prowler™ Grade on

Athletics: F

A high grade in Athletics indicates that students have school spirit, that sports programs are respected, that games are well- attended, and that intramurals are a prominent part of student life.

Nightlife

The Lowdown
ON NIGHTLIFE

Student Favorites:
The West End, the Heights, 1020, Abbey Pub

Useful Resources for Nightlife:
Citysearch, Zagat, *Village Voice*

Bars Close At:
4 a.m.

Primary Areas with Nightlife
Morningside Heights has a number of campus bars, but all of New York has booze and nighttime fun aplenty to offer.

Cheapest Place to Get a Drink
Unless it's happy hour, plan on paying four or five bucks for a pint just about anywhere you go, except of course, upscale places, where cocktails can run from $6 or all the way to $15.

Local Specialties
Because most drinking goes on in bars, the special drink is whatever you want—the bartenders are well-trained, and their bars are completely stocked.

Club Crawler
There are no clubs in the area immediately surrounding Columbia. However, if you head downtown, there is a huge scene of all-night places (frequented more by NYU students than anyone from Columbia).

Students Speak Out
ON NIGHTLIFE

"Parties in the Columbia-owned apartments are different. Since there are no security guards in most of these buildings, the celebrations can get pretty wild."

"Most on-campus parties [frats, service groups] suck; **you can't help but feel lame** at them. The bar scene is . . . a college bar scene I guess, and where you fit in depends on your level of self-respect and what you want to get out of drinking."

"Feeling like a dive? Go to the West End or the Heights. Want to get that downtown feel uptown? Go to Sip, or SoHa. There is a bar or club on every block in the Village, and the bonus is you get to interact with NYU hotties. **Go to Soho if you need a celebrity fix**."

"There's **something for everyone** in New York. Columbia is not known for its party scene, which is, quite frankly, pretty low-key. Venturing out into the city always promises a new adventure. There are great dives and bumping clubs in every neighborhood from Williamsburg and Brooklyn, to the Lower East Side and Chelsea. Winsomeness will get you a long way."

"The school-sponsored parties including barbecues and picnics are almost always fun, provided that they do not run out of food. Each college of Columbia has **special events geared to their students such as casino nights, career dinners, and cocktail parties**. Many students attend the school-run events, and for the most part, they enjoy themselves."

"Some parties suck because there are a few kegs of cheap beer, but there is not even a bag of chips to share, so you have lots of hungry drunk students. Not a good combination. A word to the wise—**have a snack before you go to a party** unless you know the host supplies grub for his guests."

"I did not go to many parties or bars. I am paying outrageous tuition here so **how can I waste my time like that**?"

The College Prowler Take
ON NIGHTLIFE

Comb the world over, and it is impossible to find a place with as happening a nightlife scene as New York. There are enough restaurants, cafès, clubs, museums, galleries, exotic movie houses, theaters, and sporting events to keep even the most extreme party animal/night owl occupied. The Morningside Heights neighborhood alone has bars and hangouts aplenty to fill the desires of the majority of the student population. Private student parties can be fun, as well, provided that the people there are interesting. The various schools at Columbia schedule many events for their students that are designed for mingleing, eating, and on occasion, light drinking.

The weekend officially begins on Thursdays around Columbia, and the bars can be busy. As fun as the city can be, it is very expensive and tiring—bars are open till 4 a.m., and many clubs stay open even later. Some prefer the local scene just because it can be less-costly than going downtown. Others live on Ramen Noodles for a week just to be able to have one night out in the city, but most would probably agree that it was worth the sacrifice.

The College Prowler™ Grade on
Nightlife: A

A high grade in Nightlife indicates that there are many bars and clubs in the area that are easily accessible and affordable. Other determining factors include the number of options for the under-21 crowd and the prevalence of house parties.

Greek Life

The Lowdown
ON GREEK LIFE

Number of Fraternities:
15

Number of Sororities:
12

Undergrad Men in Fraternities:
15%

Undergrad Women in Sororities:
9%

Fraternities on Campus:
Alpha Epsilon Pi, Delta Sigma Phi, Kappa Delta Rho, Phi Epsilon Pi, Phi Iota Alpha, Lambda Phi Epsilon, Pi Kappa Alpha, Sigma Chi, Sigma Nu, Sigma Phi Epsilon, Zeta Psi

Sororities on Campus:
Alpha Chi Omega, Alpha Kappa Alpha, Delta Gamma, Kappa Alpha Theta, Delta Sigma Theta, Lambda Pi Chi, Sigma Delta Tau

Multicultural Colonies:
Alpha Delta Phi

Other Greek Organizations:
Greek Council, Greek Peer Advisors, Interfraternity Council, Order of Omega, Panhellenic Council, Intergreek Council

Did You Know?

Columbia has a chapter of St. Anthony's Hall, a semi-secret literary society that has only a few chapters at elite schools in the United States. While they're known at other schools as being snobby intellectuals, their reputation at Columbia is simply snobby. Typically, they're among the wealthiest students at Columbia. But before you turn up your nose, remember, they throw parties with open bars every Thursday night at their beautiful brownstone on 116th and Riverside Drive, so it's best to befriend them if you can.

Students Speak Out
ON GREEK LIFE

"It's there if you want it, but it definitely does not dominate the social scene."

"Frats and sororities are around campus, but they definitely don't control the social scene. The thing about the social life around campus is that, because we're in the biggest city in the world, people spend a lot of time exploring New York and less time around campus. **Don't come to Columbia expecting to go to big-time frat parties** every night or anything like that. Most of the social life at Columbia is found outside of campus in the city."

"Greek life at Columbia is **pretty lame**."

"The **frats and sororities are jokes**, as are their members. Who the hell pays to associate with a group of frat 'friends' when you have all of New York to explore? What defect of imagination causes this?"

"Believe it or not, I actually rushed a sorority first semester. Unfortunately, I didn't decide to go through with the pledging process. Greek life is not big at all on campus. There's **really no presence**."

"Fortunately, Greek life does not dominate the social scene. When we first got here, everyone thought it was pretty lame. I have no idea what the sororities are . . . except for Theta—supposedly, that's the one for all the hottest chicks on campus. But anyway, I think Greek life is lame. There are tons of frat parties and events, but it's definitely not the focus of social life. Come to think of it, I guess they do have some pretty cool events, like AmJam—it's just **utter and total debauchery**."

"**Greek life exists here**—although quietly."

"It doesn't really dominate unless you want to. However, I think that there were record amounts **girls who rushed for sororities** recently."

"Greek life definitely does not dominate here, but it is around. **Once in a while, they have some great events**. We are actually known for only having a small percentage of our students in frats and sororities, but they are totally there and available for your enjoyment."

The College Prowler Take

ON GREEK LIFE

Students agree that there is not much of a Greek life at Columbia. While there are fraternities and sororities, they do not dominate the social scene. Those involved in the Greek system, however, seem to really enjoy it. Perhaps because there is so much going on at Columbia in the way of academics and extracurricular activities, and with the whole city of New York as a playground, the Greek life does not have much to add to the overall environment and the nightlife scene. Since you don't have to be in a frat or go to a frat to drink beer and meet people, most Columbia students choose not to.

The Greek system does exist at Columbia, but it's very self-contained. It's not the kind of school where people think you're cool if you made it into Pi Kappa Alpha, and most Columbia kids couldn't name more than one fraternity or sorority, if they could indeed name that many. The Greek system is also linked closely to the athletic world—athletes are Greeks and the Greeks are athletes!

Planning to go Greek? Read what other students have to say about Columbia's Greek life in the full-length guidebook available at *www.collegeprowler.com*.

The College Prowler™ Grade on

Greek Life: C-

A high grade in Greek Life indicates that sororities and fraternities are not only present, but also active on campus. Other determining factors include the variety of houses available and the respect the Greek community receives from the rest of the campus.

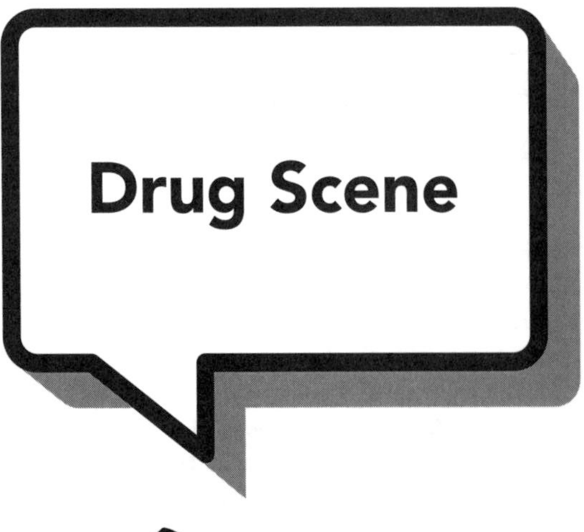

The Lowdown
ON DRUG SCENE

Most Prevalent Drugs on Campus:
Alcohol, marijuana

Liquor-Related Referrals:
31

Liquor-Related Arrests:
0

Drug-Related Referrals:
22

Drug-Related Arrests:
0

Drug Counseling Programs

Health services offers smoking cessation seminars, which meet weekly for eight weeks each semester and discuss relaxation techniques, behavioral condition, and medication options.

In addition to Counseling and Psychological Services Nightline (x7777), a student-run all-night phone line, provides an outlet for students who need a safe and anonymous person to talk to.

Students Speak Out
ON DRUG SCENE

"I don't think the drug scene is that prevalent, but if you want drugs, you can definitely get them. I don't think there's that much hard drug usage. Mostly, it's weed and ecstasy."

"If you want them **you'll find them**."

"Marijuana is the illegal drug of choice, and it is almost always available. It's tough not to be exposed to a possible contact high at most parties. There's **very little peer pressure**, though.The potheads would rather keep their stash than waste it on someone who does not even want to try it. This drug is highly visible in the social scene, but it is the individual's choice on whether or not to partake in this vice."

"**Alcohol, nicotine, and caffeine** are the drugs of choice on campus, and they are available in great abundance."

"There are **lots of uppers**, especially in the scientific realm."

"Word has it that study drugs like Ritalin and cocaine dominate the scene during exam periods, but I have yet to see anything of the sort. Caffeine seems to be the drug of choice, as all of the coffee shops and tea houses tend to be overcrowded all semester long. **Columbia comes off as being a very serious place**."

"Drugs are very popular. But many people I know, myself included, swore off drugs by the end of the year. **They get old**, and the serious abusers are such jerks that I want nothing to do with them."

"**Lots of people do drugs**, but some don't."

"If you're into it, you'll know about it; if you're not, then you won't. There's no pressure to do anything, and you don't have to worry about being tricked into taking something. Almost everybody drinks—**it could be a problem if you're a recovering alcoholic**."

The College Prowler Take
ON DRUG SCENE

Consensus among students regarding drugs at CU is that, if you want them, you can get them. Caffeine is the drug of choice—alcohol, nicotine, and marijuana are not far behind. Harder drugs are not unheard of and are very possible to attain, but they are not as visible, and unless you're sniffing them out (no pun intended), you'd never know cocaine, ecstasy, or acid were present. Study drugs are rumored to thrive in certain disciplines, as well.

For those who do not wish to imbibe or get stoned, you do not have to be exposed to those things if you choose your friends wisely. However, it is commonplace to see even the squarest of students guzzling vodka and/or sharing a joint at a party. Despite the fact that many students cut loose with some kind of substance, nobody will mock you if you choose to opt out. Columbia is chock full of very hard-working ambitious kids who would choose a good night's sleep over seven Kamikazes and a hangover that won't allow any reading to get done the next day.

The College Prowler™ Grade on
Drug Scene: B-

A high grade on Drug Scene indicates that drugs are not a noticeable part of campus life, drug use is not visible, and no pressure to use them seems to exist.

Campus Strictness

The Lowdown
ON CAMPUS STRICTNESS

What Are You Most Likely to Get Caught Doing on Campus?
Drinking from an open container

Students Speak Out
ON CAMPUS STRICTNESS

"Campus police are a rather non-intrusive entity in campus life. That's not to say that they tolerate drug use, but they by no means pry into the lives of the students."

"It depends on your RA and how out-of-control you get. Most students who get busted get **second chances**, and security is more concerned with keeping you safe and healthy than enforcing law. They would call an ambulance if they think you could have alcohol poisoning, instead of calling the cops."

"Don't get caught with an open container on campus, even if you are legal. It's not appreciated by campus security, and you may be put on report. **As long as campus security cannot see alcohol or drug use, then you are okay**. If you are caught, especially with illegal substances, your tenure at Columbia may be revoked."

"I'd say the **campus police are pretty lax** about drugs and drinking and stuff. When dorm parties get busted, no one ever really gets in trouble. The worst thing that will happen is that the people who live in the suite throwing the party might get probation, so they can't throw another party for the rest of the semester, but even that's rare. A lot of it depends on your RA. Some RAs are stricter than others about drinking and drugs. However, I think it's mainly the freshman RAs that are strict."

"They give you a warning if you get into huge trouble. Resident assistants (RAs) are usually pretty cool. **You just need to be discreet** about breaking the rules."

"There's this **group called CAVA** in case of emergencies. They came to your room and rush you to the hospital if there is any kind of dangerous drug or alcohol situation. Columbia is a pretty wet campus, I'd say. But as long as you drink discreetly, there should be no problems."

"I haven't had a problem. **Many smoke pot on campus right in the open**."

"Mostly RAs and building people deal with stuff like drugs and drinking. When there is a huge problem, campus police will get called. No one is too strict; **you get away with a lot here**."

The College Prowler Take

ON CAMPUS STRICTNESS

Students agree that campus security is willing to look the other way concerning first time alcohol and marijuana offenses. Within the dorms, the RAs have the power to enforce drug and underage drinking policies, but most do not. If you get caught, expulsion is a possibility.

Since most alcohol and drug use is limited to the rooms or apartments, it is less likely that students will get caught. There is a big difference between four people drinking in a dorm room and a wild kegger, and the latter tends to be hard to achieve in Columbia's tiny dorm rooms and apartments. If you are obviously not intoxicated, then you can get away with just about anything. If you live in a dorm and are too drunk to hand the security guard your ID yourself (i.e. your friend does), the guard is required to call CAVA (the student-run emergency care group). It's always health over legality at CU, and an underage drunk student who is taken to the hospital will rarely face disciplinary actions. Use discretion. While security is rather lenient, the safety of students is a priority.

The College Prowler™ Grade on

Campus Strictness: A+

A high Campus Strictness grade implies an overall lenient atmosphere; police and RAs are fairly tolerant, and the administration's rules are flexible.

Parking & Transportation

The Lowdown
ON PARKING & TRANSPORTATION

Student Parking Lot?
No

Freshmen Allowed to Park?
No

College Parking Services:
Absolutely none

Public Transportation:
MTA operates the subway and bus
Check out *www.mta.info* or ask attendants at subway stations for maps and schedules.

Students Speak Out
ON PARKING & TRANSPORTATION

"Parking is all but impossible. This is New York. There's no need to have a car."

"**Don't bring a car.** There is no parking and lots cost an upwards of $200 per month. Former car owners may temporarily suffer from car envy—that is, until they hear horror stories of people taking two hours to find a parking spot that happens to be 10 blocks away from their destination."

"The subway is your friend, and you will quickly learn how to maneuver and transfer like a pro. Cabs are also abundant and inexpensive if you are going with other people. There is also the trusty old bus. Any of the choices are **quick, usually inexpensive, and pretty user-friendly**."

"The subway and bus lines take some getting used to, especially for people who love the independence associated with having access to a car, but they are simple to use. Public transportation in New York is cheap, and it takes you within a block or two of where you want to go at any time. The only problem is that Murphy's Law often comes into play when waiting for a subway. When you are running late, so is the train. When you have all the time in the world, the train is there to greet you. This makes planning meeting times a bit difficult. You need to **give yourself a 15-minute time cushion to get anywhere** because you never know if the trains will be there right when you need them."

"Cabs are a good alternative for those who hate to wait for the subway. If you have a few people with you, **splitting a cab ride downtown is not a great expense**."

"Parking? **There's parking on campus**?"

"I commute to Columbia. It's really hard to find parking unless you get monthly parking at a garage; but for that, you need to sign up months in advance. Otherwise, **you can find parking on the street if you come in early enough**."

The College Prowler Take
ON PARKING

Four words vital to living in New York City: Don't bring a car. There is no parking on campus, and local garages are very expensive. Those used to owning a car might find the inability to drive to be quite nerve-racking, but after a while, it is a blessing in disguise. There is very little street parking near campus, so those who do drive to school often have to park upwards of 20 blocks away. It is not worth the heartache or expense to bring a car to Columbia. When you need a car fix, take a cab or daydream about being able to afford a driver.

The College Prowler™ Grade on
Parking: F

A high grade in this section indicates that parking is both available and affordable, and that parking enforcement isn't overly severe.

The College Prowler Take
ON TRANSPORTATION

Just outside of Columbia's gates are a subway station and a bus stop. You can get anywhere in New York by using public transportation, and it's open 24/7. A cab is worth the extra expense if you hate lines and want to get somewhere faster. Unlike many schools, Columbia students rely on public transportation and their feet to get around the city. You can really get anywhere in the city with a Metrocard, as long as you have time, a map, and a couple of bucks—Metrocards are available at any subway station, just two dollars for one trip on the subway or bus.

The College Prowler™ Grade on
Transportation: A+

A high grade for Transportation indicates that campus buses, public buses, cabs, and rental cars are readily-available and affordable. Other determining factors include proximity to an airport and the necessity of transportation.

Overall Experience

Students Speak Out
ON OVERALL EXPERIENCE

"Sometimes I wish I was somewhere more relaxed and warmer, but right now, I wouldn't trade anything for the city. It takes effort; the school doesn't really help you much, so you have to do a lot on your own."

"**It's still exciting just to walk through the gates** knowing that I am part of such a grand institution. I have enjoyed almost everything about attending this school, and there is nowhere else I would rather be."

"I love Columbia. Think **I'll force my kids to go**—once they are born, of course!"

"I am really happy with Columbia. I love pretty much everything about it! I don't think that I could be happier anywhere else. The school is awesome, classes are hard but not impossible, and the **core is a pain, but a blessing in disguise**—I have learned so much because of it, and sometimes, it can actually be fun."

"Columbia has been like a dream to me. There's no place I would rather be. It truly is **the consummate urban campus**, and I have really grown to love the city."

"All I can say is that **New York City is a great place**. The bars, clubs, and people are really cool. They call it 'The City That Never Sleeps.' Well, that's definitely true."

"If I had known, I probably would have gone to Smith or Vassar instead. The academics are really good, but in many ways, **you do not learn enough for the amount of money that you are paying**. I wish I had more caring counselors and people to tailor my program for me. I was one of those people who slipped through the cracks and had to struggle in the advanced classes because I never got my basics down-pat. I learned a lot and had a good experience, but I probably would have decided differently had I known different."

"I love Columbia. I feel like I've made the right choice. There is red tape to get through and a **sometimes-distant administration**, but there are tons of ways to get involved, and the people you will meet are incredible."

"Columbia is great. It's very bureaucratic, and the faculty is not very responsive, but there are so many opportunities in New York. It can be **a bit overwhelming, but it's really amazing nonetheless**."

The College Prowler Take

ON OVERALL EXPERIENCE

Most students absolutely love Columbia. They discovered the school that filled their academic, social, and professional needs. Since Columbia is so selective, most people who attend are thrilled to be here and would never wish to be anywhere else. Columbia has the potential to give any student what they are looking for—be it prestige, socialization, culture, or simply a degree from one of the finest schools in the world. However, the city is not for the weak-hearted. Those who need hand-holding may not find that kind of support here, but then again, they might, if they look in the right place. It takes time to find and access the things you want and need (and often students at Columbia discover fulfillment in things they never thought they'd like before, like exploring the city late at night or finding joy in medieval Italian literature), but if you're willing to work a little bit and leave a little up to chance, you may get more out of college than most of your high school friends who went to smaller, less diverse schools with fewer opportunities. Sure, there are some disappointments and shortcomings, but on the whole, there is no place like Columbia in the city of New York—a place where you can not only get an Ivy League education, but also enjoy everything that the most exciting city in the world has to offer.

The Inside Scoop

The Lowdown

ON THE INSIDE SCOOP

Columbia Slang:

Know the slang, know the school.
The following is a list of things you really need to know before coming to Columbia. The more of these words you know, the better off you'll be.

CC – "Contemporary Civilizations," required political and philosophical thought course for second-year students

Courseworks at Columbia – An online chat room where the faculty posts syllabi and students can learn about assignments and grades. Some teachers are religious about this and others ignore it completely, but knowing how to access it can to lead you to a valuable tool: *www.columbia.edu* (double click on Courses).

CULPA – This is the online resource for students wishing to glean what others think about professors at Columbia. Just type CUPLA in the Columbia search engine and you will find stuff about nearly every professor.

Hammie's – Hamilton Deli on 116th Street and Amsterdam, producers of all kinds of hangover-curing hoagies. Don't worry, they deliver.

L&R – Your freshman composition course, a.k.a. "Logic & Rhetoric"

Lit Hum – "Literature Humanities" in the bulletin; everybody, even the freshmen enjoying this required first-year literature course, calls it Lit Hum. They do not, however, abbreviate the *Iliad* or the *Odyssey*, the two first books on the reading list. And beware of any potential friends who refer to Homer as "H-dawg."

The 'Stend – An affectionate, albeit dorky, slang term for the bar and restaurant, the West End

Jay – John Jay is the dormitory, and its dining hall has the same name. But to all, it's Jay, and if you ask your Carman suite mates if they want to go to Jay at 6 p.m., they'll know you mean to have dinner, not just kick it in the lounge (with the world's ugliest furniture).

Lutomski – Rob Lutomski is, in fact, a real person and is even spotted frequently on campus. But most CU students know him as the man who controls their fate—their housing fate, that is. We usually only see him once a year, during the 10 minutes that we select our room. But wielding that red pen, he might as well be God . . . or "a" god anyway.

Star-Sixing – The ROLM phone system is the cornerstone of Columbia culture. Each student living on campus (i.e. every undergrad at Columbia) has one, and many use them to do amazing things, like record messages and send them to their friends or lovers, without ever making a phone ring.

Urban Legends

Probably the biggest rumor is that it's in Harlem, and it's dangerous. Columbia does border Harlem, but it's in a separate neighborhood. Furthermore, Harlem, contrary to popular belief, is a fairly safe neighborhood—there are a lot of families there, as well as Columbia students who've spilled over into slightly less-expensive housing. Acting like a snotty Ivy League kid won't make you friends in any neighborhood, but common courtesy and human respect will all but guarantee your safety.

The alma mater statue in front of Low Library doubles as a mythical matchmaker. It is rumored that the first boy to spot the owl hidden within her robes will be valedictorian, and the girl who finds it will marry him. Of course, this is an antiquated and sexist tradition, especially since many valedictorians are women, but members of the lonely hearts club seek out this elusive owl anyway.

"Barnard to bed, Columbia to wed." You'll have to come test-drive that one yourself.

School Spirit

Students are often very proud of going to such a well-respected university, but you won't hear anyone screaming "Go Fighting Lions" on game day. It's an intellectual spirit, not necessarily an athletic one.

Traditions

On midnight, the night before finals begin, you can hear Columbia students lean out their windows and scream at the top of their lungs. To some it's a stress reliever; to others it's an unpleasant sleep disturbance.

Things I Wish I Knew Before Coming to Columbia:

- The core curriculum takes a lot of time to fulfill, but it is worth every second. You will spend two years fulfilling your core requirements, but you'll be a better person when you're done—and a lot smarter.
- Columbia is an intimidating place. A lot of kids have a hard time settling in at Columbia because there's a feeling that everyone else knows what's going on when you don't. It's a lie—nobody knows what's going on at Columbia; everyone just makes it up.
- You can really do whatever you want at Columbia, and in New York, and as long as it's not illegal, you can probably get away with it.
- New York is absolutely the most expensive place you could ever go to college, and fun has a pretty big price tag. Flip some extra burgers before the summer ends; you'll need some cash lying around.
- While Columbia is a safe place to live and go to school, it is important to let people know where you will be. Let a friend know if you will be staying out all night. While it sounds silly, it's good to know that someone will know if you are missing.
- Financial aid is readily available for those who need it. While an application process is required, it's rather simple to get some extra help from the oft-generous Columbia coffers.
- Although there are two no-charge Citibank ATMs in Lerner Hall, the lines are excruciatingly long on Thursday afternoons and Friday nights. Get your cash ahead of time or be prepared for a long wait.

Tips to Succeed at Columbia:

- Don't be afraid to march into any administrator's office if you need help or guidance. Nobody will ask you if you're doing okay, but they will stand up and listen if you shout that you need help, whether it's with academics, your personal health, your roommate, or your boyfriend/girlfriend.
- Explore. The more adventurous you are at Columbia and in New York, the more little and big gems you'll discover. The city contains lots of thrills and charms, just waiting to be stumbled upon by you.
- Study what you want and how you want. Columbia isn't really a grade-grubbing place, especially compared to Harvard or Princeton, but you may sense occasionally that everyone around you is stressing out constantly and studying all the time. The less you pressure yourself, the better you'll do, and all Columbia kids will say that they are in the library working on their thesis or studying for finals because they like the subject they're working on, not just because they have to.
- Be who you are, and trust that you will find people that you like and who like you. It won't happen overnight, but it will happen—there are all kinds at Columbia.
- Do not wait until the last semester of your senior year to take all of your difficult classes. While some participate in the graduation events with one class left to go, there is something far more fulfilling about walking with your class knowing that you are a free (well, probably not debt-free) citizen.
- Utilize the campus tutorial services before you actually need them.

Finding a Job or Internship

The Lowdown
ON FINDING A JOB OR INTERNSHIP

Career Center Resources & Services

You can get interview advice, cover letter and resume help, counseling about your future careers, and see career counselors for any other concerns you may have. Check out *www.cce.columbia.edu* for the full lowdown on career services.

The Lowdown

The Career Center at Columbia has a lot of meetings and workshops, but most importantly, they have a comprehensive Web site of job listings. Employers looking for smart kids usually list on Columbia's Web site, which usually has 20 new listings during off-peak hiring moments, and up to a hundred if it's internship season (which starts in February and lasts clear on through April). You can have someone critique your resume at drop-in hours or attend many of the job fairs they arrange in Lerner Hall. Columbia is a great professional choice, even for undergrads, because you have fascinating work opportunities available to you in the big city. The Career Center definitely helps you take advantage of them.

Advice

The Career Services Web site always has good job listings, but that's only half the battle. Don't expect the fact that you go to Columbia to get you a job. You have to look professional and act professional (a lot of New York employers can be wary of snobby Ivy Leaguers, so watch that it doesn't work against you). Take advantage of interviewing workshops at CU if you're not so comfortable in interview situations.

The Lowdown
ON ALUMNI

Web site:
www.columbia.edu/cu/alumni

Office:
Office of University Development and Alumni Relations
475 Riverside Drive, MC 7720
New York, NY 10115
(212) 870-3100

Services Available:
The alumni office maintains the alumni network, eCommunity, and solicits donations.

Major Alumni Events:
Seminars and conferences are sponsored in cities all over the country and world to reunite CU alums. They also sponsor major reunions and events at homecoming and graduation.

Alumni Publications:
Columbia Magazine comes out four times a year and is sent to Columbia alumni all over the world.

Famous Alumni:
Lots of famous people go to and have gone to Columbia. Alexander Hamilton went to Columbia, but he never graduated. On the other hand, Julia Stiles, Joseph Gordon Levitt, Anna Paquin, and Rider Strong are all pursuing undergraduate degrees at Columbia. Unfortunately though, they don't live in beautiful apartments or have glamorous lives—Julia Stiles ate in the freshman dining hall with her buddies during her freshman year, and Anna Paquin is often seen at the West End drinking draft beer. So much for stardom.

The Ten BEST Things About Columbia:

1. The core curriculum
2. New York City
3. Diversity of student body and opinion
4. Access to smart professors and curious peers
5. Culture, excitement, and danger
6. Internship opportunities
7. Under-21 friendly
8. Nightlife
9. Subways
10. New York City!

The Ten WORST Things About Columbia:

1. Its sometimes sluggish bureaucracy
2. Cost of education and cost of living
3. The eternal dilemma—studying or doing something cool and interesting in NYC
4. Cramped housing
5. The time it takes to settle into your niche
6. Lerner Hall—the ugliest, most useful building on campus
7. The fact that it's not as conveniant as NYU
8. Never being able to get a seat in Butler Library
9. The very slow and disorganized mail system and package rooms
10. Going home to your high school friends who haven't had nearly as interesting a year

Visiting Columbia

Admissions Phone:
(212) 854-2522

Take a Campus Virtual Tour:
www.studentaffairs.columbia.edu/admissions/virtualvisit

To Schedule a Group Information Session or Campus Tour:
Undergraduate information sessions and tours are offered Monday through Friday. Information sessions begin at 10 a.m. and 2 p.m., followed by tours at 11 a.m. and 3 p.m. An information session and campus tour is also offered the second Saturday of each month, beginning at 10 a.m.

Hotel Information:

The following hotels offer discounts when you mention Columbia University while making a reservation. Keep in mind that hotels can be quite pricey in Manhattan, so consulting a discount hotel Web site may also be advisable. Rates below are based on double occupancy during peak season; they are subject to change.

Beekman Tower Hotel
3 Mitchell Place, 49th Street & 1st Avenue
(212) 355-7300 or (800) 637-8483
$180/night

Belvedere Hotel
319 West 48th Street, between 8th & 9th Avenues
(212) 245-7000 or (888) HOTEL-58
belvedere@newyorkhotel.com
$175/night

Empire Hotel
44 West 63rd Street, between Broadway and Columbus Avenue
(212) 265-7400 or (888) 822-3555
reservations@empirehotel.com
$160/night

Hotel Beacon
2130 Broadway at 75th Street
(212) 787-1100 ext. 623
info@beaconhotel.com
$145/night

For more information on all hotel accomodations on and around Columbia's campus, check out the College Prowler book on Columbia available at *www.collegeprowler.com*.

Directions to Campus

Driving from the North

- Take the New York Thruway (I-87) or the New England Thruway (I-95) south to the Cross Bronx Expressway (I-95) in the direction of the George Washington Bridge.
- Take the exit for the Henry Hudson Parkway south (the last exit before the bridge).
- Exit the Parkway at West 95th Street and Riverside Drive. Go north on Riverside Drive to 116th Street.
- Turn right and go two blocks to Broadway and the University's main gate.

Driving from the South or West

- Take the New Jersey Turnpike north or I-80 east to the George Washington Bridge.
- As you cross the bridge, take the exit for the Henry Hudson Parkway south.
- Exit the Parkway at West 95th Street and Riverside Drive and follow the directions.
- Go north on Riverside Drive to 116th Street.
- Turn right and go two blocks to Broadway and the University's main gate.

* *Please note that the main gate is not open to traffic.*

Cornell University

410 Thurston Avenue, Ithaca, NY 14853-2488
www.cornell.edu (607) 255-5241

DISTANCE TO...
Boston: 330 mi.
Hartford: 276 mi.
New York: 223 mi.
Buffalo: 151 mi.

Setting: Rural U
New Yo

"My experience at Cornell has been rewarding. The academic opportunities are immense, and the resources at your disposal are not to be overlooked."

Table of Contents

Total Enrollment:
13,655 - Extra large
Acceptance Rate:
27%
Tuition:
$31,467
Top 10% of High School Class:
85%

SAT Range

Verbal	Math	Total
650 – 730	690 – 740	1340 – 1470

ACT Range

Verbal	Math	Total
27-33	27-33	28-32

Most Popular Majors:
18% Engineering
12% Agriculture and Related Sciences
12% Business, Management, and Marketing
12% Social Sciences

Students Also Applied To:*
Harvard University, Princeton University, Stanford University, University of Pennsylvania, Yale University

*For more school info check out *www.collegeprowler.com*

College Prowler Report Card

Academics	B+
Local Atmosphere	C+
Safety & Security	B
Computers	A
Facilities	A-
Campus Dining	A+
Off-Campus Dining	B
Campus Housing	B
Off-Campus Housing	B+
Diversity	B
Guys	B+
Girls	C-
Athletics	B-
Nightlife	C+
Greek Life	B+
Drug Scene	B+
Campus Strictness	C-
Parking	C+
Transportation	B-

Academics

Special Degree Options

Dual-Degree Programs, Independent Study, Research, College Scholar Programs, Study Abroad

Sample Academic Clubs

Cornell Finance Association, Cornell Entrepreneurship Organization, Digital Video Club, Democracy Matters, Shadows Dance Troupe, Ski and Snowboarding Club

The Lowdown

ON ACADEMICS

Degrees Awarded:
Bachelor, Master, Doctorate

Undergraduate School:
Agriculture and Life Sciences; Arts and Sciences; Engineering; Hotel Administration; Human Ecology; Industrial and Labor Relations; Architecture, Art, and Planning

Full-Time Faculty:
1,437

Faculty with Terminal Degree:
89%

Student-to-Faculty Ratio:
10:1

Average Course Load:
5 courses, 15 credits

AP Test Score Requirements:
Possible credit for scores of 4 or 5

IB Test Score Requirements:
Possible credit for scores of 6 or 7

Did You Know?

Cornell is the only Ivy League university that is also its state's federal land-grant institution.

Cornell's Uris Hall displays brains in jars. One of the brains is of murderer Edward Rulloff (now the name of a Collegetown restaurant). Also among the 70 pickled brains is a pickled piece of the pumpkin mentioned above.

Best Places to Study:
Uris Library, Olin Library, Mann Library, Catherwood Library

Students Speak Out
ON ACADEMICS

"When you're lucky enough to have an actual professor instead of a TA, you really are receiving an education from the best of the best."

"The teachers are excellent. However, the thing you must keep in mind about college teachers is that they are not there to teach. They are at Cornell to do research, and they just teach on the side. I am speaking mostly of physics, math, and engineering professors. Government and economics teachers are probably not like that. Another thing about college is that **you have TAs in addition to professors**. So if you are taking a big government class, you will have a government professor for your big lectures and a government TA for your small sections."

"Teachers suck. **They don't care about students** or teaching. Math, economics, and engineering professors don't speak English very well. Many are from other countries, and there are a lot of visiting professors, which means they could care less about their students. Professors only care about their research."

"The professors are good depending on the class. I've had some really good professors, but then again, I've had some pretty bad ones. I think **it all depends on the subject**."

"I'm in the electrical engineering department, and I really like the professors. They are often very busy, but they do the best they can to **make time for you**."

"Professors are generally very good, though rather boring. **TAs are almost always useless** and don't speak English. They teach writing seminars, sections, and labs."

"It depends on the school you are in. Personally, I have found the teachers to be quite brilliant in their fields of study. All the professors that I have encountered are quite **approachable and friendly**, as well."

"All of the professors, TAs, and grad assistants are very capable, knowledgeable individuals within their field. Most of the **classes were very stimulating**, which is a direct result of the teacher's influence on the class."

"Teachers are non-existent. They teach, and you really have no other contact with them. You interact more in-depth with TAs who happen to **know their material inside and out**."

The College Prowler Take
ON ACADEMICS

Cornell University provides access to some of the best professors anywhere in the world. Cornell attracts so many terrific professors thanks to its impressive student population, its state-of-the-art resources and facilities, and its top-notch reputation throughout America's academic circles. However, some students say that professors are more focused on their own personal research than on their students.

All professors are highly qualified, and they are experts in their respective fields. TAs, on the other hand, may not be so proficient. Overall, it is up to the student to pursue his or her interests to the fullest, and to take the initiative to visit professors and TAs in office hours, where they will be happy to explain material in depth. With Cornell's intellectually dynamic faculty base, it's hard not to get one of the best educations around. However, Cornell is notorious for its intense workload. Most professors are unsympathetic and, while willing to accommodate personal needs, they make sure their students are kept very busy. Realistically, you should expect to work harder here than anywhere else.

The College Prowler™ Grade on
Academics: B+

A high Academics grade generally indicates that professors are knowledgeable, accessible, and genuinely interested in their students' welfare. Other determining factors include class size, how well professors communicate, and whether or not classes are engaging.

Local Atmosphere

The Lowdown

ON LOCAL ATMOSPHERE

Region:
Northeast

City, State:
Ithaca, New York

Setting:
Rural upstate New York

Distance from Philadelphia:
5 hours

Distance from New York City:
4 hours, 30 minutes

Points of Interest:
Buttermilk Falls, R.H. Treman Park, Taughannock Park, Cayuga Lake, Wineries, Herbert F. Johnson Museum of Fine Art

Closest Shopping Malls or Plazas:
Pyramid Mall, Commons, Carousel Mall (Syracuse, NY)

Closest Movie Theater:
Cornell Cinema
104 Willard Straight Hall (lowest level)

Famous People from Ithaca:
John Lithgow, Rod Serling, Carl Sagan, Gavin McLeaod, Gillian Anderson, Christopher Reeve

City Web sites:
http://visitithaca.com
http://www.ithaca.ny.us

Fun Facts About Ithaca:

1) Ithaca is home to the Ithaca Gun Company, established in 1880. Shotguns and rifles are still produced by this famous company for sportsmen all over the world.

2) Before the New Year, almost all of Ithaca can see the Ithaca College tower windows with their 300-watt lights shine the last two digits of the current year. At the stroke of midnight on December 31, the 10-story-high numbers change to show the new year.

3) Cayuga Lake splits the upper half of Tompkins County in two. The lake stretches about 40 miles northward from Ithaca, is the longest of the Finger Lakes, and is one of the deepest lakes in the eastern United States at 435 feet.

4) Newfield Covered Bridge was built in 1853 to protect those crossing the Cayuga Inlet Creek in Newfield. It is still standing and is the only covered bridge in the Finger Lakes District.

5) An alternative currency called Ithaca Hours was founded in 1991 by Paul Glover. Ithaca Hours are honored locally by over 400 businesses and are known internationally as an important innovation.

Students Speak Out
ON LOCAL ATMOSPHERE

"Ithaca is decent-sized. Ithaca College is on the other side of town. There's really not much to do in town, but there's so much offered on campus."

"Ithaca is a great place. It's small, but there are tons of things to do. Ithaca College is close, and students come to Cornell a lot on the weekends. But honestly, you don't have to leave campus. **There's always so much going on**—movies, plays, a cappella groups, performances—you'll always find something to do no matter what your taste."

"I love Ithaca. **It is so diverse** and has amazing waterfalls and gorges, and nice parks. Ithaca College is also fairly close."

"Ithaca College is across the hill, but the two campuses don't interact that much. The town is relatively lively and has lots of shopping and events during the warmer periods. **Cornell is a college town** with students everywhere."

"The atmosphere surrounding Ithaca varies seasonably. During the early fall semester and late spring semester, the number of students walking around campus increases. The area referred to as Collegetown is a great hangout spot regardless of the time of year. In general, Cornell prides itself on its diversity and consequently creates a very accepting atmosphere within the student body. **Cornell does not typically fraternize with Ithaca College**."

"You live in 'Cornell World.' **There is no reason to leave campus**, since everything is around you. There is a college town with bars and restaurants to entertain each and every college student. Ithaca College is located about a mile away, and you can meet IC students all around—they also have prettier girls."

"There are a couple of other colleges and universities around. We don't really mix with them, since they're separated. The parks near us are really nice, and **there are many waterfalls**."

The College Prowler Take
ON LOCAL ATMOSPHERE

While Ithaca may be sheltered from certain aspects unique to urban life, the town is actually quite dynamic and teems with action. With two college campuses, there is always something going on, and the outdoor scenery is quite stunning (even in the winter months, however unpleasant). Interaction with students and residents outside of the Cornell community is relatively limited. New York City, Philadelphia, and Montreal are all within reasonable driving distance, which allows for the possibility of leaving campus.

Despite its limited access, Ithaca does offer a beautiful outdoor setting, which allows for many fun recreational activities. Cornell University and Ithaca College create a synergy that makes Ithaca the place that it is, slightly isolated and dreary at times, but unique and special in its own right. Those seeking a more fast-paced lifestyle, characteristic of city living, might be disappointed.

The College Prowler™ Grade on

Local Atmosphere: C+

A high Local Atmosphere grade indicates that the area surrounding campus is safe and scenic. Other factors include nearby attractions, proximity to other schools, and the town's attitude toward students.

Safety & Security

The Lowdown
ON SAFETY & SECURITY

Number of Cornell Police:
77

Phone:
(607) 255-1111

Safety Services:
Cornell University Police Force, blue-light phones, campus shuttles, escort service, van call service, self-defense PE courses

Health Services:
Gannett Health Center offers a wide variety of services ranging from immunization to alcohol and other drug clinics.

Health Center Office Hours:
Fall and Spring Semesters: Monday-Friday 8:30 a.m.-5 p.m., Saturday 10 a.m.-4 p.m.
Winter Session (in January): Monday-Friday 8:30 a.m.-4:30 p.m.
Summer Session: Monday-Friday 8:30 a.m.-4:30 p.m.

Students Speaks Out
ON SAFETY & SECURITY

"Safety is pretty good. It isn't a city or anything, so when you are on campus, you are pretty much safe. There are random incidents, but everyone feels safe on campus."

"I always feel really safe and secure at Cornell. Part of the reason is because Ithaca is such a safe area. There haven't really been that many reported crimes; however, there have recently been **some reported hate crimes** toward African Americans and Asians. This is not the norm, though. I'd have to say that, overall, security and safety is great."

"**I always feel pretty secure on campus**. There are escorts and blue light phones that are available if you're walking at night, so you feel better. I've never had to deal with any crimes, but there have been some racial issues in the past. Nothing too bad, though."

"I never personally had any problems, but in the past few years there has been **a major problem with minorities being harassed**."

"The **campus is really safe**. Ithaca doesn't really have that much crime."

"I felt pretty safe walking around late at night and early in the morning. Cornell has **blue-light phones and other precautionary measures** in place."

"Security is great. I've never felt unsafe at any time at all. With the North Campus Initiative, **you always find someone to walk home with**."

"In four years here, **I've never had a problem with anything**. I feel totally safe walking anywhere within Cornell and Ithaca at any given time. Occasionally, you'll hear about something like a robbery or a sexual assault against a woman, but it rarely happens."

The College Prowler Take
ON SAFETY & SECURITY

Most students agree that Cornell is a very safe campus having had few seriously consequential incidents in the past, the worst of which have been a few muggings and some recent, racially-based crimes. Usually, the culprits aren't Cornellians, but Ithaca "townies." In general, Ithaca is a very safe area, perhaps as a result of its small size and small-town values, and some students think that this campus is safer than most other schools.

With Cornell's alert and diligent police force, safety hazards and security issues have been kept to a minimum. No college campus, however, is immune to incidents all of the time, and, even with all of the precautionary measures, Cornell will suffer a few blemishes from time to time.

The College Prowler™ Grade on
Safety & Security: B

A high grade in Safety & Security means that students generally feel safe, campus police are visible, blue-light phones and escort services are readily available, and safety precautions are not overly necessary.

Computers

The Lowdown
ON COMPUTERS

High-Speed Network?
Yes (in campus housing and on-campus University facilities)

Wireless Network?
Yes (in libraries and some computer labs)

Number of Labs:
9

Operating Systems:
Windows, Mac OS, Unix

24-Hour Labs:
Clara Dickson Community Center, Noyes Community Center

Discounted Software:
The Cornell Store sells computer software at student discounts.

Charge to Print?
Net Print: 10 cents per black and white page.

Did You Know?

Signing up for courses at Cornell is now a cinch. Sign on to "Just the Facts" to pre-register for the upcoming semester.

Students Speak Out
ON COMPUTERS

"Computer labs are rarely crowded, but most people do have their own computers. You'll probably want to bring your own. All of the dorm rooms are wired for Ethernet."

"Computer labs are crowded in Uris Library. Most of the other buildings have tons of computers, and some aren't very crowded. There are also some labs in the dorms. **You don't need to buy a computer**, but it would make your life that much easier. Also, a printer might help because it costs 10 cents per page to print at most places; sometimes, it can be 15 cents."

"You should definitely bring your own computer. **E-mail is very important here**, and it's a pain if you have to check it somewhere else all the time. You'll have many papers to write, and it would be easier just to work in your room."

"Computer labs are really nice. There is a wireless network around campus, and **all rooms have Ethernet connections**."

"Although there are many computer labs around Cornell, there is also a high demand for them, especially at libraries. **Almost everyone on campus has a computer**, so it's advisable to bring one if you can."

"Computer labs are everywhere. You can get into one at almost any reasonable hour of the night. The networks are good, and **lab technicians can help you with any problems**. You don't need to bring a computer, but it is nice to have one at your disposal at all times."

"Computer labs are abundant and always accessible, but I recommend students bring their own computers. **Most of your work involves using a computer**, so having one will make your life easier."

The College Prowler Take
ON COMPUTERS

Cornell's computing capabilities are top-of-the-line. Most students agree that computer labs are easily accessible, convenient, and well-equipped. All labs are outfitted with high-speed Internet access (some with wireless), and any software you can think of. Operating systems include both Windows and Mac OS. Furthermore, the Cornell Information Technologies staff is extremely efficient about resolving problems and troubleshooting personal computing issues.

All libraries are outfitted with computer terminals where you can check e-mail on the run or send an instant message to a friend between classes. Even though Cornell takes computing very seriously and recognizes the educational benefits of staying up-to-date on cutting-edge technologies, students will still benefit from having a personal computer, which will make their work that much more convenient and efficient. With a personal computer, you may still check in with on-campus services such as the Library Gateway.

The College Prowler™ Grade on

Computers: A

A high grade in Computers designates that computer labs are available, the computer network is easily accessible, and campus computing technology is up-to-date.

Facilities

Favorite Things to Do

Catch a tan on Libe Slope, meet friends at Libe Café in Olin Library, eat lunch at the Terrace, work out at Helen Newman, watch a hockey game in Lynah Rink, have drinks at the Regent Lounge, see a movie at Cornell Cinema, watch the spectacular sunset atop the Johnson Museum of Fine Art, and examine the stars at Fuertes Observatory

Popular Places to Chill

Olin Library Student Lounge, Trillium, Big Red Barn, Willard Straight, Terrace, Mac's

The Lowdown ON FACILITIES

Student Center:
Appel Commons, Robert Purcell Community Center, Noyes CC, Willard Straight

Athletic Center:
Friedman Strength and Conditioning Center, Teagle Hall, Helen Newman, Barton Hall, Reis Tennis Center

Libraries:
18

Movie Theater on Campus?
Yes, Cornell Cinema at 104 Willard Straight Hall and one in Uris Hall auditorium

Bowling on Campus?
Yes, Helen Newman Bowling Lanes

Bar on Campus?
Yes, Big Red Barn has beer on tap on weeknights. The Regent Lounge in the Statler Hotel has a fully stocked bar where you may get Cornell Card alcoholic beverages and food

Coffeehouse on Campus?
Yes, Uris and Olin libraries have coffee lounges; Mac's in the Hotel School does as well. Also, few students know about Green Dragon at Sibley Hall. International Coffee Hour takes place at the Big Red Barn every Thursday from 3:30 p.m.-5:30 p.m.

Students Speaks Out ON FACILITIES

"The facilities are pretty nice. The varsity athletic facilities are state-of-the-art. Computers are all modern, as are student centers and classrooms."

"The facilities are great all over campus. Cornell really takes care of its students. The gyms are pretty nice. The computers in the labs are modern, and the student centers are **either new or recently remodeled**."

"The gym is sufficient, and they have aerobics and other similarly fun classes. The **gym courses are very interesting**!"

"The on-campus gyms suck, as they are way too overcrowded. The student centers are pretty cool and have **a good amount of stuff to offer**. There are brand-new computers everywhere now—a huge upgrade from when I first started out here."

"The facilities are nice. Cornell has **one of the best indoor tracks in the nation**. The student centers are also nice. The gyms are another plus; they have nice equipment."

"The facilities and buildings here at Cornell are pretty good. Most of them are new, and **many others are being replaced** to keep up with the strong demand for a high-end campus."

"The makeup of campus can be described as a mix between Gothic and modern architecture. Most of the athletic facilities are up-to-date and very impressive. The computer **labs stay current with new programs and software**, as well."

"There are many fitness centers and a variety of places for recreation—ropes course, racquetball, tennis, squash, hiking, wall climbing, billiards, and dance. **Nearly everything is covered**."

The College Prowler Take

ON FACILITIES

Most students seem very satisfied with Cornell's facilities. Construction is continually in progress to improve older buildings and revamp outdated ones. This includes a project in the Engineering Quad, which involves renovations and the addition of a new building. This project, among others, indicates the importance that the Cornell administration places on the modernity of its facilities in order to promote learning, foster intellectual growth, and make for a more pleasant college environment overall. The architecture of many of these facilities lends itself to a traditional, Gothic, "Ivy League" atmosphere.

Many students happily commend Cornell's recreational facilities, which include state-of-the-art gyms, basketball courts, an indoor track, a cinema on campus, and numerous student centers. In general, students feel that Cornell's innovative facilities help foster its multitude of research, academic, and recreational opportunities.

The College Prowler™ Grade on

Facilities: A-

A high Facilities grade indicates that the campus is aesthetically pleasing and well-maintained; facilities are state-of-the-art, and libraries are exceptional. Other determining factors include the quality of both athletic and student centers and an abundance of things to do on campus.

Campus Dining

The Lowdown

ON CAMPUS DINING

Freshman Meal Plan Requirement?
No

Meal Plan Average Cost:
$2,594–$4,410 annually

24-Hour On-Campus Eating?
Vending machines in student centers

Student Favorites:
Trillium, Appel Commons, Big Red Barn, Terrace, Mac's

Did You Know?

With the City Bucks meal plan option, you can eat off-campus at a variety of places.

Your meal plan comes with a set amount of Big Red Bucks, a declining balance account you use can use at eateries, which you can add to anytime throughout the semester.

Students Speak Out

ON CAMPUS DINING

"The food is actually pretty good on campus. Trillium is the best, in my opinion, but it's open only for breakfast and lunch on weekdays."

"**The food on campus is fabulous**. Cornell's dining is literally rated as one of the very best in the country as far as universities are concerned. As a freshman, you will live on North Campus. The two main dining halls on North Campus are Appel Commons and the Robert Purcell Marketplace. They're all-you-care-to-eat facilities, and the food is quite good. Other than the two cafeterias already mentioned, Trillium and Hughes are pretty good places to eat. I'm a senior, and I'm still on a meal plan because I'm completely certain that their food is a heck of a lot better than anything I can cook!"

"The food, as you have probably heard, is amazing—it's number one in the country for college dorm food. I am seriously **excited to go to dinner everyday**. On North Campus you will eat at RPCC for dinner or brunch on Sundays, Appel Commons for lunch and dinner everyday, or Bear Necessities for breakfast, lunch, and dinner. All of the on-campus dining halls are really good. I would watch out for Trillium, Ivy Room, and Cascadeli, but you do not have to worry about food at Cornell."

"It's very diverse. The food is good, but **a bit expensive**. You can get anything you want from pizza to sushi."

"The food here is supposedly the best in the country, I think partly because we have such a good hotel school. For dining hall food, it's great. We make fun of it anyway, though. **The best dining halls are on North** where the freshmen are. I like RPU on North and Okenshield's on Central Campus."

"Food on campus is awesome. There's lots of variety. I think **there are over 20 places to eat on campus**. RPU, North Star, Okenshield's, and Ivy Room are all great. Some of the dining halls are all-you-can-eat, while others are à la carte. You have different varieties of food from Chinese to Italian to all-American. I have to give an A+ for food at Cornell. But watch out . . . lots of people gain a substantial amount of weight their first year."

"**Cornell dining is second to none**. The dining halls are impeccable, and the food is scrumptious. Any dining facility is good, particularly Okenshield's, Noyes, Harvest Buffet, and Robert Purcell."

"The dining halls are excellent. I find it difficult to get better food than that which you find here on campus. I've **never heard people complain about the food** from the dining halls on North campus."

"Cornell has **one of the highest ratings for on-campus dining**. It's really great! The community centers have the best dining halls."

The College Prowler Take
ON CAMPUS DINING

Campus dining is first-rate and totally compensates for hefty meal plan pricing. Diversity of selection is impressive, and some of the all-you-can-eat facilities offer a variety of different buffet assortments: deli, pasta bar, grill, stir-fry, chef's corner, Kosher corner, waffle bar, salad bar, smoothie stop, and freshly baked dessert area. The atmosphere in most dining rooms is very pleasant and conducive to a refreshing social experience. Each dining hall has a unique atmosphere. Ivy Room, for example, provides a traditional Ivy League atmosphere with a jukebox that loudly plays old-time favorites. Cascadeli offers outdoor seating on Willard Straight's balcony overlooking downtown Ithaca and Cayuga Lake.

Chefs at the dining halls really take pride in their work and reputation, and they keep students happy and coming back for more. Even those who live off campus are continually tempted to visit on-campus eateries for all-you-can-eat dinners and Sunday brunch. A caveat: With such great food and unlimited portions, many students quickly put on the "Freshman 15." But, thanks to the Cornell Fitness Centers, at least you can justify your indulgences.

The College Prowler™ Grade on
Campus Dining: A+

Our grade on Campus Dining addresses the quality of both school-owned dining halls and independent on-campus restaurants as well as the price, availability, and variety of food.

Off-Campus Dining

The Lowdown
ON OFF-CAMPUS DINING

Student Favorites:
Plum Tree, John Thomas Steakhouse, Just a Taste, Pangea, Rulloff's, Bistro Q, Coyote Loco, Maxie's, Regent Lounge, Madeline's, The Nines

Closest Grocery Stores:
Wegman's, PNC Market, Jason's Deli (in Collegetown)

Best Pizza:
Mama Teresa's

Best Chinese:
Jade Garden

Best Breakfast:
Hughes Dining

Best Wings:
Wings over Ithaca

Best Healthy:
Aladdin's/Moosewood

Best Place to Take Your Parents:
Just a Taste, the Heights, Benn Conger Inn, Lost Dog Café

Fun Facts:

1) Purity Ice Cream, founded by Leo Guenert who graduated from Cornell in 1920, is produced in Ithaca and sells 40 different flavors of ice cream.
   700 Cascadilla Street, 11 a.m.-11 p.m.
   (607) 272-1545

2) D.P. Dough, located in downtown Ithaca, makes for a great late night snack

3) *http://www.campusfood.com* allows you to conveniently order food directly from your computer's Internet browser and offers daily specials and discount prices.

4) Moosewood Restaurant is an acclaimed vegetarian restaurant that also makes famous cookbooks. It was named one of the 13 most influential restaurants of the 20th century by *Bon Appetit* magazine—*http://www.moosewoodrestaurant.com/index.html.*

Students Speak Out
ON OFF-CAMPUS DINING

"The off-campus restaurants are very diverse, from Pita Pit to Indian cuisine, and most of these can be found in Collegetown, as well."

"The restaurants in Collegetown are **pretty good for quick food**—Mama T's, Collegetown Pizza, Smoothie Hut, Collegetown Bagels, Pita Pit, Hong Kong. Other places in Collegetown are decent for a nice sit-down dinner—Rulloff's and Aladdin's. Ithaca Commons also has decent sit-down dinner places, and the local malls have the standard fast food courts."

"The restaurants around here are all right. They're **good for college students**. Go there with people who like to eat. In Collegetown; there are tons of places to eat fast. It's great!"

"It's surprising and especially pleasing to find that excellent restaurants are plentiful around the Finger Lakes region. Pangea in downtown Ithaca offers an **exotic menu of Asian-Infusion**. Plum Tree, the 'in spot' on weekends, serves first rate Japanese and has the best sake ombs around. John Thomas is renowned for its steaks, and Just a Taste is famous for its Tapas menu and diverse wine selection. The options are numerous, so make sure you start looking around early as an underclassman, and save up leftover beer money for some quality and enjoyable dining experiences."

"When you have the money to eat off campus, any restaurant in Ithaca is nice. **It's really expensive**, though."

"Off-campus restaurants are good. It's your typical college town, so there are all kinds of restaurants—just about everything imaginable. There's a Chinese restaurant that's supposed to be rated as one of the best in New York. There's also a **vegetarian restaurant, Moosewood, that's literally world famous**. If you tell people that you go to school in Ithaca, often you'll find someone who will ask you if you've ever been there. There are really too many restaurants to name."

"The restaurants off campus are pretty good and varied. We have McDonald's, Burger King, and Wendy's, but we also have nice places that have different kinds of food. It's not too expensive either. **Billy Bob Jack's is good for BBQ**."

"In Collegetown there is Plum Tree [Japanese], College Cafe [Korean], Mama Teresa's [pizza], Stella's [coffeehouse], Lemon Leaf [Thai], Collegetown Bagels [bagels and coffee], and Rulloff's [for brunch, lunch, and dinner, with a bar]. **Ithaca also has some really cute places to eat**: Moosewood, Lucatelli's, and the Station—a really cute, old train station—are all great."

"There are **definitely some nice restaurants** around. I suggest Madeline's, Maxi's, Pangea, Boatyard, and Plum Tree."

The College Prowler Take
ON OFF-CAMPUS DINING

Off-campus dining options are substantial, and most students are very pleased with Ithaca's offerings, especially given the fact that one wouldn't expect such quality dining in rural upstate New York. If you're looking for a particular food or atmosphere, Thai or vegetarian, romantic or rowdy, Ithaca is sure to have it. Many students enjoy the Boatyard Grill, Coyote Loco, and Plum Tree. Off-campus dining makes for a great change of scenery and pace from on-campus eating experiences.

Collegetown, which is in walking distance from Central Campus and most student residences, has an impressive selection of menus for either a quick stop or a sit-down lunch or dinner. Pricing varies from place to place but isn't typically exorbitant. The fact that everything is in such close proximity makes off-campus dining very convenient and satisfying.

The College Prowler™ Grade on
Off-Campus Dining: B

A high Off-Campus Dining grade implies that off-campus restaurants are affordable, accessible, and worth visiting. Other factors include the variety of cuisine and the availability of alternative options (vegetarian, vegan, Kosher, etc.).

Campus Housing

The Lowdown
ON CAMPUS HOUSING

Undergraduates living on-campus:
54%

Number of Dormitories:
34

Room Types:
Singles, doubles

Best Dorms:
Donlon, Mews, High Rise 5, Cascadilla Hall, Sheldon Court (for upperclassmen only)

Worst Dorms:
Balch, Low Rise 7, Townhouses

Bed Type:
Twin, bunk beds

Available for Rent:
Microwaves, refrigerators

Cleaning Service?
Yes—Appel Commons, RPCC, Noyes Community Center

You Get:
Bed, desk, night table, closet, desk lamp, dresser, desk chair, phone, Internet access, cable

CORNELL UNIVERSITY

Did You Know?

On the first day of finals week, freshmen emerge from their dorms on balconies and dreadfully shriek into the darkness of the night (also called Midnight Howl).

If you are a first-year student, you will reside on North Campus in one of the program houses or traditional residence halls, where you will find an abundance of resources, delicious foods, fun things to do, and many other social and academic opportunities.

Students Speak Out

ON CAMPUS HOUSING

"The dorms for the freshmen are very nice. Mews and Court are the newest and have air conditioning throughout. After first year, most students tend to live off campus."

"I happen to be a huge fan of the Dickson Complex. It's mostly singles, and I think it's the most beautiful dorm on North Campus. It's also coed. **Balch is also quite beautiful** and has quite nice rooms, but it's a women's dorm."

"I think the two new residence halls, Mews and Court, are nice, but I think that they're fairly ugly. The dorms are great, though. They really offer a very fun atmosphere. They have study lounges and kitchens. The RAs [resident advisors] also put on programs--**activities for the residents when they're not busy studying**. These programs can range from movie and popcorn nights to trips to New York for Broadway shows."

"Pray that you get Donlon! It's not the nicest in terms of quality, but it's the most social—**you'll meet tons of people** and make great friends. I loved living there this year. The new dorms, Court and Mews, are really nice too. Dickson is okay. Balch isn't very fun because it's so quiet."

"Dorms vary, but most are okay. I lived in Clara Dickson and the Townhouses—both on North Campus. I hated the Townhouses, which aren't even really dorms, but more like four person on-campus apartments that are located so far away they aren't even in Ithaca, they're actually in Cayuga Heights. Dickson was a lot of fun, though; I loved freshman year there. **Most of the dorms on North are good**, but as I said, avoid the Townhouses; they're all freshmen now."

"There are a wide variety of dorms at Cornell. **Freshmen get the new, modern dorms** on North Campus, while upperclassmen are typically stuck down on West Campus in the older, Gothic looking buildings."

"Dorms are state-of-the-art, since major renovations have been in progress on North Campus where all freshmen are now housed. The dorms are much different from when I was a freshman. **Try to get into a coed dorm**, of course."

"Since I've lived in the dorms for four years, I obviously like them a lot. **As a freshman, you will live on North Campus**. All of the freshmen live there."

"There are two types of dorms: program houses and traditional halls. **Program houses have a specific theme**, like music or culture, for instance. If you are interested in a program house, then you apply to that house, and hopefully, you'll get accepted. The traditional halls are regular. They're all quite nice, although some are better than others."

The College Prowler Take
ON CAMPUS HOUSING

Students tend to agree that campus housing for freshmen is much more convenient and enjoyable than on-campus housing for upperclassmen. This might be the direct result of a recent initiative that has permanently situated all freshmen on North Campus. Mews and Court Halls, two new dorms, are the envy of every freshman, so consider yourself lucky if you end up there. Donlon, although not as nice, is one of the most social dorms, a result of its long stretching hallways. Whether you have a single or a double, you'll be sure to meet many peers in your suites and hallways. Also, each dorm has its own creature comforts: student lounges, computer stations, kitchens, balconies, and TV rooms.

Resident advisors on each floor coordinate programming and activities with their residents and organize trips to places like the Big Apple and Montreal. Cascadilla, a unique dorm that houses non-freshmen, is located right in the center of Collegetown and is the dorm of choice for those who don't move off campus or into a fraternity or sorority house.

The College Prowler™ Grade on
Campus Housing: B

A high Campus Housing grade indicates that dorms are clean, well-maintained, and spacious. Other determining factors include variety of dorms, proximity to classes, and social atmosphere.

Off-Campus Housing

The Lowdown
ON OFF-CAMPUS HOUSING

Undergrads in Off-Campus Housing:
46%

Average Rent for a Studio Apartment:
$700/month

Average Rent for a 1BR Apartment:
$600/month

Average Rent for a 2BR Apartment:
$900/month

Popular Areas:
312 College Avenue, Collegetown Plaza, Eddygate Park Apartments, Ravenwood Apartments, Gun Hill Residences, Valentine Park Apartments

Best Time to Look for a Place:
November; housing options quickly decrease over time and especially after winter break.

Students Speak Out
ON OFF-CAMPUS HOUSING

"I think off-campus housing is best. After freshman year in the dorms, I moved into a house. Most people move to off-campus housing after freshman year."

"There's lots of off-campus housing, and **everything is about a 10-minute walk** away from campus."

"I'm actually living off-campus next year because it's **easy to lose out in the housing lottery** for sophomore year. But don't worry; as long as you start early, off-campus housing is easy to find."

"**There's plenty of it if you don't mind living further away**. People usually want to live as close to Collegetown as possible, so those places go the fastest, and they are the most expensive. I live about 10 minutes from campus, I and have no problem with the walk. It's a really nice house, and I pay less than people who live in houses far worse and are only five minutes closer to campus."

"Roughly one-third of freshmen students will become part of the Greek system, so that offers one housing solution. If freshmen plan on living off-campus, they should **start looking early** for two reasons: 1) off-campus housing goes fast [middle of first semester] and 2) there is a lottery based on seniority to determine who gets which dorms. Think, and prepare ahead!"

"There are many apartments around campus that are **easy to find and quite affordable**—only a short walk away from class. I think it's most important to live solely with the people who you are closest with—your best friends."

"Most people live off campus following freshman year. Word to the wise: **Start early, in November**, and look at many different places."

"Housing off-campus is very convenient and definitely worthwhile. However, having to deal with Cornell's ridiculously complicated and stringent housing regulations are a hassle. Although Cornell tries to regulate off-campus housing, you have much more freedom, allowing for a **more relaxing and enjoyable living situation**."

The College Prowler Take
ON OFF-CAMPUS HOUSING

Many students at Cornell tend to live off campus after freshman year. Those who do, agree that off-campus housing is the best choice, allowing for much more of a social, independent, and unrestrained living environment. While options are abundant, it's advisable to begin searching as early as possible. The hot spots, clustered directly in Collegetown and within walking distance from campus, are snatched up quickly. These options are also probably the most expensive, but by far the most luxurious and convenient, as well. Other possibilities that are not as close are generally a lot more affordable.

Regardless of living preference, Ithaca has numerous options, all of which are feasible, and each of which has its own perks (utilities inclusive, gym, parking, etc.). Some students even live on Cayuga Lake, which offers spectacular views—at the expense of a nasty commute to campus.

The College Prowler™ Grade on

Off-Campus Housing: B+

A high grade in Off-Campus Housing indicates that apartments are of high quality, close to campus, affordable, and easy to secure.

Diversity

The Lowdown
ON DIVERSITY

White: 66%

Asian American: 16%

African American: 5%

Hispanic: 5%

Native American: 0%

International: 7%

Out-of-State: 60%

Need help finding the right campus organization for you? For a detailed listing of all minority affiliated clubs on campus, check out the College Prowler book on Cornell available at *www.collegeprowler.com.*

Students Speak Out
ON DIVERSITY

"The campus is extremely diverse. I can guarantee that people on your floor will be from all over the country and possibly from all over the world."

"It's pretty much **white, Asian, and Indian**."

"Geographically, there are a lot of New York City and Long Island students. Interest-wise, it's extremely diverse. Racially, it's **pretty diverse and getting better**."

"The campus is very diverse. You see **people from all walks of life** here, and it's a lot of fun getting to explore different cultures and ethnicities."

"Cornell offers a very diverse student body with a club for each. It's impossible for one not to **find a club or group** that he or she doesn't fit in."

"**All types of diversity**. I estimate 30 percent Asian, 40 percent white upper-class from NYC, 10 percent African Americans, and 20 percent from everywhere else."

"You can find people from all over the world; however, I would say **Cornell is predominantly white** and Asian."

"Demographically, the campus is very diverse, but **people tend to hang out with others similar to themselves**. In this respect, there isn't much social integration."

"Campus is very diverse. International students are numerous, and it's hard not to **encounter students with unique backgrounds or clashing interests** in your classes. That exposure, though, in my experience, builds tolerance and develops new insights."

The College Prowler Take
ON DIVERSITY

Overall, students are ambivalent in regard to diversity at Cornell. Some feel that the school is populated by a majority of Asians and whites from the New York City and Long Island area. Certain Cornellians feel separated from minority groups, while others quote having an ethnically and culturally diverse mix of friends. One thing is certain though—with its vast population, Cornell is a melting pot of different students with unique intellectual interests and extraordinary talents. Without a doubt, the student body represents a broad range of ideas and backgrounds.

Although integration with minority groups may be less likely in common social scenarios, in class you're certain to interact with many different types of people from diverse international origins and cultures.

The College Prowler™ Grade on
Diversity: B

A high grade in Diversity indicates that ethnic minorities and international students have a notable presence on campus and that students of different economic backgrounds, religious beliefs, and sexual preferences are well-represented.

The Lowdown
ON GUYS & GIRLS

Women Undergrads: 49%

Men Undergrads: 51%

Birth Control Available?
Yes—Gannet Health Center

Social Scene
Cornell's diverse student body affords the chance for various unique interactions with many groups of guys and girls from a wide array of different backgrounds. It's not hard to meet friendly students with similar interests as yours. In general, the people at Cornell are very social, and you'll always find fraternity parties and bars packed to the brim with a very good ratio of guys to girls.

Hookups or Relationships?
With its large student population, you'll find a little bit of everything: lots of non-committal, random hookups, as well as many serious, long-term relationships. If you're looking for an evening fling, it's not hard to find, especially at an after-hours fraternity party. Interestingly, rumor has it that an estimated and staggering 75 percent of couples who leave Cornell together find themselves married thereafter. So, if you're still in that relationship at graduation, then carefully consider the possibilities and realities of a wedding date in the near future!

Best Place to Meet Guys/Girls

Meeting guys and girls is not difficult at Cornell, especially since you'll find yourself in close proximity during sections and seminars. Initially, for freshmen, the best place to meet is in the dorms and at the dining halls that promote a relaxed and social ambience.

Dress Code

Students tend to dress very casually when they go out. With the exception of some girls who flaunt their expensive purses on campus, most students dress down for class. In the evening, everyone makes a concerted effort to look half-decent. Of course, there are special occasions that might necessitate a more formal dress code. Fraternities and sororities have semi-annual formals and other fancy occasions to which anyone might be invited. The University also hosts several formal special events throughout the year.

Top Three Places to Find Hotties:

1. The Gorges
2. The Hotel School
3. Ithaca College

Top Places to Hook Up:

1. McGraw Tower
2. The Suspension Bridge
3. Olin Library Stacks
4. The Arts Quad
5. Libe Slope

Students Speak Out
ON GUYS & GIRLS

"You'll find someone if you look extremely hard—harder than you've ever looked before, anywhere!"

"I forget where we ranked, but I think Cornell is **rated fifth for having the hottest guys**. They didn't rank the girls. I kind of agree with that, but I've had no problem finding cuties."

"There are **good-looking guys on campus**, as well as pretty girls. There is a lot of diversity on the campus. At parties, I would see a cute guy, and then I would question, 'Is he from Cornell or Ithaca College?' A lot of Ithaca College students go to Cornell frat parties."

"I am a guy, and to me, there seems to be **several good-looking women** on campus."

"Good-looking guys, average women who **think they're better than the rest of the population**."

"I hope you like books, snow, and alcohol because the **girls offer very little** at Cornell. However, if you're a girl looking for a guy, Cornell could easily be described as heaven."

"Some guys are cool, and some are dorks. Most hang out with guys like themselves (i.e. fraternities), and isolate themselves from those unlike them. This increases hostilities between different groups on campus. Feuds between fraternities are common. The **girls are mostly ugly and annoying**. In an exceptional case, you may find a cool, attractive female, but that is extremely rare."

"It's no secret that the quality of females around campus is seriously lacking. That may even be an understatement. Maybe this comes at the cost of an Ivy League education. Everyone has his or her own unique niche, but the Greek scene entirely pervades the social scene around campus. If you're a good-looking girl in a sorority, then you'll have the time of your life. For guys, unfortunately, **be prepared to put on your Cornell goggles**. If Greek life is up your alley, then you'll find many of your cohorts at the bars on weekends. If you prefer to steer clear of that scene, house parties and places like Stella's might be more enjoyable."

The College Prowler Take
ON GUYS & GIRLS

Although the guys seem to be rated slightly higher than the girls, the University is huge so there are plenty of choices. There's no need to worry that all the males and females are complete dorks, either. There are some dorks, if that's what you're looking for, and some frat boys and some sorority girls.

There are also lots of organizations to meet gay, lesbian, bisexual, questioning, or transgender students if that's what you are looking for too. At Cornell, like anywhere else, there are plenty of fish in the sea. Some you'll catch, some will get away. It's that simple.

The College Prowler™ Grade on

Guys: B+

A high grade for Guys indicates that the male population on campus is attractive, smart, friendly, and engaging, and that the school has a decent ratio of guys to girls.

The College Prowler™ Grade on

Girls: C-

A high grade for Girls not only implies that the women on campus are attractive, smart, friendly, and engaging, but also that there is a fair ratio of girls to guys.

Athletics

The Lowdown
ON ATHLETICS

Athletic Division:
NCAA Division I

Conference:
Ivy League

School Mascot:
Big Red—Contrary to popular belief, the Big Red Bear is not the official Cornell mascot, since the University doesn't have any official mascot and is simply the Big Red.

Getting Tickets
Call the ticket office at (607) 254-BEAR for information on all ticket availability.

Gyms/Facilities
Andrew P. Stifel Fencing Salle, Bartels Hall, Barton Hall, Belkin Squash Courts, Charles F. Berman Field, David F. Hoy Field, Doris Robison Shell House, Friedman Strength and Conditioning Center, Helen Newman Hall Recreation Center, James Lynah Rink, John Collyer Boathouse, the Moakley Course, Newman Arena, Niemand-Robison Softball Field, Oxley Equestrian Center, Reis Tennis Center, the Richard M. Ramin Multipurpose Room, Robert J. Kane Sports Complex, Robert Trent Jones Golf Course, Robison Alumni Fields, Schoellkopf Field, Teagle Hall

Most Popular Sports
Men's hockey, football, men's lacrosse, women's lacrosse, women's soccer

Overlooked Teams
Men's wrestling, women's field hockey, women's gymnastics

Students Speak Out
ON ATHLETICS

"There are lots of IM sports—soccer, softball, basketball, and inner tube water polo. Varsity sports aren't so big, except for hockey. We're not too good at anything else."

"**Hockey is unbelievable**. You will never see any school cheer for a team more than it does for Cornell hockey. You should definitely get season tickets. It's worth it."

"Varsity hockey is huge; the games are fun. Lacrosse is also really big. Other sports just can't cut it here. My high school football team has more enthusiasm than the football team does here. **Our basketball team also stinks**. I think our hockey support is probably as big as at any college in the country. If you're an athlete, you have to be really good to play a sport, but IMs are popular if you don't make a team. There are also club teams."

"There are many varsity sports on campus. Men's ice hockey is very big here. We have a football team, but they never do very well. Lacrosse is also good; the men and women's teams did very well this year. **There is a big IM program**, and I don't think it's too hard to get involved."

"It's not a big sports school—except for hockey! We're awesome, and it's the only sport anyone cares about. **Go to a game; it's an experience**!"

"Varsity sports are present, but there's not all that much school spirit—although **homecoming is pretty fun**. I've done IM soccer, and I found that it was fun."

"Varsity athletics are big, since Cornell is a Division I school. **Some of the most nationally talented teams** are hockey, wrestling, lacrosse, and water polo. As for IM, it all depends on the sport. For some leagues like basketball, soccer, or softball, there are tournaments that last weeks at a time."

"Varsity sports are big, especially hockey and football. Everything else gets a normal share of attendance. IM sports always have participants, and **you can play any sport, including curling**."

The College Prowler Take
ON ATHLETICS

Although Cornell isn't seriously focused on its athletics program, we have come to dominate in several sports, including hockey, lacrosse, wrestling, and polo. In the future, it is without a doubt that Cornell will become increasingly more competitive and progressively more powerful. As a result, the next few years will be a very exciting time for Big Red sports, and the future has big things in store as Cornell continues to catch a bigger glimpse of the national spotlight!

Cornell is most well-known for its men's hockey team, which constantly ranks in the national top ten. Lynah Rink is consistently packed for home games, and students camp out days in advance just to secure season tickets. Most of the other teams, however, fail to draw so much attention. Many students have a liking for intramural sports. Intra-school competition is fierce, especially amongst Greek members, and IMs are a great way to stay active, get some exercise, and meet new people with similar interests.

The College Prowler™ Grade on
Athletics: B-

A high grade in Athletics indicates that students have school spirit, that sports programs are respected, that games are well-attended, and that intramurals are a prominent part of student life.

CORNELL UNIVERSITY

Nightlife

The Lowdown
ON NIGHTLIFE

Student Favorites:
The Palms, Dino's, Rulloff's, Johnny O's, Republica

Useful Resources for Nightlife:
http://www.visitithaca.com/nightlife.htm

Bars Close At:
Last call is 1 a.m., but bars usually kick out people around 1:30 a.m.

Primary Areas with Nightlife:
Collegetown, Commons, West Campus

Local Specialties:
Dr. Pepper Shot: Amaretto with Bacardi 151 lit on fire, then dropped into a glass of beer. The rest you can figure out for yourself.

What To Do If You're Not 21:
If you're under 21, not to worry. You'll spend your weekends at massive frat parties with special themes and live DJs. Underage drinking, of course, is overlooked. House parties in Collegetown are also popular; so are non-alcoholic activities (as a detox alternative) at some of the student centers. After two years, the fraternity bashes tend to get old, and students of age prefer to break into the bar scene.

Students Speak Out
ON NIGHTLIFE

"The bar scene is all the same, but Rulloff's is my bar of choice. Any bar in Collegetown is pretty nice if it is not crowded."

"There are about six or seven bars in Collegetown and a bunch more in downtown Ithaca. They are pretty good, depending on your scene, but **they are somewhat strict with IDs**. I guess it depends where you go and who you know."

"There are a bunch of bars in Collegetown. They're all pretty cool. **They all have different atmospheres**; this is good because you can probably find one that you like. There aren't a staggering number of dance clubs here, but there are a few. One notable club is called Republica."

"I do not know much about the bars since I am not 21. However, the clubs in Collegetown and near Ithaca College are a lot of fun. **I definitely suggest going to Republica and Semesters**. You probably will not go to them too often since you can just go to a frat party to dance for free."

"There are a ton of bars in Collegetown that I really like, particularly Rulloff's and Palms. The problem is that **you need a great fake ID to get into just about all of these places**, except maybe Dunbar's. I wasn't able to hit up the bars until I turned 21. There are some clubs, but I think they aren't any good."

"I don't really go to the bars, but **people have fun there**. I haven't been to any clubs, but I have heard that they aren't too bad. Chapter House is a good bar to go to."

"The **bars and clubs really don't meet my standards**, but I'm spoiled from being used to the ones in New York City. The best places to go are Dino's, Bear Lodge, and Rulloff's. The bars close at 1:30 a.m."

"**The Nines is a pizza place in the center of Collegetown**. They have live bands, drinks, and pizza to die for."

"There are not too many clubs except for some **shady ones like Republica and the Haunt**. Freshman year, you'll spend most of your time at frat parties, but after that, bars are a must."

"There is a lack of clubs, but **the bar scene is very popular**. The one down side is that last call is at 1 a.m. House parties give those who wish to stay out later somewhere to go."

The College Prowler Take
ON NIGHTLIFE

Nightlife is not lacking at Cornell, bearing in mind Ithaca's remote location and detachment from urban life. Students go out on any given night of the week, including Sundays, and many students routinely start their weekends on Thursday. With its abundant Greek life and bar scene, there's always action and a place to go to socialize with friends and meet new people. Ithaca, however, is certainly missing a variety of different options and is really limited to the two major above-mentioned components of nightlife. Even with a decent selection of bars in Collegetown and in the Commons, nightlife becomes routine and lackluster after a while.

With last call at 1 a.m. (a chief complaint of most students 21 and older), nightlife continues at after hours parties until the wee hours of the morning. Parties may feasibly carry over to dormrooms, as well. Furthermore, Ithaca really doesn't have much of a club scene. Regardless, you'll hear good music (mostly hip-hop) as live DJs craftily orchestrate the dance floors. Local bands are a hot commodity at places like the Nines, Johnny O's, and the Haunt. Cornell also attracts some of the most popular bands for campus-wide concerts. In past years, some popular bands that have been featured include Incubus, Moby, No Doubt, Stone Temple Pilots, A Tribe Called Quest, Dave Matthews Band, and Bob Dylan!

The College Prowler™ Grade on
Nightlife: C+

A high grade in Nightlife indicates that there are many bars and clubs in the area that are easily accessible and affordable. Other determining factors include the number of options for the under-21 crowd and the prevalence of house parties.

Greek Life

The Lowdown
ON GREEK LIFE

Number of Fraternities:
44

Number of Sororities:
18

Undergrad Men in Fraternities:
21%

Undergrad Women in Sororities:
19%

Other Greek Organizations:
Greek Council, Greek Peer Advisors, InterFraternity Council, Order of Omega, Panhellenic Council

Did You Know?

Most chapters have their own parties, formals, and football tailgates.

Students Speak Out
ON GREEK LIFE

"About one-third of students are Greek, but each of the houses has its own niche. I didn't go Greek, but I have had no problems going to their events or being friends with those who are in the system."

"**For about the first two years of college, Greek life controls** the social scene. That is, of course, until students become of age when they typically explore the local Collegetown bar scene for the next two years."

"**Greek life has gone from great to good and is still deteriorating** as a result of Cornell's unnecessary policies, procedures, and regulations. It used to dominate the social scene, but now I think that bars and fraternities are equally dominant."

"Greek life pretty much takes over the social scene. That doesn't mean you can't do your own thing. The Greek student body tends to become fragmented by house, and **brothers or sisters stick with their own**. It's really up to the individual to recognize his or her own unique interests and most comfortable niche. Many students choose to join the Greek system, the second largest in the country, but you don't necessarily have to be a member to be social."

"I personally hate frats, but I must admit they do dominate the social scene if you're not 21. Alcohol is the blood that flows through this school's veins, and **frat parties supply almost all the kicks to underclassmen**, especially freshmen. When you're 21, frat parties are totally forgotten, unless you're in a fraternity, of course."

"Greek life is pretty big. I'm actually in a frat. It doesn't overwhelm social life, but sometimes there's **not much to do for people who aren't in frats or sororities** during second semester, when frats no longer hold many open parties."

"**It's a big part of the school**, but I wasn't part of it. I didn't think I missed anything. I had friends who joined and enjoyed it, but in the end, it just matters how good you are at meeting people and socializing. If it's difficult for you, the Greek system may make it easier."

"Greek life is awesome! I'm in a frat, and I think it was the **best decision I ever made here**."

The College Prowler Take
ON GREEK LIFE

Greek life at Cornell is the second largest in the nation, and most students agree that it has a very significant and influential presence on campus. This might be more the case for underclassmen, whose nightlife will consist primarily of fraternity parties. Most students who join a frat or sorority are very grateful that they did, and they make friends who they stay in touch with for life. Students who are not a part of the Greek system, however, cite that joining a fraternity or sorority is not essential to having a good time and being social.

Many of the biggest parties of the year are sponsored by Greeks and take place at fraternity houses. Some are even registered with the school (the legal ones, at least). These parties no doubt fill up some of the social void that inevitably exists in a rural upstate town.

The College Prowler™ Grade on
Greek Life: B+

A high grade in Greek Life indicates that sororities and fraternities are not only present, but also active on campus. Other determining factors include the variety of houses available and the respect the Greek community receives from the rest of the campus.

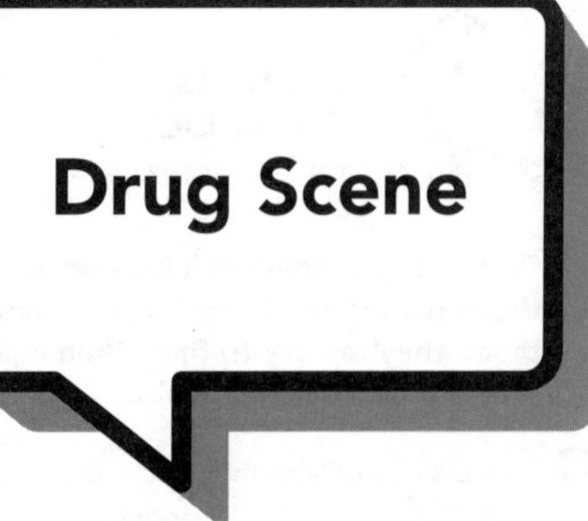

Drug Scene

The Lowdown
ON DRUG SCENE

Most Prevalent Drugs on Campus:
Marijuana, Ritalin

Liquor-Related Referrals:
85

Liquor-Related Arrests:
3

Drug-Related Referrals:
16

Drug-Related Arrests:
5

Drug Counseling Programs

BASICS: A service available for students who may want to explore their alcohol and drug use. It's designed to assist the student in examining his or her own behavior in a judgment-free environment.

EARS: Empathy, Assistance, and Referral Service—counseling and psychological services

Students Speak Out
ON DRUG SCENE

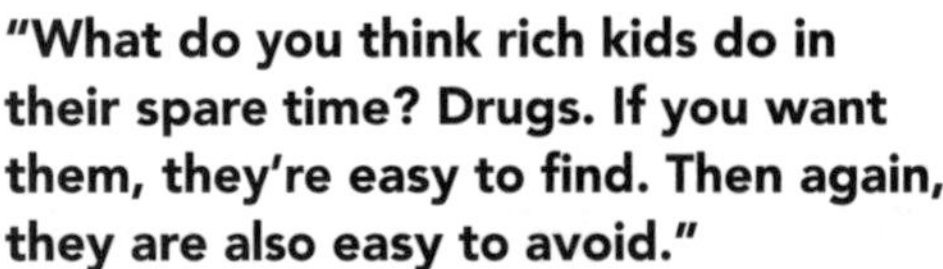

"What do you think rich kids do in their spare time? Drugs. If you want them, they're easy to find. Then again, they are also easy to avoid."

"Drugs are actually pretty rare, unless you go to some of the shadier frats. Don't worry about running into drugs. I am extremely anti-drugs. **People may smoke in their dorm rooms**, but it's pretty easy to get caught, unless you duct tape your door shut."

"The drug scene is barely even noticeable. Luckily, **Cornell isn't a drug school**; the most you'll encounter is pot. If you want to do drugs, you can find them; however, it's not very common at all."

"There's not much of a drug scene. I don't do drugs, and I've never really been confronted with them at school. Again, it depends on the crowd. **There is a lot of drinking**, though."

"I personally do not think that the drug scene is that big here at Cornell. I never run into many problems, and **I'm never pressured** by any of my friends to do drugs."

"In my experience, there is either **not much of a drug scene** on campus, or I never saw it firsthand."

"The **drug scene is pretty much underground**, and it's not as bad as some issues at your normal university."

"I have never done any drugs, so I do not know too much about them. I try to stay away from that, but I am fairly certain that there are plenty of drugs being passed around. **You can pretty much get whatever you want**, whenever you want it if you need it."

"Just like any other college campus, drugs are present. If you look hard enough, you can find pretty much anything. Alternatively, however, **alcohol is Cornell's predominant substance of choice**."

The College Prowler Take
ON DRUG SCENE

Most students say that drugs at Cornell are not a problem and that what little problems exist stay underground. Everyone will most likely meet your stereotypical pothead, and that's probably the most common drug-related issue you'll find here. Some students also use amphetamines and prescription drugs like Ritalin to stay up on late-night cramming sessions.

Although drugs are by no means prominent on campus, some say that if you want them, they're easy to find. Fortunately, there isn't a lot of pressure to get involved in drug use, and Cornell has much less of a problem than many other schools. Students tend to agree that they have never witnessed an obvious drug culture at this school.

The College Prowler™ Grade on

Drug Scene: B+

A high grade on Drug Scene indicates that drugs are not a noticeable part of campus life; drug use is not visible, and no pressure to use them seems to exist.

Campus Strictness

The Lowdown
ON CAMPUS STRICTNESS

What Are You Most Likely to Get Caught Doing on Campus?

Open containers on public property in Collegetown

Public urination (if you can't hold it!)

Drinking underage

Parking illegally

Streaking

Students Speak Out
ON CAMPUS STRICTNESS

"It depends on the situation, but for the most part, I think security is pretty lenient. Parties will get busted, but I've never heard of any long-lasting academic repercussions."

"They are pretty strict with drugs. They're **less strict about drinking**, although it is still an issue for many."

"They're not all that strict. I mean, it's all about using discretion. If people are inattentive, they'll get in trouble. **The campus police won't really go out of their way to bust you**. Alcohol is not allowed in the residence halls. This policy is taken seriously, but for those who are underage and want to go to parties to drink, it is not difficult to do so. I wouldn't say drugs are very big here. At least, they're not nearly as prominent as alcohol."

"The whole point of the Cornell police is that you can get into trouble and not have to deal with real Ithaca police. You are pretty much **guaranteed to be safe from police at frat parties**. If you drink in the dorm, you can get caught by resident assistants [RAs] and get turned into JAed [judicial administrator]. Just be careful and smart about what you do. I won't say police are loose about it, but they are definitely not extremely strict."

"They're not that strict, to be honest with you. My RA knew we were drinking in the dorm, but as long as he didn't catch us, he was cool with it. They're **pretty strict when it comes to drugs**, though."

"For the most part, campus police are not very strict. They will arrest you for drinking in public, but most **underage kids can drink all they want** at frat parties. Occasionally the cops will break one up, but it doesn't happen often. If it does, there aren't usually any arrests."

"Depending on the offense, if you are caught there is a campus judicial system, which typically awards community service fines. I'd advise that if you or friends decide to break the law, don't do it in your room. **The housing office is generally harsher than the police**."

"I can't say much about the drug scene because I don't know. I think that the **administration is pretty relaxed about alcohol**, unless of course, you're a moron and get caught with an open container. Other than that, the cops are pretty relaxed."

The College Prowler Take
ON CAMPUS STRICTNESS

Over the last few years, the administration has become progressively more strict in regards to campus social activities. Each year, at least one or two fraternities are kicked off campus for a variety of different misdemeanors. Part of the reason that the administration has moved all freshmen to North Campus is to isolate them from the majority of fraternities and sororities that are located on West. Slope Day has become highly regulated, and students are now required to present valid ID in order to drink, a policy that previously was taboo on this special day. Cornell police also strictly regulate open container rules. If you're on Cornell property conspicuously drinking, police will be quick to write you up to the judicial administrator.

What it all boils down to is using discretion and being smart. Cornell police are in place to keep things orderly and safe. They do their jobs very well, but to unwary freshmen and other unsuspecting students they can be a royal pain. Recently, more fraternity parties are being broken up as a result of underage drinking. Although fairly uncommon, it does happen every now and then. All in all, explicit offenses are dealt with accordingly. Although consequences are not particularly severe, repeat offenders will certainly suffer more grave repercussions.

The College Prowler™ Grade on

Campus Strictness: C-

A high Campus Strictness grade implies an overall lenient atmosphere; police and RAs are fairly tolerant, and the administration's rules are flexible.

Parking & Transportation

The Lowdown
ON PARKING & TRANSPORTATION

Student Parking Lot?
Yes

Freshmen Allowed to Park?
Yes

Approximate Parking Permit Cost:
$2,000 per year

Ways to Get Around:

On Campus:
Bus, car, taxi, bicycle, CU Transit Charters, VanSolutions, Tompkins TCAT (607) 277-RIDE

Airport:
The Ithaca Tompkins Regional Airport is conveniently located three miles northeast of Ithaca just off of NYS Route 13 on Brown Road. Cornell University is just a short, 10-minute drive from the airport. US Airways has regular flights to and from Philadelphia and New York City.
Call (607) 257-0456 for more information.

Syracuse Airport is an hour out of Ithaca and serves a variety of domestic locations. Call (315) 454-4330 for more information.

Students Speak Out

ON PARKING & TRANSPORTATION

"There are tons of buses all over campus that can take you wherever you have to go. They are free after 6 p.m. or just $1 if you don't have a bus pass."

"**It's easy to park but expensive**. The thing about Cornell is that you don't need a car. Everything is a 15-minute walk away. If you want to go into Ithaca, you can just take a taxi."

"Parking is a tad expensive, and it can get crazy at times. **The 'Ticket Monsters' do their jobs well**. I've adjusted, and you learn where you can park and where you can't. Some apartments have parking included in the rent—it's something you have to check out. There is a lot of on-street parking."

"Parking is terrible. **There is absolutely nowhere to park legally on campus** if you're a student. You get a permit for your dorm lot, but that aside, there's almost nowhere to park during the day or evening before 10 p.m. There are lots of spaces, they're just reserved. You will, however, always have a spot in your dorm lot. The North Campus and West Campus lots are never full."

"There is a regular bus schedule and a taxi service that is easily accessible to students. **They keep pretty regular hours**, but you must really know which bus is going where. It's complicated but understandable."

"Transportation is okay. **I am very glad I have friends with cars on campus** because it is a much more convenient way of getting around town."

"Public transportation is **efficient and convenient**, especially if you're a freshman isolated from Central Campus on North. Buses stop in Collegetown during late-night weekend hours to escort stranded freshmen back home."

The College Prowler Take

ON PARKING

While having a car is convenient, it is pretty much useless if you expect to use it primarily to drive to class. Even if you're willing to shell out the cash for an expensive parking pass, you will still be hard pressed to find a favorable place in the vicinity of one of your lecture classrooms. Cornell faces a serious space crunch in regards to on-campus parking. Don't expect any mercy from Cornell's Transportation Department (a.k.a. "The Ticket Monsters").

The College Prowler™ Grade on

Parking: C+

A high grade in this section indicates that parking is both available and affordable, and that parking enforcement isn't overly severe.

The College Prowler Take

ON TRANSPORTATION

Most students say that transportation in and around Ithaca is very convenient, although schedules take a little time to get used to. Tompkins TCAT provides shuttle service that regularly commutes between Central and other parts of campus. Bus passes are also very affordable. While students don't really have the need to take advantage of the cab service, it's available if you need it.

The College Prowler™ Grade on

Transportation: B-

A high grade for Transportation indicates that campus vehicles are readily-available and affordable. Other determining factors include proximity to an airport and the necessity of transportation.

Overall Experience

Students Speak Out

ON OVERALL EXPERIENCE

"Overall, I wish I had gone to a smaller, more personal school with smaller classes, fewer TAs, and a less competitive environment. Students here are very cutthroat, so get ready."

"**People here are cold, unfriendly, and extremely competitive**. Most classes grade on the bell curve. Notes are stolen all the time. People will not help you with homework unless you're great friends with them. Some people even lie if you ask for help, so you'll get an answer wrong. People are very showy here in terms of the kinds of cars they drive, the brand names of clothes they wear, and what their parents do. Overall, the atmosphere is depressing. However, it does prepare you for the real world, depending on what you want to do. Most people here are superficial and way too uptight. Honestly, I've had some ups, but sometimes I wish I didn't come here."

"**I really love it here**. I'm graduating this year, and I'll miss it."

"Sometimes I regret coming here, but I have met and befriended some very cool and interesting people. Cornell, **despite all of its negative aspects, is a good place** to expand your horizons and learn a lot more about life."

"I like it here; I like it a lot. **The school is beautiful over the summer**. You can take so many awesome classes—classes on wines, scuba diving, and sailing. I also like skiing, so that is a plus. The nightlife is lacking as far as I am concerned; however, I'm usually very busy with schoolwork, so it's kind of nice to not be so tempted. Bottom line, I like it here, and I would not want to be anywhere else."

"I wouldn't want to be anywhere else. I love my Cornell experience and have made lifelong friends. I love the Ithaca area and would like to live here if I could find a job. **It's really what you make of it**, so be outgoing and cater it to your likings."

"I've had great years, good years, and bad years. Overall, I'm quite happy with my time here. I was able to get a really good job and meet some amazing people. I don't think I would have been much happier at any other school, certainly not any of the others I was looking at. The one thing I can say about Cornell is that **nothing is handed to you**. There are incredible resources out there, but you have to take the initiative to go out and find them. If you expect anything to be spoon-fed to you, you'll be in for a disappointment."

"It's all right; I am happy I went here. Out of the Ivy League schools, **Cornell is known for giving the most work**. It's perhaps the most difficult. This school makes you work your butt off, and it is no joke. It is a good school, but be prepared to work hard."

"I loved my first year at Cornell. I do not wish I went anywhere else. **I made great friends, went to a lot parties, took some great classes**, and I couldn't have been happier anywhere else. I strongly suggest coming to Cornell. You won't regret it."

"I spent the last five years at Cornell and found them to be the best times of my life. I left with two degrees, a fulfilling job, hundreds of very close friends, and an **uncountable number of memories and connections**. Your experience depends on how involved and outgoing you are."

"I **enjoyed my Cornell experience**, and in retrospect, I don't think I would have gone anywhere else."

The College Prowler Take
ON OVERALL EXPERIENCE

Students express both praise and criticism when speaking of their overall experience at Cornell University. Comments on the whole, however, seem to suggest that most students have had more positive experiences than negative ones. The general response indicates that Cornell teaches serious and essential life lessons that will provide graduates an advantage over the course of their lives. Students claim that Cornell experiences give them vital exposure to hard work, intensity, and cut-throat competition, which are certainly aspects relevant to the real world. Many students are very grateful for the discipline and work ethic that they have developed here, which has become integral to their progress and success. One student clearly articulates, "The one thing I can say about Cornell is that nothing is handed to you." These words accurately summarize the Cornell experience.

Despite its shortcomings, Cornell has fulfilled many of the needs and desires of current students who are very glad that they chose Cornell, though many admit that the experience is really what you make of it. If you have a tendency to coast and bring out the negative in things, you're bound to be unhappy. If you're willing to take the time to try new things, get involved in the community, and stay open-minded, you're guaranteed to be in for an unparalleled and highly rewarding college journey.

The Inside Scoop

The Lowdown
ON THE INSIDE SCOOP

CORNELL UNIVERSITY

Cornell Slang:

AAP – College of Architecture, Art, and Planning

AEM – Applied Economics Management, the business major

Arch Sing – When a cappella groups sing under one of the many campus arches, usually near the dorms

Bear Access – CIT's package of network services

CAPS – Counseling and Psychological Services; offers free short-term on-campus counseling

Chalkings – Advertisements for events that are drawn in chalk on the roads and sidewalks of Cornell

CIT – Cornell Information Technologies; Cornell's computer and network services

Cocktail Lounge – Underground reading room in Uris Library; a great place to sleep . . . I mean, study

The Commons – Downtown Ithaca, containing cute shops and restaurants, very hippie style

COE – Cornell Outdoor Education

DOS – Dean of Students

EARS – Empathy, Assistance, Referral Service, a student-run help line for short-term counseling

FWS – Federal Work Study . . . or *"First-Year Writing Seminar"* (required for all freshman)

CORNELL UNIVERSITY

Gannett – Cornell's health care center

Haven – Peer support for lesbian, gay, bisexual, and transgender students

Hotelies – Students in the Hotel Administration college

IC – Ithaca College (sometimes instead called IK)

ILR – Industrial Labor Relations College

ISSO – International Students and Scholars Office

JA – Judicial administrator (the people who get you in trouble if you're drinking under 21, etc.)

LGBTRC – Lesbian, Gay, Bisexual, Transgender Resource Center

Libe Slope – The hill between Uris Library and West Campus dorms

Louie's Lunch – Truck on North Campus that serves fast food

Midnight Howl – The night before finals students yell as loud as they can at midnight to let out all of that studying aggression

OL – Orientation leader

POST – Pre-Orientation Service Trips

Prelim – Preliminary exam—any full-length exam that's not a final, often scheduled at night instead of during class

Quarter Cards – Advertisements handed out on one-quarter of a piece of paper

Program House – Residences organized around a theme

RA – Residence advisor

RHD – Residence hall director

RPCC – Robert Purcell Community Center

SA – Student Assembly, Cornell's student government

SAO – Student Activities Office

SAFC – Student Assembly Finance Commission, gives funds to student organizations

SHIP – Student Health Insurance Plan

The Sun – The *Cornell Daily Sun*, student-run newspaper (free in freshman dorms!)

TCAT – Tompkins Consolidated Area Transit, the public bus system

WSH or the Straight – Willard Straight Hall, the student union

Zeus – The Temple of Zeus, a café in Goldwin Smith Hall

Urban Legends

Cornell has one of the highest suicide rates. This is not true. It does, like any school, have some suicides, but in proportion to the student population the rate is not excessively higher than at other schools.

When a virgin crosses the arts quad at midnight the statues of AD White and Ezra Cornell get up and meet each other in the center of the quad to shake hands and congratulate each other on the chastity of Cornellians. (I don't know anyone who has tried it, but there are footprints on the quad, so maybe it's true.)

If a couple walks around all of Beebe Lake holding hands, they will get engaged.

If you are asked for a kiss at midnight on the suspension bridge and say no, the bridge will fall into the gorge.

School Spirit

All Cornellians undoubtedly take pride in their school. Especially as alumni, former students feel even more connected to the school after having put things in perspective and reflected upon past experiences. Students don't, however, necessarily have a tremendous amount of "rah-rah" spirit in support of the athletic teams. School spirit seems to be more contained to specific groups, like colleges (the Hotel School, in particular), departments. (applied economics and management), organizations and clubs, and fraternities and sororities.

Traditions

Dragon Day

Every year, the architecture students make a huge dragon to parade around campus and then burn. Some years, the engineers also make a large phoenix, and the event becomes a contest (other years it's just the dragon). The event begins with the architecture students selling Dragon Day T-shirts. Then, the night before Dragon Day, the architecture students toilet paper the arts quad (it looks beautiful!). The next day the parade of the dragon begins.

The Chimes

McGraw Tower has become the symbol of Cornell University. It is visible from much of Ithaca and contains the Chimes, which are played every day (occasionally ringing out the Beatles, Disney songs, or Jingle Bells).

Freshman/Seniors on the Field

On the first home football game of the season, the freshmen rush the field; on the last, the seniors do the same.

Slope Day

On the last day of classes, students gather on Libe Slope to celebrate the end of the year. It used to be an unstructured event full of very drunk students, but, now that it is organized by the University, only those over 21 can easily drink. On Slope Day there are vendors selling food, a carnival area, and famous bands playing (one year it was Rusted Root, another it was OAR and Kanye West).

Things I Wish I Knew Before Coming to Cornell:

- When it snows, it blizzards.
- Booze cruises are tons of fun.
- Olin Library has the best study lounges.
- If you don't get along with your roommate from the get-go, find another.
- Used books are cheaper than new ones.
- Walking up steep hills is good exercise.
- Buying the bed sheets and linens from the school catalog is a waste of money.
- Wegman's has the best subs.
- Senior Week rocks.
- Country music is popular in upstate New York.
- A picture is worth a thousand words.
- Take five courses first semester of freshman year.
- It gets better after the first semester.
- Don't forget to sleep!
- Explore the campus and meet new people right at the beginning.

Tips to Succeed at Cornell:

- Seek professors and TAs out in supplementary office hours.
- Take advantage of study areas, library stacks, and computer labs.
- Consult the librarians for comprehensive information on indispensable research.
- Plan ahead of time and develop a course of action first semester of freshman year.
- Find an advisor you get along with and can talk to candidly.
- Stay in touch with professors.
- Take advantage of the Cornell Career Services office.
- Don't limit yourself to specific groups.
- Explore everything Cornell has to offer.
- Don't ever fall behind.

Finding a Job or Internship

The Lowdown

ON FINDING A JOB OR INTERNSHIP

Career Center Resources & Services:

Cornell Career Center
103 Barnes Hall
Monday–Friday 8:00 a.m.–4:30 p.m.
Walk-in hours: Monday–Friday 1:30 a.m.– 3:30 p.m.
(607) 255-5221

The Lowdown

Cornell Career Services provides all of the crucial resources you can think of that might be helpful in finding your ideal job or internship. Barnes Hall has a library stocked with numerous books on different career paths and specific industries. Career counselors will conduct mock interviews with willing students and advise them on appropriate strategies and successful methods. One service available uses a series of computer tests to assess a student's interests and recommend an ideal industry fit.

Advice

Start early, and take advantage of all that the Cornell Career Services office has to offer. Sign up for Cornell's custom MonsterTrak service, and register your career profile as soon as possible to receive e-mails on job postings and obtain updates on campus recruiting.

The Lowdown
ON ALUMNI

Web site:
http://www.alumni.cornell.edu/

Office:
Office of Alumni Affairs
Alumni House
626 Thurston Avenue
Ithaca, NY 14850-2490
(607) 255-2390
Fax: (607) 255-7533
alumniaffairs@cornell.edu

Services Available:
Lifetime e-mail forwarding, career services, reunions, regional events in your area

Major Alumni Events

The biggest events for alumni are homecoming and class reunions. Since Cornell has people from all over the world, there are clubs and alumni associations all over the United States and the world. On the Web site there is more information on all Cornell has to offer for alumni. Alumni give huge donations to start projects, build buildings, and fund sports teams, so Cornell treats alumni well.

Alumni Publications

Cornell Alumni Magazine—six yearly issues for $29. *http://cornell-magazine.cornell.edu*

Various other publications for specific majors and colleges, such as the *Bulletin of Cornell Hotel Society* for Hotel School alumni: *http://www.hotelschool.cornell.edu/alumni/*bulletin/)

Famous Cornell Alumni:

Pearl S. Buck (Cla. 1926) - author of the Pulitzer Prize winning novel, *The Good Earth*, and Nobel laureate (1938, literature)

Adolph Coors (AB 1907) - cofounder of the Coors beer brewing company

Joseph Coors (BS 1939) - cofounder of the Coors beer brewing company

Ken Dryden - NHL Hockey Hall of Fame goalie

Dave Edgerton - cofounder of Burger King restaurant chain

Allen Funt (AB 1934) - producer, created *Candid Camera*

Ruth Bader Ginsburg (AB 1954) - U.S. Supreme Court justice

Sheldon Lee Glashow - Nobel laureate (Physics 1979)

Jeff Hawkins (1979) - inventor of the PalmPilot and founder of Palm, Inc. and Handspring

Bill Maher (AB 1978) - comedian and host of *Real Time with Bill Maher*

Jim McLamore - cofounder of Burger King restaurant chain

Toni Morrison - author and Nobel laureate

Bill Nye (BS, MEng 1977) - the Science Guy

Janet Reno (BA 1960) - U.S. attorney general under President Clinton

Christopher Reeve (AB 1974) - actor, best known for *Superman*

William P. Rogers - U.S. attorney general and secretary of state

E. B. White (AB 1921) - American essayist, author of *The Elements of Style*, *Charlotte's Web*

The Ten BEST Things About Cornell:

1. Outdoor scenery
2. Slope Day
3. Great friends
4. Appel Commons
5. Fridays off
6. Sledding down Libe Slope on cafeteria trays
7. Club management
8. Orientation Week (after freshman year)
9. Wine tours
10. Greek life

The Ten WORST Things About Cornell:

1. The weather
2. Hills covered with ice
3. Early morning classes
4. Townies
5. Finals Week
6. Parking tickets
7. Computer Science 101
8. Course registration
9. Ivy Room pricing
10. Construction

Visiting Cornell

The Lowdown
ON VISITING CORNELL

Hotel Information:

Benn Conger Inn
206 West Cortland Street, Groton 13073
3 Suites, 1 Room, $90-$320
(607) 898-5817

Best Western University Inn
1020 Ellis Hollow Road (at East Hill Plaza), Ithaca 14850
101 Rooms, $89-$209
(607) 272-6100 or (800) 528-1234

Clarion University Hotel & Conference Center
1 Sheraton Drive, Ithaca 14850
106 Rooms, $69-$250
(607) 257-2000

Comfort Inn
356 Elmira Road, Ithaca 14850
79 Rooms, $65-$155
(800) 228-5150 or (607) 272-0100

Econo Lodge Ithaca
2303 North Triphammer Road, Ithaca 14850
(Rte.13 & N. Triphammer Road Exit)
72 Rooms, $46-$115
(607) 257-1400

Economy Inn
658 Elmira Road, Ithaca 14850
13 Rooms, $36-$115
(607) 277-0370

Embassy Inn
1083 Dryden Road (Rt. 366), Ithaca 14850
25 Rooms, $45-$85
(607) 272-3721

Take a Campus Virtual Tour

http://www.explore.cornell.edu/tour_home.cfm
(This site contains tons of pictures, 3-D tours, and lots of other fun stuff!)

To Schedule a Tour

The Information and Referral Center offers guided walking tours of the campus throughout the year, except from late December through early January. The tours are an enjoyable and informative introduction to Cornell and its history, student life, and Cornell's combined roles as an undergraduate teaching institution, an international research university, and New York state's land-grant institution.

Tours begin at the Information and Referral Center in the Day Hall lobby and appointments are not required. The tours are mostly outdoors; each lasts about one hour and 15 minutes and includes information about Cornell's undergraduate, graduate, and professional schools and colleges. The Information and Referral Center can be reached at (607) 254-INFO, Monday through Friday, 8 a.m.-10 p.m. and Saturday 8 a.m.-5 p.m. Visit *http://www.admissions.cornell.edu/visit/* for more information.

Cornell Days

These give prospective students a chance to spend a day, and possibly a night, on campus to get a better sense of life at Cornell. Activities are arranged to show you the University from a student's perspective.

Directions to Campus

From the South

- Route 79 W will bring you into Ithaca on State Street. From State, make a right turn onto Mitchell at the stop sign.

- Follow Mitchell up the hill and bear left onto Ithaca Road. Ithaca Road will become Dryden Road at the stoplight. From Dryden Road, turn left onto Hoy Road at the blinking light. Follow Hoy to the entrance to campus.

From the North

- Use local roads to I-81. Go south on I-81 to Exit 12 at Cortland-Homer. Take Rt. 281 south to State Route 13. Go south on State Route 13 to Ithaca, NY.

- Once in Ithaca there will be signs directing you to campus. Use these in conjunction with the directions below to find Cornell University.

- Once on State Rt. 13, continue south to State Rt. 366. Turn left after the NYSEG complex onto State Rt. 366. Follow State Rt. 366 east until you reach the intersection with Hoy Road. Turn right onto Hoy Road, and it will lead you straight into campus.

From the West

- Travel east on I-90 (the New York State Thruway) to Exit 42. Travel south on Rt. 14 for approximately one-quarter mile to Route 96. Travel south on Rt. 96 for approximately 45 miles to Ithaca, NY. Travel south on Route 13 for approximately one-quarter mile to Route 79 and Green Street.

- Travel east on Route 79/Green Street. Green Street becomes East State Street. Continue to travel east on Rt. 79/East State Street. Turn left onto Mitchell Street/ Route 366. Follow Mitchell up the hill and bear left onto Ithaca Road. Ithaca Road will become Dryden Road at the stoplight. From Dryden Road turn left onto Hoy Road at the blinking light. Follow Hoy to the entrance to campus.

From the East

- Go west on I-90 (the New York State Thruway) to I-88. Go west on I-88 for 76 miles to Exit 8 for State Route 206 at Bainbridge, NY. Go west on State Rt. 206 for 25 miles to State Rt. 79 at Whitney Point, NY. Go west on State Rt. 79 for 35 miles to Ithaca, NY.

- Rt. 79 W will bring you into Ithaca on State Street. From 79 W/State Street, make a right turn onto Mitchell at the stop sign. Follow Mitchell up the hill and bear left onto Ithaca Road. Ithaca Road will become Dryden Road at the stoplight. From Dryden Road, turn left onto Hoy Road at the blinking light. Follow Hoy to the entrance to campus.

Dartmouth College

6016 McNutt Hall, Hanover, NH 03755
www.dartmouth.edu (603) 646-2875

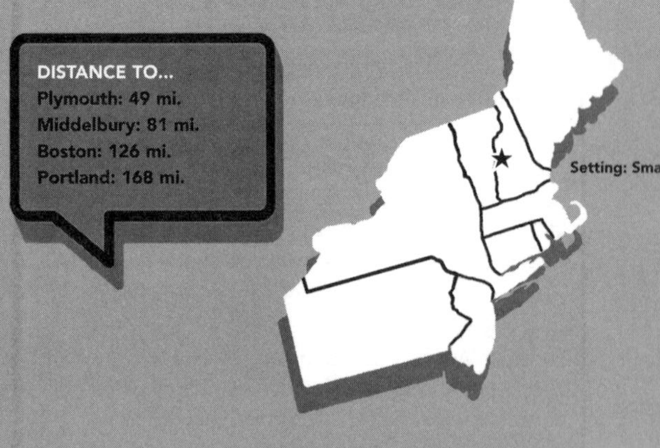

"Dartmouth is truly undergraduate. Professors teach every class and generally treat students like royalty."

Total Enrollment:
4,027 - Medium
Acceptance Rate:
19%
Tuition:
$31,965
Top 10% of High School Class:
88%
Average GPA:
3.7

SAT Range

Verbal	Math	Total
660 – 760	670 – 770	1330 – 1530

ACT Range

Verbal	Math	Total
N/A	N/A	27-33

Most Popular Majors:
13% Economics
11% Political Science and Government
9% History
7% Psychology
7% English Language and Literature

Students Also Applied To:*
Brown University, Harvard University
Princeton University, Stanford University
*For more school info check out *www.collegeprowler.com*

Table of Contents

College Prowler Report Card

Academics	A
Local Atmosphere	C-
Safety & Security	A+
Computers	A
Facilities	B
Campus Dining	B
Off-Campus Dining	C-
Campus Housing	B+
Off-Campus Housing	B
Diversity	B
Guys	A-
Girls	B-
Athletics	B+
Nightlife	D
Greek Life	A
Drug Scene	B
Campus Strictness	B
Parking	C-
Transportation	C

Academics

Did You Know?

According to the Institute of International Education, Dartmouth has the highest percentage of students who study abroad (47 percent).

Best Places to Study:
Novack Café, the Stacks, Baker Tower Room, the Collis Center, dorm lounge/study spaces

The Lowdown
ON ACADEMICS

Degrees Awarded:
Bachelor, Master, Doctorate

Full-Time Faculty:
485

Faculty with Terminal Degree:
82.7%

Student-to-Faculty Ratio:
9:1

Average Course Load:
3 courses

AP Test Score Requirements:
Possible credit for scores of 3, 4, or 5

IB Test Score Requirements:
Possible credit for scores of 6 or 7

Special Degree Options:
Combined Bachelor of Arts and Bachelor of Engineering

Sample Academic Clubs:
College Bowl, Mock Trial Society, Forensic Union, Daniel Webster Legal Society, Club of Dartmouth Entrepreneurs

Students Speak Out
ON ACADEMICS

"It's pretty easy to understand why Dartmouth is so alluring. The student body has top-notch academics available without any competition for resources from graduate students."

"Academics at Dartmouth are unbeatable. Since **we aren't in the classroom very much compared to students at other schools**, there is a lot of independent work, and it moves quickly. If you like to be challenged and move at a quick pace, you'll love Dartmouth."

"With **teaching-centered professors across the board**, Dartmouth's academics are challenging and personal. They are tailored for the intellectual development of individual students."

"One nice thing is that other than an English class that you can test out of and a freshman writing seminar, there are **no mandatory courses**. The distributive requirements are very general, and they give you a chance to take some really fun classes."

DARTMOUTH COLLEGE

"Small classes are a huge plus. Intro courses that might have a few hundred students elsewhere have 50 at Dartmouth. While some social science departments are bigger, **most upper-level classes have enrollments of a couple dozen or so**."

"Honestly, there's **not enough discourse in classes**. I've lost my ability to speak in groups from being out-of-practice in class. Some professors are wonderful and have become mentors and friends, but on the whole I'm disappointed by the academics. The history department is an exception—I've enjoyed 90 percent of the classes there. College courses are a waste of time."

"The Student Assembly maintains a **Web site where students review classes they've taken** (*sa.dartmouth.edu/guide*). It's a great way to see whether a course you're interested in is good or bad."

Want to hear more about Dartmouth courses? Visit *www.collegeprowler.com* and pick up *Darthmouth College Off the Record.*

The College Prowler Take
ON ACADEMICS

Attending Dartmouth is a surefire way to avoid those troublesome TAs, as all classes are taught by professors. While there are some duds to be avoided, students consistently cite their profs as the most outstanding part of their academic experience. Professors are rarely sidetracked by research, and a low student-to-faculty ratio makes getting to know your instructors a breeze. Various study abroad programs are another student favorite—whether strolling the hallowed halls of Oxford or chasing sheep in New Zealand is more your cup of tea, Dartmouth will provide you with the opportunity for either, and everything in between. The Dartmouth Plan facilitates taking a variety of exchange programs and terms abroad. With 10-week terms, students enjoy modest three-term course loads, and that pesky organic chemistry class will be over in no time. Sophomore Summer (sounds better than "summer school," right?) is a blast, but scattered off-terms are hard on amorous and platonic relationships alike.

As would be expected of an institution of Dartmouth's caliber, classes are challenging, professors are brilliant, and academic experiences are positive in the vast majority of cases. "Work hard, play hard" is an apt motto. While Dartmouth students let loose on weekends and remain surprisingly non-competitive when it comes to grades, most study more than they let on, particularly as finals draw near.

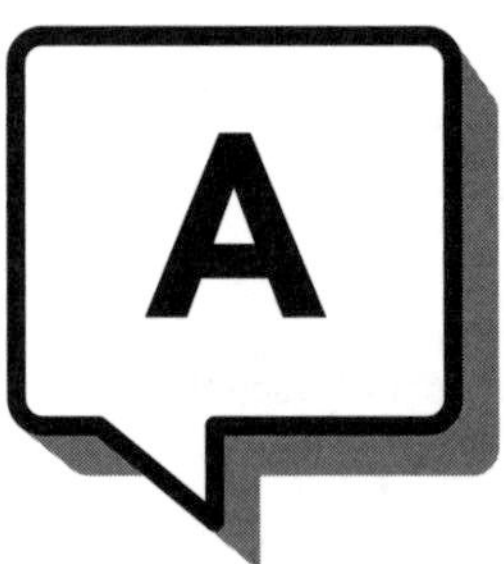

The College Prowler™ Grade on
Academics: A

A high Academics grade generally indicates that professors are knowledgeable, accessible, and genuinely interested in their students' welfare. Other determining factors include class size, how well professors communicate, and whether or not classes are engaging.

Local Atmosphere

The Lowdown
ON LOCAL ATMOSPHERE

Region:
Northeast

City, State:
Hanover, New Hampshire

Setting:
Small town

Distance from Boston:
2 hours, 30 minutes

Distance from Montreal:
2 hours, 30 minutes

Points of Interest:
Simon Pearce Glassblowing and Restaurant, Ben & Jerry's Factory, New England Transportation Museum, The Ledges

Closest Movie Theaters:
The Nugget on Main Street, the Loew Auditorium in the Hopkins Center

Major Sports Teams:
Boston Red Sox (baseball), Boston Celtics (basketball), Boston Bruins (hockey), New England Patriots (football)

City Web sites:
www.hanovernh.org

Famous Hanoverians:
Bill Bryson, author of *A Walk in the Woods*. Some say J.D. Salinger is cooped up right outside of Hanover, but no one can know for sure.

Fun Facts about Hanover:

1) Hanover is located in a scenic region known as the Upper Valley, which includes the scenic area in both New Hampshire and Vermont that borders the Connecticut River.

2) Eager for a hike? The Appalachian Trail runs right through town.

3) The town charter was granted in 1761 by King George III to settlers from Connecticut.

4) Hanover and Norwich, Vermont formed the first interstate school district in the United States.

5) Hanover was recently ranked the seventh best college town in the nation by *Outside* magazine.

Students Speak Out
ON LOCAL ATMOSPHERE

"The town life revolves around the college. This is one of the coolest things about Dartmouth—being immersed in an environment that is totally devoted to education."

"Hanover is a quaint little college town. If you want to get a good feel of what the campus is like without visiting, imagine the stereotypical 'college' atmosphere—large grassy lawns, distinguished brick buildings, and a feeling of knowledge and history. **Dartmouth is essentially the archetypical New England college**, nestled into the almost unbearably picturesque Connecticut River Valley."

"**There's no culture in Hanover**, but thankfully, Dartmouth brings culture to you. I think there's an average of three artistic events a day on campus, including movies. Best of all, everything's just five bucks for students."

"Dartmouth's atmosphere blends New England architecture and history with southern hospitality and West Coast relaxation. This creates the perfect environment for a successful and happy college career. The city of Hanover has a fruitful partnership with Dartmouth, and the local atmosphere promotes friendly, interpersonal interaction. While Hanover doesn't have the hustle and bustle of the Big Apple, it does have **a pervasive 'feel good' atmosphere that is infectious**."

"There's really nothing except for some restaurants and stores, scenic New England stuff, and a very pretty campus. There's not really anything to stay away from either. Dartmouth is 'in the sticks,' which **can be pleasant, but it can also suck**."

"Hanover is pretty dull. **Unless you're a big outdoorsy person**, **the local area won't be a big bonus**. The school's atmosphere is quite nice and idyllic—it's hard, even as a jaded senior, to not think warmly of the campus."

The College Prowler Take

ON LOCAL ATMOSPHERE

The town of Hanover is unfailingly described as "small." However, with a full-service school like Dartmouth, who needs anything else? In fact, most Dartmouth students are so busy that they rarely ponder what's beyond Wheelock Street. Those who do are usually thrilled by their placid surroundings. Situated just across the Connecticut River from Vermont, in the scenic Upper Valley, Hanover is consistently praised for its peaceful New England beauty. Unless you're satisfied donning apparel from the Gap, you'll have to hitch a ride to nearby West Lebanon, or another of Hanover's less ritzy neighbors, to find chain stores of any kind.

Hanover's isolation facilitates the insular community that is a Dartmouth hallmark. With nowhere to go and little to do, students form tight-knit bonds that foster love for the "college on the hill." Given the long travel time to major cities, "the Dartmouth bubble" is difficult to burst, though road trips are common. While culture junkies should expect boredom, the rugged type will enjoy the region's unparalleled outdoor opportunities.

The College Prowler™ Grade on

Local Atmosphere: C-

A high Local Atmosphere grade indicates that the area surrounding campus is safe and scenic. Other factors include nearby attractions, proximity to other schools, and the town's attitude toward students.

DARTMOUTH COLLEGE

Safety & Security

Did You Know?
According to the FBI, Hanover is the safest town in New Hampshire, which is, in turn, the safest state in the United States.

The Lowdown
ON SAFETY & SECURITY

Number of Dartmouth Public Safety and Security Officers:
30

Phone:
(603) 646-2234

Safety Services:
Bicycle registrations, BlitzMail bulletins, engraving of valuable items, escort service, Rape Aggression Defense, weapons storage

Health Center Office Hours:
8 a.m-4 p.m., seven days a week

Health Services:
Appointments, pharmacy, X-rays, specialty clinics, fall vaccine, Counseling and Human Development department, Women's Health program, STD and HIV/AIDS testing, Sexual Assault Peer Advisors, Planned Parenthood

Students Speak Out
ON SAFETY & SECURITY

"Dartmouth College is probably one of the safest colleges anywhere. There aren't exactly a lot of random, sketchy people wandering about like you find on urban campuses."

"To be blunt, security is really not an issue. They put locks on the front doors of our dorms, and everybody thinks that it is a big joke. Virtually **everyone leaves their doors unlocked all the time**. College-sponsored campus safety officers patrol all the time, and there are blue-light phones every 20 feet—at least it feels that way—but they're nearly always unneeded. I lost my key on the third day of school, and I never worried about locking my door again."

"Coming from the big city, it was quite a shock to be **able to stroll around campus at the wee hours of the morning** with impunity. Many people don't even lock the doors to their rooms. Neither myself nor anyone I know has ever felt threatened on campus, although the graveyard can be kind of spooky at night."

"We have blue-light emergency phones all over the place, and campus security officers patrol the campus. There is also an escort service at night. The biggest cases usually deal with **keg confiscation, inebriates, and the occasional bike theft**. The crime scene at Dartmouth is minimal."

"The college has installed security cards in all the residence halls. Personally, I think it is stupid and unnecessary, since **I find the campus to be extremely safe**. If it weren't for the Greek system, campus security would likely have nothing to do at all. They mostly handle drunk frat boys."

"As for security and safety, there's no need to worry. **The biggest crime at Dartmouth is bike theft**, and the perpetrators usually return your bike when they're done with it. Dorms are always open; no one locks their doors. It's probably one of the safest campuses around, and even so, there is an awesome safety and security force that patrols and can help you out."

"You may have heard about the two professors who were murdered a couple of years back, but that happened at their home off campus. The entire Upper Valley, not just Dartmouth, is **a very safe place, generally**."

The College Prowler Take
ON SAFETY & SECURITY

Because of Hanover's isolation and small size, most everyone on and around campus is associated with Dartmouth. With no outside crime, occasional theft is virtually the only security concern. Blue-light safety phones are numerous in case you need a late-night escort or feel unsafe, and campus security has a vigilant presence on campus, just in case trouble arises.

With classes, activities, and friends to keep up with, college students shouldn't have to worry about personal safety. At Dartmouth, you don't have to. The campus evokes a simpler time (when crime wasn't an issue), as students freely stroll campus at all hours, most rooms are left unlocked, and all dorms can be accessed with your student ID.

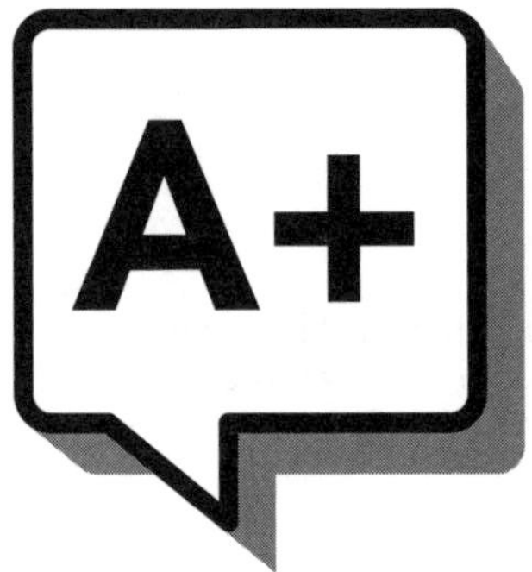

COLLEGE PROWLER™

Want to know more about campus safety services? Check out the complete College Prowler book on Dartmouth at *www.collegeprowler.com*.

The College Prowler™ Grade on

Safety & Security: A+

A high grade in Safety & Security means that students generally feel safe, campus police are visible, blue-light phones and escort services are readily available, and safety precautions are not overly necessary.

Computers

Did You Know?

The first school to have a campus-wide wireless network, Dartmouth was named the nation's "Most Wired" campus by Yahoo! in 1998.

The Lowdown ON COMPUTERS

High-Speed Network?
Yes

Wireless Network?
Yes

Number of Labs:
4, plus departmental labs

Number of Computers:
Approximately 100

Operating Systems:
Mac, Windows, Unix

24-Hour Labs:
Novack, in Berry Library

Free Software:
Adobe Acrobat Reader, Adobe Photoshop, ArcView, BlitzMail, GreenPrint, Kerberos, QuickTime, Maple, Matlab, Mathematica, Netscape, SPSS 11, Stata 7

Charge to Print?
Every student is allowed to print 600 pages for free each term, with exemptions given to thesis writers. After that, every page costs five cents.

Students Speak Out ON COMPUTERS

"Dartmouth has a great computer network. Bringing your own computer is required. Blitzmail, our e-mail system, has basically taken over the role of the telephone for most students."

"The computer access at Dartmouth is ridiculous. **I often wonder what we need so many computers and so much technology for**. We have every convenience and are spoiled rotten when it comes to this, so Get excited!"

"They're everywhere—literally. You can't walk down a hallway without finding public BlitzMail terminals that will soon dominate your life. Plus, WiFi access everywhere means that with a laptop, the world is at your fingertips from the entire campus; **doing research for a paper while sitting under a tree on the Green** is not just an image plastered on brochures."

"**All students are required to have computers**, which are connected to one of the fastest Ethernet connections in the country. There really aren't computer labs, but there are public computers all over campus, so you never should have trouble finding one."

"There are a handful of 24-hour machines by Novack Café, but **the college still lacks a central computer lab**. First floor Berry is the biggest, but it's literally impossible to get any work done there with all the people traipsing through."

"As one of the most wired campuses in the country, we have no shortage of computer access. **Every student is required to have a computer**, and there are computer terminals littered throughout campus. BlitzMail, the college e-mail system, is the dominant form of communication on campus, supplanting the use of the phone almost entirely. The college has put BlitzMail terminals [computers solely devoted to 'blitzing'] in basically every building."

"**Laptops are extremely popular at Dartmouth**, and students frequently take advantage of the campus-wide wireless Internet by working on their laptops in a cafe, in a classroom, or lying on the Green."

"Everyone on campus uses Blitzmail and **students check it 'round the clock, practically**. Laptops are increasingly popular because Dartmouth has installed a wireless network so laptops can access the Internet from just about any building on campus."

The College Prowler Take
ON COMPUTERS

Dartmouth's campus-wide, wireless network is incredibly convenient and widely acclaimed, providing Internet and e-mail access to everywhere from dorm lounges to the Green. Just don't let your professor catch you following your hometown team during class! All dorm rooms and many public spaces are equipped with Ethernet ports. Computers are used most often for the ubiquitous BlitzMail, and the Dartmouth Name Directory makes it easy to e-mail everyone from professors to that girl in your history class. All freshmen are required to bring or purchase a computer, and most choose to buy one from the school for convenience.

Dartmouth students enter with their computers and use them obsessively, so much so that room phones are never used and cell phones are just beginning to have a presence on campus. Since the college just switched from Macs to PCs, computer labs now contain both Dell and Apple machines. Kiewit Computing Services, though uniformly unhelpful, provides support for both types of computers. While the labs are too small and overcrowded, Dartmouth's online registration and public printing systems are both very easy to use.

The College Prowler™ Grade on

Computers: A

A high grade in Computers designates that computer labs are available, the computer network is easily accessible, and campus computing technology is up-to-date.

Facilities

The Lowdown
ON FACILITIES

Student Center?
Collis

Athletic Center?
Alumni Gym, with the Kresge Fitness Center located inside

Libraries?
8

Movie Theater on Campus?
The Loew Auditorium

Bowling on Campus?
No, but there is a hot bowling alley in White River Junction, 10 minutes away.

Bar on Campus?
Lone Pine Tavern

Coffeehouse on Campus?
Big Green Bean

Popular Places to Chill:
Collis Commonground, the Green, Novack Café

What Is There to Do?

For quick fun, shoot some pool in the basement of Thayer Dining Hall or Collis Student Center. Not sweaty enough for you? Swim or lift weights at Alumni Gym for indoor exercise or explore the great outdoors with an afternoon of skiing or hiking. Go to a light night "AREA" student art exhibit, or watch one of the many a cappella groups tear up a Greek house or random street corner.

Favorite Things to Do

There's always an event going on at the Hopkins Center. Movies are popular, or you can rent your own from Jones Media Center in Berry Library. Students mob the Green when it's warm enough to be outside, particularly at the beginning of spring. Collis Commonground is home to everything from conferences to volunteer fairs to dance parties.

Students Speak Out
ON FACILITIES

"On the whole, the infrastructure is a bit old, if well-maintained. Most of the dorms date from the 1920s and have not been changed much since. But what is lost in modernity is made up for in charm."

"Everything's very nice and new. I have almost no complaints, and **anything I would want to change is probably being renovated** within the next few years."

"**The gym is really nice**. I work out often, so I'm there a bunch. Squash courts, basketball, tennis, swimming, weight lifting, and a whole lot more."

"Facilities are for the most part very good. The gym is often criticized, but, beyond that, the facilities here are top-notch. The great thing is that undergraduates have access to anything the college owns. If you want to **do some research with the MRI Dartmouth owns**, you don't need to wait till you're a med school student. You can sign up to use it."

"The college has two land grants. The Dartmouth Outing Club maintains **hundreds of miles of trails, as well as a bunch of cabins** all over New Hampshire. I guess the Skiway and the Connecticut River would be considered nice facilities, and you can rent the stuff you need for either."

"A lot of people don't like Berry Library, but I don't mind it. There are plenty of places to study, and **be sure to check out the Tower Room** when you visit. It's on the third floor of Baker, and it provides the most ideal Ivy League setting anywhere on campus."

The College Prowler Take
ON FACILITIES

Students are generally satisfied, but not thrilled, with Dartmouth's facilities. While Alumni Gym meets the needs of many, the cramped weight room, also known as Kresge Fitness Center, provides the perfect reason not to work out. The enormous Baker and Berry libraries, combined with satellite libraries, provide plenty of study space, although many students despise the antiseptic look of Berry's interior. The modern-looking Hopkins Center, the central location for performing arts, which includes the spacious Spaulding Auditorium, is adjacent to the Hood Museum, and even contains a dining hall.

Baker Tower is the most notable architectural feature of Dartmouth's aesthetically pleasing campus, while the white buildings of Dartmouth Row date to the 18TH century and almost make you want to don some colonial garb. Most structures are classy brick and stone structures that remain well-maintained on the inside despite their age. Newer buildings, such as the Rockefeller Center, generally fit in well, although the soon-to-be-destroyed "Shower Tower" is an albatross. While Dartmouth has poured millions into new buildings, including Berry and the adjacent Carson, the college is in need of more dorm space. While Collis is passable as a student center, with its dining options, TV room, and common space, Dartmouth lacks a true central gathering place for students once the Green is overcome by snow.

The College Prowler™ Grade on
Facilities: B

A high Facilities grade indicates that the campus is aesthetically pleasing and well-maintained; facilities are state-of-the-art, and libraries are exceptional. Other determining factors include the quality of both athletic and student centers and an abundance of things to do on campus.

The Lowdown
ON CAMPUS DINING

Freshman Meal Plan Requirement?
Yes

Meal Plan Average Cost:
$2,400 per year

24 Hour On-Campus Eating:
None

Student Favorites:
Food Court, Collis, Courtyard Cafe

Off-Campus Places to Use Your Meal Plan:
None

Places to Grab a Bite with Your Meal Plan

Collis Café
Location: Collis Student Center
Food: Various
Favorite Dish: Custom omelet, chicken stir-fry with peanut sauce
Hours: Monday-Friday 7 a.m.- 3 p.m.

Courtyard Café
Location: Hopkins Center
Food: Greasy American
Favorite Dish: French fries
Hours: Monday-Friday 7 a.m.- 7 p.m.

Food Court
Location: Thayer Dining Hall
Food: Various/American
Favorite Dish: Ranch chicken sandwich
Hours: Monday-Sunday 11 a.m- 3 p.m and 5 p.m.- 11 p.m

Homeplate
Location: Thayer Dining Hall
Food: Healthy
Favorite Dish: Sunday breakfast buffet
Hours: Monday-Friday, 11:45 a.m.- 2:30 p.m., 4:45 p.m.- 7p.m.; Saturday-Sunday, 6:45 a.m.- 9:45 a.m.

Lone Pine Tavern
Location: Collis Student Center
Favorite Dish: Mushroom chardonnay chicken
Hours: Monday-Sunday, 8 p.m.- 1 a.m.

Novack Café
Location: Berry Library
Food: Snack
Favorite Dish: Chocolate chip cookies
Hours: Monday-Friday, 7:30 a.m.- 2:30 a.m.

The Pavilion
Location: Thayer Dining Hall
Food: Kosher/Halal/Sakuhara
Favorite Dish: Cheese bread
Hours: Monday-Friday, 11:30 a.m.- 7:30 p.m.

Other Options

Grab a snack from Brace Commons in East Wheelock or from Topside Convenience Store in Thayer. While in Thayer, stop by the Blend for delicious specialty smoothies. Eager to eat on the run? Try Colonel Bogey's at Hanover Country Club or the Skiway Café on the slopes. Students can also spend their DA$H discretionary accounts at Café North or Byrne Hall, which primarily serve graduate students.

Did You Know?

The Pavilion serves Kosher meals during the Jewish holidays.

Students Speak Out
ON CAMPUS DINING

"Aside from the fact that the food is overpriced, Dartmouth dining services offer more variety and higher quality food than most colleges do."

"The food on campus is really good. They have anything from healthier food and stir-fry to buffet style. There's the Hopkins Center, where most of the artsy people eat, since it's in the art building. There's also the main Food Court, and Homeplate, a healthier version of the regular stuff. **There are a ton of options, and the food is really good**. There's also a convenience store on campus where you can buy food with your meal card."

"The food is one of the best aspects of being a college student at Dartmouth. Dartmouth Dining Services [DDS] gives **innumerable options about 20 hours a day**. Inside Thayer dining hall alone, there is a plethora of options, including a grill/sandwich bar area, an exquisite Kosher dining section, an upscale specialized-entree section, a smoothie and juice bar, and a small college-owned convenience store. Food Court, the above mentioned 'grill/sandwich bar area,' is the most popular dining option for students, generally serving American food, like cheeseburgers—and they are delicious burgers at that."

"The smoothie bar, the Blend, is a tremendously popular option. Best of all, you can **charge all food to your student card** without having to worry about how many meals you have available."

"Dartmouth is awesome as far as food goes! The food is honestly really good. **Homeplate is probably my favorite**. They have a great grill and sandwich bar and always have awesome hot meals and other stuff. There are a lot of good dining halls, though, not just that one. The food is pretty expensive, but you just subtract money from your meal card, so you can eat whatever you want, whenever you want, and you don't need cash. There are no set meal times or anything so you can just go grab some food whenever and subtract the price from your meal plan. It's a pretty cool system."

"There's **an abundance of greasy/fried food** if that's your thing. Dining Services also does a good job of providing healthy meals, especially at the always trendy Collis. What we seem to lack is the more 'normal' food. The Kosher dining facility is great though—never any lines, and food of outstanding quality."

"You're forced to get a meal plan by the college, so you just have a card to eat at the various dining halls, and they subtract it from your account. **It's kind of a rip-off**, unless you shop smart. There is also a Dartmouth convenience store where you may also spend your meal plan dollars, but the prices are pretty high there."

The College Prowler Take
ON CAMPUS DINING

Dartmouth is an anomaly in that students actually speak fondly about their campus food. While all cafeteria offers are certain to get old, sumptuous options like the nutritious Homeplate or the greasy Courtyard Café will almost make you forget about Mama's secret-recipe lasagna.

Variety and flexibility are the name of the game. Students can eat at any establishment on campus. With no set meal times, they can do so whenever they want. Moreover, students can spend their declining balance account however they wish, meaning no meals are lost once you stop waking up during traditional breakfast hours. The food is expensive, and each item must be purchased individually, but savvy students know how to stretch their DBAs like pros.

The College Prowler™ Grade on

Campus Dining: B

Our grade on Campus Dining addresses the quality of both school-owned dining halls and independent on-campus restaurants, as well as the price, availability, and variety of food.

Off-Campus Dining

The Lowdown
ON OFF-CAMPUS DINING

Student Favorites:
EBA, Ramunto's, Dirt Cowboy, Molly's

Closest Grocery Stores:
Dartmouth Co-op on Lebanon Street

24-Hour Eating:
Fort Lou's in Lebanon, Food Stop on Main Street

Best Pizza:
Ramunto's

Best Chinese:
Panda House

Best Breakfast:
Lou's Restaurant

Best Place to Take Your Parents:
Hanover Inn

DARTMOUTH COLLEGE

Did You Know?

Looking to stay up all night? Head to Fort Lou's. Watch area truckers start their day with a fantastic breakfast as you prepare to go to bed.

Subway and Ben & Jerry's are the only chain establishments in Hanover.

Restaurant Prowler: Popular Places to Eat!

Dirt Cowboy Cafe
Food: Coffee,
Address: 9 South Main Street, Hanover
(603) 643-1323
Price: Moderate

Everything But Anchovies
Food: Pizza
Address: 5 Allen Street, Hanover
(603) 643-6135
Price: Cheap

Molly's Restaurant & Bar
Food: American
Address: 43 South Main Street, Hanover
(603) 643-2570
Price: Moderate

Ramunto's
Food: Pizza
Address: 68 South Main Street, Hanover
(603) 643-9500
Price: Moderate

Students Speak Out
ON OFF-CAMPUS DINING

"This is fairly limited, but considering Hanover's a small town in New Hampshire, we're not doing too bad. Pretty much any type of food can be found, and everything's open really late."

"Restaurants around here aren't bad. The campus runs right into Main Street and there are a few good ones there. **Molly's is my personal favorite**, but Murphy's and Rosey's are good, too."

"If you have a car you can drive to West Lebanon, where there's a McDonald's, a Burger King, and some good non-fast-food options. Without a car you still have access to Subway, Ben and Jerry's, and a number of decent sit-down places. Most of them aren't usually that crowded. **There's some great pizza places too**, but if you're from Chicago or New York City you probably won't agree."

"DIning options are severely limited for those without a car. Restaurants in Hanover are generally mediocre and expensive. Only **Murphy's On the Green** is really worth it. I'm salivating over their sweet potato fries as I write."

"This is one of the weaker aspects of Dartmouth life, although thankfully the on-campus dining makes up for the shortcomings of off-campus dining. **Ethnic food offerings are limited**: there is one Japanese food option [Bamboo Garden], one Chinese food option [Panda House], two Indian food options [India Queen and Jewel of India], and a few other nearby restaurants, including an Italian restaurant in West Lebanon."

"For upscale dining off campus, **Zin's Winebistro and the Hanover Inn provide high-quality classic fare** like prime rib and lamb. The most notable restaurant in the area is Lou's Diner. Lou's has been serving Dartmouth students for over 50 years, and has perfected the art of huge portions and delicious food. Some students stay up until Lou's opens at 6 a.m. and get an early breakfast."

"Restaurant quality varies. There is one Thai restaurant that is not particularly good and one Chinese place that is awful. Don't misunderstand; by 'one' I mean that it is literally the only Thai restaurant and only Chinese food in Hanover. Still, we have **two very good pizza joints: Everything But Anchovies [EBAs] and Ramunto's**."

"Molly's Restaurant and Murphy's On the Green are two notable restaurants on Main Street, if you don't feel like fast food. **Café Buon Gustaio is out of most student's price range** for the average meal, but it is a great place to take a date—it is an excellent Italian restaurant that serves great, fresh food."

The College Prowler Take
ON OFF-CAMPUS DINING

While the campus food is good enough to keep students eating in the dining halls most of the year, one can only physically take-on so many Food Court Double Burger Deals. When you finally venture off-campus to satisfy your appetite, you'll find a surprisingly large selection of establishments for a town as small as Hanover. Everyone has their favorite restaurants and some they despise, and there's always somewhere to take your parents, or a date, should you be so lucky.

With a few pizza places, a breakfast joint, and the token ethnic establishments, Hanover has the essential eats. There are a few surprises, as well—for instance, you can even find African food in the area. Variety is really what is lacking in Hanover—if the local Chinese or Thai restaurants don't sit well with you, then . . . Well, you don't eat Chinese or Thai (they're the only ones). You can turn to nearby West Leb for fast food or other chains, but such trips are usually well-planned excursions rather than everyday experiences. Hanover doesn't have any truly genuine eating experiences, and even the ethnic offerings smack of suburbia. However, the area provides sufficient sustenance for students making the occasional escape from the dining halls.

The College Prowler™ Grade on
Off-Campus Dining: C-

A high Off-Campus Dining grade implies that off-campus restaurants are affordable, accessible, and worth visiting. Other factors include the variety of cuisine and the availability of alternative options (vegetarian, vegan, Kosher, etc.).

Campus Housing

The Lowdown
ON CAMPUS HOUSING

Undergrads on Campus:
87%

Number of Dormitories:
32 (plus 6 Treehouses)

Room Types:
One-room singles; one-, two-, and three-room doubles, two- and three-room triples, and three-room quads

Best Dorms:
Gold Coast, East Wheelock, Mass Row

Worst Dorms:
River, the Choates, the Lodge, Treehouses

You Get:
Bed, desk, chair, bookshelf, dresser, closet, Ethernet port, cable jack

Cleaning Service?
In public areas—Cleaning of rooms is available only in East Wheelock.

Also Available:
Affinity housing: French and Italian (in East Wheelock), Asian Studies Center, Shabazz Center for Intellectual Inquiry (home of the Afro-American Society), Foley Cooperative, International House, La Casa, Latin American/Latino/Caribbean House, Native American House, smoke-free, substance-free

Students Speak Out
ON CAMPUS HOUSING

"The dorms are pretty nice, but some really suck—stay away from the River dorms, and the Choates. Otherwise, they're pretty sweet. Some have big rooms. I had a fireplace last year, and personal bathrooms are common."

"The dorms are nice. I like the Gold Coast and Mass Row. The River is the farthest away from campus, about a 10-minute walk, but that's about it. The Choates aren't that great, but I think the dorms are generally nice. A lot of them have extra amenities, **bathrooms, carpeting, fireplaces**, etc., so they can be really nice."

"In terms of housing, the **dorms are really nice**. Most of them are old buildings with a lot of character. Some even have working fireplaces in the rooms. I lived in Wheeler last year in a small, one-room double with a fireplace. My room was probably the smallest out of all my friends,' but it was in a great location. A lot of the rooms have two rooms for three people so you can have a sleeping room and a common room."

"Housing is amazing. I have had incredible rooms and rooming situations. I also think that **Residential Life works really hard to make living on campus a great experience**, and it is. Most people choose to live on campus because it's a great deal."

"**Dorms really vary**. East Wheelock is the nicest dorm cluster on campus; it's really like a three- or four-star hotel. The Choates [dorms], on the other hand, suck. They are an architectural nightmare, plain and simple, they are just ugly as all hell. The River is even worse—it's ugly and in the back of beyond. It is located behind the business and engineering schools, away from anything of use."

"**Big rooms, great locations**—what more could a college student want? Dartmouth employs the cluster system, typically putting three or four dormitories together in a group. These clusters often form individual identities, and students generally associate themselves as being from the Choates, the River, Mass Row, etc., as opposed to their individual dorms."

"Since Dartmouth is organized around the Green, all dorms are within easy walking distance of each other. That means **there really aren't any poorly-located dorms**. While the sizes of rooms vary, the smallest rooms at Dartmouth are generally the size of the biggest rooms at larger schools. People in the Choates and the River will have slightly smaller rooms than usual, but most other dorms have incredibly spacious rooms. East Wheelock, in particular, has gigantic rooms with terrific views."

"Greek houses play an integral part in the housing situation. **Many Greek-associated students choose to reside in their respective houses**."

Did You Know?

All Dartmouth students receive free cable and free long-distance calls.

The College Prowler Take

ON CAMPUS HOUSING

Of Dartmouth's residential clusters, the Choates and the River are uniformly regarded as the worst digs. However, half of the freshmen who are stuck there often say that the bonding experience of single-class housing makes up for the cramped quarters. The Choates' proximity to "Frat Row" and River's wild parties aren't half bad either. East Wheelock has far and away the nicest dorms, although its students are known for their teetotaling ways and 10 p.m. bedtimes. Freshmen in mixed-class housing frequently land spacious rooms in Wheeler-Richardson or New Hamp, and many get singles in Ripley-Woodward-Smith. The upperclassman favorite Massachusetts Row cluster has the best location, while the recently renovated Gold Coast dorms are regarded as the nicest.

Dartmouth's community is made stronger by the fact that almost all Dartmouth students, even seniors, live on campus in dorms or Greek houses. And, with the spacious size of most dorms, it's easy to see why. Most residence halls are of equal quality, and none is more than a 10-minute walk from anywhere on campus. Students don't develop strong cluster allegiances, but placing freshmen in the River and Choates may be a step toward a campus-wide residential college system. The competitiveness of sophomore room draw makes it hard to wind up near your friends and lands many students on the waitlist. However, while we can't guarantee you'll avoid that nightmare roommate, at Dartmouth it is a good bet that you'll have a large enough room that you can keep your distance.

The College Prowler™ Grade on

Campus Housing: B+

A high Campus Housing grade indicates that dorms are clean, well-maintained, and spacious. Other determining factors include variety of dorms, proximity to classes, and social atmosphere.

Off-Campus Housing

Students Speak Out
ON OFF-CAMPUS HOUSING

"I know a bunch of people that have moved off campus. It seems pretty convenient, although I don't find it as practical as it would be at a big university. The dorms at Dartmouth are good enough."

"Don't believe anyone who says there isn't a lot of it. **You can find housing in Hanover anywhere** as long as you're looking. I live off campus now for Sophomore Summer, and it's been fabulous."

"There really isn't much off-campus housing, so most people live in the dorms all four years at Dartmouth. Some off-campus housing exists, of course, but **nothing off campus is connected to the computer network**, and that's a significant drawback."

"**It's great to live off campus and feel more independent.** You can cook your own meals, live with your closest friends, and get away from campus when things get stressful."

"If you want to live off campus, it is a definite possibility after your freshman year, but there is not a ton of housing in town, so you have to plan early. I actually have a house already for my junior year with nine other people. **Usually off-campus housing is pretty nice**—if you can get a place."

"There isn't a lot of housing off campus because there isn't a lot of anything off campus. Hanover is pretty darn small. Cost will vary, convenience will vary, and **landlords are generally rotten**, but they vary, too."

The Lowdown
ON OFF-CAMPUS HOUSING

Undergrads in Off-Campus Housing:
13%

Average Rent for a Studio Apartment:
$500-$700/month

Average Rent for a 1BR Apartment:
$600-$1,000/month

Average Rent for a 2BR Apartment:
$1,000+ month

Popular Areas:
School Street and Lebanon Street. Hot spots include 8 School, 7 West, 30 Lebanon, the Red Barn, the Loveshack, and the Moontowers

Best Time to Look for a Place:
As early as possible, generally a year in advance.

For Assistance Contact:
Dartmouth College Real Estate Office
www.dartmouthre.com
(603) 646-2446

The College Prowler Take
ON OFF-CAMPUS HOUSING

While many students live off campus for a term or two, there's no mass exodus from the dorms like at any many other schools. The choice between the apartments adjacent to campus and the bigger houses deep in Hanover comes down to whether or not students want to drive to school every day.

Off-campus housing varies wildly in price and quality, as well as in distance from campus. The dorms are as nice as, or nicer than, most apartments and cost about the same on average. But because of changes in the college's blocking policy, however, it is difficult to live with a group of friends in the same dorm after freshman year. That is the main appeal of off-campus houses—a chance to spend a lot of quality time with close friends in a secluded setting.

The College Prowler™ Grade on
Off-Campus Housing: B

A high grade in Off-Campus Housing indicates that apartments are of high quality, close to campus, affordable, and easy to secure.

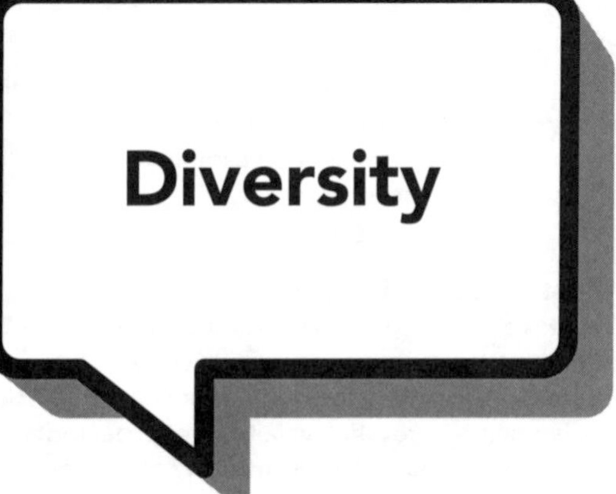

The Lowdown
ON DIVERSITY

White: 64%

Asian American: 13%

Hispanic: 6%

African American: 7%

Native American: 4%

International: 5%

Unknown: 7%

Out-of-State: 96%

Minority Clubs
AfriCaSO, Dartmouth Asian Organization, Dartmouth Chinese Culture Society, Hokupa'a, International Students Association, La Alianza Latina, Movimiento Estudiantil Chicano/a de Aztlan), MOSAIC, Native Americans at Dartmouth, Shamis

Political Activity
While the conservative *Dartmouth Review* is an established institution and the relatively new *Dartmouth Free Press* has added a liberal perspective to the campus debate, most students are apathetic. However, since New Hampshire is the first primary state, all Dartmouth students are guaranteed to get an up close view of at least one Presidential election.

Gay Pride

Openly gay students fare quite well, while those still in the closet often have a tougher time. Gays are becoming more prominent on campus, and acceptance is generally growing.

Most Popular Religions

There is a presence on campus for Catholics, Muslims, Jews, and Protestants of several denominations, while the non-denominational Tucker Foundation ensures that all faiths are respected and acknowledged. Only a small minority of Dartmouth students practice their religion fervently.

Economic Status

That half of students aren't on any financial aid speaks to the general wealth of people here. But despite the Ivy League prestige, there is little old money at Dartmouth—few affluent students flaunt their wealth or act in an elitist manner. There are many middle-class students partially working their way through college, and there are few working-class students.

Students Speak Out

ON DIVERSITY

"People complain about Dartmouth not being diverse. In some ways, this complaint is completely justified. In others ways, I think people are missing what is really around them."

"Well, campus is very white. There are minorities of all kinds: gay, black, Indian, Native American, Hispanic, and Jewish. Dartmouth is actually the most diverse school I've ever been to, but I think that after 200-plus years of being a predominantly white, heterosexual male environment, **the college still has some work to do on improving life for minorities**."

"I think the college needs to create an environment in which **everyone around you is unique in their personality**, yet similar as far as intellectual values."

"This is a tough question to answer, because, even though the college is numerically very diverse, I think the administration has gone about it in exactly the wrong way. The notion is that I should make up for centuries of white male privilege by feeling guilty and being sensitive. While changing with the times certainly in order, I think the college is really losing its identity in **a sea of politically-correct mumbo jumbo**."

"Dartmouth is approaching a 40-to-60 minority-to-non-minority ratio and has **improved in the area of diversity by leaps and bounds**. Despite a small natural minority recruiting pool—New Hampshire is one of the whitest states in the nation—Dartmouth has succeeded in bringing people of different races, ethnicities, religions, and perspectives together for an explosion of discourse."

"While racial self-segregation is a minor problem at the college, students consciously identify artificial barriers to relationships—like race—and act to overcome them. While very few people are 100 percent free of preconceived notions at Dartmouth, just as in most other areas of the world, **Dartmouth students take advantage of their diversity** in exploring new intellectual and personal areas together."

"**As far as being gay at Dartmouth, I find the school to be unacceptable**. I could talk about this for a while, but just know that, as a minority, I don't feel like Dartmouth is doing as much as they can for me. With the two billion dollar endowment that the school has, you'd think they could do more."

"Diversity is a problem that the college is addressing now. **Personally I think the campus is diverse**—some think otherwise, but I have friends from all races and a whole bunch of foreign countries."

The College Prowler Take
ON DIVERSITY

As an Ivy League institution, Dartmouth has a centuries-old tradition of being straight, white, and male. Despite fervent administration efforts to promote diversity, the "average" Dartmouth students are still crusty New England types sporting North Face. But special programs abound for traditionally underrepresented groups. Efforts to recruit Native Americans, whom Dartmouth was originally founded to educate, have been particularly vigorous. Students also report a sizable international population on campus.

While women and minorities are now proportionally represented on campus, many still feel like outsiders in the rugged New Hampshire woods. Meanwhile, other students feel racial minorities frequently self-segregate into "affinity housing" and homogenous Greek houses. Race notwithstanding, Dartmouth is still dominated by upper-middle-class students from the East Coast, although most students mix easily with people from other regions and/or varying socioeconomic status. Despite occasional tension, a strong sense of school spirit often prevails over individual differences.

The College Prowler™ Grade on

Diversity: B

A high grade in Diversity indicates that ethnic minorities and international students have a notable presence on campus and that students of different economic backgrounds, religious beliefs, and sexual preferences are well-represented.

Guys & Girls

The Lowdown
ON GUYS & GIRLS

Female Undergrads: 48.9%

Male Undergrads: 51.1%

Birth Control Available? Yes

Social Scene

With no notable divisions among its student body, Dartmouth has a vibrant social scene. While some students initiate love affairs with their laptops and others go out every night of the week, most know when to hit the books and when to let loose—usually two or three nights each week. Students are usually very friendly in class and in extracurricular activities. As opportunities to meet others abound in daily interactions and most students are linked by about two degrees of separation, building an ample social network is often as easy as lingering in the dining halls. While people usually associate by degrees of coolness, and the strength of athletes' bonds tends to make them exclusive groups, most students do have a wide cross-section of casual friends.

Hookups or Relationships?

Commitment-free hookups are extremely prevalent, to the frustration of many guys and girls. Those who enter relationships often do so seriously, to the point that casual dinner-and-movie relations are about as common as pterodactyls around campus. Many students enter Dartmouth with hometown significant others, but most of these relationships quickly fade away.

Dress Code

The protocol definitely calls for preppy, although with a North Woods twist. One glance at the Hinman Box mailroom indicates that J. Crew is the manufacturer of choice, but be sure to bring along that North Face or Columbia jacket for when the weather turns cold. While students may throw on jeans and a decent sweater for class, they don't overdo it. That goes for parties as well, over which guys and girls rarely fuss—and who could blame them, with a night of mucky basements and a disinclination to remember ahead. Moreover, when it's time for one of many theme parties, dress codes go out the window. Color Dartmouth students "refined outdoorsy."

Best Place to Meet Guys/Girls

Most hookups are initiated at weekend parties. Many students are acquainted with their "random" partner from an activity or through a mutual friend and use alcohol to bypass that extensive, unnecessary "getting-to-know-you" stage. The campus is small enough that you can see your crush almost every day with minimal effort. Extracurricular activities are a great way to expand your pool of friends, which becomes a pool of potential hookup partners come Friday night. Beer pong (played with paddles, unlike Beirut), is used universally as a poor man's invitation to a date. Who says romance is dead?

As with birds, grass, and everything else, relationships tend to blossom anew come spring. Everybody becomes infinitely hotter when all that winter clothing is shed. Studly men and buxom ladies commonly trot out to the Green to study, toss a Frisbee, and flash their hot bods.

Top Three Places to Find Hotties:

1. The Green in spring
2. Webster Ave. on Wednesday, Friday, or Saturday
3. Kresge Fitness Center on weekday afternoons

Top Places to Hook Up:

1. BEMA (Big Empty Meeting Area)
2. Baker Stacks
3. Football Field—50-Yard Line
4. The Green
5. Top of the Hop
6. President Wright's Lawn
7. The Graveyard

Students Speak Out
ON GUYS & GIRLS

"It's hard to generalize when it comes to looks. I think that the stereotypical Dartmouth male would be a beer-guzzling football-playing frat boy, but you will find that the guys are all very different."

"**Supposedly the guys are 'above average'**—I have had girls tell me this—and the girls are 'below average.' All the guys I know agree. The girls are not so hot, but then again, Dartmouth isn't a state school, so this is to be expected."

"**The girls here are quite different**—the stereotypical girl would be a ditsy blonde sorority girl, but obviously they're not all that way. Both the guys and the girls are pretty attractive, I'd say. All in all, we have a good-looking campus."

"Well, it's a mixed bag. We tend to attract a ton of athletic girls, so we get a mix of hyper-attractive athletes and relatively unattractive 'butch women.' The good thing is that they're generally all **confident, smart, witty, and classy**. Although dating can be difficult in the party-oriented atmosphere, it is comforting to know that it's easy to make friends with girls no matter what they look like."

"Dartmouth girls are generally regarded as some of the ugliest in the Ivy League. Lookers are few and tend to be snapped up by jocks and frat boys. The almost exactly equal gender ratio destroys any advantage guys would normally have in dating, and the result is almost cutthroat competition. Still, there are **diamonds to be found in the rough**."

"**Nice, cute, fun guys are everywhere**, but the campus seems to fall into two categories when it comes to dating: random hookups that leave people confused, hurt, and make for awkward situations, but can be a lot of fun; and the married-since-they-met crowd, which couples up and tends to live together. There doesn't seem to be a middle ground of adult dating."

"Everyone says the girls aren't that hot, but I think **they are the same as at other colleges**. They just wear more clothing because it is cold in Hanover a lot of the time."

The College Prowler Take

ON GUYS & GIRLS

Don't drop that high school sweetheart just yet, but Dartmouth students seem to think they look all right. The disparity between guys and girls is very real, although recent female classes are quickly closing the gap, regardless of whether or not the Dartmouth Beautification Project actually exists. Hookups—drunken or otherwise—dominate an otherwise nonexistent dating scene. With beer goggles or without, most students are able to locate a hottie or two.

While Ivy Leaguers are known more for brain than brawn, Dartmouth students defy the stereotype. Students in general, and particularly freshman guys, sometimes complain about the slim pickings, but most everyone is relatively normal looking, not to mention in fantastic shape. However, if Hanover winters weren't depressing enough, just imagine trying to determine who's hot under all that clothing.

The College Prowler™ Grade on

Guys: A-

A high grade for Guys indicates that the male population on campus is attractive, smart, friendly, and engaging, and that the school has a decent ratio of guys to girls.

The College Prowler™ Grade on

Girls: B-

A high grade for Girls not only implies that the women on campus are attractive, smart, friendly, and engaging, but also that there is a fair ratio of girls to guys.

DARTMOUTH COLLEGE

Athletic Division:
NCCA Division I (I-AA for men's football)

Conference:
Eastern College Athletic Conference

Fields:
Memorial Field, Sachem Field, Scully-Fahey Field

Men's Varsity Teams:
- Baseball
- Basketball
- Crew Lightweight/ Heavyweight (plus Freshman team)
- Cross Country (plus JV team)
- Football (plus JV team)
- Golf
- Ice Hockey
- Lacrosse
- Skiing
- Alpine and Cross Country
- Soccer (plus JV team)
- Squash
- Swimming & Diving
- Tennis
- Track & Field (Indoor/ Outdoor)

Women's Varsity Teams:
- Basketball
- Crew (plus Novice team)
- Cross Country (plus JV team)
- Field Hockey
- Golf
- Ice Hockey
- Lacrosse
- Skiing
- Alpine and Cross Country
- Soccer (plus JV team)
- Softball
- Squash
- Swimming & Diving
- Tennis
- Track & Field (Indoor/ Outdoor)
- Volleyball

Coed Teams
Equestrian, Sailing

Club Sports
Badminton, Biathlon, Boxing, Cheerleading, Football, Cricket, Cycling, Dressage, EMS, Fencing, Figure Skating, Ice Hockey, Pom, Rugby, Snowboarding, Table Tennis, Tae Kwan Do, Tang Soo Doo, Tennis, Triathlon, Ultimate Frisbee, Volleyball, Water Polo, Wresting

Intramurals (IMs)
Basketball, Eight Ball, Free Throw Shooting, Flag Football, Golf, Handball, Ice Hockey, Lacrosse, Racquetball, Ski Races, Soccer, Softball, Squash, Table Tennis, Tennis/Team Tennis, Turkey Trot Fun Run, Volleyball, Wallyball, Water Polo, Whiffle Ball

Physical Education
Ballroom Dance, Basketball, Fencing, First Aid/ CPR, Fitness (FLIP), Fly Fishing, Goju-Ryu Karate, Golf, Horseback Riding Ice Skating, Ice Hockey, JuJitsu & Aikido, Mountain Biking, Kayaking, Learning at Dartmouth, Peer Health Education, Polocrosse, Racquetball, Rape Awareness/Defense, Red Cross Lifeguard, Rock Climbing, Sailing, Scuba Diving, Skiing: Alpine, Skiing: Nordic, Snowboarding, Snowshoe Hiking, Squash, Swimming, Tae Kwon Do, Tai Chi, Tennis, Tumbling, Volleyball, Wellness Works

Getting Tickets
All students receive free entry to all sporting events simply by flashing their IDs. Additional planning is unnecessary.

Most Popular Sports
Men's rugby, football, and both ice hockey teams have the largest following. Rugby, crew, and ultimate Frisbee all have large squads.

Overlooked Teams
Women's basketball had a solid yet overlooked season, while, at the club level, the cycling team is fantastic.

Best Place to Take a Walk

Occom Pond, Golf Course

Gyms/Facilities

Alumni Gym
The primary exercise facility for non-athletes (NCAA competitors frequent Davis Varsity House), Alumni Gyms and the adjoining Berry Sports Center contain squash and basketball courts, a pool, and a weight lifting facility (Kresge Fitness Center). Additionally, the gym complex houses Leede Arena, home court of the Big Green basketball squads.

Leverone Field House
The chief indoor facility on campus includes a track and batting cages.

Thompson Arena
This 3,500-seat hockey arena is occasionally open for free skating.

Dartmouth Skiway
Just a short drive from campus, the Skiway boasts a 3 lifts, 16 trains, and a lodge.

Hanover Country Club
Scenic golf course adjacent to campus.

Tennis Courts
Six indoor courts compose the Boss Center, while an additional 17 courts, four or them clay, are part of Dartmouth's athletic facilities.

Boathouses
Allen Boathouse, home of the sailing team, adjoins Mascoma Lake, while the Friends of Dartmouth Rowing Boathouse is on the Connecticut River.

Students Speak Out
ON ATHLETICS

"The varsity sports are not so big. If you're looking for a school where athletics are an integral part of campus life, then Dartmouth isn't going to be your first choice. IM sports exist, but they aren't huge."

"The main draws are football and hockey, although we have great success in several other areas, including nationally-ranked lacrosse and crew teams. Our football team draws huge crowds, especially for the homecoming and Harvard games. **While our teams, as of late, have not been terribly successful, a good time is had by all**."

"When it comes to hockey, Dartmouth has seen a great deal of success. Our women's team has been ranked in the top 10 nationally for several years and makes regular appearances in the last stages of the NCAA tournament. Club and intramural sports are enormously popular, with **nearly all students participating in some type of athletics**."

"**Athletes are a dominant force on campus**. The resulting furor when the administration tried to cut the swim team far exceeded the mumbles of discontent over the closing of satellite libraries. While hockey comes close, there is no dominant sport on campus . . . but people here are always exercising. Sometimes I wonder if the admissions office specifically rejects obese people."

"Some sports are better than others, but no matter how badly the football team does, and it is usually bloody awful, there is always a big audience at games. IM sports are popular; most organizations have their own teams—College Bowl's basketball team or **the 'God-squad'** in softball, a combination of Aquinas House [Catholic organization] and Hillel."

"My Dartmouth interviewer told me that he knew **only a few people who weren't involved in sports in some way**. I've certainly found that to be true, even if we don't have many teams that the whole school rallies behind."

The College Prowler Take
ON ATHLETICS

Very few students watch Dartmouth sporting events religiously, but don't let that fool you into thinking they can't distinguish between football and futbol. This small school supports an amazing number of NCAA teams, meaning that a full half of Dartmouth students are varsity athletes. While basketball and football haven't fielded dominant teams for years, winter hockey games at Leverone Field House are a favorite.

There is sometimes a divide between athletes and their egghead peers, but all the sweating that goes on at Dartmouth generally promotes a friendly atmosphere for the student-athlete. Even students not on a varsity squad are usually very active. Some play intramurals, while others join popular club teams like rugby, crew, and ultimate Frisbee. Additionally, most hike, ski, or otherwise enjoy the great outdoors.

The College Prowler™ Grade on
Athletics: B+

A high grade in Athletics indicates that students have school spirit, that sports programs are respected, that games are well- attended, and that intramurals are a prominent part of student life.

The Lowdown
ON NIGHTLIFE

Organization Parties:
While most college-sanctioned parties are thoroughly lame (especially if at Fuel), cultural events in Collis Commonground or elsewhere can be a decent night-starter.

Frats:
See the Greek Section!

Students Speak Out
ON NIGHTLIFE

"A few places around town turn into bars around 10 p.m. If you're over 21, they're a lot of fun. If not, your only real option is Greek houses and private parties."

"On campus entertainment, varies from decent to awful. **This year, I caught a couple of offbeat movies** like *Dogtown* and *Z-Boys* and a documentary about Jerry Seinfeld, which were pretty cool. For those of age, Lone Pine is a decent place to grab a drink, but Fuel nightclub is beyond lame, as are most college-sponsored parties."

"I think **there's one club in the area**, but it's probably a joke. New Hampshire isn't really the 'hippest' place on earth. Same goes for bars. The restaurants in Hanover have bars, but that's about it."

"The nightlife is mainly focused on the fraternity scene, although the campus provides strong supplements and alternatives. Options include free or extremely inexpensive movies, free food options, discussion groups, speakers, pool and billiards, and more."

"Unfortunately, Hanover is small, and **there are no clubs in the area**. The bars are anal about underage drinking, so not many people hang out there, however, the fraternities make up for the lack of town nightlife."

"It's Hanover. There are no bars or clubs anywhere nearby. Instead there are frats. **We do, however, have Lone Pine Tavern in Collis**, which serves alcohol to people of age and has pretty good food."

"No clubs. **There are a couple bars**, but mostly, the Greek system is the source of nightlife. There are sponsored concerts there and parties every weekend sponsored by the frats and sororities themselves, and they take the place of clubs. However, the Greek system is under attack right now, so things may change."

"For those that don't like the party scene, **there are always cool events to go to**. Dartmouth attracts a lot of interesting speakers. I've seen Ehud Barak, Bishop Desmond Tutu, Alison Brown, and Charles Ogletree. NASA astronauts have come to speak about their past mission repairing the Hubble space telescope. There are music groups, plays, comedians, and other things to hear all the time. I got to see Itzhak Perlman for only five bucks! A cappella is also very popular on campus."

"**Every person who has come to visit me has had a blast at night**. There is a lot to do, considering our location, and people seldom complain about options. It's more common to hear people whine about having too much work to go out."

The College Prowler Take

ON NIGHTLIFE

Bars are extremely rare, save for 5 Olde and restaurants. You'll also have to hold that groove thang, as clubs are non-existent. Most weekends will feature a house party or two, although they are often hit-or-miss and require a long walk down Lebanon Street. Unless you count a NASA lecture as a party, most school-sponsored events don't get too crazy, although a cappella shows do attract sizable crowds. It is worth noting that Dartmouth is one of the few colleges in the country where fake IDs are entirely unnecessary. Anyone who wants beer can get it at fraternities, where there is no carding—and it's easy to find an upperclassman to go on a liquor run to West Lebanon.

As with Hanover in general, no nightlife exists apart from Dartmouth-sponsored events, parties, or otherwise. While it's sometimes fun just to chill in the dorms with your friends, be prepared to swill cheap beer in crowded frat basements if you choose to venture "out" for entertainment.

DARTMOUTH COLLEGE

The College Prowler™ Grade on

Nightlife: D

A high grade in Nightlife indicates that there are many bars and clubs in the area that are easily accessible and affordable. Other determining factors include the number of options for the under-21 crowd and the prevalence of house parties.

Greek Life

The Lowdown
ON GREEK LIFE

Number of Fraternities:
17

Number of Sororities:
10

Number of Coed Houses:
3

Number of Undergraduate Societies:
2

Undergrad Men in Fraternities:
28% of men, 37% of eligible men (non-freshmen)

Undergrad Women in Sororities:
22% of women, 30% of eligible women (non-freshmen)

Fraternities on Campus:
Psi Upsilon (national), Kappa Kappa Kappa (local), Alpha Delta (local), Zeta Psi (national; permanently de-recognized by the college), Theta Delta Chi (national), Phi Delta Alpha (local), Chi Heorot (local), Bones Gate (local), Sigma Nu (national), Sigma Alpha Epsilon (national), Chi Gamma Epsilon (local), Gamma Delta Chi (local), Sigma Phi Epsilon (national), Alpha Chi Alpha (local; non-residential), Alpha Phi Alpha (national; non-residential), Kappa Alpha Psi (national; non-residential), Lambda Upsilon Lambda (national; non-residential)

Sororities on Campus:
Sigma Delta (local), Kappa Kappa Gamma (national), Epsilon Kappa Theta (local), Alpha Kappa Alpha (national; non-residential), Delta Sigma Theta (national; non-residential), Delta Delta Delta (national), Kappa Delta Epsilon (local), Alpha Xi Delta (national), Sigma Lambda Upsilon (national; non-residential), Alpha Pi Omega (national; non-residential)

Coed Houses:
Phi Tau (local), Alpha Theta (local), The Tabard (local)

Undergraduate Societies:
Panarchy, Amarna

Other Greek Organizations:
Greek Leaders Council, Interfraternity Council, Order of Omega, Panhellenic Council (residential sororities), Pan-Hellenic Council (some non-residential organizations), Coed Council

Did You Know?

Animal House writer Chris Miller based the famous Delta chapter after Dartmouth's own Alpha Delta.

Students Speak Out
ON GREEK LIFE

"It can be overwhelming and all-encompassing at times, but it's a great social option if you choose to join a house. There is a sense that everyone on campus is welcome, so openness is a positive feature."

"Most houses can be stereotyped, but there are many exceptions to each rule. **Greeks provide most of the social space and programming on campus** outside of college-sponsored events, which tend to be lackluster. Come with an open mind—I never planned to be Greek, and I ended up running a fraternity!"

"Frats are the dominant social scene on campus. Despite the presence of sororities and coed organizations, when people go out on the weekends, they go to frats. **You can find somewhere to party at any time on any night of the week**. I nearly didn't come to Dartmouth because of the strength of the Greek system, but now I'm glad I did. While I came on to campus as a freshman vowing to never join a frat, I found out that their reputations are generally ill-deserved."

"Frat parties are fun, and **the camaraderie and closeness that develops between members is incredible** and well-worth the disgust from looking at the floors of the basements. The Greek system is one of the last remnants of Old Dartmouth—the way that college life was supposed to be."

"Each houses is vastly different from the next, and they change every year. **Sorority rush is awful**, but it's worth the outcome of 50 to 80 potential new friends and a place that you're always welcome."

"The Greek system dominates; a large percentage of the student body is a member of a frat or sorority. The campus is completely rural, so without any clubs people go to frat parties. Wednesday, Friday, and Saturday are the biggest nights. They're fun but completely informal. Usually, it's **dancing and DJ upstairs, beer pong downstairs**."

"Greek life on campus is very influential, and many men and women decide to become affiliated with a Greek organization. Alcohol often plays a role in Greek life and activities. However, to say that this is a defining characteristic of Greeks is untrue. Greek houses frequently sponsor **community service opportunities**, concerts, and speakers.Greek life at Dartmouth also serves to foster community relations by increasing the support network available to students."

The College Prowler Take
ON GREEK LIFE

While half the eligible students—those in their sophomore winter or later—pledge a fraternity or sorority, you don't have to be Greek to partake. Almost all frat parties are open to all students, and cheap beer—Keystone or Milwaukee's Best—flows freely to all. Beer pong is the official Dartmouth sport, but most weekend nights feature at least once dance party. Students may drink like fish, but even those on the wagon frequent frats to socialize with their friends.

While the days of *Animal House* can be relived only on celluloid, Greek houses dominate the social scene at Dartmouth. The frats remain an entrenched part of Dartmouth culture, despite administration's efforts to diminish their influence. While a few students don't care for the frats and some upper-classmen grow weary of the monotonous scene, the Greek system is a binding tie for most. Three nights a week, most of the action can still be found on good ol' Webster Aveue.

The College Prowler™ Grade on

Greek Life: A

A high grade in Greek Life indicates that sororities and fraternities are not only present, but also active on campus. Other determining factors include the variety of houses available and the respect the Greek community receives from the rest of the campus.

Drug Scene

The Lowdown
ON DRUG SCENE

Most Prevalent Drugs on Campus:
Marijuana, cocaine, ecstasy

Liquor-Related Arrests:
Campus Safety and Security reports about 250 alcohol related arrests per year.

Drug Counseling Programs
Counseling and Human Development
(603) 650-1442
Services: Assessment, individual counseling, group counseling

Students Speak Out
ON DRUG SCENE

"If you aren't into drugs, you won't know they're there. If you want drugs, you'll always be able to find them."

"There isn't much of a drug scene that I know of. If you want drugs, you can certainly get them, but it's **not a huge deal at Dartmouth**, and I think most students like it that way."

"They're **basically non-existent**. There's a little weed here and there and a few other drugs, but you have to actively look for drugs other than pot to find them. I partied frequently last year and only saw alcohol, weed, and one time, I saw mushrooms. Nothing more."

"The two biggest drugs are **pot and ecstasy**. Quite a few people smoke up, but it's not a big deal. Personally, I don't smoke, and I have never been pressured into smoking at Dartmouth."

"The drug scene is pretty low-key; but it does exist. Most people stick to alcohol, although I've seen **tons of pot**, and ecstasy is starting to become popular."

"There are drugs in Hanover, but not many. **It's not like they're selling crack in the library** or anything."

"Drugs are surprisingly present, despite the remoteness of Hanover. Hard drugs are available, though you won't witness much unless you specifically seek them, so it's easy to avoid. **Most people aren't into it**."

The College Prowler Take
ON DRUG SCENE

While the average student may run across quite a bit of pot, Dartmouth's drug scene has a very low profile. While ecstasy or the occasional mushrooms might show up at parties, students generally pass on everything but the grass.

People "in the know" claim that the hard drugs are out there, and certain fraternities at Dartmouth have reputations as being hot spots for those who dabble in substance abuse. While the fact that drugs are available may not comfort your parents (or the authorities for that matter), most Dartmouth students are not bothered by the few drugs they encounter.

The College Prowler™ Grade on

Drug Scene: B

A high grade on Drug Scene indicates that drugs are not a noticeable part of campus life, drug use is not visible, and no pressure to use them seems to exist.

Campus Strictness

The Lowdown
ON CAMPUS STRICTNESS

What Are You Most Likely to Get Caught Doing on Campus?

Public intoxication

Drinking underage

Having an unregistered keg

Creating a fire hazard (read: leaving anything) in the hallway

Keeping books from the reserve desk for too long

Engaging in a vicious "blitz" war

Streaking across the Green

Speaking your politically incorrect mind

Students Speak Out
ON CAMPUS STRICTNESS

"For the most part, there is not much strictness on campus. Dartmouth students generally do what they please, within the bounds of the law, and have a great time doing it."

"I got **fined for everything** last year. Leaving shoes outside my door, unspecified hall damage, turning in my practice room key too late. It got to be rather ridiculous."

"They're not very strict. If you get really sick from drinking and have to go to the medical center, you won't get in trouble. **I don't think they bust down on drugs very much** because it would make Dartmouth look bad and heaven forbid that happen. I've never had a problem with either. If need be, though, safety and security will call in the Hanover police."

"Lots of people get picked up by safety and security when they're drunk, but it's not a big deal, really. Just make sure you don't get caught twice, and **your parents will never know**."

"Punishment for drinking can be severe **depending on what campus police officer you get in trouble with**. You aren't thrown in jail for underage drinking, everyone knows what goes on in frats, and campus police just need to make sure no one is seriously in danger, or else they get in trouble. If you are caught for underage drinking you must speak to the class dean, and possibly they talk to your parents, you get a fine, I don't know. I was never caught. Hanover police are different story: they suck. They are less frequent than the ubiquitous Dartmouth campus police, luckily."

"While frats aren't supposed to serve minors, the wristband system they use is a joke. When safety and security walks into a party, people just calmly put down their drinks until they leave. However, while rules aren't so strict for individuals, **frats have to jump through a ridiculous number of administrative hurdles to throw a party** and often get in trouble for minor violations."

The College Prowler Take

ON CAMPUS STRICTNESS

Opinions are clearly mixed, but students most frequently encounter campus authorities while inebriated. While visibly sloshed students are frequently detained, safety and security usually won't bug those who, at the very least, *act* sober. While they conduct walkthroughs at parties, S&S looks the other way at mass underage drinking, as long as containers are kept inside. Detox trips to "Dick's House" involve a fine and a chat with a dean. Unless hitchhiking from the Grafton County Jail is your idea of Sunday morning fun, stay away from the Hanover Police. Older students report that the increasing administration exercise of *in loco parentis* is just plain *loco* and depriving Dartmouth of valuable traditions. Gone is the rope swing, as well as Psi Upsilon fraternity's keg jump.

While the administration rarely sweats the small stuff, fines for everything from parking violations to leaving shoes in the hall are annoying. The powers that be have also attempted to debilitate the Greek system through increasing strictness, banning kegs and placing all but a handful on probation for minor violations. More troubling, politically correct buzzwords often dominate the exercise of free speech. Despite the unending list of rules, regulations, and violations, a remotely savvy student can get away with most forms of illegal activity. Overall, the bulk of the college's disciplinary weight falls on organizations (usually Greek) as opposed to individuals.

The College Prowler™ Grade on

Campus Strictness: B

A high Campus Strictness grade implies an overall lenient atmosphere; police and RAs are fairly tolerant, and the administration's rules are flexible.

Parking & Transportation

The College Prowler Take
ON PARKING & TRANSPORTATION

"Students park in A-Lot, which is about a 10-minute walk from campus. During the weekends, though, you can park on campus without getting a ticket."

"Students mostly park in A-Lot, the student parking lot. Beyond that, parking is very difficult. **Hanover is extremely vigilant about checking meters** and giving tickets to offenders, and the metered spots are only good for two hours, so parking is no picnic."

"Unless you're in a house or negotiate to park at one, forget about it. **A-Lot is a mile away from the far end of campus**, and cars get plowed in under snowdrifts. Guessing which one's yours isn't an easy task."

"It exists, somewhere beyond the third star on the left and straight on till morning. Seriously, though, I don't have a car, and I don't concern myself with parking. **Most students don't have cars**."

"**Freshmen can't have cars on campus**, but there are plenty of lots/permits available for upperclassmen. The lots aren't terribly close to the center of campus, but they aren't inconvenient either."

"There isn't any public transportation—it's not necessary. There is public transportation that takes you into town, but by the time you need to get there, you'll have friends with cars and won't need it. On campus, everything is within walking distance. If you need to go somewhere at night that's across campus, **safety and security will drive you**."

"**There's free transportation**—the college pays to let Dartmouth students use it for free—to West Lebanon, but it takes six times as long as it would by a normal car."

The Lowdown
ON PARKING & TRANSPORTATION

Student Parking Lot?
A-Lot

Freshmen Allowed to Park?
No

Approximate Parking Permit Cost:
$20 per term

Parking & Transportation Services:
(603) 646-2204
Robin Guay@dartmouth.edu
www.dartmouth.edu/~parking

Parking Permits
Permits are plentiful for upperclassmen, but parking near the center of campus is impossible for undergraduates to obtain.

Ways to Get Around Town:

On Campus:
Walk or bike

Public Transportation:
Advance Transit: (802) 295-1824;
www.advancetranit.com

Taxi Cabs:
Apex Car Service: (603) 252-8294
Big Yellow Taxi: (603) 643-8294
Upper Valley Taxi: (802) 295-9455

"**Free local buses are great and easy to use**, though most people don't take advantage of them. Riding the bus to Boston can be expensive, but Dartmouth Coach is comfortable."

"Dartmouth Coach to Boston is mainly for the airport and kind of expensive, as well. **Make friends with people who have cars** for those trips to Wal-Mart in West Leb."

The College Prowler Take
ON PARKING

Freshmen can't have cars on campus, so do keep that '91 Geo Prism at home. While spaces are available for upperclassmen, a good portion keeps their vehicles at home. A-Lot and other official parking is far off the beaten path, and don't even think of parking that car outside your dorm. S&S and H-Po are hyper-vigilant about tickets and will nail cars left unattended for a few minutes or on the street overnight. Parking is surprisingly scarce for a school located in as small a location as Hanover. While students can comfortably walk anywhere on campus, the plethora of tickets is annoying, not to mention a waste of perfectly good paper. The best bet for a spot is Greek houses with lots, where even freshman can land a spot for the right price. Perhaps it's better that many students choose not to bring cars, however, as the New Hampshire winter will destroy your vehicle.

The College Prowler™ Grade on
Parking: C-

A high grade in this section indicates that parking is both available and affordable, and that parking enforcement isn't overly severe.

The College Prowler Take
ON TRANSPORTATION

Students attest that the only subway in town serves sandwiches. An Amtrak train runs from nearby White River Junction. Greyhound-affiliate Vermont Transit services locations as near as the Dartmouth Skiway and as distant as New York or Montreal. Vermont Transit buses also run to Manchester Airport, while Dartmouth Coach goes to Boston's Logan Airport. While Lebanon Airport is just miles from campus, flights run very infrequently and are very expensive. Local Advance Transit buses, while free to students, are unbearably slow. All buses depart from the Hanover Inn, just south of the Green. Foot power is sufficient to get around campus, and, as isolated as Hanover is, it takes a long time to get anywhere. While easily accessible buses and trains make it easy to leave town, a bus ride and a couple of connecting flights make for a long day's travel when all you want is to sleep in your own bed. While local transportation exists, hitching a ride from a friend remains the best way to get around the area.

The College Prowler™ Grade on
Transportation: C

A high grade for Transportation indicates that campus buses, public buses, cabs, and rental cars are readily-available and affordable. Other determining factors include proximity to an airport and the necessity of transportation.

Overall Experience

Students Speak Out
ON OVERALL EXPERIENCE

"I love Dartmouth! I've seen so many schools, and I can't think of a single substantial change I would like to see on our campus."

"Academically, I think I've learned a lot at Dartmouth. I went on their **Foreign Study Program in Paris** last winter, and that was amazing. I think that the professors are all really nice and really intelligent and Dartmouth is definitely a giant step up from high school."

"If you want to find out more about campus life, you can go to ***www.thedartmouth.com***. The school newspaper is pretty helpful with assessing what life is like and how important frats are."

"**The school honestly cares about the students' social lives**. The Dartmouth Outing Club program helped me meet a bunch of nice kids before school ever started. Then, from the moment I left the woods, they have been planning activities for us."

"I felt the campus was very safe. **People were incredibly friendly**. The dining hall food was pretty good compared to most other colleges, but after I moved off campus, when I finally had some money, I ate out a lot because the local restaurants were great."

"Most college students like their colleges. **Dartmouth students are often in love with their school**. My personal passion for Dartmouth has exceeded my own expectations, and I have found myself enormously happy at Dartmouth, despite initial misgivings. The people, resources, and general campus activity have made my Dartmouth experience (so far) entirely successful, and I am utterly content at Dartmouth. I can't wait for my summer to end so I can get back!"

The College Prowler Take
ON OVERALL EXPERIENCE

According to popular opinion, Dartmouth students are among the happiest in the land. And with a gorgeous campus, great food, spacious dorms, and a vibrant party scene, why shouldn't they be? There are certainly a host of minor drawbacks to attending school in Hanover—isolation, no parking, no more rope swing, to name a few. However, the unique positives like the study abroad program, top-notch academics, and numerous outdoor opportunities blow these negatives out of the water for most students.

Dartmouth students share perhaps the strongest sentiment for their school out of any college kids in the country. Such passion is what motivates alums to trek to Hanover for big weekends and party like teenagers, long after their heyday has passed. Dartmouth is a friendly, pleasant place, providing the vast majority of its students with a genuine Ivy League experience and, if all goes well, a big-name Ivy League diploma.

The Inside Scoop

The Lowdown

ON THE INSIDE SCOOP

Dartmouth Slang:

Know the slang, know the school. The following is a list of things you really need to know before coming to Dartmouth. The more of these words you know, the better off you'll be.

AT – Appalachian Trail; runs through Dartmouth's campus

Banner Student – Online Web site containing personal academic information

Blitz – E-mail; can be used as any part of speech

CD – Community director; no one's sure what they do, except boss around the UGAs.

Coco – College Courses, interdisciplinary in nature

***D* (the)** – Student newspaper; the nation's oldest and, many allege, worst

DA$H – An account used for on-campus, non-food purchases; it's not real money.

Dick's House – Student health center

Direct Connect – System for exchanging music and movies.

EBAs – Everything But Anchovies; they deliver until 2 a.m..

FO&M – Facilities Operations and Management

***Free Press,* (the)** – Liberal, school-supported newspaper

FSP – Foreign study program

Green, (the) – Huge grassy rectangle at the center of campus

HB – Hinman Box, where you pick up your mail; located in the Hop

H-Po – Hanover Police; really avoid when drunk

Hop, (the) – Hopkins Center; performing arts center of campus

HTH – Hometown honey, with whom you will break up shortly after arriving on campus

LSA – Language Study Abroad

NRO – Non-recording option; when invoked, allows you to receive an "NR" if you fail to achieve a desired grade in a class

ORL – Office of Residential Life

Parkhursted – Suspended; named after the administration building, Parkhurst.

Pong – Beer pong; played exclusively with handle-less paddles

PUBLIC – Name of network for Apple users

***Review,* (the)** – Independent conservative student newspaper.

Robo – Robinson Hall; home of the Dartmouth Outing Club and other student organizations

Rocky – Rockefeller Center; government center

Senior Fence – Surrounds part of the Green; don't sit on it if you're not a senior

'Shmenu – The Green Book; contains pictures of all the freshman

'Shmob – The large group in which most freshman travel.

Sketchy – All-purpose word to describe anyone or anything about which you are skeptical; use liberally.

SA Cash – Debit account that can be used in town

Sphinx – Large, tomb-like home to a secret society, located in the middle of campus

S&S – Safety and security; should be avoided when drunk

Term – Used most often in place of "quarter"; saying "semester" will give you away as a newbie in a heartbeat.

Thayer – Dining hall and engineering school. Pay attention to context clues.

Treehouses – Hastily constructed and undesirable dwellings near the river

Tripee: Fellow member of your freshman trip

UGA: Undergraduate assistant; a supposedly less mean version of RA

Webster Ave: Fraternity (and sorority) row

WILSON: Name of network for PC users

Tips to Succeed at Dartmouth:

- Always go to class when midterms or finals are coming up.
- Take naps in the afternoon.
- Have at least one good friend in every class.
- Use distributive requirements to take fun classes.
- Avoid morning classes or Tuesday/ Thursday classes all together.
- Plan a break or fun extracurricular activity into your schedule.
- Find two or three good study spots and move around.
- Don't let BlitzMail consume your life.

Things I Wish I Knew Before Coming to Dartmouth:

- Orientation is by far the best time to meet people . . . and go to Frat Row.
- All that time I procrastinated could have been spent having fun.
- I only have time for two or three extracurricular activities.
- How few nice clothes I need and how many crazy clothes I could use.
- The Choates were nothing to worry about.
- How cold a New Hampshire winter really is.
- How to ski . . . or camp.

DARTMOUTH COLLEGE

Urban Legends

Any Native American admitted will receive full a scholarship to Dartmouth. (While this is untrue, Dartmouth has renewed its original commitment to Native Americans and now has more of them than the other Ivies combined.)

Students caught drinking during orientation and before matriculation will have their admission rescinded.

Playboy once ranked Dartmouth's guys the second-hottest in the country.

Beer pong was invented at Dartmouth; students believe their paddle version is a purer game than the oft-played Beirut.

School Spirit

Love for "the College on the Hill" extends far beyond the Dartmouth jock-wear most students are perpetually sporting. From Freshman Trips forward, Dartmouth students are imbued with a fierce love of their unique and historic institution. The college's small size fosters a single Dartmouth community, and students often make the trek to Hanover during their off terms. Dartmouth alumni are fiercely loyal and noted for being generous with pocketbooks and connections. However, there is a sense among even recent graduates that the school is being slowly transformed into a cookie-cutter research institution. For now at least, Hanover is filled with students who love their school and are sublimely happy.

Homecoming

Each term has one "big" (read: party) weekend, and in fall, the chief celebration is homecoming. Freshmen are the focus of the weekend, as they are officially welcomed into the Dartmouth family. On Friday night, upperclassmen collect all the pea-greens during a Freshman Sweep. Everyone marches en masse to the center of the Green, where a giant bonfire ensues. Freshmen run around it one hundred times plus the last two digits of their class year while older students and alumni egg them on.

Winter Carnival

Back before Dartmouth was coeducational, the long winter was warmed on this weekend as hundreds of women were bused in from all over the country. Now that women have populated the Hanover campus for three decades, Winter Carnival focuses more on seasonal festivities.

Tubestock

Another three to four day round of carousing culminates when the thousand or so students on campus don their bathing suits and head to the Connecticut River, where they float themselves and large quantities of beer on homemade rafts and inner tubes. Unlike the other three "big" weekends, Tubestock is not supported by the college, and whether or not it will happen hangs in the balance until only days before.

Sophomore Summer

Summer school sounds less than glamorous, but it means three months of fantastic weather and class bonding for each sophomore class. Students often take only two courses while lounging the summer away at "Camp Dartmouth."

Ledyard Challenge
Before graduation, students are supposed to swim naked across the Connecticut River to Vermont (where nudity is legal), and then scamper in the buff back across the Ledyard Bridge.

The "Indian"
Dartmouth was originally founded for the education of Native Americans, and Indians became embedded in college lore. The college failed to follow through on their original charter, with fewer than 20 Native Americans graduating before the 1960s, but in the last few decades Dartmouth has built one of the strongest Native American studies programs in the country. While the school has never had an official mascot, the "Indian"-head logo graced the *Dartmouth* masthead, as well as athletes, for decades. Since the "Indian" was banned in 1974, the Clay Pipe Ceremony has been canceled, while only a few seniors carry "Indian"-head canes at graduation. While students are currently attempting to replace the nebulous Big Green moniker, the outcome of current efforts is uncertain.

Green Key
With temperatures finally mild, Dartmouth students take to the great outdoors to celebrate. Green Key is arguably the biggest party weekend of the year as students bask in the sun for three or four straight days. Barbecues and concerts abound, with some fraternities throwing annual parties.

DARTMOUTH COLLEGE

Finding a Job or Internship

The Lowdown
ON FINDING A JOB OR INTERNSHIP

Career Center Resources & Services:
Job/Internship Search Workshops
Job and Internship Listings (MonterTRAK)
On-Campus Recruiting
Blitz Bulletin
Graduate Advising
Electronic Portfolio

The Lowdown
If your connections via Uncle Harold fail—or should you need some additional assistance—seek out Career Services, which has a generally positive reputation around campus and provides comprehensive career help. Each fall, dozens of companies trek up to Dartmouth to woo seniors during Corporate Recruiting.

Advice
Career Services can be of help from the first summer onward, so attending a first-time users session immediately after arriving on campus can be especially helpful. Always keep a resume on file and monitor the Career Services BlitzMail Bulletin for interesting opportunities. Also, students interested in government should seek out the resources of the Rockefeller Center, which has a number of specific listings and internships.

The Lowdown
ON ALUMNI

Web site:
www.dartmouth.edu/alumni

Office:
6068 Blunt Alumni Center
Hanover, NH 03755
(888) 228-6068
alumni.relations@dartmouth.edu

Blunt Alumni Center:
Blunt is located just northwest of the Green and often hosts alumni in a tent on big weekends.

Services Available:
Online directory, e-mail account

Major Alumni Events:
The three regular-year party weekends—Homecoming, Winter Carnival, and Green Key—bring a multitude of alums back to Hanover. Additionally, class reunions are held every five years the week after commencement. Turnout for these reunions is very high, and the events raise a great deal of money for Dartmouth.

Alumni Publications:
Dartmouth Alumni Magazine
(603) 646-2256
Alumni.Maganize@dartmouth.edu

Famous Dartmouth Alumni:

Daniel Webster (Class of 1801) – secretary of state under three Presidents

Robert Frost (Class of 1896) – Pulitzer Prize-winning poet

Theodore ("Dr.") Seuss Geisel (Class of '25) – world-famous children's author

Nelson Rockefeller (Class of '30) – Vice-President under Gerald Ford

Dr. C. Everett Koop (Class of '37) – U.S. surgeon general under President Reagan

(Mister) Fred Rogers (Class of '50) – children's television entertainer

H. Carl McCall (Class of '58) – former New York comptroller and gubernatorial candidate

Louis Gerstner (Class of '63) – former IBM CEO

Paavo Lipponen (Class of '64) – former Finnish Prime Minister

Robert Reich (Class of '68) – U.S. secretary of labor under President Clinton

Paul Gigot (Class of '77) – Pulitzer Prize-winning journalist

Dinesh D'Souza (Class of '83) – political journalist and cultural critic

Jay Fiedler (Class of '94) – Miami Dolphins NFL quarterback

DARTMOUTH COLLEGE

The Ten BEST Things About Dartmouth:

1	Tight-knit community
2	Beer Pong
3	The D-Plan
4	Wireless
5	Outdoor opportunities
6	Big weekends
7	Three classes
8	Friendly professors
9	The Green on a beautiful day
10	EBAs at 2:15 a.m.

The Ten WORST Things About Dartmouth:

1	Dark winter days
2	Isolation
3	The D-Plan
4	Wrangling for diversity
5	Parking
6	Fines
7	Hanover nightlife
8	Kresge Fitness Center on a crowded afternoon
9	Student apathy
10	Administration crackdown on the Greeks

Visiting Dartmouth

Overnight Visits

Hosting is available for juniors in May and seniors in October and November. Students will stay with a current Dartmouth student on a Monday through Thursday night and must bring a sleeping bag and spending money. Please call the admissions office to schedule your stay.

Dimensions Weekend, which takes place every spring, invites all accepted students to stay at Dartmouth for a weekend. It is an incredible time, and almost every student who goes ends up matriculating at Dartmouth.

Admissions Phone:
(603) 646-2875

Take a Campus Virtual Tour:
www.dartmouth.edu/~tour

Campus Tours

Campus tours are conducted at various times throughout the year. During most of the fall, winter, and spring terms, they are given at 10 a.m. and 2 p.m. Monday through Friday and at 10 a.m and 12 p.m. on Saturday. Additional tours are conducted during summer term and peak times.

Information Sessions

From January through mid-November, half hour group sessions are conducted at 10 a.m. Monday through Friday. Information sessions are also held at 10 a.m. and 11 a.m. on Saturdays from mid-September through mid-November.

On-campus Interviews

On-campus interviews are available to rising seniors from mid-June through mid-November. Please call the admissions office at least three weeks in advance of your visit to schedule an interview.

Hotel Information:

1830 Shire Town Inn
Woodstock, VT
(802) 457-1830
Distance/Time to Campus: 30 min.

Adairs Motor Inn
Danbury, NH
(603) 768-9872
Distance/Time to Campus: 45 min.

Airport Economy Inn
West Lebanon, NH
(603) 298-8888
Distance/Time to Campus: 7 miles/ 10 min.

Alden Country Inn
Lyme, NH
(800) 794-2296
Distance/Time to Campus: 20 min.

Ardmore Inn
Woodstock, VT
(802) 457-3887
Distance/Time to Campus: 30 min.

Bed & Breakfast of Bank Street
Lebanon, NH
(603) 448-2041
Distance/Time to Campus: 15 min.

Best Western at the Junction
White River Junction, VT
(802) 295-3015
Distance/Time to Campus: 15 min

Best Western Sunapee
Lake Sunapee, NH
(800) 528-1234
Distance/Time to Campus: 30 min.

Best Western Sunapee
Lake Sunapee, NH
(800) 528-1234
Distance/Time to Campus: 30 min.

Bradford Motel
Bradford, VT
(802) 222-4467
Distance/Time to Campus: 20 miles

Breakfast on the Connecticut
Lyme, NH
(603) 353-4444
Distance/Time to Campus: 12 miles/ 20 min.

Burkhaven Motel
Sunapee, NH
(800) 567-2788
Distance/Time to Campus: 30 min.

Carriage House of Woodstock
Woodstock, VT
(802) 457-4322
Distance/Time to Campus: 30 min.

Chieftain Motor Inn
Hanover, NH
(603) 643-2550
Distance/Time to Campus: 2.5 miles

Coach an' Four Motel
White River Junction, VT
(802) 295-2210
Distance/Time to Campus: 4.5 miles/ 15 min.

Colonial Farm Inn
New London, NH
(603) 526-6121
Distance/Time to Campus: 30 miles/ 35 min.

Columns Motor Lodge
Sharon, VT
(802) 763-7040
Distance/Time to Campus: 20 min.

Comfort Inn
White River Junction, VT
Toll free: 800-628-7727
(802) 295-3051
Distance/Time to Campus: 10 min.

Coolidge Hotel
White River Junction, VT
(802) 295-3118
Distance/Time to Campus: 5 miles/ 10 min.

Days Inn/Holiday Inn Express
Lebanon, NH
(603) 448-5070
Distance/Time to Campus: 3 miles/ 5-10 min.

Deer Brook Inn
Woodstock, VT
(802) 672-3713
Distance/Time to Campus: 30 min.

Dowds Country Inn
Lyme, NH
(603) 795-4712
Distance/Time to Campus: 10 miles/ 10 min.

Fairlee Motel
Fairlee, VT
(802) 333-9192
Distance/Time to Campus: 8 min.

Fairway
New London, NH
(603) 526-6040
Distance/Time to Campus: 30 min

Fireside Inn
West Lebanon, NH
(603) 298-5906
Distance/Time to Campus: 10 min.

Gibson House Gallery and Bed & Breakfast
Haverhill, NH
(603) 989-3125
Distance/Time to Campus: 25 min.

Goddard Mansion Bed & Breakfast
Claremont, NH
(603) 543-0603
Distance/Time to Campus: 30 min.

Half-Acre Motel
Sharon, VT
(802) 763-8010
Distance/Time to Campus: 25 miles/ 15-20 min.

Hampton Inn
White River Junction, VT
(802) 296-2800
Distance/Time to Campus: 15 min.

Hanover Inn
Hanover, NH
(603) 643-4300
Distance/Time to Campus: On Campus

Hilltop Motel
Newport, NH
(603) 863-3456
Distance/Time to Campus: 35 min.

Home Hill French Inn and Restaurant
Plainfield, NH
(603) 675-6165
Distance/Time to Campus: 20 min.

Inn at Ragged Edge Farm
Wilmot, NH
(603) 735-6484
Distance/Time to Campus: 45 min.

Jackson House Inn
Woodstock, VT
(802) 457-2065
Distance/Time to Campus: 30 min.

Juniper Hill Inn
Windsor, VT
(802) 674-5273
Distance/Time to Campus: 20 min.

Lake Morey Resort
Fairlee, VT
(802) 457-3312
Distance/Time to Campus: 15-20 min.

Lamplighter
New London, NH
(603) 526-6484
Distance/Time to Campus: 25-30 min.

Lincoln Inn
Woodstock, VT
(802) 457-3312
Distance/Time to Campus: 30 min.

Mary Keane House
Enfield, NH
(603) 632-4241
Distance/Time to Campus: 12 miles/ 15-20 min.

New London Inn
New London, NH
(603) 526-2791
Distance/Time to Campus: 30-45 min.

Newport Motel
Newport, NH
(603) 863-1440
Distance/Time to Campus: 35 miles

Norwich Inn
Norwich, VT
(802) 649-1143
Distance/Time to Campus: 2 miles

October Country Inn
Bridgewater Corners, VT
(802) 572-3412
Distance/Time to Campus: 25 min.

Ottauquechee Motor Lodge
Woodstock, VT
(802) 672-3404
Distance/Time to Campus: 35 min.

Parker House Inn
Quechee, VT
(802) 295-6077
Distance/Time to Campus: 15 min.

Pierces Inn
Etna, NH
(603) 643-2997
Distance/Time to Campus: 5.5 miles/ 12 min.

Piermont Inn Old Church
Piermont, NH
(603) 272-4820
Distance/Time to Campus: 30 min.

Pine Crest Motel
White River Junction, VT
(802) 295-2725
Distance/Time to Campus: 10 miles/ 10-15 min.

Pleasant View Motel
White River Junction, VT
(802) 295-3485
Distance/Time to Campus: 5 miles

Quality Inn at Quechee Gorge
Quechee, VT
(802) 295 7600
Distance/Time to Campus: 15 min.

Quechee Inn at Marshland Farm
Quechee, VT
(802) 295-3133
10-12 min.

Ramada Inn
White River Junction, VT
(802) 295-3000
Distance/Time to Campus: 5 miles/ 10 min.

Residence Inn by Marriott
Lebanon, NH
(603) 643-4511
Distance/Time to Campus: 5 min.

Shire Motel
46 Woodstock, VT
(802) 457-2211

Silver Maple Lodge & Cottages
Fairlee, VT
(800) 666-1946
Distance/Time to Campus: 17 miles/ 20 min.

Sunset Motor Inn
Lebanon, NH
(603) 298-8721
Distance/Time to Campus: 5 min.

Super 8 Motel
White River Junction, VT
(802) 295-7577
Distance/Time to Campus: 15 min.

The Woodbridge Inn of Woodstock
Woodstock, VT
(802) 672-1800
Distance/Time to Campus: 30-35 min.

Three Church Street
Woodstock, VT
(802) 457-1925
Distance/Time to Campus: 30 min.

Trumbull House B & B
Hanover, NH
(800) 651-5141
Distance/Time to Campus: 4 miles

Village Inn of Woodstock
Woodstock, VT
(802) 457-1255
30 min.

Warren Village Inn, LLC
Warren, NH
(603) 764-5600
Distance/Time to Campus: 25 min.

Woodbridge Inn
Bridgewater, VT
(802) 672-1800
Distance/Time to Campus: 20 min.

Woodstock Inn & Resort
Woodstock, VT
(802) 457-1100
Distance/Time to Campus: 30 min.

Woodstocker Bed & Breakfast
Woodstock, VT
(802) 457-3896
Distance/Time to Campus: 20-25 min.

Directions to Campus

From the Boston Area (2.5 hours)

- Take I-93 north to I-89 north at Concord, NH.
- Get off I-89 at Exit 18 in Lebanon, NH onto Route 120. (A sign says that it is the exit for Dartmouth College.)
- Bear right off the exit, heading north on Rt.120 into Hanover.
- 4.1 miles from the exit, Rt. 120 forks at a traffic light.
- Bear right at the fork, following Rt. 120 one-half mile on South Park Street to the second traffic light.
- Turn left at the light, onto East Wheelock Street.
- Follow East Wheelock for two-tenths of a mile, when you will come to the Hopkins Center (left) and the Dartmouth Green (right).

From Burlington, VT (1.5 hours)

- Take I-89 south to I-91 north in White River Junction, VT. See following description.

From New York (5 hours), Southern New England, and Points South

- Take I-91 north to exit 13 at Norwich, VT.
- Bear right off the exit, across the Ledyard Bridge spanning the Connecticut River.
- Continue up the hill (West Wheelock Street) to the top of the hill and to the traffic light in the center of town—nine-tenths of a mile from the interstate exit.
- To your left at the light is the Dartmouth Green; to your right is the Hanover Inn.

Harvard University

University Hall Cambridge, MA 02138
www.college.harvard.edu (617) 495-1551

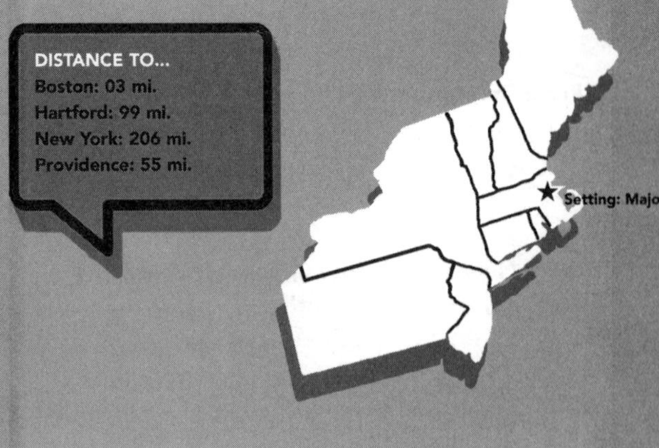

"Harvard's reputation alone makes the school an attractive, and sometimes intimidating, place to earn a college education."

Total Enrollment:
6,562 - Large
Acceptance:
11%
Tuition:
$32,097
Top 10% of High School Class:
96%

SAT Range

Verbal	Math	Total
700 – 800	700 – 790	1400 – 1590

ACT Range

Verbal	Math	Total
30-35	30-35	31-34

Most Popular Majors:
14% Economics
11% Political Science and Government
8% Social Sciences
7% Psychology

Students Also Applied To:*
Columbia University, Princeton University, Stanford University, Yale University

*For more school info check out *www.collegeprowler.com*

Table of Contents

College Prowler Report Card

Academics .... **A**
Local Atmosphere .... **A-**
Safety & Security .... **B+**
Computers .... **A-**
Facilities .... **B**
Campus Dining .... **D+**
Off-Campus Dining .... **A**
Campus Housing .... **A**
Off-Campus Housing .... **F**
Diversity .... **B+**
Guys .... **B**
Girls .... **B-**
Athletics .... **C+**
Nightlife .... **A-**
Greek Life .... **D+**
Drug Scene .... **B+**
Campus Strictness .... **A-**
Parking .... **C-**
Transportation .... **A**

Special Degree Options

History and Literature, History and Science, MBB (Mind, Brain and Behavior), a diverse array of professional degrees from the professional schools

Sample Academic Clubs

Model U.N., Women in Economics and Government, Harvard Venture Capital and Entrepreneurial Organization

The Lowdown
ON ACADEMICS

Degrees Awarded:
Bachelor, Master, Doctorate

Undergraduate Schools:
Harvard College

Full-Time Faculty:
1,555

Faculty with Terminal Degree:
99%

Student-to-Faculty Ratio:
7:1

Average Course Load:
4 courses per semester

AP Test Score Requirements:
4 or 5 on AP Language Test exempts student from the one-year language requirement; four AP Test Scores of 4 or 5 allows student to enroll in an Advanced Placement three-year degree program.

IB Test Score Requirements:
Advanced Placement granted for full IB diploma holders with three higher-level test scores of 6 or 7.

Did You Know?

The Harvard University library collection contains more than 14.6 million volumes. That makes it the second largest library collection in the United States, falling behind only the Library of Congress.

Best Places to Study:
Lamont Library, House Dining Halls, and the myriad coffee shops around the square

Students Speak Out
ON ACADEMICS

"The teachers are amazing. Some of them are a bit pompous and hard to deal with, but they're all brilliant. With a little initiative, you can forge a strong relationship with them."

"The teachers are **incredibly passionate, deep individuals**. Sure, they often can be difficult to understand and obnoxiously tough, but if you take the time to talk with them, their passion is inspiring. The teaching fellows [TFs] are often better than the professors, because they are more realistic and reachable."

HARVARD UNIVERSITY

"Most professors are terrific. Sure, there were a few I hated, but for the most part, **they're excellent lecturers** and make themselves available to all of their students. Most classes also have graduate assistants [teaching fellows, or TFs] who can be extremely helpful. In some classes, I think the professors rely too much on the TFs—if they're not good, that can be a huge problem."

"It all depends on what class. Nearly all of my teachers this year were really amazing, except for my math teacher who was just horrid. You should **definitely take foreign language classes**—they rock. If you take math, you should make sure your professor speaks English, unless you know another language, or two, fluently."

"I've had some wonderful professors, some who were very dull, some who couldn't speak English well, some who can't teach, and some who did not really care about the students. **It varies**. You'll have some big classes and some really small ones, but you can usually pick some good ones."

"Professors are good. The biggest piece of advice I can give you is to **pick classes based on the professors and not the subject and subject material**. I didn't figure this out until my junior year and wasted a lot of time in bad classes. Ask around and read the *CUE [Committee on Undergraduate Education] Guide*, which is a student-compiled guide to courses that you'll get at the beginning of each year. There is also a two week 'shopping period' for classes. Again, student-professor contact is often hard to come by in larger classes, but I do know that the new president is very committed to changing that."

"You're lucky if you ever meet your professor in almost every class. **Graduate students do the majority of the instruction**. Some of them are good teachers, and some of them are not. Classes can be interesting, but those are often the hardest ones. A lot of requirements are painful experiences, like statistics."

The College Prowler Take
ON ACADEMICS

"Unparalleled," "world-class," and "exciting" are just a few of the words used to described the constellation of academic stars you will find leading class discussions and lecturing on a huge breadth of topics at Harvard. The school's unmatched resources and wide array of studies make it the ideal place to pursue nearly any academic interest. However, some students complain that professors are too far removed from undergraduate life and that teaching assistants are left with too much responsibility in some cases.

Despite a small number of complaints, Harvard University provides a fertile ground for intellectual growth. Renowned faculty, a treasure trove of resources, and undergraduate motivation all combine to make the Harvard a terrific place for higher education. Even if some students have trouble attaining "A" grades, the University passes with flying colors.

The College Prowler™ Grade on

Academics: A

A high Academics grade generally indicates that professors are knowledgeable, accessible, and genuinely interested in their students' welfare. Other determining factors include class size, how well professors communicate, and whether or not classes are engaging.

Local Atmosphere

The Lowdown
ON LOCAL ATMOSPHERE

Region:
Northeast

City, State:
Cambridge, Massachusetts

Setting:
Major city

Distance from New York:
4 to 5 hours

Distance from Providence:
1 hour

Points of Interest:
Boston Common, Fenway Park, Quincy Market, Fanueil Hall

Closest Movie Theatres:
Loews Harvard Square, Loews Boston Common

Major Sports Teams:
Boston Red Sox (baseball), Boston Celtics (basketball), Boston Bruins (hockey), New England Patriots (football)

Famous People from Boston:
Matt Damon, John F. Kennedy, Benjamin Franklin, Robert Frost

City Web sites:
http://www.boston.com
http://www.bostonglobe.com

Local Slang:

Frappe – A milk shake

Wicked – Colloquial adjective used to mean "very"

Yankees – Refers to the New York Yankees baseball team; Bostonians exhibit a venomous hatred for anything having to do with this team

Fun Facts about Boston:

1) Boston boasts the nation's first subway, built in 1897.
2) The first paid fire department started after the 1697 fire in Boston.
3) Boston is home to over 30 colleges and universities.

Students Speak Out
ON LOCAL ATMOSPHERE

"I've loved it. The museums are great; there's the symphony orchestra, the opera, and the ballet. Walking around Boston is wonderful. There are a lot of other schools around."

"Boston is neat, and it's all fairly accessible by subway. **There are a few bad areas**, but it is a pretty safe city overall. There are historic things, museums, sporting events—whatever you want—all about a 15-minute subway ride away from campus."

"I really like Cambridge as a city. **There's a good balance** between feeling like you're in a city and not feeling too overwhelmed by it. Then, of course, downtown Boston is nearby enough, which is nice. There are tons of other universities in the Boston area, including Boston University, Boston College, and Tufts."

"Boston has Boston University, Boston College, Tufts, Wellesley, Northeastern, and about 10 smaller schools. Right in Cambridge, one stop away, is MIT, filled with the techno-geniuses of tomorrow. **There are no places too dangerous to stay away from** except Jamaica Plain; but that's on the far side of Boston—you will never get close, unless you lose your mind."

"**Cambridge is a great college town**. Even in Harvard Square, there are tons of things to do. My friend from Yale is always in awe of Harvard Square every time she comes to visit. I was in Princeton for several years, and I can tell you that Harvard Square is, hands-down, much livelier and more interesting. It also caters more to college students. Boston is also just a short train ride away. Students go into the city all the time to party."

"Boston is amazing! **The the city is so young**. There are at least four other colleges that have buses that go right to Harvard Yard, and there is never a dull night, ever."

"The community here is very college-oriented, which is nice. There are special restaurants and bars that **stay open until weird hours** to correlate with a typical college schedule."

"Boston is the **best college city in the world**. BC, BU, Northeastern, Tufts, are all there, plus countless others. The only problem is the city shuts down at 2 a.m."

HARVARD UNIVERSITY

The College Prowler Take
ON LOCAL ATMOSPHERE

The quintessential college area, Cambridge and Boston provide Harvard undergraduates with a variety of outlets for their creative, cultural, and social needs. Students laud the art museums and theatricals found throughout the city. Boston's four major sports teams also make the city a haven for sports nuts. For the party animal in all college students, Boston serves as a venue for a number of clubs and bars. Note to night owls: beware of the 2 a.m. closing time at all bars.

In addition to the excitement and variety of activities in Cambridge and Boston, Harvard undergraduates also have the opportunity to socialize with college-aged students from the numerous other universities surrounding the city. Most students find nothing wrong with the local atmosphere, but all of Boston's vivacity does come at a price. And most students will find out the hard way after a month or two of eating out and club hopping, that the city does carry a hefty cost of living.

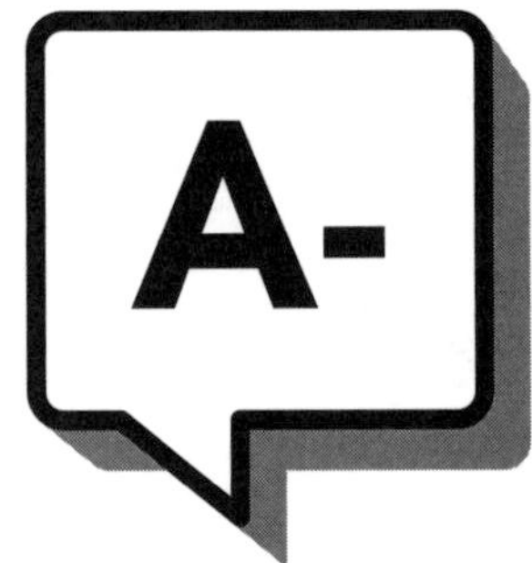

The College Prowler™ Grade on

Local Atmosphere: A-

A high Local Atmosphere grade indicates that the area surrounding campus is safe and scenic. Other factors include nearby attractions, proximity to other schools, and the town's attitude toward students.

Safety & Security

Students Speak Out
ON SAFETY & SECURITY

"The campus, itself, is fairly safe, but I don't suggest wondering too far off when it's dark. A few muggings do happen, but nothing more serious."

"It's unsurpassed. **The Harvard police are expertly trained**. Many are ex-marines and SWAT members. They are extremely approachable and friendly. Also, the blue-light phone system is all over campus and very easy to use. Crime happens, but the HUPD prevents almost everything, and if they don't prevent it, they catch the criminals who are responsible."

"Unlike many colleges, Harvard actually has its own police department. It is still in a city, but **safety is taken very seriously**, and you are never out of sight of an emergency phone. Keycard access is still a bit of a problem, but they're pretty close to fixing that."

"Campus security is really good. The Harvard University Police Department is really dedicated, and the blue-light phone emergency system ensures that police can readily arrive to help any students in need. From personal experience, **I've found the Harvard campus to be very safe**. Surrounding Cambridge is also a pretty safe city, although just like anywhere else, it's probably not the best idea to go walking alone late at night. For the most part, though, I've felt very safe and very comfortable."

"Incidents do happen here, and the lack of good lighting on campus pathways and the scarcity of patrolling HUPD officers make it **less safe than it could be**."

"Harvard does a stellar job of protecting its students. **Blue-light emergency phones cover the campus**, allowing students to make a direct call to emergency response at any time of the day or night. Additionally, all dorms require a keycard to gain access to the dorms, so unwanted individuals rarely ever cause much of a disturbance."

The Lowdown
ON SAFETY & SECURITY

Number of Harvard Police:
50

Phone:
(617) 495-1215

Web site:
www.hupd.harvard.edu/

Health Center Office Hours:
8:00 a.m.-5:30 p.m. Monday-Friday;
24-hour Urgent Care, seven days a week

Health Services:
University Health Services (UHS)

Safety Services:
Harvard University Police Department (HUPD), Cambridge Police Department (CPD)

Did You Know?

To provide extra safety, the campus is littered with blue-light telephones that have direct lines to both health and police response teams.

"I won't try to tell you that at Harvard no one gets robbed or mugged and crime doesn't happen; students should always be mindful that **Harvard is located in an urban area**. So, if you are like my roommate—who had one too many drinks and hopped a ride with someone he didn't know—then you would probably end up getting mugged just like him."

The College Prowler Take

ON SAFETY & SECURITY

Harvard students generally feel safe while roaming the streets of Cambridge, and they have good reason. The Harvard University Police Department and Cambridge Police Department do a commendable job of safeguarding the University's best asset—its students. Students also have access to multiple blue-light security phones on nearly every block and must swipe into dorms with keycards, preventing burglars from ever endangering students.

However, Cambridge, like all cities, is not completely safe from crime. Students should always keep in mind they are in an urban setting and be alert, especially when walking alone at night. A recent rash of crime in Cambridge has alarmed local citizens, but law enforcement is working to combat this trend with an increased presence. In general, Harvard students rightly feel safe, but prospective students should not be lulled into believing that Cambridge and Boston are crime-free.

The College Prowler™ Grade on

Safety & Security: B+

A high grade in Safety & Security means that students generally feel safe, campus police are visible, blue-light phones and escort services are readily available, and safety precautions are not overly necessary.

Computers

The Lowdown

ON COMPUTERS

High-Speed Network?
Yes

Wireless Network?
Yes

Number of Labs:
22

Operating Systems:
Mac OSX, Windows 2000, UNIX, Linux

24-Hour Labs:
Each upperclass house has a small 24-hour lab, and the Science Center's computer labs are open 24 hours, as well.

Free Software:
Acrobat, DreamWeaver, Eudora, Macafee Virus Scan, Photoshop, Telnet protocol for e-mail access; course-relevant software is also available.

Discounted Software:
See *http://www.uis.harvard.edu*

Charge to Print?
Five cents a page if you print from computer lab printers

Did You Know?

Harvard College offers nearly 12,000 high-speed connections, including Ethernet and wireless. User assistants will also come to your dorm room to troubleshoot any computer problems you might have.

Students Speak Out
ON COMPUTERS

"You don't need your own computer, but it's very convenient. Anything you ever have to do on campus could be done on the computer."

"Definitely do **bring your own computer**; the labs aren't generally crowded at all, and they've got a great network, but they're way over in the Science Center and can be a pain to get to in the middle of the night. I've never had too much trouble, but I've been really grateful for my computer."

"I'd suggest that you bring your own computer if you have one. All dorm rooms are wired with 24/7 high-speed and free Internet connections. There are also labs in all houses, most freshman dorms, and several in the Science Center. Except for the peak hours—right around lunch—**they generally aren't too crowded**, but I think most people find it easier to write papers in their own rooms rather than in a lab."

"Every college kid needs his or her own computer. E-mail and word processing are extremely important. Computer labs are fine, but they're a hassle. Usually they aren't too crowded. **The network is a bit slow** because of the firewall, but the roaming Internet connection is outstanding."

"**The network is fine**. There are occasional problems with connections, but it works well for regular everyday purposes like e-mail and the Web and AIM, of course."

"Definitely bring your own computer. Computer labs are abundant, but there is nothing like checking your own e-mail in your own room. Plus, **many classes have their lectures and other course materials online**, and having your own computer makes things much more convenient. Harvard also has tons of work, so the more access you have to a computer at all hours of the night, the better."

"Computer labs are available with both Macs and PCs, but the vast majority of people bring their own computers just because **it's a lot more convenient that way**. I would definitely recommend bringing your own computer. I've found a laptop to be the most convenient. If you'd rather not bring your own computer, though, the labs are definitely workable."

The College Prowler Take
ON COMPUTERS

Technology is increasingly important in today's colleges and universities, and Harvard certainly realizes that. Students have access to a number of computer labs and every upperclass house has its own computer lab in the basement. Students also benefit from a first-rate, high-speed Ethernet network, as well as the recently installed Wi-Fi (wireless) network.

Despite these positive highlights, the majority of students recommend that you bring your own computer to Harvard. Access to computer labs can be troublesome at times because of overcrowding, and having to print out an assignment at the last minute can be nerve-wracking when you have to wait for a computer to open up. The hardware is there, just be patient—factor waiting time into your schedule—if you plan on relying on Harvard's computer labs.

The College Prowler™ Grade on

Computers: A-

A high grade in Computers designates that computer labs are available, the computer network is easily accessible, and campus computing technology is up-to-date.

HARVARD UNIVERSITY

What Is There to Do?

Students have innumerable opportunities because of Harvard's vast resources and facilities. Activities range from workouts and ballroom dancing, to film screenings and scuba diving.

Favorite Things to Do

Run or bike along the Charles River, Attend guest lectures at the Institute of Politics (located at the Kennedy School of Government). See the hundreds of annual student performances held at Sanders Theatre or the Harvard Dance Center.

The Lowdown ON FACILITIES

Student Center:
None

Athletic Center:
Yes, the Malkin Athletic Center (the MAC)

Libraries:
There are over 90 libraries in Harvard's system—many are open until 2 a.m. During exams, some even offer 24-hour service.

Movie Theater on Campus?
Yes: Loews Harvard Square, 10 Church St.

Bowling on Campus?
No

Bar on Campus?
Yes, nearly a dozen are sprinkled throughout Harvard Square.

Coffeehouse on Campus?
Yes, there are nearly two dozen throughout Harvard Square.

Popular Places to Chill:
Harvard Yard, House courtyards, on the bank of the Charles River, Loker Commons and the Greenhouse, coffeehouses around campus

Students Speak Out ON FACILITIES

"There's no student center. Housing tries to make up for it, but doesn't always. We need one. Athletic facilities are good and convenient."

"The facilities are nice, new, and there are plans for a new student center. The center would have pool tables and the like, however **social life on campus really focuses around our house system**—something to definitely read up on, and something which makes Harvard so unique. They really are very successful at fostering a sense of community amongst the students at Harvard—it definitely made my first year really amazing, and it definitely distinguishes Harvard from other schools in Boston."

"There are decent facilities for non-athletes and excellent facilities for athletes. **We don't really have a student center**. Loker Commons, which is below the freshmen dining hall was intended to be a student center, but not many people hang out there. Student organization offices are scattered across campus."

"Facilities are generally state-of-the-art. **Harvard has the nation's largest endowment and most of the time it shows**. Nearly all classrooms are equipped with amazing technology, some of which seems like it's never used, but was added just so they could write about it in their admissions guide."

HARVARD UNIVERSITY

"The facilities are nice. **There can always be more, though**—more space for non-varsity athletes to work out, more dance studio space, and more space, in general!"

"The athletic facility is **outdated and crowded**. In general, the facilities are old, but the technology is updated, and the buildings have nice architecture. That is, if you ignore the few buildings built in the '70s."

"**The athletic facilities, in all honesty, are pathetic**. Unless you are a varsity athlete who has access to the first-class varsity athletic facilities, you will be left to fight for time at one of the machines or stations at the Malkin Athletic Center."

The College Prowler Take
ON FACILITIES

Harvard's classrooms are equipped with state-of-the-art technology and the Harvard library system is the largest in the world. Students wisely recognize these resources and praise the University for spending its enormous endowment on constantly improving existing facilities.

Students do complain that the Malkin Athletic Center should be expanded to meet the increase in demand. Harvard also loses points due to the lack of a true student center and the absence of any concrete plans to resolve the student center issue. Regardless of these complaints, Harvard receives high marks for providing top-notch facilities to aid undergraduates in their pursuit of improving the life of the mind—as well as the body.

The College Prowler™ Grade on
Facilities: B

A high Facilities grade indicates that the campus is aesthetically pleasing and well-maintained; facilities are state-of-the-art, and libraries are exceptional. Other determining factors include the quality of both athletic and student centers and an abundance of things to do on campus.

Campus Dining

The Lowdown
ON CAMPUS DINING

Freshman Meal Plan Requirement?
Yes

Meal Plan Average Cost:
$2,520

Student Favorites:
The Greenhouse and Loker Commons

24-Hour On-Campus Eating?
Nothing, besides 7-11 (convenience store)

Off-Campus Places to Use Your Meal Plan:
None

Other Options:
Students are only able to use their meal plan at the dining hall and a handful of other places. For this reason, there are very few options available for those strictly sticking to the meal plan.

Students Speak Out
ON CAMPUS DINING

"I won't lie—freshman dining is awful. Annenberg is rightly called 'Annenbarf.' But once you're assigned a house at the end of first year, the food is much better."

"It's not bad, although there is only one meal plan option [a full, 21-meal plan]. **Freshmen all eat together in Annenberg,** which is a really impressive and huge dining hall. Each of the 12 upperclassmen houses has its own dining hall; they are generally very good as far as cafeteria-style places go. With the board plan, you also get credit to eat a certain amount at a number of on-campus restaurants."

"I'd say **it's better than average dorm food**. I've had some pretty terrible cafeteria food in my life, and Harvard food is definitely better than that. When it comes down to it, it's still dorm food, though—some of it is less than fantastic. But there are also days when it's actually pretty good."

"On campus, **you're fairly limited**, since you'll eat most meals in a dining hall. There is a restaurant in the Science Center called the Greenhouse, a pizza restaurant, Chick-fil-A, and a snack shop."

"The food is fine. There is always plenty of variety during each meal, with a full salad bar, cereal bar, cold cut bar at lunch, soups, and pastas every meal. The dining services are also very accommodating of personal needs and preferences. The only bad thing is that they don't serve cookies at dinner time—**their cookies are amazing**."

"All freshman—and only freshman, except at breakfast—eat in Annenberg Hall. It's a huge, beautiful, building which looks much more like a church than a dining hall. Granted, the building is **more impressive than the food**, but the food is not bad at all. Plus, once you become a sophomore and you're living in your upperclassmen house, the food is much better, because they are only cooking for about 200 people or so."

"First-year food is tolerable. Upperclassmen houses are a little better. You are stuck with the meal plan all four years, so you have to be able to accept it. **The best dining hall is Adams House Dining Hall**. They are a bit pretentious there, and they only let non-Adams residents eat there at certain hours."

"Within walking distance from the Yard, **there are literally hundreds of restaurants** and cafes that cover just about every possible type of cuisine."

The College Prowler Take
ON CAMPUS DINING

Opinions on the quality of campus dining at Harvard run the gamut from total disgust to lavish praise. In general, students admire the beautiful architecture of Annenberg and most of the house dining facilities, but many students don't believe that the ambience of the dining halls makes up for the less-than-stellar cuisine served up by Harvard University Dining Services (HUDS). Since fall 2003, students have been able to use their Crimson Cash at a select number of restaurants in Harvard Square, making Harvard's dining opportunities look a bit brighter.

Most of the complaints about food quality come from first-years that are victims of Annenberg, where food is mass-produced to serve 1,600 freshmen. Upperclassmen note that food quality does improve after freshman year, and even though they love to complain about Harvard cuisine, the on-campus offerings are actually above average in the pantheon of college dining.

The College Prowler™ Grade on

Campus Dining: D+

Our grade on Campus Dining addresses the quality of both school-owned dining halls and independent on-campus restaurants as well as the price, availability, and variety of food.

HARVARD UNIVERSITY

Off-Campus Dining

The Lowdown
ON OFF-CAMPUS DINING

Student Favorites:
Pinocchio's, Tommy's House of Pizza, John Harvard's Brew House, Pho Pasteur

24-Hour Eating:
7-11 on the corner of JFK and Mt. Auburn

Closest Grocery Stores:
Star Market, Porter Square (one T-stop outbound)

Best Pizza:
Pinocchio's Pizza

Best Chinese:
Hong Kong

Best Breakfast:
Henrietta's Table

Best Wings:
Tommy's Pizza

Best Healthy:
The Wrap and Smoothie Joint

Best Place to Take Your Parents:
Harvest or Henrietta's Table

Fun Fact:
Within a 10-minute walk from the center of campus, Harvard students can choose from over 75 restaurants, offering every type of atmosphere and cuisine a student could ask for.

Students Speak Out
ON OFF-CAMPUS DINING

"Food outside of the dining hall is really good, but I find it hard to justify spending money out when the dining hall food is pretty good and already paid for."

"There are some pretty good restaurants around Harvard Square. **One of the favorites is called Spice**, which is really good but relatively inexpensive Thai food. There's also John Harvard's, which is known for classic American grill-type food. Cambridge One is a great gourmet pizza restaurant, too. There are lots more in the Square, and even more good restaurants in surrounding Boston, especially in North End."

"We really benefit from the many amazing restaurants in Cambridge. **There are too many to name**, but some of my favorites are Henrietta's Table, Border Cafe, Sandrine's, and Spice (it's really good), not to mention the billion awesome restaurants in the North End of Boston, especially Little Italy."

"There are **great restaurants in Harvard Square**. Some popular choices for college students are Spice (Thai), Bombay Club (Indian), John Harvard's (brew pub), and RedLine (chic new bar/bistro which opened last year). Off campus, there are just so many."

"There are tons of restaurants in the Square, and several dozen within a few minutes of my dorm. **I definitely recommend Mr. and Mrs. Bartley's Burger Cottage**, Iruña, Charlie's Kitchen, Café of India, and Burdick's Chocolate."

"The always-popular John Harvard's offers a good variety of quality foods and really gets bumpin' during its Monday night half-appetizer-special hours. Keep in mind that Cambridge tends to be an expensive city, so **eating out often can be a bit pricey**."

"The off-campus stuff is good, but expensive, and is **usually not open late**. There's a lot of variety. Pinocchio's has good pizza, and Hong Kong offers edible Chinese food. There are also the chains like Pizzeria Uno, Chili's, Au Bon Pain, and all kinds of smaller places everywhere."

The College Prowler Take
ON OFF-CAMPUS DINING

Though Harvard's on-campus dining can lack the zest that most students find necessary to satisfy their appetites, the cities of Cambridge and Boston provide a richly diverse environment to fulfill any gastronomic craving. Students especially praise the college-oriented Noch's Pizza, Tommy's Pizza, and a number of other local haunts all within walking distance of most dorms. Undergraduates also enjoy the opportunity to indulge in the fine cuisine of a major cosmopolitan center such as Boston. Specifically, the authentic Italian cuisine found in the North End pleases even the most difficult critics.

The diversity of Harvard's off-campus dining opportunities provide cuisine and price ranges that are certain to satisfy even the most picky appetites and wallets. The off-campus dining more than makes up for the slim pickings on campus. The off-campus dining experience at Harvard will never leave undergraduates without choices, but too many nights out and you'll quickly learn just how easy it is to pack on the "Freshman 15" and a hefty credit card bill.

The College Prowler™ Grade on
Off-Campus Dining: A

A high Off-Campus Dining grade implies that off-campus restaurants are affordable, accessible, and worth visiting. Other factors include the variety of cuisine and the availability of alternative options (vegetarian, vegan, Kosher, etc.).

Campus Housing

The Lowdown
ON CAMPUS HOUSING

Undergrads on Campus:
95%

Number of Dormitories:
13 upperclass houses,16 freshman dorms

University-Owned Apartments:
2,500 apartments, but only a limited number are available to undergraduates.

Room Types:
Everything from singles to 10-person suites are available.

Best Dorms:
For freshman, anything in the Yard

For upperclassmen, Kirkland House and Adams House

Worst Dorms:
For freshman, the Union Dorms

For upperclassmen, Mather House

Bed Type:
Extra-long

Cleaning Service?
Weekly cleaning of all bathrooms

Dormitories

Harvard approaches on-campus living unlike any other college in the nation. After being carefully assigned roommates and dorm accommodations by the college during their first year, students get to choose whom they'll live with for the remaining three. They do this by means of a blocking group. Blocking groups are composed of up to eight people and can be coed. Every group is then entered into a random housing lottery and assigned to an upperclass house for the next three years—so you will live with your blockmates together in one house. Don't worry, although you stay in the same one, you get assigned to a different room each year and they get better as you go along!

There are 13 independent houses, and each has its advantages and disadvantages. They all feature all types of room sizes and the number of floors and bathrooms per room varies greatly, even within the same dorm. All houses and freshman dorms are coed and the male-to-female ratio is tweaked to match the overall composition of the college as closely as possible.

But, before you get ready to move into your house, you'll spend your first year in one of the freshman dorms. All of the freshman dorms, with the exception of Apley Court, Greenough, Pennypacker and Hurlbut, are located in Old Harvard Yard. The type of room and number of students each dorm holds varies from year to year, depending on the size of the freshman class and the planning of the Harvard Housing Office. What's different about Harvard dorms is that rather than rows of double rooms along hallways, like so many other colleges have, the setup is based on suites.

Did You Know?

You can search the past inhabitants of every freshman dorm room at *http://www.hcs.harvard.edu/~dorms/*.

You Get

Many rooms include fireplaces and large common areas, while others offer larger bedrooms, but smaller common rooms. Harvard provides each student with a bed, a dresser, a desk, a bookcase, some closet space, and an Ethernet connection.

Also Available

Another housing option is the Dudley Co-Op. This "do-it-yourself house" is home to about 32 undergrads who share the duties of cooking and cleaning. They pay about half what other students pay for room and board.

Students Speak Out

ON CAMPUS HOUSING

"The dorms, overall, are probably the best anywhere. There are a few that are sort of ugly and institutional, but most are old brick buildings with large, comfortable suites."

"I think that Harvard has some of the best dorms around. There are very few that aren't, in relative dorm terms, they're spacious and nice. There are many different arrangements, but **almost everyone I know likes their dorm** and develops a good deal of house pride!"

"All of the freshmen live in Harvard Yard, or close by, in the Union, for their first year. After that, **you're able to choose a group of seven other people**—collectively called a blocking group—who you want to live with for the following years, and all of you are assigned to the same upperclass house—you don't get to choose. I think it's a pretty good system."

"Dorm rooms are amazing. Just check out the Web and see pictures of some of the rooms. Most people live in suites with common rooms as freshmen, and **many people even have private bathrooms**. Nobody can complain about Harvard housing."

"You'll have **no choice in dorms**. All the freshman ones are great, if only for their location in the Yard. Once you're moved into upperclassmen houses, you'll have a one-in-four chance of drawing a Quad House. These are farther from the Yard than the others—about a 20-minute walk, as opposed to five—but they are also a bit more ornate and have great private libraries."

"Harvard students are spoiled by how nice the living arrangements are. The worst of Harvard housing is amazing in comparison to most other schools. You cannot really avoid dorms because all housing is random. However, **the overflow housing as upperclassmen is quite spacious**, carpeted, and has a kitchen and cable, but some complain that you lose the house feel by living there."

"Harvard's unique housing system does not allow students to preference any particular dorm. At some point during the August before your freshman year, you will get your rooming assignment. Nearly all the freshmen live in what is known as Harvard Yard, the University's historic central hub that has witnessed over 350 years of history. You will spend the next three years in your house. **Students tend to develop a sense of house pride**, mainly because you eat your meals with and participate in a number of events, such as intramural sports, with the people in your house."

"It's by far **the nicest housing** out of anything that my friends have at other schools. You can't pick your dorm, but if you could, it would be a toss-up—they all have their strengths and weaknesses."

The College Prowler Take

ON CAMPUS HOUSING

When 95 percent of undergraduates at Harvard *prefer* to live on campus, you know there must be something desirable about the housing opportunities. From its rich history and beautiful architecture, to the close-knit house communities and central location, the quality of Harvard campus housing is matched by few, *if any*, universities in the country. Freshmen live in the Old Yard and the Union, while upperclassmen move towards the Charles River and out towards the Quad after their first year. But, regardless of location, the rooms at Harvard tend to be spacious, and almost all rooms feature common rooms and private bathrooms. Many of the houses also offer features such as darkrooms, music practice rooms, workout facilities, and late-night grills.

However, all dorms have their pros and cons, and you will hear undergraduates living in the river houses complain about smaller rooms, while students in the Quad complain about the long trek to classes. The complaints are few, but do exist. The general sentiment of the Harvard undergrad is resoundingly in favor of campus housing at Harvard. House communities are integral parts of student social life, and because of this, few would relinquish their rooms on campus just because of a long walk or slightly smaller living quarters.

The College Prowler™ Grade on

Campus Housing: A

A high Campus Housing grade indicates that dorms are clean, well-maintained, and spacious. Other determining factors include variety of dorms, proximity to classes, and social atmosphere.

Off-Campus Housing

The Lowdown
ON OFF-CAMPUS HOUSING

Undergrads in Off-Campus Housing:
5%

Average Rent for a Studio Apartment:
$1,200

Average Rent for a 1BR Apartment:
$1,425

Average Rent for a 2BR Apartment:
$1,750

Best Time to Look for a Place:
Start looking early—try during the summer if you're looking for term-time housing and by spring break if you're searching for a summer spot.

Popular Areas:
Central Square, Porter Square, Somerville

For Assistance, Contact:

The Harvard Housing Office (HHO)

http://www.fas.harvard.edu/%7Euho/offcampus.htm

(617) 495-1942

E-mail: uho@fas.harvard.edu

Students Speak Out
ON OFF-CAMPUS HOUSING

"I wouldn't really want to live off campus. Living on campus, and in Kirkland, is the best part of my Harvard experience."

"It's **not very convenient**. Like Cambridge and Oxford in England, Harvard has a house system. More than 90 percent of students stay in the houses all four years. Those who don't are rich, and they can afford the high housing prices! But the houses are great, and the community is very friendly."

"Almost nobody lives off campus because the dorms are, for the most part, really good, and Cambridge housing is both expensive and difficult to find. However, during the summer, a lot of students stay around Cambridge doing various things, and they are able to find cheap and nice sublet apartments. During the year, though, **I would definitely advise against off-campus housing**."

"Usually, they make you live on campus the first year. I personally prefer to live off campus because **I can get more work done**, and I don't have to deal with the constant dormitory melodrama that goes on."

"There is no reason to live off campus. Most Harvard kids live on campus because **housing off campus is so expensive** and the Harvard rooms are so nice."

"Off-campus housing is **farther away from classes than on-campus housing** and tends to be ridiculously expensive. Additionally, hardly anyone chooses off-campus housing options because of their affinity towards their house."

The College Prowler Take
ON OFF-CAMPUS HOUSING

With a housing system that offers the best location and rooms in the Cambridge/Boston area, few students choose to live off campus. Most students complain that off-campus housing is too expensive and nearly impossible to find anywhere near Harvard Square.

Even those undergraduates with the resources to live off campus choose to live on campus because the house system offers unparalleled resources and a close-knit community. It is the centerpiece of many students' college experience. If you absolutely must live off campus, then plan ahead, be open-minded, and take advantage of the Harvard Housing Office and tips (or hand-me-downs) from fellow students.

The College Prowler™ Grade on
Off-Campus Housing: F

A high grade in Off-Campus Housing indicates that apartments are of high quality, close to campus, affordable, and easy to secure.

Diversity

The Lowdown
ON DIVERSITY

Native American: 1%

Asian American: 17%

African American: 8%

Hispanic: 8%

White: 57%

International: 9%

Out-of-State: 85%

Minority Clubs
Undergraduate minority students have the opportunity to join many clubs that focus on improving the status of minority students. Most notable are the Black Students Association (BSA) and the BGLTSA.

Political Activity
There is a largely liberal political base, but conservative political groups do make their presence felt on campus. Nearly every student has an informed opinion, and the Institute of Politics provides an excellent forum for discussion and debate of current political topics.

Gay Pride

Harvard is tolerant of homosexuality, and the Bisexual, Gay, Lesbian, Transgender, and Supporters Alliance (BGLTSA) constantly rallies to increase tolerance for homosexuality on campus.

Most Popular Religions

Harvard is certainly a secular university, and no one religion dominates the University. Christianity and Judaism appear to be the most represented religions. Religiously-focused organizations have very little visibility on campus.

Economic Status

The economic status of Harvard students covers the entire spectrum. Some students work their way through school, while others never worry about finances. Most students probably come from upper-middle-class homes.

Students Speak Out

ON DIVERSITY

"Harvard's diversity is one of its biggest assets. I have friends from every imaginable racial, ethnic, and geographical group."

"It depends on where you're coming from. For me, it was much **more diverse than my high school**, but I've heard other people say that it's not as diverse as theirs was. You can pretty much find any type of person, though."

"I think that the campus is diverse. There are people from all over the world and of every different race, and religion. Some people think that minorities are still underrepresented here, but I think that it's **full of tons of different cultures** that make Harvard a very exciting place to be."

"There are exchange students from, well, nearly everywhere. Occasionally, you'll find a bigot, too, but there is **plenty of diversity**, and racial tension is fairly rare."

"Harvard is ethnically very diverse. But **financially, the students at Harvard aren't so diverse**. In terms of political views of students, the extremes do not have a large presence."

"The campus is **incredibly diverse** in more ways than just race. One night on my way to a party, I found out that a guy I was walking with was previously in the circus, we passed a piano and learned that another guy was a concert pianist, and then another got drunk and started speaking Hindi. You never know what you're gonna get."

The College Prowler Take

ON DIVERSITY

Harvard undergraduates thrive on diversity because it presents alternate approaches and opinions on topics ranging from politics and religion to culture and sexuality. Harvard students tend to be among the most open-minded in all of higher education. Students of all races, backgrounds, and beliefs will find a forum in which they can express and discuss their opinions. Despite the wealth of diversity, some students do complain that most of the undergraduates come from a very narrow socioeconomic bracket.

Students hail from across the globe, and though this facilitates expression and individuality, it often fuels controversies that captivate the entire student body. (Check out *http://www.thecrimson.com* for recent controversies and debates across campus.) If diversity is a must, then Harvard is certainly the right fit, but for close-minded souls, culture shock will certainly await you around every corner here.

The College Prowler™ Grade on

Diversity: B+

A high grade in Diversity indicates that ethnic minorities and international students have a notable presence on campus and that students of different economic backgrounds, religious beliefs, and sexual preferences are well-represented.

Top Three Places to Find Hotties:

1. Downtown Boston
2. Parties
3. RedLine

Top Places to Hook Up:

1. Your dorm room
2. Other people's dorm rooms

The Lowdown
ON GUYS & GIRLS

Female Undergrads: 48%

Male Undergrads: 52%

Birth Control Available?
University Health Services provides free condoms and physicians will provide prescriptions for various methods of birth control.

Hookups or Relationships?
Random hookups do happen on the weekends (and weekdays see their share, as well). However, most people are extremely busy and often are so focused on their work that relationships either die out or become serious within a short period of time. This isn't to say you'll never see lasting relationships: annoyingly cute couples walk the Yard surprisingly often. And the *Harvard Magazine*—the alumni pub—is always filled with news of another couple of Harvard newlyweds.

Best Place to Meet Guys/Girls
Through extracurricular organizations, friends, and finals clubs.

Dress Code
On the weekends, most people dress up to go out, but during weekday study breaks or hangout sessions, most anything goes. (Though throughout the winter, dress code really doesn't matter because everyone is so bundled up to keep warm.) In general, Harvard tends to be a bit more formal than average. On the weekends, guys generally sports khakis with a button down or knit-shirt, with a sweater or leather jacket. Girls' dress combinations vary greatly and will often depend on the weather to determine if a skirt or pants are appropriate for the evening.

Students Speak Out
ON GUYS & GIRLS

"Most girls at Harvard aren't that 'hot,' but there's a fair share of 'cute' girls. It's pretty much the same situation at any top 15 school, I think."

"We have the full range of the human spectrum. **Most people are very interesting**, though, regardless of their other physical traits. It's what's inside that counts, and the guys and girls at Harvard have a lot inside!"

"**There are some 'beautiful people**,' though I'd say all of the Ivies have more than their share of people that could stand to get out of the library a little more."

"There are some very hot Harvard girls, but there are also some really unattractive girls. Trust me, **you'll find your own group**, and regardless of appearances, the students are definitely Harvard's biggest asset."

"The people here, in general, are really great. Of course, there are the occasional people I dislike, but **the group of students, as a whole, is a great one**. If you're worried about people constantly talking about their academic accomplishments or something, don't worry, it doesn't happen here."

"There are dorks everywhere! However, the women in Boston have impressed me. The **guys are jerks**."

The College Prowler Take

ON GUYS & GIRLS

Don't let "Van Wilder" or "Girls Gone Wild" give you any crazy ideas about college and what girls and guys will look like at Harvard. If physical attractiveness on campus is essential in your college selection process, then you might want to steer clear of Harvard University. Though most students believe that the student body is of average attractiveness, very few report a significant number of hot guys or girls on campus. Additionally, girls tend to accept the male population as average or better, while guys have a less positive outlook towards the female student population.

The lack of looks at Harvard shouldn't get you down just yet though, because Boston is home to a myriad of other universities to find potential partners. But, for those who believe looks are not exactly everything, Harvard students' individuality should provide plenty of options for single guys and girls.

The College Prowler™ Grade on

Guys: B

A high grade for Guys indicates that the male population on campus is attractive, smart, friendly, and engaging, and that the school has a decent ratio of guys to girls.

The College Prowler™ Grade on

Girls: B-

A high grade for Girls not only implies that the women on campus are attractive, smart, friendly, and engaging, but also that there is a fair ratio of girls to guys.

Athletics

The Lowdown

ON ATHLETICS

Athletic Division:
NCAA Division I

Conference:
Ivy League

School Mascot:
John Harvard

Fields:
Harvard Stadium, Jordan Field, Club Sports Field

Men's Varsity Sports:	Women's Varsity Sports:
Baseball	Basketball
Basketball	Crew
Crew	Cross Country
Cross Country	Fencing
Fencing	Field Hockey
Football	Golf
Golf	Ice Hockey
Ice Hockey	Lacrosse
Lacrosse	Skiing
Skiing	Soccer
Soccer	Softball
Squash	Squash
Swimming	Swimming
Tennis	Tennis
Track	Track
Volleyball	Volleyball
Water Polo	Water Polo

Students Speak Out
ON ATHLETICS

"Varsity is not too big at all, except within the team. IM [intramural] sports are big among people who do them. It's all relative, but you don't hear much about either unless you're really into them."

"We offer dozens of sports and play over a thousand IM games per year. **Freshmen play in their own league**, and upperclassmen houses compete against each other. Harvard has more varsity teams than any other school, and many survive on 'amateurs,' so if you want to play a varsity sport, it is much more open than other D-1 schools. Attendance at athletic events is, unfortunately, fairly light."

"Varsity sports can be big, depending on the sport and the team. **Attendance is very poor**, except for 'the Game,' which is the annual football rivalry with Yale. Hockey is also mildly popular, and basketball draws some, as well. We have a ton of varsity teams, so if you do want to play competitively, chances are Harvard offers it."

"If you would rather just compete in a more relaxed setting, Harvard **IMs offer a variety of sports** in a much more friendly setting. Many people use them as a way to meet other people, but there are some fairly competitive teams."

"We are definitely lacking in the team spirit department, however we still get big crowds at some football and basketball games. **Rowing is really popular**, and our teams are always pretty good. IMs are very popular, which is another great side effect of the house system. Men's IMs get more participation and are more competitive than the women's, but even the women's teams are really fun."

"Varsity athletes aren't revered like at other places. Athletes do tend to be the more social students. **Hockey and football games get decent turnouts**. And sports like crew and squash are among the best in the nation. Harvard offers a lot of intramural sports. They're well-organized and there's a lot of variety, such as crew, fencing, softball, Frisbee, football, volleyball, and basketball. People of all skill levels can participate, and many students do."

The College Prowler Take
ON ATHLETICS

Originally founded as an athletic league, the Ivy League, including Harvard, has lost its reputation as an athletic powerhouse in major sports. However, Harvard is home to more varsity sports than any other institution in the nation. Additionally, Harvard offers an array of club sport opportunities that will satisfy the desires of any wannabe rugby, fencing or Frisbee players, to name just a few. And for those not interested in organized sports or their accompanying time commitments, Harvard offers intramural sports that often generate heated battles and spawn a number of house rivalries.

However, Harvard does lose points because of the lack of support for its varsity programs. Men's ice hockey, football, and lacrosse garner quite a few fans, but the only time Harvard fans even resemble true college sports fans is on the day of the Harvard-Yale football game. Overall, the college offers the resources for just about any level of activity.

The College Prowler™ Grade on
Athletics: C+

A high grade in Athletics indicates that students have school spirit, that sports programs are respected, that games are well-attended, and that intramurals are a prominent part of student life.

HARVARD UNIVERSITY

Nightlife

Students Speak Out
ON NIGHTLIFE

"There are tons of bars in Cambridge and Boston. Living so close to a metropolitan city is incredibly convenient."

"**They've cracked down on this a lot in Cambridge** because everyone's old favorite place, the Grille, served one too many underagers. In Boston, you have it all—my favorite is the Pavolo. Underage booze is easy to get."

"There are a few bars: Daedalus, RedLine, Temple Bar. **The bars are okay, but they are kind of hard on fake IDs**. There are final clubs which some people go to—my favorite is the Phoenix. Basically, they are like fraternities, just more elitist—girls are always invited; non-member males are not."

"The most important thing to know about the bars and clubs is that they, for the most part, are strict with IDs. For example, **you must have identification that says you are 21**. If it is an out-of-state ID, you must also have a backup. There are also clubs which are 19-and-over."

"In Harvard Square, **the most popular bars are the Hong Kong, Daedalus, and RedLine**. In Boston, there are many great dance clubs—each with a different feel—it depends on your preference. Avalon is a huge, generic college-crowd dance club that is popular. Some of the more chic places are Pravda and Club Nicole."

"**We're a subway ride away from Boston, so obviously, the nightlife is amazing**. It's a great little getaway from campus when you want to relieve some stress and get your party on!"

The Lowdown
ON NIGHTLIFE

Student Favorites:
RedLine, Daedalus, Grafton Street

Useful Resources for Nightlife:
www.unofficialharvard.edu
www.boston.com

Bars Close At:
1:30 a.m. or 2:00 a.m.; depends on the bar

Primary Areas with Nightlife:
Harvard Square, Lansdowne Street

Cheapest Place to Get a Drink:
Hong Kong

Local Specialties:
The Scorpion Bowl

Favorite Drinking Games:
Beer Pong, Card Games (A$$hole), Century Club

"John Harvard's is known for its Monday night half-price appetizers. **A lot of students go there for their home-brewed beer, but they definitely card**. I'm not such an expert on clubs and bars, but I know there are definitely some pretty good places in Boston."

The College Prowler Take

ON NIGHTLIFE

Though Cambridge is home to quite a few bars, Harvard students remain a bit dissatisfied with the Puritanical laws that halt alcohol sales after 10:45 p.m. and on Sundays, as well as the law forcing bars to close at 2 a.m. However, Harvard students still manage to spend plenty of time and money at local bars like RedLine, Daedalus, and the Hong Kong ("the Kong," in Harvard vernacular).

If the local bar scene does not sound appealing, just take the short T-ride to Boston and you will find a cornucopia of activities, ranging from bars and clubs to theaters and coffee shops. All in all, Boston and Cambridge provide Harvard students with enough nightlife opportunities to make most other college students jealous.

The College Prowler™ Grade on

Nightlife: A-

A high grade in Nightlife indicates that there are many bars and clubs in the area that are easily accessible and affordable. Other determining factors include the number of options for the under-21 crowd and the prevalence of house parties.

Greek Life

The Lowdown

ON GREEK LIFE

Number of Fraternities:
4

Number of Sororities:
3

Undergrad Men in Fraternities:
Less than 1%

Undergrad Women in Sororities:
Less than 1%

Did You Know?

Fraternities and sororities are not officially recognized on campus, although in recent years Greek life has been unofficially gaining a stronger presence.

Students Speak Out
ON GREEK LIFE

"There are no official fraternities, but there are finals clubs, which are the same thing, and they throw really fun parties. But by no means are they the dominating thing on campus."

"It's almost non-existent. There are a few off-campus fraternities and sororities, but **they definitely do not dominate the campus**. There are also all-male finals clubs and all-female societies that are sort of Greek-like, but none of these are sanctioned by the college. I went through four years perfectly happy without joining any of these, although I have several good friends in one of the off-campus fraternities."

"With very few frats and sororities, the Greek life is completely avoidable. Finals clubs are a little harder to hide from if they're not your things, but after freshmen year they don't have as big of a presence if you're not in one. The **finals club parties are great for freshman girls**, but bad for just about everyone else not in the club."

"We don't have a Greek life. The University does not officially recognize fraternities and sororities. On the other hand, **we do have finals clubs where most girls go**, but not the boys, since they can't get in. If people really want to socialize, you go to the parties in the upperclass houses or in the Quad—it's infamous for parties."

"The Greek life is minor at Harvard because the frats and sororities are relatively new additions to campus that have been initiated in the hopes of creating a fuller social scene. **Greeks have to rent out spaces to throw their functions**, so they're shadowed in comparison to older establishments with their own space such as the finals clubs. However, some frats do throw a mean party."

"There isn't any official Greek life at Harvard. Instead, there are finals clubs, which kind of work like frats minus a house. Actually, some sororities are getting started just in recent years, and **they're growing in popularity**, I think. But it's not nearly enough to dominate the social scene."

"Fraternities and sororities exist unofficially at Harvard and really have no major presence on campus. **There's no Greek week or crazy frat parties**. Instead, Harvard features final clubs, an upscale version of fraternities. These clubs are over one hundred years old and members meet in multi-million dollar clubhouses around campus. These clubs are also unofficial, but they throw a good number of parties and tend to be late night hangouts for people once the bars close at 2 a.m."

The College Prowler Take
ON GREEK LIFE

Enamored by the ridiculous antics of the frat boys from *Animal House*? If so, then Harvard probably is not the place for you. Fraternities and sororities are not officially recognized on campus, though in recent years they have increased their presence as unofficial organizations. Without houses, these organizations do not have the ability to throw the parties one expects of a healthy Greek system, although they occasionally rent out Boston clubs or take over dorm rooms to throw enormous bashes.

In place of a Greek system, Harvard has the controversial institution known as the "finals club." These clubs are often criticized as the remnants of the "Old Boys" network of Harvard days of yore. They selectively offer membership after a student's freshman year, and they serve an important role in an otherwise lean on-campus social scene.

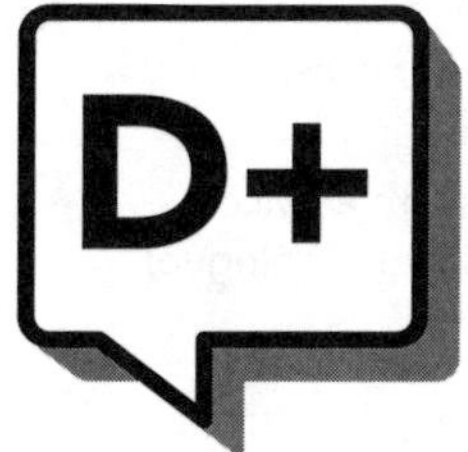

The College Prowler™ Grade on

Greek Life: D+

A high grade in Greek Life indicates that sororities and fraternities are not only present, but also active on campus. Other determining factors include the variety of houses available and the respect the Greek community receives from the rest of the campus.

Drug Scene

The Lowdown
ON DRUG SCENE

Most Prevalent Drugs on Campus:
Alcohol, marijuana

Liquor-Related Referrals:
123

Liquor-Related Arrests:
12

Drug-Related Referrals:
3

Drug-Related Arrests:
9

Drug Counseling Programs:
Harvard University Health Services:

Center For Wellness and Health Communication, mental heath aervices, Project ADD (Alcohol and Drug Dialogue), Bureau of Study Counsel

Students Speak Out
ON DRUG SCENE

"I know people that smoke weed, and I've heard of people doing cocaine, but my friends weren't really into it, so I don't know much about the scene."

"I never was involved with it, which means that in four years **I never really came across it**. I know it exists, but it's not rampant."

"I know some drugs are there, but it kind of seems like the kind of thing where **if you're looking for it, you can find it**, but if you aren't, it's not going to be something you'll notice. I wouldn't say it's a big thing."

"Okay, let me preface this by saying that I don't do drugs, but I have acquaintances who have tried various things. **Pot is pretty common**, and it's not that hard to get. There is a small scene, often associated with specific finals club that does ecstasy. Also, if you really want, you could find coke. But drugs are by no means a dominant scene on campus."

"If you weren't interested in drugs, **you wouldn't even know they existed on campus**. People are very respectful if you don't drink or don't do drugs."

"People smoke a lot of weed, but still not very much compared to national or even high school scenes. Although other drugs are around, **they're not everywhere**."

"Harvard certainly has its fair share of weed smokers, but it is not that prevalent. I also know that **some people do cocaine** and other hard drugs, but I doubt Harvard's drug habits are that much different from any other college or university."

The College Prowler Take
ON DRUG SCENE

Drugs have a very small presence at Harvard. Marijuana is certainly the most prevalent, while harder drugs such as cocaine are often rumored to be the drug of choice for a small minority. However, these tend to be rumors and should not be trusted completely. The overwhelming majority of students avoid all drug use, and they enjoy the ability to engage in a drug-free social life.

Students also note that for those interested in drug use, there are a number of outlets, especially within the city of Boston. All in all, Harvard receives high marks for its ability to keep drug use to a minimum and facilitate an academic and social life that is not inhibited by drugs.

The College Prowler™ Grade on
Drug Scene: B+

A high grade on Drug Scene indicates that drugs are not a noticeable part of campus life; drug use is not visible, and no pressure to use them seems to exist.

Campus Strictness

The Lowdown
ON CAMPUS STRICTNESS

What Are You Most Likely to Get Caught Doing on Campus?

If you're underage, you are most likely to be caught drinking in your dorm room. If you are 21 or older you're most likely to get caught with a hangover. Regardless, here's a list of things that you will most likely get caught doing:

Drinking underage

Parking illegally

Public urination or indecency

Smoking marijuana

Making too much noise in your dorm

Students Speak Out

ON CAMPUS STRICTNESS

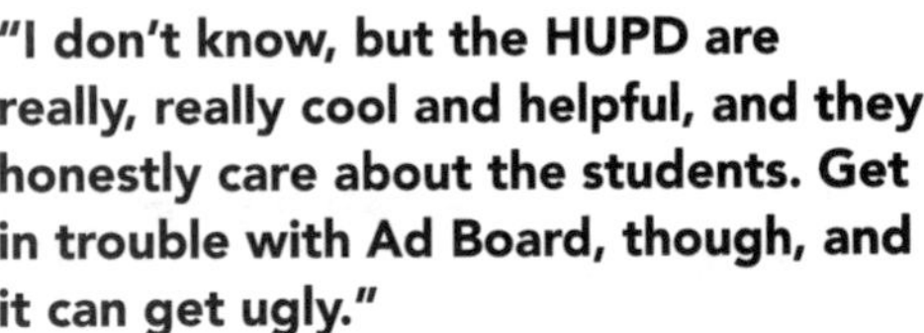

"I don't know, but the HUPD are really, really cool and helpful, and they honestly care about the students. Get in trouble with Ad Board, though, and it can get ugly."

"**I never had a problem** with how the HUPD handled parties or drinking. I didn't ever drink or do drugs, however, but my friends did, and they haven't had any problems."

"The official campus drug and alcohol policy is **very strict**. Repeated violations usually result in a forced year away from Harvard or expulsion, but I don't know of anybody who that's happened to."

"Drugs obviously get you in trouble if you get caught, but **you can pretty much get around anything**, if you are smart."

"Campus police are **not strict at all**. Even if you call them at 4 a.m. because you are drunk and locked yourself out, they'll still be super nice and understanding."

"Harvard University police do not care about drinking at all. Often times **they'll break up parties that are too rowdy**. Even while busting the parties, the HUPD tend to be quite jovial and only care about quieting down the party, not busting underage drinking. As a prime example, after Harvard won the Ivy League championship in football, a couple cops even showed up to joke around at the football team's keg party."

"Sometimes, **an officer will try to scare an underage drinker** by taking their name and ID number down, but rarely will they actually bust anyone. They are there to protect the students, not to get them in trouble."

The College Prowler Take

ON CAMPUS STRICTNESS

Other than freshmen, Harvard students have few worries about campus strictness. University police are present to protect the safety of students, not detain or punish every underage drinker or noisy reveler. Most students feel free from punishment because almost all students are given at least one warning before any official disciplinary actions are taken.

For those unfortunate students who frequently abuse school policy, punishments can range from probation to expulsion. However, many students realize that the University is reluctant to expel a student and often grants them readmission after a certain amount of time. While Harvard may be a bit lax, don't fall into a false sense of security, because Cambridge and Boston police are strict, and they will punish any act of underage drinking. Students should just keep in mind that with independence comes responsibility and that frequent abuse of the rules does not come without punishment at Harvard.

The College Prowler™ Grade on

Campus Strictness: A-

A high Campus Strictness grade implies an overall lenient atmosphere; police and RAs are fairly tolerant, and the administration's rules are flexible.

Parking & Transportation

The Lowdown
ON PARKING & TRANSPORTATION

Student Parking Lot?
Yes

Freshmen Allowed to Park?
No

Approximate Parking Permit Cost:
$800 a year

Ways to Get Around:

On Campus:
Harvard Shuttle
http://www.uos.harvard.edu/transportation/shu.shtml

Public Transportation:
MBTA Bus System
MBTA T (subway system)

Taxi Cabs:
Ambassador-Brattle Taxi Cambridge (Yellow) Taxi Co.: (617) 492-1100

Students Speak Out
ON PARKING & TRANSPORTATION

"No one has cars here, but if you bring one, then you will likely pay a lot for parking."

"**Don't try to bring a car**. There is parking at the stadium, but it is expensive and not very convenient. As a junior or senior, you may be able to get a spot in a garage closer to campus, but definitely not as a freshman."

"There is a T [subway] stop and **many bus stops** within two minutes of my dorm. It's very efficient."

"I'm **very impressed**. I only use my car maybe three times per month."

"I live by it. **Traffic around Boston is horrible**, and public transportation is pretty inexpensive. They have special buses and stuff for college students to get around the campus and community."

"You would probably be **less than a minute walk from your dorm room to the subway or buses**, and from there, you can get just about anywhere in Boston or Cambridge."

"Parking is **basically nonexistent**. Freshmen aren't allowed to bring cars, and the upperclassmen who do often find it really inconvenient to find places to keep their cars. Most things are within walking distance, though, and the subway leaves right from Harvard Square."

"You don't need a car because the Boston **mass transportation is really good**."

The College Prowler Take
ON PARKING

Nearly every student interviewed discouraged bringing a car to college. Students cite the enormous expense of parking and the relative scarcity of parking in Cambridge as the major reasons to avoid keeping a car on campus. For practical purposes, students do not need parking because Boston's public transit system provides students with subway and bus transportation to nearly every place in the city.

The College Prowler™ Grade on
Parking: C-

A high grade in this section indicates that parking is both available and affordable, and that parking enforcement isn't overly severe.

The College Prowler Take
ON TRANSPORTATION

Students frequently utilize public transportation in Boston, and they almost always give nothing but high marks for the system. Boston's public transportation provides Harvard students with a reliable and safe method of reaching almost anywhere they wish to go. The local T has frequent stops throughout Cambridge and Boston, while the commuter rail takes students throughout Massachusetts and as far as Providence, Rhode Island. Moreover, the MBTA bus system provides additional routes throughout the area.

The College Prowler™ Grade on
Transportation: A

A high grade for Transportation indicates that campus buses, public buses, cabs, and rental cars are readily-available and affordable. Other determining factors include proximity to an airport and the necessity of transportation.

HARVARD UNIVERSITY

Overall Experience

Students Speak Out
ON OVERALL EXPERIENCE

"My advice to prospective students: state school. State school students have less work and more fun. As one of my friends said, state school girls are cooler, hotter, and have fewer inhibitions. Harvard is hard."

"I like Harvard. It is a challenge, but that is to be expected. The class sizes are often too large, but **every now and then a professor will prove to be human** and make himself accessible outside of class. I like the campus, as it is very alive and very well-kept. If you want a good education and want to have a good time all in one, Harvard is best."

"In one word: unimaginable. In every sense, Harvard has fulfilled my highest expectations. The academics, people, resources, and opportunities are unbeatable. **I wouldn't go anywhere else**. But a word of warning, and this kind of depends on your concentration . . . you do have to do a good amount of work if you want to do well. You can't really fail out, but you have to work hard to do well and get anywhere above a B- or B average."

"I love it at Harvard. It can be challenging at times, but the resources and people available to you are unmatched. I would not want to be anywhere else. **The best part of the school is your peers**—the students you are here with are some of the most amazing individuals, yet very few are cocky, too proud, or conceited. Everyone is really on level ground here, and it's great. You'll learn a lot in your classes, but you'll learn even more from your peers. And who knows, you might make friends with a future president, CEO, or actor."

"I love it. The things I thought I would look for in a school—a lot of school spirit, good professor-to-student ratio, prestige—ended up not mattering at all. What is important is the location and the people. **Harvard has the best of both**."

"I hate the weather, and I think the students can be a bit pretentious and too career-oriented, but overall it is simply amazing. **Professors and courses are thought-provoking and creative**. Even though I might not have individual conversations with most of my professors, they are generally the experts in their field and simply listening to them is quite engaging. While binge drinking can be fun, Harvard's student theater productions, speaker events on campus, and Boston's various attractions offer [other] opportunities to enjoy yourself, no matter what your idea of fun is."

"**I can't imagine being anywhere else**. I love my classes, my dorm, and my friends. The resources available to me (as an earth and planetary science major) are unbelievable, and I have no doubt that I would not be able to do the research I am doing at many other schools. Sure, sometimes the stereotype of Harvard kids being stuffy and nerdy is true, but for the most part, it is a very fun and admirably impressive group of people."

The College Prowler Take
ON OVERALL EXPERIENCE

Challenging, rigorous, and positive all describe students' overall experience at Harvard. The academic challenge initially seems daunting to many students, but the intellectual output facilitated by this academic powerhouse leaves students pleasantly surprised. The social life of most Harvard students acts as a counterbalance to the intellectual challenge, and not surprisingly, students forge lifetime memories and friends throughout their four years at Harvard.

The Harvard experience leaves most students yearning for more. The University provides undergraduates with a rich history, unparalleled cultural diversity, and intellectual rigor that challenges each student to fulfill every ounce of their potential. Students leave the University satisfied, prepared, and as a stronger, more aware global citizen than ever.

The Lowdown
ON THE INSIDE SCOOP

Harvard Slang:

Know the slang, know the school. The following is a list of terms you really need to know before coming to Harvard. The more of these words you recognize, the better off you'll be.

ABP – Au Bon Pain, the popular French fast food stop in Harvard Square, on the Mass Avenue side of the Holyoke Center

Ad Board – A faculty committee charged with interpreting and enforcing the rules of the Faculty of Arts and Science

Af-Am – Afro-American Studies

B-School – Harvard Business School

Concentration – Harvard's word for "major"

Coop – The Harvard Cooperative Society, the bookstore located at Harvard Square Pronounced as in "chicken coop"

The Core – A set of courses that composes approximately one-quarter of the undergraduate program; students choose seven courses from eleven broad areas of academic inquiry

Crimson – The name of the student daily newspaper, the *Harvard Crimson*; also the nickname of any Harvard sports team

Crimson Cash – A declining debit account system that uses your Harvard ID. You can put cash on electronically in order to purchase copies, food, and other sundries.

CUE Guide – The *Harvard University Course Evaluation Guide*, published by the Committee on Undergraduate Education

Div School – Harvard Divinity School

Ed School – Also known as HUGSE (Harvard University Graduate School of Education)

FAS – Faculty of Arts and Sciences, composed of Harvard College, the Graduate School of Arts and Sciences, and the Division of Continuing Education.

GSAS – Graduate School of Arts and Sciences

GSE – Harvard Graduate School of Education

HASCS – Harvard Arts and Sciences Computer Services

HBS – Harvard Business School

Head of the Charles – The annual October regatta held on the Charles River

HLS – Harvard Law School

HMS – Harvard Medical School

HOLLIS – Harvard's libraries' online catalog and now also a directory to the suite of electronic resources that the libraries make available

House – The residences of sophomores, juniors, and seniors. Harvard houses were modeled on the college systems of Oxford and Cambridge, in England.

HUL – Harvard University Library (the entire library system)

HUPD – Harvard University Police Department

ICG – Instructional Computing Group (technical support)

IOP – Institute of Politics, at the Kennedy School of Government

KSG – Kennedy School of Government

K-School – Kennedy School of Government

Let's Go – The series of travel books written and published by Harvard students

MAC – Malkin Athletic Center

Masters – Faculty members who lead and administer each undergraduate house

MBTA – Massachusetts Bay Transportation Authority (i.e. the subway and buses)

MIT – Massachusetts Institute of Technology. The other university in Cambridge.

OCS – Office of Career Services

Pit – The area immediately surrounding the Harvard Square T stop, one of the Square's hubs of street entertainment

Proctors – Graduate students or officers of the university who live among freshmen, serve as academic advisors, and direct the events and programs of an entryway

QRAC – Quadrangle Recreational Activities Center at 66 Garden Street

Quad – An area separated from the main campus by about a fifteen-minute talk, composed of three undergraduate houses, a library, and an athletic facility

Radcliffe Institute for Advanced Study – An interdisciplinary center offering non-degree instruction and executive education programs. The Institute was created when Harvard and Radcliffe formally merged in October 1999.

Reading Period – That 10-day period of anxiety in which students prep for final

Resident Tutors – Graduate students or faculty members who live in the houses with students, and provide them with a range of informal advice and counsel

Shopping Period – The first five or so days of an academic term at Harvard, before Study Cards are submitted for formal enrollment in a course, when students can visit classes, sit in on lectures, and review syllabi and readings.

Statue of Three Lies - The John Harvard Statue (see Urban Legends)

The "T" – Short for MBTA (see definition on previous page)

Tercentenary Theater – The part of Harvard Yard bounded by Widener Library, University Hall, Sever Hall, and Memorial Chapel. It is the site for commencement.

TF – Teaching Fellow (like other colleges' TAs)

UHS – University Health Services

Veritas – The Harvard motto. Latin for "truth"

The Yard – Most universities have a quadrangle, but Harvard has its Yard, divided into two parts. The freshman dormitories border the Old Yard; Widener Library and Memorial Church border the New Yard.

Things I Wish I Knew Before Coming to Harvard:

First of all, Harvard is not completely made up of rich, snobby kids who got in because of their parents' alumni status. Instead, Harvard students are diverse in every way and no matter who you are, you will find people similar to you. Secondly, I wish I'd realized that even though Cambridge is the quintessential town for college students, it is extremely expensive. Finally, do not be scared away from Harvard because you think you won't be smart enough or because you think the classes will be too difficult. Practically all Harvard students think its tough and think everyone else is smarter than they are. The University offers plenty of study groups and tutoring services, so that even if you are struggling, there is a place to turn to.

Shopping period—a week or week-and-a-half in which you can visit classes before registering for them—is a great opportunity, take advantage of it.

The workload is intense, think about how you can manage your time efficiently.

Though Harvard students have fun, the majority are at Harvard for academics and a crazy social life is not a top priority.

If you are not from a place where it snows, then prepare for a cold winter.

Freshman week (a.k.a. Camp Harvard) is amazing—don't be shy because everyone is new to the school just like you.

Tips to Succeed at Harvard:

Pick classes you actually like.

Actually go to class.

Get advice from upperclassmen.

Check your final exam dates before you register for classes.

Join study groups if at all possible.

Harvard's Urban Legends

School lore has it that the John Harvard Statue, located outside of University Hall is a statue of the founder of the University. In reality, the story of this statue contains three lies. Lie #1: John Harvard didn't found Harvard (the Massachusetts Bay Colony government did). Lie #2: Harvard started in 1636 not 1638. Lie #3: It's not even John Harvard. No one knows what he looked like since there are no surviving portraits of the man. Daniel Chester French, the sculptor, used a 19th century undergraduate for his model.

School Spirit

Harvard students are proud, almost snobbishly arrogant, when it comes to their university reputation, though athletics receive little support, if any. Students wear their colors proudly, especially on the weekend of the Harvard-Yale football game. However, after freshman year, students find themselves wearing less and less apparel with the Harvard name or crest, though the color crimson becomes increasingly present in student's wardrobes. Overall, student spirit brims high when it comes to Harvard.

Finding a Job or Internship

The Lowdown

ON FINDING A JOB OR INTERNSHIP

Career Center Resources & Services:

The Office of Career Services (OCS) offers a number of resources and services to help you figure out what you plan to do with your college education. The following list is just a sampling of the numerous opportunities to be found at OCS:

Career Self-Assessment

Resume, Interview and Networking Workshops and Case-studies

Career Library with books and guides to finding summer and full-time careers

Professional Connection—a tool to link alumni with undergraduates pursuing similar fields

OCS also provides access to a number of online job listing sites such as MonsterTrak.

For a complete listing of resources and opportunities at the Office of Career Services stop by their Web site at *http://www.ocs.fas.harvard.edu/index.htm*

The Lowdown

Placing the Harvard name on your resume certainly gives you an advantage for applying to jobs or internships. However, it's not an automatic acceptance. The Harvard name is more like a foot in the door and your success at the college can help determine whether you ultimately find the job that you want.

Advice

If you are interested in finding jobs or internships, then stop by the Office of Career Services. At OCS you can meet with one of the many career counseling experts who will help you search out the perfect job match, help edit your resumes, and even review your interview technique through videotaped mock interviews.

Average Salary Information

The Office of Career Services and the Harvard Alumni Association does not maintain data on average salary information of Harvard University graduates. The salary of Harvard undergraduates just out of college varies enormously. A number of students pursue high-paying, six figure salaries in consulting or investment banking, while other students earn very little monetary compensation while pursuing graduate degrees or public service opportunities.

The Lowdown

ON ALUMNI

Web site:
http://www.haa.harvard.edu/

Office:
Harvard Alumni Association
University Place
124 Mt. Auburn St.
6th Floor
Cambridge, MA 02138

Services Available:

The Harvard Alumni Association (HAA) offers a variety of services, ranging from reunions and symposiums throughout the country, to the ability to search through the alumni database to find professional connections, and even access to chat rooms and message boards.

HAA also offers the Travel/Study Program, in which alumni can gather together to vacation and learn simultaneously. This fall, alumni can register for trips throughout the world that will be led by an expert who will explain the local customs, and architecture.

Alumni Publications
The *Harvard Magazine*
Alumni also keep up to date on Harvard through the *Harvard Gazette* and the undergraduate daily, the *Crimson*.

Famous Harvard Alumni:

Michael Crichton (Class of 1964) – Author of *Jurassic Park*

Matt Damon (Class of 1992) – Star of *Good Will Hunting* and numerous other hit films

Al Gore (Class of 1969) – Former Vice President and Democratic nominee for President

Tommy Lee Jones (Class of 1969) –Star of *The Fugitive*

John F. Kennedy (Class of 1940) – Former President of the United States

John Lithgow (Class of 1967) – Actor and star of hit TV show *Third Rock from the Sun*

Yo-Yo Ma (Class of 1976) – Famous composer and musician

Conan O'Brien (Class of 1985) – Host of the *Late, Late Show with Conan O'Brien*

Franklin D. Roosevelt, (Class of 1904) – Former President of the United States

The Best & Worst

The Ten BEST Things About Harvard:

1	Professors
2	Student motivation and ambition
3	Opportunity to pursue any interest
4	Alumni dedication to helping students find jobs
5	Boston
6	Campus housing
7	The Harvard Library System
8	Diversity
9	State-of-the art technology
10	R-E-S-P-E-C-T

The Ten **WORST** Things About Harvard:

1. Students focusing too much on the future
2. Inaccessible professors
3. Classes are tough!
4. Lack of sleep during exam period
5. Weather
6. Massachusetts liquor laws
7. No crazy college stories
8. Rejection from student organizations
9. New England winters
10. Disdain from people who think everyone at Harvard is an arrogant jerk

Visiting Harvard

The Lowdown
ON VISITING HARVARD

Hotel Information:

The Charles Hotel
1 Bennett Street, Cambridge, MA 02138
(617) 864-1200

The DoubleTree Guest Suites Hotel
*Less than a mile from Harvard Square
400 Soldiers Field Road, Cambridge, MA
(617) 783-0090

Harvard Square Hotel
110 Mount Auburn Street, Cambridge, MA 02138
(617) 864-5200

The Inn At Harvard
1201 Massachusetts Ave., Cambridge, MA 02138
(617) 491-2222

Sheraton Commander
16 Garden Street, Cambridge, MA 02138
(617) 547-4800

Take a Campus Virtual Tour:
http://www.hno.harvard.edu/tour/

To Schedule a Group Information Session or Interview:
Call the admissions office at (617) 495-1551 or check out the admissions office Web site at *http://www.college.harvard.edu/admissions*

Campus Tours:
Campus tours are offered year-round, Monday through Friday at 11 a.m. and 3 p.m.

Overnight Visits:
To schedule an overnight visit contact the admissions office at (617) 495-1551.

Directions to Campus

From I-90 (Massachusetts Turnpike)

- Get off at Cambridge (exit 18).
- Turn left immediately onto Soldiers Field Road (west).
- Take Harvard Square exit, bear right across Anderson Bridge, and drive straight into Harvard Square.
- For Byerly Hall, proceed through two lights—the first just before the Square (and Out of Town News), the second after passing through the Square.
- After the second light, get in the left-hand lane, bearing to the far left.
- Upon taking a sharp left turn at the next light, move directly to the right-most lane and follow it onto Garden Street.
- The admissions office is across the street on your left at 8 Garden Street, in Radcliffe Yard.

From Logan Airport

By Subway (the "T")

- Take the shuttle bus to the Airport T stop (Blue Line).
- Take the Blue Line inbound four stops to Government Center.
- Change to the Green Line westbound and go one stop to Park Street.
- Switch to the Red Line outbound (toward Alewife), go four stops and get off at Harvard.
- The subway ride from Logan Airport can take 45 to 60 minutes. (Tokens cost $1).

By Taxi

- The ride to Harvard Square from Logan Airport takes about 20 to 30 minutes, depending on traffic.
- Typically, the ride costs about $25.

From South Station (Trains and Buses):

By Subway

- Take the Red Line toward Alewife.
- From South Station it is six stops to Harvard Square.

Princeton University

Box 430 Princeton, NJ 08544
www.princeton.edu (609) 258-3000

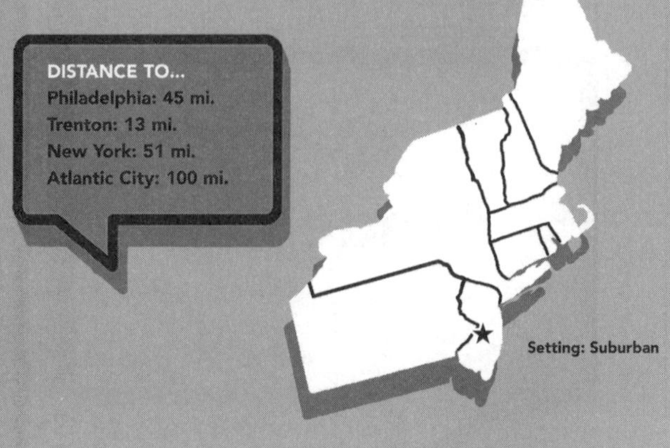

"Some of the best professors in the world reside here at Princeton, and unlike other schools, they actually teach other undergraduate courses."

Total Enrollment:
4,801 - Medium
Acceptance Rate:
13%
Tuition:
$31,450
Top 10% of High School Class:
94%
SAT Range

Verbal	Math	Total
700 – 790	700 – 800	1400 – 1590

SAT II Requirements
Any three SAT II subject tests.
Most Popular Majors:
12% Political Science and Government
9% Economics
9% History
8% English Language and Literature
8% Public Policy Analysis
Students Also Applied To:*
Columbia University, Harvard University, Stanford University, Yale University

*For more school info check out *www.collegeprowler.com*

Table of Contents

College Prowler Report Card

Academics	A+
Local Atmosphere	C+
Safety & Security	A
Computers	A-
Facilities	B+
Campus Dining	B+
Off-Campus Dining	B
Campus Housing	C+
Off-Campus Housing	D-
Diversity	B
Guys	B
Girls	B
Athletics	B
Nightlife	C
Greek Life	C-
Drug Scene	B
Campus Strictness	B+
Parking	B
Transportation	C+

The Lowdown
ON ACADEMICS

Degrees Awarded:
Bachelor, Master, Doctorate

Undergraduate Schools:
Arts and Sciences, Engineering

Full-Time Faculty:
799

Faculty with Terminal Degree:
95%

Student-to-Faculty Ratio:
5:1

Average Course Load:
4 for AB students, 5 for BSE students

Special Degree Options
Cross-Registration, Independent Study, Study Abroad, Interdisciplinary certificate program in addition to departmental concentration, Independent Concentration, Teacher Certificate Program

Sample Academic Clubs
American Institute of Chemical Engineers, Engineering Council, Finance and Economic Forum, Ivy Leaguers For Freedom, Pre-Business Society, Princeton Association of Women in Science

AP Test Score Requirements
AP Test Scores may be used to 1) enter upper-level courses, 2) fulfill the foreign language requirement, 3) become eligible for graduation in three or three and one-half years (advanced standing). Generally, a score of 4 or 5 is needed to receive recognition.

IB Test Score Requirements
A score of 6 or 7 on the International Baccalaureate (higher level) qualifies students for advanced placement in most subjects.

Did You Know?

? Princeton University's sixth president, John Witherspoon, was one of the signers of the Declaration of Independence.

In May 1970, colleges around the nation adopted the "Princeton Plan" (fall recess) in response to the student unrest following the Cambodian incursion in Southeast Asia.

The faculty currently includes five recipients of the Nobel Prize in physics, and one each in literature, economic sciences, and medicine.

Princeton is one of the only American institutions to mandate a senior thesis, which has been a requirement for graduation since 1925.

Best Places to Study:
Empty classrooms in the Frist Campus Center, Firestone Library, Small World Coffee, Café Vivian, Architecture Library

Students Speak Out
ON ACADEMICS

"Princeton is all about the undergrad program. The classes are great, and the professors actually teach them. You can really get to know your professors here if you try!"

"The professors at Princeton are pretty good. Some TAs don't speak English too well, but **office hours are very helpful**."

"The professors and preceptors are remarkably concerned with the academic life of the undergraduate, both in theory and practice. The **University requirements for independent work** mandate close student-teacher contact and in practice professors generally make themselves easily available to meet outside of the classroom, regardless of the size of the class."

"Princeton hosts a **Freshmen Seminar Program**, which creates a variety of seminars open only to freshmen. While the topics are narrowly tailored, depending upon the professor's personal academic interests, this program allows freshmen to participate in intensive discussion groups and helps to ease them into the increased academic expectations of sophomore year."

"I loved my professors. They are world-famous, yet they would take me to dinner to discuss the means of educating inner city youth, the meaning of Melville's short stories, or even why New York was on one of the largest fault lines. The personal attention is ridiculous, and **I still turn on my TV and see my professors** on there all the time. It really is pretty cool."

"Our academic programs are first-rate, and many of our professors are highly regarded in their fields. Also, because of **Princeton's commitment to undergraduate education**, the professors are accessible to students. Of course, some of them are quite dull, but that is the exception. The academics are hands-down outstanding."

"Princeton is **primarily an undergraduate institution**, so the professors are there for us. Professors are required to have a certain number of office hours, so students can drop by at any time during those times to talk about class, and papers. Most professors have more than the required hours."

"The academics are world-renowned here. Just **be prepared to work your butt off**!"

The College Prowler Take
ON ACADEMICS

As a school that has been repeatedly ranked first in the nation by just about any national educational syndicate, there is no question that the level of Princeton's academics make it one of the best—if not *the* best—schools in the nation for undergraduate education. Princeton's professors not only have great credentials, they also place an emphasis on personal accessibility. All professors are required to teach, and no graduate students are allowed to lead lecture courses. What results is an institution that thrives on the education of undergraduates, not the research of professors. Some professors, such as the famed religion professor and recent star of *Matrix Reloaded* and *Matrix Revolutions*, Cornel West, even ask students not to send e-mail but instead to stop by office hours to facilitate interaction out of the classroom.

While some students gripe about some of Princeton's academic requirements, including a diverse selection of distribution requirements, demanding independent work both junior and senior year, and mandatory weekly preceptorial sections, it is these features of the undergraduate education at Princeton that make its students some of the best prepared for graduate work and demanding jobs. Princeton's rigorous academic demands encourage independent thought and efficiency. Even though the work is demanding, there are many resources available to undergraduates, such as an extensive network of tutors and a staff of well-trained Writing Center advisors, to ensure that few are left behind.

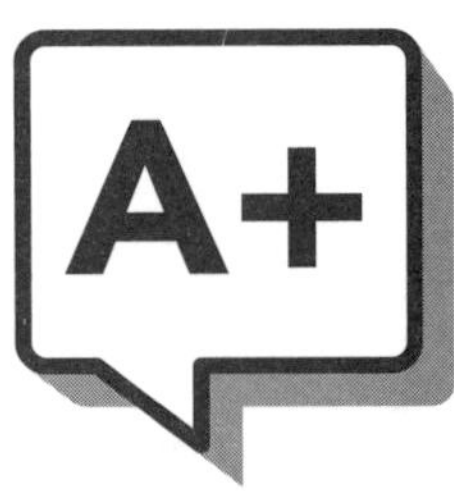

The College Prowler™ Grade on
Academics: A+

A high Academics grade generally indicates that professors are knowledgeable, accessible, and genuinely interested in their students' welfare. Other determining factors include class size, how well professors communicate, and whether or not classes are engaging.

Local Atmosphere

The Lowdown
ON LOCAL ATMOSPHERE

Region:
Mid-Atlantic

City, State:
Princeton, New Jersey

Setting:
Suburban

Distance from Philadelphia:
1 hour

Distance from New York City:
1 hour

Points of Interest:
Albert Einstein's house,
Art Museum, University Chapel

Famous People from Princeton:
Albert Einstein (lived here after leaving Germany), Woodrow Wilson, Grover Cleveland, Toni Morrison, John Chancellor, Paul Robeson

Major Sports Teams:
Philadelphia Phillies, New York Yankees, New York Mets (baseball); Philadelphia 76ers, New Jersey Nets, New York Knicks (basketball); New York Rangers, New Jersey Devils, Philadelphia Flyers (hockey)

City Web sites:
www.princetonol.com
www.pacpub.com

Fun Facts about Princeton:

1) The house next door to Einstein's house is identical to his. This has not always been true. When the movie producers of *I.Q.*, a film chronicling Einstein's time at Princeton, did not receive permission from the current residents of Einstein's to film there, they bought the house next door and remodeled it to look exactly like Einstein's.

2) Contrary to popular belief, the cannon scars on the side of Nassau Hall are not the result of British cannon fire. Because Nassau Hall served as a British garrison during part of the Revolution, the marks are in fact the result of cannon fire from the rebel colonists.

3) Princeton briefly served as the location of the nation's capitol when the Continental Congress met at Nassau Hall between June and November of 1783.

4) The Academy Award-winning *A Beautiful Mind* was filmed on Princeton's campus and used many of the University's students as extras. The number of applications to Princeton increased the following year.

5) Princeton University's campus houses an impressive outdoor sculpture garden, including a piece by Pablo Picasso.

Students Speak Out
ON LOCAL ATMOSPHERE

"Princeton is a pretty, quiet, and wealthy town, but there isn't a great deal of interaction between school and town."

"It's a nice town. It's quiet, and it has **good shopping** if you prefer pricier stores and trendy fashions. The town's people do not seem to be a problem. It's rather safe, as well."

"It's a fairly small town. **Most things are done either on campus or nearby**; you have to drive at least 15 minutes to find stuff away from campus. There is a nice town center at Nassau Street and Palmer Square with lots of shops and restaurants. There's also a movie theater right at the edge of campus. Philly and New York are pretty close, too."

"New Jersey is the heart of everything, in the sense that, from where you will be, you are an hour-and-a-half from the beach, **two hours from Atlantic City**, three hours from DC, and 30 minutes from Trenton."

"Rutgers University and the College of New Jersey are the closest other schools, but we really don't have anything to do with them. The town is very quaint and community-oriented. There are lots of little stores and restaurants, and the campus is one of the most beautiful places I've been to. **The architecture and greenery is really breathtaking**, especially in the spring and fall."

"**The town and University are fairly separate** entities, but the town is small enough that most errands can be done conveniently on foot. The towpath that runs by Lake Carnegie is beautiful. There are some great, but pricey, restaurants."

"It's a nice atmosphere. There's a big main street with shops and stores right on campus, but it's still a small town setting. **The people here are extremely friendly**."

"No student should pass through Princeton without an expresso or cappuccino from **Small World Coffee**. It's the heart and soul of the town, and true love of the student body."

The College Prowler Take
ON LOCAL ATMOSPHERE

Princeton, New Jersey is a small town with a rich history. Many students complain that Princeton is trapped in time, essentially because of its older buildings and small-town atmosphere. Students expecting an urban campus are sorely disappointed when they arrive on campus by way of the "Dinky," the two-car train that connects Princeton to the main New Jersey Transit rail connection.

Perhaps because of its relatively isolated nature, members of the town and campus communities co-exist rather peacefully. Princeton undergraduates are generally well received by "townies," but there have been recent tensions between students and local authorities because of proposed changes to the town's alcohol policy. Each year, to help mend any bruised relations, town and gown come together for "Communiversity," a day-long street fair that invites both students and townies to enjoy the closed-off Nassau Street and participate in activities such as a 5K run and sidewalk drawing. Despite strong ties to the community and a historically rich atmosphere, the university leaves much to be desired by way of a varied social life, so students are forced to look elsewhere for excitement—such as to New York and Atlantic City.

The College Prowler™ Grade on

Local Atmosphere: C+

A high Local Atmosphere grade indicates that the area surrounding campus is safe and scenic. Other factors include nearby attractions, proximity to other schools, and the town's attitude toward students.

Safety & Security

The Lowdown
ON SAFETY & SECURITY

Number of Princeton Public Safety Officers:
57

Phone:
911 (emergencies)
(609) 258-3134 (non-emergencies)

Health Center Office Hours:
Monday-Friday 9 a.m.-4:30 p.m., Tuesday 10 a.m.-4:30 p.m.; open at all times for emergencies

Safety Services:
Rape Aggression Defense System (RAD), Bike Registration, Bike Lock Program, Operation I.D., Escort Service, Emergency Phones, Campus Shuttle Service, Assault Prevention Education, Laptop Registration

Health Services:
Clinical Services, outpatient services, inpatient services, sexuality education counseling and health office (annual exams for women, including breast and pelvic exams, care for infections and STDs, "morning after pills," preconception advising, pregnancy testing and options, HIV and STD testing, discounted contraception), sexual harassment/assault resources and education program, eating concerns counseling, alcohol and other drugs counseling

Students Speak Out

ON SAFETY & SECURITY

"There's not much to worry about in terms of safety. There are occasional thefts, but common sense, like locking your door, is enough to prevent it."

"I felt secure walking around by myself—as a female, at that—at any hour of the day. **I wouldn't wander to the outer edges of campus, though**. They tend to be darker and less secure."

"**Campus security is very good**. I had to walk late at night from the library to my dorm, and I had no problems. Public safety is open 24/7, so if you ever need to call them for any reason, they are available. The Princeton town is pretty small and very safe, so I never had to worry."

"The campus is pretty safe. It is a pretty isolated campus in a small town, so there really isn't any danger to walking around at night. There are a few instances of people being followed, but these are pretty rare. **The school is very responsive to safety**. We have public safety officers and a lot of phones on campus that you can use to call for help. We used to have rows of bushes by the tennis courts, but these were cut down because people could hide in there and attack people walking by."

"If anything, **public safety has too much of a presence** on campus. As long as you use common sense and stay out of certain parts of town by yourself after dark, there is nothing to worry about."

"Our ID cards, or prox cards, that let us into buildings are overrated. They are probably more of a scare tactic than anything. **You can almost always get someone to let you in** if you forget your prox in your room, and if you are persistent enough, you can usually pull the doors open."

"The one piece of advice I would offer about campus safety is to **buy a lock for your laptop and bike**. Also, don't take anything you like too much out to the Street with you. I lock my laptop and bike and have been lucky with both, but I have had four or five jackets taken out at the eating clubs. There's not much you can do about lost jackets except post notices in coat rooms and never expect to see lost possessions again."

"I feel very safe here: almost **too safe** . . . ."

"The biggest risk you'll have here is getting an expensive bike stolen. Princeton is a small town, and **the University is fairly isolated**. I guess this can be a good or a bad thing."

Did You Know?

Historically, Princeton has had the lowest campus crime rate in the Ivy League.

Lyle Menendez was initially rejected from Princeton in 1987, but later gained admission to Princeton's Class of 1991. During his first semester at Princeton, Menendez supposedly received a one-year suspension for plagiarizing a classmate's psychology lab report. After returning to Princeton, Menendez subsequently was placed both on academic and disciplinary probation and was convicted of murdering his parents before he could graduate.

The College Prowler Take
ON SAFETY & SECURITY

Princeton has 24-hour campus security. There is a strong presence of these public safety officers, whether it is breaking up a noisy room party or assisting in medical emergencies. Because of Princeton's small size as both a town and a university, most students feel safe enough to walk alone in the middle of the night to the 24-hour WaWa convenience store for a cup of coffee or wrap sandwich after everything else is closed. The most common crime seems to be theft of unattended items, namely laptop computers, bicycles, and jackets. Recently, however, there has been more attention placed on campus sexual violence in the form of date rape, thanks to an intensive Take Back the Night program initiated by the Organization for Women Leaders (OWL), a women's issues group founded by several members of Princeton's Class of 2003.

As a town, Princeton is extremely safe. Some may even lament that the constant presence of public safety officers makes it difficult to have too much fun on campus, but the university has made personal safety a top priority, particularly through the installation of a personal ID system for getting into dormitories and other university buildings.

The College Prowler™ Grade on
Safety & Security: A

A high grade in Safety & Security means that students generally feel safe, campus police are visible, blue-light phones and escort services are readily available, and safety precautions are not overly necessary.

The Lowdown
ON COMPUTERS

High-Speed Network?
Yes

Wireless Network?
Yes

Number of Labs:
36

Number of Computers:
254

Operating Systems:
Windows 95/98/NT/2000/XP, Macintosh OS, Unix, PUCC

24-Hour Labs:
1942 Hall Basement, Butler Apartments, Carl A. Fields Center Basement, OIT Computing Center, Edwards Hall Basement, 21/22 Forbes College, Gauss Hall Basement, B-9-B Graduate College, Hibben-Magie Apartments, 106 Lawrence Apartments, Lower Madison Hall Common Room, B59 McCosh Hall, McDonnell Hall's Brush Gallery, 33/34 New Graduate College, Julian Street Library

Charge to Print?
No

Free Software

Norton AntiVirus, Outlook Express, Microsoft Office, Microsoft Internet Explorer, Aladdin (Stuffit) Expander, Adobe Acrobat Reader, RealPlayer

Discounted Software

Adobe Acrobat, After Effects, Illustrator, InDesign, PageMaker, PhotoShop, CorelDraw Graphics Suite, Vector Effects, FileMaker Pro, Macromedia Dreamweaver MX, Fireworks MX, Flash MX, Freehand MX, ColdFusion MX Developer and Flash Player 6, Microsoft Office 10, Norton SystemWorks

Students Speak Out

ON COMPUTERS

"Definitely bring your own computer. There are, however, lots of computer facilities around campus. It only gets really crowded around exam time and around JP and thesis due dates."

"The computer facilities are very good. They all have high-speed Internet connections and loads of applications. In the new engineering building there is even a classroom with laptops on every desk. Because everyone lives on campus all four years, **all rooms have Ethernet connections**. Libraries also have Ethernet outlets, so you can bring your laptop and work there. The school offers some subsidized deal to buy computer equipment, and pretty much everyone has their own computer. If not, you can still get by."

"The computer labs at Princeton are quite sufficient and **will satisfy even the nerdiest of computer nerds**."

"**Computer clusters aren't always crowded**, but everyone I knew had their own computer simply because you are almost always writing papers, conjuring up problem sets, e-mailing, or researching. You just spend a lot of time on the computer, so I would really recommend you bring your own. It's certainly more convenient, but the clusters are also available."

"Every room is hard-wired for Internet access with a T1 connection. As for the computer clusters, they usually aren't that crowded, except maybe at **finals time when everyone tries to write their papers at once** on the last day. Many students bring their own computers, which leaves the rather nice computer clusters unused most of the time."

"Computer clusters are crowded during peak times, like right before senior theses are due and right before Dean's Date, when all papers are due at the end of a semester. Other than those three times a year, you should be able to access computers easily, especially since there are so many clusters on campus. Every room has Ethernet ports, and pretty much wherever you are on campus, a cluster shouldn't be too far away. **Your dorm may even have one** in the basement. They're not crowded at all and are usually close-by."

Did You Know?

Princeton's Student Computer Initiative offers discounted desktop and laptop computers, both Windows and Mac, to students. Each student can take advantage of the prices once during his or her four years at Princeton.

Princeton's Department of Public Safety offers laptop registration in an effort to curb the rampant computer theft of the past few years.

The Office of Information Technology (OIT) offers "H-Drive" access to students so that undergraduates can access their files from any computer on the campus network.

The College Prowler Take
ON COMPUTERS

A Princeton professor once started his first lecture on the history of Africa by saying, "Princeton students have the worldwide reputation of being both voracious readers and avid writers." Then he proceeded to assign several thousand pages of reading for the semester in addition to three papers and a final exam. While this course is definitely the exception rather than the rule, it does emphasize the role of Princeton's workload on the average student's daily life.

The University provides students with access to 24-hour computer support resources, including residential computer consultants who live in the dorms and are able to help students work out computer problems, such as a virus, before they have to bring their computers to a technician. Princeton even has a computer initiative that makes both laptop and desktop computers more affordable to students. For students who opt not to bring a computer, however, all hope is not lost. There are 24-hour computer clusters all over campus. Generally, the computer labs are not crowded except around major deadlines, such as the infamous "Dean's Date," the deadline at the end of the semester for all written work. Some students will camp out in the clusters during these intense periods, leaving only to eat, shower, or sometimes shave.

The College Prowler™ Grade on
Computers: A-

A high grade in Computers designates that computer labs are available, the computer network is easily accessible, and campus computing technology is up-to-date.

The Lowdown
ON FACILITIES

Student Center:
Frist Campus Center

Athletic Center:
Dillon Gym (Stephens Fitness Center, Dillon Pool, Squash Courts), DeNunzio Pool, Pagoda Tennis Courts, Jadwin Gym

Libraries:
19

Campus Size:
500 acres

Movie Theater on Campus?
Yes—Frist Campus Center Film/Performance Theater, Frist Campus Center

Bowling on Campus?
No

Coffeehouse on Campus?
Yes—Café Vivian, Frist Campus Center

What Is There to Do?
Without even leaving campus, students can take a run around Carnegie Lake, go to a movie for $2, watch excellent live theater, including the famous Triangle Club kick line (of cross-dressing men), work out in the state-of-the-art gym facilities, practice their musical instruments or have a music lesson, develop photos in one of several campus dark rooms, or sip a latte in the Campus Center's Café Vivian, named for the wife of former University President Harold Shapiro.

Students Speak Out
ON FACILITIES

"Most facilities are excellent, and there are lots of new buildings, centers, and libraries. The new student center is excellent and gives a nice dining alternative to dining halls."

"**The main athletic facility for non-varsity athletes is Dillon Gym**. It is pretty old, but there are four basketball courts, two aerobics rooms, and a fitness center, so I guess it's okay. There are computer clusters located all over campus that are very nice. The student center is only a couple of years old, so it is also pretty nice—it's becoming a place for people to eat, hang out, and study. The classrooms are okay, as well."

"A **new engineering building**, the Friend Center, was finished recently, and its classrooms all have projection TVs with the latest audio/video equipment, as well as some really nice chairs. The older classrooms are pretty standard."

"They're great. Princeton just got a new track two years ago, and the student center was remodeled and looks great! Everything is excellent. There's a new gym fitness room, new computers, and nice housing. **The old buildings are all fixed up**, and there are a lot of new buildings. They are all kept clean and safe, and there is a lot of history to them."

"The Frist Student Center can get really crowded, especially during exams. The third floor study room used to be a fantastic refuge for those seeking silence, but people have started to bring in their Ipods and food and camp out for what seems like days. If you're looking for a good place to study in Frist now, it is a good idea to seek out an empty classroom or **go next door to the East Asian Library**."

"They're pretty darn good. They're all first-rate and are kept in good shape, too—partly because **the University has money out the wazoo** and partly because vandalism isn't much of an issue. The new exercise center in Dillon Gym is amazing."

"Café Viv was really nice when it first opened. It was never too crowded. Now, even with a larger staff, **people are always there**, so it is not always the best place to study."

"**The newly renovated Marquand Library is quite phenomenal**. The study carrels are huge, and the building is in the middle of campus. Art history majors certainly can't ask for more out of their library."

The College Prowler Take
ON FACILITIES

Common student facilities, such as the gym and student center, are state-of-the-art. The student gym, Stephens Fitness Center in Dillon Gym, was recently renovated and the machines were updated. The student government continues to battle with the issue of gym overpopulation, and machines are added to the limited space on a regular basis. The Frist Campus Center opened in 2000, increasing student space dramatically. Students now have a campus coffee shop, convenience store, food court, and smoothie stand where they can charge everything to their student account, much to the chagrin of many Princeton parents suffering from the phenomenon known as "Frist sticker shock."

Princeton has made a lot of recent strides to catch up with other major universities in terms of campus facilities. Students were once forced to cram into the small but character-filled Chancellor Green, which is now undergoing renovation. Perhaps it was poor planning or just not realizing how popular new facilities would be, but Frist Campus Center and Stephens Fitness Center both face overcrowding problems, which will only get worse as the University expands its student body.

The College Prowler™ Grade on
Facilities: B+

A high Facilities grade indicates that the campus is aesthetically pleasing and well-maintained; facilities are state-of-the-art, and libraries are exceptional. Other determining factors include the quality of both athletic and student centers and an abundance of things to do on campus.

Campus Dining

The Lowdown

ON CAMPUS DINING

Freshman Meal Plan Requirement?
Yes

Meal Plan Average Cost:
$3,816

Student Favorites:
Forbes College Dining Hall, the Grill, Villa Pizza

Other Options

After sophomore year, most students elect to move out of their residential colleges, forfeit their meal plan, and move into upperclass housing. In upperclass housing, they must decide whether they want to join an eating club, one of the campus co-ops, or "go independent." For those who go independent, they have the option to move into Spelman Hall, a group of dormitory buildings designed by I.M. Pei that contain suites of four singles, a kitchen, bathroom, and common room. This is also where the married students live. There are two campus co-ops—2D, a vegetarian co-op, and Brown, named for its kitchen in Brown Hall.

Did You Know?

In 2003, Princeton's Dining Services won a prestigious Ivy Award with five other groups, including the famous New York sushi institution, Nobu.

Students with a meal plan may request to organize a cookout, and all food and supplies are available at the contract holders' dining unit.

Sledding, anyone? Students "borrow" trays from Frist to go sledding on the hills of the golf course behind Forbes College.

Once a semester, Dining Services organizes to have a local restaurant come to each of the residential colleges and cook a gourmet meal. Recent cuisines have ranged from Ethiopian to French.

COLLEGE PROWLER™

Need help finding the finest campus grub? For a detailed listing of all on-campus eateries, check out the College prowler book on Princeton available at *www.collegeprowler.com*.

Students Speak Out
ON CAMPUS DINING

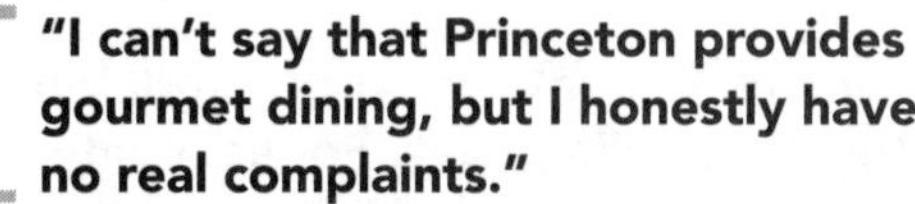

"I can't say that Princeton provides gourmet dining, but I honestly have no real complaints."

"Food is **generally very average**. It's your basic dining hall buffet food—we got sick of it pretty quickly. At the end of sophomore year, you join an eating club. There are 10 eating clubs on Prospect Street ['the Street']. They are where you will eat your meals and hang out. It's similar to a frat, I guess. The food at eating clubs is generally much better than the dining halls. The club I was in, Charter, probably had the best food on the Street."

"The food is good. The dining halls have a huge selection, and the Frist Campus Center is awesome. Meal times are a really **good time to hang out with friends**."

"The food in the dining halls is pretty good. After graduation, you'll quickly miss the unlimited amounts and varieties of food! This year, I think **the food situation has gotten even better** since they built a brand new student center."

"**Eating clubs do not offer as many dining options** as the University-run dining halls, but the food is generally better. Also, students in eating clubs spend more time with a smaller group of people, thus making the club system open to stereotypes of exclusivity, as perpetuated by classic works such as F. Scott Fitzgerald's *This Side of Paradise*."

"Initially, students are split into five residential colleges that provide them with a set of dorms, a college staff, and a dining hall. Students may eat in any dining hall on campus, regardless of their own residence. Each dining hall consists of a main hot line, a salad bar, a grill, and a cold buffet. There are **always vegetarian options besides the salad bar**."

"There are five **bicker clubs**, and to gain membership, students must participate in what is essentially a three-day rush period. Once a student decides to bicker, he or she can only bicker [attempt to join] a single club."

The College Prowler Take
ON CAMPUS DINING

The strength of Princeton's dining hall facilities is that they have many options. While the food in the hot line tends to be somewhat tasteless and boring—although that is changing—events such as the visiting restaurant night more than make up for it. Sunday brunch is by far the best meal of the week, and students are more than willing to struggle out of bed on Sunday mornings to get to the dining halls for made-to-order omelets and bagels and lox.

Eating in the dining halls does get boring after two years, so the vast majority of students opt to go independent, join a co-op, or join an eating club. The food quality at the co-ops and the eating clubs is varied. While some clubs brag award-winning chefs, others complain about a constant barrage of fried foods. The common thread that students enjoy in both the eating clubs and the dining halls is an active social scene and, oftentimes, meal time at Princeton is seen generally more as a social hour than a period of nourishment.

The College Prowler™ Grade on

Campus Dining: B+

Our grade on Campus Dining addresses the quality of both school-owned dining halls and independent on-campus restaurants, as well as the price, availability, and variety of food.

Off-Campus Dining

The Lowdown

ON OFF-CAMPUS DINING

Student Favorites:
Annex Restaurant, Hoagie Haven, Panera Bread Bakery and Café, PJ's Pancake House, Sakura Express, Small World Coffee, Teresa's Cafe Italiano, Thomas Sweet Ice Cream, Triumph Brewing Company

Best Pizza:
Old World Pizza

Best Chinese:
Golden Orchid

Best Healthy:
Moondoggie Café

Best Wings:
Chuck's Spring Street Café

Best Breakfast:
PJ's Pancake House

Best Place to Take Your Parents:
The Ferry House, Mediterra Restaurant, Blue Point Grill

Students Speak Out

ON OFF-CAMPUS DINING

"The restaurants are very good, but they're a little pricey. For economy-style dining, Hoagie Haven and the WaWa convenience store are both very good bets."

"There are some really nice off-campus restaurants because Princeton is a wealthy town. I didn't eat off campus very much because I'm too cheap and all our meals were provided for us. These restaurants can be pretty pricey at about **$10 to $20 per entrée**. There are some fast food places like Burger King, but the best spot is Hoagie Haven—they make subs, hamburgers, and fries, and they make it cheap. It's open late, and it's near the engineering building. A lot of students swing by if they're working late at night."

"**Blue Point Grill and Ajihei** are the best for seafood and sushi, respectively. The Ferry House is also incredible for seafood."

"The Annex is a bar and restaurant located on Nassau Street across from the main library. Also reasonably priced, the Annex becomes a popular haunt for seniors who will leave the library and the dreaded senior thesis only for **last call, which coincides with the closing of the library**."

"Food around here is **good, but expensive**. Be sure to bring your appetite along with your pocketbook!"

"Hands-down, the most popular restaurant among students is **Sakura Express**. The friendly owners serve sushi rolls and other Japanese dishes that are relatively cheap and extremely fast."

"**Thai Village** serves up an excellent pad Thai. It is BYOB and a popular meeting place for birthday parties or large groups."

PRINCETON UNIVERSITY

"There are some good places within easy walking distance of campus. There are plenty of $25-a-plate places, but there are also some other **good restaurants that are within a college student's budget**, such as Zorba's—really good gyros, Old World Pizza—they use whole basil leaves in their pizza, and Sakura Express."

Fun Facts:

With the recent influx of sushi restaurants into Princeton, there are several "Princeton rolls" and "Tiger rolls" around town.

Some of the town's seafood restaurants, including the Blue Point Grill, have amazingly fresh fish, thanks to Nassau Street Seafood Market, which purchases its fish at the famous Fulton Fish Market in New York.

Triumph Brewing Company brews its own beer, which is served in the restaurant. While a pint may be steeper in cost than one at the Annex or the Ivy Inn, there is something to be said for being able to watch the brewing of the beer as you drink it.

The College Prowler Take

OFF-CAMPUS DINING

Recently, Princeton restaurants have started to diversify. Now it is possible to sample a wide variety of ethnic cuisines, whereas a few years ago, selection was limited. New Jersey's top rated sushi restaurant, Ajihei, is a two-minute walk from campus. Students have made a cult of Witherspoon Street's Sakura Express, sending postcards from around the world to the two sushi chefs. Aside from the inexpensive Burger King on Nassau Street, students also favor the take out Greek deli, Olives, and the take out Greek restaurant, Zorba's. Several mid-range options, such as the popular Italian Teresa's, provide options for nicer nights out. High-end restaurants, including the Ferry House and Mediterra, are popular amongst wealthy "townies" and parents in for the weekend.

For a town its size, Princeton offers dozens of restaurant options. Some restaurants in town are certainly too expensive for a student's budget, but those restaurants are generally saved for special occasions, such as Parent's Weekend. If there is a cuisine that is not represented by Princeton's restaurants, it is easy enough to get on a train and find something in New York.

The College Prowler™ Grade on

Off-Campus Dining: B

A high Off-Campus Dining grade implies that off-campus restaurants are affordable, accessible, and worth visiting. Other factors include the variety of cuisine and the availability of alternative options (vegetarian, vegan, Kosher, etc.).

Campus Housing

The Lowdown

ON CAMPUS HOUSING

Undergrads on Campus:
97%

Number of Dormitories:
41

Room Types:
Housing runs the gamut at Princeton, and there is no general formula. Many of Princeton's dorms were built before modern amenities were standard in homes, so older buildings have been heavily renovated in order to accommodate changing times.

Best Dorms:
Patton Hall, Little Hall, Witherspoon Hall, Blair Hall, 1915 Hall, 1903 Hall

Worst Dorms:
1940 Hall, 1941 Hall, Forbes Annex, Cuyler Hall, Brown Hall, Wilcox Hall

Also Available:
Substance-free areas, smoke-free areas, special needs housing, independent housing

Cleaning Service?
Yes, in public areas only

You Get:
Bed, dresser, Internet access, desk, chair, telephone jack

Did You Know?

The dorm where John F. Kennedy lived before transferring to Harvard is no longer standing.

In the mid-twentieth century, Princeton students were responsible for bringing all of their own furniture.

F. Scott Fitzgerald's *This Side of Paradise* depicts, in part, residential life at Princeton at the start of the twentieth century.

Students Speak Out

ON CAMPUS HOUSING

"The residential colleges for underclassmen vary. Some have bathrooms; some don't. Some are new; some are old and crappy. Upperclassmen housing also ranges."

"Pack your **shower shoes**. The shower itself may not be too bad, but you may have several flights of stairs to walk down before reaching a bathroom."

"If you want newer rooms with air-conditioning, **Scully Hall is a good bet**. In terms of central location, 1903 Hall, Brown Hall, and Cuyler Hall are all good places."

"Dorms here are all rather nice and offer lots of **Gothic-type architecture**. Appearance-wise, some of the newer buildings are not as impressive as others, but all have similar living conditions. I enjoy it very much. The social scene is a little monotonous, and some of the fellow students are a little pretentious, but on the whole, it's a great place to have a college experience."

"Generally, **freshmen rooms are not that bad**. You may have to share a bedroom and closet with two other people, but you usually have a common room as a buffer."

"If you have allergies, try to draw into Scully, because it is the only air-conditioned dorm on campus. If you have serious medical problems, try drawing in **special-needs housing**. The housing office will pick your room for you, but they will at least take your needs into account."

"Dorms are fine. Everyone lives on campus, so everyone is in the same boat—it's just fun to live with everyone. Mathey, Rocky, and Wilson are great residential colleges. **Butler is yucky**, although people really like the people that live down there. You'll probably love it wherever you live. We still argue over who had the best residential college experience."

"You don't get much choice freshman year—it's random—but you can choose how many roommates you want. Sophomore year, you choose within the same college by lottery. Junior year, you can move into the nicer, upperclassmen dorms. Forbes College is perhaps the nicest, but it's further from everything. **Rocky and Mathey are both nice and have the old Gregorian style**. Butler and Wilson are more 'modern' and ugly, in my humble opinion."

Need help choosing a dorm? For a detailed listing of all dorms on campus, check out the College Prowler book at *www.collegeprowler.com*.

The College Prowler Take

ON CAMPUS HOUSING

Generally, Princeton students are pleased with their housing experiences, but they realize that is more a reflection of the experiences themselves than the actual accommodations. While the upper-campus residential colleges, Rocky and Mathey, are attractive on the outside, students in the lower-campus residential colleges, Butler, Wilson, and Forbes, complain about "waffle ceilings" and far walks. As far as upperclass housing, the quality of your dorm depends on your draw time and personal preference. While one student may prefer the air-conditioning of Scully, others would complain about its lack of proximity to the rest of the upperclass dorms and prefer to live in a smaller, non-air-conditioned room in Brown or Edwards.

Princeton's housing options could be better—a lot better. Still, students view campus housing as a bonding experience, and only three percent opt out of it. With few affordable options within walking distance to campus, the University has little incentive to improve the conditions in the dorms, as it knows the students have few other options. In a recent move to improve living conditions on campus, however, the University has started to renovate one large dorm or two small dorms a year. This is a long-awaited improvement, considering that many students in some of the older Gothic dorms still have to walk down four flights of stairs to use a washroom.

The College Prowler™ Grade on

Campus Housing: C+

A high Campus Housing grade indicates that dorms are clean, well-maintained, and spacious. Other determining factors include variety of dorms, proximity to classes, and social atmosphere.

Off-Campus Housing

Students Speak Out
ON OFF-CAMPUS HOUSING

"It's not that it isn't convenient, it's just that nobody really lives off campus."

"Just about **everyone lives on campus**. Off-campus housing is very expensive due to the nature of the Princeton area, but on-campus housing is really good."

"**Barely anyone lives off campus**!"

There's not much off-campus housing available, but no worries, you're guaranteed on-campus housing for all four years. Generally, it gets better as you get older. Your best chance of living off campus in a really nice room is to **become an eating club officer** and live there—you get awesome rooms then!"

"Students are **guaranteed on-campus housing for four years**, so you don't have to worry about finding an apartment."

"Off-campus housing basically does not exist. Apartments off campus are **very expensive**, and there's so much going on that no one ever wants to leave anyway. I don't know anybody who doesn't live on campus."

"There's really **no reason to live off campus**. It's expensive and really inconvenient. Almost everyone, without exception, lives in on-campus housing all four years. Housing at Princeton is pretty good. You will live comfortably, but do not expect the Ritz Carlton. The new fitness center in the gym is incredible, to say the least."

The Lowdown
ON OFF-CAMPUS HOUSING

Undergrads in Off-Campus Housing:
3%

Average Rent for a Studio Apartment:
$825/month

Average Rent for a 1BR Apartment:
$1,100/month

Average Rent for a 2BR Apartment:
$1,570/month

Popular Areas:
Princeton, Princeton Junction

Best Time to Look for a Place:
Spring

The College Prowler Take
ON OFF-CAMPUS HOUSING

Students cannot elect to live off campus until junior year, so most students grow accustomed to the daily housekeeping service in communal dorm areas, particularly bathrooms and hallways, during their freshman and sophomore years. Because Princeton is such an affluent town, particularly in the areas surrounding the campus, off-campus housing is not financially feasible to the majority of the undergraduate population.

To find an affordable option, a student would need access to a car, which is problematic because parking near the academic buildings can be close to non-existent. Then, once the student found off-campus housing, he or she would have to install necessary features that are provided in on-campus housing, such as Ethernet—and then have to cope with the utter isolation of living off campus. In short, until graduation, on campus is "where home is" for most Princeton students.

The College Prowler™ Grade on

Off-Campus Housing: D-

A high grade in Off-Campus Housing indicates that apartments are of high quality, close to campus, affordable, and easy to secure.

Diversity

The Lowdown
ON DIVERSITY

White: 63%

Asian American: 13%

African American: 8%

Hispanic: 7%

Native American: 1%

International: 8%

Out-of-State: 85%

Minority Clubs

Campus groups, such as Princeton South Asian Theatrics and Naacho, have helped raise awareness of minorities on campus. The Black Student Union has a board in Frist that allows for better publicity of minority events on campus.

Political Activity

The majority of Princeton students do not engage in campus political activity on a regular basis, but there is an active debate group, the Whig-Cliostrophic Society. The College Republicans and College Democrats also draw energetic membership.

Gay Pride

Generally, the Princeton community is accepting of gay students, as seen by the popularity of Pride Alliance events.

Religion

Princeton has several very visible campus religious groups, such as Agape, Athletes in Action, and the Center for Jewish Life.

Economic Status

Even though Princeton has the reputation of being an elitist institution, Princeton attracts students of all economic backgrounds because of its recent no-loan program.

Students Speak Out

ON DIVERSITY

"It is predominantly white upper-class, but I'm Hispanic, and I know lots of people who are also Hispanic, African American, and Asian. I don't really find it to be much of an issue, though."

"The campus is mostly white, but there is a **decent percentage of minorities**. I guess the diversity could be a little better, but they are working on it."

"It's extremely diverse here. There are people here from all over—different states, different countries—they are just from all over the place. It's pretty cool. You get to see a lot of different cultures out there, and **people are very proud of their ethnicities**."

"It's somewhat diverse, **depending on your definition of diversity**. People come from everywhere, from all walks of life, from all countries. It actually is hugely interesting. The campus is working to admit more minorities, but I felt like my experience was diverse. My best friends were from all over and of many ethnicities."

"The students represent most of the world, and because of the scene, **you will pretty much interact with everyone** from a wide array of different backgrounds."

"What makes the Princeton experience so exceptional is not necessarily the racial diversity, but the diversity of student experience. While some students come from very isolated parts of the United States, such as rural Kansas, **others come from cosmopolitan international centers**."

"It's pretty diverse. I met a lot of people during **various social events and at parties**."

The College Prowler Take

ON DIVERSITY

Depending upon students' personal experience, some students think that Princeton is very diverse, and others think that there are relatively few minorities present. While not all students believe that Princeton is diverse, it is impossible to deny the range of student groups available to promote diversity awareness.

Princeton is not as diverse as some other Ivy League schools, but the school's demographics are diverse considering the racial and economic standing of the surrounding town. Diversity at Princeton is starting to improve because the university has recently instituted a no-loan financial aid program, which ensures that all financial aid will be given in the form of grants that do not need to be repaid. An increasing number of discussion forums have also helped raise awareness of campus diversity issues.

The College Prowler™ Grade on

Diversity: B

A high grade in Diversity indicates that ethnic minorities and international students have a notable presence on campus and that students of different economic backgrounds, religious beliefs, and sexual preferences are well-represented.

The Lowdown

ON GUYS & GIRLS

Female Undergrads: 48%

Male Undergrads: 52%

Birth Control Available?

Yes—Sexuality Education Counseling and Health Office (S.E.C.H.), McCosh Health Center. Female students who have had an annual exam with their home doctor or have an exam with the S.E.C.H. office can have their birth control prescriptions filled at health services for a discounted fee. S.E.C.H. offers all forms of birth control: birth control pills, patches, diaphragms, contraceptive gel, and Depo-Provera injections. S.E.C.H. also sells discounted condoms.

Social Scene

Like any university, Princeton students range from studious ones who rarely go out to those who can hardly be called students. For some students, Princeton provides a "work hard, party hard" environment, which is initially surprising because of the rigor of Princeton's academic program. Contrary to popular belief, not all Princeton students are nerds or trust fund kids, so most find their niche quickly. Unfortunately, the Greek scene, strong athletic teams, and eating clubs slightly fragment the student body, but they also help some students gain some sort of identity on campus.

Hookups or Relationships?

The Princeton hookup scene is relatively isolated to underclass women and upperclass men. By junior and senior year, Princeton women generally date or get involved in serious relationships, while Princeton men play the field more. Because male Princeton freshmen are at the absolute bottom of any dating hierarchy, they tend to remain in relationships from high school rather than face rejection from the women on campus.

Dress Code

Generally, Princeton students are a happy medium between preppy and fashionable. It is rare to see a student show up to class in sweatpants or anything resembling pajamas. Few students have what could be called an "urban, edgy" look. Guys usually wear polo shirts and khakis, and girls wear comfortable, stylish clothes. Recent uniforms have included Lilly Pulitzer attire, Longchamp bags, and jeans by Seven and Paper Denim & Cloth.

Best Place to Meet Guys/Girls

The best place to meet other students initially is in residential colleges, whether it is in the dining hall or in one's RA group. Fraternity and sorority rush starts several weeks after the freshmen arrive on campus, and the Greek scene draws a small fraction of students into Greek life. For everyone else, social interaction can occur on a regular basis anywhere from "the Street" to campus religious gatherings. Princeton students are notorious for getting spring fever or simply frolicking whenever the weather is warm. Mysteriously, the rate of random hookups seems to increase during warm weather periods, such as Freshman Week and in the spring. (This may also correlate to relatively slow work periods.)

Top Three Places to Find Hotties:

1. Eating clubs
2. Frist Campus Center
3. Dining halls

Top Places to Hookup:

1. Eating clubs
2. Empty classrooms—Frist and the E-Quad
3. Tennis court pagoda
4. Firestone Library carrels
5. Athletic fields

Students Speak Out

ON GUYS & GIRLS

"On the whole, there are attractive people here. After visiting, a friend of mine described Princeton as being full of 'beautiful, disgruntled people."

"There's probably a pretty big spectrum, but hot guys are definitely available. I'm quite satisfied with the guys on campus. As for the girls, well, I think **we're really good-looking**, as well."

"A lot of people at Princeton are pretty wealthy. It is also mostly white. There can be **a lot of stuck-up snobs**, but most of the people I met were very cool and down-to-earth. The girls are okay, although they definitely don't compare to some other schools in terms of looks. The guys pretty much agree that there aren't a lot of hot chicks on campus."

"The guys are cool but **a little pretentious**, and the girls are very pretentious. The majority of the student body is ugly as sin—only a few good-looking students exist, half of which have boyfriends. The idea of 'importing girls' is widely used."

"People here are pretty diverse and run the gamut from **bookish nerds to party animals**."

"Not only are the girls cute, but they are also smart, nice, and non-threatening. The only downside is that, as Princeton tends to have people who are used to success, **guys tend to fear the whole asking-out thing**. We have a lot of serious couples and hookups here, but minimal dating."

"I found the majority of girls here to be attractive. It seemed that there were an **abnormally large percentage of hot girls**. I didn't pay much attention to the guys."

"The guys are **50/50**. As for the girls, they are split, too. You have the stuck-up rich snobs, and then you have the everyday girl who is friendly and loves to go out and make some new friends."

"You have to remember that there are three other major colleges within 30 minutes of you, so you can always meet people form other schools when you go out. You are not limited to just Princeton kids—you have Rutgers, College of New Jersey, and Rider. And, within an hour, you have all the New York and Philly schools, too."

"You have a nice selection of good-looking guys and girls if you go to the right places. Generally, if you **go to the eating clubs on a Thursday or Saturday night**, you'll find the best-looking people on campus."

The College Prowler Take
ON GUYS & GIRLS

People often joke that we are all nerds deep down at Princeton. With the pressures of getting into a top school like Princeton, many of the matriculating students missed some of the more active social lives that their high school classmates had the opportunity to experience. Socializing freshman year is awkward at best. Freshman girls are pursued by the more experienced upperclassmen while freshman boys wait for their turn to come. After a freshman year of casual dating or hooking up, Princeton women plunge to the bottom of the dating totem pole by senior year when they see their male classmates attempt to chase the younger women on campus.

It is difficult to place a single stereotype on the Princeton man or Princeton woman. Many of us would like to think that we resemble alumni Dean Cain ('88) or Brooke Shields ('87), but the diversity of student character and experience makes it difficult to pigeonhole anyone. As a gross generalization, Princeton students are very health-minded, are relatively thin, and many students joke that the average height is about three inches over the national average. Is everyone tall, thin, and good-looking at Princeton? No, but we can dream, can't we?

The College Prowler™ Grade on
Guys: B

A high grade for Guys indicates that the male population on campus is attractive, smart, friendly, and engaging, and that the school has a decent ratio of guys to girls.

The College Prowler™ Grade on
Girls: B

A high grade for Girls not only implies that the women on campus are attractive, smart, friendly, and engaging, but also that there is a fair ratio of girls to guys.

Athletics

The Lowdown
ON ATHLETICS

Athletic Division:
NCAA Division I

Conference:
Ivy League

School Mascot:
Tiger

Men's Varsity Teams:
- Basketball
- Baseball
- Crew
- Cross Country
- Fencing
- Football
- Golf
- Hockey
- Lacrosse
- Soccer
- Squash
- Swimming & Diving
- Tennis
- Track & Field
- Volleyball
- Water Polo
- Wrestling

Women's Varsity Teams:
- Basketball
- Crew
- Cross Country
- Fencing
- Field Hockey
- Golf
- Hockey
- Lacrosse
- Soccer
- Softball
- Squash
- Swimming & Diving
- Tennis
- Track & Field
- Volleyball
- Water Polo

Getting Tickets

Students do not need to pay for many sporting events, and tickets are not difficult to obtain. Occasionally, it is necessary to get tickets ahead of time, but only for major events, such as a Princeton-Penn home basketball game.

Most Popular Sports

On the varsity level, the most visible teams are the football, basketball, baseball, ice hockey, and lacrosse teams. Football games draw in droves of alumni, especially for games against Big Three rivals Harvard and Yale. A strong rivalry with Penn in basketball gives Princeton students something to get heated up about during the icy winters. Both lacrosse teams—men's and women's—have collected multiple national titles in recent history and are a great source of school spirit.

Overlooked Teams

The squash program is probably one of the most successful, but underappreciated, athletic programs on campus. Each year, the team places well in national tournaments, but gets little exposure on campus, perhaps because few students even know what squash is by the time they get to campus freshman year. On the club level, both rugby teams have had great runs in national tournaments recently, but, because of its status as a club sport, rugby does not get the same sort of exposure as the football or lacrosse teams.

Best Place to Take a Walk

Towpath around Lake Carnegie, Princeton Battlefield

Students Speak Out

ON ATHLETICS

"Sports on campus are huge! It seems that nearly half, or more, of the student body participates in some form of athletics—varsity or IM."

"Varsity sports are pretty big. Our football team isn't that good, so basketball gets a lot of fan support, as does lacrosse. A very high percentage of the student body plays varsity sports. Everyone else plays club sports or intramurals [IMs]. **Intramurals are pretty big** and cover sports from hockey, to flag football, to basketball, etc. I played in a lot of IMs, and they were always competitive and a lot of fun."

"**I love going to basketball games**! Sometimes they can be very exciting, especially if we are having a good season."

"There are **lots of opportunities**. Varsity sports are pretty big, and fairly good. Field hockey, lacrosse, swimming, some individual track events, basketball, squash—all are competitive on the national level and some have several national titles. Football has been less consistent, although they won the Ivy League champs my first year. There are also club sports, which are sort of like varsity, but officially a step below."

"IM sports are huge and so much fun! We have everything from **broomball—it's the best sport ever, hockey using brooms instead of sticks**—soccer, basketball, to inner tube water polo. They were a huge part of my Princeton experience. Not only did I have an awesome time and get great exercise, but I also met a lot of my close friends through them."

"We have a ton of varsity athletes—it blows me away. IM sports are fairly big, as well. **Not too many students attend football games**, but a hell of a lot attend men's basketball games. Our basketball team is always first or second in the Ivy League. Our lacrosse team has won the national championship in recent years. Varsity sports are very big, and a lot of people get involved in at least one of them."

"I have been to all the pool events and a couple football and basketball games, and they seem to be pretty good, especially the water polo games. There are **really hot guys in tight Speedos**—it is great!"

The College Prowler Take
ON ATHLETICS

Athletics (varsity, club, and intramural) play an important role on campus. At some point in their Princeton career, most students will have some exposure to campus athletics, whether it is attending a game of the title-winning men's lacrosse team at Class of 1952 Stadium, or participating in a yoga class at Dillon Gym. For students who are not up to varsity level, there are still plenty of opportunities to participate on a team, whether it is on one of the spirited IM teams or one of the University's 34 club teams. Scenic features such as the wooded towpath and Lake Carnegie also encourage students to take a break from their work and go jogging along one of the university's trails.

As a small Ivy League school, Princeton's athletic prowess is almost surprising. Unable to offer athletic scholarships or any other prequisites, the University draws athletes who come to Princeton not only because of some of the award-winning athletic teams, but also because of the top-notch academics. The Ivy League provides some fantastic rivalries and gives Princeton students another venue for bragging about their abilities on and off the field.

The College Prowler™ Grade on
Athletics: B

A high grade in Athletics indicates that students have school spirit, that sports programs are respected, that games are well- attended, and that intramurals are a prominent part of student life.

Nightlife

The Lowdown
ON NIGHTLIFE

Student Favorites:
Triumph Brewing Company, the Annex, T.I., Colonial, Cottage, Cap and Gown, Ivy Inn, Tower

Bars Close At:
12 a.m.-2 a.m.

Primary Areas with Nightlife:
The Street

Cheapest Place to Get a Drink:
The Street

Students Speak Out
ON NIGHTLIFE

"The bars are okay; they're not really a big scene here. The majority of the social scene is on campus. Most of the off-campus bar and club scene occurs in New York City."

PRINCETON UNIVERSITY

"Because Princeton is a small town, there aren't many bars and clubs off campus. If you want to go clubbing, you probably have to go to New York—it's about an hour away by train. Ivy is a bar that's close to campus. Seniors will go there occasionally, but **most of the social life revolves around 'the Street**.'"

"On weekends, **eating clubs will have DJs, bands, parties, and free beer**, so this is where people party. Clubs are usually open to everyone, although some clubs may have passes for special nights."

"We don't really do clubs and bars off campus. **The major social scene at Princeton revolves around the eating clubs** on Prospect Street and basically on campus. There are 11 clubs, and every Thursday and Saturday, and some Fridays, they each have bands, DJs, or something going on. It's all free, all so much fun, and all very campus-orientated."

"There are some nice spots in Princeton, but remember that New York is only an hour-and-a-half away from Princeton. Philly is an hour away, and Trenton is only 30 minutes away. New Brunswick is where Rutgers University is—there is a whole bunch of college stuff to do around there, too. **Princeton is like a central location for almost every party and college spot in New Jersey**, because it is right in the middle of things."

"Generally, **students don't venture off campus to go to bars** and clubs. Sometimes we'll go in to New York, but there really isn't much in the town. The bars that are there are very strict about IDs, but once you're legal, some kids do go to Triumph or another bar called Ivy Inn."

"I've never been to any bars or clubs. Most people don't go because of the eating club system. They function kind of like frats—most **eating clubs are 'on tap'** Thursday, Friday, and Saturday nights, and a few will always be open to anyone with a Princeton ID."

"**Triumph and the Annex** are the bars that people go to, although most people stick to the social scene on campus—the eating clubs."

The College Prowler Take

ON NIGHTLIFE

Princeton hardly has dozens of social options available, but between the Street, room parties, the bars of Nassau Street, and convenient transportation to both New York and Philadelphia, options certainly exist. While a night out at Princeton's clubs and bars tends to be quite average, legendary Princeton "holidays," such as Newman's Day and Dean's Date, which encourage late nights out, more than make up for the otherwise monotonous social scene. Annual, special events hosted by the eating clubs, including house parties and winter formals, also provide a nice break from just going out to get wasted.

Despite the proximity to New York and Philadelphia, public transportation is somewhat inflexible, as the last train on a Saturday night leaves New York's Penn Station around 1 a.m., leaving students stranded in Princeton Junction unless they are willing to pay the hefty late-night cab fare.

The College Prowler™ Grade on

Nightlife: C

A high grade in Nightlife indicates that there are many bars and clubs in the area that are easily accessible and affordable. Other determining factors include the number of options for the under-21 crowd and the prevalence of house parties.

PRINCETON UNIVERSITY

Greek Life

Students Speak Out
ON GREEK LIFE

"Greek life has a minimal role at Princeton. I wasn't involved in it at all and rarely saw it, but there are a few sororities and fraternities. Greek life is really minor."

"Frats and sororities aren't a big part of campus because of 'the Street.' There are some, but they aren't that big because they're **not recognized by the University**."

"There is a **growing presence of Greek life**, although no houses exist. The majority of social scene is found at the eating clubs."

"There are fraternities, but they are not officially recognized by the university. You'll find some dorm 'frat' parties, but the frats are usually strongly linked to one or more of the eating clubs. Most of the social life is dominated by the eating clubs, where there is a **fair amount of drinking that goes on**."

"There is Greek life on campus—it is pretty popular, although **not absolutely essential to the University**. It is growing in popularity. I am in a sorority, and I love it."

"Technically, I guess we have Greek life, but it's not too big, and the University doesn't acknowledge it. The eating clubs have nearly eradicated the need for Greek life, since being a member is **like being in a coed frat**. Their parties are usually better than lame, University-run entertainment. They're run by students, while the University looks the other way."

The Lowdown
ON GREEK LIFE

Number of Fraternities:
14

Number of Sororities:
4

Undergrad Men in Fraternities:
20%

Undergrad Women in Sororities:
15%

Fraternities on Campus:
Beta Theta Pi, Chi Phi, Delta Kappa Epsilon, Delta Phi, Delta Psi, Kappa Alpha Order, Phi Kappa Sigma, Pi Kappa Alpha, Sigma Alpha Epsilon, Sigma Chi, Sigma Phi, Theta Delta Chi, Zeta Beta Tau, and Zeta Psi

Sororities on Campus:
Delta Delta Delta, Kappa Alpha Theta, Kappa Kappa Gamma, and Pi Beta Phi

Multicultural Colonies:
Alpha Epsilon Pi, Delta Sigma Theta, Alpha Kappa Alpha, Lambda Upsilon Lambda, Zeta Phi Beta, Sigma Lambda Upsilon

Other Greek Organizations:
Panhellenic Council

The College Prowler Take
ON GREEK LIFE

Princeton University does not officially recognize the fraternities and sororities that exist on campus. Unofficially, the University has been trying for years to figure out whether to incorporate the existing Greek system into campus life, or to rid the campus of any form of Greek system. Fraternities initially started on Princeton's campus in the 1840s, but fearing the deterioration of Princeton's celebrated debate societies, the administration forbade any Greek presence on campus.

To do this, Princeton's administrators required students to sign a pledge that they would not go Greek for the next hundred years. Without houses and without recognition from the University, Princeton's modern Greek system does not have much of a presence on campus and most students are disinterested in the system.

The College Prowler™ Grade on
Greek Life: C-

A high grade in Greek Life indicates that sororities and fraternities are not only present, but also active on campus. Other determining factors include the variety of houses available and the respect the Greek community receives from the rest of the campus.

PRINCETON UNIVERSITY

Drug Scene

The Lowdown
ON DRUG SCENE

Most Prevalent Drugs on Campus:
Alcohol, marijuana, cocaine, Ritalin, Dexedrine, Adderall

Liquor-Related Referrals:
244

Liquor-Related Arrests:
28

Drug-Related Referrals:
22

Drug-Related Arrests:
3

Students Speak Out
ON DRUG SCENE

The College Prowler Take
ON DRUG SCENE

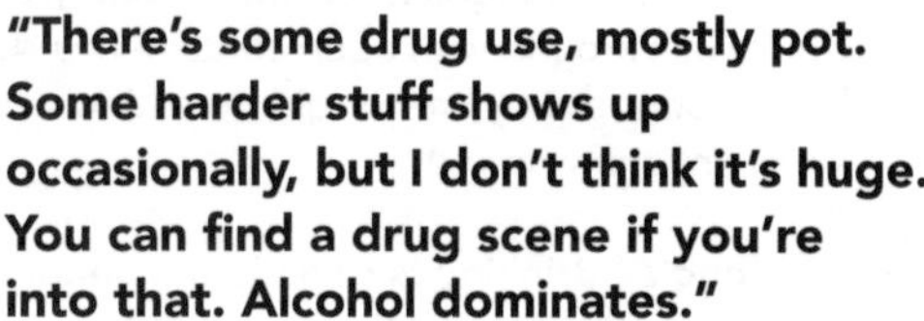

"There's some drug use, mostly pot. Some harder stuff shows up occasionally, but I don't think it's huge. You can find a drug scene if you're into that. Alcohol dominates."

"The drug scene isn't that bad. Marijuana is the dominant drug here. I think **very few people do the hardcore drugs**."

"It's present like at anywhere else. It **depends on the crowd**. There is a lot of wealth, so designer drugs are popular."

"Honestly, I tried to avoid the drug scene and succeeded. I think it's pretty safe to say that it's there, but **only if you choose to be part of it**, although pot is the most abundant."

"I'd say there's not really a drug scene. I mean, I would think that there would be some, like at any place you go, but I have never heard of any bad things in Princeton. I think I heard of something only once and it had to do with pot. **All the drug scenes are in the big cities** like Philly, New York, Trenton, and so on."

"As far as I can tell, **the 'scene' is pretty small**. There's a fairly large drinking scene, but as far as drugs go, I'd say it's only among a certain group of people."

"I'm not really sure. I have **never encountered any drug-related issues**."

Like almost any other university, there are drugs present on Princeton's campus. The drug scene on Princeton's campus is not very visible, but it is present. With the strong presence of eating clubs as the main dining and social option for students, alcohol is the source of the majority of strain in the relationship between administrators and students. Each weekend, a number of students have to visit McCosh Health Center, or "get McCosh-ed," for alcohol-related issues. Other than alcohol, marijuana is the most prevalent drug on campus.

A small minority of Princeton students have started to use drugs other than alcohol and marijuana. A recent article in the *Daily Princetonian* reported an increasing presence of drugs such as cocaine and Adderall on campus. Because of the academic pressures, some students opt to use prescription drugs, such as Ritalin, to stay awake to do work. Most students at Princeton do not use drugs, and it is by no means a widespread problem.

The College Prowler™ Grade on

Drug Scene: B

A high grade on Drug Scene indicates that drugs are not a noticeable part of campus life, drug use is not visible, and no pressure to use them seems to exist.

Campus Strictness

The Lowdown
ON CAMPUS STRICTNESS

What Are You Most Likely to Get Caught Doing on Campus?

Drinking underage

Drinking in common areas

Public urination or indecency

Parking illegally

Making too much noise in your dorm

Having candles or other contraband items in your dorm room

Students Speak Out
ON CAMPUS STRICTNESS

"Campus police aren't too strict on drugs and drinking. There are lots of room parties on campus that aren't broken up until things get too loud or out of control."

"They're rather relaxed in nature as long as the students are not way too loud or **blatently disregarding the rules**."

"I'll give you a little parable. When I was pre-fresh and came to visit, I attended a party with **a pool filled with beer**."

"They are **pretty leniant about drinking**. Just don't walk around with open containers. I don't know about drugs; I never did them and never knew anyone who did."

"**As long as drinking is done in a manner that doesn't disturb others**, and as long as people don't start passing out and calling ambulances, things are fine."

"Drugs are really not an issue and are considered unacceptable throughout the student body, so it's **not an issue with police**. A lot of drinking goes on, and the University has been trying to crack down on it in recent years, but with little success. For people who like to go out, drinking is a large part of the social culture."

"They **won't tolerate drugs if they find out**. With drinking, they tend to look the other way unless someone is hospitalized or something. They bust room parties sometimes, but no one is ever arrested. Drinking is a different thing, but campus police will look the other way. They're not strict at all; there are parties outside all the time."

The College Prowler Take
ON CAMPUS STRICTNESS

Few Princeton students will find themselves under the scrutiny of Princeton's campus police or administration. Those students who do, can be called in for any number of reasons, from climbing tent scaffolding at reunions, to breaking into a dining hall after hours to get a scoop of ice cream. Room parties tend to be broken up, not because of presumed underage drinking, but because of noise complaints. Just as long as those students who choose to drink do so without breaking noise and open container regulations, campus security does not give them too much of a problem.

Campus police rely mostly on the town police for taking care of major issues. The campus police focus more on problems such as noise complaints, which may result from parties where alcohol is served. The majority of calls they receive are about thefts and alcohol-related issues, such as drunken students needing transport to McCosh Health Center in the middle of the night.

The College Prowler™ Grade on

Campus Strictness: B+

A high Campus Strictness grade implies an overall lenient atmosphere; police and RAs are fairly tolerant, and the administration's rules are flexible.

Parking & Transportation

The Lowdown
ON PARKING & TRANSPORTATION

Student Parking Lot?
Yes

Freshmen Allowed to Park?
No

Parking Permit Cost:
$135/year for automobiles,
$50/year for mopeds

Best Place to Find a Parking Spot:
Lot 23

Ways to Get Around:

On Campus

Campus Shuttle, 5 p.m.-10:40 p.m.,
(609) 258-6861

Dial-a-Ride, 10:40 p.m.-2 a.m.,
(609) 258-6861
Tiger Tram, 5:30 a.m.-6:45 p.m.

Students Speaks Out
ON PARKING & TRANSPORTATION

"It's all very convenient. New Jersey Transit trains stop literally on the edge of the campus. For $16, you can go between Princeton and New York City without using a car."

"Parking sucks because **there aren't a lot of places you can park without incurring a $20 fine**. There are a few big lots where everyone parks, but these are generally pretty far from the living areas."

"**The train actually runs through Princeton's campus**, so it is pretty convenient for getting to New York City or the rest of New Jersey. It also connects to Amtrak should you want to go further. I've been able to get from Princeton to Boston by train, and it was very convenient."

"Public transportation is pretty good. There is a train station on campus, the Dinky, that connects directly to the main New Jersey Transit train line. The Princeton 'Airporter' also comes right on campus for transportation to the airport, and there are campus shuttles that go to the grocery store. The buses are pretty good, too. **You can probably get anywhere in the state** using public transportation."

"Parking is not really a problem, but **the lot is relatively far from your dorm**, so it's always kind of a big deal to go get your car for something. There's only temporary parking near the dorms. A lot of students don't have cars because you don't really need to go off campus if you don't want to."

"Parking for freshman is pretty far, but it's available. **It gets better as you get older**."

The College Prowler Take
ON PARKING

One major strength of Princeton's parking program is that it is possible to walk nearly everywhere on campus, so parking is a non-issue. There are plenty of restaurants, shops, and small grocers within walking distance of the dorms. When students need to go off campus, there are plenty of shuttle buses between the dorms and parking lots throughout the day.

The College Prowler™ Grade on

Parking: B

A high grade in this section indicates that parking is both available and affordable, and that parking enforcement isn't overly severe.

The College Prowler Take
ON TRANSPORTATION

Princeton's public transportation is very accessible, but it is somewhat inconvenient for students. The train connecting Princeton and Princeton Junction runs only once an hour throughout most of the day, and stops running for several hours during the night, which puts huge constraints on nights out in New York City. There are plenty of airport options, which allows students to comparison shop for airline tickets home and for vacations.

The College Prowler™ Grade on

Transportation: C+

A high grade for Transportation indicates that campus buses, public buses, cabs, and rental cars are readily-available and affordable. Other determining factors include proximity to an airport and the necessity of transportation.

Overall Experience

Students Speak Out
ON OVERALL EXPERIENCE

"My overall experience has been very positive. You get used to the uniqueness of the school. I got involved in sports, and I had a great time."

"I found the pre-med process at Princeton very frustrating. The people in my required courses were **extremely competitive**. It took me a few semesters to find a group of other students who felt the same way, who were willing to work together to make it through the tough intro level courses."

"I love it here. **It's a little conservative**, but the opportunities are fabulous. I love Princeton and have had incredible experiences. It's not the perfect place for me, but I don't think that any college is perfect for anyone. Princeton is the kind of place that should be totally amazing but somehow, it's not. There is a weird vibe, but it also completely depends on who you know, where you end up, and what kind of person you are, because most people love it."

"Initially, like many others, **I wasn't that thrilled with the school** because it is very much a closed campus, and there's not tremendous choice in terms of the social scene. But freshman year, I made some really close friends with people in my hallway, and from there, I started to like it more and more. The four years have gone so fast, and I'm actually a little sad that it's time to move on."

"It is impossible to love every second at Princeton, because the work is simply too demanding. In the midst of all of the work, however, **you will make some of the strongest bonds of your life**, whether it is with professors, graduate students, administrators, support staff, or your fellow students. The Princeton bond is not limited to just that population either. Alumni are more than willing to share their wealth of knowledge and experience with students, so that they can get the best opportunities in the workplace. A friend of mine networked during his sophomore year and got an offer for a paid internship at one of the country's top investment banks before his junior year, a year earlier than the official recruitment process even begins!"

"Princeton has challenged me in ways that I could have never imagined. **My first obstacle was my freshman-year roommate** who kept weird hours and who I could find clacking away on her computer keyboard while I was trying to sleep. The next obstacle was finding ways to make the meals in the dining hall bearable, but the reward of good eating club food was totally worth it."

"While my intro level courses were difficult, it was a different kind of difficult from the upper level ones. Whereas my intro level courses **were a challenge to my academic endurance,** the upper level ones always left me thinking. In the end, it was a privilege to get to work with some of the greatest minds and most influential people of our time."

The College Prowler Take
ON OVERALL EXPERIENCE

Once students get past the relative isolation of Princeton, they immerse themselves in the multitude of campus academic and social activities, from political and humor publications to debate societies to eating clubs. The academic program is demanding, which students appreciate, and it prepares students for not only the work force but also top-notch graduate schools. The historic buildings and eating clubs give Princeton its own sort of feel that may not mesh well with all students, but certainly provides Princeton undergrads with a plethora of traditions and opportunities that are characteristically Princeton.

Princeton is not just a school, it is an experience. Students who take full advantage of what Princeton has to offer have the opportunity to work with some of the most talented professors and scholars in the world on an idyllic campus. They graduate with one of the best undergraduate educations in the country, not to mention all the connections the alumni experience has to offer. Some students may not realize the significance of the Princeton experience until they march onto Elm Drive for their graduating P-rade, but the majority of students know how special the Princeton experience is by the time they are back from the woods on their pre-frosh Outdoor Action trip.

The Inside Scoop

The Lowdown
ON THE INSIDE SCOOP

Princeton Slang:

Know the slang, know the school. The following is a list of things you really need to know before coming to Princeton. The more of these words you know, the better off you'll be.

Alexander Beach - Central New Jersey's answer to a beach, the grassy area between Blair, Witherspoon, Alexander, and West College where students suntan

Bicker - The five-day period at the start of second semester during which sophomores wishing to join selective eating clubs go through a rush-like process to gain invitation

Big Three - Harvard, Princeton, and Yale, becomes an issue mostly during football season

Cannon Green - Green behind Nassau Hall with a cannon partially buried in the center, location of coveted Big Three bonfire

Communiversity - Day-long event each April that tries to unify town and gown through activities along Nassau Street and on Nassau Green

Dean's Date - The last day of reading period when all written course work is due. If a student cannot complete his work, he has to go see a dean. This is also one of the biggest nights out at the eating clubs.

Dinky - Two-car New Jersey train that connects Princeton to Princeton Junction

E-Quad - Engineering quadrangle

Freshman Week - Also called "Frosh Week," time for sophomores and upperclassmen to settle in while freshmen attend events organized by university administrators to help them learn more about campus life.

Honor Code - Princeton institution that is taken very seriously. Student sign a pledge at the end of every paper and exam, and are expected to turn in students that they witness cheating.

Hose - Reject from a bicker club

Houseparties - Three-day party weekend at the end of spring semester. On Friday, students go to a formal, followed by a semi-formal on Saturday, and then Lawnparties on Sunday.

Independent - Upperclassman who is not a member of an eating club, University dining hall, or co-op

JP - Short for junior paper, the independent paper to be completed by all A.B. students. Some A.B. departments only mandate one JP, while others ask for two.

Newman's Day - Popular student "holiday," April 24. Participating students try to drink 24 beers in 24 hours without going to sleep, vomiting, or missing class.

Nude Olympics - Now-banned tradition, the tradition dictated that sophomores would participate in naked frolicking in Holder courtyard during the first snowfall of the year.

Old Nassau - Nickname for Princeton University and title of Princeton's alma mater, which is sung at most campus events

P/D/F - Short for Pass/D/Fail. Students are given four P/D/Fs to use during the course of their Princeton education. They can only use one at a time and must pay attention to the strict deadlines associated with this option.

Proctor - Public Safety officer

Prospect 11 - Popular campus drinking challenge; Students must drink a beer at each of the eating clubs during the course of a night.

Reading Period - Week-and-a-half period at the end of classes for students to work on independent work and catch up on reading before exams

Room Draw - Computerized lottery that assigns draw times to students for picking rooms each spring for the following academic year; Students have tried for years to figure out how the draw is "randomized" with very little success.

U-Store - Abbreviation for University Store, the campus bookstore; Even though it claims to be unaffiliated with the University, the U-Store is the only place where students can find the few rare appliances that are approved by the Fire Safety Code.

Wa - Short for the WaWa Food Market

'Zees - Short for advisees, the freshmen in an RA group; There are usually groups of approximately 15 to 20 'zees for each RA.

Things I Wish I Knew Before Coming to Princeton:

- Get on the smallest meal plan possible.
- Unless you like living in a cave, you should bring several lamps.
- Outdoor and Community Action programs really are a great way to meet people and learn about Princeton while doing something fun and useful.
- The U-Store will give you the lowest price on a textbook. For example, you can bring a listing from Barnes and Noble, including the cost of shipping, and the U-Store will match their price.
- Opportunities are available as long as you seek them out and talk to people.
- Walking to review sessions in January will make you colder than you have ever felt before. Pack warm clothes!
- Meet as many people as possible during Freshman Week.
- Cinder blocks are essential in a small dorm room.

Tips to Succeed at Princeton:

- Use all resources that are available to pick your classes—RAs, Student Course Guide—and do not believe everything your academic advisor says.
- Pick classes you actually like.
- Take advantage of as many special lecture series as possible.
- Research your professors before choosing your classes.
- Go to class. Never miss precept.
- Check your e-mail constantly, but do not spend all your time on the Internet.
- Ask the TAs tons of questions.
- Try to complete your distribution requirements as early as possible. If you can't find a class you want to take in a given semester that fills a distribution requirement, look at the Bulletin to see if something more interesting is going to be offered the following semester.
- Take advantage of Princeton's student networking events and alumni events that are open to undergrads. Connections made while casually networking may eventually net a job offer or fantastic internship.
- Actually use reading period, and go to all review sessions.

Princeton Urban Legends

A curse placed on the University when it was originally founded brought bad luck and death to all of the University presidents, which is why there were so many presidents in Princeton's first years.

Butler College was designed in such a depressing manner to remind students of the horrors of the Holocaust, which explains the barbed-wire-esque structures atop each of the buildings.

The eating clubs were formed to promote better understanding of gourmet food amongst the uncouth Princeton men.

James Buchanan Duke offered Princeton a large sum of money in the 1920s to change its name to Duke. When the University refused, he donated the money instead to Trinity College in North Carolina, which is why Duke is now called the Princeton of the South.

The black squirrels that roam around campus are a biology project gone wrong.

School Spirit

Princeton students and alumni can never be accused of not having school spirit. From making endless jokes about Harvard and Yale, to coming back for annual reunions, Princeton is more than a four-year education, it is a lifetime legacy. An alumnus at a recent P-rade said, "The toughest thing about Princeton is not getting in. It is getting over it." While Princeton is not a school where all undergrads attend all of the football games, there is a constant aura of Princetonia. It is nearly impossible to pass through Fitz Randolph Gates at graduation without owning at least one vibrant orange and black article of clothing. This spirit does not stop at the school level. Princeton undergrads also rally behind their residential colleges and continue to discuss who had the best experience. For example, Butler residents brag about their intramural prowess while Rocky residents make fun of Butler for its dorms and claim superiority because of their Gothic ones.

Traditions

Baccalaureate Address

Baccalaureate is one of Princeton's most time-honored traditions. Originally referred to as a sermon, the Baccalaureate Address marks the end of reunions and the start of commencement activities for graduating seniors. Held in the University Chapel, recent speakers have included retiring Dean of Admission Fred Hargadon and e-Bay CEO Meg Whitman ('77).

Beer Jackets

Traditionally made of white denim, beer jackets are part of the reunions uniform for each class. This tradition began with a few members of the Class of 1912, who noticed that the foam from their beers would spot their clothing. To avoid pricey cleaning charges, they developed the idea of a beer jacket, a jacket that could be worn to protect clothing from stains while drinking. The following year, the Class of 1913 adopted this tradition and wore their signature beer jackets throughout the spring. In recent times, the graduating class will vote on a design for their jacket, which is distributed during the reading period of their final exams.

Big Three Bonfire

The Bonfire is by no means a regular occurrence on Princeton's campus. According to tradition, a bonfire is to be built after Princeton's football team beats both Harvard and Yale, thus serving as a celebration of the much-coveted Big Three Title. Students construct the bonfire in the center of Cannon Green behind Nassau Hall and usually include an outhouse and effigies of both John Harvard and the Yale Bulldog.

Nude Olympics

Shortly after women began to enroll as Princeton undergraduates in the fall of 1969, the tradition of the Nude Olympics was born. During their sophomore year, the first completely coed class, the Class of 1973, participated in naked revelry in Holder Courtyard. Over the years, some aspects of the Nude Olympics have changed, except for the central rules: the Nude Olympics would occur at midnight in Holder Courtyard during the first major snowfall of the year, and sophomores would participate. After much debate, the Nude Olympics were banned several years ago, and incoming students must sign a pledge agreeing not to participate in the event.

Old Nassau

Princeton's alma mater is sung at the end of most campus events, including athletic events and Triangle shows. The song was composed in 1859 by a freshman, Harlan Page Peck, Class of 1862.

Finding a Job or Internship

The Lowdown
ON FINDING A JOB OR INTERNSHIP

Career Center Resources & Services:
Career Library
CareerNews Listservs
TigerTracks

Princeton's Office of Career Services offers plenty of resources to students who are looking for a job or internship, but students definitely have to take a proactive approach during the process. Because Princeton students are so heavily recruited for banking and consulting positions, it often seems as if Career Services focuses all of their resources on students interested in those positions, but there are many services available to students who do not fall into those categories. Because of Princeton's strong alumni network, however, it is frequently networking that helps students get sought-after jobs and internships.

Advice

When you get to campus, make an appointment with an advisor at the Career Services Office to discuss your interests and develop a resume. Your advisor may be able to put you in touch with alumni who can advise you on good classes to take for your desired career and possibly invite you to trail them in their jobs for a day. Also, make sure to put yourself on the career e-mail listserv so that you can get weekly updates about internships and jobs as well as upcoming programs, including career fairs and resume building workshops.

Alumni

The Lowdown
ON ALUMNI

Web site:
www.alumni.princeton.edu

Office:
Alumni Council of Princeton University
Maclean House
P.O. Box 291
Princeton, NJ 08544-0291
alco@princeton.edu
(609) 258-1900

Services Available:
Online Alumni Directory
E-mail Services
Transcript Requests

Major Alumni Events

Princeton's biggest alumni events include Alumni Day, reunions, and homecoming. Homecoming takes place in the fall and includes class gatherings and tailgates before some Tiger football. Alumni Day is considered a mid-winter alumni celebration during which alumni return to campus for lectures by distinguished faculty. The Woodrow Wilson Award and James Madison Medal are given , and the day ends with a Service of Remembrance. Reunions, lasting several days, are Princeton's biggest alumni event. From fireworks to lectures to the P-rade, Princetonians take reunions very seriously, and attendance is always impressive.

Famous Princeton Alumni:

James Baker (Class of '52) - Former secretary of state

Jeff Bezos (Class of '86) - Founder of *Amazon.com*

Bill Bradley (Class of '65) - Basketball star and politician

Dean Cain (Class of '88) - Actor in *Lois and Clark*

David Duchovny (Class of '82) - Actor in the *X Files*

John Foster Dulles (Class of '35) - Former secretary of state

Steve Forbes (Class of '70) - *Forbes Magazine* president and editor-in-chief

Bill Frist (Class of '74) - Current Senate Majority Leader

Lisa Najeeb Halaby (Class of '76) - Queen Noor of Jordan

James Madison (Class of 1771) - Former President of the United States

Ralph Nader (Class of '55) - Consumer advocate

Donald Rumsfeld (Class of '54) - Secretary of defense

Brooke Shields (Class of '87) - Actress in *The Blue Lagoon*

George Shultz (Class of '42) - Former secretary of state

Jimmy Stewart (Class of '32) - Actor in *It's a Wonderful Life*

Meg Whitman (Class of '77), CEO of eBay

The Best & Worst

The Ten BEST Things About Princeton:

1	The academic program
2	Focus on campus undergraduate life
3	Renovated dorms
4	Tradition and strong alumni programs
5	Sunday brunch at Forbes
6	Eating clubs for upperclass dining
7	Senior nights at the Annex
8	Safe campus
9	Houseparties
10	Sitting out on Alexander Beach on a sunny day

The Ten **WORST** Things About Princeton:

1	The relative isolation of the town
2	Rainy springs
3	Old, outdated dorms
4	Crowded Stephens Fitness Center
5	Rare Big Three Bonfires
6	Academic advising system for underclassmen
7	High price of stores and restaurants in town
8	Boring precepts
9	Pizza night in the dining halls
10	Non-English speaking TAs and preceptors

Visiting Princeton

Hotel Information:

In Princeton:

Nassau Inn
www.nassauinn.com
Palmer Square
Princeton, NJ
(609) 921-7500, (800) 862-7728
Distance from Campus: Walking distance
Price Range: $190-$230

Peacock Inn
www.peacockinn.com
20 Bayard Lane
Princeton, NJ
(609) 924-1707
Distance from Campus: Walking distance
Price Range: $125

Route 1, North of Campus:
Courtyard by Marriott
www.marriott.com
U.S. Route 1 and Mapleton Rd.
(609) 716-9100, (800) 321-2211
Distance from Campus: 2 miles
Price Range: $170

Days Inn
www.daysinn.com
U.S. Route 1 and Raymond Road
Monmouth Junction, NJ
(732) 329-4555, (800) 325-2525.
Distance from Campus: 4 miles
Price Range: $60

Route 1, South of Campus:
AmeriSuites
www.amerisuites.com
3565 U.S. Route 1
Princeton, NJ
(609) 720-0200, (800) 833-1516
Distance from Campus: 3 miles
Price Range: $130-$150

Take a Campus Virtual Tour

www.princeton.edu/~okkey/tourstart.html

To Schedule a Group Interview

Call (609) 258-3060 on any weekday. During the summer, hours are from 8:30 a.m.-4:30 p.m., and hours are 9 a.m.-5 p.m. for the rest of the year.

Overnight Visits

Princeton has a weekend for accepted students each April, commonly called Pre-Frosh Weekend. Accepted students have the opportunity to sleep in a dorm room and are paired with underclassmen so they have the chance to attend classes, eat in the dining halls, and experience residential college life. Usually, the eating clubs go off-tap for the weekend, so pre-frosh don't actually get an accurate portrayal of Princeton's social life.

Directions to Campus

Driving from the North

- Take the New Jersey Turnpike south to Exit 9 (New Brunswick).
- After the toll booths, take the first right turn onto the ramp for Route 18 north.
- Soon after you enter Route 18, take the left side of a fork in the road, staying in the right lane.
- Immediately bear right for an exit to U.S. Route 1 south/Trenton.
- Drive south on Route 1 for about 18 miles to the Alexander Road, exit and follow signs for Princeton.
- At Faculty Road (traffic light, gas station) turn right, and proceed to the traffic circle.
- Go three quarters of the way around the circle and turn right onto Elm Drive.
- At the next traffic circle, go half-way around and proceed to the traffic kiosk.

Driving from the South

- If you are coming from southern New Jersey, take Interstate 295 north (instead of the New Jersey Turnpike), exiting at Route 1 north (exit 67).
- Travel about three miles north on Route 1 to the Alexander Road exit, and follow signs for Princeton.
- At Faculty Road (traffic light, gas station) turn right, and proceed to the traffic circle.
- Go three quarters of the way around the circle and turn right onto Elm Drive.
- At the next traffic circle, go half-way around and proceed to the traffic kiosk.

Driving from the East

- Take Interstate 195 west (toward Trenton) to the exit for Interstate 295 north.
- Drive seven miles to the exit for Route 1 north (exit 67).
- Travel about three miles north on Route 1 to the Alexander Road exit, and follow signs for Princeton.
- At Faculty Road (traffic light, gas station) turn right, and proceed to the traffic circle.
- Go three quarters of the way around the circle and turn right onto Elm Drive.
- At the next traffic circle, go half-way around and proceed to the traffic kiosk.

Driving from the West

- Drive east on Interstate 78 into New Jersey. Exit onto southbound Interstate 287 (toward Somerville).
- Follow signs for Routes 202/206 south.
- Go south on 202 for a short distance and then follow signs to 206 south, which will take you around a traffic circle.
- Go south on 206 for about 18 miles to Nassau Street (Route 27) in the center of Princeton.
- Turn left onto Nassau Street, and follow it to the third traffic light.
- At the next traffic circle, go half-way around and proceed to the traffic kiosk.

University of Pennsylvania

3451 Walnut Street Philadelphia, PA 19104
www.upenn.edu (215) 898-7507

"Penn allows a perfect combination of work and play. I love the people here, and I have found plenty of extracurricular activities to keep me busy."

Total Enrollment:
9,719 - Large
Acceptance Rate:
21%
Tuition:
$32,364
Top 10% of High School Class:
94%

SAT Range

Verbal	Math	Total
660 – 750	680 – 780	1340 – 1530

ACT Range

Verbal	Math	Total
28-33	28-34	28-33

Most Popular Majors:
12% Finance
8% Economics
7% History
5% Psychology

Students Also Applied To:*
Columbia University, Cornell University, Georgetown University, Harvard University, Yale University

*For more school info check out *www.collegeprowler.com*

Table of Contents

College Prowler Report Card

Academics	A-
Local Atmosphere	A-
Safety & Security	C+
Computers	B+
Facilities	A-
Campus Dining	C-
Off-Campus Dining	A-
Campus Housing	D
Off-Campus Housing	A
Diversity	B+
Guys	B
Girls	C+
Athletics	B+
Nightlife	A-
Greek Life	A-
Drug Scene	B
Campus Strictness	A
Parking	D-
Transportation	B+

Academics

The Lowdown
ON ACADEMICS

Degrees Awarded:
Bachelor, Master, Doctorate

Undergraduate Schools:
College of Arts and Science, School of Engineering and Applied Science, School of Nursing, Wharton School of Business

Full-Time Faculty:
1,286

Faculty with Terminal Degree:
100%

Student-to-Faculty Ratio:
6:1

AP Test Score Requirements:
Possible credit for scores of 5

IB Test Score Requirements:
Possible credit for scores of 6 or 7

Average Course Load:
CAS: 4, Wharton: 4.5, Nursing: 4.5, Engineering: 5

Sample Academic Clubs
(For full listing see *pobox.upenn.edu/homepages/group_homepages.html*)
American Medical Students Association, Black Wharton Undergraduate Association, The Engineering Peer Advising Council, and the Golden Key National Honor Society

Did You Know?

In 1778, University Provost William Smith was serving time due to a political struggle with the Provincial Congress of Philadelphia, and chose to continue teaching his moral philosophy class from Philadelphia's Old City Jail.

Penn is home to America's first medical school (1765), business school (1881), and law classes (1850).

Best Places to Study:
Fisher Fine Arts Library, Van Pelt Library, Houston Hall, Huntsman Hall

Need help finding the right major? For a detailed listing of all academic programs at UPenn, check out the complete College Prowler book on UPenn at *collegeprowler.com*.

UNIVERSITY OF PENNSYLVANIA

Students Speak Out
ON ACADEMICS

"There are both big lecture courses—which I never had a problem in—and courses with a small number of students, so don't let people tell you that you'll get lost in the system."

"Penn stands out among most universities in that it has great teachers available. In an effort to generalize, I'd say that **not all the teachers are great at teaching**—aren't professors supposed to be good at teaching?!—but it's clear that most are pretty brilliant in their field. My classes are always interesting because I take classes dealing with subject matter that I'm interested in."

"**Professors vary by subject**. The three big lectures I was in—PoliSci001, Microeconomics, and Introduction to Experimental Psychology—were all taught by amazing professors. All of them knew their subjects, but some could hold my attention and some couldn't. I never felt that any of them were underqualified by any means."

"The professors at Penn are amazing. They're all extremely knowledgeable, and all of the professors that I have had have been really easy to talk to. Usually, **there's no problem meeting with them during office hours** or communicating through e-mails. They're all pretty fair, too. There are, of course, difficult ones, but even they are rational."

"The teachers are so-so. A lot of them pretty much give their lectures and assign textbook problems. The only problem is that once you get to the exam, it's about a million times harder than the basic material covered in class. Students learn to survive though. **Study groups are a must**! I'd say I learn the most from late-night cramming with a group of friends where we would explain different sections to one another."

"All the **humanities classes are fantastic**. The professor will usually focus on a general subject and take a really interesting angle on it, which allows the class to examine the subject from many different perspectives. That way, it is much easier to relate to the course work."

The College Prowler Take
ON ACADEMICS

Penn students tend to be genuinely impressed with the knowledge and commitment of their professors, but they concede that, now and then, an uninterested and/or uninteresting teacher can slip into one's schedule. While members of the faculty are usually more than willing to get to know their students, in larger classes the student must take the initiative by attending office hours or requesting research opportunities. Penn students who speak to upperclassmen and "shop around" for courses usually end up enjoying their course load immensely. The enormous number of classes offered at Penn (the course book is the size of a phone book) practically guarantees ample opportunities to find ideal classes and professors for each student.

The business program may be unsurpassed, but practically every department at Penn is strong and will provide students with knowledgeable professors and a wide area of relevant classes. Despite the fact that the undergraduate school is populated by almost 10,000 students, the majority of classes are comprised of less than 20 students. However, it is not impossible to find yourself in a history lecture with 300 other students, and in many courses you must make an effort to get to know your professor. Overall, Penn provides an incredible educational experience, but more opportunity for intellectual discussion in some of the larger classes would make the school even better.

The College Prowler™ Grade on
Academics: A-

A high Academics grade generally indicates that professors are knowledgeable, accessible, and genuinely interested in their students' welfare. Other determining factors include class size, how well professors communicate, and whether or not classes are engaging.

Local Atmosphere

The Lowdown
ON LOCAL ATMOSPHERE

Region:
Northeast

City, State:
Philadelphia, Pennsylvania

Setting:
Major city

Distance from New York:
2 hours

Distance from Washington, DC:
2 hours

Points of Interest:
Rittenhouse Square, Philadelphia Museum of Art, South Street, Old City

Closest Shopping Malls or Plazas:
The shops at Liberty Place, The Gallery at Market East, The Bellevue, King of Prussia

Major Sports Teams:
Phillies (baseball), 76ers (basketball), Eagles (football), Flyers (hockey)

City Web sites:
www.phila.gov/
www.onebigcampus.com/html/flash.htm

Famous People from Philadelphia:
Marian Anderson, Donald Bartholomew, John Barrymore, Ed Bacon, Boyz II Men, Alexander Calder, Wilt Chamberlain, Bill Cosby, Stuart Davis, Walter E. Diemer, Oliver Evans, Margaret Mead, Cecil B. Moore, Man Ray, Betsy Ross, Will Smith, the Three Stooges

Local Slang:
Hoagie – outside of Philly commonly known as a sub or a hero
Wawa – found in Philly and south New Jersey, this is basically a convenience store where you can get a "fresh" sandwich 24 hours a day.
Wiz-with – the proper way to order a cheesesteak with Cheese Wiz and onions. (For no onions, simply say, "Wiz-without.")

Fun Facts about Philadelphia:

1) Philadelphia is a city of firsts; the city is home to the first insane asylum, the first electronic computer (ENIAC developed at Penn), America's first university (yes, Penn itself), and the nation's first zoo.
2) The stairs that Rocky Balboa climbs victoriously in the first Rocky movie are none other than those which lead to the main entrance of the Philadelphia Museum of Art.
3) King of Prussia Mall, located in a suburb right outside of Philly is the East Coast's largest mall and the second largest in the country, dwarfed only by the Mall of America.
4) Philly's official nickname is "The City of Brotherly Love" because it was founded by William Penn (whose statue stands on top of city hall), and perhaps the first city in the world to tolerate all religions. In fact, Penn's mascot, the Quaker, was picked in homage to Billy Penn himself to reflect this aspect of Philadelphia's history.
5) Philadelphia boasts over one hundred art museums, many of which can be found along the Ben Franklin Parkway, designed to mimic the Champs-Elysees.

Students Speak Out
ON LOCAL ATMOSPHERE

"It's in a city, but Penn is pretty self-contained. In theory, you could never have to leave, but at the same time, you are so close to museums and other universities, why wouldn't you?"

"Over the last few years, the University has made advancements in improving the surrounding community and strengthening relations with our neighbors. Although, one **shouldn't attempt to wander too far** beyond campus limits. Downtown, like most other major urban centers, offers a number of distractions, ranging from the symphony to the ballet, to clubs, pubs, and upscale shopping."

"It's a city atmosphere, but at the same time one could be in the middle of campus, standing on a green, and not know he or she was in a city. **There are more than a few universities present**—Drexel being the closest, with Temple, La Salle, St. Joseph's, and Villanova relatively close by. As far as stuff to stay away from, I'd say that it's probably a good idea to steer clear of much of West Philly. Stuff to visit? It's Philly, there are a lot of historical places to visit and cheesesteaks to eat."

"West Philadelphia has a bad reputation, but I feel very safe on and around campus. It's definitely a city atmosphere and everything you need is within walking distance. **There isn't much to do uptown** besides see the neighborhoods, but downtown in Center City there are a lot of clubs and stores, theaters, museums, and more."

"Penn probably has the most amazing campus and location I have ever seen. The campus itself is a very warm and cozy environment. Best of all, unlike most colleges in the city, **it actually has a campus**. University City is great, because there are so many stores, restaurants, and other schools within short walking distance."

"Philadelphia is a great city. **Drexel and Temple are located within the city**. Plus, Villanova is only a short drive away. West Philadelphia, the neighborhood in which Penn resides, tends to get an undeserved bad rap."

The College Prowler Take
ON LOCAL ATMOSPHERE

Students at Penn love Philadelphia. Most wanted to study at an urban college for the excitement and opportunity that only a city can provide, and their wishes are more than fulfilled by Penn's West Philly location. Center City, with its streets full of restaurants, theaters, and other hot spots, is a short walk away, and the historical richness of Old City is just a hop, skip, jump, and a cab ride from the heart of Penn's campus. Speaking of campus, unlike most urban schools, Penn actually has one, which allows students to relax, play sports, toss a ball, ride a bike, or catch some sun on the grassy expanses of college green or the many courtyards around the dorms.

Unique, vibrant, and artsy, the city of Philadelphia has absolutely everything a student could want. On a given weekend, a Penn student could easily take a walk along Walnut Street, spend some time at the zoo, enjoy a meal at one of Philadelphia's excellent restaurants, and then spend some time at trendy South Street's many shops. While Philadelphia offers all of this and more, it lacks the crowded jostle of New York, providing a comfortable college setting for even those students without any previous urban experience.

The College Prowler™ Grade on
Local Atmosphere: A-

A high Local Atmosphere grade indicates that the area surrounding campus is safe and scenic. Other factors include nearby attractions, proximity to other schools, and the town's attitude toward students.

UNIVERSITY OF PENNSYLVANIA

Safety & Security

Did You Know?

The University of Pennsylvania was honored with the "Clery Award for Campus Safety Improvements." This honor recognizes the University's innovative technological programs and outstanding campus police patrols.

In the past decade at Penn, overall crime has decreased by 31 percent. Robberies have decreased by 62 percent, thefts by 31 percent, burglaries by 24 percent, and assault by 23 percent. In addition, 2,500 outdoor light fixtures have been installed, plus eight public gardens and 450 trees have been planted.

The Lowdown

ON SAFETY & SECURITY

Number of UPenn Police:
104

Phone:
(215) 573-3333

Health Center Office Hours:
Seven days a week including weekends and evenings during the school year; Hours are subject to change during summer and winter breaks.

Safety Services:
Blue-light phones, rest room alarms, bike registration, safer living seminars, walking escorts, PennBus, LUCY (loop through University City), Handivan

Health Services:
Alcohol and other drug abuse services, allergy, dental problems, dermatology, ophthalmology, medication services, orthopedics, sports medicine, podiatry, routine physicals, student awareness of safer sex supplies, surgery, victim support, women's health, STD screening, counseling and psychological services.

Students Speak Out

ON SAFETY & SECURITY

"I never really feel unsafe on campus, but I know some people have. Security's decent compared to most schools."

"You'll definitely get approached by homeless people, but there's enough security on campus so **no one will hassle you** as long as you don't go wandering around the streets of West Philly at 3 a.m. alone."

"Security is surely present. Sometimes, so present that it becomes extremely aggravating, especially when it takes half an hour to sign in a guest on a regular weekend afternoon. But **you always feel safe**, which is ultimately the most important thing."

"Even though West Philadelphia has a horrible reputation for crime and violence, the campus has a safe feeling to it. **There are obvious areas to avoid**, and safety precautions are good to keep in mind. Usually traveling with a group during the evening is a smart thing to do, but during the day, you can feel free to travel about as you wish without much worry."

"There are PennCops [UPenn police] on almost every corner, on bikes, in cars, and sometimes even horses. **Safety is not an issue** in the least. I lived off campus this past year and even felt safe there. The Penn police are all over the campus, and even a few blocks off campus."

"Although campus itself is said to be safe, as a female, I would be careful. There have been a few incidents within the past few years. Although security is getting tighter, you are in West Philadelphia. **Try not to walk alone at night**. There is a walking escort or van that you can call; do not be afraid to use it."

The College Prowler Take

ON SAFETY & SECURITY

Students are well aware of the supposedly dangerous reputation of West Philadelphia, but most feel very secure walking around campus at any time. Most believe that the campus is in as safe of a neighborhood as a large city can provide and believe that the less-than-perfect safety record is a small price to pay if you want an urban campus. Students appreciate the strong efforts made by the university administration to improve security in recent years, which include a increased police force, technological security innovations, and the use of a Penn ID Card for access to most buildings after certain hours.

The College Prowler™ Grade on

Safety & Security: C+

A high grade in Safety & Security means that students generally feel safe, campus police are visible, blue-light phones and escort services are readily available, and safety precautions are not overly necessary.

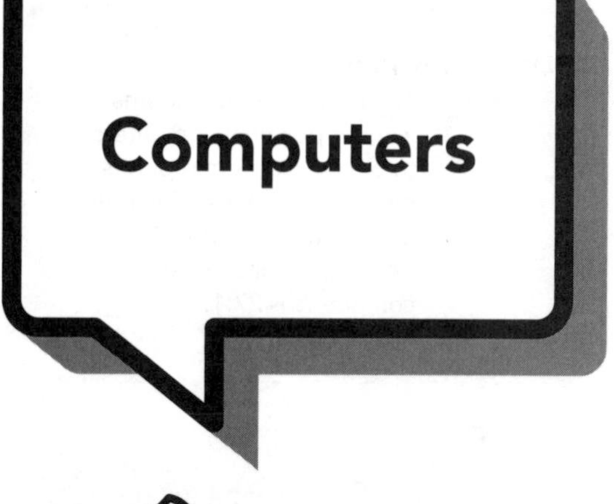

The Lowdown

ON COMPUTERS

High-Speed Network?
Yes

Wireless Network?
Yes

Number of Labs:
28

Numbers of Computers:
1,150 (including laptops on loan)

Operating Systems:
Mac, Windows

24-Hour Labs:
Rosengarten Lab, Long Island Friends of Penn Computer Area, Towne PC Labs, Charles Adams, Huntsman Hall, Harrison College House Computing Lab

Discounted Software:
FileMaker Pro, Microsoft Office (PowerPoint, Excel, Word), Dreamweaver

Charge to Print?
Yes

Did You Know?

The ratio of Penn students without personal computers to public access computers on campus is 1:1.4. The ratio of students with or without personal computers to computers is 27:1.

Students Speaks Out

ON COMPUTERS

"Everyone here seems to have a million things to do, and barely enough time to do them. Writing a paper is stressful enough, why pile computer rental issues on top of that?"

"There are ample computer labs on campus and most students bring their own PC setup, so the **labs are hardly ever crowded**. As a matter of ease, I recommend that students bring their own computer equipment, as printing in the labs can be costly."

"**Almost everybody I know brought their own computer** to campus, and I would recommend doing the same. On the flip side, that means that computer labs usually aren't crowded and I don't imagine that it would be difficult to gain access to a computer at any hour. The network gives virus protection and most of the online functions are really helpful."

"About the computer labs, I have absolutely no clue because I never use them. I would say **your own computer is a must**. There are obviously ways to work around not having a computer. You can always rent one at the library, and I would assume that the computer labs have fabulous accommodations. But seriously, why make life more confusing?"

"There's no one main computer lab, a lot of **computers are spread out at different places on campus**, so you should definitely bring your own to work with in your room. Once you are online, it is easy to access Penn resources."

"Finding a computer lab that's open may not be the easiest thing to do early in the morning. However, when you do need a computer during regular hours, **computer labs are all over campus**. Most are occupied by a good number of students, but usually there are a few computers available to use. The network on campus seems pretty free to use."

The College Prowler Take

ON COMPUTERS

Approximately 95 percent of Penn students bring their own computer to school. Most would agree that possessing a personal system makes life easier when it comes to late-night work sessions and last-minute assignments. A computer also allows students to download music and movies, a common procrastination tool at Penn. On the other hand, the fact that so many people own a computer means that those who don't have more than their share of public computer stations. There are many more public computers on campus than there are students without one of their own.

Wireless Internet is available in some areas of the school, but even in parts of campus where a wireless connection is not available, most study lounges and libraries provide outlets for an Ethernet connection. The fast connection proves to be important, as the school largely bases its communication system around the computer.

The College Prowler™ Grade on

Computers: B+

A high grade in Computers designates that computer labs are available, the computer network is easily accessible, and campus computing technology is up-to-date.

Facilities

Did You Know?

College Hall is rumored to have been the inspiration for Alumnus Charles Adams's *Addams Family* mansion.

Houston Hall was the first student union in the United States.

Irving Auditorium houses an 11,000-pipe Curtis Organ, the only early 20th century civic pipe organ that remains in its original condition.

The Lowdown
ON FACILITIES

Student Center:
Houston Hall

Athletic Center:
Pottruck Fitness Center, Hutchinson Gymnasium

Libraries:
There are 15 on campus. There's a fine arts library, a library of Jewish studies, and science and engineering libraries.

Movie Theatre on Campus?
Yes, The Bridge and Cinemagic both show recently released films throughout the week.

Bar on Campus?
Yes, Smokey Joe's, Billy Bob's are popular campus hangouts.

What Is There to Do?
When a friend is starring in a new production, check it out at the Iron Gate Theater. Start a club and hold meetings at Houston Hall. Enjoy jazz concerts at the Annenberg Center for Performing Arts. If you're a sports buff, watch a football game at Franklin Field or the big Penn vs. Princeton game at the famed Palestra.

Students Speak Out
ON FACILITIES

"Facilities on campus are beautiful. Some of the buildings are old, others are new. There is constant renovation to make Penn a better place to be."

"**The athletic facilities are amazing** because sports are so huge on campus, especially for an Ivy League school. Computers are spread out, so you should have your own in your room. The student center is awesome because it is open really late and has a lot of space to sit, talk, relax, and study."

"The heart of campus extends a mere six blocks. **Penn has undergone a number of remodeling projects** during the past five years, improving both the interior and exterior of a number of buildings on campus, making the University both an attractive and exciting place to learn."

"Facilities are more than adequate, but projects are always being undergone to improve them. The only main problem that I've seen is that all club sports are allotted one field to practice on, so **getting access is extremely difficult**. Otherwise, we have a gorgeous new gym and the administration is relatively receptive to student input."

"There are good facilities, but we need more space that we're allowed to play on. They should open Bower field to the general student population, especially since they're building on Hill field. **Franklin Field is great**, Houston Hall is great; in fact, all I've seen is pretty good."

"The libraries have a lot of books; almost any book that you could ever need for a research project. **There are several libraries** on campus: Van Pelt, Lippincott, the fine arts library, the law library, the biomedical library. It just goes on and on. All the libraries are nice places to study with comfortable couches."

The College Prowler Take

ON FACILITIES

Penn facilities make it convenient for students to exercise, grab a bite to eat, play a game of pool, or simply round up a study group. Construction is a constant on campus. The renovation of the high-rises, a new Hillel building, and a beautified Hill Field (now called Hill Square) are among the newest improvements on campus. The buildings range from ugly to beautiful. Huntsman Hall is one of the most technologically advanced buildings in the world, while the music building is a dilapidated mess.

Construction is a blessing and a curse on campus. If the building you live in is being worked on, the noise can be quite a headache, but construction is part of every city, and the finished product only contributes to the already impressive scenery. Again, the best facilities on campus (i.e. Pottruck Fitness Center, Huntsman Hall, and Houston Hall), require little improvement, while others desperately need a face lift.

The College Prowler™ Grade on

Facilities: A-

A high Facilities grade indicates that the campus is aesthetically pleasing and well-maintained; facilities are state-of-the-art, and libraries are exceptional. Other determining factors include the quality of both athletic and student centers and an abundance of things to do on campus.

Campus Dining

The Lowdown

ON CAMPUS DINING

Freshman Meal Plan Requirement?
Yes

Meal Plan Average Cost:
$2,806

24-Hour On-Campus Eating?
Wawa, Fresh Grocer, McDonald's, Philly Diner

Student Favorites:
La Petite Creperie in Houston Hall, Beijing, La Terasse, Fresh Grocer, the Real Le Ahn food truck, and Hemos food truck are all student favorites.

Want to know more about campus dining? For a detailed listing of all eateries on campus, check out the College Prowler book on UPenn available at *www.collegeprowler.com*.

UNIVERSITY OF PENNSYLVANIA

Students Speak Out
ON CAMPUS DINING

"Dining halls are okay. I suggest eating from the food carts—they're inexpensive, in wide variety, and have good food. It's 'cool' to be on a first name basis with the food cart guys."

"Campus food is not very good, but they're trying a completely new system based upon student input, so it should improve drastically. The dining halls are nice, though **they do get crowded around dinner time**. Penn students can also use Dining Dollars at certain retail locations if they get sick of campus food."

"The food in the cafeterias is **nothing to brag about**, but it definitely satisfies your hunger. There's something for everyone, and if you can't find what you like, there's a grill that's available for customized dinners, such as cheeseburgers and hotdogs, along with other special items. Restaurants litter the border of the campus, and that's only in the vicinity of the school."

"**The food is decent**, particularly compared to most other college dining halls. Houston Hall is a little expensive. Everyone should go to the Creperie at least once. It's great!"

"I'm really not a fan of on campus dining. I would definitely not recommend getting a meal plan. **The food is really expensive**, and, I mean, it is okay, but for the price that you are paying, it should be really good. Plus, you have to mold your schedule around the dining hall hours."

"The dining halls have **limited selections if you are vegetarian or vegan**. If you are, then be prepared for a horrible year of food. Instead, go to the supermarket nearby, buy your own food, and plan on cooking!"

The College Prowler Take
ON CAMPUS DINING

Some Penn students are impressed by the quality and variety of food, while others get sick of the dining options extremely quickly. For the most part, students acknowledge both positive and negative aspects of the dining program. At Penn, students on a meal plan have three options to pay for food: 1) they can use a specific number of allotted meals per week or semester at the dining halls, 2) use Dining Dollars, which can be continuously replenished at most retail locations around campus, or 3) use PennCash, which works somewhat like a debit card.

Whether you like the food or not, there is certainly enough to eat, facilitated by multiple all-you-can-eat locations. In addition, there's something to eat at all hours. Wawa is a popular place to grab a made-to-order sandwich. Freshmen are required to purchase a meal plan, but as long as you purchase the smallest plan available and you make an effort to find places with food that suits your tastebuds, your freshman dining experience should be more than bearable.

The College Prowler™ Grade on
Campus Dining: C-

Our grade on Campus Dining addresses the quality of both school-owned dining halls and independent on-campus restaurants as well as the price, availability, and variety of food.

Off-Campus Dining

The Lowdown
ON OFF-CAMPUS DINING

Student Favorites:
Bubble Tea House, Allegro's, Izzy and Zoe's, Mad 4 Mex, Beijing

Best Pizza:
Allegro's, College Pizza, Famous Famigla

Best Chinese:
Beijing, Susanna Foo,

Best Breakfast:
Izzy & Zoe's, Philly Diner

Best Wings:
Lee's, Moriarty's

Best Cheesesteaks:
Pat's, Jim's, Geno's

Best Ice Cream:
Scoop DeVille

Best Place to Take Your Parents:
Buddakan, White Dog Café, La Terrasse, Bookbinders

Food Specials:
Mad 4 Mex: Monday-Thursday 2 p.m.-4 p.m., half price food with a college ID

Abner's: Students get free cheesesteaks when the UPenn basketball team scores 100 points, and coupons are distributed at many athletic events.

24-Hour Eating:
Pat's King of Steaks, Geno's Steaks, Philly Diner, Fresh Grocer

Closest Grocery Stores:
Fresh Grocer
4001 Walnut Street
University City
(215) 222-9200

Fun Facts:

1) Pat's and Geno's are located directly across the street from each other, and, as a result, they have had the most famous rivalry in the world of cheesesteaks. If you go to one, you have to go to the other, simply to see which one really is better.

2) In the summer, Philly is home to many farmer's markets, the closest to Penn being the one at Clark Park. Here, in the summer months, you can buy fresh baked goods, flowers, fruits, and vegetables.

3) The Ritz Carlton in Center City has a weekend all-you-can-eat chocolate buffet for $15. You don't have to stay at the hotel to hoard cookies and brownies galore, so this is definitely something to check out.

Students Speak Out

ON OFF-CAMPUS DINING

"My friends and I always go down to Chinatown on the weekend to eat. There's great grub there for like $4. And it wouldn't be Philly without the cheesesteaks!"

"Off campus is host to a wide variety of dining options. **Chinatown is an interesting diversion**. In Rittenhouse square, Alma de Cuba, Rouge, and Bleu are tasty."

"Cheesesteaks are everywhere: Pat's, Geno's, and Jim's are the best. I had all three in a span of an hour and a half once, but I'm a fat kid. Pat's is a messy cheesesteak but my favorite. I particularly enjoy it for the quality of its steak; it's a little sparse with its onions though. **Geno's is a more refined cheesesteak**, more onions, not as messy, but also not as good. Jim's is like a cheesesteak one would see on a billboard. It has the soft, fluffy bread, the steak that is diced into a million little pieces so that it's easy to chew, with just enough, but not too much onions or cheese. If you want to talk cheesesteaks, just give me a call."

"Center City, a quick subway ride from campus, provides **a huge variety of foods** from all different cultural backgrounds. Italian, Chinese, Cuban, and Caribbean are just a few types you might find. Of course, a few Penn favorites are always great places to visit, such as Abner's, Allegro's, and the New Deck Tavern."

"Moriarty's is **home to some of Philly's finest wings**. Pat's and Geno's have a long-standing rivalry over who has the best cheesesteaks in Philly."

"I haven't been many places, but **Geno's is always good**, and there are a million other places to go. There's even a Hawaiian restaurant with waitresses in Hula skirts and everything!"

"Most restaurants on or off campus come at a price unless you go to Chinatown, where **you can get pretty full for $20**. Philly has a lot of good Italian places. Don't try the seafood unless it's Cajun."

The College Prowler Take

ON OFF-CAMPUS DINING

Philly restaurants are a staple of the Penn experience for their variety and convenience. On a normal day, students usually opt to eat somewhere close and cheap, but on the weekends it is not uncommon for students to migrate east of the river or west of the high-rises to treat their taste buds to some authentic Ethiopian or upscale Asian cuisine. Places to eat vary not only in fare, but also in price. Whether you have to save up or wait for your parents to take you out, definitely try a Stephen Starr restaurant at some point before you graduate.

The food in Philadelphia is definitely one of the best things about Penn's location. Since the school is immersed in West Philly, the line between off campus and on campus is blurred. As a result, some places considered "off campus" are across the street from your dorm, next door to a classroom, or behind the bookstore. Since nightlife at Penn usually doesn't get started until around 11 p.m., there is always ample time to grab some eats as a pre-party activity. There is no doubt that Philadelphia restaurants will fulfill your needs, whether you want a place to take a date, to celebrate a birthday, to people watch at a trendy spot, or simply to enjoy an immensely satisfying, yet affordable, meal.

The College Prowler™ Grade on

Off-Campus Dining: A-

A high Off-Campus Dining grade implies that off-campus restaurants are affordable, accessible, and worth visiting. Other factors include the variety of cuisine and the availability of alternative options (vegetarian, vegan, Kosher, etc.).

Campus Housing

Did You Know?

The three high-rise dorms are positioned in such a way that the space between them forms a wind tunnel, an architectural blooper that makes this part of Locust Walk a place to avoid in cold winter months.

All residents get free access to the Penn Video Network, which includes more than 65 channels, including many satellite, cable, and international stations.

The Lowdown
ON CAMPUS HOUSING

Undergrads on Campus:
62%

Number of Dormitories:
11

Room Types:
Traditional room – singles, doubles

Suite-Style (w/ common room, private bathroom, and sometimes kitchen) – singles, doubles, triples, quads

Best Dorms:
Spruce, Ware, Fisher Hassenfeld, Hill

Worst Dorms:
Gregory, Stouffer
(These dorms have spacious rooms and may be right for you if you prefer a quiet, relaxed environment)

Cleaning Service?
Yes, in public areas (hallways, lobbies, laundry rooms, shared bathrooms). Bathrooms are cleaned once a week on weekends. Suite bathrooms are not cleaned. There is also an laundry service for a fee.

You Get:
Bed, desk, chair, wardrobe or built-in closet, mattress, book shelf, window shades, Ethernet connection, phone jack and free local calls

Students Speak Out
ON CAMPUS HOUSING

"Hill House definitely has a personality all its own. Hill House nearly coerces new students to socialize with one another with open lounges just a few steps away from each dorm room."

"If you want to meet a lot of people, live in the Quad. Most freshman live there. The bad thing is **you don't get your own bathroom**. I need my own bathroom; that's why I chose one of the high-rises. There are mostly upperclassmen in the building, but they reserve something like two floors for freshman. I was lucky enough to have a very social floor, and I met a lot of people."

"Penn's on-campus housing system is based around the concept of 'College Houses.' These houses are meant to integrate the Penn community by sex, age, race, and interest, and as a result, every dorm is coed and there are no exclusively freshmen dorms on campus."

"**For freshmen, living in the Quad is a must**. Thanks to a comprehensive renovation, the exterior is exquisitely manicured and landscaped. The dorm rooms are comparatively large, with a number of singles available to freshmen. Almost all come equipped with a sink and air conditioning."

"The Quad [Spruce, Ware, and Fischer Hassenfeld Houses] is the best place to live for freshmen. It's absolutely beautiful, **the rooms are decently sized**, it's in the middle of campus, and they recently installed air conditioning. Hill also gives a very social setting."

"King's Court/English House, Stouffer, Gregory, Mayer, and a few others provide quiet settings that allow people to study if they want to. The high-rises [Harrison, Harnwell, and Hamilton Houses] are mainly used by upperclassmen and are set up apartment-style. I don't know many people who liked living there freshman year."

"Dorms are varied, though none are unbearable. Some are clearly better than the rest. Living in the Quad is the best because of all the people, but singles in the Quad are really small. Hill and Kings Court/English House are isolated but have dining halls conveniently on their first floors. **Rooms in Hill aren't air-conditioned** though, and most Quad rooms are. Stouffer and the high-rises have big rooms but are isolated for freshman because mostly upperclassmen live there."

The College Prowler Take

ON CAMPUS HOUSING

Freshmen have little trouble meeting people whether they are in Kings Court/English House, Hill, or the Quad. Most people apply for the Quad as freshmen because they want a social atmosphere, but since many of these first-year students get placed in Kings Court/English House or Hill, these dorms end up being filled with friendly and social people, as well. Ultimately, the Quad is the most popular because of its central location, air conditioning, and relatively nice rooms. Kings Court and Hill, however, are self-sufficient. Both have dining halls and activity rooms that the Quad lacks.

The high-rises appeal to upperclassmen because they provide these students with kitchens and private bathrooms and bedrooms, as well as a close proximity to Fresh Grocer and the row of restaurants between Locust and Walnut. The amenities of each dorm are fairly ample; every dorm has laundry rooms, lounges, residential programs that sponsor trips and speakers, and much more. The quality of the rooms varies enormously. Some have carpet, some hardwood floors, and others linoleum. Some have sinks and fireplaces while others could be used as a storage closet during the summer. They also vary greatly in size, ranging from so small you can hardly fit the bed in, to so large it should hardly be called a dorm, but rather a warehouse.

The College Prowler™ Grade on

Campus Housing: D

A high Campus Housing grade indicates that dorms are clean, well-maintained, and spacious. Other determining factors include variety of dorms, proximity to classes, and social atmosphere.

Off-Campus Housing

The Lowdown
ON OFF-CAMPUS HOUSING

Undergrads in Off-Campus Housing:
38%

Average Rent for a Studio Apartment:
$629/month

Average Rent for a 1BR Apartment:
$725/month

Average Rent for a 2BR Apartment:
$1,102/month

Popular Areas:
University City (West Philly)

Best Time to Look for a Place:
Fall, almost a year in advance

For Assistance Contact:
Office of Off-Campus Living
www.business-services.upenn.edu/offcampusliving/
(215) 898-8500
E-mail: farcas@pobox.upenn.edu

Students Speak Out
ON OFF-CAMPUS DINING

"Off-campus living is worth it if the idea appeals to you. At the most, you'll have a 15-minute walk to class."

"After freshman year, most sophomores will live in either a high-rise apartment or in a frat house. But even sophomore year, loads of people start to get off campus. It's cheaper, nicer, and really useful if you plan on staying around over the summer. **Most upperclassmen chose to live off campus**, either in a house or in a Hamilton Court apartment. If you want to live off campus you had better start looking early because come February most decent off-campus housing is gone."

"I've seen a lot of people who are very happy living off campus, and it seems to cost about the same price. **People, generally, seem happy either way**, and the amount of people on and off campus is about equally split in numbers."

"**It's really convenient**. Lots of people live off campus. University City has tons of apartments and houses for students to rent. It can be a little expensive, but not that bad."

"**I recommend living on campus for social reasons, mostly**. There is a lot of off-campus housing, though. Popular among students is Hamilton Court on 39th, and a little more upscale is Chestnut Hall, also on 39th. Houses are also popular; Beige Block is the party area. Be wary of going past 42nd Street."

"If you can, try to find off-campus housing. Off-campus housing is pretty convenient and much cheaper. **On-campus housing is ridiculously expensive**, but it saves you the trouble of having to look for an apartment."

The College Prowler Take

ON OFF-CAMPUS HOUSING

Many students opt to live off campus as their years at Penn progress, although most don't go far, staying almost exclusively in the surrounding area that comprises University City. As a result, student's living off campus are not at all isolated from campus life. Many students take pleasure in the freedom of not being told when to move in and out and of not having RAs and GAs to monitor their activity. The Office of Off-Campus Living can assist students with everything from finding a place to live, to settling disputes with landlords. There are also local real estate companies that cater to members of the Penn community.

The school is, in one way, forced to make off-campus living a convenient option for students because Penn is only equipped to house about 70 percent of students. The school responds to this need by providing shuttles and other forms of transportation around campus and also by offering an Internet connection to those students who decide not to live in dorms. There is an abundance of houses, including spacious Victorian style homes and apartment buildings, in close proximity to Penn's official campus. So many inhabitants of these buildings are Penn students and faculty that the few streets west of campus are actually regarded as being part of Penn's campus by most who travel there for parties or dinner.

The College Prowler™ Grade on

Off-Campus Housing: A

A high grade in Off-Campus Housing indicates that apartments are of high quality, close to campus, affordable, and easy to secure.

Diversity

The Lowdown

ON DIVERSITY

White: 61%

Asian American: 18%

African American: 6%

Hispanic: 6%

Native American: 0%

International: 9 %

Out-of-State: 81%

Political Activity

On a campus with almost 10,000 undergraduate students from 50 states and countries all over the world, it is not likely that you will find one political viewpoint to be overwhelmingly popular. In reality, almost every political viewpoint is represented, and the campus is pretty much split down the middle as far as conservatism and liberalism. Many students are relatively apathetic, and, although they may have strong opinions, choose not to be an active force for any cause.

Gay Pride

There are many on-campus groups run by and for the gay community of Penn. In fact, there are probably more groups than most people realize; although the majority of students are very accepting of the gay community, students do not tend to be extremely aware or involved.

Most Popular Religions

Judaism is a very popular religion among Penn students. Hillel's membership lies in the thousands, and there are services offered for all Jewish denominations. Christianity is also common, although there is a much lower percentage of Christian people on campus than at most other schools. There is a church on campus, as well as many other local places of worship. There are also Christian clubs including a Christian a cappella group.

Minority Clubs

Penn's minority organizations contribute to the social character of Penn's campus. Many throw parties and cultural activities, usually welcoming the entire community, no matter which race, to come participate in the festivities.

Economic Status

There are students of all economic standing at Penn. However, many, if not most, undergraduate students enjoyed a relatively privileged upbringing.

Students Speak Out

ON DIVERSITY

"A lot of the diversity comes from within Wharton and the engineering school, as they both having big Asian and Indian populations. But, the campus, in general, is very diverse."

"Because of the portion of upper-middle-class students, **the Caucasian population seems to dominate**. There aren't too many people from the Midwest or the South. There also exists a sizable Asian population. However, some other minority groups are highly underrepresented."

"**Penn is definitely diverse**, but there's still a lot of self-imposed segregation. Even though there are all types of inter-ethnic friendships, you'll often find, with ample exceptions, the black people at one table, the Asian people at another, and the Jews everywhere. White Christians? Where?"

"The crowd here is very diverse. You'll probably meet **some of the craziest people** here. What I always appreciated is that although people party hard and get carried away, they are very intelligent and goal-directed. Work always gets done, but not at the expense of social life."

"It's not incredibly diverse, but **it's not completely white**, either. There's also a student union or club for just about every nationality you can think of. There just aren't very many."

"There's an African American interest dorm that I find rather segregated. But, if you're open and you seek out people of different backgrounds, you'll find them. **I have a really diverse group of friends**, not only ethnically, but also in terms of where they're from regionally, and what kind of interests they have. I love it! It's just another benefit of attending a large school."

"All types of people go to Penn, but **there could be stronger diversity**. I think that we were only six percent African American this year. I've met people from countries all over the world and from all sorts of backgrounds."

Want to know more about diversity at UPenn? For a detailed listing of all cultural organizations on campus, check out the College Prowler book on UPenn available at *www.collegeprowler.com*.

The College Prowler Take
ON DIVERSITY

Although Penn students come from a range of economic and racial backgrounds and have varying political viewpoints, African American and Hispanic students make up a meager six and seven percent of the student population, respectively. Some students find this to be a problem, asserting that the large Asian and non-Christian populations do not make up for the fact that other minority groups are not adequately represented.

Students are not the only ones who believe that certain minority groups should have a stronger presence on campus. The admissions office has stated that they take race into account when deciding whether or not to grant admission to a high school student, and last year the school launched an initiative to attract more African-American students to apply and matriculate as undergraduate students at Penn. Furthermore, overall diversity is strong, and students are granted a rich and eye-opening experience if they are open, as are most, to exposing themselves to people with lifestyles and backgrounds dramatically different from their own.

The College Prowler™ Grade on
Diversity: B+

A high grade in Diversity indicates that ethnic minorities and international students have a notable presence on campus and that students of different economic backgrounds, religious beliefs, and sexual preferences are well-represented.

The Lowdown
ON GUYS & GIRLS

Women Undergrads: 48%

Men Undergrads: 52%

Birth Control Available?
Yes. Women with a prescription can receive refills for birth control medication at Student Health services. Condoms are also available for sale from Women's Health, or for free at the Office of Health education and in many dorms from the RAs.

Social Scene
Penn has been called the "Social Ivy," and this designation might very well be accurate. People tend to be extroverted and love to have fun. Freshmen orientation is probably social interaction at its most extreme. New freshmen and upperclassmen returning early from summer vacation go out practically every night before classes start and feel free to introduce themselves to random people outside on the street. However, this does not at all mean that you must find your lifelong buddies during the first week of school.

Hookups or Relationships?

Both random hookups and committed relationships occur. However, it seems that the most common occurrence is what some of us like to call "the college relationship." The college relationship is the hookup that turns into "a person to hang out with," more or less a friend with benefits. This is a person whose company you sincerely enjoy, and you choose to spend extra time both hanging out and hooking up with, but there is no spoken commitment involved.

Dress Code

Penn students tend to sport a "calculated casual" attire. Jeans are standard for both class time and weekends.

Top Three Places to Find Hotties:

1. Frat parties
2. Recitation
3. Pottruck

Top Places to Hook Up:

1. Under "the button"
2. In the stacks of the library
3. Dorm rooms
4. By the Bio-pond
5. At a frat house (on the dance floor, in a bedroom)

Students Speak Out
ON GUYS & GIRLS

"A large percentage of students tend to hail from the Northeast and tend to be upper-middle-class. The guys are better looking than the girls, though."

"The people at Penn are pretty good-looking. **Everyone here seems to be pretty trendy**—people seem to dress up in the Banana Republic style a lot—very sleek."

"Penn students, in general, are very good-looking. **Yes, they're hot**. Unlike on many smaller, liberal arts school campuses, hot is not defined by how good you can look without even trying or who's the sexiest bohemian. Penn hot for the girls usually centers around who can wear the most expensive ensemble while still sporting a relatively casual appearance. As for the guys, it's buff abs, preppy clothes, and hair gel all the way."

"Since it's cold most of the time, you don't see much of the actual person, just a heap of sweaters and pants. Of course, underneath all of that cotton and wool, there are **wonderful people with great ambitions and ideas**. If you take the time to learn about your classmate's dreams, you might see a glimpse of the type of company into which you've fallen."

"**The variety of girls is crazy**. You have the bookies that stay in their rooms studying forever on end. If you can get them to take a break and talk to you, they aren't as dull as they seem. In fact, usually they are the coolest people to talk to. Then there are the stuffy rich girls that privately hold their noses up above everyone else while acting politely to fend off insults."

"**Everyone at Penn is different**. Some are nice, some not, some hot."

"I'm going to be honest: the guy selection wasn't the greatest this year. Now, I'm not saying it was horrible, but you had to look around a little, and **some of the guys were kind of cocky**. I think the girls are better than the guys, but my guy friends would most certainly disagree."

The College Prowler Take

ON GUYS & GIRLS

One student surveyed for this book stated that "the intellects of the world are typically not the same as the beauties." No one would argue with the statement, but at Penn, people certainly make the best of what they were born with. In addition to the fact that people make an effort to enhance their appearance, the personality beneath the designer jeans and styled hair is often quite intriguing, as well. Girls tend to like the selection of guys better than vice-versa. This may be due to the fact that Penn is chock-full of clean-cut, intelligent, athletic, and wealthy men. The guys may complain that the girls' looks aren't quite up to par with what they would be at a West Coast or southern school, but the complaints usually come to an abrupt halt the moment they find "their type," which occurs at Penn almost without exception.

Even if you had trouble finding someone of the opposite (or same) sex who really appealed to you in high school, the increased student enrollment can only help a students' chances of finding the right person, or in most cases, people, for them. As picky as you may be about who you choose to "spend time with," at Penn you pretty much automatically know the person hitting on you at a party is, at least, somewhat intelligent and has some good qualities, otherwise he or she would not be here. As far as promiscuity goes, most people here are definitely not prude, but if you do happen to arrive at school a virgin, you will not be alone. And guys, if you really can't find a girl here, there's always Bryn Mawr, a prestigious all-girls college, right outside of Philly. And, believe me, some of those girls are starved for some male companionship.

The College Prowler™ Grade on

Guys: B

A high grade for Guys indicates that the male population on campus is attractive, smart, friendly, and engaging, and that the school has a decent ratio of guys to girls.

The College Prowler™ Grade on

Girls: C+

A high grade for Girls not only implies that the women on campus are attractive, smart, friendly, and engaging, but also that there is a fair ratio of girls to guys.

The Lowdown

ON ATHLETICS

Athletic Division:
NCAA Division I

Conference:
Ivy League

School Mascot:
Quaker

Men's Varsity Sports:
Baseball
Basketball
Cheerleading
Fencing
Football
Sprint Football
Golf
Lacrosse
Rowing (heavy and light)
Soccer
Squash
Swimming
Tennis
Track/Cross-Country
Wrestling

Women's Varsity Sports:
Basketball
Cheerleading
Fencing
Field Hockey
Golf
Gymnastics
Lacrosse
Rowing
Soccer
Softball
Squash
Swimming
Tennis
Track/Cross-Country
Volleyball

UNIVERSITY OF PENNSYLVANIA

Students Speak Out
ON ATHLETICS

"There's definitely school pride, especially against rival Princeton. In playoff games against them, students all over campus wear their 'Puck Frinceton' shirts."

"Basketball is our biggest varsity sport, followed by football. People wait in an overnight line to get basketball season tickets. **The games are always packed**, but campus life doesn't completely stop for them. Intramural sports are plentiful, and everybody who wants to play gets to."

"Varsity sports are huge. A lot of people get recruited to play on a varsity sports team, so it's no wonder we have so much school spirit. It's exciting to go to a football game or a basketball game because **we always win**. IM [intramural] sports are very popular too. People at Penn tend to be very athletic and well-rounded, so it's not very hard to find a new sport to pick up and some more-than-worthy competition to get involved in."

"Varsity sports are **part of the lifeblood of this campus**. Football games draw huge crowds, which are dwarfed by the immensity of Franklin Field. Both the Palestra's and Franklin Field's historical value lends excitement to every game, and the traditions that have lasted for so many years, such as the throwing of toast, allow the audience to have its own fun at the expense of the opponents. If you're having trouble getting into the game, chants and roll outs will spark your Penn pride."

"Athletics here are decent, but not spectacular. Penn is competitive and often wins against other Ivies, as well as non-Ivies. **Intramural sports are substantial**, and club sports cover almost every sport that varsity does, plus much, much more."

"**Football and basketball are good**. We made the tournament in basketball this year. IM sports are there for you, but aren't huge. I have a lot of friends who play rugby and water polo, and they love it."

"**Varsity sports are good on campus**, and spirit usually rises when we have big games and homecoming. I don't know much about intramural sports, but I know that some actually compete nationwide."

The College Prowler Take
ON ATHLETICS

One thing that sets Penn apart from other Ivy League schools is the intense school spirit that radiates throughout the student body. Students definitely support the varsity teams, many of which are among the best in the league. Home football games are heavily attended, and some basketball fans wait in "the line" overnight to get season tickets for the men's basketball team, which often competes in the NCAA tournament. One important tradition involves frenzied students tearing down the goal posts after a victorious championship football game and throwing them into the Schuylkill River.

Intramural and club sports are participated in relatively widely. Students have the chance to compete in a wide selection of sports. Club sports are taken seriously by those involved, while intramural athletes, though often extremely competitive, tend to have a more laid-back practicing and training schedule. Anyone can start an intramural team simply by recruiting a specified number of people and registering the squad. Penn athletics provides impressive facilities, most noticeably the new Pottruck Fitness Center, and ample opportunity for absolutely everyone to participate as both an athlete and a spirited fan.

The College Prowler™ Grade on

Athletics: B+

A high grade in Athletics indicates that students have school spirit, that sports programs are respected, that games are well-attended, and that intramurals are a prominent part of student life.

Nightlife

Student Favorites:
Smokey Joe's, Billy Bob's, Egypt, Chrome

Useful Resources for Nightlife:
www.digitalcity.com/philadelphia/bars
www.philadelphia.citysearch.com
Philadelphia Magazine (*www.phillymag.com*)

Bars Close At:
2 a.m.

Primary Areas with Nightlife:
University City, Center City

Cheapest Place to Get a Drink:
Blarney Stone

What to Do if You're Not 21:
The following places permit students ages 18 and above either regularly or for special events: Cavanaugh's, Smokey Joe's, Woody's, Egypt Nightclub, Shampoo

Students Speak Out
ON NIGHTLIFE

"If Greek life isn't your scene, there are a million dance clubs, pubs, and hot night spots around campus and in Philly."

"Penn has an active Greek system, and the **parties are generally good**, though they can get packed. There are numerous clubs downtown. On-campus spots for a drink include Smokey Joe's, Billy Bob's, White Dog, and La Terrasse."

"Most of the campus parties revolve around the Greek system and are a lot of fun. Drinks and access are free, and they're all within walking distance. **There are only two bars on campus**—Billy Bob's and Smokey Joe's. Both are very popular. I only go to the clubs downtown when Penn is sponsoring a party, but they're usually really nice and show students a good time."

"The bars and clubs off campus are pretty good. Places like Egypt, Envy, Chrome, Adrenaline, and Paradigm are all fun. **Carding in Philly is pretty strict**, so either have a fake ID, or expect to get cozy with the bouncers."

"We have Billy Bob's and Smokey's on the campus; they are pretty good bars, if you have an ID. There are **plenty of bars and clubs off campus**. There are clubs like the Locust Club, 8th Floor, and Envy—these ones are promoted basically every week."

"C'mon! You're in Philly! Of course there are awesome bars and clubs! The best and most popular bars on campus are Smokey Joe's and Billy Bob's. **My favorite is the Blarney Stone**, and there's Cavanaugh's, but that's mostly an upperclassmen and grad students' bar."

"One thing I hate about Philly is that clubs tend to close at 2 a.m. The really good clubs like Transit and Evolution sometimes stay open until 3:30 a.m. **There are 'after hours' clubs**, but they don't advertise to the public. Usually, they roam bars at about 1 to 2 a.m. and pass their fliers around."

The College Prowler Take ON NIGHTLIFE

Students really enjoy the endless array of nightlife possibilities that Penn's location has to offer. Bars like Smokey's and Billy Bob's are the staples for many students, while others venture further into the city to dance to every type of dance music from disco to techno. For a change of pace, some students enjoy karaoke or concerts, but no matter how you choose to spend your weekend nights, being under 21 years of age can definitely narrow your options.

If you're into the bar or club scene, then going to school in Philadelphia is probably a smart decision. There are a number of bars scattered around University City, and clubs all over Center City and downtown. Most fraternities and sororities will have an event at a city club at some point, so if you are planning to join the Greek system, plan to experience this part of city nightlife, as well. Because most Greek organizations strongly encourage their new members to attend all the events (even at over-21 venues), and because bars and clubs tend to be strict about carding, a fake ID is about as valuable as a rhino horn at an Asian Bazaar.

The College Prowler™ Grade on

Nightlife: A-

A high grade in Nightlife indicates that there are many bars and clubs in the area that are easily accessible and affordable. Other determining factors include the number of options for the under-21 crowd and the prevalence of house parties.

Greek Life

The Lowdown ON GREEK LIFE

Number of Fraternities:
29

Number of Sororities:
7

Undergrad Men in Fraternities:
23%

Undergrad Women in Sororities:
16%

Fraternities on Campus:
Alpha Chi Rho, Alpha Epsilon Pi, Alpha Tau Omega, Beta Theta Pi, Delta Kappa Epsilon, Delta Phi (St. Elmo's), Delta Psi (St. Anthony's Hall), Delta Tau Delta, Delta Upsilon, Kappa Alpha, Kappa Sigma, Lambda Chi Alpha, Phi Delta Theta, Phi Kappa Psi, Phi Kappa Sigma, Phi Sigma Kappa, Pi Lambda Phi, Pi Kappa Alpha, Pi Kappa Phi, Psi Upsilon, Sigma Alpha Epsilon, Sigma Chi, Sigma Nu, Sigma Phi Epsilon, Sigma Pi, Tau Epsilon Phi, Theta Xi, Zeta Beta Tau, Zeta Psi

Sororities on Campus:
Alpha Chi Omega, Alpha Phi, Chi Omega, Delta Delta Delta, Kappa Alpha Theta, Sigma Delta Tau, Sigma Kappa

Students Speak Out
ON GREEK LIFE

"The frat parties range from lively dance parties with loud music and cheap beer to more cozy gigs with hard liquor and frat brothers who are ever so eager to give you a tour of the upstairs."

"The **parties on campus are unusually plentiful and enjoyable**, especially for an Ivy. All of the 30 or so frat houses try to sponsor parties on a regular basis. Some of my favorite host frats are SAE, AEPi, Pike, and Tep. And you can find parties regularly in the high-rise apartments and in non-Greek houses on and around campus."

"Greek life is a popular option for many students. I would approximate that about 30 percent are involved, to some extent. Because of the number of fraternities and sororities and the students who partake, it seems that **Greek life is a large factor in the social scene**. Parties, generally, do not exclude non-Greek students unless they are closed or mixers."

"Greek life on campus is pretty big. Freshman year, the Greek scene is huge with tons of frat parties each weekend. However, **the scene gets kind of old** once you are a sophomore, and most people end up drifting away and throwing their own parties in their rooms. You can go Greek or not; either way, you should be fine."

"I was very skeptical about Greek life but ended up rushing, and it was the best decision I have ever made. You can definitely have fun and survive on campus without joining, but **it's such a great experience**."

"Greek life isn't that important, and this is coming from someone in a fraternity. You can find friends in fraternities, and you can find a lot more outside the fraternity. **Frats and sororities are really just in the background**, although there are a lot of Greek parties all the time."

"Greek life is big, but **I wouldn't say that it dominates** the social scene. You can do whatever you want at Penn."

The College Prowler Take
ON GREEK LIFE

Students at Penn, Greek and non-Greek alike, make a weekly habit of visiting frat houses for some good old-fashioned college fun. On big party weekends like Spring Fling, there could be over 20 parties to choose from in one night. The number of fraternities, the individual personality of each one, and the frequency with which parties occur give Penn students a choice of gatherings including everything from loud and exciting, to small and personal.

Although becoming involved in the Greek system at Penn can be a rewarding and memorable experience, it rarely monopolizes the sisters' and brothers' social lives. At Penn, members of fraternities and sororities have friends outside of their organization, and many of them, more-so in sororities, do not live in the house. Subsequently, these students remain well-rounded, and they do not isolate themselves from the rest of campus, making the Greek system something everyone can benefit from, whether they choose to become affiliated or not.

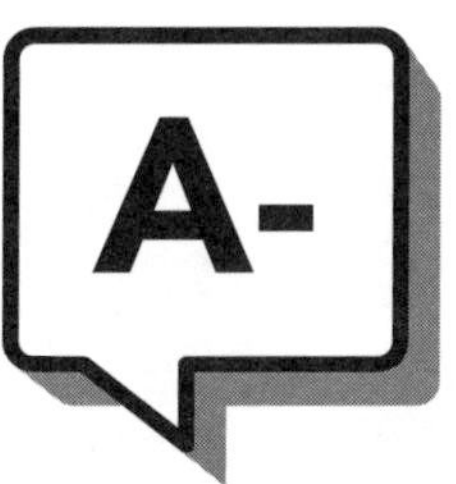

The College Prowler™ Grade on
Greek Life: A-

A high grade in Greek Life indicates that sororities and fraternities are not only present, but also active on campus. Other determining factors include the variety of houses available and the respect the Greek community receives from the rest of the campus.

Drug Scene

The Lowdown
ON DRUG SCENE

Most Prevalent Drugs on Campus:
Alcohol, marijuana, Ritalin

Liquor-Related Referrals:
23

Liquor-Related Arrests:
28

Drug-Related Referrals:
17

Drug-Related Arrests:
1

Drug Counseling Programs

Counseling and Psychological Services
(215) 898-7021
Services: Screening and intervention, free, confidential, and professional services

Drug and Alcohol Resource Team
(215) 573-3525
Services: Workshops and other educational activities.

Students Speak Out
ON DRUG SCENE

"Drugs are there. Alcohol is obviously the biggest. After that is stuff like Ritalin or caffeine pills for focus and energy, especially during finals."

"I would say that drugs on campus are relatively remote. **Weed is everywhere**, obviously. Compared to a lot of other campuses, Penn kids don't do drugs, but it's all relative. Unless you consider alcohol a drug—then forget everything I just said."

"Lots of people smoke weed. There are a few rich kids who insist on doing coke. Other than that, **it's your normal college thing**—mostly weed, some shrooms, whatever. It's not a really big deal."

"It's easy to get and easy to avoid. There's a lot of weed and shrooms around, but if you aren't into it, **it's not central to the social scene**. There's not much hard stuff, but you are in Philly—if you really are into that, you are in one of the bigger cities in the country, and you can find it if you want to."

"The problems with drinking and drugs are baseline; **people are smart about not getting caught**, especially with drugs. There are occasional alcohol-related incidents but nothing major, in my memory."

"I had heard rumors of drugs like coke before I got to Penn, but at no point was I exposed to it directly. Drugs are present, but **they aren't something that is forced upon you**."

"There's a big misconception that because Penn is a top-caliber university, there are fewer drugs circulating around campus. This is Tom Clancy fiction at its best. **Penn kids like their drugs just like other college-age kids**. Weed is ubiquitous, but not the problem. X and coke are everywhere. It's a shame, but college is just a microcosm of the real world."

The College Prowler Take
ON DRUG SCENE

Not surprisingly, alcohol and marijuana are common and easily obtained at Penn. However, students feel that the drug scene is easy to avoid if you simply do not make an effort to become involved in it. Since very few people have cars on campus, designated drivers are not necessary, which may down the number of sober people at parties.

There are, of course, other drugs of choice among smaller groups of students. Cocaine, ecstasy, and opium are among those that can be found on campus in some instances, but it seems that most students make it through their Penn career without coming in contact with any of these.

The College Prowler™ Grade on
Drug Scene: B

A high grade on Drug Scene indicates that drugs are not a noticeable part of campus life; drug use is not visible, and no pressure to use them seems to exist.

Campus Strictness

The Lowdown
ON CAMPUS STRICTNESS

What Are You Most Likely to Get Caught Doing on Campus?

- Underage drinking
- Parking violations
- Running a red light
- Trying to sneak into a dining hall without your Penn card
- Downloading copyrighted materials
- Leaving garbage in the hallway of your dorm
- Making too much noise during "quiet hours"

Students Speak Out
ON CAMPUS STRICTNESS

"Often, they'll confiscate alcohol, and occasionally a frat will get in trouble for it, but that's not a big deal. Weed is a little worse. Anything harder than weed is harshly punished."

"It depends on the incident, I suppose. Although, a large percentage of drinking- or drug-related offences are handled within the housing system, rather than involving the police. In the end, it seems the **policies tend to be a bit lax**."

"**The Penn police are extremely helpful**. They'll only break up a party if it's disrupting the surrounding neighborhoods. Penn has a rule that if you get sick at a party and call the Penn police, then you can't get in trouble with the University for it."

"Drinking still goes on, although most **on-campus parties get busted** after a while. They are stricter in dorms than in other places."

"They're **not at all strict about drinking**. They usually break up most big parties around 2 a.m., but if they see you drinking on the street, they'll probably just ask you to pour it out. They're getting a little stricter about fake IDs at bars. Sometimes they scan them, but if you get rejected, 99 percent of the time they don't actually take the ID away."

"Campus police are pretty lenient about the drinking policy. Their main goal is just to prevent the students from getting hurt, so they normally only intervene if there is a fight. Other than that, **they pretty much leave the students alone**. The only time that they really become strict is during Spring Fling weekend—a weekend full of drinking and debauchery."

"Penn's still **the party school of the Ivies**! The police are pretty lenient about letting students have their parties, unless there are noise complaints or fighting. Then they just disperse the crowd and send everyone home."

The College Prowler Take

ON CAMPUS STRICTNESS

On campus, safety comes first and discipline comes later—much, much later. Students feel that campus police are not very strict, and only enforce rules if they feel that the infraction is putting students in danger or if the violation is particularly obvious.

The situation with RAs tends to be the same. If you walk into your RAs room with a bottle of alcohol in your hand, you will most likely get written up, but if you keep it in a room with the door closed, the chances of getting in trouble are very low. The official alcohol policy at Penn says, "In cases of intoxication and/or alcohol poisoning, the primary concern is the health and safety of the individual(s) involved. No student seeking medical treatment for an alcohol or other drug-related overdose will be subject to University discipline. This policy shall extend to another student seeking help for the intoxicated student." In closing, Penn's alcohol policy is there to help students, not to damage their reputations or academic careers.

The College Prowler™ Grade on

Campus Strictness: A

A high Campus Strictness grade implies an overall lenient atmosphere; police and RAs are fairly tolerant, and the administration's rules are flexible.

Parking & Transportation

The Lowdown
ON PARKING & TRANSPORTATION

Student Parking Lot?
Yes

Freshmen Allowed to Park?
Yes

Approximate Parking Permit Cost:
$870-$1,092 per year

Best Places to Find a Parking Spot:
If you have a permit, in these student lots:
Walnut St. between 32nd and 33rd Streets
38th and Spruce Streets (enter off of 38th)
NE corner of 34th and Chestnut Streets
32nd and Walnut Streets

Good Luck Getting a Parking Spot Here:
Hamilton Shops

Ways to Get Around:

On Campus:
Penn Shuttle Services, 6 p.m.-3 a.m., (215) 898-RIDE
PennBus Services, 4:45 p.m.-12 a.m., schedule at *www.upenn.edu/transportation/bus.html*

Public Transportation:
Septa (Commuter Train, Bus, Subway), (215) 580-7852, all information found at *www.septa.org/*

Students Speak Out
ON PARKING & TRANSPORTATION

"The subway is pretty easy to follow, cabs are everywhere, and regional rail is available only five minutes from Penn's campus."

"**Parking is terrible**. I wouldn't recommend bringing a car on campus. There's no need since Philadelphia is accessible through taxis and public transportation."

"There are few parking garages, making parallel parking the only option. **Most spots are metered**, which is a hassle, and often there are no open spaces to begin with."

"The subway and trolley system makes getting around Philadelphia easy and inexpensive. **Cabs are also omnipresent**."

"Honestly, public transportation could be better. The buses are lousy, and the subway routes are inane. Still, **the subways are cheap** and will get you pretty much anywhere you need to go in a reasonable amount of time. However, if you're lazy, I would have to say that the taxis are just phenomenal."

"**Public transportation is one of the easiest ways to get around** Philadelphia. The subway, buses, taxis, or even walking can get you to nearly everywhere in the city. Granted the prices might be a bit steep—$2.60 round-trip into the heart of the city on the subway—but the rides are welcomed."

"**Finding a parking space isn't easy** if you live on campus. Most underclassmen don't bring their cars to school."

"The **parking scene is pretty good at Penn**; however, you would have to pay for a regular parking spot. See, Penn is not a closed campus—cars travel through the streets. So, naturally, parking on the side streets for a whole semester would not be practical."

The College Prowler Take
ON PARKING

You do not want to park on campus. As a matter of fact, there are not very many places in Philadelphia that you would want to park either. Even if you can afford the expensive cost of a permit, subsequent parking meters, and the occasional ticket, the average Penn student cannot spare the time to make sure the meter is fed or the car is in and out of the garage at the right time.

Some people do bring a car to school, but most of them live in Philadelphia or a local suburb and find a personal vehicle useful for bringing home laundry and picking up mom's home-cooked meals. However, if you are far enough from home that you can not simply drop the car off and take a cab back to campus, a car will usually prove to be a bigger hassle than it is worth.

The College Prowler™ Grade on

Parking: D-

A high grade in this section indicates that parking is both available and affordable, and that parking enforcement isn't overly severe.

The College Prowler Take
ON TRANSPORTATION

Parking in the city is a nightmare, and the convenience of cabs, regional rail, subways, buses and trolleys is one greatly appreciated by students.

One great thing about Penn's location is that Center City and South Street, two great places to venture out to, are in easy walking distance. If it's late, or you are going to somewhere further like Old City, splitting a cab with a couple friends makes the ride affordable and easy. The school is also within close proximity to a Greyhound bus station, and some thriftier students take advantage of the Chinatown bus, which travels to other big cities on the East Coast, often for incredibly cheap fares. The 30th Street Station, from which Amtrak and Septa trains depart, is within blocks of campus and provides an easy way to get home for students from northeastern states.

The College Prowler™ Grade on

Transportation: B+

A high grade for Transportation indicates that campus buses, public buses, cabs, and rental cars are readily-available and affordable. Other determining factors include proximity to an airport and the necessity of transportation.

Overall Experience

Students Speak Out

ON OVERALL EXPERIENCE

"I really love it here. It's excellent. Nobody has ever told me anything interesting about their school that can surpass Penn."

"Going into my senior year, I can honestly say I would not rather be anywhere else. **Penn has truly become a home away from home**, and I'm hopeful that I can continue the Penn experience, if accepted to the law school. Its location is unmatched, its facilities are beautiful, and it remains home to a brilliant faculty, including a number of Nobel Prize winners. Its number four ranking, in combination with everything else, makes Penn number one to its students."

"I've had a great experience at school so far. **It's a 'work hard, party hard' environment** with a big interest in sports. The cheesesteaks are reason enough to come here."

"I'm absolutely in love with this school, and I couldn't imagine going anywhere else. I think that **Penn allows for a perfect combination of work and play**. I love the people, I have found plenty of extracurricular activities to keep me busy, and I cannot wait for classes to start up again in the fall. Come here. You'll have fun. I promise."

"My overall experience at Penn has been marvelous. Penn is huge. I would have to say that it's more difficult to avoid making friends with good people than it is to do so. There are **so many different types of people with interesting personalities** all over campus, and a wide range of activities to help you meet them. The classes are truly exciting, and you'll learn a lot more from them than what's on the syllabus. Living in a city, on a vast campus, and attending one of the finest universities in the country is rarely disappointing, and never boring. You can always fine something interesting to do, and someone splendid to do it with."

"I wanted to go to school in a big city, so Penn definitely fits that role well, as it's nearly in the middle of Philadelphia. I enjoyed my freshman year and **I'm enthusiastic about my major, chemical engineering**, having been through my first classes and meeting the professors of the department. They all are such brilliant professors, and I'm incredibly glad to have their knowledge at my disposal."

"It's definitely a great experience. I love the city and the school. **I would never want to be anywhere else**. It has the stellar academics of an Ivy, a great city with tons to do, and wonderful people. What more could you want out of college?"

The College Prowler Take

ON OVERALL EXPERIENCE

Students seem to be extremely content and do not regret their decision to come to Penn, even though the school definitely has a pre-professional feel. Despite this fact, it is extremely common to find yourself in an intellectual conversation, and the students really do work hard, while remembering that college is about fun, as well. The opportunities provided at Penn are astounding. In fact, there is almost too much to do here. Most students base the reason for their happiness around the people, the academics, the urban environment, and the endless opportunities. People who enjoy their experience at Penn tend to appreciate city life, socializing, and an active schedule. Usually, students do not hesitate to endorse Penn, and many feel that everyone should love the school as much as they do.

Many adults call their years as an undergraduate the best four years of their lives. Penn students certainly cannot make that prediction so soon, but most would agree that their experiences at Penn have led to the best years of their lives so far. Obviously, Penn is not the school for everyone, but the student body consists of interesting, intelligent, and well-rounded people, which creates a stimulating and fun environment for most. If you come to Penn, rest assured, you will eventually meet fascinating people, find something to be passionate about, and enjoy the benefits of living in a vibrant city. You can also feel confident that an education from Penn will prepare you for what lies beyond your undergraduate years. The Penn overall experience is defined by the combination of the rich history and academic rigor of an elite Ivy League school, and the school spirit and propensity for socializing of a state school, which forms the "work hard, play hard" mentality that many Quakers, and prospective Quakers, find so appealing.

The Inside Scoop

The Lowdown

ON THE INSIDE SCOOP

UPenn Slang:

Know the slang, know the school. The following is a list of things you really need to know before coming to UPenn. The more of these words you know, the better off you'll be.

Baby Quad - A small section of Spruce College House in lower quad including the south courtyard and the rooms around it

The Bridge - Either the bridge on Locust Walk between Huntsman Hall and 1920 Commons or the Bridge Cinema on Walnut

The Button - A sculpture of a split button in front of the Van Pelt Library. The rumor is that every Penn student is supposed to have sex under the button before they graduate.

The Castle - Psi Upsilon Fraternity

The Compass - The circle pointing you in the right direction in the middle of Locust Walk. It serves as a common place to meet friends coming from different directions.

DP - The *Daily Pennsylvanian*, the official newspaper of the University of Pennsylvania

Fro-Yo - What Penn students call frozen yogurt at the Hill dining hall

Fro-Gro - A nickname for Fresh Grocer

Ghetto-magic - The Cinemagic Theater

M&T - Management and Technology, an undergraduate program combining Engineering and Wharton

Smokes - Smokey Joe's Bar on 40th St.

The River - The Schuylkill River located next to Franklin Field

The Wa or Wa Squared - Nicknames for Wawa

Whartonite - Nickname for a typical Wharton student, describes a business-like, conservative, and overly wealthy student

Things I Wish I Knew Before Coming to UPenn:

- Get the smallest meal plan offered.
- Party hard during Freshmen Orientation.
- Skip the "Penn Reading Project."
- Get a random roommate freshman year.
- Computers are better when portable.
- You don't need half the things you want to bring.

Tips to Succeed at UPenn:

- Shop around for classes during the add/drop period.
- Talk to upperclassmen for advice.
- Go to office hours.
- Do your homework.
- Learn how to manage your time effectively (alternate solution: learn how to function on two hours sleep).
- Get on as many school mailing lists as humanly possible.
- Work hard, but remember to have fun.
- Success is not always measured by grades, so don't get too stuck on the numbers.

Urban Legends

People seem to believe that *Playboy* ranked the boys at UPenn #4 in the nation, and the girls #352. The nerve!

Everyone has sex under "the button" before they graduate.

If you walk on the compass before your first midterm freshman year, you're doomed to fail the test.

School Spirit

School spirit is incredibly strong at Penn, especially at sporting events. The pinnacle of students' spirit is shown at the Penn vs. Princeton basketball game, where our long rivalry with the Princeton basketball team is displayed with chants and banners bearing clever anti-Princeton slogans. Even outside of the basketball season, students can constantly be seen wearing Penn paraphernalia and bringing high school friends by to partake in the Penn experience that students seem to enjoy so thoroughly.

Traditions

Here's a Toast!

Toast Throwing: During football games, Quaker fans sing the traditional school song "Drink a Highball" and toss toast onto the field. Bonus points if you can hit the cheerleaders. If you can't get your hands on toast, bagels, donuts, or French bread work just as well.

What's That Floating in the River?

Goal Post Tossing: When the Quaker football team wins the Ivy League championship, frenzied fans (attempt to) tear down the goal post and hurl it into the Schuylkill River, which is right next door to Franklin Field.

Ahhhh!

Econ Scream: "Economics 001" is one of the most common classes for freshmen to take at Penn. On the eve of the course's first midterm, stressed students gather in the Quad at midnight and release some frustration by collectively screaming. Feel free to streak across the courtyard if you feel so inclined.

You Sexy Fling

Spring Fling: Considered to be the best weekend of the year at Penn by most students and the best spring festival in the country by some, Spring Fling is an incredible three days of vendors, bands, performances, and all out partying. Recent acts at the annual Spring Fling Concert were Busta Rhymes, the Donnas, Jurassic 5, and OK Go.

The Meet Market

Penn Relays: If you are a track fan, even a tiny little bit, you have heard of the Penn Relays, the biggest track meet in the world. This yearly event draws visitors and athletes from all over the world to Penn's campus to watch the best high school, college, and professional athletes of the day compete against one another.

The Lowdown

ON FINDING A JOB OR INTERNSHIP

Career Services is an essential tool for snagging interviews for jobs and internships. Career advisors can help you organize a resume and give you tips for nailing an interview. If you're not sure where to apply, Career Services also provides a job and internship database where you can search by region, type of job, and salary, among other criteria, to help find places to approach.

Advice

Go over your resume with someone at Career Services. They will tell you which points to highlight, and useful tips for formatting. Also, go to see guest lecturers who are involved with something you are interested in. You may get to meet them afterwards and gain an excellent opportunity, or you could simply learn something that will make you an even better candidate during an interview.

Bonus Quote

"UPenn has many, many helpful services for students, especially for those trying to locate jobs or discover a path to pursue. Career Services helped me develop my first respectable resume as I applied for a job with a small research company located a couple blocks from the campus. They were courteous and knowledgeable; they help numerous students every year, if not every day."

The Lowdown

ON ALUMNI

Web site:
www.upenn.edu/alumni

Office:
E. Craig Sweeten Alumni House
3533 Locust Walk
Philadelphia, PA 19104

Services Available:
Education, Travel Program, Career Services, Insurance, Library Portal, Online Community

Famous UPenn Alumni:

(Note: C=College, W=Wharton, SEAS=Engineering, ASC=Annenberg School of Communications, M=Medical School, G=Graduate School, L=Law, E=Education, H=Honorary degree)

Sadie Alexander (E'18, G'21, L'27) – First African American woman in U.S. to earn a Ph.D.

Candice Bergen (2 yrs., early '60s, H'92) – Actress *Murphy Brown*

William Brennan (W'28) – Supreme Court Justice

Harold E. Ford, Jr. (C'92) – U.S. Congressman

Doug Glanville (SEAS'93) – Philadelphia Phillies center fielder

Rabbi Israel Goldstein (C'14, H'76) – A founder of Brandeis University

William Henry Harrison (1789-91) – Ninth President of the United States

Duncan Kenworthy (ASC'73) – Producer, *Four Weddings and a Funeral* and *Notting Hill*

Andrea Mitchell (CW'67) – NBC News correspondent

Rob Perelman (W'64, WG'66) – Financier

Maury Povich (W'62) – Talk show host

Dr. Stanly Prosiner (C'64, M'86) – Recipient of the 1997 Nobel Prize in Medicine

Alan Rachins (W'64) – *L.A. Law* and *Dharma and Greg* actor

Ed Rendell (C'65) – Former Mayor of Philadelphia and current Governor of Pennsylvania

Martin C. Smith (C'64) – Author of *Gorky Park*

Arlen Specter (C'51) – U.S. Senator, Pennsylvania

Donald Trump (W'68) – Entrepreneur

John Edgar Wideman (C'63, H'86) – Author, Rhodes Scholar

The Ten BEST Things About Penn:

1	Spring Fling
2	Penn Relays
3	High-speed Internet
4	The Quad
5	The libraries (over 5 million volumes)
6	Philly
7	Cheesesteaks
8	The dual-degree and interdisciplinary programs
9	"Puck Frinceton" T-shirts
10	Pottruck Fitness Center

The Ten WORST Things About Penn:

1	Parking
2	Inconvenient hours at the dining halls
3	Cold winters
4	Teachers with indecipherable accents
5	Stereotypical Ivy League students
6	The wind tunnel between high-rises
7	Slow elevators
8	Frat hopping in the winter
9	Constant construction
10	Tough workload

Visiting Penn

For more hotel information and travel discounts, you may also contact "Campus Visits" at (877) 88-PHILA or *www.onebigcampus.com*.

Take a Campus Virtual Tour:
www.upenn.edu/admissions/tour

The Lowdown
ON VISITING PENN

The following hotels offer special "University of Pennsylvania" rates and/or discount packages. Hotels marked with an asterisk (*) are located on or walking distance from campus.

University City

***The Hilton Inn at Penn**
www.theinnatpenn.com
3600 Sansom Street
Philadelphia, PA
(215) 222-0200, 800-Hiltons
Distance from Campus: 0 miles (on campus)
$149-$169/night (ask for best available rate)

***Sheraton – University City Hotel**
www.sheraton.com/universitycity
36th and Chestnut Streets
Philadelphia, PA
(215) 387-8000, (800) 325-3535
Distance from Campus: less than 1 mile
Price Range: $129-$159/night

Center City

Philadelphia Downtown Courtyard
www.courtyard.com
21 North Juniper Street (at Filbert)
Philadelphia, PA
(215) 496-3000
Distance from Campus: 2.4 miles
$99/night

To Schedule an Interview

Alumnus will most likely contact you for an off-campus interview in your area. On-campus interviews are usually only granted to legacy applicants.

Overnight Visits

Contact the Office of Admissions two weeks prior to your visit if you wish to stay overnight. Overnight housing is available Monday through Wednesday nights during the months of October, November and February. Students need to bring a sleeping bag for their one evening stay. You will be housed with a volunteer who will offer you a view of Penn that will not be covered on a tour or in an information session. You should plan to arrive at the Admissions Office no later than 4 p.m. to meet your host.

Directions to Campus

Driving from the Northeast via the New Jersey Turnpike South

- Use Exit 4. Bear right out of the toll following signs to Philadelphia and Ben Franklin Bridge.
- After crossing the bride take I-676 West to I-76 East, the Schuylkill Expressway.
- Follow I-76 East to Exit 346-A – South Street (a left exit lane).
- Turn right onto South Street to enter campus.

Driving from the South via I-95 North

- Use the I-676/Center City Philadelphia Exit which is approximately seven miles north of the airport.
- Follow I-676 West, the Vine Street Expressway, until I-76 East, the Schuylkill Expressway.
- Follow I-76 East until Exit 346-A – South Street (a left lane exit).
- Turn right onto South Street to enter campus.

Driving from the West via the Pennsylvania Turnpike

- On the PA Turnpike use Exit 326, the Valley Forge Interchange.
- Take I-76 East for approximately 17 miles until Exit 346-A – South Street (a left lane exit).
- Turn right onto South Street to enter campus.
- To find parking, turn right at the second light onto 33rd Street.
- Take the first left onto Walnut Street, and there will be a lot on the right at 38th and Walnut.

Driving from the North via I-95 South

- Use the I-676/Center City Philadelphia Exit. (Follow signs to I-676 West, the Vine Street Expressway).
- Take I-676 West until I-76 East, the Schuylkill Expressway.
- Follow I-76 East until Exit 346-A – South Street (a left-lane exit).
- Turn right onto South Street to enter campus.

Yale University

38 Hillhouse Avenue New Haven, CT 06511
www.yale.edu (203) 432-9300

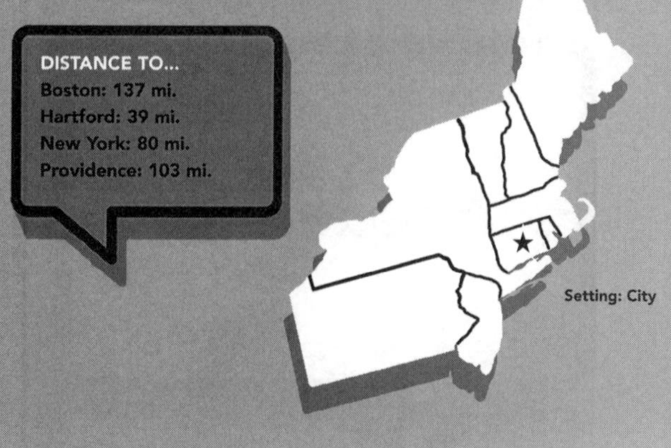

"Yale University is a brand name that inspires instant recognition, confidence, and esteem."

Total Enrollment:
5,319 - Large
Acceptance Rate:
10%
Tuition:
$29,820
Top 10% of High School Class:
95%

SAT Range

Verbal	Math	Total
690 – 790	690 – 790	1380 – 1580

ACT Range

Verbal	Math	Total
N/A	N/A	30-34

Most Popular Majors:
14% History
11% Economics
10% Political Science and Government
7% English Language and Literature
7% Psychology

Students Also Applied To:*
Columbia University, Dartmouth College, Harvard University, Stanford University

*For more school info check out *www.collegeprowler.com*

Table of Contents

College Prowler Report Card

Academics	A
Local Atmosphere	C-
Safety & Security	B-
Computers	A
Facilities	A-
Campus Dining	C+
Off-Campus Dining	B+
Campus Housing	A-
Off-Campus Housing	B
Diversity	B
Guys	B
Girls	B+
Athletics	C
Nightlife	B-
Greek Life	D+
Drug Scene	B+
Campus Strictness	A
Parking	C-
Transportation	C-

The Lowdown
ON ACADEMICS

Degrees Awarded:
Bachelor, Master, Doctorate

Undergraduate School:
Yale College

Full-Time Faculty:
1054

Faculty with Terminal Degree:
91%

Student-to-Faculty Ratio:
6:1

Average Course Load:
4 to 5 courses

AP Test Score Requirements:
Possible credit for scores of 4 or 5

IB Test Score Requirements:
Possible credit for scores of 6 or 7

Sample Academic Clubs:
The Yale College Bioethics Society, Yale Psychological Society, Objectivist Study Group, Yale Entrepreneurial Society, Yale Film Society, Yale Political Union

Did You Know?

75 percent of Yale courses enroll fewer than 20 students.
29 percent of courses enroll fewer than 10 students.

Sterling Memorial Library is the second largest college library in the country.

All tenured professors of the Faculty of Arts and Sciences teach undergraduate courses.

There isn't a traditional credit system at Yale. Instead, students must complete 36 equally weighted courses.

Looking to find out more about Yale academic programs? Read College Prowler's complete Yale guidebook available at *www.collegeprowler.com*.

Students Speak Out
ON ACADEMICS

"I haven't seen much competition at Yale. I think the sciences tend to be the hardest classes. However, nothing is impossible, and everyone here is very supportive."

"**I haven't been thrilled with my professors** or my classes this year. I really liked three out of the nine classes I took. This surprised me because, well, it's Yale. But I really think that it will get better as I get into the more advanced courses."

"As an English major, **I've been lucky to love almost all of my professors**, as well as the seminar leaders. Several stand out—in particular, my professor who was about 70 years old and came to lectures wearing short, tight miniskirts with knee-high, black leather, four-inch stiletto boots. She would comfortably lean against a table at the front of the lecture hall, or perhaps perch herself on the table, and then talk to us, rather than at us. It was a highly intellectual environment, yet simultaneously laid-back and comfortable. I loved her!"

"As a pre-med student, the science classes I have taken have, for the most part, been strong, well-taught and structured. I have learned an immense amount of material. Unfortunately, the classes are all large, and therefore, **they're inevitably more impersonal**. You have to make a fairly big effort to get to know the professor—ha, even to get him to know you exist."

"Most professors are excellent scholars and teachers. They communicate effectively, engagingly, and with authority. It's hard to construct a schedule that isn't mostly composed of classes taught by great professors. That said, **there's the occasional professor who is incoherent**, either due to limited command of English, or poor organizational skills. Those professors can be identified and easily avoided, thanks to Yale's 'shopping period.'"

"Yale is known for their undergraduate focus, and **all professors are required to teach undergrads**. This is a huge advantage, since either way you are paying for their salaries; you might as well have access to them."

The College Prowler Take
ON ACADEMICS

Although students seem happy with their education at Yale, most realize that a successful course load depends not only on the professors and the material, but also on the careful selection of classes. There are amazing lectures and seminars in every department, but there are also those few professors and classes that will be disappointing. The key is to choose the right class for you. Some people soon realize they love lectures, but not seminars. Some students don't like to deal with TAs. Some want professors who dominate the class, while others want to interact with the material more directly. Once you figure out what you want, Yale becomes filled with opportunities to learn.

Most students come to Yale for a "name brand" education, hoping the school's reputation will be enough to carry them smoothly into their future. What these students might not realize is that they must choose to make the name stand for something. If you talk to students here, some will say Yale is a breeze, and some will say it's the most challenging experience of their lives. This difference of opinion does not depend on the students' intelligence or the ease or difficulty of their majors—it has to do with how many learning opportunities they are willing to accept.

The College Prowler™ Grade on

Academics: A

A high Academics grade generally indicates that professors are knowledgeable, accessible, and genuinely interested in their students' welfare. Other determining factors include class size, how well professors communicate, and whether or not classes are engaging.

Local Atmosphere

The Lowdown
ON LOCAL ATMOSPHERE

Region:
Northeast

City, State:
New Haven, Connecticut

Setting:
City

Distance from Boston:
2 hours, 30 minutes

Distance from New York City:
1 hour, 30 minutes

Points of Interest:
Chapel Street, Yale University Art Gallery, Peabody Museum of Natural History, New Haven Green, Wooster Square, East Rock State Park

Closest Shopping Malls or Plazas:
Chapel Street, Broadway

Closest Movie Theater:
The York Square Cinema
61 Broadway, New Haven
Phone (203) 776-6300
http://www.yorksquare.com

Major Sports Teams:
New Haven Ravens (baseball), New Haven Knights (hockey), New Haven Ninjas (football)

Famous People from New Haven:
Charles Goodyear (inventor)
Joe Lieberman (politician)
Eli Whitney (inventor)

City Web site:
http://www.cityofnewhaven.com

Fun Facts About New Haven:

1) In 1879, Walter Camp, then the Yale football captain, developed the game of football as we know it today.
2) Two legendary foods began in New Haven establishments still operating today—the hamburger by Louis Lassen of Louis' Lunch in 1895 and pizza by Frank Pepe of Pepe's Pizzeria Napoletana in 1900.
3) Legend has it that Yale students invented the game of Frisbee using empty pie plates from Mrs. Frisbie's pies to sail across the New Haven Green.
4) New Haven is home to not one but three Tony award-winning regional theaters—Long Wharf, Yale Repertory Theater, and the Shubert—where such classics as *My Fair Lady* and *The Sound of Music* premiered before they went to Broadway.
5) New Haven is the home of the International Festival of Arts and Ideas during which the city becomes the home of performances and activities ranging from an annual performance of the Metropolitan Opera Company, to children's storytelling.

Students Speak Out
ON LOCAL ATMOSPHERE

"Yale is redeveloping lots of the surrounding neighborhoods. We have a Broadway with our bookstore, Urban Outfitters, J.Crew, and many pizza places."

"Even though people sometimes say that New Haven is dangerous, I haven't had any trouble. **There's an escort service available** to walk you back to your dorm when you're at the library late and have a laptop with you or if you just feel a little nervous. I haven't felt uncomfortable walking around at night as long as there's someone else with me. I guess New Haven isn't as much of a city as some places, but it is still great."

"New Haven has started to become more of a college town, so **the parts closest to the colleges are really nice**. You have to walk for a bit to get into the rougher parts, and no one really goes there because there's nothing there for us. Overall, it's fine."

"Yale students' lives are centered around Yale, which has enough variety and things to do to keep you busy for years. And I like that for a university, it's really pretty close-knit; **we're all about Yale**. I think that's great. Stuff to stay away from: sketchy neighborhoods, of course, but that's really it. There are tons of things to do. There is stuff for everyone."

"I love New Haven, despite the bad reputation it sometimes gets. Actually, the only people who say negative things about the city are people who don't actually live here. Once you move in, you realize that, like any city, you need to take precautions and use common sense. If you do, then you'll feel totally safe. **New Haven has so much going on**—from the repertory theaters to the arts festivals—and there are cool little blues and jazz cafes within walking distance—so much stuff, you'd never be able to get around to it all."

The College Prowler Take
ON LOCAL ATMOSPHERE

New Haven is unlike any other place in the world. Yale, the bastion of wealth and privilege, is surrounded by an urban and impoverished area. Although Yale tries to hide this element (while urging that they help to fix it), this atmosphere can still be depressing, especially on cold, gray days. However, it affords the student the opportunity to interact with a real, urban city—a real plus if you want to make a difference. There are an unlimited amount of volunteer opportunities, as well as chances to meet people outside of Yale's somewhat sheltered campus.

On a different note, the area immediately around Yale is a great, bohemian, college town. The shop fronts look more like SoHo than Connecticut, the restaurants are mostly ethnic, and sometimes there are small street fairs. The college is not contained in one place; the dorms and classrooms are pretty scattered, but definitely within walking distance. Everywhere you go there are Yalies, but rarely students from other colleges. Yale has an amazing art gallery that is often overlooked by the students, even though it is free to the public and very close. Across the street is the British Art Center, which is a great space in which to study, but sometimes a bore to visit for its art. At Yale, there is a real range of things to do, just not enough time to do it all!

The College Prowler™ Grade on

Local Atmosphere: C-

A high Local Atmosphere grade indicates that the area surrounding campus is safe and scenic. Other factors include nearby attractions, proximity to other schools, and the town's attitude toward students.

Safety & Security

The Lowdown
ON SAFETY & SECURITY

Number of Yale Police:
35+

Phone:
(203) 432-4400

Health Center Office Hours:
Urgent Care is open 24 hours a day.

Safety Services:
Blue phones, night escorts, minibus service

Health Services:
Birth control, STD testing, physicals, urgent care, mental hygiene

Students Speaks Out
ON SAFETY & SECURITY

"Be careful. Buy mace. Don't walk alone. But that goes for anywhere. New Haven isn't in that bad of an area at all."

"The campus is really safe. You need to have an ID card and keys to get into dorms and onto the freshman part of campus after hours. **Yale Police are always around**, and they're very friendly. You can always call the minibus to take you back to campus if it's late, and you don't feel safe. Or you can call for an escort. They're really on-point about that. Also, there are blue phones everywhere which will immediately connect you to security."

"Security is good. There are always campus police officers on their bikes or just standing around, and I guess their presence makes us feel safe. **I feel very safe on campus** and in the area around campus, but if you stray too far, you probably should walk in a small group of people rather than by yourself, as with any other unfamiliar city."

"It is necessary to have common sense when you're on campus. School is pretty much contained, but New Haven is also a regular city, so I guess you could say **one must have a sense of 'street smarts.'** There were about two incidents of students from the various schools being mugged. They weren't harmed, but their wallets were taken. The criminals were apprehended, and those people were also walking by themselves pretty late at night—that's never a good idea."

"There are countless blue-light phones all around campus, from which you can dial a friend or security. **There are panic buttons on each phone**, and you can also get in touch with security to come pick you up. I feel safe on campus, but I usually try to walk with someone wherever I go late at night. All you need is common sense on any urban campus. The minibus will pick you up from certain locations, but I walk everywhere."

"**I haven't had any problems** personally, and I leave my door unlocked and open almost all of the time."

The College Prowler Take
ON SAFETY & SECURITY

Although New Haven is an urban setting with its share of crime, students agree that they generally feel safe on campus and in town. Because of the area, it is easy to end up in a bad part of town simply by walking three blocks in the wrong direction. But, you quickly learn what and where these places are, and when to avoid them. Yale has its own police force, separate from the New Haven Police Department, and its presence is felt. There are also many services for student safety, such as police escorts to walk you home after late-night study sessions.

Although New Haven can be dangerous, it is usually so only when a person is unwise (i.e., walks home alone late at night). Most students agree that the safety services and security are a great resource and ought to be used. As long as you use common sense, there is rarely a reason to feel in danger.

The College Prowler™ Grade on

Safety & Security: B-

A high grade in Safety & Security means that students generally feel safe, campus police are visible, blue-light phones and escort services are readily available, and safety precautions are not overly necessary.

Computers

The Lowdown
ON COMPUTERS

High-Speed Network?
Yes

Wireless Network?
Yes

Number of Labs:
11 open clusters, 12 restricted access (one in each residential college)

Operating Systems:
PC, UNIX, Macintosh

24-Hour Labs:
All labs are open 24 hours.

Free Software:
Yale offers a variety of free software ranging from Norton Antivirus to statistics programs.

Discounted Software:
Through ePortal, Yale has considerable discounts, particularly Microsoft.

Charge to Print?
Yes, seven cents per page

Did You Know?

Yale partially subsidizes computer purchases made through their Web site.

Students Speak Out ON COMPUTERS

"Most kids I know bring their own PC. Yale has a cool deal with Dell to subsidize. I've never heard of the computer labs being crowded."

"I always think **everyone should bring their own computer**! I've only used the G4s in the art building at Yale and a couple of dinosaur PCs in the library, but the labs were never crowded. It's probably safe to say that they get crowded during finals."

"Bring your own computer if at all possible. You will be glad not to have to leave the room to work. **Each residential college dorm at Yale has computer labs**, but who wants to stay up all night in a place with fluorescent lighting, when you could be lounging in your pajamas with a cup of hot chocolate? It's much easier to concentrate that way."

"I think the computer labs here are adequate. I've never had a problem getting a computer when I've needed one. But, **there's a bit of an e-mail culture here**, so I've found it very convenient to have my own computer in my room."

"I love having a laptop. Having your own computer gives you the freedom to work wherever you feel comfortable, and bringing your laptop to the library is very helpful. The computer clusters are useful but **typically crowded**. I use them to print sometimes, but it's easier to link to a roommate's printer and share."

"**Computer labs can get crowded** during midterms and finals period, so it would probably be better to bring your own computer. There's usually one that is available to use, but it's just easier and more convenient to have your own."

The College Prowler Take ON COMPUTERS

Students agree that although it is convenient to have a personal computer, it is unnecessary. Everywhere you look, there is a computer kiosk or lab, and every residential college has its own computer lab. Very rarely is it impossible to find a computer to work on or check e-mail (except during the chaos of midterms or finals). As a plus, labs provide a quiet place—away from roommates and your television—where work can actually be done.

If you want to bring a computer, students agree that laptops are the best choice. Their mobility makes them easy to take to the library, to class, or outdoors on a nice day. All dormrooms are fitted with Ethernet (high-speed) connections, so it is as easy as buying a cord to connect to the network. Also, every residential college has a team of computer assistants available to fix your computer for free, practically anytime. This is an invaluable resource that comes in handy at the beginning of the year when you have to install Yale software or, God forbid, if you tragically lose a paper the night before it is due.

The College Prowler™ Grade on

Computers: A

A high grade in Computers designates that computer labs are available, the computer network is easily accessible, and campus computing technology is up-to-date.

YALE UNIVERSITY

Favorite Things to Do

Yale theater can often rival most off-Broadway shows, offering an astounding amount of talent for little or no money. If you want to experience a slightly more upscale evening, there are often art show openings where you can rub elbows with Yale's "artsy" crowd while drinking wine and looking at often amazing artwork. If you feel like relaxing during the week, you can always see an independent film at the York Square Cinemas.

Facilities

The Lowdown
ON FACILITIES

Student Center:
None

Athletic Center:
Payne Whitney Gymnasium; also, most residential colleges have their own gyms.

Libraries:
There are eight major libraries, as well as one in each residential college.

What Is There to Do?
Occurring throughout the year there is theater, art shows, student readings, improv comedy, a capella singing, basically almost anything you want.

Movie Theater on Campus?
Yes

Bowling on Campus?
No

Bar on Campus?
Gypsy; also many bars near campus—Rudy's, the Anchor, BAR

Coffeehouse on Campus?
There are many near campus, ranging from Starbucks to the local mainstay, Koffee.

Popular Places to Chill:
Koffee, East Rock State Park, the New Haven Green

Students Speaks Out
ON FACILITIES

"The buildings are hundreds of years old and incredible to look at, let alone live in and use."

"The library is gorgeous, and the **gym is huge**. There are computers everywhere—even outside the dining halls. The facilities are definitely up-to-par."

"Our facilities are great. We have a gigantic gym, seriously. It's one of the biggest, or *the* biggest—although I can't really remember, since there's a sort of competition to be the world's biggest gym. **The computer clusters are up-to-date**. I don't think we really have a student center, though."

"**The facilities are decent**. I don't have much to compare them to. The gym is huge. Each residential college has some special features, and some are better than others."

"Awesome! **There's no real student center**, but that's not a problem. There are tons of places to gather and do stuff."

"The facilities are pretty nice, especially in the renovated colleges. Payne-Whitney Gym is the scariest place on campus because it is large and intimidating, but the smaller residential college gyms are user-friendly. **Each residential college has special features**. For example, Saybrook College has a darkroom, and Branford College has squash courts. Each college has its own buttery, kitchen, TV room, gym, laundry room, common room, dining hall, and library."

The College Prowler Take
ON FACILITIES

Most students agree that the facilities at Yale are pretty nice. The residential colleges are beautiful architectural wonders, and those that have been renovated are equally beautiful on the inside. The classroom buildings are often as picturesque as cathedrals, affording students the opportunity to learn amidst stained glass and Gothic stonework. However, if you ask students about facilities, the first thing that comes up is the Payne Whitney Gym, which is amazing both inside and out. It is huge—the second largest gymnasium in the world, and fully-equipped. In addition, the gym offers dozens of free and pay classes every semester, including yoga, dance, and kick-boxing.

There is no student center at Yale, but students agree that the lack of one is rarely, if ever, missed. Each residential college has a common room for meetings or just hanging out, as well as a library (or two in the case of Davenport), dining hall, TV room, laundry room, and features such as private gyms, kitchens, darkrooms, or music rooms. Essentially, they are self-contained units where students are bound to socialize with one another.

The College Prowler™ Grade on
Facilities: A-

A high Facilities grade indicates that the campus is aesthetically pleasing and well-maintained; facilities are state-of-the-art, and libraries are exceptional. Other determining factors include the quality of both athletic and student centers and an abundance of things to do on campus.

Campus Dining

The Lowdown
ON CAMPUS DINING

Freshman Meal Plan Requirement?
Yes

Meal Plan Average Cost:
$3,222-$4,120

24-Hour On-Campus Eating?
No

Student Favorites:
The Law School Dining Hall, Berkeley

Other Options:
After your freshman year, you can trade in your 20-meal plan for a 14-meal plan with 100 "Flex" dollars. Flex can be used at a small variety of off-campus places including Au Bon Pain and Naples Pizzeria. If you have a heartier appetite, you can opt for the unlimited meal plan, which includes guest passes and 20 "Eli Bucks" per semester.

Did You Know?

If you live on-campus, you must have a meal plan.

Students Speak Out
ON CAMPUS DINING

"The food on campus is decent and probably as good as you can expect out of a college dining hall. Some days are better than others, of course, but there's a pretty wide selection, so you can always find something."

"We have many dining halls, and the food is pretty good. You'll have a meal plan that allows you to eat at Commons, which is our main dining hall, and 12 residential colleges—each has its own dining hall. **There are 'Pan Geos' stations at each college** that prepare things like wraps, pasta, and Asian food right in front of you."

"**Campus food is not good**—unless you go to one of the newer residential colleges, then you'll get some fresh stuff. Stay away from JE at all costs. We can also transfer and eat at the med school, law school, SOM, wherever. The med school has the best food, though."

"The newly-renovated colleges seem to have good food. Branford, Saybrook, and Berkeley seem to have better options. **I like eating at Commons because it's open longer**. Each college has its own personality, and it shows in its dining halls. You can also have a different meal plan that gives you Flex Dollars to spend at local places like Au Bon Pain, Yorkside Pizza, and more."

"The dining hall food is mediocre at best. **The food is repetitive and fattening**. Its main downfall is self-serve, unlimited portions, so students have a tendency to consume mass quantities of food at each meal. The vegetables and fruits are usually not very fresh and a limited selection is available. For late-night snacking, each residential college has a buttery, where fried foods and other treats can be purchased for cheap prices."

"Food on campus is fine, but I'm not picky. It's obviously not the highest quality, but **there are tons of choices**. Don't worry about it. The dining halls all pretty much serve the same food. You'll slowly find out about little differences of each place."

"Dining halls are dining halls. **The food here is nothing special, but it's fine**. The School of Management actually is pretty great—well worth the trek halfway up Science Hill. And there are about a trillion great off-campus places, particularly Thai and Indian. Although, my favorite place to go is still the Educated Burger. Recently I've been going to the Whole Enchilada, this amazing health-food Mexican place on Whitney."

The College Prowler Take

ON CAMPUS DINING

The dining hall food at Yale is surprisingly decent, with a large selection of entrees every day and a salad bar and sandwich bar, if all else fails. There are dining halls in each college, and they are all beautiful, decorated with crystal chandeliers, stained glass windows, and portraits of famous Yalies of the past (including Bill Clinton and George Bush). Furthermore, because most people take most of their meals in their residential college, the students and staff become a makeshift family. Although all residential dining halls serve the same menu, each dining hall has its own special differences. Some have frozen yogurt machines, some have "Pan Geos," specially made dishes cooked right in front of you, and some have blenders for smoothies. Students can go to whichever dining hall is most convenient. There is also Commons, a popular choice for freshman and for a quick lunch because of its central location and extended hours. Although this large "cafeteria" has extended hours, beware of recycled leftovers.

However, no matter how many options a dining hall presents, it can still be monotonous day in and day out. Moreover, the limited hours can be inconvenient for busy students whose schedules might be a bit unorthodox. Unlike many universities, Yale does not have on-campus restaurants for further options, and the dining hall plan is mandatory for those living on campus (although there are some plan choices). All in all, dining hall food is still the most convenient option, and often it is pretty good.

The College Prowler™ Grade on

Campus Dining: C+

Our grade on Campus Dining addresses the quality of both school-owned dining halls and independent on-campus restaurants as well as the price, availability, and variety of food.

Off-Campus Dining

The Lowdown

ON OFF-CAMPUS DINING

Student Favorites:
Thai Taste, Claire's, Yorkside

Closest Grocery Stores:
Shaw's
150 Whalley Ave.
495-9608

Best Pizza:
Pepe's or Sally's

Best Chinese:
It is hard to find good Chinese around Yale. Your best bet is Main Garden.

Best Breakfast:
Copper Kitchen

Best Wings:
The Anchor Bar

Best Healthy:
Claire's

Best Place to Take Your Parents:
Scoozi

Fun Facts:
New Haven is the birthplace of the hamburger.

On Chapel Street, there are five Thai restaurants within a block of each other.

During the International Festival of Arts and Ideas (summer), there is a Pizza Fest where all the local pizza places come out to the New Haven Green and let you sample their fare. This is a great opportunity to conduct a taste test between Sally's and Pepe's.

Students Speak Out
ON OFF-CAMPUS DINING

"It's great. There's Thai food, Italian, everything. Good places include Pad Thai, Sally's, Abate, Clarie's, and Hot Tomatoes. There are so many."

"There are a bunch of **great restaurants** in the area. I'd recommend Hot Tomatoes, Roomba (a personal favorite), and Thai Taste (another personal favorite) to name a few."

"We usually just go to **an organic grocery store** called Out of the Woods. There's a place that we affectionately call 'Basement Thai' that is across the street from the art building at 1156 Chapel. Also, a bookstore/cafe called Book Trader has used books for sale, as well as coffee and sandwich-type stuff."

"The restaurants around campus are great! There are tons of Thai restaurants that are all great. There is such a variety—Japanese, Chinese, cafes, pizza places, grills, Mexican, Ethiopian, and Indian. Some names of some good spots include Samurai, Thai Taste, Rainbow Cafe, Yorkside Pizza, Naples, Hot Tomatoes, and Ivy Noodle. **There are so many places.**"

"**New Haven is famous for pizza**, so there are a bunch of those types of places. Gourmet Heaven is great too; it is open for 24 hours, and there's pretty much anything you could ask for. It's like a convenience store/grocery store, and there's a buffet and someone who makes sandwiches. It's an awesome place for late-night snacks!"

"There are tons of food places on the streets around campus, and no taxi is ever necessary. Yorkside Pizza, Ivy Noodle, Thai Taste . . . the list goes on and on. There are **lots of ethnic** Thai, Chinese, Japanese, Ethiopian, and Italian places plus organic food type places, too. There are expensive places like Hot Tomatoes if you really want them."

"New Haven has an amazing food scene! For every budget, there is a restaurant that has great food. The upscale, atmospheric restaurants with fabulous food include Zinc, Roomba, and Miso. For fantastic pizza, try BAR—they also brew their own beer on premises—or the infamous Wooster Square pizzerias: Sally's and Pepe's. Chapel Street has Thai restaurants across from each other, as well as Rainbow Café for the informal BYOB crowd. **Naples has cheap pizza to go by the slice** but does not serve liquor anymore. Wonderful Indian, Ethiopian, Malaysian, and Japanese eateries also line the streets."

The College Prowler Take
ON OFF-CAMPUS DINING

Sometimes, you might want to get away from the Yale atmosphere or catch a meal between dining hall hours. Students agree there are many reasonably priced places within walking distance from Yale, particularly for pizza, Thai (Thai Taste is best), or Indian food. If you feel like taking a longer walk or a cab ride, New Haven has the two "best" pizza places in America—Pepe's and Sally's—less than a block away from each other. Conduct an independent taste test to choose your favorite. And if your parents are in town or you have a special date, there are many pricier options such as Caffé Adulis (French and Ethiopian cuisine), Scoozi (fine Italian food), and Roomba (Latin fusion).

If ethnic food is your thing, New Haven will be like food heaven, but if your palate is a bit more sedate or if you like fast food, it is a little more difficult to find good food. Because Yale favors little independent restaurants, there are very few fast food places in the area. In addition, while there are lots of little burger places, there are few options for the diner crowd. (Don't be fooled by Tandoor. While it looks like a diner on the outside, it is actually an Indian restaurant!) However, there is so much good ethnic food to choose from, hopefully your tastebuds will evolve!

The College Prowler™ Grade on

Off-Campus Dining: B+

A high Off-Campus Dining grade implies that off-campus restaurants are affordable, accessible, and worth visiting. Other factors include the variety of cuisine and the availability of alternative options (vegetarian, vegan, Kosher, etc.).

Campus Housing

The Lowdown
ON CAMPUS HOUSING

Undergraduates Living On-Campus:
86%

Number of Dormitories:
20

Room Types:
Suites—Students live in singles or doubles that surround a main common room.

Singles—Student has their own private room, but there is no common room.

Note: There are no private bathrooms.

Best Dorms:
Saybrook, Berkeley, Branford, Timothy Dwight

Worst Dorms:
Trumbull, Calhoun

Bed Type:
Twin extra-long

Available for Rent:
Mini refrigerators

Cleaning Service?
In public areas only (i.e., bathrooms, hallways, laundry rooms, etc.)

You Get:
Bed, dresser, desk, basic cable, Internet access, phone line with voicemail.

Did You Know?

The residential college system is the foundation of Yale's social structure, fostering a sense of community and creating a vibrant social and intellectual environment on a more manageable scale.

Students are randomly assigned to their residential colleges. However, if one of your relatives was/is in a particular residential college, you can choose to be or not to be assigned to that college.

All freshman, except those in Silliman and Timothy Dwight, live in freshman dorms on Old Campus their first year. Although you are housed with freshman from your college, you will have greater opportunity to interact with other colleges.

Students Speak Out

ON CAMPUS HOUSING

"You don't have much choice over where you're living; you're randomly assigned to a college freshman year, and you live there all four years."

"They assign you to one of 12 residential colleges—it's like your home for the next four years. **Each college is like a little community**, so they have their own master (a professor who lives there and is responsible for ensuring good social life) and a dean (a professor responsible for overseeing academic matters). The houses also contain a dining hall, computer cluster, kitchen, TV room, and more. You also play intramural sports for your college and participate in special house events."

"My dorm this year was superb. Durfee is on Old Campus; it's an excellent, excellent dorm with huge windows and a great view of Old Campus for all sorts of activities. Dorms, in general, are really good. **Morse's dorm rooms are also huge**. Other dorms are not as huge, and you might not get singles until later on, but you get other perks, as well, for being in that college."

"The dorms are generally really nice—some more than others. There are 12 residential colleges, and **you're assigned to one randomly**. Freshman year, you'll be on Old Campus unless you're in Silliman or TD. All the dorms on Old Campus are nice except for Lanman-Wright—those rooms are a little small, but they're in a great location. They have been renovating each of the colleges—one per year. They've renovated four now, and those are obviously the nicest—Saybrook, Branford, Berkeley, and TD."

"I consider the college housing system one of Yale's most important assets. Which college you end up in isn't really that important. My college house is usually considered one of the 'ugly' ones, but I've had a wonderful experience with the dean, master, and most importantly, the students. There are about 100 students per year in each college, so over the course of your college years at Yale you get to know them pretty well. Since most people at Yale are busy doing lots of different activities, **it's really nice to have a home base of 'dorm friends'** that are always familiar faces in the dining hall, even if you don't spend all of your time with them."

"All the dorms have their perks. There are either small rooms with good location or awesome rooms off in the corner. A lot have been renovated. I was in Bingham; **it has a huge tower for one entryway** and nine stories! It has an elevator and an 'off-limits' roof with an amazing view—we had barbecues up there!"

The College Prowler Take
ON CAMPUS HOUSING

Most students agree that Yale's residential college system provides students a place to live and learn that surpasses any other dorm experience. By combining social activities, extracurriculars, and academics, the residential colleges eventually begin to feel like home for students during the four years they are at Yale. Each college is a microcosm of the University, creating the feel of a small college within a larger institution. The residential colleges are beautiful on the outside, mostly Gothic structures, but some are Georgian and have a modern outward appearance.

On the inside, however, many colleges are in dire need of renovations—frequent power outages, plumbing problems, and more. Most students live in suites with three to 12 students, although there are some singles. The suites have a common room and usually many doubles. Due to housing crunches, many of these doubles are supposed to be singles, so living quarters can be really tight. Some dorms were recently renovated, however. These include Berkeley, Branford, Saybrook, and Timothy Dwight. Unfortunately, you can't choose your dorm because students are randomly assigned to colleges. But, in the end, most students are happy. When you look around at your college courtyards, sometimes you can't help but be amazed—"I live here!?!"

The College Prowler™ Grade on

Campus Housing: A-

A high Campus Housing grade indicates that dorms are clean, well-maintained, and spacious. Other determining factors include variety of dorms, proximity to classes, and social atmosphere.

Off-Campus Housing

The Lowdown
ON OFF-CAMPUS HOUSING

Undergrads in Off-Campus Housing:
14%

Average Rent for a Studio Apartment:
$700/month

Average Rent for a 1BR Apartment:
$850/month

Average Rent for a 2BR Apartment:
$1,100/month

Popular Areas:
Chapel Street, Broadway, Science Hill

Best Time to Look for a Place:
Spring semester

For Assistance Contact:
University Properties
rental.feedback@yale.edu

Students Speak Out
ON CAMPUS HOUSING

"It depends on how much you want to spend. Some apartments are right across from dorms, some are four or more blocks away."

"There are lots of people who live off campus, and **it seems pretty convenient to me**. I personally like on-campus housing because it's more of a central social space. But if you plan to live away from campus, it's pretty easy to find a nice space that's nearby."

"Off-campus housing is pretty convenient. There are some houses and apartments that are popular spots. **Most people stay on campus**, since the housing is generally really nice."

"You will not want off-campus housing. On-campus housing is excellent, and residential college life is at the center of the Yale experience. If you are not a part of residential college life, **you will be more isolated** from fellow students."

"Housing off campus is **abundant but pricey**. The closer to Yale and New Haven, the more expensive or potentially dangerous is can be at night. It's better if you can get a group together that you can share a place. I believe that a lot of places offer student pricing or have places reserved. The more people you have, the better things are in terms of expenses."

"A lot of my friends think it is worth it to live off campus, and I love their places—most live in the Chapel Street area, or on High Street. It's not that expensive, and **you can get huge apartments**, but I wanted to be on campus because I like the college atmosphere and the camaraderie of living with my class. Plus, it's nice to pad down to brunch in PJs and slippers on the weekends and to have laundry right downstairs. We have our whole lives to be grown-up and live in apartments. Why not take advantage of this perfect little bubble tailored exactly to our needs? None of us will ever have the chance again!"

The College Prowler Take
ON OFF-CAMPUS HOUSING

While students admit that off-campus housing is available and close to campus, most choose to stay on campus for all four years. Because students must house on campus until their junior year, by the time they have the opportunity to move, they have made connections to their college and enjoy the social scene it creates. The decision to move off campus means a separation from the Yale community. You don't have Ethernet, and you do have more responsibility.

That being said, those who choose to move off campus are usually very happy with their decision. Yale basically owns all the property around campus, including apartments, so you deal directly with them. This makes things easier and more organized (especially if you are on financial aid). Decisions are made by lottery. In the end, everyone who applies gets an apartment, usually one of their top three choices. It is a personal decision to live off campus or on. The pluses of off-campus living include no more meal plan, more privacy, and a break from the academic environment.

The College Prowler™ Grade on

Off-Campus Housing: B

A high grade in Off-Campus Housing indicates that apartments are of high quality, close to campus, affordable, and easy to secure.

YALE UNIVERSITY

The Lowdown
ON DIVERSITY

White: 62%

Asian American: 14%

African American: 8%

Native American: 1%

Hispanic: 7%

International: 8%

Out-of-State: 91%

Students Speak Out
ON DIVERSITY

"New Haven is like a mini New York at times. It's very much the melting pot, although Mediterranean cultures seem to be predominant here, as well as the Irish. For the most part, everything is just mixed."

"Geographically, ethnically, and politically, we have a great representation from all states and countries. **I have lots of international friends**. It's great! There are people with different sexual orientations, personalities, ideas, life experiences, talents, and even ages. There are even students here who will graduate at 19! I guess it's not only important that a campus is diverse, but it's also important that there is acceptance, tolerance, and interaction between groups."

"The 'Yale part' of New Haven is quite radically different from the 'New Haven part' of New Haven. Basically, the Yale campus and immediate surroundings are primarily wealthy and white. **The rest of New Haven is actually quite poor**, and it's primarily people of color. It's quite an astonishing separation."

"It's extremely diverse. One of the best things about Yale is the diversity and open-mindedness. This is another good reason to be in the residential colleges—**you will meet the most amazing people from all walks of life**, all cultures, and all backgrounds."

"I think Yale is a diverse place, but that **diversity isn't always apparent**. There's a noticeable tendency for students to self-segregate a little bit according to racial/ethnic/religious background. I don't mean that everyone has friends exactly like themselves, but there is a strong sense of shared cultural identity fostered by clubs and other programs that has a visible effect on the friendships that people form when they come here."

"Very diverse. I feel about as exotic as white bread—and I'm half Polish, half Puerto Rican! However, despite the open vibe and the conspicuous diversity, **de facto segregation is still inevitable in some regards**. There are definitely cliques of Hispanic kids and black kids, as well as Jewish cliques. But maybe that's human nature, and I think that Yale is a pretty amazing place to find a good mix of all different types of people with all different types of interests."

The College Prowler Take
ON DIVERSITY

Yale prides itself on its diversity and the freedom of expression on campus, and most students agree that the student body is diverse racially, ethnically, religiously, and geographically. This wide spectrum of people transforms Yale into a dynamic microcosm of the world, where students are exposed to an unlimited amount of perspectives. These opinions are heard everyday at discussions during dinner, and seen on campus in the form of protests and activist group events. Not only does this diversity make student life more exciting, it also makes classes much more interesting. Everyone brings in a totally new perspective, so that classes become more like heated debates than boring lectures.

In addition, every element of the student body is represented in clubs and associations. Here, new students can meet members of the Yale community with similar backgrounds. Unfortunately, students note that while the campus is diverse, sometimes people stay in factions or cliques rather than branching out.

The College Prowler™ Grade on

Diversity: B

A high grade in Diversity indicates that ethnic minorities and international students have a notable presence on campus and that students of different economic backgrounds, religious beliefs, and sexual preferences are well-represented.

Guys & Girls

The Lowdown
ON GUYS & GIRLS

Women Undergrads: 49%

Men Undergrads: 51%

Birth Control Available?
Yes, you can find it at Yale University Health Services.

Social Scene
The residential college system at Yale makes it easy to make connections between students. By transforming Yale into smaller social units, the colleges make interactions less overwhelming and intimidating, and by sponsoring social activities (like study breaks, dances, etc.), they provide opportunities to make new friends. In addition, campus organizations provide a place to meet people of similar interests.

Hookups or Relationships?
Because students at Yale are so focused on their academics and activities, hookups are more convenient and more popular than relationships. However, some people do develop these random encounters into serious relationships.

Dress Code

There is no official style at Yale. Instead, everybody does his or her own thing, from punk to trendy to preppy. The only time there is a more uniform look is during finals, when most people walk around in their pajamas or sweats.

Best Place to Meet Guys/Girls

At Yale, students study hard and party hard, so most people meet either in academic settings or at bars, clubs, and parties. Classes and clubs provide a setting in which you can slowly get to know someone and become friends first. As a bonus, you know off the bat that you have something in common, such as a love for Russian literature or similar political beliefs.

While academic connections often flourish into serious relationships, students meet each other at bars, clubs, and parties. In drunken hazes, students dance, kiss, and sometimes go home with each other, but these hookups rarely develop further, and often result in awkward sightings in the future.

Top Three Places to Find Hotties:

1. Cross-campus
2. Toad's Place
3. Naples

Top Places to Hook Up:

1. The Stacks
2. Toad's Place
3. Risk
4. BAR
5. The Frats

Students Speak Out
ON GUYS & GIRLS

"I'm not wealthy, and I was afraid of that infamous 'Ivy league/private school atmosphere' of over-privileged kids, but everyone at Yale is so nice."

"The guys are very nice, and chivalrous, too. People hold the door for each other all the time! And when I started doing that in other places, people sort of stared at me. There are many hot guys, but you have to make sure they're straight. **The gay/lesbian/bi/trans scene is out there and open**. The girls are also very nice. Are girls hot? I wouldn't really know; my friends who are lesbians are happy here. I think the people here are the friendliest, most amazingly smart, and modest people ever. I think we convert many pre-frosh into coming to Yale with just how great, open and friendly our people are!"

"All the guys seem hot at first, but then it sort of dies down. It depends on your standards, though. Most of them are really nice, fun, and cool. I love all the friends I've made at school—they're great. For the most part, everyone is very friendly and easy to get along with. Also, **people aren't usually too cliquish**. You know how girls can be kind of catty? The girls at Yale totally aren't at all. You can walk into any party or room and make new friends."

"I'm being perfectly honest; the common rhetoric is that the dating scene at Yale stinks. Some people do date, and some do have boyfriends or girlfriends, but mostly, **people like to complain about the dating scene** and say that it's usually more random hookups. I don't know how much this is true. I know a large number of people in every category. As always, there are the hotties, and there are the not-so-hotties. I'd say we're pretty average in the looks department."

"I guess **guys range from 'average' to 'not bad**.' Some are ugly, and some might be hot, though my preference runs towards women. The women fall in the same range, but I would say that, for the most part, they are 'good' to 'hot.' They range from all around the world and in a variety of features. Whatever your preference, I am sure that you won't be disappointed at all."

"It's very hard to come up with a 'typical' Yale guy or girl, but I suppose that's part of the fun of being here. We're probably not significantly hotter or less hot than similar schools. A lot of Yale girls are prettier than they think they are, and are fun and interesting to boot. Yale guys are harder to characterize, but I'd say there is a fair mix of attractive but sometimes dumb jocks, self-conscious and average frat boys, and urbane/sensitive/sophisticated/probably gay other guys. I mean, **we're no Florida State**. But there are some surprisingly beautiful people here."

The College Prowler Take
ON GUYS & GIRLS

Students agree that Yale is a pretty attractive school. While many students do not have the time to put into primping (makeup, clothes selection, shaving), the rumor that beauty is inversely proportional to intelligence is proven wrong at Yale. Not only are many guys and girls hot, they are talented, smart, funny, and interesting to boot.

Unfortunately, Yale students are also busy—too busy to have relationships. Instead, most of them partake in random hookups that occur during drunken blurs. To many, hooking up is just another kind of stress relief. But for those who are looking for love, there is hope. Some students do find real love. Some even get married!

The College Prowler™ Grade on
Guys: B

A high grade for Guys indicates that the male population on campus is attractive, smart, friendly, and engaging, and that the school has a decent ratio of guys to girls.

The College Prowler™ Grade on
Girls: B+

A high grade for Girls not only implies that the women on campus are attractive, smart, friendly, and engaging, but also that there is a fair ratio of girls to guys.

Athletics

The Lowdown
ON ATHLETICS

Athletic Division:
NCAA Division I

Conference:
Ivy League

School Mascot:
Bulldog - Handsome Dan

Fields:
Yale Bowl, Johnson Field, Smillow Field Center, DeWitt Family Field and Baseball Stadium

Men's Varsity Teams:
Baseball
Basketball
Crew
Cross country
Fencing
Football
Golf
Ice Hockey
Lacrosse
Sailing
Soccer
Squash
Swimming
Tennis
Track

Women's Varsity Teams:
Basketball
Crew
Cross country
Fencing
Field Hockey
Golf
Gymnastics
Ice Hockey
Lacrosse
Soccer
Softball
Squash
Swimming
Tennis
Track
Volleyball

YALE UNIVERSITY

Most Popular Sports:
Football, Crew

Overlooked Teams:
Women's Fencing (Yale fencer Sada Jacobson is number one in the world!)

Best Place to Take a Walk:
East Rock State Park

Students Speak Out
ON ATHLETICS

"Varsity sports and intramural [IM] sports are very popular here. If you want to join, definitely go for it!"

"Varsity sports are not that big. Yeah, you can probably make out the jocks because they are always wearing sports gear, sweatpants, and Yale gear. The football game against Harvard is obviously huge. Other than that, it's not that big. We had a good men's basketball season, so that gained some attention. **IM sports depend on your college**. Saybrook and Calhoun try hardcore to win, but others such as Trumbull don't really try."

"Varsity sports are as big as you can expect at an Ivy League school. I am actually on the varsity golf team, and it's definitely growing and improving, but it does not compare to a big state school. When **our basketball team tied for Ivy League champions**, everyone got really excited and pumped up about that. It almost felt like we went to a big basketball school. It was a fun atmosphere."

"Varsity sports are pretty big, but it's not like everyone goes to every game. IM sports are also cool and are played between the residential colleges. **There are club sports, as well**, which are not as rigorous as varsity sports but more intense than the mostly-for-fun IMs. I play a club sport, which is awesome; you need no experience at all."

"No one really cares about stuff like football games, probably because we're not that great of a team—the only thing that seems to get mass support is basketball, lots of people go to the guys' b-ball games. I've actually never been, but I go to the girls' b-ball games a lot to cheer on my roommate. And I've been to a few hockey games, but only to sing the national anthem, so that shouldn't really count. A lot of people play IMs, though. But, in some colleges, they tend to be kind of competitive to the point that **if you're not very good, you don't have that much fun**—that is if you're allowed to play at all. I have had a particularly infuriating Ping-Pong experience, so I've kind of boycotted IMs since then."

"It's all about what you're into. **Varsity is big if we're winning**. Football is always big. Harvard-Yale games are ridiculously fun."

The College Prowler Take
ON ATHLETICS

For a school with such a strong academic reputation, Yale has a pretty strong athletic program. From IMs to varsity sports, Yale offers options for every level of sports enthusiast. Our varsity sports often do reasonably well, and most colleges compete actively in IMs. While not everybody participates in sports, practically everybody comes out for the Yale-Harvard football game, even when it is in Boston. During this one weekend of revelry, the students express their support for the team. However, some students don't even know sports exist—this is Yale after all! Essentially, sports are as important as most other activities at Yale, such as volunteer projects, a cappella, drama, and the school newspaper.

The College Prowler™ Grade on
Athletics: C

A high grade in Athletics indicates that students have school spirit, that sports programs are respected, that games are well-attended, and that intramurals are a prominent part of student life.

The Lowdown
ON NIGHTLIFE

Student Favorites:
Toad's, Alchemy, Risk, Bar, Rudy's, Viva Zapata's

Primary Areas with Nightlife:
Downtown New Haven (Crown Street, Chapel Street)

Bars Close At:
2 a.m.

Cheapest Place to Get a Drink:
Rudy's

Club Crawler

Because most students do not have a car, they are limited to the few clubs around Yale. These include Risk, Alchemy, and the mainstay, Toad's Place.

Alchemy

223 College Street

(203) 777-9400

Alchemy is divided into two sections. One section is a bar/café known for its "conversation menu;" the other section is home to New England's largest dance floor.

This club is one of the few that often hosts international talent.

Friday: Happy Hour, 2 for 1 drinks until 9 p.m.

Risk

230-232 Crown Street

Across the street from Alchemy is Risk, a great place to go next if you are club hopping. Sometimes radio stations such as 105.1FM broadcasts live from the location.

Bar Prowler:

Yalies like to drink. Luckily, Yale is surrounded by a variety of bars ranging from the dive to the upscale.

BAR

254 Crown Street

(203) 485-8924

BAR serves excellent pizza and beer brewed on the premises. On Tuesday and Saturday nights, the dance floor is open.

Rudy's

372 Elm Street

(203) 865-1242

Rudy's is a New Haven Bar not a Yale Bar. There you will get to mix and mingle with the townies and listen to great local bands. At Rudy's you can get a $2 beer and some of the best French fries in New Haven.

What to Do if You're Not 21

Almost every club around Yale holds occasional all-ages nights. And if you want to see a great show, Toad's often has all-ages concerts. But when it comes to underage fun, its best to stick to Yale parties, ranging from the traditional frat fiesta to all-out theme parties (casino night, winter balls, and dance parties).

Students Speak Out
ON NIGHTLIFE

"As for the party scene, I know that Yalies usually party on Thursday, Friday, and Saturday nights."

"The popular clubs are Toad's, Alchemy, Risk, and there are a few more that just opened. **I think Toad's is kind of creepy, though.** It depends what kind of music and dancing you're into."

"I'm a closet fan of frat parties. I know they're gross, but **I inevitably have a great time whenever I go to Beta late-night**. Toad's is also always fun, although not for more than an hour or so—like between 12:30-1:30 a.m. is usually best."

"Toad's is cool. I've never been to Risk or Alchemy, but I hear they're usually fun. And I'm excited to start going to Bar this year with my society, cause **it looks like a relaxed and cozy place to hang and drink**."

"On campus parties are frequented by underclassmen and can be entertaining. **Bars and clubs off campus are more for the older crowd**. Toad's Place is the Saturday night dance party, where people revel in the sketchiness. BAR is the premier Thursday night hangout."

"**People go to Viva's and El Amigo's for chips and margaritas**, Kavanaugh's for rail drinks, and Hot Tomatoes for fancy martinis."

"**Yale parties generally suck**, unless you know the people throwing them. I've only been clubbing once (Alchemy), but I had a good time there."

The College Prowler Take
ON NIGHTLIFE

Starting Thursday night, there are many parties ranging from Fraternity kegs, to room parties, to organized theme balls. The room and frat parties are pretty much comprised of people packed like sardines around a warm keg of cheap beer listening to bad house music. Some people frequent these until they graduate (free alcohol), but many tire of them by their junior year, opting instead to go to bars or clubs or stay home with friends. While these parties can be disappointing, Yale is notorious for its theme parties. In fact, Yale's "Casino Night" made the *Rolling Stone*'s top 10 best college parties, and the Lesbian/Gay/Bisexual/Transgender Cooperative (The Co-op) holds several dances a year (for both straight and gay students) that draw not only a tremendous Yale crowd but also attract people from other universities and the local New Haven area. As for clubs, students are limited to a few places near campus, most notably Toad's Place.

Many students come to college with the idea that they will work until their cerebral cortexes bleed, and party until they don't know who they are. At Yale, you can go out every night or you can choose to never go out, but no one will hold your hand. Most soon figure out that an intermediate approach to partying is best—the "work hard, play hard" mantra can be applied here. Just know that, at Yale, there are many social outlets to choose from, so you certainly won't go bored, no matter how socially inept you are.

The College Prowler™ Grade on
Nightlife: B-

A high grade in Nightlife indicates that there are many bars and clubs in the area that are easily accessible and affordable. Other determining factors include the number of options for the under-21 crowd and the prevalence of house parties.

Greek Life

The Lowdown
ON GREEK LIFE

Number of Fraternities:
8

Number of Sororities:
3

Fraternities on Campus:
Sigma Chi, Alpha Delta Phi, Delta Kappa, Beta Theta Pi, Zeta Psi, Sigma Alpha Epsiolon, Sigma Nu, Lambsa Upsilon Lamda

Sororities on Campus:
Kappa Alpha Theta, Kappa Kappa Gamma, Pi Beta Phi

Other Greek Organizations:
Pan-Hellenic Council

Did You Know?

Delta Kappa Epsilon is famous for Butthole Week in which its new pledges walk around campus, unwashed, performing degrading tasks.

Students Speak Out
ON GREEK LIFE

"There's no real Greek life at Yale. Social activities mostly center around clubs and residential colleges."

"We have fraternities and some sororities, but most of the time, you probably wouldn't even know they existed. **They do throw popular parties at their houses**. Some have houses, some don't. But there's just so much to do on and off campus that Greek life is insignificant. In fact, I think that the a cappella scene sort of replaces that. If you're looking for parties, there are plenty of parties that are advertised by signs or by e-mail that are not Greek. Social life is really what you make of it."

"Sororities are almost nonexistent; you'll hardly know anyone in one. As for frats, they're bigger if you want them to be. There are maybe four houses that consistently throw parties, but **it tends to be the same crowd at these parties**. If it's your thing, it's really cool, if not, there is plenty more to do around here."

"The Greek system is kind of small and doesn't dominate the social scene. I am actually in a sorority, but **it's very low-key** and just another social outlet. It's nice, though, since everyone is very supportive and fun. The fraternities are mostly associated with certain sports. DKE is mostly football and baseball players. There is always a frat party on Thursday, Friday, and Saturday, and sometimes they have big parties with themes and fun drinks."

"Greek life really isn't that big here. There are lots of sororities and fraternities, but they don't dominate. They do throw a bunch of parties, and one frat has a weekly party—this drinking thing—and another is known for Tang, its **annual drinking competition**. Everyone loves it."

"Greek life does not dominate the social scene; it is a minority, although **you can find 'Greeks' if you look**. It took me until my senior year to make a friend who happened to be into the Greek scene and attend a few parties. There's definitely no pressure to be a part of that, although there are some nice sorority and fraternity houses near campus."

The College Prowler Take
ON GREEK LIFE

With the exception of a few frat parties, the Greek scene at Yale is almost nonexistent. For those few who are involved, it is mostly seen as another social activity, a place where you can hang out, and find some support. The fraternity scene is more prominent than the sororities (there are eight fraternities, but only three sororities). This is mostly because they serve as clubs for Yale's varsity athletes.

While the Greek scene is very small, most Yalies see the a cappella groups as a replacement. Like most fraternity and sorority pledges, the singing groups' potential members rush and go through an initiation. These groups are together a lot for rehearsals and tours, so they become a kind of family of their own.

The College Prowler™ Grade on
Greek Life: D+

A high grade in Greek Life indicates that sororities and fraternities are not only present, but also active on campus. Other determining factors include the variety of houses available and the respect the Greek community receives from the rest of the campus.

Drug Scene

The Lowdown
ON DRUG SCENE

Most Prevalent Drugs on Campus:
Alcohol, marijuana, stimulants (Ritalin, Adderall, cocaine), ecstasy

Liquor-Related Referrals:
2

Liquor-Related Arrests:
0

Drug-Related Referrals:
1

Drug-Related Arrests:
3

Drug Counseling Programs:
Substance Abuse Counseling (Mental Hygiene Department)

Students Speak Out
ON DRUG SCENE

"I know people who smoke marijuana, but I can't comment on anything harder than that. The drug scene is not very big around here."

"I'm not a part of it, so **I wouldn't know a thing about it**. The pot smokers have to get their pot somewhere, but I don't know where. They get it somehow, so it must exist."

"**The drug scene isn't huge**, but you've definitely got your group of stoners and druggies. I feel like few people do things beyond smoking weed, though. I know some people who do coke occasionally, but that's all I know."

"**Pot is easy to get** and easy to smoke. That's about my level of involvement in the drug scene, I don't know about anything else."

"I guess as in any place, if you're looking for drugs, you'll find them. **I've never been pressured** or exposed to them."

"Some people at Yale use drugs. I'm just guessing here, but I think most Yale students either have never used drugs, or have used pot socially a few times. **There are some more serious drug-users**, of course. But, even among those, I think you often find very serious students who do great academic work and contribute to the community here. I think the quality of the experience you have here has very little to do with whether or not you choose to use drugs."

The College Prowler Take
ON DRUG SCENE

The drug scene on campus is surprisingly prevalent. Many of the students have the money to support a thriving drug habit and the stress to warrant one. Furthermore, the administration is very lax about their drug policies and punishments. The most popular drugs on campus are marijuana, which seems easily attained if you want it, and stimulants (cocaine, speed, and Ritalin), which are becoming more and more prevalent as study drugs.

However, while the drug scene exists, it is easily avoided. It is generally present within certain cliques. Overall, If you don't interact with that element, you might never even encounter drugs on campus. Students at Yale do not have to succomb to "peer pressure."

The College Prowler™ Grade on

Drug Scene: B+

A high grade on Drug Scene indicates that drugs are not a noticeable part of campus life; drug use is not visible, and no pressure to use them seems to exist.

Campus Strictness

The Lowdown
ON CAMPUS STRICTNESS

What Are You Most Likely to Get Caught Doing on Campus?

Drinking underage

Public urination or indecency

Parking illegally

Making too much noise in your dorm

Downloading copyrighted materials

Sending unsolicited e-mail (spam)

Running around on rooftops of buildings

Having candles and incense sticks in your dorm

Students Speak Out
ON CAMPUS STRICTNESS

"It's not very strict. The Yale police are there to basically protect you from the New Haven police. Drinking is pretty big, although if you don't want to, there is really no pressure."

"Basically, Yale's policy is 'we know you're going to drink, so please do it safely and on campus.' They pay for kegs for the quad parties—it's amazing. **The only strict rule is 'no kegs on Old Campus**.' But we would walk by with our beer and liquor in front of the police, and it would be fine. They just don't want you being obvious about it on freshman campus, but you can walk around with it in the colleges, no problem."

"If you need medical attention, there is the campus facility whose policy is that as long as you are out by 8 a.m., **it will not go on your record**. If you stay later, your dean and master are notified. Of the few kids I know who have had to do that, none of them have stayed past 8 a.m., so it's an awesome policy."

"I would say that the **campus police aren't very strict on drinking and drugs**, or at least they're not as strict as they could be. There's a lot of drinking on campus, and I do know a few pot smokers, but I wouldn't want to jump to conclusions about how well they're doing their job. Maybe we just slip by."

"The campus police are not strict at all. You really can't get in trouble for any of that. Yale just doesn't want you to die or get sick. **They usually never break up parties** or anything. When my friend who goes to a state school visited, she was shocked at how the alcohol was roaming around so freely. It's cool, though, because you don't have to worry about getting in trouble for having some fun."

"Yale really has no big policy against drinking. My college actually had a cookout, and there was a keg and wine. Yalies, for the most part, are responsible, so the school doesn't really have to worry about anything. **There's also a place where you can go if you think you or your friend has had too much to drink**—the Undergrad Department of Health—and they take care of you, and your parents don't know. Your parents only find out if you get really sick and, for whatever reason, have to go to the Yale-New Haven hospital."

"**You can get away with a lot here**, and I think students tend to forget that. Yale police will certainly shut down rowdy parties, but it's more unusual for them to start arresting kids for drinking, or getting warrants to search for drugs. I think there's some degree of understanding that college students will break these laws no matter what, but the police will get involved in the event that these activities [parties, sporting events, or protests] are disturbing other students."

The College Prowler Take

ON CAMPUS STRICTNESS

As long as illegal things aren't done recklessly and publicly, the campus police are willing to look the other way. Police do not usually raid houses unless there are noise complaints or fighting. Underage drinking is ignored by the administration, which even allows alcohol at public social events within the college. Yale treats its students as adults who are capable of taking care of themselves and making wise decisions.

Essentially, the campus police follow the spirit of the law not the letter of the law; they care only about the students' safety. In fact, the campus police officers often protect students from getting caught by the "real" police. For example, if a student is walking down the street with an open beer can—this is illegal in New Haven—campus police will warn him/her not to. Students have been known to "smoke" right in the courtyard of their college. Most students applaud this relaxed approach and feel comfortable and safe despite the leniency.

The College Prowler™ Grade on

Campus Strictness: A

A high Campus Strictness grade implies an overall lenient atmosphere; police and RAs are fairly tolerant, and the administration's rules are flexible.

Parking & Transportation

The Lowdown

ON PARKING & TRANSPORTATION

Student Parking Lot?
Yes

Freshman Allowed to Park?
Yes

Approximate Parking Permit Cost:
$550-1000 per year

Ways to Get Around Campus:

Daytime Campus Shuttle
7:20 a.m.-6:00 p.m.
Monday through Friday

Nighttime Minibus
6:00 p.m.-7:30 a.m., (203) 432-6330

Students Speak Out
ON PARKING & TRANSPORTATION

"Parking is not abundant at Yale, so I would not bring a car. From what I have seen, there really is no need for a car—everything is pretty close."

"Most freshmen don't have cars, not even many upperclassmen do. **Everything you need is within walking distance**. A cab to the train station is four bucks, so New York City and Boston are easily accessible. Plus, parking for the year is really expensive."

"I don't have a car, nor do I know how to drive, but I do know people who have cars, and **it seems pretty simple**. There are parking lots right on campus, and they're very convenient. It looks easy enough to park."

"**You want to get a spot in a garage**—that's the most efficient way to have a car. You can get info online if you want official Yale places, or you can just shop around with other garages on campus."

"Ha! Can't say I've used New Haven public transportation more than once. **Can't say I'd use it again**."

"Public Transportation is **a pain in the behind**. The bus never comes when you think it's supposed to. It is always easier to just walk rather than wait indefinitely. There seems to be a new trolley type thing, but I have yet to figure out exactly what it is or where it goes."

"You can basically walk everywhere you need. I think I took a bus once in the past three years, and **it was okay**."

The College Prowler Take
ON PARKING

While on-campus parking permits are available to students, most do not have a car or think one is necessary. Most places are within walking distance, and most social activities are contained on-campus. And New York and Boston are just a train ride away. However, if you are the type of person who easily gets bored in one location, or who likes to explore new places as a hobby, it could be helpful to have a car.

The College Prowler™ Grade on
Parking: C-

A high grade in this section indicates that parking is both available and affordable, and that parking enforcement isn't overly severe.

The College Prowler Take
ON TRANSPORTATION

While most places are within walking distance, there are also many options for getting around elsewhere. Most students prefer Yale Transit, which will take students to destinations on campus and in New Haven (most conveniently, the train station), and it's free and easy to use. However, if you need to go somewhere off the beaten path, you can take the city bus or even a cab. Beware—taxi service is often unreliable.

The College Prowler™ Grade on
Transportation: C-

A high grade for Transportation indicates that campus buses, public buses, cabs, and rental cars are readily-available and affordable. Other determining factors include proximity to an airport and the necessity of transportation.

Overall Experience

Students Speak Out
ON OVERALL EXPERIENCE

"I've read somewhere that Yale was described as 'intense,' and it really is. There's so much to do here that you really have to sit down and think about what to do the next day to make the most of your time."

"I love Yale! **There's just so much to do here**. I have great friends, inspirational classes, and great photos to prove it. My friends all love Yale—they're all down-to-earth, quirky people who have exceptional talents and interesting perspectives on everything. I've had so many long discussions—about everything— that ran late into the night. You will meet new people every day, really nice ones. You won't believe it when your freshman year is over so quickly!"

"I've had a great experience at school, both socially and academically. **I definitely couldn't imagine being anywhere else**. I think there is a place for everyone at Yale, since the University offers so much and is so diverse. We're not completely cutthroat either. It is much more laid-back than some Ivy League schools, but it's still competitive. There's a good balance. And the people are great. You'll meet so many interesting, fun, quirky, and cool people. Everyone loves the student body. You'll get a great academic experience, but the people you meet and your friends will complete the entire experience."

"I enjoyed aspects of Yale. **A lot depends on which program you are interested in** and what your study interests are. Some programs are great. You will find that there is a certain level of depersonalization present at any large university. I came from a small liberal arts high school and was used to a lot of individual personal attention—you will most likely have to fight for that."

"I like practically every single person I've met at Yale. They're all very smart, of course, but they're also down-to-earth. We all understand that there's something bigger than ourselves, and that we're not the center of the universe. There's more to life than studying all the time and trying to knock others down. All I've heard from Yalies is praise. **I personally adore the school**, and I would recommend that anyone who gets in should go here."

"I love Yale, and I haven't for a moment wished I were somewhere else. Sure, Yale has problems, just as every school does, but **I'm grateful for the dozens of fascinating and truly talented friends I've made**, the inspiring professors I've worked with, the opportunities I've been offered, and the incredible personal development that I've experienced here. I'm a much different, much better person than I was three years ago. I consider myself very lucky to go here, and I wouldn't trade that privilege for anything."

The College Prowler Take
ON OVERALL EXPERIENCE

Students are enthusiastic about their love for Yale. Some even claim that they have never been happier in their lives. Although students often complain about their piles of work or their small dorm rooms, in the end, all these problems fade into the background of the overall picture. Instead, all they see are the gorgeous buildings, amazing classes, brilliant faculty, and endless lists of cool things to do.

When it comes down to it, however, students are most in love with the people they have had the opportunity to meet. Students at Yale are smart, down-to-earth, dynamic, fun, interesting, and amazingly talented. When they get together, they have fascinating discussions and produce incredible work. At Yale, you have the opportunity to grow academically and personally. Most Yalies agree that this personal development is the most important and rewarding part of their college experience.

The Inside Scoop

The Lowdown
ON THE INSIDE SCOOP

Yale Slang:

Know the slang, know the school. The following is a list of things you really need to know before coming to Yale. The more of these words you know, the better off you'll be.

Blue Book - This Bible of class listings and descriptions is your shopping guide to academics.

Bursar - A method of charging bookstore goods, food, and miscellaneous Yale services to your ID card. The Bursar and your parents should become good friends because this bill gets sent home!

CCL - Cross Campus Library. This is the underground home of weenie bins and lots of '70s furniture. Almost as popular a place for socializing as for studying. Also, late hours mean lots of snoozing studiers.

Couch Duty - There are two people in your bedroom and you are not one of them. Guess where you get to sleep? Also known as "sexile."

D.S. - Directed Studies. Also known as Directed Suicide and Deep Sh*t. This is a freshman program that comprises three of your classes every semester (Philosophy, Literature, and History/Politics). Now when someone mentions Kant, you can say in all honesty, "Metaphysics of Morals? I hated Metaphysics of Morals!"

DUH - Acronym still used to refer to the old Department of University Health, even though they changed the name to University Health Services about 20 years ago. Have a stomach ache? According to these professionals, either you're pregnant or you're probably pregnant.

Durfee - The Durfee Sweet Shoppe. This Bursar-billable coffee and snack shop is located in the basement of Durfee on Old Campus. A great place to score late-night snacks.

Gut - An easy class that takes the pressure off a busy schedule and fulfills distributional requirements. See "Listening to Music," better known as "Clapping for Credit."

Legacy - A Yalie who is here because his or her parent or other miscellaneous relative went here.

Machine City - A subterranean oasis connecting CCL and Sterling. It's a common place for study groups and TA meetings, and is home to vending machines that fulfill your wildest junk-food fantasies.

Science Hill - The location of most science classes. A half-mile from Old Campus, this is God's way of punishing physics and bio-chemistry majors who would otherwise get no exercise.

Shopping Period - During the first two weeks of classes, Yale gives you the chance to preview potential classes without any commitment. Why do only four classes of reading when you can do 15? Still, it is a good opportunity to make sure your calculus teacher speaks English.

Spring Fling - During this campus-wide party the weekend before reading week, students blow off steam basking in the sun and listening to famous bands like Rusted Root or Wyclef.

Swing Space - Officially Boyd Hall. This relatively new dorm temporarily houses students while their colleges undergo renovations.

Weenie Bin - Similar to isolation tanks, the weenie bins are study carrels in CCL.

The Whale - Purportedly a hockey rink, but it looks like a whale.

Urban Legends

The movie *The Skulls* is based on Yale's secret society, Skull and Bones (whose past members include President George W. Bush and his father).

The basic idea for Federal Express was submitted as a term paper at Yale . . . and only got a C.

Campus pundits Porn 'n Chicken (a club devoted to watching pornography and eating fried chicken) made the first Ivy League pornographic film. *The Staxxx* is set in Sterling Memorial Library's Stacks (home to millions of dusty books), and it has a cast comprised of Yale students.

When the Vanderbilt family donated the money to fund the building of Vanderbilt Hall on Old Campus, it was stipulated that whenever a relative came to be educated at Yale, he would stay in the luxurious "Vanderbilt Suite." However, in 1969 it was decided that the castle-like hall would house and protect the first class of female Yale students—against the siege, so to speak, of Yale men's advances. As it turned out, though, that very same year a Vanderbilt descendent attending the college somehow received word of the old "Vanderbilt Suite Clause" and threatened to take the University to court unless he and a friend were given permission to live among the newly-admitted young women. Permission was finally granted, and the two came to be known as the "happiest young men at Yale."

School Spirit

School spirit is strong at Yale. When you walk down the street, you see students parading in Yale clothing and accessories. This might be because there are few clothing stores near campus, but it still creates a sense of solidarity amongst the student body. Students are proud of the Yale name, and they are willing to defend it to the death against Harvard and Princeton. This becomes most apparent during the Harvard-Yale weekend. In preparation for this surge of school spirit, students buy shirts saying insults such as "Harvard sucks, and Princeton doesn't matter," and they party for their school. Alumni flock, and practically the entire student body goes to the game to cheer the football team to victory in New Haven or Boston.

Traditions

Yale is a school steeped in tradition. In fact, there is a sense of the people who have come before you in almost every activity, from walking down the street to drinking a cup at Mory's. These traditions become most apparent during age-old ceremonies like Commencement, and Class Day. However, Yale's real tradition is having traditions create traditions. For example, during Class Day (the ceremony the day before Commencement) it is tradition for students to smoke a special tobacco blend out of a clay pipe and to wave good-bye to Yale with a white handkerchief. Today, students do this while wearing the silliest hats imaginable. Now, this is a new tradition.

Things I Wish I Knew Before Coming to Yale:

- During the winter, New Haven can get colder than you ever thought possible . . . ever!
- No matter how much you like a class, odds are you won't go if it is before 9:30 a.m.
- Don't pack too much. You do not need your entire ballerina figurine collection! But you will need lots of lamps (Yale has very bad overhead lighting), a shower basket, rugs, posters, and lots of underwear (no one wants to laundry!).
- Yale students aren't that intimidating.
- Don't buy sheets or lamps from Yale. In the end, they are rip-offs.
- Most importantly, you can do anything you want at Yale. If you want a class that is restricted to juniors and seniors, plead your case and beg if you have to, your enthusiasm will win you a spot. If you want to travel abroad but you do not have the money, just apply for all grants or ask financial aid creatively.

Tips to Succeed at Yale:

- Explore different majors before committing to your (parents') dream of becoming a doctor/lawyer/engineer. There are so many options out there, and Yale is a great place to discover some of them.
- Don't take on too much. As freshman, the temptation is to do everything because everything seems so darn cool. But, in the end, no matter how cool all 15 of your extracurricular activities are, eventually they will seem like the bane of your existence, when compared to academics.
- Try to quickly learn what type of class structure suits you best. Do you like large lectures, or do you crave personal interaction with your professors? Do you want to talk or listen? Do like to take tests or write papers?
- See your freshman counselor as the resource he/she is. This senior knows the ins and outs of Yale and can give you advice on everything from good classes to take, to where to take your parents when they come. They also remember what it is like to be a freshman and truly want to help you through it.
- Go to Masters' Teas. These opportunities to spend the afternoon drinking tea and eating little sandwiches while listening to great and famous people speak is invaluable. Some recent guests include singer/songwriter Carole King, actor Bronson Pinchot, writer Tobias Wolff, and political commentator Arianna Huffington.
- Don't party too much. Freedom is great, but just because you can go out and get wasted every night does not mean you should.
- That said, don't study all the time. Yale is a strong academic school, but it is also so much more. What you can learn about life is often just as valuable as what you can learn about astronomy. Remember, there is only so much information your brain can retain at once.

The Lowdown
ON FINDING A JOB OR INTERNSHIP

Career Center Resources & Services

The Career Center provides individual counseling appointments, a career resource library, different workshops, panels, career fairs, practice Interviews, on-campus interview programs, resume referral programs, as well as internship/summer job listings and graduate/professional school information.

The Lowdown

Finding a summer job, internship, or career (gasp!) can be an incredibly overwhelming experience, especially when you have no idea what you want to or can do. This is where Undergraduate Career Services steps in. While they can't do the deciding for you, they offer a variety of resources—from personal guidance appointments, to access to job databases, to career fairs and on-campus interview programs. There is no reason to struggle alone; they are there to help.

Advice

Although as competitive students, we are eager to use every opportunity to add padding to our resume, it is important to take some time off to travel or just relax. So many students choose to do a painful unpaid internship their summer after freshman year, but the benefits are sometimes outweighed by a summer of suffering. As a freshman, it is very difficult to get a worthwhile internship (most good ones are reserved for sophomores or higher), so you may end up standing by a photocopier all summer without being paid or learning. This early experience is unexceptional in the long run. Most are better off resting or traveling.

However, once it is time to decide your real future post-graduation, it is important to start at the beginning of senior year (if not earlier), when most early applications for jobs and graduate schools are accepted. Also, it is important to pursue all possible opportunities during that year. For example, if you are pretty sure you want to go to law school, it is still a good idea to apply for a few jobs. It is amazing how many people change their minds during this time; the closer you are to the reality of a decision, the less or more appealing it might seem.

Major Alumni Events

The biggest events for alumni are the Yale-Harvard football game and class reunions. The game takes place usually the weekend before fall recess and alternates between Yale's campus and Harvard's. Class reunions take place year-round. Information can be found on the alumni Web site.

Alumni Publications

Yale Alumni Magazine

The *Yale Alumni Magazine* covers the entire university, including research, university policy, and student affairs. Being both separate and inseparable from Yale, the magazine's writers create a unique perspective on current campus affairs.

AYA Blue Print

The *Blue Print* is the newsletter of the Yale alumni. It includes AYA news, class news, club news, and Grad/Pro news.

The Lowdown
ON ALUMNI

Web site:
http://www.aya.yale.edu

Office:
Association of Yale Alumni
232 York Street
New Haven, CT 06511
aya@yale.edu
(203) 432-2586

Services Available:

Some services and amenities available for Yale alumni are lifetime e-mail forwarding, educational travel discounts, sporting event ticket packages, and library borrowing privileges. Also, several lectures and reunions will be held on a regular basis.

The AYA provides a channel for communication between the alumni and the university, oversees the direction of alumni organizations and programs, provides the means for examination of university policies, and maintains the stature of Yale University. Rose Alumni House is open regularly on weekdays between 8:30 a.m. and 5:00 p.m., as well as during many special alumni weekends.

Famous Yale Alumni:

President William Howard Taft (Class of 1878)

Benjamin Spock (Class of '28), revered author of *Baby and Child Care*

Supreme Court Justice Potter Stewart (Class of '33)

President Gerald Ford (Class of '41)

Supreme Court Justice Byron White (Class of '46)

President George H.W. Bush (Class of '48)

Sam Waterston (Class of '62)

Senator Joseph Lieberman (Class of '64)

Governor George Pataki (Class of '67)

President George W. Bush (Class of '68)

President Bill Clinton (Class of '73)

Senator Hillary Clinton (Class of '73)

Supreme Court Justice Clarence Thomas (Class of '74)

Sigourney Weaver (Class of '74)

Meryl Streep (Class of '75)

Angela Bassett (Class of '80)

Jodie Foster (Class of '84)

Ed Norton (Class of '91)

The Ten BEST Things About Yale:

1. Shopping period
2. Master's teas
3. Brilliant professors
4. Beautiful architecture
5. Yale in London (Study Abroad)
6. Residential college system
7. Pepe's and Sally's Pizza
8. Computer clusters
9. Yale University Art Gallery
10. Toad's Place

The Ten WORST Things About Yale:

1. The weather
2. Bad neighborhoods
3. Lack of time
4. Meal plan requirement
5. Weenie bins
6. Legacies
7. Finals on Sunday
8. The Group IV (Math and Science) requirements
9. Parking
10. The dating scene

Visiting Yale

The Lowdown
ON VISITING YALE

Hotel Information:

The Colony Inn
1157 Chapel Street
(800) 458-8810
Distance from Campus: 3 blocks
Price Range: $80-$90

Holiday Inn at Yale
30 Whalley Avenue
(800) HOLIDAY
(203) 777-6221
Distance from campus: 3 blocks
Price: $89

Omni New Haven Hotel at Yale
155 Temple Street
(800) THE-OMNI
(203) 772-6664
Distance from Campus: 4 blocks
Price Range: $150-up

Quality Inn
100 Pond Lily Avenue
(800) 228-5151
(203) 387-6651
Distance from Campus: 4 miles
Price Range: $55-$75

Residence Inn by Marriott
3 Long Wharf Drive
(800) 331-3131
(203) 777-5337
Distance from Campus: less than 5 miles
Price Range: $99-up

Three Chimneys Inn
1201 Chapel Street
(800) 443-1554
(203) 789-1201
Distance form campus: 4 blocks

Take a Campus Virtual Tour

http://www.yale.edu

To Schedule a Group Information Session or Interview

Call (203) 432-9300 on any weekday from 8:30 a.m. to 4:30 p.m. Eastern time.

To schedule an interview, send a request to student.interviews@yale.edu

Campus Tours

Campus Tours are offered:

Monday - Friday, 10:30 a.m., 2 p.m.

Saturday and Sunday, 1:30 p.m. only.

Call for holiday schedule.

Special tours by appointment.

Overnight Visits

Requests for accommodations should be submitted to student.interviews@yale.edu well in advance (no earlier than August 11th).

In addition, Yale hosts Bulldog Days for accepted students. During a couple of days in April, you will be able to experience the life of a college student. You can not only stay in a dorm room (remember a sleeping bag!), you can eat in the dining halls, attend classes, and meet other Yale prospective students, faculty, and deans. Expect to receive an invitation with your acceptance package.

Directions to Campus

Interstate 95

From the North

- Connect to I-91 North in New Haven.
- Take Exit 3 (Trumbull Street) and follow directions below for I-91.

From the South

- Connect to I-91 North in New Haven (left exit).
- Take Exit 3 (Trumbull Street) and follow directions below for I-91.

Interstate 91

From the North or South

- Take Exit 3 (Trumbull Street).
- Stay in the middle lane and continue straight onto Trumbull Street to the fifth traffic light.
- Turn left onto Prospect Street and continue for one block.
- Prospect Street becomes College Street at this point.
- Continue for two blocks and turn left onto Elm Street.
- The Visitor Center is located on the left hand side of the street, opposite the New Haven Green.

Route 15

(Wilbur Cross/Merritt Parkways)

From the North

- Take Exit 61.
- Drive south on Whitney Avenue for approximately five miles.
- Turn right on Sachem Street at the Peabody Museum traffic light.
- Continue to next traffic light and turn left onto Prospect Street.
- At the second traffic light, Prospect Street becomes College Street.
- Continue for two blocks and turn left onto Elm Street.
- The Visitor Center is located on the left hand side of the street, opposite the New Haven Green.

Route 15

From the South

- Take Exit 57.
- Drive east on Route 34 (Derby Avenue) for approximately five miles past the Yale Athletic Fields.
- Turn left onto Route 10 North, Ella T. Grasso Boulevard.
- Proceed to the fifth traffic light and turn right onto Whalley Avenue.
- Whalley becomes Broadway in one mile, and Broadway becomes Elm Street in another two miles.
- Continue on Elm for two to two and a half blocks.
- The Visitor Center is located on the left hand side of the street, opposite the New Haven Green.

Route 34

From the West

- Follow directions from Route 34 above.

REPORT CARD SUMMARY

Academics

Academics are graded based on the quality of professors and their accessibility. **Ivy League Universities love to boast about superstar professors and faculty Nobel laureates**, but are these educational icons always available to teach? The academic grade also reflects class size, how easy it is for students to get into the classes they want, and the use of teaching assistants—who can be a mixed bag—instead of actual professors.

PRINCETON UNIVERSITY

BROWN UNIVERSITY

DARTMOUTH UNIVERSITY

HARVARD UNIVERSITY

YALE UNIVERSITY

COLUMBIA UNIVERSITY

UNIVERSITY OF PENNSYLVANIA

CORNELL UNIVERSITY

REPORT CARD SUMMARY

Local Atmosphere

When prospective students imagine the stereotypical college campus, they're probably picturing an Ivy League school. In truth, Ivy League campuses can be found positioned in the middle of an urban metropolis—like Penn—and in the middle of nowhere—like Dartmouth. **The local atmosphere grade considers a number of factors** including the proximity to cosmopolitan areas (as well as other colleges), the geographical features, things to do, and the local attitude towards students.

BROWN UNIVERSITY

COLUMBIA UNIVERSITY

HARVARD UNIVERSITY

UNIVERSITY OF PENNSYLVANIA

CORNELL UNIVERSITY

PRINCETON UNIVERSITY

DARTMOUTH COLLEGE

YALE UNIVERSITY

REPORT CARD SUMMARY

Safety & Security

The presence of crime on campus is something to consider when choosing a college. Your school might look like Pleasantville when the tour guide shows you around campus, but there could be more to the picture. **Your safety and security should not be taken for granted**. This grade considers not just the safety of the school and its surrounding neighborhood, but also the administration's security measures. Is the campus open to strangers? How many security guards and officers are employed? And do students feel safe?

DARTMOUTH COLLEGE

PRINCETON UNIVERSITY

HARVARD UNIVERSITY

CORNELL UNIVERSITY

YALE UNIVERSITY

BROWN UNIVERSITY

COLUMBIA UNIVERSITY

UNIVERSITY OF PENNSYLVANIA

REPORT CARD SUMMARY

Computers

While many Ivy students find themselves faced with up-to-date and top-of-the-line technology, don't get to school and kick yourself for leaving your computer at home. Don't forget to **consider the abundance, accessibility, and dependence of computers**. If the school has tiny computer labs packed with people, you might want to bring or buy your own machine (it'll make printing out assignments 10 minutes before class much easier).

CORNELL UNIVERSITY

DARTMOUTH COLLEGE

YALE UNIVERSITY

HARVARD UNIVERSITY

PRINCETON UNIVERSITY

BROWN UNIVERSITY

UNIVERSITY OF PENNSYLVANIA

COLUMBIA UNIVERSITY

REPORT CARD SUMMARY

Facilities

With some of the largest endowments in the nation, **one would expect the Ivy League campuses to offer students the best of the best**. While this may be accurate in some aspects of campus living, it can be misleading in others. Waiting for a seat in the library or an empty bench in the weight room may seem like small potatoes to some, but the quality, size, and availability of these resources can seriously affect your overall college experience. See how each Ivy fared.

CORNELL UNIVERSITY

UNIVERSITY OF PENNSYLVANIA

YALE UNIVERSITY

PRINCETON UNIVERSITY

BROWN UNIVERSITY

DARTMOUTH COLLEGE

HARVARD UNIVERSITY

COLUMBIA UNIVERSITY

REPORT CARD SUMMARY

Campus Dining

It might not come as a shock that mass-producing food for thousands normally results in lower quality grub than Mom's home cooking. Afterall, there are **two things college students love to complain about: their workload and campus dining**. In order to find out who does best, we look at a number of factors including quality, variety, and attention to special eating needs. In addition, cost and meal plan requirements also factor into each Ivy League school's grade.

CORNELL UNIVERSITY

PRINCETON UNIVERSITY

DARTMOUTH COLLEGE

YALE UNIVERSITY

BROWN UNIVERSITY

UNIVERSITY OF PENNSYLVANIA

COLUMBIA UNIVERSITY

HARVARD UNIVERSITY

REPORT CARD SUMMARY

Off-Campus Dining

Many restaurants on and around Ivy League campuses have their own distinct and long-standing traditions. **Some local favorites include lobster, New England clam chowder, and Philadelphia cheesesteaks**. Fast food restaurants are also popular among busy Ivy Leagers who don't always have time to sit down and eat. Whether the Ivy League student has access to these culinary pleasures, however, and whether their pocketbooks can carry the strain, is another matter altogether.

COLUMBIA UNIVERSITY

HARVARD UNIVERSITY

BROWN UNIVERSITY

UNIVERSITY OF PENNSYLVANIA

YALE UNIVERSITY

CORNELL UNIVERSITY

PRINCETON UNIVERSITY

DARTMOUTH COLLEGE

REPORT CARD SUMMARY

Campus Housing

Dorm life can be a magical couple of years. You are at the prime of your life, living mostly unsupervised, with hundreds of people your age, from both sexes, with almost no responsibilities. Sure, some dorms—even at Ivy League schools—might resemble Motel 6 more than the Four Seasons, and **air-conditioning is not always a guarantee**, but no matter what the conditions, dorm life is an experience you'll remember for the rest of your life.

HARVARD UNIVERSITY

YALE UNIVERSITY

BROWN UNIVERSITY

DARTMOUTH COLLEGE

CORNELL UNIVERSITY

COLUMBIA UNIVERSITY

PRINCETON UNIVERSITY

UNIVERSITY OF PENNSYLVANIA

REPORT CARD SUMMARY

Off-Campus Housing

From state to state and region to region, what's available to students varies greatly in quality, convenience, and cost. **Here, each college is graded not only on the local real estate market, but also on their attitude towards off-campus housing**. Will they help you find a place? Do you need special permission to live outside the dorms? We also take into account the proximity of housing to campus, cost, and whether or not living off-campus interferes with campus life.

UNIVERSITY OF PENNSYLVANIA

BROWN UNIVERSITY

CORNELL UNIVERSITY

DARTMOUTH COLLEGE

YALE UNIVERSITY

PRINCETON UNIVERSITY

COLUMBIA UNIVERSITY

HARVARD UNIVERSITY

REPORT CARD SUMMARY

Diversity

College isn't just supposed to be high school with more buildings. It's supposed to be an experience that broadens your horizons, and it's hard to do that if you only meet people exactly like you. While some **Ivy League universities can seem homogenous**, many, as of late, have implemented "need-blind" policies and other programs that actively recruit minorities and students from a wide range of backgrounds. Just keep in mind that diversity isn't just about race.

COLUMBIA UNIVERSITY

HARVARD UNIVERSITY

UNIVERSITY OF PENNSYLVANIA

BROWN UNIVERSITY

CORNELL UNIVERSITY

DARTMOUTH COLLEGE

PRINCETON UNIVERSITY

YALE UNIVERSITY

REPORT CARD SUMMARY

Guys

Don't make the mistake of labeling each and every guy who gains admission to the Ivy Leagues a "nerd." Just think of it this way: come fall, **you'll be attending classes with some of the most able-minded young males in the country**. A high grade for guys means not only attractive men, but also a smart, friendly, and engaging group. A good campus dating scene and the ratio of guys to girls can also play a role in the assessment of the male student body.

DARTMOUTH COLLEGE

BROWN UNIVERSITY

CORNELL UNIVERSITY

HARVARD UNIVERSITY

PRINCETON UNIVERSITY

UNIVERSITY OF PENNSYLVANIA

YALE UNIVERSITY

COLUMBIA UNIVERSITY

REPORT CARD SUMMARY

Girls

Sure Ivy girls are smart, but are they hot, nice, and fun to be around? Afterall, you might have a hard time enjoying your next four years if there aren't any worthwhile people on campus. College should offer a new and engaging social scene, and with that comes members of the opposite (or same) sex who are **not just attractive, but personable** as well. Here's how the Ivies rank when it comes to girls.

B+	YALE UNIVERSITY
B	BROWN UNIVERSITY
B	PRINCETON UNIVERSITY
B-	DARTMOUTH COLLEGE
B-	HARVARD UNIVERSITY
C+	COLUMBIA UNIVERSITY
C+	UNIVERSITY OF PENNSYLVANIA
C-	CORNELL UNIVERSITY

REPORT CARD SUMMARY

Athletics

Considering their academic stature, and the fact that they don't offer any kind of athletic scholarships, most **Ivy League sports programs are actually quite competitive**. But do Ivy League students support their varsity teams? How about intramural participation? These are both factors in a school's athletics grade. Other things to keep in mind are the administration's stance on athletics, the funding available, and the quality and availability of facilities and equipment. Even a school that doesn't compete at a national level can get a good grade if the campus actively promotes its athletic scene.

DARTMOUTH COLLEGE

UNIVERSITY OF PENNSYLVANIA

PRINCETON UNIVERSITY

CORNELL UNIVERSITY

BROWN UNIVERSITY

HARVARD UNIVERSITY

YALE UNIVERSITY

COLUMBIA UNIVERSITY

REPORT CARD SUMMARY

Nightlife

You might have to surrender some of your social life in order to do well academically at an Ivy League school, but **that does not mean that the "work hard, play hard" mantra doesn't apply at these colleges**. A high grade in Nightlife indicates that there are many bars, clubs, and other opportunities for entertainment on and around campus. Other determining factors include affordability, accessibility, the number of options for the under-21 crowd, and the prevalence of house parties in the area.

COLUMBIA UNIVERSITY

HARVARD UNIVERSITY

UNIVERSITY OF PENNSYLVANIA

BROWN UNIVERSITY

YALE UNIVERSITY

CORNELL UNIVERSITY

PRINCETON UNIVERSITY

DARTMOUTH COLLEGE

REPORT CARD SUMMARY

Greek Life

Whether or not you plan on joining a fraternity or sorority, it is possible that Greek life could still be a part of your college experience. At some schools, Greek events are major social functions. **The Greek scene varies across the Ivies**, so be sure to learn about the type of role it has at each school. A high grade means that Greek organziations are not only active and visible, but also welcome and respected by the other students.

DARTMOUTH COLLEGE

UNIVERSITY OF PENNSYLVANIA

CORNELL UNIVERSITY

BROWN UNIVERSITY

COLUMBIA UNIVERSITY

PRINCETON UNIVERSITY

HARVARD UNIVERSITY

YALE UNIVERSITY

REPORT CARD SUMMARY

Drug Scene

Drugs have been an issue ever since people discovered that they could grind up, inject, smoke, melt, or swallow various stuff to change the way they feel. This grade addresses the prominence of the drug scene on campus, along with the student attitudes, to let you know how visible the threat of drug use actually is at each school. **Here, a high grade means that drugs are not a noticeable part of campus life**.

CORNELL UNIVERSITY

HARVARD UNIVERSITY

YALE UNIVERSITY

BROWN UNIVERSITY

DARTMOUTH COLLEGE

PRINCETON UNIVERSITY

UNIVERSITY OF PENNSYLVANIA

COLUMBIA UNIVERSITY

REPORT CARD SUMMARY

Campus Strictness

Ivy League schools run the gamut from progressive or radical to practically sheltered. Some institutions have even been known to change when a new dean comes into office or an embarrassing story makes its way into the headlines. Regardless, most colleges have developed their own distinct character, and the College Prowler grade on campus strictness reflects this. Here, a high grade implies an overall lenient atmosphere.

COLUMBIA UNIVERSITY

UNIVERSITY OF PENNSYLVANIA

YALE UNIVERSITY

HARVARD UNIVERSITY

BROWN UNIVERSITY

PRINCETON UNIVERSITY

DARTMOUTH COLLEGE

CORNELL UNIVERSITY

REPORT CARD SUMMARY

Parking

If a school scores a good mark in this area, parking is available and isn't too expensive; the school offers some form of student parking, be it a separate student lot or the availability of permits for use in specific areas. Another factor is the severity of parking enforcement. (**Are there parking lot monsters, or good spot Samaritans?**) A low grade, therefore, means that you'll never find a spot, you'll never be able to afford one if you do, and by the time you get back to your car, it'll look like a ticker-tape parade came marching by . . .

PRINCETON UNIVERSITY

BROWN UNIVERSITY

CORNELL UNIVERSITY

DARTMOUTH COLLEGE

HARVARD UNIVERSITY

YALE UNIVERSITY

UNIVERSITY OF PENNSYLVANIA

COLUMBIA UNIVERSITY

REPORT CARD SUMMARY

Transportation

This section takes into account the expense, convenience, and availability of student buses and public transportation systems. It also addresses the accessibility of the school from elsewhere in the country (via trains, planes, or buses). In addition, the the actual necessity of transportation also plays a role—**A school with bad transportation can be somewhat redeemed if the system is largely unnecessary**. If you have to shell out $35 for a cab ride to your apartment, the grade won't be so hot.

COLUMBIA UNIVERSITY

HARVARD UNIVERSITY

BROWN UNIVERSITY

UNIVERSITY OF PENNSYLVANIA

CORNELL UNIVERSITY

DARTMOUTH COLLEGE

PRINCETON UNIVERSITY

YALE UNIVERSITY

REPORT CARD SUMMARY

Weather

If you live in the Northeast, then you're probably familiar with the region's erratic weather patterns by now—you'll experience all four seasons, but year after year, one seems longer and more intense than the next. However, if you're coming from the South or the West Coast, you may be in for a rude awakening. During colder seasons, many students choose to wear layers of clothing. The winters can get excruciatingly cold, especially toward northern New England, and temperatures can and will dip below 0°—that's Fahrenheit, not Celsius!

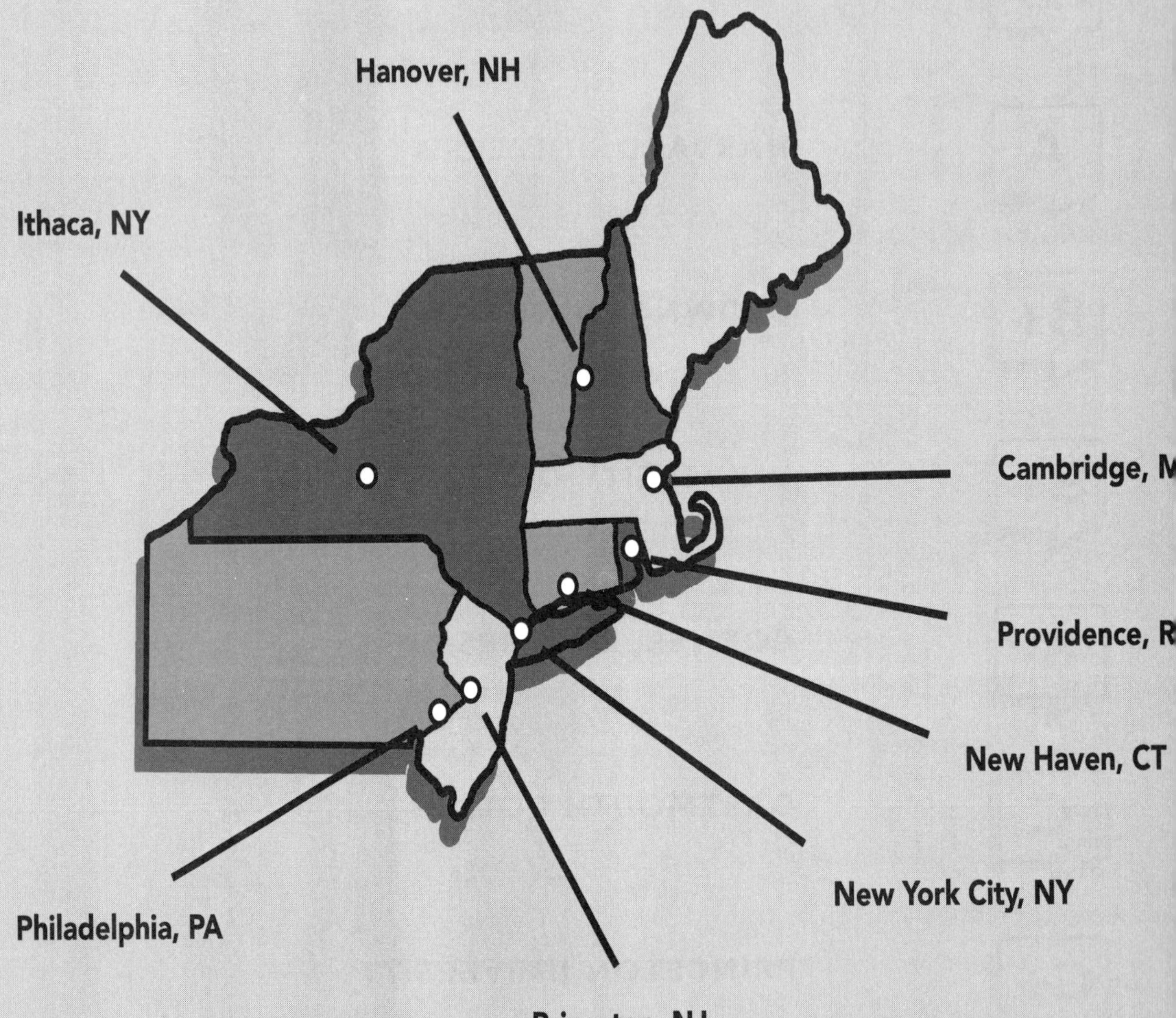

Weather Information by City

Cambridge, MA (Harvard University)

Average Temperature

Fall:	55° F
Winter:	32° F
Spring:	49° F
Summer:	71° F

Average Precipitation

Fall:	3.7 in.
Winter:	3.6 in.
Spring:	3.6 in.
Summer:	3.2 in.

New Haven, CT (Yale University)

Average Temperature

Fall:	52° F
Winter:	28° F
Spring:	47° F
Summer:	71° F

Average Precipitation

Fall:	4.6 in.
Winter:	3.9 in.
Spring:	4.7 in.
Summer:	4.4 in.

Hanover, NH (Dartmouth College)

Average Temperature

Fall:	59° F
Winter:	34° F
Spring:	65° F
Summer:	80° F

Average Precipitation

Fall:	3.4 in.
Winter:	2.7 in.
Spring:	3.6 in.
Summer:	3.5 in.

New York, NY (Columbia University)

Average Temperature:

Fall:	58° F
Winter:	32° F
Spring:	53° F
Summer:	77° F

Average Precipitation:

Fall:	3.1 in.
Winter:	3.7 in.
Spring:	4.5 in.
Summer:	4.2 in.

Ithaca, NY (Cornell University)

Average Temperature

Fall:	50° F
Winter:	21° F
Spring:	43° F
Summer:	69° F

Average Precipitation

Fall:	3.4 in.
Winter:	2.5 in.
Spring:	3.3 in.
Summer:	4.0 in.

Philadelphia, PA (University of Pennsylvania)

Average Temperature

Fall:	58° F
Winter:	35° F
Spring:	53° F
Summer:	75° F

Average Precipitation

Fall:	3.3 in.
Winter:	3.2 in.
Spring:	3.7 in.
Summer:	3.8 in.

Princeton, NJ (Princeton University)

Average Temperature

Fall: 54° F
Winter: 32° F
Spring: 50° F
Summer: 72° F

Average Precipitation

Fall: 3.8 in.
Winter: 3.4 in.
Spring: 4.1 in.
Summer: 4.6 in.

Providence, RI (Brown University)

Average Temperature

Fall:	54° F
Winter:	28° F
Spring:	47° F
Summer:	79° F

Average Precipitation

Fall:	3.4 in.
Winter:	3.9 in.
Spring:	4.2 in.
Summer:	4.0 in.

SECTION 5

Random Facts

Encore Ivy

In the process of creating *Untangling the Ivy League*, we stumbled across many random facts and miscellanneous data that were just too good to leave out—thus leading to the creation of "Section 6: Random Facts." In the following section, you will find many true, yet knee-slapping, facts and figures about the Ivies that could indeed be useful during an important admissions interview or, at the very least, spice up a seemingly insignificant elevator conversation.

In the following chapter, we'll provide information on a number of things about your favorite Ivy League institution, including:

- How each school got its start in acadamia and the factors that led up to it.
- The most random facts and figures that might shock you about each institution.
- Famous individuals—both real and fictional—associated with each of the Ivies.
- The latest information and updates on each Ivy that many elite academic officials haven't even heard of yet!

BROWN UNIVERSITY
In deo speramus
(In God we hope)

How Brown Came to Be

In 1763, James Manning, a Baptist minister, was sent to Rhode Island by the Philadelphia Baptist Church Association with the sole purpose of founding a college. At the same time, local Congregationalists, led by James Stiles, were working toward a similar goal. On March 3, 1764, a charter was filed to create Rhode Island College in Warren, Rhode Island, reflecting the work of both Stiles and Manning. The charter had more than 60 signatories, including John and Nicholas Brown of the Brown family—the namesakes of the University. James Manning, the minister sent to Rhode Island by the Baptists, was sworn in as the College's first president in 1765.

Rhode Island College moved to its present location on College Hill (East Providence) in 1770, and shortly after, construction began on the first building, The College Edifice. This building was renamed University Hall in 1823. The Brown family—Nicholas, John, Joseph, and Moses—orchestrated the move to Providence, organizing and funding a great majority of the construction of the new buildings. The family's ties with the college were strong: Joseph Brown became a professor of Physics at the University, and John Brown served as treasurer from 1775 to 1796.

In 1804, a year after John Brown's death, the University was renamed in honor of John's nephew, Nicholas Brown, Jr., who was a member of the class of 1786 and contributed $5,000 (which, adjusted for inflation, is approximately $59,500 in 2005, though it was 1,000 times the roughly $5 tuition) toward an endowed professorship. In 1904, the John Carter Brown Library was opened as an independent historical and cultural research center based around the libraries of John Carter and John Nicholas Brown.

The Brown family was involved in various other business ventures in Rhode Island, including slavery, which has led to some discussion of the role of slavery in Brown's legacy in recent years. In recognition of this history, the University has recently established a special Committee on Slavery and Justice (*http://www.brown.edu/Research/Slavery_Justice/index.html*).

Juicy Tidbits About Brown

Brown was the first college in the nation to welcome students of all religious affiliations.

Brown is notable for, among other things, having the only egyptology and history of mathematics departments in the United States.

Brown was one of the first institutions to emphasize media studies, with its department in modern culture and media, where students undergo in-depth film study courses such as film criticism, critical theory, and many more.

Brown's school colors are seal brown, cardinal red, and white.

Brown was recently named "the most fashionable school in the Ivy League" by the fashion trade journal, *Women's Wear Daily*, on the basis that students on campus seem to have the strongest sense of personal style.

Spring Weekend

Starting in 1960, Brown replaced a traditional Junior Dance with a **Spring Weekend concert** on the college's main green, which has, in the past, brought in acts such as Bob Dylan, Ella Fitzgerald, Bo Diddley, The Fugees, Peter, Paul and Mary, James Brown, Janis Joplin, Ray Charles, Bruce Springsteen, U2, R.E.M., Afrika Bambaata, Elvis Costello, George Clinton, and Sonic Youth. Some of the more recent acts include Joan Jett & the Blackhearts, Jurassic 5, Bela Fleck & the Flecktones, Reel Big Fish, and Sleater-Kinney.

Yum

At the end of each semester, on the last day of "**reading period**," when students study for exams, naked students walk into the Rockefeller and Science Libraries and hand out donuts to their peers.

There are over 240 registered student organizations on campus with diverse interests. Student Activities Night, during the orientation program, is an opportunity for first-years to become acquainted with the wide range of clubs.

Naked Party

Every fall, the Brown University Co-Ops (BACH) throw an invitation-only "naked party," where all guests remove their clothes upon entry. **The party is known for good times, but not for lewdness**. The hosts aim to create a comfortable setting where people of all body types can celebrate the naked human body.

The Chug 'N Run

One evening during each year's Spring Weekend, athletic/alcoholic Brown students gather down at the India Point Park walking path, lugging countless 30-packs of inexpensive light beer. The entrants in the Chug 'N Run chug a beer, run a mile, chug a beer, run a mile, chug a beer, run a mile, then chug one last victory beer. Not everybody makes it to beer number four, and much comic beer explusion occurs along the way. Less adventurous students can walk the course alongside the runners as part of the "Sip&Stroll." This annual tradition, started by Brown women athletes, involves a surprisingly high number of gung-ho female students.

Students often rub the nose of **the bust of John Hay** for good luck on exams.

People associated with Brown University are often referred to as "Brunonians."

Seniors sometime sleep, and supposedly even fornicate, in the Sciences Library before graduation.

Students can pass through the Van Winkle Gates only twice (once upon entering the University, and once again during Commencement). Superstition has it that students who pass through the gates for a second time before graduation do not graduate.

Beware the Seal!

Students avoid the Brown seal on the steps leading to the Pembroke green for a variety of reasons:

- *Female students avoid the seal to ward off pregnancy, although avoiding the Sciences Library would seem to be more effective.*
- *Previously, Pembroke students avoided the seal to ensure that they would get married.*
- *Previously, male Brown students avoided the seal to ensure they would graduate in four years.*

Brown has the oldest engineering program in the Ivy League.

Notable Brown Alumni

Athletics

John Spellman (BA, 1924) - Olympic gold medalist for light heavyweight freestyle wrestling, 1924.

Norman Taber (BA, 1913) - Olympic gold medal-winning team member for the 3,000-m relay, 1912.

Wallace Wade (BA, 1917) - American football coach at the University of Alabama and then Duke; namesake of Duke's football stadium.

Other

Kate Borstein (MA, 1989) - Transgender activist/performance artist/author, *Gender Outlaws & My Gender Workbook.*

Barnaby Evans (MA, 1975) - Creator of the environmental art installation "WaterFire."

Kathryn S. Fuller (AB, 1968) - President and CEO, non-profit World Wildlife Fund.

Samuel Gridley Howe (AB, 1821) - Physician, abolitionist, advocate of education for the blind.

Kerry Kelly (MD, 1977) - Chief medical officer, New York City Fire Department.

Elliot Maxwell (AB, 1968) - Educational reformer.

Donna Zaccaro (AB, 1983) - President, non-profit WhatGoesAround Inc..

Fictitious Alumni

Otto Mann - The zany bus driver from *The Simpsons.*

Special Agent Monica Reyes - From The *X-Files.*

Julianne Potter - The main character of the movie, *My Best Friend's Wedding* (played by Julia Roberts) and her "best friend" (played by Dermot Mulroney) met and made their marriage pact while attending Brown.

Attended Brown (did not graduate)

Sidney E. Frank (Class of 1942) - Founder, CEO, and chairman of Sidney E. Frank Importing Co.; brand builder responsible for American success of Grey Goose vodka, Jägermeister, and Gekkeikan sake.

John W. Heisman (Class of 1891) - Namesake of the Heisman Trophy.

Lois Lowry (Class of 1958) - Author, *The Giver.*

Leelee Sobieski (currently enrolled, Class of 2006) - Actress, *Eyes Wide Shut* (1999), *Never Been Kissed* (1999), *Here on Earth* (2000), *Joy Ride* (2001), *The Glass House* (2001); nominated for Emmy for *Joan of Arc.*

Ted Turner (Class of 1960) - Founder of CNN.

Princess Theodora of Greece (currently enrolled, Class of 2006) - Princess of Greece and Denmark.

Allegra Beck (currently enrolled, Class of 2008) - Daughter of Donatella Versace and 50 percent owner of Versace fashion house.

Notable faculty

Ama Ata Aidoo (Drama) - Poet/playwright

David Berson (Medical) - Discovered 3rd photoreceptor in the eye (in addition to rods and cones).

Fernando Cardoso (International Relations/Business) - Former President of Brazil.

Leon Neil Cooper (Physics) - Nobel Prize in physics 1972; father of superconductivity.

Robert Coover (English) - Post-modern writer, *Spanking the Maid & The Origin of the Brunists*; notable for his metafiction; electronic writing pioneer.

Robert Creeley (English) - Poet, *Pure Shit.*

Anne DeGroot (Medical) - Likely to be the first to create an effective globally-relevant AIDS vaccine.

Notable faculty (continued . . .)

John Donoughue (Computer Science) - Founder of Cyberkinetics, a company that recently won FDA approval to test brain/robot interfaces in humans.

Oskar Eustis (Drama) - Famous theater director, *Angels in America* (original production).

Carlos Fuentes (Literature) - Mexican writer, *The Death of Artemio Cruz*.

James Head (Geology) - Planetary geologist, trained astronauts during Apollo missions.

Stephen Houston (Archeology) - World-famous archeologist, expert on Mayan hieroglyphics.

Sergei Khrushchev (Government) - Son of Nikita Sergeyevich Khrushchev.

Otto Neugebauer (Mathematics) - Highly-respected historian of mathematics.

Robert Scholes (English) - President, Modern Language Association; author, *The Rise and Fall of English*.

Leslie Thornton (Film) - Lauded experimental film-maker, *Peggy and Fred in Hell*.

Andries "Andy" Van Dam (Computer Science) - Computer graphics pioneer and creator of hypertext; inspiration for "Andy" character in Pixar's *Toy Story* movies.

Paula Vogel (Drama) - Pulitzer Prize winning play-wright, *How I Learned to Drive*.

Xu Wenli (Government) - Founder of Chinese Democratic Party.

John Edgar Wideman (African-American Studies) - Writer; two time PEN/Faulkner Award winner, *Philadelphia Fire*.

Gordon Wood (History) - Pulitzer Prize winner, *Radicalism of the American Revolution*.

C. D. Wright (English) - Poet, String Light; MacArthur "genius grant" winner.

Brown's New Curriculum

In the late '60s, Brown students weren't happy with their University and were ready to do something about it. The Brunoians of this era simply felt that there were too many distribution and core requirements and that the educational autonomy of each individual student was lacking because of this.

In 1969, Brown adopted a "New Curriculum," marking a major change in the University's institutional history. The curriculum was the result of a paper written by Ira Magaziner and Elliot Maxwell, called "Draft of a Working Paper for Education at Brown University." This paper was the result of a year-long Group Independent Studies Project (GISP) involving 15 professors and over 80 students. The group was inspired by student-initiated experimental schools, especially San Francisco State College, and sought ways to improve education for students at Brown. The philosophy they formed was based on the principle that "the individual who is being educated is the center of the educational process." Way back in 1850, Brown President Francis Wayland wrote: "The various courses should be so arranged that, insofar as practicable, every student might study what he chose, all that he chose, and nothing but what he chose."

The paper made a number of suggestions for improving education at Brown, including a new kind of interdisciplinary freshman course that would introduce new modes of inquiry and bring faculty from different fields together. Their goal was to transform the survey course, which traditionally sought to cover a large amount of basic material into specialized courses which would introduce the important modes of inquiry used in different disciplines.

The New Curriculum that came out of the working paper was significantly different from the paper itself. Its key features were:

- Modes of Thought courses aimed at first-year students
- Interdisciplinary University courses
- Students could elect to take any course Satisfactory/No Credit
- Distribution requirements were dropped
- The University simplified grades to ABC/No Credit, eliminating pluses, minuses, and D's. Furthermore, "No Credit" would not appear on external transcripts.

Except for the Modes of Thought courses, a key component of the reforms which have been discontinued, these elements of the New Curriculum are still in place. And as it turns out, 21st century Brunoians couldn't be happier with their college experiences.

(http://www.browndailyherald.com)

COLUMBIA UNIVERSITY

In lumine tuo videbimus lumen (In thy light we shall see light)

How Columbia Came to Be

Columbia's history can be traced back to its first president, Samuel Johnson (1696–1772). Johnson was a dedicated clergyman who held classes in the schoolhouse of Trinity Church. The growth of King's College (the name it was given upon its foundation in 1754) was placed on the back burner due to the American Revolution, as the college was temporarily shut down. It re-opened as Columbia College in 1784 in a new building in lower Manhattan. The title was first vested in the regents of the University of the State of New York, but in 1787, it was transferred to the trustees of the college, who elected William Samuel Johnson president. In 1857, under Charles King (1789–1867), the college moved to a site at Madison Ave. and 49th St. In 1897, under Seth Low, the move was made to the University's current location at Morningside Heights.

The gradual addition of professional and graduate schools resulted in the assumption of the name Columbia University in 1896. Then, in 1912, the name became Columbia University in the City of New York. Columbia College remained the name of the undergraduate school and, in 1919, originated the modern Contemporary Civilizations Core Curriculum requirements (or the 4C requirements), for which it is still well-known.

Juicy Tidbits About Columbia

Columbia has formal educational ties to the Juilliard School of Music and the American Museum of Natural History in New York City. Internationally, CU has academic connections with Oxford and Cambridge universities in England, the University of Paris in France, Kyoto and Tokyo universities in Japan, and many other global educational institutions.

Notable CU Presidents

- F.A.P. Barnard
  (Pioneer for co-education)
- Nicholas Murray Butler
  (Formal Presidential Advisor)
- Dwight D. Eisenhower
  (34th President of the U.S.)
- William J. McGill
  (Distinguished Psychologist)
- George E. Rupp
  (IRC Chairman)

While recently on the decline, the Columbia football team is one of the nation's oldest and played a major role in the development of the sport. It won the Rose Bowl in 1934.

Columbia's wrestling team is the oldest in the nation.

Two major publications at Columbia include the *Columbia Daily Spectator*, the nation's second-oldest student newspaper, and *The Jester*, a campus humor magazine established in 1899 and edited at one point by Allen Ginsberg**.**

The annual Varsity Show, once led by Rodgers and Hammerstein, is a student-produced musical that satirizes traditions at Columbia and its rival colleges.

Lou Gehrig *played baseball while he was a student at Columbia.*

In 1902, New York newspaper icon **Joseph Pulitzer** donated a substantial sum to Columbia for the founding of a school to teach journalism. Ten years later, the Graduate School of Journalism opened—the only journalism school in the Ivy League. The school remains the nation's most prestigious, and is the administrator of the coveted **Pulitzer Prize** and **The DuPont-Columbia Award** in Broadcast Journalism.

Columbia's football team set an NCAA record for playing the most consecutive football games without a win. After losing 44 straight games, it broke the streak by beating Princeton at Columbia's homecoming game in 1988.

Crew was Columbia's first sport.

Columbia is among the **top 20** universities in terms of its number of NCAA Division I varsity sports offerings.

The current Columbia University campus was formerly the site of a mental institution.

Columbia, when it was still known as ***King's College****, established the first American medical school to grant the MD degree in 1767.*

Columbia's alumni include actress Amanda Peet, singer Art Garfunkel, and former president Franklin Delano Roosevelt.

Notable Columbia Alumni

Athletics

Annie Duke (MA, 1991) - Professional poker player.

Sid Luckman (BA, 1937) - American football quarterback; enshrinee of the Pro Football Hall of Fame.

Paul Robeson (Law, 1923) - American football All-American; attorney, musician, activist.

David Stern (Law, 1966) - NBA Commissioner.

Marcellus Wiley (MA, 1997) - American football player (Nickname: Dat Dude); Pro-Bowl defensive end.

Other

Madeleine Albright (MA, 1968; Ph.D., 1976) - Secretary of State under President Clinton.

Pat Buchanan (MA, 1962) - Conservative commentator, speechwriter, senior advisor to three U.S. presidents.

DeWitt Clinton (BA, 1790) - Former governor of New York State, former mayor of New York City, main proponent of the Erie Canal.

Leon N. Cooper (BA, 1951; MA, 1953) - Pioneer in the realm of physics.

Simon S. Kuznets (BS, 1923; MA, 1924) - Notable economic scientist.

Bhimrao Ramji Ambedkar (MA, 1920; Ph.D., 1926) - architect of India's constitution; Minister of Law.

Norman F. Ramsey (Ph.D., 1935) - Pioneer in the realm of physics.

Theodore Roosevelt (Law 1884) - The 26th president of the United States.

Fictitious Alumni

Thomas Babington Levy - Dustin Hoffman's character in *Marathon Man*—involved in one of the most agonizing torture scenes ever portrayed.

Oliver Slocumb - Ryan Phillippe's character in the film, *Igby Goes Down*. Phillipe plays Kieran Culkin's "fascist" older brother, for whom the most important thing is outward success.

Attended Columbia (did not graduate)

Amelia Earhart (Class of 1923) - The world's most famous aviatrix.

Art Garfunkel (Class of 1965) - Half of the folk duo Simon and Garfunkel.

Lou Gehrig (Class of 1925) - Baseball player for the New York Yankees; enshrinee of the baseball hall of fame.

Anna Paquin (Currently Enrolled, Class of 2006) - Actress, *X-Men* (2003), *25th Hour* (2002), *She's All That* (1999), and *The Piano* (1993).

Notable Faculty

Alfred Aho (Computer Science) - The "A" in the programming language AWK.

Jagdish Bhagwati (Economics) - Author of *In Defense of Globalization.*

Alan Brinkley (American history and University Provost) - Son of legendary newscaster David Brinkley.

Richard Bulliet (History professor and Middle East scholar) - Author of *Kicked to Death by a Camel.*

Charles Frederick Chandler (Chemistry) - President of the New York Metropolitan Board of Health; inventor of the flush toilet.

Dwight Eisenhower (Former president) - Supreme Commander; Allied Expeditionary Force; 34th president of the United States.

Milos Forman (Film) - Film director, *One Flew Over the Cuckoo's Nest*, *Amadeus*, and *The People vs. Larry Flynt.*

Not in Our Backyard

In 1968, students protested over the issue of whether Columbia would build its gymnasium in neighboring Morningside Park—the barrier separating Columbia from Harlem. This offended many people, and one day in April, some students went to Morningside Drive and tore down the fence, attempting to break into the construction site. They were restrained by police, and some were arrested. The whole Morningside gym project was seen by the protestors to be an act of aggression aimed at the black residents of neighboring Harlem. **For several days, students took over administration buildings, occupied classrooms, and even attacked the Columbia ROTC detatchment.** Order was eventually restored when, with the assistance of NYPD, the university president snuck back into his office through a secret tunnel. The riots that rocked Columbia University during the memorable year of 1968 remain the most notorious of the student rebellions of that tumultuous time.

The episode is generally seen as a marking point where the student body's and administration's values appeared to diverge most sharply. Eventually, Columbia ended up scrapping the plans for the gym and built a subterranean "Physical Fitness Center" under the north end of campus. This facility is still in use today. However, the plans for Morningside gym were not all for nothing; the architectural plans drawn up for the abandoned Morningside Park gym project were eventually used at Princeton University to build Dillon Gym.

(http://www.gfsnet.org)

CORNELL UNIVERSITY

"I would found an institution where any person can find instruction in any study." – Ezra Cornell, 1865

How Cornell Came to Be

Cornell University was established in 1865 by Ezra Cornell, a farmer, mechanic, and inventor, shortly after the Civil War ended. The youngest of the Ivies, Cornell is portrayed by academics around the globe as a university where the classics and more practical subjects, such as engineering and agriculture, are taught in equal allotment and with equal dedication. The University can also be described as a "pioneer institution" for many reasons—it was the first major institution in the eastern United States to admit women along with men, when the first women enrolled in 1872. It awarded the first university degrees in veterinary medicine and journalism and, in 2001, established the first American medical school outside of the United States. Cornell has set so many precedents that, educational historian Frederick Rudolph once dubbed it "the first American university." Among other firsts, it taught the first course in American history, formed the first university publishing company, and awarded the nation's first doctorates in electrical engineering and industrial engineering. Also, The School of Hotel Administration and New York State School of Industrial and Labor Relations are the first four-year schools devoted to those particular fields.

Juicy Tidbits About Cornell

"This place is so incredibly beautiful, and my favorite times are the fall, when all the leaves are turning, and the spring, after a long winter, when the glorious sun warms us and turns everything green. Thank goodness for the winter months or people would never be able to get through their courses."

—Justice R.B. Ginsburg

When asked about Cornell and the surrounding area of Ithaca and Central New York.

Cornell was the first major institution in the eastern United States to promote coeducation.

Cornell awarded the first university degree in veterinary medicine and taught the first course on the American Civil War.

Cornell University has both **public and private affiliations.** Cornell is both a privately-endowed university and a federal land-grant institution of the state of New York. The University is also a partner of the State University of New York.

Cornell now has a medical campus in Doha, Qatar, in the Middle East.

(The Weill Cornell Medical Center).

Penn is the only Ivy with an undergraduate school of business.

However, Cornell also has an accredited undergraduate business program.

Congresswoman Cynthia McKinney has taught at Cornell.

Slope Day

Cornell's modern-day "Slope Day" celebrations started in 1901 as "Spring Day," a celebration of the end of winter. After the national drinking age limit was changed to 21 in 1984, Slope Day became an unofficial event on Libe Slope on the last day of the spring semester, involving lots of alcohol. Starting with 2003, Slope Day was retooled to become a **University-sponsored event with live concerts and catered alcohol** to those over the age of 21.

Notable Cornell Alumni

Athletics

Bruce Arena (BS, 1973) - Coach of the United States men's national soccer team.

Gary Bettman (BS, 1974) - Commissioner of the NHL.

Keith Olbermann (BS, 1979) - Television sports and news commentator.

Dick Schaap (BS, 1955) - Late sports newscaster on ABC and ESPN; twice winner of the Emmy Award; author and co-author of 33 books.

Other

Dr. Robert Atkins (MD, 1955) - Creator of Atkins Diet and an author on health and nutrition.

Sandy Berger (BA, 1967) - National Security Advisor to Bill Clinton.

Dr. Joyce Brothers (BS, 1947) - Author, psychologist, and television personality.

Barber B. Conable (AB, 1942, LL.B., 1948) - President of the World Bank from 1986 to 1991, Congressional Representative (R-New York) for nine consecutive terms.

Pete Coors (BS, 1969) - Coors brewery executive and 2004 senatorial candidate.

Stephen Friedman (AB, 1959) - Assistant for economic policy to President George W. Bush, and director of the National Economic Council.

Ruth Bader Ginsburg (AB, 1954) - U.S. Supreme Court justice.

Charles Lee (BS, 1962) - CEO of Verizon.

Toni Morrison (MA, 1955) - Novelist; Nobel Prize, Pulitzer Prize for *Beloved*, author of *Song of Solomon.*

Janet Reno (BA, 1960) - United States Attorney General under Bill Clinton.

Jimmy Smits (MFA, 1982) - Actor, *NYPD Blue.*

Fictional Alumni

Gabrielle Ashe - Character in Dan Brown's *Deception Point.*

Charles Foster Kane - Played by Orson Welles, title character of the film *Citizen Kane.*

Vicky Lathum - Played by Tara Reid in the *American Pie* movie trilogy.

Sideshow Mel - Character on *The Simpsons*; Sideshow Bob's brother.

Ling Woo - Character in *Ally Mcbeal* who was the editor of the *Cornell Law Journal.*

Attended Cornell (did not graduate)

Huey Lewis (Class of 1973) - Rock musician for Huey Lewis and the News.

Joe Nieuwendyk (Class of 1989) - NHL Champion; did not graduate as a result of going pro.

Kurt Vonnegut (Class of 1945) - Author of *Slaughterhouse-Five* and *Breakfast of Champions.*

Notable faculty

Hans Bethe (Physics) - Also known for nuclear physics, notably nuclear fusion and stellar nucleosynthesis; Nobel Prize winner.

Allan Bloom (Government) - Author of *Closing of the American Mind.*

Joan Jacobs Brumberg (Human Development) - Feminist, Gender, and Sexuality Studies; scholar in adolescence, body image, and eating disorders.

John Cleese (Professor at-Large) - Comedian and actor.

Richard Feynman (Physics, nuclear physics, especially quantum electrodynamics) - Nobel Prize winner.

Allen Hatcher (Mathematics).

Roald Hoffman (Chemistry, theoretical chemistry) - Nobel Prize winner.

Cornell's Weill Medical Center

Qatar may intitially seem like an unlikely country to be leading education reform in the Gulf region. The country's ruler, Sheik Hamad bin Khalifa al-Thani, tolerates no political dissent, and many areas of public life remain off-limits to debate.

Yet Doha, Qatar's capital city, has become home to one of the boldest experiments in higher education in the world, and certainly the boldest in the Middle East. Along with Cornell's Weill Medical School, three other schools—Virginia Commonwealth, Carnegie Mellon, and Texas A&M—have opened branch campuses in this tiny Gulf country (slightly smaller than Connecticut) over the past few years.

The four universities are located in a development called Education City, overseen by one of Sheik Hamad's three wives, Sheika Mozah. Mozah is leading the overhaul of the country's entire school system, including Qatar University, the largest in the country. The 2,500-acre site includes a 300-bed teaching hospital, and a science and technology park.

Many of the students were attracted by the combination of a Western education in a Middle Eastern setting. **"It's a lot like Saudi Arabia, it's just a smaller version of it,"** said Anaya Sarkar, a first-year pre-med student at Cornell.

Although far from home, the branch universities in Doha maintain close contact with their home campuses. Some classes, like Cornell's radiology class, are taught by videoconference via New York State. In order to maintain academic standards, the universities maintain complete control over staffing and admissions.

(http://www.cornell.edu/visiting/qatar/)

DARTMOUTH COLLEGE

Vox Clamantis in Deserto
(The voice of one crying out in the wilderness)

How Dartmouth Came to Be

The "Big Green," Dartmouth College, is one of the nation's most prestigious universities, but it started out in a log hut with a total enrollment of four students. Dartmouth was founded in 1769 by Reverend Eleazar Wheelock, a Congregational minister from Connecticut. Wheelock had earlier established Moor's Charity School in Lebanon, Connecticut, primarily for the education of Native Americans. In seeking to expand his school into a college, Wheelock relocated his educational enterprise to Hanover, in the Royal Province of New Hampshire. The move from Connecticut followed a lengthy and sometimes frustrating effort to find resources and secure a charter. One of Wheelock's first students, Samson Occom, a Mohegan Indian, was instrumental in raising substantial funds for the College. The Royal Governor of New Hampshire provided the land upon which Dartmouth would be built and on December 13, 1769, got the "ok" from King George III, thus officially establishing the College. That charter created a school "for the education and instruction of Youth of the Indian Tribes in this Land . . . and also of English Youth and any others." Named for William Legge, the Second Earl of Dartmouth—an important supporter of Eleazar Wheelock's efforts—Dartmouth is the nation's ninth oldest college and the last institution of higher learning established under Colonial rule.

In 1819, Dartmouth College was the subject of the historic Dartmouth College Case, in which the State of New Hampshire attempted to amend the College's royal charter to make the school a public university, claiming that the initial charter (before national independence was won) was therefore invalid. Daniel Webster, an alumnus of the class of 1801, presented the school's case to the Supreme Court. The Courts eventually found the amendment of Dartmouth's charter to be an illegal impairment of a contract by the state and prevented New Hampshire from taking over the college. Webster concluded his fiery, yet somber, oration with the following words: "It is, Sir, as I have said, a small college. And yet there are those who love it."

Juicy Tidbits About Dartmouth

While gathering background for a movie in Hanover, **writer F. Scott Fitzgerald** became extremely drunk at a fraternity party and was forced to leave the project. Although portions of his work were used in the film, he was never given a writer's credit.

Dartmouth Outing Club, founded in 1909, organized a winter weekend "field day" in 1910. This was an athletic event centered on skiing, a sport which the Outing Club helped to pioneer and publicize on a national scale. In 1911, the event was named Winter Carnival; social events were added, and women were invited to attend. Special trains made runs to transport women guests to Dartmouth, and *National Geographic* magazine referred to it as "**the Mardi Gras of the North**." The event became famous, much like Spring Break in Fort Lauderdale was during the 1950s and 1960s.

The Dartmouth Film Society is one of America's oldest student-run film societies.

In 2002, Dartmouth College was forced to cut both the men's and women's swim teams as a result of the school's financial troubles. The cutting of the swim teams received national attention after a member placed the team on eBay in an effort to raise money for the team.

After significant lobbying and fundraising by students, alumni, and supporters, both the men's and women's teams were reinstated.

The men's varsity swim team at Dartmouth began in 1920, making it one of the oldest swim programs in the United States.

The tradition of rushing the football field during the Homecoming game was discontinued in 1986, after a group of freshmen injured several players.

Women's rowing at Dartmouth was founded as a varsity sport in 1975. Each year, the team avidly recruits inexperienced freshmen to walk on, welcoming them to make an impact on the team. These walk-ons make up more than half of the team while the rest are recruited women, totaling nearly 60 at the beginning of the fall. Through cuts and self-selection, the freshmen compete in two or more eights by the time spring season comes around. They are led by a varsity team made up of around 30 women.

"I would insist that the person who spends four years in our north country and does not learn to hear the melody of rustling leaves or does not learn to love the wash of racing brooks . . . has not reached out for some of the most worthwhile educational values accessible at Dartmouth."

—Ernest Martin Hopkins,
Late president of Dartmouth

Dartmouth was involved in the 1819 landmark Supreme Court case, ***Dartmouth College v. Woodward***, in which Chief Justice John Marshall ruled that the charters of business corporations are contracts and are guaranteed under the U.S. Constitution.

Currently, as many as three-quarters of Dartmouth undergraduates participate in some form of athletics.

Dr. Seuss (Theodor Geisel) graduated from Dartmouth in 1925.

Dartmouth was the last university established under colonial rule.

The green light atop Dartmouth's Baker Tower is only lit on special occasions, such as Dartmouth Night, which kicks off Homecoming weekend. The custom was formalized in 1975.

Dartmouth was the first Ivy to provide its students with free, campus-wide, wireless Internet.

Now, students are required to have their own personal computers; they must be compatible with the school's network.

Notable Dartmouth Alumni

Athletics

Brad Ausmus (BA, 1991) - Major League Baseball player for the Houston Astros.

Jay Fiedler (BA, 1994) - NFL Quarterback.

Mike Remlinger (BA, 1988) - Major League pitcher for the Chicago Cubs.

David Shula (BA, 1981) - NFL coach; son of legendary Miami Dolphins coach Don Shula.

Other

Michael Arad (BA, 1991) - An architect who was selected to design the World Trade Center Memorial.

Kanichi Asakawa (BA, 1899) - The first Japanese professor at a major university in the United States (Yale University).

Salmon P. Chase (MA, 1826) - An American politician and jurist in the Civil War era who served as Chief Justice of the United States.

Theodor Seuss Geisel, aka Dr. Seuss (MA, 1925) - American writer of many children's books.

Laura Ingraham (BA, 1986) - Worked as a speech-writer in the Reagan Administration and has served as a law clerk to U.S. Supreme Court Justice Clarence Thomas.

Norman Maclean (BA, 1924) - An American novelist and academic most noted for his novel, *A River Runs Through It*, published in 1976.

Nelson Rockefeller (BA, 1930) - A governor of New York and the 41st vice president of the United States of America from December 19, 1974 to January 20, 1977.

Paul Tsongas (MA, 1962) - A United States senator from Massachusetts and a member of the United States Democratic Party.

Daniel Webster (Law, 1801) - American politician and orator; defended Dartmouth in the famous Dartmouth College Case.

Fictitious Alumni

Josiah Edward "Jed" Bartlet - A fictional president of the United States played by Martin Sheen on the television serial drama, *The West Wing*.

Michael Corleone - Character in Mario Puzo's novel, *The Godfather*. He was also the main character of the film trilogy that was directed by Francis Ford Coppola. Michael Corleone was played by Al Pacino in all three films.

Harlan Siler - Played the overbearing father of Zach Siler (Freddie Prinze Jr.) in the movie, *She's All That*. Zach didn't want to go to his dad's alma mater, Dartmouth. His dad was played by Tim Matheson. Coincidentally, Matheson also starred in *Animal House* (1978), which was partly inspired by one of its writers who was a **Dartmouth** alum.

Attended Dartmouth (did not graduate)

Robert Frost (Class of 1896) - American poet famous for his lyrical poems on country life in New England; *The Road Less Traveled*.

Fred Rogers (Class of 1954) - Transferred to enroll in the seminary.

Notable faculty

Robert Fogelin (Philosophy) - A preeminent Hume scholar, Professor Fogelin also teaches classes on Plato, Kant, and Wittgenstein.

Thomas Nichols (Government) - Former *Jeopardy* champion/Russian specialist. One of the few remaining Dartmouth professors who demands that papers be handed in on time.

John Rassias (French) - His innovative theories on the teaching of foreign languages led to Dartmouth's LSA programs, drill sessions, and language lab.

We Will Survive!

In 2005, Booz Allen Hamilton, a prestigious, international management consulting firm selected Dartmouth College as **one of the World's 10 Most Enduring Institutions**, based on its ability to overcome crises that threatened its survival. (Remember the Dartmouth College Case?)

Other institutions on the list included Oxford University, the Sony Corporation, General Electric, the Rolling Stones, the Salvation Army, and the modern Olympic Games. Dartmouth was the only U.S. university or college on the list, and with Oxford, one of only two universities in the world to be so named.

When conducting the study, Booz Allen Hamilton selected each of the institutions based on their uncanny abilities to meet—or sometimes even exceed—seven specific criteria: innovative capabilities, governance and leadership, information flow, culture and values, adaptive response, risk structure, and legitimacy.

According to panelists, **it was Dartmouth's risk-management structure that clinched their spot on the list**—taking into account the institution's often-challenged, yet ultimately triumphant, existence of a set of internal systems for managing risk. Dartmouth has literally had to fight for survival from its earliest days, time and again emerging a more viable institution whether facing a legal threat to the college charter, or an internal threat from misguided leadership. Its flexible risk structure has enabled and empowered Dartmouth to survive these crises and emerge the stronger for it.

(http://www.ameinfo.com/56439.html)

HARVARD UNIVERSITY

Veritas (Truth)

How Harvard Came to Be

On September 14, 1638, John Harvard, a 31-year-old clergyman from Charlestown, Massachusetts died, leaving his library and half of his estate to a local college. The young minister's bequest allowed the college to firmly establish itself, and in honor of its first benefactor, the school adopted the name Harvard College. Founded just 16 years after the arrival of the Pilgrims at Plymouth, the University has grown from nine students with a single teacher to an enrollment of more than 18,000 degree candidates, including undergraduates and students in 10 principal academic units.

During its early years, the College offered a classic academic course based on the English university model, all-the-while remaining consistent with the prevailing Puritan philosophy of the first colonists. In the 18th and 19th centuries, the college diversified, turning away from Puritanism towards intellectual independence. Under the leadership of president Charles W. Eliot, from 1869-1909, Harvard revitalized its law and medical schools and established schools of business, dental medicine, and arts and sciences, and transformed itself into a major modern university.

Juicy Tidbits About Harvard

Why Harvard Crimson?

The color was unofficially adopted by an 1875 vote of the student body, although the association with some form of red can be traced back to 1858, when Charles William Eliot, a young graduate student who would later become Harvard's president, bought red bandanas for his crew so they could more easily be distinguished by spectators at a regatta.

Let's Go travel guides, a travel guide series and a division of Harvard Student Agencies ***(http://www.hsa.net/)***, is run solely by Harvard students who research and edit improved versions of the books every summer—like College Prowler!

Seven United States presidents received graduate degrees from Harvard.

The radio station WHRB (95.3FM Cambridge), is run exclusively by Harvard students. Known throughout the Boston metropolitan area for its top-notch classical, jazz, underground rock, and blues programming, WHRB is also home of the notorious radio "Orgy" format, where the entire catalog of a certain band, record, or artist is played in sequence.

In 1995, Harvard cut funds to ROTC, saying that the military's "don't ask, don't tell" standpoint violated their non-discrimination policy.

Mr. Burns of *The Simpsons*, identified by Lisa Simpson as *"the worst man in the world,"* **is a Yale graduate and a member of a secret society. Sideshow Bob, guilty of several attempted murders, was also a Yalie.**

A side note:
***The Simpsons* writing staff includes several Harvard graduates.**

Harvard's first director of physical education and culture in 1859, Abraham Molineaux Hewlett, was black.

Actor Tommy Lee Jones and former Vice President Al Gore were once roommates at Harvard.

Cotton Mather (Class of 1678), son of Increase Mather, Harvard's sixth president, extracted what is, **until this day, the sweetest revenge on Harvard**.

Although Cotton Mather had hoped to follow in his father's footsteps, he was quickly passed over for the job three times. Frustrated, he joined a group of conservative clergymen (all Harvard alums) who founded the Collegiate School of Connecticut in 1701. In 1718, he suggested that the school was renamed Yale College.

So, in the end, **a Harvard man helped to create his alma mater's biggest rival, Yale.**

Although the University officially outlawed the filming of motion pictures on its campus since *Love Story* in the 1960s, Harvard has been featured in many films, including *Legally Blonde, The Firm, Good Will Hunting, With Honors,* and *Harvard Man.*

In one particularly cheeky stunt, former Harvard alum **William Randolph Hearst bought a jackass and snuck it into a professor's room**. When the donkey greeted the man on his arrival, hanging around the animal's neck was a card that read, "Now there are two of you."

It is believed that Harvard held the nation's first-ever spring football practice in March of 1889.

Harvard students have a tradition known as "Primal Scream," **during which they engage in a** lap around Harvard Yard in the nude.

The event, which takes place on the last night of reading period, is a way of relieving stress before finals.

Three "unpublished" hallowed rights of passage for Harvard undergrads are to:

1) pee on the John Harvard statue (whose foot visitors famously rub for good luck)

2) launch butter onto the ceiling of the Union

3) have sex in Widener (the library)

A perk of being a Harvard University Professor **(a title given to only around 10 of Harvard's preeminent professors)** is being allowed to graze cattle in Harvard Yard.

On the TV show *The Simpsons*, the Kwik-E-Mart is on 57 Mount Auburn Street, an address for the *Harvard Lampoon* Castle.

The dents on the pathway outside Harvard's Stoughton Hall are reportedly marks left by cannonballs. Nineteenth-century **Harvard undergrads warmed their rooms by heating cannonballs** (stolen from the Massachusetts State Armory down the street). To avoid receiving demerits at inspection times, students would hurl the cannonballs out their windows.

Notable Harvard Alumni

Athletics

Ted Donato (BA, 1991) - Former Harvard hockey captain; won an NCAA championship; played in the Olympic Games; and enjoyed a 13-year NHL career with the Boston Bruins and New York Rangers among other teams.

Robert T. Jones (Class of 1924) - Winner of the 1923 U.S. Open for golf.

Other

John Quincy Adams (BA, 1787) - The 6th president of the United States.

Samuel Adams (BA, 1740; MA, 1743) - Organizer of Boston Tea Party.

Michael Crichton (BA, 1964; Medical 1969) - Novelist; author of *Jurassic Park*.

Al Franken (BA, 1973) - Comedian; featured in early episodes of *Saturday Night Live*.

Al Gore (BA, 1969) - Former vice president of the United States.

Ted Kaczynski (BA, 1962) - Unabomber terrorist.

John Lithgow (BA, 1967) - Actor; *Third Rock from the Sun* and *Harry and the Hendersons*.

Conan O'Brien (BA, 1985) - Late-night talk show host.

Natalie Portman (BA, 2003) - Actress; *Star Wars* episodes 1,2,3; *Garden State*.

Henry David Thoreau (BA, 1837) - Journalist, philosopher, writer; *Civil Disobedience*, *Cape Cod*.

Kenneth G. Wilson (BA, 1956) - Physicist; Nobel Prize winner.

Fictitious Alumni

Alan Jensen - Adrian Grenier's character in *Harvard Man*.

Mitch McDeere - Tom Cruise's character in *The Firm*.

Elle Woods - Reese Witherspoon's character from *Legally Blonde* and *Legally Blonde 2*.

Attended Harvard (did not graduate)

Matt Damon (Class of 1992) - Actor, *Good Will Hunting*, *The Talented Mr. Ripley*; was actually born in Cambridge, MA in 1970.

Robert Frost (Class of 1901) - Poet; awarded an honorary degree in 1937.

Bill Gates (Class of 1977) - Co-founder of Microsoft; as of 2005, wealthiest person in the world.

William Randolph Hearst (Class of 1886) - Newspaper magnate; was known as a practical jokester up untill his dropout.

Wallace Stevens (Class of 1901) - Poet, *Sunday Morning*, *Thirteen Ways of Looking at a Blackbird*.

Notable faculty

Kenneth Arrow (Economics) - Economist; Nobel Prize winner.

Richard Clarke (Psychology, social ethics) - Diplomat; counterterrorism expert.

Walter Gilbert (Biology) - Molecular biologist; Nobel Prize winner.

Robert Putnam (Political Science) - Notable political scientist.

John Winthrop (Astronomy, math) - Astronomer; mathematician.

The Harvard Film Archive

The Harvard Film Archive (HFA) and Cinematheque is part of the Harvard University Faculty of Arts and Sciences. It is a non-profit organization located at the landmark Carpenter Center right across from the Harvard Yard. The facility includes a 210-seat theater equipped with state-of-the-art film and video equipment.

Over 25 years of age, the HFA has roots that can be traced back to 1927. It was then that the Department of Fine Arts and the Fogg Art Museum at Harvard University called for a dedicated space for film preservation and exhibition within the University. The Harvard Film Archive began its ongoing exhibition schedule on March 16, 1979 with a screening of Ernst Lubitsch's silent film, *Lady Windermere's Fan*. Thanks to the efforts of its founders, Robert Gardner, Alfred Guzzetti, Stanley Cavell, William Rothman and Vlada Petric, the HFA expanded its role, providing not only a resource for undergraduate students of film, but also developing a vast collection of 16mm and 35mm film prints, as well as rare video materials and vintage film posters and promotional materials. **To this day, the HFA remains one of the only venues in New England committed to preserving and exhibiting a diverse range of independent, international, and silent films**.

The purpose of the HFA is to further artistic and academic appreciation of the cinema and the moving image media within Harvard and the New England community by creating a setting where audiences have the opportunity to interact with filmmakers and artists alike.

The HFA has been privileged to host such renowned artists as photographer and film-maker William Klein, Swedish actress Bibi Andersson, Canadian director Atom Egoyan, independent filmmaker Harmony Korine, British director Terence Davies, African-American director Charles Burnett, Iranian filmmaker Abbas Kiarostami, actor-director John Malkovich, and the "Father of African Cinema," Ousmane Sembene.

(http://www.harvardfilmarchive.org/)

PRINCETON UNIVERSITY

Dei sub numine viget
(Under God's power she flourishes)

How Princeton Came to Be

Princeton University has long been a frontrunner of America's educational system. The University was given its charter in 1746 and was located in the town of Elizabeth for one year and the town of Newark for nine. In 1756, Prince's Town (Princeton's former name) became the home of the College of New Jersey (it wasn't called Princeton University until 1896). The entire college was housed in Nassau Hall, the largest academic building in the colonies, for nearly 50 years. During the American Revolution, it survived occupation by soldiers from both Union and Confederate sides and still today bears a cannonball scar from the Battle of Princeton.

In 1896, Princeton University adopted as its informal motto, "Princeton in the nation's service." The slogan was derived from a keynote speech by Woodrow Wilson, a former faculty member. In 1996, Princeton celebrated its 250th Anniversary and re-emphasized its historic commitment to community service. At that time, in recognition of the increased outreach of the University and its alumni all over the globe, the informal motto was extended to "Princeton in our nation's service and in the service of all nations."

Juicy Tidbits About Princeton

Princeton's Nude Olympics, the annual frolic in the first snow of the winter, is now banned.

Princeton's colors of orange and black might have referred to William of Orange (of the House of Nassau), for whom Nassau Hall, the main administrative building, was named.

Princeton's art museum is a teaching museum for the Department of Art and Archaeology as well as a cultural resource for the entire University and surrounding community.

Actor *David Duchovny*, **of *X-Files* fame, got his Bachelor's degree from Princeton and both a Ph.D. and Master's in English literature at Yale.**

Princeton University has a tradition called Newman's Day, during which students strive to consume 24 drinks in 24 hours, often going to class drunk or with beer poured into coffee mugs. The day is supposed to have derived its name from a quote attributed to the actor Paul Newman: "24 beers in a case, 24 hours in a day. Coincidence? I think not." The event is neither sanctioned by the university nor supported by Mr. Newman.

A 2003 Princeton survey found that A's made up 44-55% of undergraduate grades **at the eight Ivy League schools plus Stanford, MIT, and the University of Chicago.**

In 1783, the Continental Congress met in Princeton's Nassau Hall, making it **the capital of the United States** for a short time.

The original Princeton tradition of climbing to the top of Nassau Hall and stealing the bell clapper to prevent the bell from ringing (and starting class on the first day of the school year) was stopped after the clapper was removed for safety reasons.

Princeton's "house parties" are formal parties thrown simultaneously by its eating clubs at the end of the spring term.

The Princeton ceremonial bonfire is only held if the school beats Harvard and Yale at football in the same season.

Notable Princeton Alumni

Athletics

Hobey Baker (AB, 1914) - Famous hockey player; college hockey's top individual award is named in his memory.

Bill Bradley (AB, 1965) - Member of the Pro Basketball Hall of Fame; former U.S. senator.

Jeff Halpern (AB, 1999) - Current NHL player for the Washington Capitals.

Dick Kazmaier (AB, 1952) - Heisman Trophy winner in 1952.

Other

James Baker (AB, 1952) - Secretary of State under President George H.W. Bush.

Aaron Burr (AB, 1772) - 3rd vice president of the United States.

Dean Cain (AB, 1988) - Actor; played Superman in the television series *Lois and Clark: The New Adventures of Superman.*

Bill Frist (AB, 1974) - Senate majority leader.

Ralph Nader (AB, 1955) - Green Party presidential candidate.

John Nash (Ph.D., 1950) - Nobel laureate for economics; focal character in the 2001 film, *A Beautiful Mind.*

George Rupp (AB, 1964) - Former president of Columbia University.

Charles Schwab (AB, 1944) - founder of brokerage firm.

Adlai E. Stevenson (AB, 1922) - former governor of Illinois, Democratic presidential candidate, and United Nations ambassador.

Jimmy Stewart (AB, 1932) - Actor; played George Bailey in *It's a Wonderful Life.*

Woodrow Wilson (AB, 1879) - 28th President of the United States and governor of New Jersey.

Fictitious Alumni

Mary Jensen Matthews - The character played by Cameron Diaz in *There's Something About Mary.*

Joel Goodson - Tom Cruise's character in *Risky Business.*

Carlton and Philip Banks - From *The Fresh Prince of Bel Air.*

Sam Seaborne - Rob Lowe's character on *The West Wing.*

Attended Princeton (did not graduate)

F. Scott Fitzgerald (Class of 1917) - Author of *The Great Gatsby* and *This Side of Paradise*, which happens to be about life at Princeton.

John F. Kennedy (Class of 1939) - Left after first semester for medical reasons; 35th president of the United States.

James V. Forrestal (Class of 1915) - Secretary of Defense under Harry Truman.

Notable faculty

Alan Blinder (Economics) - Vice chairman of the Federal Reserve Board under President Bill Clinton.

Joyce Carol Oates (Creative Writing) - Accredited with many notable fictional books and essays.

Peter Singer (Human Relations) - Expert on practical ethics.

Cornel West (African-American Studies) - Also teaches theology courses at Princeton.

Andrew Wiles (Mathematics) - Proved Fermat's Last Theorem.

WPRB: King of the Collegiate Airwaves

Broadcasting live and direct from Princeton University, WPRB, Princeton's student-run radio station, is 30,000 Watts strong, making it one of the most powerful college radio stations on the planet. WPRB was founded, as WPRU, in 1940—only 20 years after public broadcasting was introduced to the United States by KDKA in Pittsburgh, PA. On November 10, 1955, the call letters were changed from WPRU to WPRB, therefore making it the first college FM station in the country. In February 1960, WPRB increased its transmitter output to 17,000 watts, making it the largest college station in America.

WPRB offers a diverse selection of music. The station has been known to play everything from Bach and Mozart, to Miles Davis and Charlie Parker on into the best that modern-day Alternative and Indie Rock has to offer. WPRB also sponsers the longest running folk show in the state. Also, during the academic year, WPRB offers sports broadcasts for Eagles, Phillies, Giants, and Yankees games.

Today, the station (103.3 FM) is situated in the studios of Bloomberg Hall (opened in 2005). **WPRB's broadcast range stretches from the outskirts of New York state through Philadelphia on into Wilmington, Delaware**. WPRB is also available to listeners everywhere on the Web. So, don't be afraid to tune in and turn the volume up . . . way up ! ! !

(http://www.wprb.com/)

UNIVERSITY OF PENNSYLVANIA

Leges sine moribus vanae (Laws without morals are useless)

How Penn Came to Be

In 1749, Benjamin Franklin wrote and circulated a pamphlet titled "Proposals Relating to the Education of Youth in Pensilvania." Unlike the other four colleges that existed in America at the time—Harvard, William and Mary, the College of New Jersey (now Princeton University), and Yale—Franklin's new school would not focus on education for the clergy. Eager to establish a college for the education of future generations, Franklin advocated an innovative concept of higher education, one which would teach both the ornamental knowledge of the arts and the practical skills necessary for making a living and doing public service. The proposed program of study became the nation's first modern liberal arts curriculum.

The doors to the University opened in 1751, when the first classes were held, and in 1786, Penn was chartered by the state of Pennsylvania as the first "university" in the United States. Penn was born with a more egalitarian vision than ever imagined before in the colonies, with members of the Board of Trustees from every denomination and the only non-sectarian faculty in the new nation.

For over a century, Penn's campus was located in downtown Philadelphia—the campus was moved across the Schuylkill River to West Philadelphia in 1872, where it has since remained. The present campus covers over 260 acres. Some recent improvements to the surrounding neighborhoods include the opening of several restaurants, a large grocery store, and a movie theater on the western edge of campus.

Juicy Tidbits About Penn

The University of Pennsylvania is home to the nation's first medical school.

The Penn Glee Club, started in 1862, is Penn's oldest performing arts group.

Benjamin Franklin, who also invented the bifocals and the lightning rod, founded the University of Pennsylvania.

The first African-American to represent the United States in any international competition was John Baxter Taylor, who won a gold medal at the 1908 London Olympics and was a Penn sprinter.

Penn is **the oldest "university"** in the United States, chartered in 1786. Harvard did not become a chartered university until 1790.

During Penn's "Hey Day," juniors walk through the campus and get covered in various condiments such as mustard and ketchup, and then congregate on the college green where the president gives a speech and officially promotes them to senior status.

Penn's alumni include Donald Trump and Martin Luther King Jr.

Penn was the first Ivy League school to establish a department in criminology.

Notable Penn Alumni

Athletics

Chuck Bednarik (BA, 1948) - Hall of Fame Linebacker; played for the Philadelphia Eagles.

Bert Bell (BA, 1919) - Former National Football League Commissioner from 1946-1959; took the league to unprecedented heights.

Andre Iguodala (Class of 2006) - NBA player for the Philadelpia 76ers (did not graduate as a result of going pro).

Billie Jean King (Ph.D., 1999) - Tennis great; defeated Bobby Riggs in the 1973 "Battle of the Sexes."

Andrea Kremer (BA, 1980) - ESPN sports correspondent.

Other

Gloria Allred (BA, 1964) - Lawyer; feminist.

Noam Chomsky (Ph.D., 1965) - Linguist and activist.

Gordon Clark (BA, 1922) - Philosopher and Christian theologian.

Leonard Lauder (BA, 1956) - Co-founder of Estée Lauder; billionaire investor.

John Legend, birth name John Stephens, (BA, 2002) - R&B singer/songwriter.

Ezra Pound (BA, 1906) - Famous Poet; *To Whistler American.*

Maury Povich (BA, 1962) - Talk-show host.

Ed Rendell (BA, 1965) - Pennsylvania Governor, former Philadelphia Mayor, and former Democratic National Committee Chairman.

Melissa Rivers (BA, 1989) - Actress and daughter of actress/comedian Joan Rivers.

Donald Trump (BS, 1968) - Billionaire investor and financier.

Attended Penn (did not graduate)

William Henry Harrison (flunked out; Class of 1791) - 9th president of the United States.

John Heisman (Class of 1894) - Football great; the Heisman Trophy is named after him.

Martin Luther King, Jr. (1949-1950) - The primary figure in the civil rights movement of the 1960s (took graduate courses; no degree).

Notable faculty

Dr. Christian B. Anfinsen (Chemistry) - Nobel Prize winner in chemistry.

Matt Blaze (Computer Science) - Associate Professor.

Thomas Childers (History) - Notable history professor.

Francis X. Diebold (Economics) - W.P. Carey Term Professor in Economics.

Dr. Gerald Edelman (Medicine) - Nobel Prize winner in medicine.

Dr. Ragnar Granit (Medicine) - Nobel Prize winner in medicine.

Kathleen Hall Jamieson (English) - University of Pennsylvania author and media analyst.

Bruce Kuklick (American History) - History department.

Dr. Simon Kuznets (Economics) - Nobel Prize winner in economics.

Dr. J. Robert Schrieffer (Physics) - Nobel Prize winner in physics.

Rogers Smith (Political Science) - Distinguished Professor of political science.

Treasures Lost and Found

It's only fitting that America's oldest university should be home to the country's largest archaeological collection. The UPenn Museum was founded in 1887 as an attraction for visitors when the University relocated from central Philadelphia to open land in West Philadelphia. There had been a small collection of antiquities at the University, and these, combined with others gathered on a late 19th-century expedition to the Middle-East, formed the basis for the museum.

The actual building was constructed in 1899 and celebrated its centennial in 1999. The museum's three floors of galleries, which range in format from tightly-packed cases of classical artifacts, to the spacious Chinese rotunda, offer enough to delight visitors of all ages and levels of knowledge and interest.

The ground floor, the Lower Egyptian Gallery, provides a stunning introduction to this culture, as it features elements from the Merenptah Palace that are claimed to be "the finest preserved part of an ancient Egyptian palace anywhere in the world."

Although nothing in the museum can top the Lower Egypt exhibition, the Mesopotamian exhibition on the top floor certainly equals it in terms of quality. It features the world's oldest wine jar and various artifacts from the Royal Tombs of Ur (one of the most important cities of Sumer situated south of Iraq, west of the Euphrates River) so fine in quality they look as if they could have easily been shipped in from the antique shops in Philadelphia's Jewelers Row.

It seems as if the musuem's sheer size is its only setback—even a quick breeze through will require several hours out of your day. And for busy Penn students, this could very well be more time than they have to spare.

(http://www.museum.upenn.edu/)

YALE UNIVERSITY

Lux et veritas
(Light and truth)

How Yale Came to Be

Yale University has graduated numerous Nobel Prize laureates and U.S. presidents, including our recent leaders William Clinton and George W. Bush. Yale's emphasis on undergraduate teaching is unusual among its peer research universities. The undergraduate College was the most selective worldwide in 2004, accepting fewer than 10 percent of its applicants, and has produced more Rhodes Scholars than any institution—except Harvard.

Yale was founded in 1701 as the **Colliegiate School of Connecticut** by a group of 10 Congregationalist ministers, all of whom were Harvard alumni—some records even describe them as "outcasts." In the late 17th century, they all met in Branford, Connecticut and compiled all of their books together—eventually leading to the formation of the school's first library. The group is now known as "The Original Founders."

Yale is the third-oldest American institution of higher education. The institution opened in the home of its first rector, Abraham Pierson, in Killingworth, Connecticut. In 1716, it was finally moved to its permanent location in New Haven. Its name was changed to Yale College in 1718 in honor of Elihu Yale—a private trader and one of the key financial contributers to the young school.

Numerous changes were made within the college during the 1800s. A variety of schools were added, including medicine (1813), divinity (1822), law (1824), graduate studies (1847), and art and architecture (1865). Women undergrads weren't admitted to Yale untill 1969. The University's youngest school, the Yale School of Management, was founded in 1976.

Juicy Tidbits About Yale

Oscar-winning actress **Jennifer Connelly** attended Yale before transferring to Stanford.

George Bush, Sr. (and G.W.) were both Yale cheerleaders.

Jodie Foster graduated magna cum laude from Yale in 1985.

"Bright College Days," Yale's unofficial alma mater, sung to the tune of a German patriotic song, "Die Wacht am Rhein" ("The Watch on the Rhine"), was penned by Henry Durand in the late 19th century. The song fell out of favor after the WWI due to anti-German sentiments.

Yale's traditions include naked parties, where **students relieve stress by drinking in the nude.**

Famous thespians have attended Yale including Angela Bassett, Jennifer Connelly, Claire Danes, Jodie Foster, Holly Hunter, David Hyde Pierce, Paul Newman, Edward Norton, Meryl Streep, and Henry Winkler.

A Yale football tradition includes the playing of "The Stripper" by the Yale Precision Marching Band, whereupon Saybrook College coeds ("college" being a Yale term for "dorm") would strip.

Notable Yale Alumni

Athletics

Walter Camp (BA, 1880) - The "Father of American Football."

Theo Epstein (BA, 1995) - Became Red Sox general manager at age 28; youngest in Major League Baseball history.

Eric Johnson (BA, 2000) - Tight end for the San Francisco 49ers.

Frank Shorter (BA, 1969) - Gold medal (1972) and silver medal (1976), Olympic marathon.

Other

Bing Gordon (BA, 1982) - Co-founder, executive vice-president, and chief creative officer of Electronic Arts.

John Kerry (BA, 1966) - U.S. senator, Massachusetts (1985-present).

Clarence King (MA, 1977) - Founder of the U.S. Geological Survey (USGS).

Art Laffer (BA, 1963) - Economist; best known for the "Laffer Curve."

Edward Lampert (BA, 1975) - Founder and chairman, ESL Investments (hedge fund), bought Kmart, Sears.

Henry Luce (BA, 1920), co-founder of *Time* magazine.

Benjamin Spock (BA, 1925) - Child psychologist.

Juan Trippe (BA, 1932) - Founder and CEO, Pan Am.

Eli Whitney (BA, 1792) - Inventor of the cotton gin.

Fictitious Alumni

Tom Buchanan - Antagonist of F. Scott Fitzgerald's *The Great Gatsby*.

"Mr. Burns" (Class of 1914) - The owner of the Springfield Nuclear Powerplant in *The Simpsons*; Homer's boss.

Nick Carraway - Narrator of F. Scott Fitzgerald's *The Great Gatsby*.

Rory Gilmore - Main character of *Gilmore Girls*.

Linus Larrabee - Protagonist in the movie *Sabrina*, played by Humphrey Bogart in 1954 and Harrison Ford in 1995.

Attended Yale (did not graduate)

Jennifer Connelly (Class of 1990) - Academy Award-winning actress.

Elia Kazan (Class of 1937) - Academy Award-winning director

Leo Laporte (Class of 1979) - Host of *The Screen Savers* on TechTV.

Oliver Stone (Class of 1966) - Academy Award-winning director.

Notable faculty

George Akerlof (Economics) - Nobel Laureate, economics, 2001.

Raymond Davis (Physics) - Nobel Laureate, physics, 2002.

John F. Enders (Physiology) - Nobel Laureate, physiology and medicine, 1954.

Tjalling Koopmans (Economics) - Nobel Laureate, economics, 1975.

James Tobin (Economics) - Nobel Laureate, economics, 1981.

Getting Involved at Yale

Timothy Dwight Hall is more than just the location for the Center for Public Service and Social Justice at Yale. Dwight Hall (as it is known to most Yalies) is the largest studen-run organization in the country, with over 60 different student-run service and advocacy groups. Their mission is "to foster civic-minded student leaders and promote service and activism in New Haven and beyond." Founded in 1886 as the Young Men's Christian Association at Yale, Dwight Hall is an independent, non-profit umbrella organization with a strong history of social justice work in the New Haven area and throughout the U.S. Built in 1935, Timothy Dwight College consists of three four-story buildings arranged around a central court, covering an entire city block.

To give you an idea of how fluent and affective the organization is run, in 2003, approximately $1.83 of volunteer service and activism was produced for every $1.00 spent by Dwight Hall. An average of over 3,000 Yale College students become involved in Dwight Hall-sponsored community service events during each academic year, with over 80 percent participating in at least one program before graduation. In 2004 alone, volunteers impacted over 20,000 people in the state of Connecticut. Among other things, **Dwight Hall offers educational and financial resources, not to mention countless publicity and networking opportunities**, especially for issues where religion plays a role.

(http://www.dwighthall.org)

SECTION 6

Straight from the Source

About Marc

Marc Zawel graduated from Cornell University in May 2004 with a Bachelor of Arts in history. Raised in Purchase, New York, he got his start in journalism as editor of his high school newspaper, the *Rye Crop*, at Rye Country Day School. It was a simple paper, published monthly, covering such important issues as the lack of student parking spaces and the quality of school lunches. By his junior year at Rye, Marc had been selected as a correspondent for *Teen People*, and his first article was published in the magazine shortly thereafter.

Once in Ithaca, he continued to pursue his interest in writing, becoming a reporter for the *Cornell Daily Sun*, the nation's second-oldest independent college newspaper. He quickly ascended the ranks there, becoming a news editor his junior year, and serving as the paper's managing editor the following year. Marc was also active in leading several other organizations at Cornell, including the Arts & Sciences Ambassadors, an admissions office outreach program, Mortar Board, a national senior honor society, and Victory Club, an annual black-tie charity fundraiser sponsored by the brothers of Alpha Delta Phi fraternity. He was a dean's list student and a recipient of the Cornell Baccalaureate Service Award.

Since graduation, Marc has experienced the inner-workings of a presidential campaign as an organizer in Orlando, Florida and also traveled across the United States. He continues to work as a freelance writer, focusing on admissions and higher education, with work appearing in the *New York Times* and several national magazines, including *Business 2.0*, *Hatch*, and *Playboy*. For fun, he enjoys running, traveling, reading, and watching movies.

More information about the author can be found at *www.marczawel.com*.

Marc Says:

I'm quick to point out that this is my first book. Heck, I've just graduated for crying out loud. But don't be mistaken; admissions, higher education, and the Ivy League are all very familiar to me. During my four years at Cornell, I experienced many facets of campus life: as managing editor of the *Cornell Daily Sun*, during which time I had regular meetings with the University president and other top administrators; as an executive board member of the Arts and Sciences Ambassadors, an admissions office outreach program; as president of Mortar Board, a national senior honor society; and as rush and philanthropy chair of Alpha Delta Phi fraternity.

Although I worked hard to leave my mark at Cornell, simply getting there was the hardest part. Unfortunately, poor, uninformed decisions characterized my college application process.

Visiting stark and empty college campuses the summer before my senior year in high school gave me little notion of the type of school that would best fit me. Coming from a small high school, there was a desire on my part to branch out into a larger community, although not at the sacrifice of losing close interaction with classmates and teachers.

With little idea of where to apply, Wesleyan University in Middletown, Connecticut was the recipient of my Early Decision application. Two rounds of the Early Decision process and a rejection letter later, I was left in a precarious situation. I devoted so much time and energy to my Wesleyan application that I spent little time exploring other options. When April rolled around, nervous anticipation filled every trip to the mailbox as the rejection letters rolled in.

From Northwestern University: "Dear Marc, Thank you for your interest in Northwestern University. The Admission Committee has completed a thorough and careful review of your application. We are sorry that we are unable to offer you a place in the freshman class."

From the University of Michigan: "Dear Mr. Zawel, After careful consideration of your application for admission to the University of Michigan, we regret that we are not able to offer you a place in the College of Literature, Science, and the Arts for the Fall 2000 term."

Then there were the wait list notifications.

From Emory University: "Dear Marc: The Emory College Admission Committee has completed an extensive review of your admission application. We are unable to offer you immediate acceptance to Emory College, but would like to extend to you a position on our Wait List."

From Washington University in St. Louis: "Dear Marc: I am writing to inform you that the Admissions Committee has placed your name on the wait list for the freshman class entering next fall at Washington University in St. Louis."

And from Cornell University: "Dear Marc: I am sure you have been anxious to learn the decision of your application to Cornell for the fall semester, 2000. The selection committee in the College of Arts and Sciences has reviewed your application carefully, but we are unable to give you a final decision at this time. Rather, we are placing your name on our waiting list."

All told, the numbers were not great. Acceptances: 2. Rejections: 2. Wait Lists: 6.

And then, several weeks later, a glimmer of hope in the form of a letter from Cornell, dated May 23, 2000: "Dear Marc, Thank you for being so patient in waiting to hear from us. Although the response to the admissions offers we made in April has made it impossible for us to admit anyone from the waiting list for the fall semester, we are very pleased to inform you that you have been admitted as a freshman entering in January, 2001."

Yes, I'd been accepted! It would be a deferred entrance, allowing me to take classes elsewhere in the fall, but come the following semester, I'd be in Ithaca.

Additional Thanks

This book would never have been possible had it not been for the help, support and confidence of countless friends, family members, professors, colleagues, and assistants. First and foremost, my parents, Susan and Daniel, and six siblings, Alex, Alyssa, Josh, Leigh, Peter, and Reva, played every role possible, from editor to cheerleader, and must be thanked. My uncle Walter Schneir and his wife, Miriam, and my grandmother, Elaine Fein, all life-long writers, were also helpful in providing direction to this first-time author.

At Cornell, Vice Provost Isaac Kramnick, the supervisor of my independent study, was insightful in his guidance and patient with an often over-worked, over-stressed senior. Richard Polenberg, one of the most brilliant professors I've ever encountered, was a wonderful and understanding advisor and friend. Dean Stephen Friedfeld, formerly in the University's academic advising and admissions office and now at Princeton, was a fantastic resource from the start and a great mentor during my time in Ithaca. And last, but certainly not least, Jeffrey S. Lehman, Cornell's president, was so kind and supportive to grant me time to discuss affirmative action with him.

Late nights spent discussing this book and its premise with my former roommate, Gautham Nagesh, gave me direction, especially when revealing the "Ivy League Myth." I'm grateful for the research assistance of several colleagues of mine at the *Cornell Daily Sun*, including Jonathan Auerbach, Owen Bochner, and Daniel Cohen, all of whom contributed considerably to the Ivy athletics chapter.

Several other Cornell undergrads must also be thanked for their help: Lauren Acker, for her research; Mikhail Agladze, for extensive research on the Ivy League's secret societies and Greek systems; Agata Gluszek, for helping to coordinate the surveying of Ivy students; Lisa Gu, for compiling statistics on the eight schools; Diana Lo, for researching Ivy pranks; Michael Morisy, for contributing to the Ivy athletics and pranks chapters; Melissa Korn, for wonderful contributions to the Ivy scandals and Skull and Bones chapters; and Erica Temel, for her contributions to the urban legends chapter.

I'm also heavily indebted to the thousands of college students who contributed their thoughts, opinions, and ideas to this book. Had it not been for them, this comprehensive work would never have been possible. In particular, Rebecca Avrutin, Kate Bossart, Kate Carcaterra, Laurie Gestal, Lizzie Maratea, and Jen Tisser all took the time to read and comment on this book's many drafts. Additional thanks to my housemates at 134 College and brothers at 777 Stewart, who were always up for a night out in Ithaca to provide a little time away from the project.

Brett Hoover, the Ivy League's assistant director for public information, was an important resource and great help to this project. Kathy Arberg, at the public information office of the Supreme Court of the United States, was so helpful in facilitating my communication with Justice Ruth Bader Ginsburg.

Finally, Chris Mason, Erik Ketzan (who contributed much to the history chapter), Adam Burns, Dana Block, Kevin Nash, and the wonderfully-talented crew at College Prowler, who placed so much trust in me in authoring this book, must be thanked. It's difficult for me to have imagined a better first publishing experience.

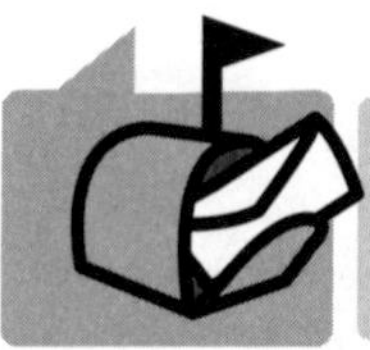

About the Contributors

Matthew Kittay—
Brown University

This book reflects a lot of time and effort, and I hope you find it as useful as I intend it to be. I picked up the project as a chance to reflect on my own experience at Brown and learn even more about the University where I spent four years of my life. I never expected to find myself writing a book.

I had a great time writing this edition of the guidebook to Brown, and I get a good deal of satisfaction knowing that people will know more about the University and what they can hope to find when they come to visit or to study at the school. Brown is a great place, and like many of the students I interviewed, there's nowhere in the world I would rather call my alma mater than Brown.

matthewkittay@collegeprowler.com

Michelle Tompkins—
Columbia University

Michelle Tompkins hails from Sacramento, California and is the youngest of four children. Prior to attending Columbia University, she worked as a disc jockey for a Santa Rosa radio station, two Sacramento Theatre Companies and founded a talent agency in Los Angeles. When academia beckoned, she attended American River College in Sacramento and for two years was the Editor-in-Chief of the college newspaper the *Current*.
At Columbia, she has served the past three years as Editor-in-Chief of the *Observer*, the literary and features magazine for Columbia School of General Studies. She will receive her BA in Film and will continue to work on creative writing projects in New York City.

michelletompkins@collegeprowler.com

Oliver Striker and Maria Adelmann—
Cornell University

I recently graduated from Cornell in May from the College of Arts and Sciences. While I pursued a major in English, I was grateful for the opportunities I had to explore a wide range of different academic disciplines. Specifically, I maintained an intensive focus in business and finance, and this summer I'll be starting a job in real estate investment banking. Shortly thereafter, I expect to reminisce about my incredible college experiences at Cornell as I slave away on Wall Street for long and endless hours.

I have no doubt, thanks to the brilliant professors I've encountered, that the skills I acquired at Cornell will serve me in good stead from here on out. I intend to stay in touch with the numerous friends I made at Cornell and meet new alums here in New York City. Cornellians have an even tighter bond with their school once they graduate, and I can't wait to visit Ithaca sometime in the near future.
If you have any questions or comments please feel free to e-mail me.

I would like to send special thanks to Mom and Dad, Clarissa Striker, Casey Becker, Tom Waldron, James Larocca, Matt Maxwell, Namita Khosla, and the entire team at College Prowler!

oliverstriker@collegeprowler.com

I am a sophomore in the College of Arts and Sciences, majoring in psychology and English. I have a great job in the Student Activities Office and have enjoyed learning how to peer counsel in EARS. I spend much of my free time writing and hope one day to be on the list of famous Cornellians. In the meantime, I just hope to do well on my finals.

mariaadelmann@collegeprowler.com

Janos Marton—
Dartmouth College

I remember the college search process as an extremely exciting time, and it's great to be able to help out future generations of (hopefully Dartmouth) students.

I graduated last year and recieved a degree in history. Born and raised in New York City, I came to Dartmouth on a whim but have loved my four years here. I'm serving my second term as student body president, am a staff writer for the *Free Press*, and a member of Chi Gamma Epsilon fraternity.

Best of luck to everyone. While I hope you find the best college for you, no matter where you end up, the next four years are going to be incredible.

janosmarton@collegeprowler.com

Dominic Hood—
Harvard University

Originally born in San Antonio and raised in New Orleans, my transition to the New England culture and weather of Harvard University challenged me beyond my dreams. I'm now a junior at Harvard College and concentrating in psychology, with my own emphasis on organizational behavior. I've been excited about writing this guide because I remember the challenge of selecting a college and I wish I had found a guide like this to provide a realistic perspective on colleges, instead of relying on the admissions office propaganda. I'm not sure what I'll be doing in the future, but I'm sure writing will play a large part in my career, so this has been a great opportunity to sharpen my writing and editing skills. If you have any questions or comments, please contact me by e-mail.

Enough about me! I want to take this opportunity to especially thank my mother who has always supported my decisions and guided me in the right direction when I was uncertain of the right path. I also want to thank my father for instilling in me the sense of independence and motivation necessary to succeed in the ever-changing, fast-paced world. And finally, above all things I thank God, for without Him this book and wonderful universities like Harvard would not be possible.

dominichood@collegeprowler.com.

Alison Fraser—
Princeton University

As a native Princetonian, it has been a privilege to work on this book, and hopefully I have been able to accurately convey my enthusiasm for both town and gown. Growing up in the Princeton area has afforded me both the "townie" and student experience, which few get to have. I initially came to Princeton, like many of my peers, with the intention of going to medical school after graduation. Three semesters of college-level chemistry quickly cured me of that plan, and I graduated from Princeton with an AB in history and a certificate in American Studies.

While at Princeton, I managed the Student *Facebook* Agency, was a member of the campus' Student Agencies—a group formed to encourage entrepreneurship on campus, and was an active member in several campus groups. I hope the shared experiences of those interviewed for this book as well as my own personal insights will help you to make the decision to come to Princeton. It is obviously not an experience for everyone, but grueling hours spent preparing thoughtful, well-researched essays for Dean's Date as well as a University-mandated senior thesis have led me to believe that Princeton provides its graduates with one of the strongest liberal arts educations in the country that effectively prepares its students for both the workplace and graduate school. I welcome any comments or questions about this College Prowler guide, so please e-mail me.

alisonfraser@collegeprowler.com

Jennifer Klein—
University of Pennsylvania

I hope you enjoyed reading this College Prowler guidebook! Writing this book was a great way to gain valuable experience and to learn more about my school. Currently, I am a junior at Penn working towards a major in visual studies, a new interdisciplinary major that combines psychology, art history, fine arts, and other subjects to create a hodgepodge of a major which is perfect for me. Outside of class, I serve as the design editor for *34th Street*, the arts and entertainment magazine of the school newspaper, the *Daily Pennsylvanian*. I can not say what lies ahead for me beyond my days as a student, but I know that wherever I end up, my experience at Penn will have been an integral part of getting me there. Hopefully, after reading this book, you feel that you are a step closer to entering your years as a college student. If you do, my goal has been achieved.

I would like to thank all the people who helped me create a book that reflects the opinions of students at Penn, not just my own. These very special people are none other than Kristen Ryan, Mike Lonegan, Rachel Firsch, Maggie Hennefeld, Michael Gertner, Dave Tompkins, Melanie Heckman, Scott Greenwald, Sandra Wang and Mary Boise.Thanks also to those who convinced me to try to write a book and helped make it a reality, including Mom, Dad, Nicky, Andrew, Jocelyn Nelson, Hazel Rushin, Kaitlin Chabina, and everyone at College Prowler.

jenniferklein@collegeprowler.com

Melissa Doscher—
Yale University

If I had to write this guide at any other time in my life, the result would have been different and biased by my perspective at the moment. But now that I have just graduated and have had the time to reflect honestly and objectively, I can step back and see the experience for what it truly was—amazing. As an English major, I have had the opportunity to immerse myself in what I love, to read the words of geniuses, and to participate in their legacies. But as a student at Yale, I have had the opportunity to grow as a person and to realize that I am not just a list of achievements or an academic machine—I am a human being. In my time at college, I have encountered people whose talents blow my mind and whose life experiences could make me laugh until I cry or cry until I laugh. These moments were some of the most important I experienced at Yale.

At this point, I feel prepared to enter my future, although I am completely unsure of what it holds for me—graduate school, publishing work, writing? I hope that this guide proves helpful whether it is assisting you in making a choice or informing you about your future. It is so exciting to be where you are, and I wish you the best of luck!

melissadoscher@collegeprowler.com.

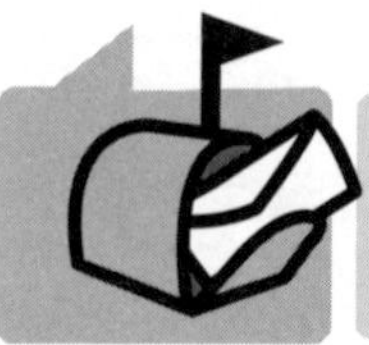

About College Prowler

Why Are We Unique?

College Prowler publishes insider reality guides on 200 different colleges across the nation. Unlike other guidebooks, the College Prowler series follows a "1 school, 1 guide" approach and dedicates one complete book to each college. Each school-specific guide is written by the students who actually go there and contains hundreds of quotes on all aspects of campus life. The company originally began as a class project.

Students Speak Out About:

- Academics
- Athletics
- Campus Dining
- Campus Housing
- Campus Strictness
- Computers
- Diversity
- Drug Scene
- Facilities
- Girls
- Greek Life
- Guys
- Local Atmosphere
- Nightlife
- Off-Campus Dining
- Off-Campus Housing
- Parking
- Safety & Security
- Transportation
- Weather

Thousands of Students Share Their Opinions

To maintain objectivity, we have refused investment from colleges. Instead, we let the students tell it like it is and fill each individual guide with over 300 student responses, both positive and negative.

Students Rank 200+ Colleges in 200+ Guides

Our rankings represent student happiness, prominence, and satisfaction for each respective category. The higher the grade, the happier, the more prominent, or the more satisfied students are with the particular category. The ranking process is in the hands of current students and recent graduates the entire time.

Over 200 Writers Dig for the Details You Care About

College Prowler has quotes from students about drugs on campus, Greek life, diversity, campus strictness and many other categories that don't usually pop up in traditional college guides. These quotes and categories are here to provide a helpful assessment of what's really happening on each campus. By including important, relevant facts and stats, like the average SAT score or the cost of a parking permit, you get a detailed look at the unique culture of each college. It's like having an older friend show you around campus.

Information Resources

We couldn't have produced this book without huge amounts of research. Below is a list of many of the sources that we would like to thank and refer you to for more information on the Ivy League.

Print Sources:
The Columbia Electronic Encyclopedia, Sixth Edition
New York Times
USA Today

Web Sites:
Ameinfo.com
AmericanCheerleader.com
Answers.com
Brown.edu
BrownDailyHerald.com
Centraldaily.com
College.hcmo.com
Collegefidential.com
Columbia.edu
Cornell.edu
Cumb.org
Dartmouth.edu
Dwighthall.org
Gfsnet.org
Gocrimson.collegesports.com
Harvard.edu
Harvardfilmarchive.org
Harvard-Magazine.com
Imdb.com
Ivyleaguesports.com
Jvibe.com
Museum.upenn.edu
News.Yahoo.com
Penn.edu
Princeton.edu
Slopeday.cornell.edu
Snpp.com
Urbanlegends.com
Wikipedia.org
Wprb.com
Yale.edu
Yalealumnimagazine.com

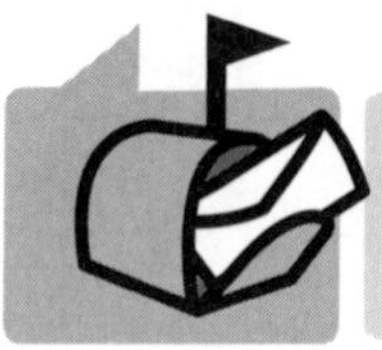

Independent Counselors

If you need additional advice, it might help to contact a counselor in your area.

ALABAMA

Kim R. Crockard Ed.D.
C3
10 Office Park Circle, Suite 212
Birmingham AL 35223
Business Phone: 205-871-1955
E-mail: drcroc@bellsouth.net

ARIZONA

Christopher Covert CEP
Sedona Educational Associates
11 Sundial Circle
PO Box 2475
Carefree AZ 85377
Business Phone: 480-575-1535
Fax: 480-575-1536
E-mail: CCovert915@aol.com
Web: www.sedonaed.com

Ceel Kenny CEP
The Ceel Kenny Group, LLC
110 Sage Drive
Sedona AZ 86336
Business Phone: 928-282-2728
E-mail: sea@sedona.net
Web: www.sedonaed.com

Nancy P. Masland Ed.S., CEP
Nancy P. Masland & Associates
PO Box 30248
Tucson AZ 85751
Business Phone: 520-749-4220
Fax: 520-749-9475
E-mail: nancy@nancypmasland.com
Web: www.nancypmasland.com

W. Judge Mason M.A.
Sedona Educational Associates
150 Devils Kitchen Drive
Sedona AZ 86351
Business Phone: 928-284-5719
Fax: 928-284-5802
E-mail: judge@judgemason.org
Web: www.judgemason.org

Adrianne G. Selbst M.Ed., CEP
College Quest
21826 N. Calle Royale
Scottsdale AZ 85255
Business Phone: 480-585-7993
Fax: 480-585-2805
E-mail: AdrianneG@cox.net
Web: www.azcollegequest.com

ARKANSAS

Thomas A. Eppley Jr., Ed.D., CEP
Thomas A. Eppley & Associates
2901 N. Grant
Little Rock AR 72207
Business Phone: 501-223-8949
Fax: 501-223-2435

CALIFORNIA

Diane Grant Albrecht M.S., CEP
Cathedral Hill Office Building
1255 Post Street
Suite 1001
San Francisco CA 94109
Business Phone: 415-928-1562
Fax: 415-928-4867
E-mail: DGA84@aol.com

Miriam I. Bodin M.A., CEP
Bodin Associates/Educ. Alternatives
1110 West C St. Suite 2108
San Diego CA
Business Phone: 858-484-7378
Fax: 650-937-0011

E-mail: mbodin@bodinassociates.com
Web: www.bodinassociates.com

Miriam I. Bodin M.A., CEP
Bodin Associates/Educ. Alternatives
5050 El Camino Real
Suite 101
Los Altos CA 94022
Business Phone: 650-937-1111
Fax: 650-937-0011
E-mail: mbodin@bodinassociates.com
Web: www.bodinassociates.com

Katherine Cohen Ph.D.
IvyWise, LLC
9744 Wilshire Blvd., Suite 312
Beverly Hills CA 90212
Business Phone: 310-246-0406
Fax: 310-246-0407
E-mail: jackie@ivywise.com
Web: www.ivywise.com

Karen Curreri M.S.
Curreri College Counseling
14035 West Tahitii Way #323
Marina del Rey CA 90292
Business Phone: 310-822-5020
Fax: 310-302-1966
E-mail: currericollegecounseling@adelphia.net

Kay Davison CEP
National Institute for Educational Planning
2042 Business Center Drive
Suite 200
Irvine CA 92612
Business Phone: 949-833-7899
Fax: 949-261-0262
E-mail: kdavisonca@earthlink.net

David Denman M.Div.
Educational Consultant
3030 Bridgeway Avenue
Ste. 233
Sausalito CA 94965
Business Phone: 415-332-1831
Fax: 415-332-6205

Paula G. Feldman M.S., CEP
Educational Consultant
4618 Dorchester Road
Corona del Mar CA 92625
Business Phone: 949-759-0330
Fax: 949-760-0888
E-mail: Paulaedcon@sbcglobal.net

Diane Geller M.A.,CEP
DeFelice & Geller, Inc.
2999 Overland Avenue
Suite 217
Los Angeles CA 90064
Business Phone: 310-202-0838
Fax: 310-202-6455
E-mail: DHGeller@aol.com

Lynn Hamilton M.A., CEP
PO Box 50724
Santa Barbara CA 93150
Business Phone: 805-969-1177 or 800-793-7506
Fax: 805-969-2973
E-mail: L.hamilton@cox.net
Web: www.schoolfinders.com

Melissa Mose M.A.
Marriage & Family Therapist
The S.T.E.P. Group
18663 Ventura Blvd. #201
Tarzana CA 91356
Business Phone: 818-222-6340
Fax: 818-222-5440
E-mail: mlmose@pacbell.net

Jill Q. Porter M.S., CEP
Educational Consultant
1850 Castellana Road
La Jolla CA 92037-3840
Business Phone: 619-284-7277
Fax: 858-454-5580
E-mail: porters@electriciti.com

Virginia Reiss M.S., CEP
Licensed Educational Psychologist
980 Magnolia Avenue
Suite 8
Larkspur CA 94939
Business Phone: 415-461-4788
Fax: 415-461-4626
E-mail: vreiss2@earthlink.net
Web: www.virginiareiss.com

Barbara Stahl M.A., CEP
3373 Jennifer Way
San Jose CA 95124
Business Phone: 408-377-3078
E-mail: barbaraestahl@earthlink.net

Toby Waldorf
Educational Consultant
212 S. Woodburn Dr.
Los Angeles CA 90049
Business Phone: 310-476-2762
Fax: 310-476-2772
E-mail: twaldorf@twaldorf.com
Web: www.destination-u.com/toby

Rachel Winston
Educators With A Vision
7700 Irvine Center Dr., Suite 800
Irvine CA 92612
Business Phone: 949-833-7706
Fax: 949-833-1450
E-mail: Educators@MathTeachers.com

COLORADO

Steven R. Antonoff Ph.D., CEP
Antonoff Associates, Inc.
1241 South Parker Rd.
Suite 203
Denver CO 80231
Business Phone: 303-745-5577
Fax: 303-745-4488
E-mail: schoolbuff@aol.com

Diane E. Arnold CEP
Educational Consultant
2733 Big Horn Circle
Lafayette CO 80026
Business Phone: 303-604-2339
Fax: 303-604-2382
E-mail: Darnold64@aol.com

Shirley Burr Darling M.A., CEP
Educational Consulting Service
1355 S. Colorado Blvd.
Ste. 300
Denver CO 80222
Business Phone: 303-757-3010
Fax: 303-757-3018
E-mail: SBDarling@aol.com

Jana P. Lynn Ph.D., CEP
Lynn Associates
6249 Songbird Circle
Boulder CO 80303
Business Phone: 303-443-7845
Fax: 303-442-3818
E-mail: drjanalynn@comcast.net

Estelle R. Meskin M.A., CEP
Educational Consultant
282 Monroe Street
Denver CO 80206
Business Phone: 303-394-3291
Fax: 303-355-7541
E-mail: EMeskin@aol.com
Web: www.EstelleMeskin.com

CONNECTICUT

Camille M. Bertram CEP
Camille M. Bertram, Educational Consultants
120 Riders Lane
Fairfield CT 06824
Business Phone: 203-255-2577
Fax: 203-255-4713
E-mail: CMBert@cmbconsultants.com
Web: www.cmbconsultants.com

Virginia J. Bush CEP
Educational Consultant
15 Agawam Ave.
Fenwick
Old Saybrook CT 06475
Business Phone: 860-388-1242
Fax: 860-388-3250

Adrienne A. DuBois M.S.Ed., CEP
Adrienne A. DuBois Associates
15 E. Putnam Avenue
Greenwich CT 06830
Business Phone: 203-629-2566
Fax: 203-629-5337
E-mail: AADuBois@aol.com

Donald M. Dunbar M.Ed.
Dunbar Educational Consultants
191 Elm Street
New Canaan CT 06840
Business Phone: 203-966-5454
Fax: 203-259-4943

Susan Edwards M.A., CEP
Susan Edwards & Associates
10 Pennoyer Street
Rowayton CT 06853
Business Phone: 203-866-2692
Fax: 203-838-5999
E-mail: SBEEduCon@worldnet.att.net

Adam R. Goldberg
Leslie S. Goldberg & Associates, LLC
10 Hunter Drive
West Hartford CT 06117
Business Phone: 860-249-5151
Fax: 617-969-5125
E-mail: adam@edconsult.org
Web: www.edconsult.org

John Greenwood
Dunbar Educational Consultants
191 Elm Street
New Canaan CT 06840
Business Phone: 203-966-5454
Fax: 203-966-5530
E-mail: dunbedc@aol.com

Alan Haas CEP
Educational Futures
191 Main Street
New Canaan CT 06840
Business Phone: 203-966-6993
Fax: 203-966-3832
E-mail: EduFutures@aol.com

Alan Haas CEP
Educational Futures
191 Main Street
New Canaan CT 06840
Business Phone: 203-966-6993
Fax: 203-966-3832
E-mail: EduFutures@aol.com

Emilie K. Hinman
Dunbar Educational Consultants, Inc.
10 Indian Chase Drive
Greenwich CT 06830
Business Phone: 203-625-6344
Fax: 203-622-0423
E-mail: EKHDunbar@aol.com
Margaret King Ph.D.
Margaret King & Associates
1895 Post Road
Fairfield CT 06430
Business Phone: 203-255-5511
Fax: 203-254-3678
E-mail: mkingec@aol.com

Carol A. Loewith M.A., CEP
Educational Consultant
191 Fairfield Woods Road
Fairfield CT 06825
Business Phone: 203-372-4222
Fax: 203-372-3538
E-mail: CALEdCon@aol.com

William M. Morse Ph.D., CEP
William Morse Associates, Inc.
260 Riverside Avenue
Westport CT 06880-4804
Business Phone: 203-222-1066
Fax: 203-222-1315

James P. Robinson
Robinson / Scholastic Objectives
281 Loon Meadow Drive
PO Box 628
Norfolk CT 06058
Business Phone: 860-542-1300
Fax: 860-524-1301
E-mail: jrobinson@scholasticobjectives.net
Web: www.scholasticobjectives.net

Daria M. Rockholz Ph.D.
Educational Consulting Services
PO Box 539
Ridgefield CT 06877
Business Phone: 203-313-0734
Fax: 203-740-1048
E-mail: drockholz@aol.com

Jan Rooker M.A.
College Coach
6 Prides Crossing
New Canaan CT 06840
Business Phone: 203-972-3487
Fax: 203-972-0654
E-mail: rookerj@msn.com
Web: www.janrooker.com

Marcia B. Rubinstien M.A., CEP
EDUFAX
345 North Main Street
Suite 317
West Hartford CT 06117
Business Phone: 860-233-3900
Fax: 860-233-3900
E-mail: edufax@edufax.com
Web: www.edufax.com

Amy Sack Ph.D.
101 Oakland Drive
Trumbull CT 06611
Business Phone: 203-261-8068
E-mail: asack2@aol.com
Web: www.admissionsaccomplished.com

Alison Pedicord Schleifer M.S.
Educational Consultant
220 Alston Avenue
New Haven CT 06515
Business Phone: 203-387-3454
Fax: 203-387-3454

Laura Seese Ph.D.
Educational Advancement Associates
14 Old Farms Lane
West Suffield CT 06093
Business Phone: 860-254-5451
Fax: 860-254-5451
E-mail: LauraSeese@edadvancement.com
Web: www.edadvancement.com

Mary Spiegel M.A.
Spiegel Educational Consulting
16 Plumb Creek Road
Trumbull CT 06611
Business Phone: 203-261-3299
Fax: 203-261-5764
E-mail: spiegels2@juno.com
Web: www.trumbullbiz.com/go2college

Susan Wexler M.S., CEP
Educational Consultant
14 Bushy Ridge Road
Westport CT 06880
Business Phone: 203-341-0599
Fax: 203-226-7758
E-mail: susanwex@aol.com

DELAWARE

Bettina G. Heiman M.A.
CollegeChoice
2408 Driftwood Drive
Wilmington DE 19810
Business Phone: 302-475-7912
Fax: 302-475-7912
E-mail: collegechoice@comcast.net

WASHINGTON DC

Kpakpundu Ezeze Ed.D.
Future Quest, Inc.
1346 Ritchie Place, NE
Washington DC 20017
Business Phone: 202-832-6339
Fax: 202-529-6836
E-mail: kezeze@aol.com

Geraldine C. Fryer CEP
Educational Advisor
5125 MacArthur Blvd, Ste. 42
Washington DC 20016-3300
Business Phone: 202-333-3230
Fax: 914-967-7966
E-mail: gcfryer@aol.com

Steven Roy Goodman M.S., J.D., CEP
Tilden Gardens 502
3020 Tilden St. NW
Washington DC 20008-3081
Business Phone: 202-986-9431
Fax: 202-986-9432
E-mail: steve@topcolleges.com
Web: www.topcolleges.com

Virginia Reynolds Vogel Ed.S., CEP
Educational Guidance Service
3006 Dent Place, NW
Washington DC 20007
Business Phone: 202-342-1979
Fax: 202-342-2646

FLORIDA

Robin G. Abedon M.A.T., CEP
12904 Mizner Way
Wellington FL 33414
Business Phone: 561-790-5462

Fax: 561-790-0593
E-mail: rabedon@takingtheNextStep.com
Web: www.takingtheNextStep.com

Betty Jean Arsenault Ed.D.
Arsenault Educational Consultants, LLC
801 International Parkway
5th Floor
Heathrow FL 32746
Business Phone: 407-562-1800
Fax: 407-869-8444
E-mail: DrBetty@bellsouth.net
Web: www.ArsenaultEducationalConsultants.com

Sandy Bercu M.A.
College Consulting Services
14043 Shady Shores Drive
Tampa FL 33613
Business Phone: 813-963-6342
Fax: 813-963-1929
E-mail: sbercu@aol.com

Mary B. Consoli B.S.Ed., CEP
Mary B. Consoli Associates
111 2nd Avenue NE
St. Petersburg FL 33701
Business Phone: 727-896-5022
E-mail: mbconsoli@aol.com
Web: www.mbconsoli.com

Leslie Goldberg M.Ed., CEP
New England Educational Advisory Service, LLC
7301-A Palmetto Park Road
Suite 206-B
Boca Raton FL 33433
Business Phone: 561-620-0050 or 800-696-5684
Fax: 781-749-2029
E-mail: leslie@edconsult.org
Web: www.teenproblem.com

Shirley H. Grate CEP
SG, Inc. (GRES)
PO Box 17623
West Palm Beach FL 33406-7623
Business Phone: 561-357-5592
Fax: 561-357-5592
E-mail: sgrate@aol.com

Janet Greenwood Ph.D., CEP
Greenwood Associates, Inc.
310 S. Brevard Avenue
Tampa FL 33606
Business Phone: 813-254-5303
Fax: 813-250-9060
Web: www.GreenwdAssoc.com

Janet I. Greenwood Ph.D., CEP
Greenwood Associates, Inc.
425 W. Colonial Drive, Suite 104
Orlando FL 32804
Business Phone: 407-835-1240
Fax: 813-250-9060
Web: www.GreenwdAssoc.com

Louise Kreiner CEP
New England Educational Advisory Service
7301-A Palmetto Park Rd.
Suite 206-B
Boca Raton FL 33433
Business Phone: 561-620-0050 or 800-696-5684
Fax: 781-749-2029
E-mail: KreinerCon@aol.com
Web: www.teenproblem.com

Midge Lipkin Ph.D., CEP
Schoolsearch
161 Orchid Cay Drive
Palm Beach Gardens FL 33418
Business Phone: 561-630-3666
Fax: 617-489-5641
E-mail: mlipkin@schoolsearch.com

Martha Moses M.A., CEP
Martha Moses & Associates
8100 SW 81 Drive, Suite 277
Miami FL 33143
Business Phone: 305-273-0014
Fax: 305-273-7879
E-mail: mmoses@gate.net

Judi Robinovitz M.A., CEP
Judi Robinovitz Associates
3010 N. Military Trail
Suite 220
Boca Raton FL 33431
Business Phone: 561-241-1610 or 888-GET-1600
Fax: 561-241-1605
E-mail: JudiRobino@aol.com
Web: www.ScoreAtTheTop.com

Judi Robinovitz M.A., CEP
Judi Robinovitz Associates
2513 Burns Road
Palm Beach Gardens FL 33410
Business Phone: 561-626-2662 or 888-438-1600
Fax: 561-626-2756
E-mail: JudiRobino@aol.com
Web: www.ScoreAtTheTop.com

Judi Robinovitz M.A., CEP
Judi Robinovitz Associates
12008 South Shore Blvd. Ste. 105
Wellington FL 33414
Business Phone: 561-333-8882 or 888-438-1600
Fax: 561-333-8840
E-mail: JudiRobino@aol.com
Web: www.ScoreAtTheTop.com

Joan Tager M.S., CEP
Educational Consultant
121 St. Edward Place
Palm Beach Gardens FL 33418
Business Phone: 561-627-3757
Fax: 561-627-4243
E-mail: capstager1@aol.com

GEORGIA

Tamara A. Ancona M.A.
Licensed Professional Counselor
5770 Lake Heights Circle
Alpharetta GA 30022
Business Phone: 678-297-0708
Fax: 770-232-0460
E-mail: tancona@tagcounseling.com
Web: www.tagcounseling.com

Leonard Buccellato Ph.D., CEP
Licensed Psychologist
3340 Peachtree Rd., NE
Suite 1125
Atlanta GA 30326
Business Phone: 404-231-9925
Fax: 404-231-0689
E-mail: leonardbuccellato@yahoo.com

Mark L. Fisher Ed.D., CEP
Fisher Educational Consultants, Inc.
10 Glenlake Parkway
South Tower, #130-182
Atlanta GA 30328
Business Phone: 678-222-3444
Fax: 770-399-9933
E-mail: drmarkfisher@bellsouth.net

Lida H. Griest M.Ed.
Lida Griest Educational Counseling
3400 Peachtree Road, Suite 1600
Atlanta GA 30326
Business Phone: 404-239-0053
Fax: 404-239-0757
E-mail: griest@bellsouth.net

Jean P. Hague M.A., CEP
400 Colony Square
1201 Peachtree NE #200
Atlanta GA 30361
Business Phone: 404-872-9128
Fax: 404-870-9093
E-mail: jeanhague@aol.com

B. J. Hopper M.Ed., CEP
Educational Consultant
3400 Peachtree Rd
Suite 1539
Atlanta GA 30326
Business Phone: 404-814-1394
Fax: 770-475-8123
E-mail: BHopper719@aol.com

George G. Kirkpatrick M.A., CEP
The George G. Kirkpatrick Co.
2970 Peachtree Rd.
Ste. 345
Atlanta GA 30305
Business Phone: 404-233-3989
Fax: 404-233-0497
E-mail: kirkeducon@aol.com
Web: www.theggkco.com

Sandra G. Lawrence M.Ed.
Independent College Consultant
2952 Foxhall Circle
Augusta GA 30907
Business Phone: 706-860-9517
E-mail: MrsL31747@aol.com

Teed M. Poe M.S.
501 Manor Ridge Drive
Atlanta GA 30305

Business Phone: 404-351-9557
Fax: 404-351-0339
E-mail: teedmp@comcast.net

J. Victor Spigener III
Spigener & Associates
8045 Sandorn Drive
Atlanta GA 30075
Business Phone: 770-650-1962
Fax: 770-650-5799
E-mail: spigenerv@bellsouth.net

Leigh Anne Spraetz LPC, NCC
Greenwood Associates, Inc.
730 Mallory Manor Court
Alpharetta GA 30022
Business Phone: 678-336-3265
Fax: 678-393-0941
E-mail: laspraetz@comcast.net
Web: www.greenwdassoc.com

Christie Theriot Woodfin M.Ed., LPC, CEP
Woodfin & Associates, LLC
1201 Peachtree Rd., 400 Colony Sq.
Suite 200
Atlanta GA 30361
Business Phone: 404-870-9105
Fax: 404-506-9660
E-mail: cwoodfin@bestschoolforyou.com
Web: www.bestschoolforyou.com

ILLINOIS

Susan J. Bigg M.P.H., CEP
Educational Consultant
1410 Wrightwood Ave #K
Chicago IL 60614-1140
Business Phone: 773-404-1699
Fax: 773-404-1620
E-mail: wbyeats@megsinet.net

Jill Burstein M.A., CEP
Jill Burstein Educational Consulting
30 W. St. Andrews
Deerfield IL 60015
Business Phone: 847-940-8090
Fax: 847-940-5507
E-mail: collegefinderjb@aol.com
Web: www.college-finder.org

Harriet R. Gershman M.S.Ed., CEP
Access Education International
1150 N. Lake Shore Drive
Chicago IL 60611
Business Phone: 312-642-4001 or 888-967-5333
Fax: 312-943-1063
E-mail: ACSGersh@aol.com

Harriet R. Gershman M.S.Ed., CEP
Access Education International
1800 Sherman Avenue
Suite 203
Evanston IL 60201
Business Phone: 847-492-3434
Fax: 847-492-3433
E-mail: acsgersh@aol.com

Nancy Gore Marcus M.A.Ed., CEP
333 Rosewood Avenue
Winnetka IL 60093
Business Phone: 847-446-7557
Fax: 847-446-5512
E-mail: ngmadvise@aol.com

Imy F. Wax M.S., CEP
Licensed Clinical Prof. Counselor
1320 Carol Lane
Deerfield IL 60015
Business Phone: 847-945-0913
Fax: 847-945-6475
E-mail: ImyWax@aol.com

KENTUCKY

Paul H. Levitch
Levitch & Associates, LLC
7508 New LaGrange Rd., Suite 9
Louisville KY 40222
Business Phone: 502-412-7244
Fax: 502-412-7247
E-mail: paul@levitch.net
Web: www.levitch.net

Jane Schoenfeld Shropshire CEP
3079 1/2 Royster Road
Lexington KY 40516
Business Phone: 859-396-9508
E-mail: jshrop@att.net

LOUISIANA

Nancy W. Cadwallader M.F.A., CEP
Collegiate Advisory Placement Serv.
P.O. Box 66371
Baton Rouge LA 70896
Business Phone: 225-928-1818
Fax: 225-928-1322
E-mail: cadwallader@worldnet.att.net

Kathie Livaudais Carnahan
Carnahan & Associates
4904 Magazine Street
New Orleans LA 70115
Business Phone: 504-269-6449
Fax: 504-894-1008
E-mail: collegepro@bellsouth.net

Farron G. Peatross M.A., CEP
Educational Placement Services, Inc.
3839 Betty Virginia Circle
Shreveport LA 71106
Business Phone: 318-869-0088
Fax: 901-685-3157
E-mail: peatross@bellsouth.net
Web: www.educplacement.com

Christie Theriot Woodfin M.Ed., LPC, CEP
Woodfin & Associates, LLC
6221 South Claiborne Ave. #439
New Orleans LA 70125
Business Phone: 866-942-0345
E-mail: cwoodfin@bestschoolforyou.com
Web: www.bestschoolforyou.com

MARYLAND

Judith Bass
Bass Educational Services
4229 Cherry Valley Dr.
Olney MD 20832
Business Phone: 240-606-4996
Fax: 240-220-0654
E-mail: judy@collegeconsulting.info

Diane E. Epstein CEP
College Planning Service, Inc.
6704 Pawtucket Road
Bethesda MD 20817-4836
Business Phone: 301-320-5311
Fax: 301-320-5310
E-mail: dianecps@comcast.net

Charlotte Klaar M.S., CEP
College Consulting Services
14 Fiona Way
Brunswick MD 21758
Business Phone: 301-834-6888
Fax: 301-834-6888
E-mail: CKlaar@ccs4college.com
Web: www.ccs4college.com

Shirley Levin M.A., CEP
College Bound
6809 Breezewood Terrace
Rockville MD 20852
Business Phone: 301-468-6668
Fax: 301-770-3833
E-mail: lev4advice@verizon.net

Irena S. Makarushka Ph.D.
School Search Group, LLC
502 Baltimore Avenue
Towson MD 21204
Business Phone: 410-494-0209
Fax: 410-494-0274
E-mail: makarushka@ssgllc.com

Susan M. Patterson M.Ed.
College Placement Consulting, LLC
8133 Elliott Rd. Suite 2
Easton MD 21601
Business Phone: 410-822-4500
Fax: 410-822-3226
E-mail: collegeplacement@mail.com

Lorine Potts-Dupré Ph.D., CEP
7006 Carroll Avenue
Suite 202
Takoma Park MD 20912
Business Phone: 301-891-8866
Fax: 301-270-8352
E-mail: LNPD@aol.com

Gail H. Ross M.A.
College Admissions Consultant
6128 Durbin Road
Bethesda MD 20817
Business Phone: 301-229-7005
Fax: 301-229-6161
E-mail: gailhross@hotmail.com

Sara Slaff J.D.
CollegePlan, LLC
1113 Hollins Lane
Baltimore MD 21209
Business Phone: 410-828-6011
Fax: 410-828-6083
E-mail: collegeplan@verizon.net
Web: www.collegeplanllc.com

Virginia Reynolds Vogel Ed.S., CEP
Educational Guidance Service
85 Bay Drive
Annapolis MD 21403
Business Phone: 301-469-6973
Fax: 301-263-4171

MASSACHUSETTS

Peter D. Adams Ed.M.
Educational Counseling
PO Box 620
Ashfield MA 01330
Business Phone: 860-233-6624
Fax: 413-628-3388
E-mail: padamsec@verizon.net

Edward L. Bigelow
Dunbar Educational Consultants, Inc.
PO Box 248
Dedham MA 02027
Business Phone: 781-329-1248
Fax: 781-329-6477
E-mail: MOE9817@aol.com

Susan Bisson Ed.M.
Advocates for Human Potential, Inc.
490-B Boston Post Road
Suite 200
Sudbury MA 01776
Business Phone: 978-261-1433
Fax: 978-443-4722
E-mail: sbisson@ahpnet.com
Web: www.ahpnet.com

Joan H. Bress LICSW, CEP
College Resource Associates
12 Southwood Road
Worcester MA 01609
Business Phone: 508-757-8920
Fax: 508-757-3383
E-mail: jbress@aol.com
Web: www.CollegeResourceAssociates.com

Stella Christine Chapman
Starr & Chapman, Inc.
1073 Long Pond Road
Plymouth MA 02360-2637
Business Phone: 617-938-3595
Fax: 617-938-3603
E-mail: chapman_christine@yahoo.com
Web: www.starreducation.com

Marilyn F. Engelman Ph.D., CEP
Educational Directions
57 East Main Street
Suite 220
Westborough MA 01581
Business Phone: 508-870-1515
Fax: 508-870-1505
E-mail: mengelman@educationaldirections.com
Web: www.educationaldirections.com

Marilyn F. Engelman Ph.D., CEP
Educational Directions
73 Lexington Street, Ste. 201
Auburndale MA 02466
Business Phone: 617-964-0440
E-mail: marilyn171@aol.com

Carol Gill M.A., CEP
Carol Gill Associates
39 Glenoe Road
Chestnut Hill MA 02467
Business Phone: 617-739-6030
Fax: 914-693-6211
E-mail: carolgill@aol.com
Web: www.collegesplus.com

Adam R. Goldberg
Leslie S. Goldberg & Associates, LLC
351 Hunnewell Street
Needham MA 02494
Business Phone: 617-969-5151
Fax: 617-969-5125
E-mail: adam@edconsult.org
Web: www.edconsult.org

Leslie Goldberg M.Ed., CEP
Leslie Goldberg & Associates, LLC
15 Sentinel Road
Hingham MA 02043

Business Phone: 781-749-2074
Fax: 781-749-2029
E-mail: leslie@edconsult.org
Web: www.edconsult.org

Renee LeWinter Goldberg Ed.D., CEP
Educational Options, LLC
175 Beacon Street, #309
Somerville MA 02143
Business Phone: 617-864-8864 or 617-287-7439
Fax: 617-864-3515
E-mail: Renee@optionsined.com
Web: www.optionsined.com

Charlotte Klaar M.S., CEP
College Consulting Services
30 Lyman Street
Suite 1
Westborough MA 01581
Business Phone: 508-836-9555
Fax: 508-836-9555
E-mail: CKlaar@ccs4college.com
Web: www.ccs4college.com

Louise Kreiner CEP
Educational Consultant
PO Box 949
Amesbury MA 01913
Business Phone: 978-388-1578
Fax: 978-388-1873
E-mail: KreinerCon@aol.com
Web: www.louisekreiner.com

Timothy B. Lee Ed.M., CEP
Advocates for Human Potential, Inc.
490-B Boston Post Road, Ste. 200
Sudbury MA 01776-3365
Business Phone: 978-443-0055 x412
Fax: 978-443-4722
E-mail: tlee@ahpnet.com
Web: www.ahpnet.com

Midge Lipkin Ph.D., CEP
Schoolsearch
127 Marsh Street
Belmont MA 02478
Business Phone: 617-489-5785
Fax: 617-489-5641
E-mail: mlipkin@schoolsearch.com

Midge Lipkin Ph.D., CEP
Schoolsearch
127 Marsh Street
Belmont MA 02478
Business Phone: 617-489-5785
Fax: 617-489-5641
E-mail: mlipkin@schoolsearch.com

Midge Lipkin Ph.D., CEP
Schoolsearch
63 Waterline Drive
New Seabury MA 02649
Business Phone: 508-477-0251
Fax: 508-477-7780
E-mail: mlipkin@schoolsearch.com

Mary Mansfield M.Ed., CEP
Mansfield Associates
20 Lincoln Lane
Sudbury MA 01776
Business Phone: 978-443-4404
Fax: 978-443-9669
E-mail: rsmansfie@aol.com

Benjamin L. Mason Ed.M., CEP
Mason & Associates
131 Crescent Street
Waltham MA 02453
Business Phone: 781-209-0048
Fax: 802-425-7601
E-mail: beemason@aol.com

Sarah M. McGinty Ph.D., CEP
McGinty Consulting Group
322 Marlborough Street
Boston MA 02116
Business Phone: 617-262-3435
Fax: 617-262-0561
E-mail: sarahmcginty@att.net
Web: www.mcgintyconsulting.com

Adam S. Metsch
The College Advisor of New England, Inc.
94 Shaker Road
East Longmeadow MA 01028
Business Phone: 413-525-9595
Fax: 413-525-9599
E-mail: Adam@College-Advisor.com
Web: www.College-Advisor.com

Bonny Musinsky M.A., CEP
Musinsky & Associates
49 Kendall Common Road
Weston MA 02493
Business Phone: 781-899-5759
Fax: 781-647-7919
E-mail: musin@attbi.com

Laurie H. Nash Ed.D., CEP
Educational Consultant
24 Cross Hill Road
Newton Centre MA 02459
Business Phone: 617-332-2794
Fax: 617-965-8338
E-mail: Laurie@LaurieNash.com
Web: www.LaurieNash.com

Michael W. Spence CEP
Howland & Spence, Inc.
266 Beacon Street
Boston MA 02116
Business Phone: 617-536-4319
Fax: 617-536-9031
E-mail: mspence@howlandspence.com

MICHIGAN

Teresa S. Lloyd Ed.S.
Grosse Point College Admissions Consulting
1020 Bishop Road
Grosse Point Park MI 48230
Business Phone: 313-882-2526
E-mail: tslloyd@comcast.net

Lynn B. Luckenbach M.Ed., CEP
Lynn B. Luckenbach, Inc.
111 S. Woodward
Suite 214
Birmingham MI 48009
Business Phone: 248-644-0749
Fax: 248-642-0136
E-mail: lynnluck@aol.com

MINNESOTA

Valerie J. Broughton Ph.D., CEP
College Connectors
100 Second Ave. NE #750
Minneapolis MN 55413
Business Phone: 612-251-1978
E-mail: valerie@collegeconnectors.com
Web: www.collegeconnectors.com

Nicky B. Carpenter
1001 Twelve Oaks Center Drive
Suite 1020
Wayzata MN 55391
Business Phone: 952-475-0330
Fax: 952-475-0362
E-mail: NCARPEN635@aol.com

Deborah Landon MBA
Educational Advisory Services
4549 Abbott Avenue South
Minneapolis MN 55410
Business Phone: 612-922-5888
Fax: 801-880-7589
E-mail: LandonEducation@yahoo.com
Web: www.susanmspain.com

Suzanne Luse M.A., CEP
Suzanne Luse & Associates
3588 Woodland Trail
Eagan MN 55123
Business Phone: 651-688-0595
Fax: 651-406-8455
E-mail: sueluse@comcast.net

Susan F. Sykes M.A.
Educational Consultant
19 Hawthorne Road
Hopkins MN 55343
Business Phone: 763-218-1030
Fax: 952-935-8675
E-mail: ssadvisor@winternet.com

MISSOURI

James C. Heryer M.A., CEP
College Guidance & Placement
705 Brush Creek Blvd.
Kansas City MO 64110
Business Phone: 816-531-2706
Fax: 816-531-2738
E-mail: jheryer@aol.com

Rosalyn S. Lowenhaupt M.A., CEP
Indep. School Placement Service
7710 Carondelet, #101
St. Louis MO 63105

Business Phone: 314-727-4909
Fax: 314-727-4340
E-mail: isps-rsl@att.net

Jane Schoenfeld Shropshire CEP
Indep. School Placement Serv.
7710 Carondelet Ave.
Suite 101
St. Louis MO 63105
Business Phone: 314-727-4909
Fax: 314-727-4340
E-mail: jshrop@att.net

NEVADA

Harriet R. Gershman M.S.Ed., CEP
Access Education International
6879 West Charleston
Suite B
Las Vegas NV 89117
Business Phone: 702-898-6911 or 888-967-5333
Fax: 847-492-3433
E-mail: aeiconsults@aol.com

James A. Nolan M.A., CEP
Access Education International
6879 West Charleston
Suite B
Las Vegas NV 89117
Business Phone: 702-898-6911 or 888-967-5333
Fax: 847-492-3433
E-mail: aeiconsults@aol.com

Virginia Reiss M.S., CEP
Licensed Educational Psychologist
Access Education International
6879 West Charleston
Suite B
Las Vegas NV 89117
Business Phone: 702-898-6911 or 888-967-5333
Fax: 847-492-3433
E-mail: aeiconsults@aol.com

NEW HAMPSHIRE

Mei-Ling Henrichson CEP
Mei-Ling Henrichson Educ. Consulting
PO Box 138
Winchester NH 03470
Business Phone: 603-239-8189
Fax: 603-239-8311
E-mail: mlhedcon@ix.netcom.com

NEW JERSEY

Amy Leib Alexander M.S.
ALA Educational Consulting
206 Claremont Avenue
Montclair NJ 07042
Business Phone: 973-655-1603
Fax: 973-655-1601
E-mail: ALAeduc@comcast.net

Judith Berg M.A., CEP
Educational Consultant
257 Monmouth St. Bldg. B #1
Oakhurst NJ 07755
Business Phone: 732-531-1300
Fax: 732-531-6493
E-mail: judyberg@optonline.net

Barbara A. Fallon Ph.D., CEP
Educational Consultant
PO Box 200
Saddle River NJ 07458
Business Phone: please contact by E-mail
E-mail: barbarafallon1@yahoo.com

Pearl Glassman P.D., CEP
Pearl Glassman Educational Counseling, Inc.
8200 Blvd. East - PHR
North Bergen NJ 07047
Business Phone: 201-854-8282
Fax: 201-854-6080
E-mail: janetloren@pipeline.com

Barbara Hannmann Ed.S.
Licensed Prof. Counselor & School Psychologist
325 Springhouse Lane
Moorestown NJ 08057
Business Phone: 609-458-2928
Fax: 856-234-1397
E-mail: bobbihann@aol.com
Web: www.barbarahannmann.com

Leonard Krivy Ph.D.
Educational Consultant
1765 Fireside Lane
Cherry Hill NJ 08003
Business Phone: 856-428-1282

Fax: 856-428-6910
E-mail: LPKPHD@aol.com

Ronna Morrison M.A., CEP
Ronna Morrison Associates
11 Maple Avenue
Demarest NJ 07627
Business Phone: 201-768-8250
Fax: 201-768-4957
E-mail: RonnaCEP@aol.com

Marylou Schaffer M.Ed., CEP
Crossroads Youth Counseling
17 Hathaway Lane
Verona NJ 07044
Business Phone: 973-857-1251
Fax: 973-857-1950
E-mail: MLSCROSS@aol.com

Anita Targan M.A., CEP
Anita Targan Associates
2 Gloucester Place
Morristown NJ 07960
Business Phone: 973-538-7607
Fax: 973-538-3713
E-mail: atargan@earthlink.net

NEW MEXICO

Whitney Laughlin Ed.D.
Educational Consultant
18 Cougar Ridge Road
Santa Fe NM 87505
Business Phone: 505-690-9054
E-mail: laughlin@rt66.com
Web: www.whitneylaughlin.com

Estelle R. Meskin, M.A. M.A., CEP
National Certified Career Counselor
Santa Fe NM
Business Phone: 505-986-8534
Fax: 505-986-8534
E-mail: EMeskin@aol.com
Web: www.EstelleMeskin.com

Alan C. Posich M.A.
CollegeMasters
4167 Montgomery Blvd. NE
Albuquerque NM 87109
Business Phone: 505-888-1701
Fax: 505-884-1798
E-mail: Aposich@earthlink.net

Kim A. Rubin M.A., CEP
Rubin Educational Resources
2205 Miguel Chavez Road
Suite B
Santa Fe NM 87505
Business Phone: 505-989-8910
Fax: 505-989-8906
E-mail: generalinfo@rubinedu.com
Web: www.rubinedu.com

NEW YORK

Virginia J. Bush CEP
Educational Consultant
444 East 86th Street
New York NY
Business Phone: 212-772-3244
Fax: 860-388-3250

Noreen Cambria M.S.
Cambria Associates, Inc.
PO Box 20608
Huntington Station NY 11746
Business Phone: 516-993-3818
E-mail: guidancepro@yahoo.com
Web: www.guidancepro.com

Kyung Yo Cho
North Shore Educational Consultants
220 S. Service Road
Roslyn Heights NY 11577
Business Phone: 516-626-1351
Fax: 516-626-6726
E-mail: CHONSA@aol.com

Katherine Cohen Ph.D.
IvyWise, LLC
140 West 57th Street, Suite 3D
New York NY 10019
Business Phone: 212-262-3500
Fax: 212-262-4100
E-mail: kcohen@ivywise.com
Web: www.ivywise.com

Marilyn G.S. Emerson M.S.W.
College Planning Services, Inc.
84 Old Farm Road, N.

Chappaqua NY 10514
Business Phone: 914-747-1760
Fax: 914-992-7818
E-mail: mgse@collplan.com
Web: www.collplan.com

Geraldine C. Fryer CEP
Educational Advisor
1066 Boston Post Road
Rye NY 10580-2902
Business Phone: 914-967-7952
Fax: 914-967-7966
E-mail: gcfryer@aol.com

Patricia B. Gildersleeve M.S., CEP
The College Advisory Service
16 Harrogate Road
New Hartford NY 13413
Business Phone: 315-732-9001
Fax: 315-738-0153
E-mail: pbgilder@aol.com

Carol Gill M.A., CEP
Carol Gill Associates
369 Ashford Avenue
Dobbs Ferry NY 10522
Business Phone: 914-693-8200
Fax: 914-693-6211
E-mail: carolgill@aol.com
Web: www.collegesplus.com

Carole Gitnik M.S.
C. Gitnik & Assoc. College Advisors
7 Yale Drive
Manhasset NY 11030
Business Phone: 516-625-9678
Fax: 516-625-9673
E-mail: CLG8640@yahoo.com

Pearl Glassman P.D., CEP
Pearl Glassman Educational Counseling, Inc.
30 White Birch Road
Pound Ridge NY 10576
Business Phone: 914-764-5153
Fax: 914-764-0922
E-mail: glassman@cloud9.net

Leslie Goldberg M.Ed., CEP
New England Educational Advisory
Service,LLC
123 East 18th Street
New York NY
Business Phone: 212-358-8095 or
800-696-5684
Fax: 978-373-4760
E-mail: leslie@edconsult.org
Web: www.teenproblem.com

Barbara Ann Kenefick Ph.D., CEP
Educational Advisor
County Route 9
Chatham NY 12037
Business Phone: 518-392-4753
Fax: 518-392-4753
E-mail: bkenefick@berkshireschool.org

Jane Kolber CEP
Educational Consultant
142 East 71 Street
New York NY 10021
Business Phone: 212-734-1704
Fax: 212-772-7397
E-mail: JEKWFK@aol.com

Louise Kreiner CEP
New England Educational Advisory Service
123 East 18th Street
New York NY
Business Phone: 212-358-8095 or
800-696-5684
Fax: 978-373-4760
E-mail: KreinerCon@aol.com
Web: www.teenproblem.com

Joette Krupa MLS
College Placement Consultants
2330 Shirl Lane
Niskayuna NY 12309
Business Phone: 518-346-1095
Fax: 518-377-6062
E-mail: hjkrupa@nycap.rr.com

Yong Moon M.S.
Empire College Bound Counseling Co.
163-10 Northern Blvd.
Suite 311
Flushing NY 11358
Business Phone: 718-661-4936
Fax: 718-661-4937
E-mail: gt1976@aol.com

Mike Musiker M.Ed., CEP
Musiker Associates
1326 Old Northern Blvd.
Roslyn Village NY 11576
Business Phone: 516-621-3713
Fax: 516-625-3438
E-mail: mike@summerfun.com

Suzan Reznick M.A., CEP
The College Connection
39 Roma Orchard Road
Peekskill NY 10566
Business Phone: 914-734-8440
Fax: 914-737-1202
E-mail: asksuzan@optonline.net

Jill Rifkin M.S.
College Options
145 Darrach Road
Delmar NY 12054
Business Phone: 518-439-1843
Fax: 518-478-0652
E-mail: jrrif@aol.com

Christine J. Scott M.S.
Scott-Deutsch Associates
PO Box 586
Ardsley NY 10502
Business Phone: 917-519-2900
E-mail: cscottbxsci@aol.com

Joan Tager M.S., CEP
Educational Consultant
577 Old Montauk Highway
(Office open mid-May to mid-Oct.)
Montauk NY 11954
Business Phone: 631-668-4239
Fax: 631-668-7054
E-mail: capstager1@aol.com

Sally M. Ten Eyck B.S.Ed., CEP
College Assistance Plus
43 Tygert Road
Altamont (Albany) NY 12009
Business Phone: 518-765-3288
Fax: 518-765-4851
E-mail: smteneyck@yahoo.com

NORTH CAROLINA

Gordon Bingham M.A., CEP
Bingham Associates
173 Tullyries Lane
Lewisville (Winston-Salem) NC 27023
Business Phone: 336-946-2819
Fax: 336-945-0909
E-mail: gbingham2@triad.rr.com

Mary Jane Freeman M.A.Ed., CEP
Davidson Center for Learning & Acad. Planning
PO Box 550
452 S. Main St.
Davidson NC 28036-0550
Business Phone: 704-892-4533
Fax: 704-892-5977
E-mail: MaryjaneF@aol.com

Linda McMullen M.Ed., CEP
Licensed Professional Counselor
3435 Lakeview Trail
PO Box 6278
Kinston NC 28501
Business Phone: 252-523-2769
Fax: 252-523-0998
E-mail: McMullen@eastlink.net

Ann Crandall Sloan M.A., CEP
Triangle Educational Planners
3820 Merton Dr., Suite 215
Raleigh NC 27609
Business Phone: 919-828-2828
Fax: 919-828-1981
E-mail: acsloan@teplanners.com
Web: www.triangleeducationalplanners.com

OHIO

Arline Altman M.A.Ed., CEP
College-Career Planning Consulting
6050 Cranberry Court
Columbus OH 43213
Business Phone: 614-864-0356
Fax: 614-864-3388
E-mail: collegecareerplan@insight.rr.com

Bill Kellerman M.A.
College 101
6467 Oregon Pass

West Chester OH 45069
Business Phone: 513-379-9521
E-mail: wlk@cinci.rr.com

Phyllis Kozokoff M.A., CEP
Licensed Professional Counselor
23811 Chagrin Blvd., Suite 307
Cleveland OH 44122
Business Phone: 216-464-3686
Fax: 216-360-8792
E-mail: Pkozokoff@aol.com

OREGON

Andrew Bryan
The Academic Institute, Inc.
1915 Main Street
Baker City OR 97814
Business Phone: 541-523-4797 or 888-385-2877
Fax: 928-244-1315
E-mail: info@eduplacement.com
Web: www.academicinstitute.com

Marilyn Petrequin
Petrequin College Consulting
2455 NW Marshall St.
Suite 8B
Portland OR 97210
Business Phone: 503-223-4429
Fax: 503-223-4429
E-mail: mpetrequin@yahoo.com
Web: www.transportlogic.com/~petrequin

Nancy E. Smith CEP
1012 SW King
Suite 101
Portland OR 97205
Business Phone: 503-226-0072
Fax: 503-350-0644
E-mail: dekesmith@aol.com

PENNSYLVANIA

Peggy Baker M.Ed.
Educational Consultant
1934 Whiteacre Drive North
Bethlehem PA 18015
Business Phone: 610-867-2477
E-mail: pegedu@yahoo.com
Web: www.PeggyBakerconsulting.com

Laurie Crockett Barclay Ed.M.
College Planning Associates
912 W. Fourth Street
Williamsport PA 17701
Business Phone: 570-322-1313
Fax: 570-322-8796
E-mail: lbarclay@suscom.net

Grant Calder CEP
Bennett Educational Resources
310 North High Street
West Chester PA 19380
Business Phone: 610-692-9096
Fax: 610-692-9132
Web: www.schoolplacement.com

Robert Cohen Ed.D.
College Admissions Services
65 E. Elizabeth Ave.
Suite 612
Bethlehem PA 18018
Business Phone: 610-867-1818
Fax: 610-867-3276
E-mail: rdcollege@enter.net
Web: www.collegeplan.com

John E. Granozio M.Ed.
College Advisory Service
355 Dreshertown Rd.
Fort Washington PA 19034
Business Phone: 215-572-1590
Fax: 215-646-5076
E-mail: palm2@dellnet.com

Dodge Johnson Ph.D., CEP
College Planning
547 S. Sugartown Road
Malvern PA 19355-2643
Business Phone: 610-647-6755
Fax: 610-647-3746
E-mail: dodge@dodgejohnson.com
Web: www.dodgejohnson.com

James A. Nolan M.A., CEP
Access Education International
1062 Lancaster Ave. #22
Rosemont PA 19010
Business Phone: 610-527-9242
Fax: 610-527-1892
E-mail: NolEduIntl@aol.com

Lloyd R. Paradiso CEP
Cresslund Farm, Box 459
Blue Bell PA 19422
Business Phone: 267-975-7580
E-mail: lparadiso@sageeducation.com
Web: www.sageeducation.com

Luisa M. Rabe M.B.A.
Pruett Rabe Associates
112 Buck Lane
Haverford PA 19041
Business Phone: 610-896-9522
Fax: 610-896-9882
E-mail: luisa@pruettrabe.com

Suzanne F. Scott Ed.M., CEP
Licensed/Certified School Psychologist
681 Meetinghouse Road - 1
Elkins Park PA 19027
Business Phone: 215-887-2201
Fax: 215-887-4624
E-mail: scottaas@comcast.net
Web: www.IECAonline.com/suzannescott

Susan Strom M.Ed.
College Selection Consultants
680 Long Acre Lane
Yardley PA 19067
Business Phone: 215-321-7019
Fax: 215-321-7019
E-mail: susanstrom@comcast.net

Barry Sysler Ph.D.
Academic Directions
509 Coachwood Court
Newtown PA 18940
Business Phone: 866-4-YOUR-ED (866-496-8733)
Fax: 215-579-9469
E-mail: bsysler@aol.com
Web: www.academicdirections.com

RHODE ISLAND

Susan M. Hanflik M.Ed.
Educational Consultant
170 Summit Drive
Cranston RI 02920
Business Phone: 401-944-4315
Fax: 401-944-4315
E-mail: smhanflik@cox.net

C. Claire Law M.S., CEP
Educational Avenues
2358 South County Trail
Suite 100
E. Greenwich RI 02818
Business Phone: 401-885-8611
Fax: 401-885-7682
E-mail: Claire@eduave.com
Web: www.eduave.com

Ruth Lipka M.A.
Academic Admissions Consultants, LLC
430 Old River Rd.
Lincoln RI 02838
Business Phone: 401-762-3675
E-mail: alllipka@cox.net

SOUTH CAROLINA

William S. Dingledine Jr., M.S., CEP
The Princeton Review
PO Box 5249
Greenville SC 29606
Business Phone: 864-467-1838
Fax: 864-467-0780
E-mail: WSDingle@educdir.com
Web: www.educdir.com

Ann Carol Price M.Ed., CEP
Educational Planning Services
3104 Devine Street
Columbia SC 29205
Business Phone: 803-252-5777
Fax: 803-252-4333
E-mail: anncarolprice@yahoo.com

TENNESSEE

Mary B. Consoli B.S.Ed., CEP
Mary B. Consoli Associates

624 Reliability Circle
Knoxville TN 37932
Business Phone: 865-675-1997
Fax: 865-671-1920
E-mail: mbconsoli@aol.com
Web: www.mbconsoli.com

Farron G. Peatross M.A., CEP
Educational Placement Services, Inc.
5130 Greenway Cove
Memphis TN 38117
Business Phone: 901-685-3156
Fax: 901-685-3157
E-mail: peatross@bellsouth.net
Web: www.educplacement.com

Bunny Porter-Shirley CEP
Educational Planning Services
801 Lynnbrook Road
Nashville TN 37215
Business Phone: 615-269-3322
Fax: 615-385-0828
E-mail: eduplanners@comcast.net
Web: www.eduplanners.com

Anne Thompson M.A., CEP
Educational Consultant
3978 Central Avenue
Memphis TN 38111
Business Phone: 901-458-6291 (x1812)
Fax: 901-323-4848
E-mail: athompson@cpcmemphis.net
Web: www.cpcmemphis.net

TEXAS

Carol G. Cohen CEP
Cohen's College Connection
4950 Keller Springs Rd.
Ste. 160
Addison TX 75001-6205
Business Phone: 972-381-9990
Fax: 972-381-9997
E-mail: carolgene@cohenscc.com
Web: www.cohenscc.com

Elizabeth Hall M.A., CEP
Education Consulting Services
2509 Hartford Road
Austin TX 78703
Business Phone: 512-476-5082
Fax: 512-477-9654
E-mail: ehh@mail.utexas.edu

Lindy Kahn M.A., CEP
Lindy Kahn Associates, Inc.
6717 Vanderbilt
Houston TX 77005
Business Phone: 713-668-2609
Fax: 713-668-4551
E-mail: lindyk23@hotmail.com
Web: www.educationalconsulting.com

Ceel Kenny
The Ceel Kenny Group, LLC
531 Rockhill Drive
San Antonio TX 78209
Business Phone: 210-804-0600
Fax: 210-804-0601
E-mail: sea@sedona.net
Web: www.sedonaed.com

Peggy Manley M.Ed.
Educational Search & Placement
2902 Bowman Avenue
Austin TX 78703
Business Phone: 512-481-0717
Fax: 512-473-2551
E-mail: espsat@austin.rr.com

Londa May M.Ed., CEP
Campus Selection, Inc.
2 Dunloggin Lane
The Woodlands TX 77380
Business Phone: 281-364-9700
Fax: 281-292-0449
E-mail: lmay@campusselection.com
Web: www.campusselection.com

Ann Montgomery M.Ed.
Sage Education Group, LLC
3730 Kirby Dr. Suite 930
Houston TX 77098
Business Phone: 713-520-5522
Fax: 713-520-0486
E-mail: ann@sageeducationgroup.com
Web: www.sageeducationgroup.com

Judy W. Muir M.Ed.
6162 San Felipe Rd.
Houston TX 77057
Business Phone: 713-819-5400
Fax: 713-784-4654
E-mail: judywmuir@yahoo.com

Marshall E. Shumsky Ph.D., CEP
Developmental & Cognitive Psychology
7887 San Felipe Road, Suite 101
Houston TX 77063-1620
Business Phone: 713-784-6610
Fax: 713-784-9565
E-mail: shumsky@flash.net

Elissa Sommerfield M.A., CEP
School Placement Services
9636 Hollow Way
Dallas TX 75220
Business Phone: 214-363-7043
Fax: 214-363-0146
E-mail: esom@techrack.com

Rhea M. Wolfram CEP
Rhea M. Wolfram Associates
13928 Hughes Lane
Dallas TX 75240-3510
Business Phone: 972-233-1115
Fax: 972-233-2666
E-mail: rwolframsis@airmail.net

UTAH

None listed.

VERMONT

Lora K. Block M.A., CEP
College Advisory Services
McIntosh Lane
Bennington VT 05201
Business Phone: 802-447-0776
Fax: 802-447-7042
E-mail: lblock@sover.net

Robert M. Kantar
Educational Resources
1041 Brown Farm Road
Lyndonville VT 05851
Business Phone: 802-626-4620
E-mail: RKantar@aol.com
Web: www.bobkantar.com

Benjamin L. Mason Ed.M., CEP
Mason & Associates
PO Box 59
2687 Greenbush Rd.
Charlotte VT 05445
Business Phone: 802-425-7600
Fax: 802-425-7601
E-mail: BEEMASON@aol.com

VIRGINIA

Samuel Barnett Ph.D., CEP
School Futures
227 Nutley St. NW
Vienna VA 22180
Business Phone: 703-938-1787
Fax: 703-938-1787
E-mail: sbarnett@schoolfutures.com
Web: www.schoolfutures.com

Shirley A. Bloomquist M.Ed.
A Second Opinion
11136 Rich Meadows Drive
Great Falls VA 22066
Business Phone: 703-406-8034
Fax: 703-406-8034
E-mail: sbloomqu@aol.com

Leslie A. Kent M.A.
Leslie Kent Consulting
2713 Verily Court
Oakton VA 22124
Business Phone: 703-620-9297
E-mail: lakent@cox.net

Joan E. Levin LCSW, M.Ed.
A+ College Counseling
2026 Rhode Island Avenue
McLean VA 22101
Business Phone: 703-359-0202
Fax: 703-533-7229
E-mail: joanendow@hotmail.com

Emily A. Snyder M.A.
Know Your Options
12731 Lady Somerset Lane
Fairfax VA 22033

Business Phone: 703-817-0797
Fax: 703-817-0514
E-mail: Emily@KnowYourOptions.net
Web: www.KnowYourOptions.net

WASHINGTON

Andrew Bryan
The Academic Institute, Inc.
13400 NE 20th Street
Suite 47
Bellevue WA 98005
Business Phone: 888-385-2877 or 425-401-6844
Fax: 928-244-1315
E-mail: info@eduplacement.com
Web: www.academicinstitute.com

Linda Jacobs M.Ed.
Linda Jacobs & Associates
5508 35th Avenue NE
Suite 104
Seattle WA 98105
Business Phone: 206-323-8902
Fax: 206-323-3635
E-mail: LinJacobs@aol.com

Kiersten A. Murphy M.Ed.
Murphy Educational Consulting
7221 Laurel Ave. SE
Snoqualmie WA 98065
Business Phone: 800-553-6402 / 425-396-5618
E-mail: kiersten@schoolconsultant.com
Web: www.schoolconsultant.com

Pauline B. Reiter Ph.D.
College Placement Consultants
40 Lake Bellevue
Suite 100
Bellevue WA 98005
Business Phone: 425-453-1730
Fax: 206-232-8153
E-mail: preiter@qwest.net

WEST VIRGINIA

Jamie Dickenson MBA
1596 Kanowha Blvd. East
Charleston WV 25311
Business Phone: 304-556-4807
Fax: 304-414-2211
E-mail: jamie@jamiedickenson
Web: www.jamiedickenson

WISCONSIN

Laurie A. Bookstein CEP
College Placement Services
9596 N. Regent Road
Milwaukee WI 53217
Business Phone: 414-351-6801
Fax: 414-351-6801
E-mail: cpsinclab@aol.com

Gisela Terner M.Ed.
Special Education Consulting & College Planning
1009 West Glen Oaks Lane, Suite 208
Mequon WI 53092
Business Phone: 262-240-2213
Fax: 262-240-2214
E-mail: gterner@execpc.com

Words to Know

Academic Probation – A student can receive this if they fail to keep up with their school's academic minimums. Those who are unable to improve their grades after receiving this warning can possibly face dismissal.

Beer Pong / Beirut – A drinking game with numerous cups of beer arranged in a particular pattern on each side of a table. The goal is to get a ping pong ball into one of the opponent's cups by throwing the ball or hitting it with a paddle. If the ball lands in a cup, the opponent is required to drink the beer.

Bid – An invitation from a fraternity or sorority to pledge their specific house.

Blue-Light Phone – Brightly-colored phone posts with a blue light bulb on top. These phones exist for security purposes and are located at various outside locations around most campuses. If a student has an emergency or is feeling endangered, they can pick up one of these phones (free of charge) to connect with campus police or an escort service.

Campus Police – Policemen who are specifically assigned to a given institution. Campus police are not regular city officers; they are employed by the university in a full-time capacity.

Club Sports – A level of sports that falls somewhere between varsity and intramural. If a student is unable to commit to a varsity team but has a lot of passion for athletics, a club sport could be a better, less intense option. If a club sport still requires too much commitment, intramurals often involve no traveling and a lot less time.

Cocaine – An illegal drug. Also known as "coke" or "blow," cocaine often resembles a white crystalline or powdery substance. It is highly addictive and dangerous.

Common Application – An application that students can use to apply to multiple schools.

Course Registration – The time when a student selects what courses they would like for the upcoming quarter or semester. Prior to registration, it is best to have an idea of several back-up courses in case a particular class becomes full. If a course is full, a student can place themselves on the waitlist, although this still does not guarantee entry.

Division Athletics – Athletics range from Division I to Division III. Division IA is the most competitive, while Division III is considered to be the least competitive.

Dorm – Short for dormitory, a dorm is an on-campus housing facility. Dorms can provide a range of options from suite-style rooms to more communal options that include shared bathrooms. Most first-year students live in dorms. Some upperclassmen who wish to stay on campus also choose this option.

Early Action – A way to apply to a school and get an early acceptance response without a binding commitment. This is a system that is becoming less and less available.

Early Decision – An option that students should use only if they are positive that a place is their dream school. If a student applies to a school using the early decision option and is admitted, they are required and bound to attend that university. Admission rates are usually higher with early decision students because the school knows that a student is making them their first choice.

Ecstasy – An illegal drug. Also known as "E" or "X," ecstasy looks like a pill and most resembles an aspirin. Considered a party drug, ecstasy is very dangerous and can be deadly.

Ethernet – An extremely fast internet connection that is usually available in most university-owned residence halls. To use an Ethernet connection properly, a student will need a network card and cable for their computer.

Fake ID – A counterfeit identification card that contains false information. Most commonly, students get fake IDs and change their birthdates so that they appear to be older than 21 (of legal drinking age). Even though it is illegal, many college students have fake IDs in hopes of purchasing alcohol or getting into bars.

Frosh – Slang for "freshmen."

Hazing – Initiation rituals that must be completed for membership into some fraternities or sororities. Numerous universities have outlawed hazing due to its degrading or dangerous requirements.

Sports (IMs) – A popular, and usually free, student activity where students create teams and compete against other groups for fun. These sports vary in competitiveness and can include a range of activities—everything from billiards to water polo. IM sports are a great way to meet people with similar interests.

Keg – Officially called a half barrel, a keg contains roughly 200 12-ounce servings of beer and is often found at college parties.

LSD – An illegal drug. Also known as acid, this hallucinogenic drug most commonly resembles a tab of paper.

Marijuana – An illegal drug. Also known as weed or pot; besides alcohol, marijuana is one of the most commonly-found drugs on campuses across the country.

Major –The focal point of a student's college studies; a specific topic that is studied for a degree. Examples of majors include physics, English, history, computer science, economics, business, and music. Many students decide on a specific major before arriving on campus, while others are simply "undecided" and figure it out later. Those who are extremely interested in two areas can also choose to double major.

Meal Block – The equivalent of one meal. Students on a "meal plan" usually receive a fixed number of meals per week. Each meal, or "block," can be redeemed at the school's dining facilities in place of cash. More often than not, if a student fails to use their weekly allotment of meal blocks, they will be forfeited.

Minor – An additional focal point in a student's education. Often serving as a compliment or addition to a student's main area of focus, a minor has fewer requirements and prerequisites to fulfill than a major. Minors are not required for graduation from most schools; however some students who want to further explore many different interests choose to have both a major and a minor.

Mushrooms – An illegal drug. Also known as "shrooms," this drug looks like regular mushrooms but are extremely hallucinogenic.

Off-Campus Housing – Housing from a particular landlord or rental group that is not affiliated with the university. Depending on the college, off-campus housing can range from extremely popular to non-existent. Those students who choose to live off campus are typically given more freedom, but they also have to deal with things such as possible subletting scenarios, furniture, and bills. In addition to these factors, rental prices and distance often affect a student's decision to move off campus.

Office Hours – Time that teachers set aside for students who have questions about the coursework. Office hours are a good place for students to go over any problems and to show interest in the subject material.

Pledging – The time after a student has gone through rush, received a bid, and has chosen a particular fraternity or sorority they would like to join. Pledging usually lasts anywhere from one to two semesters. Once the pledging period is complete and a particular student has done everything that is required to become a member, they are considered a brother or sister. If a fraternity or a sorority would decide to "haze" a group of students, these initiation rituals would take place during the pledging period.

Private Institution – A school that does not use taxpayers dollars to help subsidize education costs. Private schools typically cost more than public schools and are usually smaller.

Prof – Slang for "professor."

Public Institution – A school that uses taxpayers dollars to help subsidize education costs. Public schools are often a good value for in-state residents and tend to be larger than most private colleges.

Quarter System (sometimes referred to as the Trimester System) – A type of academic calendar system. In this setup, students take classes for three academic periods. The first quarter usually starts in late September or early October and concludes right before Christmas. The second quarter usually starts around early to mid–January and finishes up around March or April. The last quarter, or "third quarter," usually starts in late March or early April and finishes up in late May or Mid-June. The fourth quarter is summer. The major difference between the quarter system and semester system is that students take more courses but with less coverage.

RA (Resident Assistant) – A student leader who is assigned to a particular floor in a dormitory in order to help to the other students who live there. A RA's duties include ensuring student safety and providing guidance or assistance wherever possible.

Recitation – An extension of a specific course; a "review" session. Because some classes are so large, recitations offer a setting with fewer students where students can ask questions and get help from professors or TAs in a more personalized environment. As a result, it is common for most large lecture classes to be supplemented with recitations.

Rolling Admissions – A form of admissions. Most commonly found at public institutions, schools with this type of policy continue to accept students throughout the year until their class sizes are met. For example, some schools begin accepting students as early as December and will continue to do so until April or May.

Room and Board – This is typically the combined cost of a university-owned room and a meal plan.

Room Draw/Housing Lottery – A common way to pick on-campus room assignments for the following year. If a student decides to remain in university-owned housing, they are assigned a unique number that, along with seniority, is used to choose their new rooms for the next year.

Rush – The period in which students can meet the brothers and sisters of a particular chapter and find out if a given fraternity or sorority is right for them. Rushing a fraternity or a sorority is not a requirement at any school. The goal of rush is to give students who are serious about pledging a feel for what to expect.

Semester System – The most common type of academic calendar system at college campuses. This setup typically includes two semesters in a given school year. The "fall" semester starts around the end of August or early September and finishes right before winter vacation. The "spring" semester usually starts in mid-January and ends around late April or May.

Student Center/Rec Center/Student Union – A common area on campus that often contains study areas, recreation facilities, and eateries. This building is often a good place to meet up with fellow students and is most commonly used as a hangout. Depending on the school, the student center can have a huge role or a non-existent role in campus life.

Student ID – A university-issued photo ID that serves as a student's key to many different functions within an institution. Some schools require students to show these cards in order to get into dorms, libraries, cafeterias, and other facilities. In addition to storing meal plan information, in some cases, a student ID can actually work as a debit card and allow students to purchase things from bookstores or local shops.

Suite – A type of dorm room. Unlike other places that have communal bathrooms that are shared by the entire floor, a suite has a private bathroom. Suite-style dorm rooms can house anywhere from two to ten students.

TA (Teacher's Assistant) – An undergraduate or grad student who helps in some manner with a specific course. In some cases, a TA will teach a class, assist a professor, grade assignments, or conduct office hours.

Undergraduate – A student who is in the process of studying for their Bachelor (college) degree.

New England Colleges 2006

Looking for peace in the Northeast?
Pick up this regional guide to New England!

New England Colleges
7¼" X 10", 1030 Pages Paperback
$29.95 Retail
August 2005
1-59658-504-8

New England is the birthplace of many prestigious universities, and with so many to choose from, picking the right school can be a tough decision. With inside information on over 34 competive Northeastern schools, *New England Colleges 2006* provides the same high-quality information prospective students expect from College Prowler in one all-inclusive, easy-to-use reference.

Off the Record

Our growing collection of single-school guides . . .

Alfred University
Allegheny College
American University
Amherst College
Arizona State University
Auburn University
Babson College
Bard College
Barnard College
Bates College
Baylor University
Beloit College
Bentley College
Boston College
Boston University
Bowdoin College
Brandeis University
Brigham Young University
Brown University
Bryn Mawr College
Bucknell University
Cal Poly
Cal State - Northridge
Caltech
Carleton College
Carnegie Mellon University
Case Western Reserve Univ.
Clemson University
Colby College
Colgate University
College of Charleston
College of the Holy Cross
College of William and Mary
College of Wooster
Colorado College
Columbia University
Connecticut College
Cornell University
Dartmouth College
Davidson College
Denison University
Depauw University
Dickinson College
Drexel University
Duke University
Duquesne University
Elon University
Emerson College
Emory University
Florida State University
Fordham University
Franklin & Marshall College
Furman University
George Washington Univ.
Georgetown University
Georgia Tech
Geneva College
Gettysburg College
Grinnell College
Grove City College
Guilford College
Hamilton College
Hampton University
Harvard University
Harvey Mudd College
Haverford College
Hofstra University
Indiana University
Iowa State University
Ithaca College
James Madison University
Johns Hopkins University
Kenyon College
Lafayette College
Lehigh University
Lewis and Clark College
Loyola Marymount University
Loyola University - Chicago
Loyola University - New Orleans
Macalester College
Marquette University
MIT
Miami University of Ohio
Michigan State University
Middlebury College
Mount Holyoke College
Muhlenberg College
New York University
Northeastern University
Northwestern University
Oberlin College
Occidental College
Ohio State University
Ohio University
Penn State
Pepperdine University
Pitzer College
Pomona College
Princeton University
Providence College
Purdue University
Reed College
Rensselaer Polytechnic Institute
Rice University
Rhodes College
Rhode Island School of Design
Rochester Institute of Technology
Rollins College
Rutgers New Brunswick
San Diego State University
Santa Clara University
Scripps College
Seattle University
Seton Hall University
Skidmore College
Smith College
Southern Methodist University
Southwestern University
St. John's University
St. Louis University
Stanford University
SUNY Albany
SUNY Binghamton
SUNY Buffalo
SUNY Stony Brook
Swarthmore College
Syracuse University
Temple University
Texas A&M University
Texas Christian University
Towson University
Trinity College Connecticut
Trinity University Texas
Tufts University
Tulane University
Union College
University of Alabama
University of Arizona
UC Berkeley
UC Davis
UC Irvine
UCLA
UC Riverside
UC San Diego
UC Santa Barbara
UC Santa Cruz
University of Central Florida
University of Chicago
University of Colorado
University of Connecticut
University of Delaware
University of Denver
University of Florida
University of Georgia
University of Illinois
University of Iowa
University of Kansas
University of Kentucky
University of Maryland
University of Massachusetts
University of Miami
University of Michigan
University of Minnesota
University of Mississippi
University of Missouri
University of Nebraska
University of New Hampshire
University of North Carolina
University of Notre Dame
University of Oklahoma
University of Oregon
University of Pennsylvania
University of Pittsburgh
University of Puget Sound
University of Rhode Island
University of Richmond
University of Rochester
University of San Diego
University of San Francisco
University of South Carolina
University of South Florida
University of Southern California
University of Tennessee
University of Texas
University of Utah
University of Vermont
University of Virginia
University of Washington
University of Wisconsin
Valparaiso University
Vanderbilt University
Vassar College
Villanova University
Virginia Tech
Wake Forest University
Washington & Lee University
Washington Univ. in St. Louis
Wellesley College
Wesleyan University
West Point Military Academy
West Virginia University
Wheaton College Mass.
Whitman College
Williams College
Xavier University
Yale University

5½" X 8½", 160 Pages Paperback
$14.95 Retail

WWW.COLLEGEPROWLER.COM